# Food
# Cures

## Magic Foods to Help You Live Longer, Fight Disease, and Lose Weight

Reader's
Digest

The Reader's Digest Association, Inc.
New York, NY/Montreal

ISBN 978-1-60652-116-8

*Magic Foods: Live Longer, Supercharge Your Energy, Lose Weight, and Stop Cravings!*
Copyright © 2007 by The Reader's Digest Association, Inc.

Photography: Elizabeth Watt (Food Stylist: Anne Disrude); D.A. Croll; Food Collection; Getty Images: Digital Vision, PhotoAlto, Photodisc, Stockbyte

Library of Congress Cataloging-in-Publication Data
    Magic foods for better blood sugar / [editor, Marianne Wait].
        p. cm.
    Includes index.
    ISBN 978-0-7621-0755-1 (hardcover)
    1. Nutrition—Popular works. 2. Food—Composition—Popular works.
    3. Blood sugar—Popular works. I. Wait, Marianne, 1967-
    RA784.M285 2006
                      613.2—dc22
                      2006026505

---

*Food Cures: Breakthrough Nutritional Prescriptions for Everything from Colds to Cancer*
Copyright © 2007 by The Reader's Digest Association, Inc.

Food photographer: Rita Maas. Additional photography courtesy of: BrandXPictures, BananaStock, Corbis, Getty Images, Image Source, Jupiter Images, PhotoAlto, Reader's Digest Books, Stockfood, and Shutterstock.

Library of Congress Cataloging in Publication Data
Food cures : breakthrough nutritional prescriptions for everything from colds to cancer / [editor, Marianne Wait].
        p. cm.
    Includes index.
    ISBN: 978-0-7621-0730-8 (hardcover)
    ISBN: 978-0-7621-0797-1 (paperback)
    1. Nutrition--Popular works. 2. Diet therapy--Popular works.
    3. Medicine, Popular. I. Wait, Marianne, 1967-
    RA784.F62 2007
    615.8'54--dc22
                      2007024471

We are committed to both the quality of our products and the service we provide to our customers. We value your comments, so please feel free to contact us.

The Reader's Digest Association, Inc.
Adult Trade Publishing
44 South Broadway
White Plains, NY 10601

NOTE TO READERS
The information in this book should not be substituted for, or used to alter, medical therapy without your doctor's advice. For a specific health problem, consult your physician for guidance. The mention of any products, retail businesses, or websites in these books does not imply or constitute an endorsement by the authors or by the Reader's Digest Association, Inc.

For more Reader's Digest products and information, visit our website:
    www.rd.com (in the United States)
    www.readersdigest.ca (in Canada)

Printed in China

3 5 7 9 10 8 6 4 2

# CONTENTS

# Magic Foods ......5

# Food Cures ......305

# Magic Foods

### Live Longer, Supercharge Your Energy, Lose Weight, and Stop Cravings

Robert A. Barnard, coauthor of *The Volumetrics Weight-Control Plan*,
Christine L. Pelkman, Ph.D. & Densie Webb, Ph.D., R.D.

**The Reader's Digest Association, Inc.**
**New York, NY | Montreal**

# contents

A major health crisis is emerging, one that most doctors are just beginning to recognize. You may never have heard of it, but it could very well be affecting how you feel right this minute. It's not heart disease, diabetes, or obesity, although it's linked to all three. It's out-of-control blood sugar, and you may have it without even knowing it.

Chalk it up to our modern-day diets, which are loaded with foods that send blood sugar soaring, only to crash in short order. When the crash comes, you may feel listless, irritable, headachy— and ravenously, must-eat-something-sugary-this-minute hungry. Riding this blood sugar rollercoaster is a sure way to send your hunger up, your energy down, and your waistline *out*.

# introduction Magic Foods

Our love affair with sugar-raising foods, especially "white" foods such as white bread, white rice, French fries, and sugary baked goods, has led to an outbreak of insulin resistance—essentially, what happens when the body's system for handling blood sugar spikes gets worn out from overwork. Insulin resistance is linked to serious problems ranging from heart disease and memory loss to—you guessed it—diabetes. About 25 percent of adults have it. If you're overweight and over 45, the chances that you have it are nearly one in two.

Fortunately, insulin resistance is reversible. If eating the wrong foods can cause it, eating the right ones can cure it. And it's not that hard to do. We designed this book to help you get off the blood sugar rollercoaster—without turning your diet upside down.

In *Magic Foods for Better Blood Sugar*, you won't find strict eating regimens or crazy rules about carbohydrates. What you will find are 57 foods that can help you nudge your diet into sugar-friendly territory. Add just one to your plate (for instance, try barley instead of white rice), and you could see results right away. Add a few more (like avocados, which contain fats that actually improve insulin sensitivity), and you'll really be on the road to feeling better and staving off killer diseases.

Even if you already have diabetes, these strategies can help make your cells more sensitive to insulin and keep blood sugar swings in check.

You can still eat steak, if you keep it lean, as well as pasta and other carbohydrate foods if you choose the right ones (whole grains actually reduce your diabetes risk). We'll also show you how adding a few "secret ingredients" like cinnamon and vinegar to your dishes can yield amazing results.

*Magic Foods* is based on the latest nutrition science, but it's designed for regular folks like you who just want to know what to eat. For instance, you won't have to look up numbers before you choose a food. Our recipes, meal makeovers, meal plans, and cooks tips make it incredibly simple to get more of the 57 Magic foods onto your plate. Your meals will still taste delicious—and they'll leave you more satisfied, so you won't be hunting around for something else to eat.

At Reader's Digest, we take your health to heart. Here's something you can do to rein in insulin resistance, offload dangerous belly fat, guard yourself from diabetes (or help reverse it), and feel more fully charged and ready to embrace life every day. Don't wait for your doctor to say you have a problem. Turn the page now and start discovering the good foods and fun tools that await you.

Marianne Wait
*Senior Health Editor*
*Reader's Digest Books*

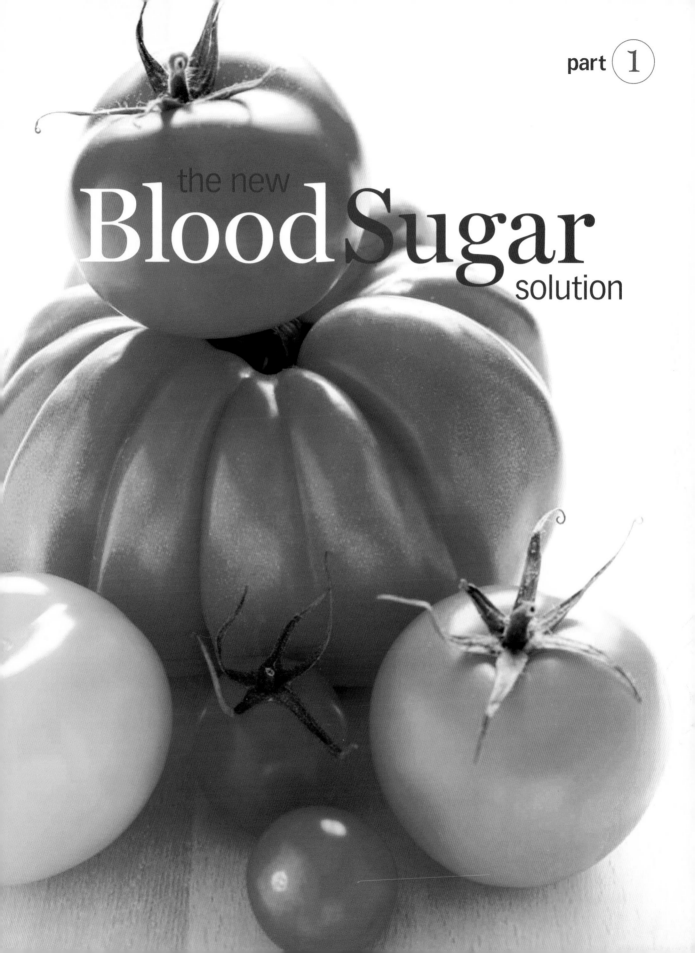

the new
# BloodSugar
solution

# chapter 1

# THE NATION'S SECRET
# healthCRISIS

If you're like most people, you've probably never given your blood sugar a second thought unless you have diabetes. But doctors and researchers have recently discovered a shocking truth: If your blood sugar levels regularly soar and crash like a radio-controlled airplane, your body may sustain damage, just as the model plane does over time. Of course, in your case, the damage will occur on the inside, where you can't see it. The consequences, like low energy or weight gain, can be bothersome—or they can be deadly.

It's no longer just certain people who need to worry about their **blood sugar.** It's pretty much **everyone.**

Whether or not you have diabetes, a diet loaded with foods that send blood sugar up high and down low can jack up your risk of heart disease by damaging your blood vessels and raising your cholesterol. It may even chip away at your memory and increase the risk of certain cancers. You may not notice a problem, but that doesn't mean it's not there. You may have started on a path that can shave years off your life.

This realization is nothing short of a revolution in the way we understand diet and health. Fortunately, none of the damage happens overnight, and even modest changes in the foods you eat every day can start you on a healthier path and make you feel more alert, alive, and energized right away.

# The Lure of "Fast-Acting" Foods

When you need a quick pick-me-up, what do you reach for? Maybe a candy bar, a handful of crackers or pretzels, or a box of raisins. It makes sense. These "fast-acting" foods take no time at all to dissolve in your stomach. Quick as light, they race into your bloodstream, flooding your body with blood sugar (glucose), and you're raring to go! The trouble is, the surge doesn't last long. In fact, it's over just as quickly as it started, leaving you feeling worse off than before—and hungry again well before your next mealtime.

Without knowing it, you may even be starting your day with foods that fizzle out in a hurry, leaving you in a slump. Think back to the last time you ate a bagel for breakfast, or a bowl of cornflakes, frozen waffles with syrup, or white toast with jam. You probably felt fine at first, but later in the morning, you may have noticed your energy level beginning to sink. Maybe you started to get irritable. Once your energy hit bottom, you may have found yourself hungry again—no, starving! So naturally, you ate a big lunch and probably a fast-acting one to boot: maybe a sandwich on a white roll the size of a softball, with a few handfuls of pretzels, a large soda or fruity drink to wash them down, and a cookie (or two) for dessert. And the cycle started over again.

Unfortunately, our diets are chock-full of foods that send us for a wild ride on the blood sugar rollercoaster. It's no wonder most of us have less energy than we'd like and feel listless too often.

It's also no wonder most of us weigh more than we want to. Yes, eating too much and exercising too little get the lion's share of the blame, but the blood sugar rollercoaster contributes by setting in motion a chain of events that eventually sends you shopping for "fat jeans."

Sound bad? Low energy and weight gain are only the tip of the iceberg in terms of what happens when your blood sugar swings high and low.

High blood sugar after meals can, over time, **damage** the body, even if it **NEVER** causes **diabetes**.

# Why Blood Sugar Matters

For most of us, even when blood sugar skyrockets after a big meal, our bodies can bring it back to normal in a few hours with no problem. Only people with untreated diabetes have blood sugar levels that stay quite high most of the time. Thus, for a long time, doctors thought that only those people needed to be concerned about the effect of food on blood sugar.

Now we know that even in healthy people, high blood sugar after meals can, over time, damage the body, *even if it never causes diabetes*.

In short, it's no longer just certain people who need to worry about their blood sugar; it's pretty much everyone. It should concern you even if you're thin and healthy, and especially if you don't get much exercise (does that describe you? It describes most people) or you carry extra weight around your middle.

By now you're wondering, "How can I get off the rollercoaster?" Take heart: It's not that difficult—and the book you're holding will show you how. Later, we'll get into much more detail about how our diets contribute to unstable blood sugar (hint: foods like white bread, white rice, potatoes, and sugary drinks are major culprits)

# Health Effects of Fast-Acting Foods

Diets full of fast-acting carbs like these send blood sugar on a wild ride, which wreaks havoc on the body.

diabetes memory loss

low energy

hunger

weight gain

fatigue

mood swings

heart attacks cancer

and which foods can help solve the problem. But for now, let's take a deeper look at why you should care and how you stand to benefit from this book.

## Energy and Weight Gain

Eating makes you feel full, right? Well, actually, that depends.

When you eat a big meal, especially one with a lot of starchy or sugary foods, the food makes its way through your stomach and intestines and then is converted into glucose, the main fuel for your muscles and even your brain. Voilá, instant energy!

But a big starchy meal can give the body more glucose than it needs. In fact, it can raise blood sugar levels twice as much as another, healthier meal would.

Most people's bodies can bring blood sugar down fairly quickly, within an hour or two of eating. The body does this by releasing insulin, a hormone produced by beta cells in the pancreas. Insulin signals the body to let that blood sugar into cells to use as fuel and to store the rest in the muscles.

But if you eat a huge pile of French fries or a big piece of bread, your body has to deal with a serious flood of blood sugar, so it overreacts, pumping out too much insulin. If you're overweight, it may pump out even more. All that extra insulin brings blood sugar down—too far. And it hangs around a long time, keeping your blood sugar low for hours. As a result, you can fall into a semi-starved state. Indeed, your blood sugar may be even lower than it was before you ate! Now you're really dragging. Your energy is low. You may get a headache.

Your body recognizes that your blood sugar is too low, so it reverses course, spewing out hormones that raise blood levels of sugars and fats (the kind that could trigger a heart attack). Your brain also sets in motion signals that tell you that you're hungry. Even though you ate more calories at lunch than you really needed, your blood sugar is so low that your body thinks it needs more food. Those doughnuts in the conference room sure look attractive right now.

### MEALS THAT MAKE YOU HUNGRY

It's not just low blood sugar but also rapidly falling blood sugar that triggers a powerful hunger signal. In 16 studies, 15 of them found that meals that raise blood sugar quickly resulted in feeling hungrier before the next meal. For example, in a study of 65 women, those whose meals were designed to keep blood sugar stable reported feeling less intense hunger and less desire to eat, especially during the afternoon.

These kinds of meals increase levels of leptin, a hormone that decreases hunger (and boosts fat burning) and lowers levels of ghrelin, a hormone that increases hunger. The women who ate blood sugar–boosting meals reported that they felt hungrier sooner.

In many studies, people who ate such meals also ate more at the next meal. In a study of overweight teenage boys, the boys ate 500 more calories within 5 hours after eating blood sugar–boosting breakfasts and lunches than they did when they ate meals that were kinder to their blood sugar. In other studies, the differences were more modest, about 150 calories. Still, eating even 100 extra calories a day may mean the difference between losing weight and gaining it.

Now, you can lose weight on any diet that cuts calories. But losing is only half the battle—and often, it's the easiest part. Sticking to a healthy eating plan that lets you keep the weight off is the hard part. Eating plenty of Magic foods is a key solution.

### A MOMENT ON THE LIPS …

When you eat a meal that really bumps up your blood sugar, your body pumps out lots of insulin to bring it down, as you've just learned. But it also stops burning fat for fuel so it can use up the blood sugar instead. Your belly (or butt or thighs) pays the price. People whose diets boost blood sugar the most tend to have more body fat, especially around the abdomen, the most dangerous place for it to accumulate.

Getting off the blood sugar rollercoaster can make losing that spare tire a lot easier. In studies involving everyone from obese men to pregnant women to children, a blood sugar–stabilizing diet led to more body fat loss (or, in the case of the pregnant women, less body fat gain during the pregnancy).

> People whose diets boost blood sugar the most tend to have more **body fat,** especially around the **ABDOMEN.**

In a cruel twist of fate, a diet that causes your blood sugar to spike and dive may even slow your metabolism. Compared to a diet that keeps blood sugar levels stable, it reduces the rate at which you burn calories when you're sitting still. In a study of 39 over-weight men and women, the difference worked out to about 80 extra calories burned each day. That's an extra pound (0.5 kg) lost about every six weeks, or more than 8 pounds (3.5 kg) a year. The more overweight you are, the greater the difference may be.

## A Threat to Your Heart

It's fairly easy to imagine how a diet that's rough on your blood sugar can contribute to weight gain. It's a little harder to understand how it can also contribute to a heart attack—yet it can. It can lead to clogged arteries and higher blood pressure, and it can raise the level of inflammation in the body, which doctors now know is intimately connected with heart attack risk.

High blood sugar produces unstable forms of oxygen called free radicals. These nasty molecules damage the arteries, making it harder for blood vessels to do their job of keeping blood pressure normal and making cholesterol more likely to stick like glue to artery walls.

The high levels of insulin that your body needs to tame all this blood sugar are pretty nasty, too.

**BLOOD SUGAR UPS AND DOWNS**

All carbs raise blood sugar. But some carb foods, like white potatoes and white rice, raise it higher and faster than others, like sweet potatoes and barley. Higher peaks mean steeper drops—your blood sugar may sink lower than before you ate—and that's when energy stalls and hunger strikes anew.

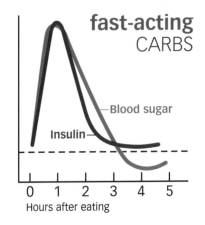

They can set in motion changes that raise blood pressure, make blood more likely to form heart-threatening clots, and increase inflammation—all of which raise your heart disease risk.

Over time, meals that cause blood sugar to spike also tend to lower "good" HDL cholesterol and raise triglycerides, fats that are toxic to cells, increasing the risk of heart disease—and of sudden cardiac arrest.

Big major studies have shown how powerful these damaging effects can be to the heart. In a study of more than 43,000 men age 40 and older, those whose diets boosted blood sugar the most were 37 percent more likely to develop heart disease in the following 6 years. In the Nurses' Health Study of more than 75,000 middle-aged women, those whose diets boosted blood sugar the most were twice as likely to develop heart disease over 10 years. For overweight women, such a diet was even more threatening. For instance, their triglycerides were 144 percent higher than those of women who ate a healthier diet, compared to 40 percent higher for women who weren't overweight.

Fortunately, the phenomenon works in reverse, too: The kinder your meals are to your blood sugar, the kinder they'll be to your heart. Several studies have found that people who ate the fewest blood sugar–boosting foods had higher levels of HDL cholesterol, lower triglycerides, and fewer heart attacks.

## The Cancer Connection

It's even harder to imagine how seesawing blood sugar levels could possibly lead to cancer, but high insulin levels seem to promote an environment that makes it easier for certain tumors to grow. Research is still ongoing, and, unlike with heart disease and diabetes, it's too early to make strong statements about the connection between blood sugar levels and cancer. But there is cause for concern with the following cancers.

**Colon and rectal cancer.** In the Health Professionals Follow-up Study conducted by the Harvard School of Public Health and involving more than 50,000 middle-aged men, those whose diets were most likely to raise blood sugar fast and high were 32 percent more likely to develop colon or rectal cancer over 20 years. The heavier the men, the stronger the effect. In the Women's Health Study, funded in part by the U.S. National Cancer Institute, the rise in cancer risk was an astounding 185 percent higher over 8 years.

**Breast cancer.** In the Women's Health Study, sedentary women who followed a blood sugar–boosting diet were 135 percent more likely to develop breast cancer over seven years than women whose diets were more blood sugar friendly. These women had not yet entered menopause. On the other hand, a Canadian study of nearly 50,000 women found no link to breast cancer before premenopause, but among postmenopausal women, there was an 87 percent increase in breast cancer risk—and it was even higher if the women did little or no vigorous exercise. A Mexican study comparing women who got breast cancer with those who didn't found the risk was 62 percent greater with blood sugar–boosting diets. A similar Italian study found an 18 percent increase.

**Endometrial cancer.** In the Iowa Women's Health Study, which involved more than 23,000 postmenopausal women, those who didn't have diabetes and followed blood sugar–spiking diets were 46 percent more likely to get this cancer over 15 years. An Italian study that compared women who developed endometrial cancer with a similar group of women who didn't found a 110 percent increase in risk linked to this type of diet.

**Prostate cancer.** An Italian study looked at men ages 46 to 74 who developed prostate cancer and compared their diets with those of a similar group of men who didn't get the cancer. Those whose diets were most likely to spike blood sugar were 57 percent more likely to have prostate cancer. A similar Canadian study found a 57 percent increase in risk.

**Pancreatic cancer.** Even the organ that produces insulin may be more prone to cancer if it's constantly bathed in that hormone. A study using data from the Nurses' Health Study over 18 years found that women whose diets raised blood sugar the most were 53 percent more likely to develop pancreatic cancer than women whose diets raised it the least. Women in the first group who were overweight and physically inactive were 157 percent more likely to get the cancer than similar women in the second.

## The Mood and Memory Connection

We began this chapter by showing how a meal that raises blood sugar fast and furiously can leave you dragging like a willow in a windstorm. Not surprisingly, it doesn't do much for your mood, either.

Our moods are intimately affected by the levels of hormones in our systems, including the hormone insulin. These hormones in turn affect neurotransmitters, chemical messengers in the brain. The different types of nutrients we eat, including carbohydrate and protein, affect these transmitters differently, triggering drowsiness or alertness. But the brain may be most sensitive to one simple compound: blood sugar.

Unlike muscles, the brain can't store sugar. It needs just the right amount of it at all times to function best, so it's not surprising that it's very sensitive to even very small differences in the amount of blood sugar available. A steady supply—which the foods in this book will help you achieve—is by far the best.

Both low and high levels of blood sugar can cause trouble when it comes to your mood and memory. People report feeling more symptoms of depression when their blood sugar is low. Memory is affected, too. In one study, people

with diabetes had more trouble processing information, remembering things, and paying attention—besides being in a bad mood—when their blood sugar was low. In people with type 2 diabetes, blood sugar swings are linked not only with poor memory but also, over time, with cognitive decline and dementia.

High blood sugar levels spell trouble, too. Long before they cause diabetes, they can impair the brain, shrinking a part that stores memories and increasing the risk of Alzheimer's disease. In one study at New York University, researchers found that in people who tended to have high blood sugar levels after meals, a part of the brain called the hippocampus, which is most associated with long-term memory, was smaller than in people whose postmeal blood sugar levels were lower.

On the positive side, keeping your blood sugar on an even keel can help you feel better and stay mentally sharp. People with diabetes who control their blood sugar well report better moods, less depression, and less fatigue than those who don't. Careful studies have found that the better they control their blood sugar, the better they are able to recall a paragraph after reading it and to remember words from a list.

In general, eating a good breakfast is the best way for anyone to improve mental functioning later in the day. Studies regularly show that eating breakfast improves mood, mental alertness, concentration, and memory. Eating the *right* breakfast, one that keeps blood sugar on an even keel until lunch, is likely to work even better.

## The Road to Diabetes

Perhaps the worst thing about eating meals heavy on fast-acting foods is that over time, they can greatly increase your risk of type 2 diabetes, the kind that's related to lifestyle. In type 2 diabetes—which we'll just call diabetes from now on—your body can't make enough insulin to keep your blood sugar levels under control.

In major long-term studies, eating fast-acting meals increased the risk of diabetes by 40 percent in middle-aged men and by a whopping 50 percent in middle-aged women. Fortunately, it doesn't happen overnight. It's not as if you eat a jelly doughnut on Tuesday and wake up with diabetes on Wednesday. It takes years, even decades, for your body to get to the point where it can't keep blood sugar under control on its own.

Most of us, though, are headed in the wrong direction.

The good news is that the slow journey toward diabetes can be redirected *at any point along the path*. The earlier you start, of course, the easier and more effectively you can change direction. Eating meals that are gentler to your blood sugar is key.

## Insulin Resistance: A Growing Epidemic

Ever strip a screw when you're in the midst of a do-it-yourself project? Suddenly, you need to use real elbow grease to turn it just a little bit. And the more it gets stripped, the harder it is to turn.

Your body can be a little like that. The more foods you eat that spike your blood sugar, the more insulin your body has to pump out to handle the load. Over time, repeated surges of insulin can strip your cells' insulin receptors, figuratively speaking, so they don't work as well, and the insulin can't be used as efficiently. When that happens, your body has to pump out more insulin to do the same job. This condition is called insulin resistance.

In the West, where the mega-meal and the electric recliner are all too pervasive, insulin resistance is increasingly common. About 25 percent of adults have it. And if you're overweight and over 45, the chances that you have it are nearly one in two. You're much more likely to develop insulin resistance if you're overweight and sedentary.

## fighting INSULIN RESISTANCE

Eating foods that keep blood sugar levels stable is key to preventing or reversing insulin resistance. To further help your cause, take these steps.

**exercise** Even if you don't lose weight, exercising reduces insulin resistance. In one study, spending 30 minutes on a stationary bike three or four times a week cut insulin levels by 20 percent while lowering blood sugar levels by 13 percent—enough to take someone from "prediabetes" to "normal."

**cut calories** Simply eating less, even before you lose any weight, can improve insulin sensitivity and reduce levels of circulating insulin (your body needs less insulin if it's more sensitive to it). In one study of sedentary men and women, eating 25 percent fewer calories than they were used to over six months resulted in significantly lower fasting insulin levels. Other studies have found that cutting calories improves insulin sensitivity.

**get enough sleep** Missing out on a full night's sleep increases insulin resistance, possibly by disturbing hormone balance. Doing so for years may increase the risk of developing diabetes. In a recent study of men, those who slept less than 6 hours a night were twice as likely to develop diabetes over the following 15 years compared to men who got about 7 hours a night. (Those who got more than 8 hours a night were also at higher risk.)

# —do you have metabolic syndrome?

quiz

Metabolic syndrome is a cluster of risk factors that often occur together and increase your risk of diabetes and heart disease. The U.S. National Institute of Health's National Cholesterol Education Program defines it by looking at five measurements, four of which any doctor can test you to determine (the first one, waist size, you can find yourself).

## Once you know your numbers, take this test.

○ **Waist size.** Check this box if yours is more than 40 inches (102 cm) for men or more than 35 inches (88 cm) for women.

○ **Triglycerides.** A normal level is below 150 mg/dL (1.70 mmol/L)*. Check this box if yours is 150 mg/dL (1.70 mmol/L) or higher.

○ **HDL cholesterol.** This is the "good" cholesterol, so a higher number is better. Check this box if yours is lower than 40 mg/dL (1.00 mmol/L) for men or 50 mg/dL (1.30 mmol/L) for women.

○ **Blood pressure.** A normal level is less than 120/80 mm/Hg. Check this box if yours is 130/85 mm/Hg or higher.

○ **Fasting blood glucose.** This is the level of blood sugar after you haven't eaten for 6 hours. A normal level is 70 to 100 mg/dL (4.0 to 5.5 mmol/L). Check this box if yours is 110 mg/dL (6.0 mmol/L) or higher.

## your score   Total **how many boxes** you checked, then find your results here.

0   Congratulations; you have no signs of metabolic syndrome. Keep up the good work.

1   You don't have metabolic syndrome, but each of these is an independent risk factor for heart disease, so you should still take action.

2   You don't have metabolic syndrome, but these risk factors intensify each other, so work with your doctor to remedy them.

3   You have metabolic syndrome. You are at increased risk of developing diabetes and heart disease in the years ahead, but you can reverse the trend by losing weight, getting more exercise, and eating better. Talk with your doctor about ways to reduce your risk factors. The dietary approach outlined in this book is particularly important to you.

4   You have metabolic syndrome and then some—the more risk factors you have, the greater your overall risk. Get medical help and follow the dietary approach in this book.

5   You have metabolic syndrome and are at very high risk of developing diabetes and heart disease. Talk to your doctor and follow the recommendations in this book.

*Canada measures blood glucose, blood cholesterol, and triglycerides by millimole per liter (mmol/L). The milligram per deciliter (mg/dL) method is the U.S. standard.

If you have insulin resistance, your blood sugar levels may still be normal, although they may be on the high side after meals. You don't have diabetes—yet. But you are going in a direction that's putting a lot of stress on your blood sugar control system, and you're doing some damage along the way.

The extra insulin your body has to churn out can raise blood pressure, cause cholesterol problems, and even make it easier for certain cancers to grow. It also paves the way for weight gain. And here's a real scare: There's growing evidence that the brain itself can become insulin resistant, which impairs the function of nerves and leads to the buildup of toxic deposits, increasing the risk of dementia, including Alzheimer's disease.

And of course, insulin resistance increases the risk of diabetes. High blood sugar and extra insulin can damage the beta cells in the pancreas—the ones that make insulin—so they become fatigued or die off. When that happens, you have diabetes.

Insulin resistance starts slowly, furtively, silently. It has no symptoms. But once you develop it, it's easier to become even *more* insulin resistant. In a vicious cycle, the more insulin your body has to produce to keep blood sugar down, the more insulin resistant you become—unless you do something to reverse the trend. Fortunately, changing your eating style to include more of the slow-acting foods in this book is one of the biggest keys to preventing or reversing the condition. (For other ways, see "Fighting Insulin Resistance" on page 17.)

## Metabolic Syndrome: The Kitchen Sink of Conditions

Insulin resistance on its own can be dangerous, as you've just discovered. But there's worse news: If you have it, you may also have a host of related problems that tend to cluster together like birds on a telephone wire. Each of these problems on its own raises your risk of heart disease, but if you have three or more of them, your risk is double what it would be if you had only one. You're practically a heart attack waiting to happen, *even if your levels of "bad" LDL cholesterol are normal.*

This cluster of problems is known as metabolic syndrome. If you have this condition, you're also an excellent candidate for diabetes, even if your blood sugar levels aren't high yet. Indeed, 85 percent of people with type 2 diabetes have metabolic syndrome.

Metabolic syndrome is incredibly common here, affecting about one in four adults. Anyone can develop it, but you're much more likely to get it as you get older. In one large study of men and women age 50 and older, 44 percent had it. If you're carrying extra pounds, you're even more likely to have it.

Getting older, gaining weight, and being sedentary all contribute to the syndrome, but in many ways, this is a condition that you eat your way into. Diets low in fiber, high in calories, full of saturated fat, and loaded with foods that boost blood sugar quickly all contribute. In the Framingham Heart Study, one of the longest and largest studies of diet and disease, people whose diets tended to send blood sugar the highest after meals were 40 percent more likely to have metabolic syndrome than those who usually ate foods like the ones in this book.

According to the U.S. National Institute of Health's National Cholesterol Education Program, you have the syndrome if you have three or more of these problems.

**Belly fat**. A big belly isn't just somewhere you've put on extra weight. From your body's

> If you have **metabolic syndrome,** you're an excellent candidate for **DIABETES,** even if your blood sugar levels aren't high yet.

standpoint, fat around the middle is a very different kind of fat than, say, fat on your thighs. It's easier for this kind of fat to get into the bloodstream, where it can wreak havoc and increase the risk of heart disease. Indeed, researchers now suspect a large waist may be a better marker for heart disease risk than being overweight or obese in general.

**High triglyceride levels.** These fats are stored in the blood, ready to be broken down for energy. Even a mild elevation can increase your risk of heart disease.

**Low HDL cholesterol levels.** You've probably heard a lot of talk about "good" HDL cholesterol. It's the kind your body uses to pull "bad" LDL cholesterol out of the blood and transport it back to the liver, where it's broken down. Levels of HDL are often low in people with metabolic syndrome.

**High blood pressure.** Blood pressure is also often elevated in metabolic syndrome. It may not be high enough for your doctor to diagnose you as having high blood pressure, but along with the other factors, it's bad for your heart.

# —do you have prediabetes?

*quiz*

Only a blood glucose test can tell for sure. If your fasting blood glucose level is between 100 and 125 mg/dL (5.5 and 7.0 mmol/L), you have prediabetes. (Some doctors prefer a different test, given after you've had a sugar-rich drink.)

## Should you ask your doctor to test you?
*Here's how to decide.*

○ If you're **45 or older,** consider being tested.

○ If you're **45 or older and overweight,** it's strongly recommended that you be tested.

○ If you're **younger than 45 and overweight,** consider being tested if you also have one or more of these risk factors.

- You have a parent, brother, or sister with diabetes.

- Your ancestry is African, Asian, Native American, Native Canadian, Pacific Island, or Spanish.

- You're a mom who has had at least one baby weighing 9 pounds (4 kg) or more at birth, or you had gestational diabetes when you were pregnant.

- Your blood pressure is 140/90 mm/Hg or higher, or you've been told you have high blood pressure.

- Your cholesterol levels aren't normal: Your HDL cholesterol is 35 mg/dL (0.90 mmol/L) or lower, or your triglycerides are 250 mg/dL (2.80 mmol/L) or higher.

- You are fairly inactive, or you exercise less than three times a week.

*Some of these numbers, such as those for blood pressure and HDL, are different from those in the quiz for metabolic syndrome. One reason is that borderline risk factors become more significant when they're combined, as they are in metabolic syndrome.*

**High fasting glucose levels**. Your blood sugar may not be high enough to qualify you as having diabetes, but it still increases your risk of developing both diabetes and heart disease. The cause is insulin resistance.

## Prediabetes

Even if you have insulin resistance and metabolic syndrome, a test of your blood sugar in a doctor's office may show perfectly normal levels. For a while—for years, really—your body may be able to cope with too much blood sugar after meals by pumping out extra insulin.

In some people, though, the insulin-producing beta cells in the pancreas just can't keep up. They become less effective (*exhausted* is the word doctors use), and some of them die. Then your body just can't make enough insulin to keep blood sugar levels under control.

Your blood sugar may be a little high when you wake up in the morning. A normal level after a fast, that is, after 6 hours of not eating anything, is between 70 and 100 milligrams (mg)

# quiz

## —do you have diabetes?

If your blood sugar level after not eating for 6 hours (fasting blood glucose level) is 126 mg/dL (7.0 mmol/L) or higher, you have diabetes. Ideally, you would have been tested when you showed any of the risk factors for prediabetes (see "Do You Have Prediabetes?" on the preceding page), but many people don't find out they have diabetes until they start to have symptoms. That's unfortunate, because even though diabetes may cause no symptoms for years, it's increasing your risk of heart disease, blindness, and nerve problems. The sooner you get your blood sugar levels under control, the better your chances of avoiding these complications.

See your doctor at once if you have any of these symptoms.

○ Increased thirst

○ Increased hunger

○ Fatigue

○ Increased urination, especially at night

○ Weight loss without dieting

○ Blurred vision

○ Sores that don't heal

of glucose for every 10th of a liter (dL) of blood/ 4.0 to 5.5 millimoles (mmol) of glucose for every liter (L) of blood. If yours is between 100 and 125 mg/dL (5.5 and 7.0 mmol/L), you have prediabetes. You don't have full-blown diabetes yet, but you're on the train that takes you there.

Your chances of developing diabetes are very high over the next few years—but you can still get off the train. That was proven in a major study, called the Diabetes Prevention Program, of more than 3,000 men and women in 27 U.S. medical centers. Their ages ranged from 25 to 85, with an average of 51. All were obese. All had prediabetes. About 11 percent of those in the study who did nothing to change their lifestyles went on to develop diabetes in *each year* of the three-year study. That is, about a third got diabetes.

Those who switched to healthier diets and lost weight, however, didn't suffer the same fate. Over three years, they started walking about 30 minutes a day, ate healthier meals, and lost about 15 pounds (7 kg) each. Although some did develop diabetes, there was a 58 percent reduction in the overall incidence of the disease.

## Diabetes

If insulin resistance has damaged your pancreas so much that you have prediabetes, and you do nothing to change your lifestyle, it's almost inevitable that you will develop diabetes. Your beta cells are exhausted and just can't produce nearly enough insulin to do their job. Your blood sugar levels are above 125 mg/dL (7.0 mmol/L) even when you wake up in the morning.

The train may have left the station, but you can still get off at the next stop. Your diet is an essential part of your treatment plan. You'll work with your doctor to take the right medication to improve your insulin sensitivity and insulin production. Losing weight, exercising, and choosing foods that are gentle to your blood sugar levels are key to the effectiveness of those medications.

Take this book to your doctor or nutritionist and discuss how to work our recommendations into your lifestyle plan. Working with your doctor, you may be able to reduce the medications you take. In some cases, under medical supervision, you may be able to stop taking them entirely.

# The Magic Foods Solution

The nation's secret health crisis—insulin resistance and the closely related threats of diabetes, heart disease, and other health problems—is a secret no more. The way we've been eating affects our moods, our appetite, our weight, and, in the end, our longevity. But once you know what to do, you can make changes without a lot of fuss that will help you feel better and be healthier in the next 20 minutes and the next 20 years.

*Magic Foods for Better Blood Sugar* isn't a radical diet. It doesn't turn basic nutrition upside down. You'll find many of the same building blocks of a healthy diet here that you've heard about for decades: whole grains, fruits and vegetables, nuts, seeds, beans, eggs, lean meats and poultry, seafood, and low-fat dairy products. But we've improved this time-honored advice to help you keep your blood sugar in balance before, during, and after each meal. And you'll do it with the Magic foods you'll discover in Part 2, the meal makeovers you'll discover in Part 3, and the recipes and meal plans you'll find in Part 4.

The differences between the Magic Foods approach and a basic healthy diet are subtle but powerful. Whether you're young or not so young, thin or not so thin, with normal blood sugar levels or high ones; whether you are insulin resistant or not; and indeed, whether you have diabetes or not, this way of eating can make all the difference in the world to your health. Read on to learn more.

# chapter 2

# THE hiddenEFFECTS OF food

The **glycemic load** is a more powerful factor in keeping you **healthy** than the amount of carbohydrate— or fat—you eat.

Now you're in on the secret: Most of us are damaging our health by eating too many foods that send our blood sugar soaring. Besides contributing to diabetes and other serious illnesses over the long haul, meals loaded with these foods also leave you tired, grumpy, and hungry again in no time after you eat them. Other foods barely move the blood sugar needle or move it gradually, keeping you feeling full and energized.

Unfortunately, foods don't come with labels explaining which is which. After reading this chapter, though, you'll know how to tell the difference.

In the end, it's as simple as choosing pasta over rice, baked beans instead of mashed potatoes, oil-and-vinegar dressing instead of Thousand Island, and other easy fixes. Read on to discover what makes these foods Magic.

First, we'll talk about the three so-called macronutrients in food—carbohydrate, fat, and protein—from which we get almost all of our calories, and we'll tell you how they affect your blood sugar. Then we'll talk about two "magic" food components you can use for amazingly effective blood sugar control: soluble fiber and acetic acid, found in sour foods.

# Carbohydrate

We'll reveal the main plot twist right now: Carbohydrates are the foods that raise blood sugar. Plain and simple, right? The trouble is, not all carb foods are created equal.

Carbohydrates are actually found in most foods except fats and oils, meats, poultry, and fish. But of course, some foods contain more carbs than others. Beans are about one-fourth protein and three-fourths carbohydrate. Rice, on the other hand, is more than 90 percent carbohydrate. Whole milk contains all three macronutrients: fat, protein, and carbohydrate.

It's the quantity of carbohydrate in foods (and of course, how much of the food you eat) that primarily affects blood sugar, but the type of carbohydrate also has an effect.

## Introducing the Glycemic Index and Glycemic Load

To figure out which carbs are best and worst for blood sugar, scientists had to do some serious detective work. First, they needed to come up with a way to measure a food's effect on blood sugar.

Nutrition scientist David Jenkins, M.D., Ph.D., developed a system called the glycemic index (GI) back in 1981 (the prefix *glyc-* means "sugar"). He had volunteers eat different foods, all containing 50 grams of carbohydrate. Then he measured the volunteers' blood sugar over the following 2 hours to see how high it went.

As a control he used pure glucose, the form of sugar that's identical to blood sugar—your body converts glucose very quickly to blood sugar—and assigned it the number 100 on his new index.

The glycemic index opened a lot of eyes. Almost everyone had assumed that table sugar would be the worst offender, much worse than the "complex carbohydrates" found in starchy staples such as rice and bread. But this didn't always prove true. Some starchy foods, like potatoes and cornflakes, ranked very high on the index, raising blood sugar nearly as much as pure glucose. That's why you won't see these foods in our list of Magic foods.

The higher the **glycemic load** in the diet, the greater the incidence of obesity, diabetes, heart disease, and cancer.

### WHERE THE GLYCEMIC INDEX FELL SHORT

Something was wrong, however. Some of the results pointed fingers at healthy foods, such as carrots and strawberries. Watermelon was just about off the top of the GI chart. But no one ever gained weight from eating carrots, nor do carrots, in the real world, raise blood sugar. What was the GI missing?

The GI measured the effects of a standard amount of carbohydrate: 50 grams, or about 1 1/2 ounces. But you'd be awfully hard-pressed to eat enough carrots—seven or eight large ones—to get 50 grams of carbohydrate. The same holds true for most other vegetables and fruits. They're full of water, so there's not much room in them for carbohydrate. Bread, on the other hand, is crammed with carbohydrate. You get 50 grams by eating just one slice.

To solve the problem, scientists came up with a different measurement: the glycemic load (GL). It takes into account not only the *type* of carbohydrate in the food but also the *amount* of carbohydrate you would eat in a standard serving. (To get a bit technical, a food's GL is the GI multiplied by the amount of carbohydrate in one serving.)

This made more sense. By this criterion, carrots, strawberries, and other low-calorie foods are clearly good to eat—they all have low GL values, since the amount of carbohydrate they contain is low.

The GL has turned out to be a powerful way to think about not just individual foods but also whole meals and even entire diets. When scientists looked at the GL of typical diets in different populations, they found that the higher the GL, the greater the incidence of obesity, diabetes, heart disease, and cancer. You may remember a study we mentioned in Chapter 1 in which men who ate the most sugar-boosting foods were 40 percent more likely to get diabetes. That's GL we were talking about. We also talked about the Nurses' Health Study finding that women were twice as likely to develop heart disease over 10 years if they ate more sugar-boosting foods. Again, the GL. The converse is also true: The lower the GL of your diet, the more likely you are to keep your weight under control and stay free of chronic disease.

When it comes to eating right, controlling weight, and preventing disease, the GL is a heavy hitter. It's a more powerful factor in keeping you healthy than the amount of carbohydrate—or fat—you eat.

## What Makes Some Carbs Better than Others

Why would one high-carb food have a different GL than another? Why does white rice, for instance, have a higher GL than, say, honey? It has to do with the way nature constructed them.

Carbohydrates consist of starches and sugars. Starch—think of starchy foods like beans and potatoes—is made up of sugar molecules bound together in long chains. When you eat a carbohydrate-rich food, your body converts those starches and sugars into glucose, or blood sugar. Some starches, like those in white rice, are extremely easy for the body to convert, and therefore blood sugar levels rise like a hot temper after you eat them. Others, like those in beans, take a lot more work to break down, so blood sugar levels simmer rather than explode.

Four factors determine how fast the body breaks down carbohydrate.

**CARB DENSITY COUNTS**

The glycemic load takes into account how much carbohydrate a serving of food contains. The amount in one bagel equals the amount in five helpings of watermelon.

### 55 grams of carbohydrate

1 bagel          =          5 cups watermelon

### THE TYPE OF STARCH—OR WHY TO AVOID STICKY RICE

Remember, starches are made of sugar molecules chained together. Some chains have straight edges, while others are branched. The straight-edged type, called amylose, is harder for your body to break down and turn into blood sugar. The branched type, called amylopectin, is much easier to break down because there are so many places for the enzymes that break down starch to get at it. Think of a tree with lots of branches—there are a lot more spots for birds to land on it compared to a simple post.

White potatoes are very high in amylopectin, the branched kind of sugar chain, which is why they raise your blood sugar in a jiffy. Peas and lentils are high in amylose, the straight kind, so they're converted to blood sugar at a snail's pace.

The more amylose a food contains, the slower it will be digested and converted into blood sugar. Take rice, for instance. Some types contain more amylose than others. In general, the softer and stickier the rice is after cooking, the lower its amylose content; this is why "sticky rice" is dastardly to your blood sugar. The firmer the rice, the higher the amylose and the harder it is for your body to turn into blood sugar quickly—making brown rice a better choice. Some genetic variants of rice—such as some sold in Australia, for example—are particularly high in amylose (as much as 25 percent), but unfortunately, most of the rice we eat is low in amylose and thus has a high GL.

### THE TYPE OF SUGAR—OR WHY FRUIT IS A-OKAY

Sugar is the molecule that makes up carbohydrates, but there is more than one kind. There's table sugar (sucrose) as well as the kind found in fruits and grains (fructose), the kind in milk (lactose), and the kind in malted barley (maltose). The sugar in milk and fruit tends to be absorbed more slowly than other sugars since it needs to be converted into glucose by the liver first, which is why these foods are gentle to your blood sugar.

Ironically, table sugar, which is half fructose and half glucose, is turned into blood sugar more slowly than some starches, like bread or potatoes. That doesn't make sugar good for you, of course. One reason is that fructose, especially in the amounts contained in packaged foods loaded with high-fructose corn syrup, raise triglycerides, blood fats that increase the risk of heart attack. (Fruit, by contrast, contains a little fructose plus plenty of water, fiber, and nutrients.) The other reason is that sugar packs a lot of carbohydrate calories in a small package.

**NOT ALL STARCHES ARE EQUAL**

Potatoes raise blood sugar fast because the type of starch they contain is easily broken down. Peas contain a type of starch that's broken down much more slowly.

potato (amylopectin)

peas (amylose)

That's why one 32-ounce (1-liter) cola drink contains a whopping 400 calories—and will send your blood sugar soaring.

## HEAT—OR WHY NOT TO OVERCOOK RICE OR PASTA

All starch, whether it's made of straight or branched chains, is composed of crystals, which don't dissolve in cold water. Think of a grain of rice or a piece of raw potato—put it in water and it stays the same. But heat breaks down those crystals so the starch can dissolve in water—a little like a snowflake that comes in from the cold. When you cook a starchy food, it absorbs water and becomes easier to digest.

The more overcooked rice or pasta is, the faster it makes your blood sugar rise. When starch is heated and then cooled, it can return, in part, to its crystal form; that's why hot potatoes have a high GL, while potato salad's is slightly lower. Just make it with olive oil instead of mayo to keep it healthier.

## PROCESSING—OR WHY TO AVOID WHITE FLOUR

Have you ever noticed that some wheat breads are as smooth as white bread, while others have crunchy kernels in them? Those kernels take a long time for your body to break down. So do any whole, intact grains, such as wheatberries (small kernels of wheat, delicious in salads).

Modern commercial flour, on the other hand—especially white flour—is extremely easy for the body to turn into blood sugar, which is why we suggest throughout this book that you choose whole grains that are still intact and foods such as beans, lentils, and wheatberries instead of those made from white flour. (Unfortunately, we're surrounded by white-flour foods. You'll need to make a conscious effort to cut back.)

Until the 19th century, the main way to turn grain into flour was to grind it between stones, sometimes powered by a water wheel. Making very fine flour took a lot of work, and it was

## pasta
### GETS A PASSING GRADE

Bread, even many whole wheat breads, can raise your blood sugar pretty quickly. Yet pasta, even if it's made from white flour, has a much lower GL. How can that be?

Imagine putting cooked pasta and a piece of bread in a bowl of water. The bread will fall apart, but the pasta won't. That's because in pasta dough, the starch granules get trapped in a network of protein molecules, so it takes more work—and more time—to get at them. That's why **pasta releases its carbs much more slowly than potatoes** or most breads do, especially if it's served al dente (slightly undercooked). Similarly, gnocchi, a pasta-like product made from durum wheat and potato flour, has a lower GL than potatoes. You'll find pastas, especially whole wheat pastas and protein-enriched pastas, on our list of Magic foods in Part 2.

Pasta is particularly good for you if you eat it as the southern Italians do: **cooked al dente,** prepared with olive oil and beans or vegetables, served in modest portions, and followed by a piece of fish or lean meat and perhaps a side of garlicky greens and fruit for dessert. A huge bowl of overcooked pasta with a butter or cream sauce is not what the doctor ordered.

available only in small amounts to the rich. Then high-speed, high-heat steel rollers, which make very fine flour quickly and inexpensively, were invented, almost instantly transforming our diets into blood sugar nightmares.

Modern manufacturing also allows grains to be turned into highly processed forms such as cornflakes or puffed corn snacks, which tend to have higher GLs than grains left intact, like popcorn, or those milled in an old-fashioned manner, like coarse, stone-ground whole wheat flour used in stone-ground wheat bread.

In a study, folks who ate a **high-protein** diet consumed 25 percent **FEWER** calories than those in the high-carb group.

# Protein

Unlike carbohydrate, protein doesn't raise blood sugar. Your body breaks it down into amino acids, which it uses as building blocks for muscles as well as many compounds such as neurotransmitters, the brain's chemical messengers. Unless you're on a diet that has no carbs, your body won't even try to convert protein into blood sugar.

That's why you'll find protein foods such as fish, chicken, beef, pork, soy, milk, eggs, and cheese on our list of Magic foods. If you substitute calories from one of these foods for some of your carbohydrate calories, your blood sugar will thank you. For instance, if you add shrimp to a rice dish, you'll eat less rice, and the meal will have less impact on your blood sugar.

While we're fans of protein, we're not suggesting a diet of fatty bacon, greasy burgers, and the like. These are packed with saturated fat, and as you'll read a bit later, saturated fat increases insulin resistance, which is bad for your blood sugar. Lean protein foods, like fat-free milk and

chicken breast without the skin, are far better choices because they contain fewer calories and less saturated fat. Fish and shellfish are definitely on the menu because they're not only low in saturated fat but also high in heart-healthy omega-3 fatty acids. Beans, peas, and lentils, all high in protein, have the added plus of being rich in fiber.

We're also not suggesting an extremely high protein, low carb diet. You'll find out why in the next chapter.

## More Pluses for Protein

There are also other benefits to protein. Some of the compounds our bodies make from protein's amino acids help regulate blood sugar, so including protein in a meal means your body will handle the carbohydrates in that meal more efficiently. That's one reason we want you to include a source of protein with every meal. Another reason: Your body takes a while to break down the protein in the foods you eat, and this slows the digestion of the whole meal, including the carbs it contains, making for a slower rise in blood sugar.

In one recent study, healthy volunteers ate a starchy breakfast (white bread) followed by a starchy lunch (mashed potatoes and meatballs). On some days, however, they got extra protein in the form of whey (dairy protein). On days when they ate more protein, their blood sugar levels were more than 50 percent lower in the following 2 hours than on days when they ate mostly carbs. Another study, of people with diabetes, found that adding whey reduced their blood sugar response by 21 percent over the following 2 hours.

Protein, especially the kind found in milk, also stimulates the pancreas to produce insulin. That may not sound like a good idea since having high levels of insulin over long periods of time is unhealthy. But the earlier your body makes insulin in response to a rise in blood sugar, the less insulin it may need to make—and the less likely you are to become insulin resistant.

## Protein and Weight Loss

Eating more protein-rich foods should even help you lose weight. Protein puts a damper on hunger, expanding the time between when you eat and when your stomach starts rumbling again. Research proves it. In a six-day study, one group of volunteers went on a low-GI, high-protein diet. The other group followed a low-protein, high-carb diet. Both groups were allowed to eat as much as they wanted—and the folks who ate the high-protein diet consumed 25 percent fewer calories than those in the high-carb group. In a longer study, lasting six months, high-protein dieters lost more weight than high-carb dieters. They ate less because they felt fuller.

Getting enough protein can also help keep your metabolism running at full speed. Usually, when you really cut back on calories—especially if you go on a very low carb diet—your body resorts to breaking down muscle tissue for energy. But muscle tissue burns up a lot of calories even when you're not flexing a thing, so breaking it down slows your metabolism. Eating plenty of protein helps your body keep its muscle tissue.

In diet studies, people on moderately high protein diets lost more body fat and less muscle. A moderately high protein diet might get as much as 30 percent of its calories from protein, rather than the 15 to 20 percent most people get. Twenty to 30 percent is the protein intake we recommend.

## Fat

Fat has gotten a bad rap, to the point where most people think the less fat you eat, the better. Research is proving that this just isn't true.

During the height of the low-fat craze, people loaded up on carbohydrates like fat-free chips and low-fat cookies—foods laden with fast-acting carbohydrates—thinking they were doing themselves good. What a mistake! They were actually wreaking havoc on their blood sugar and eating just as many calories in the bargain.

The fact is, fat's no demon. Some fats are positively good for you and your blood sugar, and they absolutely belong in your diet.

Like protein, fat doesn't raise blood sugar, so swapping carb-rich foods such as pretzels for fat-rich foods such as nuts can be an excellent trade.

Also like protein, fat takes a while to digest. Because it slows the rate at which food leaves

**THE POWER OF PROTEIN**

Adding protein to a carbohydrate dish lowers the glycemic load of the dish—assuming you eat the same amount—because you end up eating less carbohydrate. Protein itself also helps steady blood sugar.

LOWER GL

fried rice          shrimp-fried rice

your stomach, it can blunt the blood sugar effect of a whole meal, even if that meal includes carbs. Tossing your salad with olive oil or drizzling some on your pasta, adding some nuts to your rice, broiling fatty fish for dinner, or using slices of ripe avocado in your sandwich won't magically lower your blood sugar, but it will help.

## Good Fat, Bad Fat

Notice that we've talked about nuts, oils, and fish instead of other fat sources such as burgers or butter. It's true that adding fat lowers the GL of a starchy food, but adding butter or sour cream to a heap of mashed potatoes doesn't make it healthy. Quite the contrary.

Butter, which comes from cow's milk, is an animal food, and as with many animal foods, most of the fat it contains is saturated. That's the kind that clogs arteries. It's also bad for blood sugar. In both animal and human studies, a diet high in saturated fat has been shown to trigger insulin resistance, which it does in many ways. Saturated fat increases inflammation, which is toxic to cells, including those that handle glucose. It also makes cell membranes less fluid, so the insulin receptors there are less responsive to insulin; the hormone bounces off them like water off a drum rather than sticking to them.

It's clear that people who eat the most saturated fat are at the highest risk of developing insulin resistance and metabolic syndrome. And as you read in Chapter 1, these conditions increase your risk of heart disease and diabetes.

The trick, then, is to avoid the worst of the "bad" fat foods, like marbled steak, high-fat lunchmeats, butter, whole milk, full-fat cheeses, and ice cream, and choose instead lean cuts of meat and poultry, fat-free or 1% milk, low-fat cheese, and lean lunchmeats such as turkey, chicken, and extra-lean roast beef.

Even better, embrace unsaturated fats, which can actually *improve* insulin sensitivity, thus benefiting your blood sugar. These fats come mainly from plants—think avocados, nuts and seeds, olives, and olive and canola oil—and fish and seafood. The Mediterranean diet, one of the healthiest diets in the world, gets a moderately high 30 to 35 percent of its calories from fat, mostly the unsaturated kind. This is the fat ceiling we recommend.

## Protecting Your Heart

"Good" fats are also good for your heart. Swapping that cheeseburger for seafood or that butter for peanut butter (a good source of unsaturated fat) lowers your "bad" LDL cholesterol while leaving "good" HDL cholesterol alone. In fact, eating just a handful of nuts a few times a week can slash your risk of getting heart disease by 25 percent.

So can eating fish a few times a week. Seafood contains omega-3 fatty acids, which do a world of good for your heart by lowering triglycerides, helping prevent blood clots, reducing inflammation, and promoting normal heart rhythm. Eating just two servings of fish—especially fatty fish such as salmon or mackerel—a week can reduce your risk of heart disease by a third or more.

## Losing Weight

You'd think that if you want to lose weight, you should cut way back on fat, which is high in calories. Pretty obvious, right? Surprisingly, recent research has shown it's not necessarily true. A moderate-fat diet can be every bit as effective as a low-fat diet in helping you lose weight—if you choose mostly beneficial fats.

A moderate-fat **diet** can be every bit as effective as a low-fat diet in helping you **LOSE** weight.

A bit of fat also makes meals more satisfying, which can make it easier to stick to a healthy eating plan over the long haul. Try to go too low fat, and you'll most likely throw in the towel at some point, probably sooner rather than later. In one study of overweight men and women, those on a moderate-fat diet lost about 9 pounds (4 kg) over 18 months, while those on a low-fat diet actually wound up *gaining* more than 6 pounds (3 kg). One key reason was dieting fatigue: Only 20 percent of those on the low-fat diet were still actively participating by the end of the study, while 54 percent of those on the moderate-fat diet were still at it.

# Lower Blood Sugar with Soluble Fiber

Carbs, protein, and fat are all macronutrients—nutrients that provide the vast majority of our calories. Fiber doesn't count because it isn't digested by the body, so it provides not a single calorie. Nevertheless, it's an extremely important element in a Magic diet.

There are two types of fiber: soluble and insoluble. Soluble fiber is the kind that dissolves in water. It's found in oats, barley, beans, and some fruits and vegetables. Insoluble fiber is found mostly in whole wheat and some fruits and vegetables. Both types are very good for you, but only soluble fiber will help lower your blood sugar—in a big way.

How big? Researchers at a USDA Diet and Human Performance Laboratory tested oatmeal and barley (which is even richer in soluble fiber than oatmeal) on overweight middle-aged women. On days when the women ate oatmeal for breakfast, their blood sugar levels over the following 3 hours were about 30 percent lower than when they ate a sugar-laden pudding. On days when they ate barley cereal, it was about 60 percent lower.

## BEST FOODS FOR SOLUBLE fiber

Here you'll find the amount of soluble fiber per serving of various foods. Remember, you're aiming for about 10 grams a day.

### grains (1/2 cup cooked)

| | |
|---|---|
| Barley | 1 g |
| Oats | 1 g |

### beans and peas (1/2 cup cooked)

| | |
|---|---|
| Black beans | 2 g |
| Great Northern beans | 1.5 g |
| Kidney beans | 3 g |
| Lima beans | 3.5 g |
| Navy beans | 2 g |
| Pinto beans | 2 g |
| Black-eyed peas | 1 g |
| Chickpeas | 1 g |

### vegetables (1/2 cup cooked)

| | |
|---|---|
| Broccoli | 1 g |
| Brussels sprouts | 3 g |
| Carrots | 1 g |

### fruit (1 medium fruit, except where noted)

| | |
|---|---|
| Apple | 1 g |
| Blackberries (1/2 cup) | 1 g |
| Grapefruit | 2 g |
| Orange | 2 g |
| Pear | 2 g |
| Prunes (1/4 cup) | 1.5 g |

How does soluble fiber work its magic? When it mixes with water, it forms a gum. Think of oatmeal; you can pick out the grains or flakes when it's dry, but once you cook it, it's one big mush. This gooey gum forms a barrier between the digestive enzymes in your stomach and the starch molecules in food—not just in the oatmeal but also in the toast you ate with it. Thus, it takes longer for your body to convert the whole meal into blood sugar.

Eating more foods rich in soluble fiber is a key strategy for lowering your blood sugar after meals. It will also improve your health in other ways. Oatmeal is famous by now for lowering cholesterol, but it may lower high levels of triglycerides and reduce blood pressure as well. There's even a health claim allowed on oatmeal packaging: "Eating 3 grams of soluble fiber from oatmeal in a diet low in saturated fat and cholesterol may reduce the risk of heart disease." (About 1 1/2 cups of cooked oatmeal supplies 3 grams.) Lots of other foods are also rich in soluble fiber (see "Best Foods for Soluble Fiber" on page 31).

Nutrition experts tell us to aim for at least 20 grams of total fiber a day, both insoluble and soluble. A good goal for soluble fiber is 10 grams. Sound like a hard goal to reach? Here are some foods you might eat in a typical day that would add up to more than 10 grams.

*Breakfast:* A cup of cooked oatmeal with a chopped medium apple; soluble fiber: 3 grams.

*Lunch:* Add a side dish of black beans (1/2 cup); soluble fiber: 2 grams.

*Dinner:* Add a side dish of roasted Brussels sprouts (about 1 cup); soluble fiber: 6 grams.

In case you're counting, that's 11 grams. Not surprisingly, many of these fiber-rich foods also

Eating more foods rich in soluble **fiber** is a key strategy for lowering your blood sugar after meals.

have low GLs, so they can help lower the GL of a meal if you use them to replace other carbs. For instance, if you ate a combination of 1/2 cup of rice and 1/2 cup of beans instead of 1 cup of rice, you'd drop the GL by almost half.

# Pucker Power

Wouldn't it be terrific if there were a simple ingredient you could add to your meals that would act like an anchor, keeping blood sugar from rising too high? As it turns out, there is. It's acetic acid, the sour-tasting compound that gives that characteristic tang to vinegar, pickles, and sourdough bread.

The effect can be quite dramatic. In one small study, people who ate a buttered 3-ounce (85-g) bagel and orange juice—a high-GL breakfast— saw their blood sugar shoot up in the next hour. But when they also drank about a tablespoon of apple cider vinegar (with artificial sweetener added to improve the taste), their blood sugar levels after the meal were 50 percent lower! A similar 50 percent reduction in blood sugar happened when they had the vinegar along with a chicken-and-rice meal.

How does acetic acid make it happen? Scientists aren't sure, but they do know that it interferes with the enzymes that break apart the chemical bonds in starches and the kinds of sugars found in table sugar and milk. This means it takes your body longer to break down those foods into blood sugar. Other researchers believe acetic acid keeps foods in the stomach longer so they aren't digested as quickly. Acetic acid may also speed up the rate at which glucose is moved out of the bloodstream and into muscle cells for storage.

No matter how it works, it does, and taking advantage of it is as easy as adding vinegar to salads and other foods and having a pickle with your sandwich at lunchtime. Lemon juice also has "pucker power" and seems to help control blood sugar. You'll read more about vinegar, lemon juice, and sourdough bread in Part 2.

# The Secrets of a Magic Diet

Now you understand why rice raises blood sugar fast while oatmeal raises it more slowly and chicken doesn't raise it at all. And why the soluble fiber in beans and the acetic acid in vinegar help keep your blood sugar steady. If you don't feel like remembering the details, don't. You don't need to. In Chapter 4, we'll reveal the Seven Secrets of Magic Eating, and if you follow these rules, you'll be eating for better blood sugar.

You don't even need to bother with the exact GL numbers of the foods you eat (although we do supply them for some common foods on pages 55-58). In this book, we've simply classified foods according to very low, low, medium, high, and very high GL. The foods you'll read about in Part 2 have very low, low, or medium GLs—part of what makes them Magic.

It's important to note that you don't always have to choose foods in the "low" category. Eating just one low-GL food in a meal in place of a high-GL food is enough to tame your blood sugar response to the whole meal. Also remember that a food's GL is based on a moderate portion; if you eat twice as much, the effect on your blood sugar will be twice as great. Of course, the converse is also true: If you eat 50 percent less of a starchy food, your blood sugar response will be 50 percent lower. In each Magic food entry in Part 2, you'll find out the size of an appropriate serving of that food. Keeping your portions under control is of course the best way to lose weight, whether or not you choose low-GL foods.

You'll learn much more about how to focus on Magic foods later in the book. First, in case you're tempted after reading this chapter to switch to a very low carb diet, let us explain why that's a bad idea.

## WHAT ABOUT wine?

Alcohol, in the right amounts, can benefit blood sugar. Moderate drinking—from one drink a few times a week up to one a day for women or two a day for men—is associated with lower fasting insulin levels, higher levels of "good" HDL cholesterol, smaller waist circumference, and lower triglycerides ... in other words, a lower risk of metabolic syndrome (see page 19).

It also lowers the risk of developing diabetes by between 33 and 56 percent, according to a comprehensive review of more than 30 studies. And if you have diabetes, it reduces your risk of developing heart disease by 34 to 55 percent.

Wine, especially red wine, may have extra benefits. It contains antioxidants that, in animal studies, help prevent insulin resistance. Wine is also acidic, so in theory, it should reduce the blood sugar effect of foods you eat. But beer is fine, too; despite what you may have heard, even regular beer is fairly low in carbohydrates.

The main benefits come from the alcohol itself, but don't forget the moderation part. People who have three or more drinks a day have a much higher risk of diabetes and heart disease. A drink is defined as a 12-ounce (341 ml) beer, 5 ounces (150 ml) of wine, or a 1.5-ounce (45 ml) shot of distilled spirits, such as vodka.

If you have diabetes, ask your doctor about drinking. Because alcohol lowers blood sugar, it could cause hypoglycemia.

# chapter 3

# WHY low-CARB DIETS AREN'T THE ANSWER

Many **low-carb** diets have turned out to be less effective, and less healthy, than originally claimed.

What raises blood sugar? The simple answer is carbohydrates. So why not just yank them out of your diet like weeds in your garden? Why not quash blood sugar by swearing off bread, pasta, rice, and cereal? Been there, done that. The low-carb craze is on the downswing, and that's a good thing because over the long haul, very low carb diets simply aren't good for you, as you'll discover in this chapter. That doesn't mean it's not smart to cut back on carbs—but don't go crazy.

When low-carb diets first became popular, they seemed to be a breath of fresh air after the low-fat (and high-carb) diets that preceded them. Remember low-fat cookies, low-fat snack cakes, and low-fat everything else? With low-carb diets, suddenly people could load up on bacon and still lose weight as long as they were willing to eat hamburgers without buns and pretty much give up sandwiches and spaghetti. People were amazed at how effective these diets could be. Weight loss could happen very quickly, sometimes within days. And amazingly, it often seemed to come with added health benefits, including lower cholesterol, blood pressure, and triglycerides (blood fats linked to heart attacks.)

The most extreme kind of low-carb diet was pioneered by the late Robert Atkins, M.D., whose first book, *Dr. Atkins' Diet Revolution*, came out in 1972. It promised quick and long-lasting weight loss and prevention of chronic disease, all while allowing high-fat steak and ice cream. Since then, other, more moderate low-carb diets have allowed small amounts of carbohydrate-rich foods, but they still cut out most grains as well as starchy vegetables and even fruit.

# The Downsides of These Diets

The Atkins diet and the many other low-carb diets that followed in its footsteps have turned out to be less effective, and less healthy, than originally claimed. Often, the weight returned, and as it did, problems such as high cholesterol and high blood pressure came back, too. Also, in the end, many people decided they didn't want to go through life without ever eating pasta again.

Let's look at what would happen if you followed one of the more extreme low-carb diets.

## You'll Feel Terrible

Low-carb diets usually begin with an "induction" phase that eliminates nearly every source of carbohydrate. Often, you'll consume as few as 20 grams of carbohydrate a day. That's less than 100 calories' worth—about what's in a small dinner roll. On a 1,200-calorie diet, that's only about 8 percent of your daily calories. By contrast, health experts recommend that we get between 45 and 65 percent of our calories from carbs.

When carbohydrate consumption falls below 100 grams, the body usually responds by burning

muscle tissue for the glycogen (stored glucose) it contains. When those glycogen stores start to run out, the body resorts to burning body fat. But that's a very inefficient, complicated way to produce blood sugar. The body tries to do it only when it absolutely has to (such as when it's starving)—and for good reason. Turning fat into blood sugar comes at a price in the form of by-products called ketones. They make your breath smell funny. They can also make you tired, lightheaded, headachy, and nauseated. Feeling lousy is certainly one way to dampen the appetite, but not one that most people would choose.

Burning fat for blood sugar produces **ketones,** which can make you tired, lightheaded, headachy, and nauseated.

With virtually no carbs in your system, you may even have trouble concentrating. According to the Institute of Medicine of the National Academy of Sciences, the human brain requires the equivalent of 130 grams of carbohydrate a day to function optimally—and that's a minimum.

## Your Health May Suffer

If you're overweight or obese, and you have insulin resistance—and especially if you have prediabetes or diabetes—cutting way back on carbohydrates can have immediate health benefits. Your blood sugar and insulin levels will go down, your triglycerides and blood pressure may fall, and your levels of "good" HDL cholesterol may rise.

But the low-carb diet will also wreak some havoc. When your body breaks down lean body mass—muscle—for energy, your metabolism slows because muscle tissue burns up a lot of calories. This may be one reason that the weight often comes back after you've been shunning carbs for a while.

The effects on your heart are also questionable. Especially if you switch to a high-saturated-fat diet, as people do when they start eating their fill of steak and bacon, your "bad" LDL cholesterol will go up. Levels of homocysteine, an amino acid that increases the risk of heart disease, may also rise if you eat a lot of meat and too few vegetables. And to get rid of the ketones produced when your body burns fat for energy, your kidneys need to work overtime, which raises your risk of kidney stones.

Ironically, low-carb diets may even interfere with insulin sensitivity; a certain amount of carbohydrate in your diet may be needed in order for the pancreas, which produces the insulin that keeps blood sugar in check, to work well.

## You'll Miss Out

It's not just that you'll feel deprived because you've had to give up bread, fruit, and all the rest. Your body will also be deprived of foods and nutrients that are essential for good health, including the following.

**Whole grains.** These protect against metabolic syndrome, diabetes, heart disease, stroke, and cancer.

**Fruits and vegetables.** Produce helps prevent heart disease, stroke, and some cancers. Most fruits and vegetables are very filling while providing few calories, so they can help you cut calories without deprivation. Indeed, the more fruits and vegetables people eat, studies show, the thinner they tend to be.

**Beans.** Rich in protein, complex carbohydrates, and B vitamins, beans have no saturated fat and lots of soluble fiber. They also contain plant chemicals that protect against heart disease and cancer.

**Low-fat dairy foods.** Sure, you can have butter and cream on a carb-restricted diet, but you won't get much calcium or protein from them. Fat-free and low-fat versions of milk and yogurt are excellent sources of those nutrients.

**Fiber.** Getting fiber from these foods (except dairy) helps reduce the risk of heart disease and diabetes. Beans and many fruits and vegetables are particularly rich in soluble fiber, which helps lower blood sugar, curbs hunger, and lowers LDL cholesterol.

**Vitamins, minerals, and health-protective plant chemicals.** Whole grains, for example, are rich in components such as lignans, which may protect against diabetes independently of their effects on blood sugar. And without fruits and vegetables, you'd be awfully hard-pressed to get enough vitamin C or other disease-fighting antioxidants.

## You'll Eat Too Much "Bad" Fat

The original Atkins diet became popular largely because it allowed people to eat foods forbidden on most other diets, such as cheeseburgers (without buns). More recently, the diet has been revised to include sources of healthier fats, such as fish and olive oil, and other low-carb diets have shied away from saturated fats as well. But in practice, once you stop eating bread, fruit, and beans, it's all too easy to eat too many fatty animal foods. After all, how many foods can you take out of your diet?

If you load up on saturated fats—the original Atkins diet got as much as 26 percent of its calories from saturated fat versus the 10 percent or less that experts recommend—it's bad for your health. Saturated fats are still the major culprits behind elevated LDL cholesterol. The latest revisions to the diet, to be fair, do emphasize lean poultry and seafood, but in practice, many people are attracted to this diet for the bacon and butter.

What's more, saturated fats also directly impair the body's ability to react to insulin, so following a low-carb, high-saturated-fat diet may help you lose weight in the short term, but it may also speed the development of insulin resistance. Eventually, that can lead to metabolic syndrome, diabetes, and heart disease.

## The Weight Will Come Back

Two major studies of low-carb diets, published in the *New England Journal of Medicine*, looked at obese men and women who stuck with either a low-carb, high-fat diet or a low-fat, high-carb diet. Both diets were low in calories.

In one study, which lasted six months, the low-carb diet seemed to win hands down. The people on it lost nearly 13 pounds (6 kg); the low-fat dieters shed just 4 pounds (2 kg). But the second study lasted six months longer, revealing a truth about low-carb diets: The results don't last. This study too found that the low-carb dieters lost more weight in the first six months, but in the second half of the year, the weight came roaring back. By the end of a year, there was no significant difference in weight loss between the two groups. This weight "snap-back" may be one reason that extremely low carb diets have fallen out of favor.

## Take the Good, Leave the Bad

The good news? Many of the weight-loss advantages of low-carb diets may have nothing at all to do with restricting carbohydrates. The main benefit may be due to the extra protein—and you can add protein to your diet even if you don't drastically cut carbs. As you discovered in Chapter 2, protein-rich foods can really help with weight control. One reason may be that protein stimulates the body to burn slightly more calories than carbohydrates or fats do.

The main reason, though, is that protein foods curb hunger better. When people eat protein-rich foods, they feel fuller longer, and when they diet, they consume fewer calories and lose more weight when they eat a lot of protein.

One recent study puts it in perspective. Researchers at the University of Washington School of Medicine in Seattle gave volunteers a diet that got 50 percent of its calories from carbohydrates. That's certainly not a low-carb diet, though it's not a high-carb diet either. It's actually a good goal, on par with what we suggest in this book.

To start, the volunteers got only 15 percent of their calories from protein and 35 percent from fat. That's about what most people get. Then they switched: Carbs stayed the same, but fat was decreased to 20 percent of calories, and protein was doubled to 30 percent. The participants were allowed to eat as much as they wanted—but they ate less. Over 14 weeks, they lost an average of 11 pounds (5 kg), including 8 pounds (3.5 kg) of body fat, thanks to the extra protein.

The main **BENEFIT** of low-carb diets may be due to the extra **protein** in them.

## More Protein, and Carbohydrates in Moderation

No matter how you slice it, we eat too many carbohydrates. We consume many more calories than we used to, and most of those extra calories come from extra carbs (so many chips and cookies!). Thus, it makes sense to cut back some on carbs. It also makes sense to choose lower-GL carbohydrate foods instead of "fast-acting" carbs that send your blood sugar soaring. These strategies are a big part of the Magic Foods approach to eating.

That approach, which we spell out in the next chapter, provides the benefits of a drastically low carb diet with none of the hazards. You'll get the blood sugar advantages, including lower insulin levels. By eating plenty of lean protein, you'll feel satisfied and less hungry. And by choosing "good" fats and limiting "bad" ones, you'll keep LDL cholesterol from rising and protect your heart in the process. You'll also discover a way of eating that you can enjoy—rather than endure—for the rest of your life.

# chapter 4

# A BREAKTHROUGH eating APPROACH

This is not a "diet" in the dieting sense. It's a **delicious,** practical, long-term strategy for healthy eating.

Now that you know how important it is to eat foods that help keep your blood sugar steady, you're probably wondering, "So what's for dinner?" We've given you some heavy hints already, but it's time to spell it all out so you know exactly how to eat the *Magic Foods* way—and can start doing it today. Get ready for the ultimate sugar-busting, health-enhancing diet. You'll feel so good, you'll never look back.

In this chapter, you'll discover the Seven Secrets of Magic Eating and how to put them to practical use. The great news is that it's easier than you may think. In fact, changing just a few of the foods you eat every day can help you feel more energized and prevent the chronic diseases that slow us all down as we age.

This is not a "diet" in the dieting sense. It's a delicious, practical, long-term strategy for healthy eating, one that will not only help stabilize your blood sugar but also make it easier to leave that extra weight behind. The best part is that you can start by making as many or as few changes to your current diet as you'd like. You can decide to do only one or two new things—for instance, switching from rice to barley and snacking on hard-boiled eggs instead of pretzels—until you're ready for another change. Or you can be a bit more ambitious right from the start. Our goal is to give you the tools you need to eat for better blood sugar, to use as you wish.

With the *Magic Foods* approach to eating, you don't have to give up bread, although you will want to navigate the bread aisle carefully and eat a little less. You don't have to swear off potatoes and white rice, although you'll definitely eat them more sparingly than you do now. You can also have pasta, in moderation (we'll explain which types are best for better blood sugar). And we encourage you to pour yourself cereal for breakfast—assuming it's one of the kinds we describe in this chapter.

You'll enjoy eating more protein-rich foods to keep you full and help keep your blood sugar low and steady. And while you'll say goodbye to unhealthy fats, your diet will actually contain plenty of fat in the form of "good" fats to add appeal to meals and blunt the blood sugar effects of the carbs you eat.

Along the way, you'll learn a few clever tricks of the trade, such as how to finish your salad with a dressing that can lower the blood sugar impact of your entire meal, how to use a little-known Middle Eastern spice to pull the plug on blood sugar, which sour fruit has a sweet benefit, and which little seeds pack a powerful health kick.

We're not asking you to throw your current diet out the window—just to tweak it a bit. Magic eating is really a series of very small, simple steps, such as adding a chopped apple to oatmeal, choosing sourdough bread instead of regular white bread, and making sweet potato fries your fries of choice (try them; you'll love them). Whether you make one change a meal,

one change a day, or only one change in all, your blood sugar will benefit.

Although the changes are easy, the rewards are real: more energy, less weight, a healthier heart, lower risk of diabetes, protection against certain cancers, and greatly improved quality of life.

# The Seven Secrets of Magic Eating

If you remember only one strategy from this book, remember the Seven Secrets of Magic Eating. Some of them may sound unusual, while others seem like the good old rules of healthy eating you already know about. But each one was chosen for a specific reason: to keep your blood sugar levels steady throughout the day. Here's a quick summary. You may even want to jot down the seven secrets and post them on your fridge as a daily reminder to keep you on the *Magic Foods* course. You'll read more about each of these secrets shortly.

1. **Choose low-GL carbs and limit carb portions**. Carbohydrate-rich foods, especially grains and starchy vegetables, are the main contributors to high blood sugar. By choosing "slow-acting" (low-GL) carbs instead of "fast-acting" (higher-GL) carbs, you can help keep blood sugar low and steady. You'll also want to limit your portions no matter what kind of carbs you choose.

2. **Make three of your carb servings whole grains**. You're not eating as many carbs, so make those you do eat count by choosing whole grains, which help prevent heart disease and diabetes independently of their effects on blood sugar.

3. **Eat more fruits and vegetables.** Aim for at least seven to nine small servings a day. Most fruits and vegetables have little carbohydrate and are packed with vitamins, fiber, and health-protective compounds, with few calories. Eating fruits or adding vegetables to carbohydrate-rich dishes helps make your diet blood sugar friendly.

4. **Eat protein at every meal.** Protein lowers the GL of meals and helps curb hunger, making weight loss easier.

5. **Favor good fats.** "Bad" saturated fats can interfere with your ability to control blood sugar, but "good" unsaturated fats help your body control it better. Good fats also lower the GL of meals.

6. **Add acidic foods to your meals.** It's an amazingly simple way to blunt the blood sugar effect of a meal.

7. **Eat smaller portions.** We're talking not about just carb-rich foods here but about all foods. Even when you eat a low-GL diet, calories count. Cutting calories can help you fight insulin resistance—and of course, along with exercise, it's still the way to lose weight.

# SECRET 1 | Choose Low-GL Carbs and Limit Carb Portions

Most of the carbs we eat are the kind that send blood sugar soaring. We eat lots of potatoes, mostly fried. We consume enormous quantities of bread in all forms, but mostly bread that's made with refined white flour and has little fiber. We eat a lot of rice, most of it white. We treat ourselves to muffins, cakes, and pastries made with white flour. We snack on bags of potato chips and pretzels (it's true pretzels are low in fat, but they're more or less just empty carbs). And we wash it all down with sugar-sweetened sodas and fruit drinks.

If you're going to tackle your dietary weak points, this is the place to start. The good news is that it's relatively easy to make improvements. Because we eat so many of these foods to begin with, any change is a change for the better!

## "Just Say Less"

One approach is to simply eat less of these high-GL foods. In the past decade or two, we've started to eat more calories, nearly all of them from carbohydrates—and nearly all of those carbohydrates are high GL. So it's time to dial down the carbohydrate mania: Eat fewer salty snacks out of bags, fewer French fries, less bread, and fewer pastries, and drink a lot less soda and other sweetened drinks. Ask yourself, "Do I really need that sugar-coated cereal, that whole takeout container of white rice, those French fries on the 'side' (which take up half the plate), or that giant slice of leftover birthday cake?"

We're not talking about a "just say no" approach but rather a "just say less" approach.

Let's say you start your day with a great big bowl of cornflakes or Rice Krispies or Corn Chex. If you measured how much you poured, it would probably be at least twice the serving size suggested on the box. So the "just say less" approach is to pour out less cereal. Fill the rest of the bowl with berries, low-GL fruits that will bring down the overall GL of your breakfast. And like many fruits, berries are rich in fiber that can help fill you up.

## Go Low GL

Even better, why not choose a lower-GL breakfast cereal? If you fill your bowl with a single serving of a medium-GL cereal—such as Grape-Nuts, Cheerios, Special K, or Life—instead of a high-GL one, your blood sugar will be lower after breakfast. And it'll be even lower if you choose a low-GL cereal, such as All-Bran, Bran Buds, or Alpen Muesli—or, if you like hot cereal, oatmeal. Keep watching portions and slicing berries or an apple into your bowl, and you'll really lower your blood sugar response to breakfast. Plus, you'll give yourself a seriously healthy start to the day.

If you like numbers, consider this: A 2-ounce (60 g) bowlful of Kellogg's Cornflakes has a GL of 48; a 1-ounce (30 g) bowlful of All-Bran cereal plus a whole medium apple has a GL of 15—more than two-thirds less. That means your blood sugar will rise two-thirds less as well.

Here's another example. At dinner, instead of a potato, you might decide to make pasta since it has a lower GL. That's a good substitution. A 5-ounce (140 g) baked potato has a GL of 26; the same size serving of pasta has a GL of 17. So the switch itself lowers the GL of that side dish by 9 points, changing it from a "high" to a "medium" GL choice. You could serve the pasta with a little olive oil, freshly ground black pepper, and a tablespoon of Parmesan cheese and never miss the potato a bit.

Now, to lower the GL of your pasta side dish even further, you could cut some red bell peppers into strips, microwave them for a minute, and toss them with the pasta, oil, pepper, and cheese. Because the vegetables add volume to the dish, if you serve yourself the same 5-ounce (140 g) portion, you'll eat half as much pasta, so the GL of the dish has been cut in half—to 4.5. This means the GL of your side dish is only 20 percent of what it would have been if you'd had the baked potato, which means it should raise your blood sugar 80 percent less!

Take a look at "The Glycemic Load of Common Foods" on page 55 and "The Magic Carb Pyramid" on page 43. Pick out a high-GL food that you eat frequently and figure out ways to eat less of it—such as substituting a low-GL or a medium-GL food for it and eating small portions. Now you're cooking.

A final note: Even if you're choosing lower-GL foods, it's still important to watch your portion sizes. That's because if you eat twice the recommended portion of the food, the GL will double. It's a simple concept, but one that many people miss. Even if you choose beans—a low-GL food—doubling the serving size will double the GL.

## WHAT'S BOOSTING YOUR BLOOD SUGAR THE MOST?

The best way to lower the GL of your diet is to figure out which high-GL foods you eat the most and then eat less, either by cutting back on portions or choosing a different food in its place.

In a major study of middle-aged women, these five foods were the biggest contributors to GL in the diet. Together, they made up about 30 percent of the GL of the women's entire diets. Try the smart substitutions instead. Each of them has a GL that's at least 50 percent lower than that of the food it replaces. These are only a few examples; you'll find more throughout this book.

| Food | Percent of GL in the Diet | Smart Substitution |
|---|---|---|
| Cooked potatoes | 7.7 | Pasta |
| Cold breakfast cereal | 6.5 | High-fiber cereal |
| White bread | 5.2 | Sourdough bread |
| Muffin | 5.0 | Apple |
| White rice | 4.6 | Pearled barley |

For kids, studies show, the biggest contributors to a high-GL diet are often candy, soft drinks, cakes, cookies, and salty snacks. So this age group will require a different strategy. For them, encouraging fruits as snacks and low-fat milk as a beverage may be the best thing you can do.

# 2 SECRET | Make Three of Your Carb Servings Whole Grains

If we are gorging ourselves on refined carbs, we're doing it largely at the expense of whole grains. And that's a shame because when it comes to preventing chronic disease, there's nothing like whole grains. There's clear, strong evidence that if you eat at least three servings of these foods a day, you'll substantially lower your risk of developing metabolic syndrome, diabetes, heart disease, and cancer. Most of us, though, have less than one serving a day. A serving is about an ounce (30 g)—one slice of 100 percent whole grain bread or 1/2 cup of cooked grains.

Eating more whole grains has been shown to cut heart disease risk by 25 percent in women and 18 percent in men and reduce diabetes risk by 35 percent in both. One key way grains may protect against these diseases is by helping to prevent a root cause: metabolic syndrome (described on page 19). In one study of more than 750 men and women over age 60, those who ate about three servings of whole grains a day were 54 percent less likely to have metabolic syndrome than people who ate less than one serving a day. Their fasting blood sugar levels were lower, and they tended to have less body fat. They also had 52 percent fewer fatal heart attacks. In fact, just six weeks on a whole grain diet can markedly improve insulin sensitivity, according to one study of overweight men and women.

Why are whole grains so good for us? They contain all the parts of the grain, not just the starchy low-fiber center (endosperm) but also the nutrient-rich germ layer and the fiber-rich bran layer on the outside. Whole grains are rich in fiber, antioxidants, vitamins, minerals, and a wide range of plant compounds that protect against chronic disease in many different ways.

Most whole grains have lower GLs than most refined grains, but there are exceptions. Finely milled 100 percent whole wheat bread, for instance, actually has a fairly high GL, while some refined foods, like pastas made from white semolina flour, have medium GLs. In general, though, you're better off with whole grains, which offer benefits to blood sugar that are totally unrelated to their GLs.

When it comes to the grain-based carbs you eat, don't be a perfectionist. As long as you get three servings of whole grains a day, there's room for some refined grain foods, especially if they're low GL. Just watch portion sizes no matter what kind you're eating.

How many carbs should you eat in total? In the *Magic Foods* approach, your goal is to get 45 to 55 percent of your calories from carbs every day. Turn to the Magic Meal Plans in Part 4 to see what this looks like in an actual menu.

## WHAT COUNTS AS WHOLE GRAIN?

**Bread** with the word *whole* in the first ingredient (such as *whole wheat*)

**Brown rice**

**Dehulled barley** (pearled barley isn't technically a whole grain, although it is good for you)

**Oats**

**Whole wheat pasta**

**Popcorn**

**Wheatberries**

**Exotic grains**, including amaranth, buckwheat, and quinoa

# The Magic carb Pyramid

## choose least often

potatoes
French fries
white bread
overcooked pasta
udon noodles
white rice
sticky rice
rice-based cereal

cornflakes
millet
instant Cream of Wheat
most baked goods
nondiet soda
sweetened fruit drinks
dried dates
raisins

## choose more often

converted white rice
wild rice
brown rice
wheatberries
pasta cooked al dente
whole wheat pasta
rye crispbread

chocolate milk
apple juice
pineapple juice
dried figs
bananas

sweet potatoes
black-eyed peas
whole grain cereals
low-sugar cereals
regular Cream of Wheat
whole grain and sourdough
  bread

## choose most often

coarse barley bread
whole-grain pumpernickel
pearled barley
oatmeal
bran cereal
muesli
lima beans
split peas

milk
soy milk
tomato juice
dried prunes
dried apricots

popcorn
yogurt
most vegetables (except potatoes)
lentils
all dried beans (except black-eyed peas)
most fresh fruits (and 100% fruit juice
  if limited to 6 ounces)

# 3 Eat More Fruits
**SECRET** and Vegetables

It's no secret that fruits and vegetables are good for you. You probably already know some of their health benefits, such as lower blood pressure and lower risk of heart disease, diabetes, stroke, and certain cancers. You may even know that eating produce can reduce your risk of losing your vision as you age. Yes, fruits and vegetables are rich in vitamins, thousands of health-protective compounds, and fiber.

But did you know that eating more of them is a key strategy in losing weight and keeping it off? With the exception of a few very starchy vegetables—like potatoes—the vast majority are very low in calories. That's largely because they're mostly water and fiber (which has no calories). Studies show that the more fruits and vegetables people eat, the less they tend to weigh.

It can be as simple as eating a salad. In one study at Pennsylvania State University, women who started a meal with a low-calorie salad and then ate a pasta dish ate about 12 percent fewer calories in total than women who skipped the salad and started in on the pasta. In another study, adding about 6 ounces (170 g) of vegetables (in this case, carrots and spinach) to dinner helped people feel fuller on fewer calories.

> Studies show that the more **FRUITS** and **VEGETABLES** people eat, the less they tend to weigh.

With a few exceptions, you can forget anything you've heard about not eating this fruit or that vegetable because it contains sugar or will raise your blood sugar. Most fruits and vegetables are actually quite low in total carbohydrates, and they have fiber— often the soluble fiber that slows blood sugar's rise—so their GLs are quite low.

## Foils for High-GL Carbs

You'll lower the GL of a typical portion of any carb dish by mixing in almost any vegetable or fruit (again, potatoes don't count). If you add tomatoes, carrots, and spinach to a pasta salad, for example, you'll eat less pasta. If you add chopped broccoli to a rice side dish, you'll eat less rice; the same goes for adding strawberries to hot or cold cereal. And fewer carbs equals lower blood sugar.

Let's consider a rice side dish. A cup of cooked long-grain white rice has a GL of 23, making it a high-GL food. But a cup of green peas has a GL of only 6, so if you mix an equal amount of peas with the rice, a cup of the side dish would have a GL of only 15, changing it from a high- to a medium-GL food. Really, mixing any vegetable into your rice—chopped cooked onions or carrots or asparagus—similarly lowers its GL.

## Snack Perfection

Whole fruit is almost always a good snack choice. Two ounces (60 g) of corn chips, for example, has a GL of 17—making it a medium-GL food (and that's if you buy a small snack-size bag). But a medium peach or plum has a GL of only 5, and a similar-size apple's GL is 6. Plus, you're eating twice as much food, so which do you think is likely to satisfy your hunger best? Even if you ate a plum, a peach, *and* an apple, the GL would be only 16. On the other hand, if you munched 4 ounces (125 g) of corn chips instead of 2, the GL for your snack would be a whopping 34!

Raw veggies are also Magic snacks, dipped in low-fat sour cream, low-fat dressing, or one of the bean dips on pages 204–206. Pack some carrot sticks or cherry tomatoes in a sandwich bag, and you'll have no reason to hit the vending machine—practically devoid of Magic foods— in the afternoon. Fill up on veggies of different colors, since different hues indicate different health-protective compounds. You don't want to miss out on any!

You'll find plenty of tips for adding specific fruits and vegetables to your meals in Part 2, where we introduce you to all the Magic foods. The bottom line? Load up. When it comes to these nonstarchy fruits and vegetables, the more the merrier.

## A Few Exceptions

Pretty much all fruits and vegetables are good for us, but some aren't as good for our blood sugar. When we tell you to eat more fruits and veggies, we're talking about colorful veggies (not starches like potatoes) and fresh, whole fruit. Here's the scoop.

**Potatoes.** These are the big exception: They're dense in easily absorbed carbohydrates, so their GL is quite high. In fact, the more potatoes, including French fries, that people eat, the higher their risk of diabetes. Many nutritionists think potatoes should be classified with grains rather than with vegetables, and even there, they're at the top of the carbohydrate pyramid.

**Other starchy vegetables.** Sweet potatoes and winter squash are rich in carotenoids and other important nutrients as well as fiber, which is also beneficial. But they're also high in carbohydrates, although their carbs aren't as easily absorbed as those in white potatoes. That makes them a better choice than white potatoes, and we include some delicious recipes for them in Part 4. But as with other carbohydrate-rich foods, watch portions.

**Dried fruits.** Drying concentrates the sugars in fruit and can make for intensely caloric treats. It's fine to have some raisins, dried plums, dates, figs, and apricots, but don't overindulge in them. Consider what happens when grapes (GL 8) turn into raisins (GL 28) or plums (GL 5) turn into dried plums (GL 10). Two ounces (60 g) of dried dates has a whopping GL of 25.

### WHAT ABOUT TROPICAL fruits?

Some nutritionists warn against tropical fruits, which can be starchy, but mostly, these foods are fine. It's true that bananas are starchy and are a medium-GL fruit while nearly all others are low GL, so you shouldn't overeat them, but don't ban them either. And mangoes, which are extraordinarily nutritious (and oh, so good), have gotten a bad rap, but they are low GL, so keep them on the menu. Papayas are fine, too, as are pineapple and watermelon. Coconut isn't a great choice, but it has nothing to do with GL; it's high in saturated fat, which is bad for the heart and insulin sensitivity.

**Juices.** You'll miss out on most of the fiber and some of the vitamins in the whole fruit, and you'll get a lot more calories—and a higher GL. If you eat 4 ounces (125 g) of fresh pineapple, for example, the GL is 6. But if you drink a small juice glass (6 ounces or 177 ml) of pineapple juice, the GL is 12. Ditto for an orange (GL 5) versus a small glass of OJ (GL 10), and for grapefruit (GL 3) versus a small glass of grapefruit juice (GL 7). And if you go for a sweetened fruit drink, all bets are off: A 12-ounce (375 ml) serving of cranberry juice cocktail—about the size of a small soda—has a GL of 36. When you drink juices, keep portions small, and make sure they're unsweetened (read labels carefully).

# The Magic **protein** Pyramid

## choose least often

- marbled beef
- regular ground beef
- pork ribs
- pork sausage
- bacon
- bologna
- salami

- hot dogs
- chicken with skin
- whole milk
- butter
- cream
- full-fat cheese

## choose more often

- lean beef
- extra-lean ground beef
- lean pork

- lean ham
- lean lamb

## choose most often

- soy foods
- fish and shellfish
- poultry without skin
- nuts
- seeds
- low-fat cheese
- fat-free or 1% milk

- fat-free or low-fat yogurt
- eggs
- split peas
- lentils
- green peas
- All dry beans
  (except black-eyed peas)

*Note: Beans are about one-third protein and two-thirds carbohydrate, so they appear in both the protein and carbohydrate pyramids. Similarly, milk and other dairy foods also contain some carbohydrate, so they also appear in both pyramids.*

# 4 | Eat Protein at Every Meal

**SECRET**

Want to control your blood sugar and your weight? Get enough protein.

A moderately high protein diet may get as much as 30 percent of its calories from protein, rather than the 15 to 20 percent most people get. In the *Magic Foods* approach, 20 to 30 percent of the calories you eat should come from protein.

Protein has little or no effect on your blood sugar, so any time you mix protein-rich foods with carbohydrate-rich foods, you automatically lower the GL of each portion. But protein has other benefits, as you saw in Chapters 2 and 3. It helps keep hunger at bay between meals. And if you're trying to lose weight, taking in more protein will help your body hold on to its calorie-burning muscle tissue so the weight comes off more easily.

There's no need to go overboard, though. A serving of a protein-rich food like chicken breast or sirloin steak is a mere 2 to 3 ounces (60 to 85 g), although a more typical portion is 6 ounces (170 g). The main thing to focus on is having at least a small portion of a protein-rich food at *every* meal (and as part of as many snacks as you can). It can be side dish of beans, a glass of fat-free milk, a slice or two of lean turkey, a few ounces of sirloin steak in a stir-fry, a snack of unsweetened yogurt, or a handful of nuts. Among the list of Magic foods in Part 2, you'll find these excellent protein sources.

**Beans, lentils, and peas.** These "vegetarian" sources of protein are excellent: They have essentially no saturated fat, and they're very low GL, in large part because they contain so much soluble fiber. And they pack a lot of minerals in small packages. Try to eat meals based on these foods at least once or twice a week.

**Soy foods.** Like beans, these are low-saturated-fat, low-GL, high-protein foods. Try a stir-fry with tofu; experiment with soy milk on your cereal (it tastes better than it once did, so give it

a chance); and grill some tempeh, a textured soybean product with a nutty flavor. Or stock up on frozen soy-based vegetarian burgers.

**Nuts and seeds.** It's hard to find a protein-rich snack, but nuts are one of the few. These little nuggets serve up not only protein but also good-for-you fats. Just stick to a palmful, since they're high in calories.

**Fish and shellfish.** All fish and shellfish are low in saturated fat, so they're excellent protein choices. Fatty fish are also rich in omega-3 fatty acids, which help prevent heart disease and may improve insulin sensitivity. You'll make a good choice either way: low-fat fish like cod and flounder are sources of low-saturated-fat protein, while fattier fish like wild salmon and rainbow trout provide both protein and omega-3's.

## SNEAKING IN PROTEIN

It's easy to add protein to your meals and snacks.

Starting the day with **whole grain toast?** Instead of buttering it, spread it with a table-spoon of peanut butter.

When summer **berries** are in season (or frozen berries are on sale), make a quick smoothie with fat-free yogurt, a good protein source.

Making a salad? Toss in some **chickpeas** (garbanzo beans) or leftover **chicken**.

Center your lunch around **bean soup**, either vegetarian or flavored with a small amount of **pork**.

Buy single-serving packs of **nuts** to take to work for a quick snack.

Keep some hard-boiled **eggs** in your fridge as snacks or easy protein-rich additions to salads and sandwiches.

Keep **soy-based veggie burgers** in your freezer for quick dinners or high-protein, meaty boosts to pasta sauce (just crumble them into the sauce).

Look for brands of cereals and frozen waffles that contain protein sources such as **soy**.

For a healthy heart, aim for two or three servings of fish or shellfish a week.

**Chicken and turkey.** These are also low in saturated fat and quite low in calories if you choose white meat without the skin.

**Eggs.** Eggs are nutritious and versatile. A large egg has only 1.5 grams of saturated fat, and even though it's high in cholesterol, an egg a day won't raise most adults' cholesterol levels. Have eggs for breakfast or enjoy an egg salad sandwich on whole grain bread with low-fat mayo. A hard-boiled egg makes a perfect high-protein snack.

**Red meat.** Beef, pork, lamb, and other red meats are major contributors to saturated fat in our diets, but that doesn't mean you can't eat them. The key is to choose the leanest cuts, which have more protein—and less saturated fat. And don't eat red meat every day; leave room for meals centered on fish, beans, and so on.

**Dairy foods.** Fat-free or 1% milk, low-fat or fat-free yogurt, and low-fat cheeses contribute high-quality protein with very little saturated fat. Like all dairy foods, they're high in calcium, a key mineral. But full-fat cheeses, along with butter and high-fat dairy desserts like ice cream, are major contributors to saturated fat in our diets. Have milk and other dairy products every day, but go lean.

## THE LEANEST MEATS

Even red meat can be a fine source of low-saturated-fat protein if you choose the right cuts.

For **beef,** choose round steaks and roasts (eye of round, top round, bottom round, round tip), top loin, top sirloin, or chuck shoulder.

When buying **ground beef,** look for extra-lean—90 percent lean or preferably 95 percent, if you can find it.

For **pork,** choose tenderloin or loin chops.

If you like **ham,** ask for extra lean.

For **lamb,** go for leg, arm, or loin.

For **lunchmeats,** check nutrition labels. Look for less than 1 gram of saturated fat per serving.

# 5 SECRET | Favor Good Fats

With all the emphasis on low-fat foods in recent years, you might think we'd be advocating a low-fat diet. But we're not. Instead of following a low-fat diet—which is almost by necessity a high-carbohydrate diet—you can get as much as 35 percent of your calories from fat in the *Magic Foods* approach. Check out the Magic Meal Plans in Part 4 to see what this amount looks like.

Fat, as you read in Chapter 2, isn't all bad, especially where your blood sugar is concerned. Fat doesn't raise blood sugar a bit, and it doesn't require insulin in order to be metabolized, so it doesn't raise insulin levels either. Its GL is zero. Because it slows the rate at which food leaves your stomach, it can blunt the blood sugar effect of a whole meal, even if that meal includes carbs.

Including fat-rich foods in your meals can also help your body metabolize carbohydrates better—provided they're the right fats. That means monounsaturated fat (the kind in olive oil, nuts, and avocados) and omega-3 fatty acids (found in fatty fish) instead of saturated fat (the kind in red meat and dairy foods). Good fats are remarkable because they can actually help reverse insulin resistance (turn back to page 30 if you want to refresh yourself on this). Saturated fat, on the other hand, not only raises "bad" LDL cholesterol and increases heart disease risk, but we now know that it increases insulin resistance, too.

Favoring good fats means eating fish at least once a week; adding avocado instead of full-fat cheese to your salads and sandwiches; tossing your pasta salad with, say, olive oil and toasted walnuts instead of cream sauce; and putting peanut butter instead of butter on your toast (or dipping your bread in olive oil). Adding good fats to foods means each portion will have a lower GL.

# The Magic **fats** Pyramid

**choose least often**

fatty red meats
butter
cream
full-fat cheese
whole milk
premium ice cream

solid shortening
solid margarine
lard
mayonnaise
partially hydrogenated vegetable oils

**choose more often**

corn oil
soybean oil

safflower oil
sunflower oil

**choose most often**

olive oil
canola oil
nuts
nut oils

seeds
flaxseeds
fatty fish
avocados

## fats AT A GLANCE

**THE GOOD FATS**

### monounsaturated fats: Olive
oil, canola oil, avocados, peanuts, almonds,
cashews, and most other nuts. When they
replace saturated fats, they have a beneficial effect on cholesterol and help reverse
insulin resistance.

### omega-3 fats: Fatty fish. Related fats,
which the body can convert to a degree to
the more active form found in fish, are
found in flaxseed and canola oil. Omega-3
fats, especially from fish, help prevent heart
disease and may improve insulin sensitivity.

### polyunsaturated fats: Corn,
soybean, and safflower oils can be beneficial, but most of us already get plenty of
polyunsaturated fats, so don't go out of
your way to get more. You're much more
likely to need more monounsaturated fat in
your diet.

**THE BAD FATS**

### saturated fats: Red meats; full-fat
dairy foods; and a few vegetable oils, such
as coconut oil. These increase levels of
"bad" LDL cholesterol, promote heart
disease, and reduce insulin sensitivity.

### trans fats: These are found in solid
margarine; vegetable shortening; partially
hydrogenated vegetable oils; and many
deep-fried snacks, fast foods, and commercial baked goods. They raise "bad" LDL
cholesterol, lower "good" HDL cholesterol,
increase heart disease risk, and may
increase insulin resistance. Trans fats are
now listed on nutrition labels, and manufacturers are offering new foods with "no trans
fats." These are fine as long as they're also
low GL, which is rarely the case!

## Making the Switch

If you're used to steaks and butter, how do you
make the switch to better fats? With these steps.

**Cut back on the major sources of saturated
fat in your diet.** Start by identifying them: Look
at the top tier of "The Magic Fats Pyramid" on
page 49 and check out "The Top 10 Sources of
Saturated Fat" on page 51. How often do you eat
these foods? What single change do you think
you could make in the next week—using a leaner
sandwich meat at lunch, having steak instead of
ribs, choosing low-fat frozen yogurt instead of
ice cream? Make that one change, and when you
have, start thinking about your next one. Work
toward eating more foods from the bases (and
middle tiers) of the fat and protein pyramids—
and much fewer from the top tiers. Just cutting
back on cheese, full-fat yogurt, and regular sour
cream—or choosing low-fat substitutes—can
substantially reduce the amount of saturated fat
you eat with very little effort. So can switching
from whole milk to 1% or fat free.

**Eat more nonmeat protein.** We're talking
beans, lentils, peas, and soy foods. By swapping
a few meat-based meals a week for vegetarian
options, you can go a long way toward building a
healthier diet. Aim for one new vegetarian meal
each week for a month. Ultimately, turn it into a
lifetime habit.

**Eat fish or shellfish twice a week.** It can be
fresh, canned, or frozen (but skip the breaded
fish sticks). Experiment with different cooking
methods. As a start, try our recipe suggestions in
Part 4.

**When you eat red meat, choose lean cuts.**
It can make a big difference in how much saturated fat you get, and you won't need to sacrifice
taste. Three ounces (85 g) of cooked regular
ground beef has 6 grams of saturated fat, while
the same amount of extra-lean ground beef has
only 2.5 grams. Check out "The Leanest Meats"
on page 48 and try to stick with these options
whenever you can.

**Cook and season with olive oil.** Use it for sautéing, grilling, and roasting; as an ingredient in salad dressing; or drizzled over vegetables, grains, and fish. Reach for the olive oil instead of butter whenever you cook. You'll hardly notice the difference in most foods, and making this change can dramatically decrease the amount of saturated fat you add to your diet. If you simply must have the taste of butter in a dish, add a teaspoon or two to olive oil to impart that buttery flavor.

**Make canola oil your second choice.** Use it for a more neutral taste when sautéing and in baking. It's very versatile yet low in saturated fat.

**Add more nuts, seeds, and avocado to your menus.** You can add nuts to practically any main dish or baked item, and avocado is an easy addition to salads and sandwiches. Or simply carve up a few slices of avocado, drizzle with lemon juice, and enjoy as a snack. See the Nuts and Avocado entries in Part 2 for more menu suggestions.

---

## THE TOP 10 SOURCES OF SATURATED FAT

A quick glance at this list can make it easier to target the foods that are adding the most saturated fat to your diet.

| | |
|---|---|
| 1 | Cheese |
| 2 | Beef |
| 3 | Milk |
| 4 | Oils (such as palm, palm kernel, and coconut oil) |
| 5 | Ice cream/sherbet/frozen yogurt |
| 6 | Cakes/cookies/quick breads/doughnuts |
| 7 | Butter |
| 8 | Shortening, lard, other animal fats |
| 9 | Salad dressings/mayonnaise |
| 10 | Poultry with skin |

*Source: Dietary Guidelines for Americans 2005*

---

# 6 | Add Acidic Foods to Your Meals
**SECRET**

As you discovered in Chapter 2, even a little bit of pucker power from acidic ingredients can lower your blood sugar response to a carb-rich meal. Making foods more acidic slows the breakdown of starches into blood sugar, so your blood sugar rises more slowly.

Certain acidic foods, though, such as vinegar (acetic acid), seem to work in additional ways, making them more effective. So think vinegar! Toss out those creamy salad dressings and buy or make dressings that combine vinegar with olive oil, such as mustard vinaigrette. It takes just a tablespoon of vinegar per serving to substantially lower the GL of a meal.

Eat a small green salad drizzled with vinaigrette before lunch or dinner several times a week. You'll get some acetic acid in your meals *and* squeeze more vegetables into your diet.

But don't stop there. Soak fish in vinegar and water before cooking, suggests the Vinegar Institute; it'll be sweeter and more tender and hold its shape better. When poaching fish, toss a tablespoon of vinegar into the simmering water for the same reasons. Make a vinegar-based marinade for meat destined for the grill. Mix in a little vinegar when cooking canned soup to perk it up, and add some to the water in which you simmer vegetables. See the Vinegar entry in Part 2 for more suggestions.

If you like Japanese food, you can feel a little better about the rice if you're having sushi, since sushi rice is made with rice wine vinegar.

## More Ways to Add Acids

Go beyond vinegar with these tips for adding bite to your meals.

**Use mustard,** which is made with vinegar, instead of mayonnaise on sandwiches, as a base to coat chicken and meats, and in bean dishes.

**Eat that pickle** with your sandwich. It gets its sour taste from vinegar.

**Go beyond pickled cucumbers** and try pickled tomatoes, carrots, celery, broccoli, cauliflower florets, and red and green bell peppers. If you're at a Japanese restaurant, ask for *oshinko* (pickled vegetables).

**Don't throw out the pickle liquid!** It makes an excellent marinade, especially when mixed with a little olive oil and chopped fresh herbs.

**Eat sauerkraut,** which is pickled cabbage. Look for low-sodium varieties.

**Squeeze lemon juice,** which is also acidic, over fish and seafood. Fresh lemon juice can revitalize a lackluster soup or stew, and it livens up green vegetables, rice, and chicken.

**Try lime juice** on fish, turkey, avocados, melon, sweet potatoes, and black beans.

**Eat citrus fruit** such as fresh grapefruit, which, as your tongue has already told you, is somewhat acidic.

**Ask for sourdough bread.** As the dough ferments, it releases lactic acid, which, like vinegar, has a beneficial effect on the food's GL.

**Cook with wine.** It's acidic, too, and gives a tasty tang to sauces, stews, soups, and roasts. Try cooking fish in wine: Sauté garlic (and onions if you want) in olive oil, add seasoning, then pour in some wine and reduce the heat. Add the fish and cook in the simmering liquid. Squeeze in a little lemon juice at the end.

**Drink wine with your dinner.** It's another way to include an acidic liquid with your meal. Drinking wine (as well as other alcoholic beverages) in moderation—a glass a day for women, up to two for men—can help keep blood insulin levels low and is linked with a lower risk of developing diabetes. Moderate alcohol consumption also raises "good" HDL cholesterol levels and helps protect against heart disease. (If you have diabetes, check with your doctor first.)

# 7 | Eat Smaller Portions
SECRET

We've already stressed the importance of doling out smaller portions of fast-acting carb foods, such as mashed potatoes and rice, and even slower-acting foods such as whole grain cereal. But portion sizes count almost no matter what you're eating. That's because calories matter.

Eating fewer calories is one of the best ways to improve your insulin sensitivity. You'll do better if you go ahead and lower the GL of your overall diet, with the help of the Magic foods in this book, but simply eating less also helps by improving your insulin sensitivity (which ultimately lowers your blood sugar). It does this even if you don't lose weight. But of course, eating less does help you shed pounds—another key element in preventing insulin resistance, diabetes, and heart disease.

So where should you cut back on calories? Everywhere. Carbs are of course a main target, especially high-GL carbs such as rice, sodas, and sweetened drinks. But so is anything you tend to go overboard on. Yes, we want you to make protein a part of every meal, but that doesn't mean gorging on a 1-pound (450 g) porterhouse is okay. Six ounces (170 g) of a much leaner sirloin is plenty. We also recommend eating nuts, but again, the devil is in the details. An ounce (30 g) of almonds—about 25—has about 165 calories. That's fine. But if you eat a cup's worth, you're taking in more than 800 calories—more than you should get from an entire meal. Few of us have the room in our diets to eat that many extra calories without gaining weight, which increases insulin resistance. Olive oil is great for your heart and your blood sugar, but don't soak your bread in it. At 119 calories per tablespoon, you won't want to consume more than 1 or 2 tablespoons a day.

Fortunately, there's one category of food that doesn't require much portion control: nonstarchy fruits and vegetables. It's quite difficult to eat too many apples, carrots, tomatoes, salad greens, or raspberries. They'll fill you up, with few calories and a low GL, and take the place of more caloric foods.

## How Much Should You Eat?

Of course, the answer to this depends on how much you currently weigh and how active you are. If you know approximately how many calories you want to aim for each day, see our Magic Meal Plans in Part 4 to get a good sense of how much food this means.

Not sure how many calories you need each day? Here's a nifty rule of thumb. If you're trying for modest weight loss, simply add a zero to your weight to get a ballpark calorie target. For instance, if you weigh 160 pounds, your target for modest weight loss would be 1,600 calories a day.

It's worth keeping a food diary for a few days to see how many calories you're really eating; the number may well be more than you think (and aren't you a little curious?). Use the nutrition labels on packaged foods to get the calories per serving (be careful; some packages contain two servings, so you'll have to double that number if you eat the whole thing). For fresh foods, use a Web site like www.calorie-count.com, www.thecaloriecounter.com, www.calorieking.com, or www.nal.usda.gov/fnic/foodcomp/search to get the calorie counts of common foods.

Another way to get a handle on portion sizes is simply to train your eye to identify what a reasonable serving looks like (see "What Does a Serving Look Like?"). Bring these images to mind when you're serving food, ordering food, and of course, eating food. The serving sizes are quite small, so don't feel bad if your portion is twice as large. A serving of pasta or rice is 1/2 cup, but most people eat a cup, so that counts as two servings. Most of us need no more than six servings of grains a day—preferably low- or medium-GL grains—so if you're eating three

or four servings at a sitting, that's too much. A single dense bagel can equal six servings of grains—an entire day's worth!

A serving of meat or chicken is about 3 ounces (85 g), but most people can eat two servings a day—the size of two decks of cards.

## Cutting Back

Unfortunately, in this age of super-size servings, we've been trained to eat a lot. It's up to you to fight back.

Start by putting less food on your plate or in your bowl. Studies show that when large portions are put in front of us, most of us eat more—often

### WHAT DOES A SERVING LOOK LIKE?

Here are some images to keep in mind. Each is one serving.

A 3-ounce (85 g) serving of cooked **meat** is the size of a deck of cards.

A 3-ounce (85 g) serving of **fish** is the size of a checkbook.

An ounce (30 g) of **cheese** is the size of four dice.

An ounce (30 g) of **sliced cheese** is the diameter of a CD.

A half cup of **pasta or rice** is the size of a baseball cut in half.

A cup of cold **cereal** is the size of a baseball.

A medium **baked potato** is the size of a personal-size bar of soap.

Two tablespoons of **peanut butter** is the size of a Ping-Pong ball.

Two tablespoons of **salad dressing** is the size of a shot glass.

A 6-ounce (180 ml) serving of **juice** is the size of a small yogurt container.

A medium piece of **fruit,** such as an apple, is the size of a tennis ball.

50 percent more at a single meal. Put your meals on plates in the kitchen rather than putting a big plate or bowl on the table for everyone to dig into at will. Buy small single-portion bags of snacks rather than eating out of a big bag (which always disappears). If you do buy a big bag, dole out a reasonable portion onto a small plate or a napkin, then close the bag and put it away out of sight before you sit down to munch.

When you're eating out, order smaller dishes (don't be afraid to order from the children's menu at fast-food places) or ask the server to put half the dish in a doggie bag before you start to eat. It's also a good idea to share one main dish and a separate dish of vegetables or share one main dish and fill up with a salad or broth-based soup.

In general, though, try to eat most of your meals at home. It's much easier to control your calorie intake as well as the amount of fat and number of high-GL foods that go into your meal.

# Putting It All Together

Are you ready to eat the *Magic Foods* way? In the first chapter, you learned how important it is to your health and well-being to eat in ways that keep your blood sugar levels stable throughout the day. In the second chapter, you found out what makes certain foods catapult your blood sugar, while others keep it humming steadily. In the third chapter, you learned the pitfalls of a quick-fix low-carb approach. And now you've learned the Seven Secrets of Magic Eating. In the next chapter, you'll quiz yourself to see where your diet stands now, discover some fixes for your dietary downfalls, and bone up on smart strategies for eating out.

Then it's on to the real meat of the book (lean meat, of course!). In Part 2, you'll find profiles of the 57 Magic foods, from apples to yogurt. Each profile tells you how the GL of the food stacks up (either very low, low, or medium; you won't find Magic foods with a high or very high GL) plus other important health benefits it offers. You'll also learn the proper portion size—because remember, portions count—as well as menu suggestions and cooking tips.

In Part 3, the Magic Meal Makeovers show you how to make simple changes to your breakfasts, lunches, snacks, dinners, and desserts to help you make your meals more blood sugar friendly without a lot of fuss.

To really help you put Magic eating into action, in Part 4 we've supplied more than 100 Magic recipes. These make low-GL cooking come alive, incorporating the Magic foods in clever, simple, and delicious ways. Each recipe includes full nutritional information, but you don't have to worry about that if you don't want to; we've made sure the dishes are good for your blood sugar.

You'll even find meal plans that fit these recipes into a week's worth of eating based on three different calorie goals to help you manage your weight. All the tools you need are right at your fingertips!

# THE GLYCEMIC LOAD OF COMMON FOODS

The GL is the best measure of a food's effect on blood sugar. Here, we've listed some common foods and grouped them into three categories: low GL (10 and under), medium GL (11 to 19), and high GL (20 and up). You want to aim for as many low-GL foods as possible and eat high-GL foods more sparingly.

Since carbohydrate foods are the ones that contribute most to the GL of your diet, we've focused on those foods here. Foods that are mostly protein or fat—such as meats, fish, and cheeses—have little or no GL, so you won't find many of them in this list, although you will find them in the Magic foods entries in Part 2. Including protein-rich foods and "good" fats in your meals and snacks will help keep your GL score for the day moderate.

Remember that portion size makes a big difference: If you eat two servings of a medium-GL breakfast cereal, it suddenly qualifies as a high-GL food. On the other hand, if you just love a food in the high-GL category, go ahead and eat a small portion, preferably along with a small portion of a low- or medium-GL food.

## LOW (GL = 10 or less)

| Breads, Tortillas, Grains | Serving size | GL |
| --- | --- | --- |
| Coarse barley bread (75% intact kernels) | 2 slices | 10 |
| Soy and flaxseed bread | 2 slices | 10 |
| Whole grain pumpernickel bread | 2 slices | 10 |
| Pearled barley | 1 cup | 8 |
| Popcorn | 2 cups | 8 |
| Wheat tortillas | 2 6" (15 cm) | 6 |

| Breakfast Cereals | Serving size | GL |
| --- | --- | --- |
| Alpen Muesli | 1/3 cup (1 oz [30 g]) | 10 |
| Oatmeal, instant | 1 cup prepared (1 oz [30 g dry]) | 10 |
| All Bran | 1/2 cup (1 oz [30 g]) | 9 |
| Bran Buds | 1/3 cup (1 oz [30 g]) | 7 |
| Oatmeal made from rolled oats | 1 cup prepared (1 oz [30 g dry]) | 7 |

| Beans and Peas | Serving size | GL |
| --- | --- | --- |
| Lima beans | 1 cup | 10 |
| Pinto beans | 1 cup | 10 |
| Chickpeas | 1 cup | 8 |
| Baked beans | 1 cup | 7 |
| Kidney beans | 1 cup | 7 |
| Navy beans | 1 cup | 7 |
| Butter beans | 1 cup | 6 |
| Green peas | 1 cup | 6 |
| Split peas, yellow | 1 cup | 6 |
| Lentils, green or red | 1 cup | 5 |

# LOW (GL = 10 or less)

| Dairy and Soy Drinks | Serving size | GL |
|---|---|---|
| Low-fat yogurt with fruit and sugar | 7 oz (200 ml) | 9 |
| Soy milk | 1 cup (8 oz [250 ml]) | 7 |
| Low-fat chocolate milk, sweetened with aspartame | 8 oz (250 ml) | 3 |
| Low-fat yogurt with fruit, sweetened with aspartame | 7 oz (200 ml) | 2 |

| Fruits and Vegetables | Serving size | GL |
|---|---|---|
| Prunes, pitted, chopped | 1/3 cup (2 oz [60 g]) | 10 |
| Apricots, dried, chopped | 1/3 cup (2 oz [60 g]) | 9 |
| Peaches, canned in light syrup | 1/2 cup (4 oz [125 g]) | 9 |
| Grapes, medium bunch (about 50) | 4 oz (125 g) | 8 |
| Mango, sliced | 2/3 cup (4 oz [125 g]) | 8 |
| Pineapple, diced | 2/3 cup (4 oz [125 g]) | 7 |
| Apple | 1 small | 6 |
| Kiwifruit, sliced | 2/3 cup (4 oz [125 g]) | 6 |
| Beets, sliced | 1/2 cup | 5 |
| Orange | 1 small | 5 |
| Peach | 1 small | 5 |
| Plums | 2 small | 5 |
| Pear | 1 small | 4 |
| Strawberries | about 6 medium | 4 |
| Watermelon, chopped | 2/3 cup (4 oz [125 g]) | 4 |
| Carrots, raw | 1 large | 3 |
| Cherries | about 16 (4 oz [125 g]) | 3 |
| Grapefruit | 1/2 | 3 |

| Beverages | Serving size | GL |
|---|---|---|
| Orange juice, unsweetened | 3/4 cup (6 oz [180 ml]) | 10 |
| Grapefruit juice, unsweetened | 3/4 cup (6 oz [180 ml]) | 7 |
| Tomato juice | 3/4 cup (6 oz [180 ml]) | 4 |

| Sweets | Serving size | GL |
|---|---|---|
| M&Ms with peanuts | 25 (1 oz [30 g]) | 6 |
| Nutella (chocolate hazelnut spread) | 4 Tbsp | 4 |

| Nuts | Serving size | GL |
|---|---|---|
| Mixed nuts, roasted | 1/3 cup (1.5 oz [45 g]) | 4 |
| Cashew nuts | about 13 (1.5 oz [45 g]) | 3 |
| Peanuts | 1/3 cup (1.5 oz [45 g]) | 1 |

# Medium (GL =11–19)

| Bread, Tortillas, Crackers, Chips | Serving size | GL |
|---|---|---|
| Coarse barley bread (50% intact kernels) | 2 slices | 18 |
| High-fiber white bread | 2 slices | 18 |
| Corn chips | 2 oz (60 g) | 17 |
| 100% whole grain bread | 2 slices | 14 |
| Sourdough rye bread | 2 slices | 12 |
| Stone-ground wheat thins | 4 | 12 |
| Corn tortillas | 2 6" (15 cm) | 11 |
| Rye crispbreads | 2 1/2 | 11 |

| Grains | Serving size | GL |
|---|---|---|
| Converted long-grain white rice | 2/3 cup cooked | 16 |
| Brown rice | 2/3 cup cooked | 18 |
| Quinoa | 2/3 cup cooked | 16 |
| Wild rice | 2/3 cup cooked | 18 |
| Wheatberries | 2/3 cup cooked | 14 |
| Bulgur | 2/3 cup cooked | 12 |

| Pasta | Serving size | GL |
|---|---|---|
| Spaghetti (cooked 15 minutes) | 1 cup | 17 |
| Whole wheat spaghetti | 1 cup | 13 |
| High-protein spaghetti | 1 cup | 12 |

| Beverages | Serving size | GL |
|---|---|---|
| Low-fat chocolate milk | 8 oz (250 ml) | 12 |
| Pineapple juice, unsweetened | 6 oz (180 ml) | 12 |
| Apple juice | 8 oz (250 ml) | 8 |

| Fruits, Vegetables, Beans | Serving size | GL |
|---|---|---|
| Sweet corn | 1 cup | 18 |
| Sweet potato | 1 medium (5 oz [140 g]) | 17 |
| Figs, dried, chopped | 1/3 cup (2 oz [60 g]) | 16 |
| Banana | 1 small (4 oz [125 g]) | 11 |
| Black-eyed peas | 1 cup | 11 |

| Breakfast Cereals | Serving size | GL |
|---|---|---|
| Nabisco Cream of Wheat, regular | 1 cup prepared (1 oz [30 g]) | 17 |
| Post Grape-Nuts | 1/2 cup (1 oz [30 g]) | 16 |
| Cheerios | 1 cup (1 oz [30 g]) | 15 |
| Life | 3/4 cup (1 oz [30 g]) | 15 |
| Special K | 1 cup (1 oz [30 g]) | 14 |

# High (GL = 20 or higher)

| Potatoes | Serving size | GL |
|---|---|---|
| Baked russet Burbank potato | 1 medium | 26 |
| French fries | 5 oz (140 g) | 22 |

| Grains | Serving size | GL |
|---|---|---|
| Sticky white rice | 2/3 cup cooked | 31 |
| Millet | 2/3 cup cooked | 25 |
| Couscous | 2/3 cup cooked | 23 |
| Long-grain white rice | 2/3 cup cooked | 23 |

| Pasta | Serving size | GL |
|---|---|---|
| Udon Japanese noodles | 1 cup cooked | 25 |
| Spaghetti (cooked 20 minutes) | 1 cup | 22 |

| Breads | Serving size | GL |
|---|---|---|
| French baguette | 2 slices | 30 |
| Middle Eastern flatbread | 1 large | 30 |
| Italian white bread | 2 slices | 22 |
| Hamburger roll | 1 | 21 |
| Light rye bread | 2 slices | 20 |
| Mini-bagel (Lender's) | 1 | 20 |
| Wonder Bread | 2 slices | 20 |

| Breakfast Cereals | Serving size | GL |
|---|---|---|
| Kellogg's Cornflakes | 1 cup (1 oz [30 g]) | 24 |
| Rice Chex | 1 1/4 cups (1 oz [30 g]) | 23 |
| Nabisco Cream of Wheat, instant | 1 cup prepared (1 oz [30 g]) | 22 |
| Rice Krispies | 3/4 cup (1 oz [30 g]) | 22 |
| Corn Chex | 1 cup (1 oz [30 g]) | 21 |

| Dried Fruit | Serving size | GL |
|---|---|---|
| Raisins | 1/3 cup | 28 |
| Dates, dried, chopped | 1/3 cup | 25 |

| Beverages | Serving size | GL |
|---|---|---|
| Ocean Spray Cranberry Juice Cocktail | 12 oz (375 ml) | 36 |
| Coca-Cola | 12 oz (375 ml) | 24 |

| Sweets | Serving size | GL |
|---|---|---|
| Mars Bar | 2 oz (60 g) | 26 |
| Jelly beans | 20 | 22 |
| Betty Crocker chocolate cake with chocolate icing | 4 oz (125 g) | 20 |

Source: "International Table of Glycemic Index and Glycemic Load Values 2002," Kaye Foster-Powell, Susanna H. A. Holt, and Janette C. Brand-Miller, *American Journal of Clinical Nutrition* vol. 76, no. 1 (2002), 5–56. Additional data from www.glycemicindex.com, www.mypyramid.gov, and www.ars.usda.gov.

# chapter 5

# THE MAGIC FOODS
# approach
# in ACTION

Now that you're armed with the Seven Secrets of Magic Eating, where do you go from here? Altering your diet can seem dizzyingly difficult, but it doesn't have to be, especially if you make one tiny change at a time. A good first step is to take stock of your eating habits and find out what you're doing right—and where you could stand to make some gentle adjustments.

You'll be **amazed** how the simple act of acknowledging your eating habits can make you more open to **changing** them.

In this chapter you'll:

• **Quiz yourself** to find out how Magic your diet is. You'll be amazed how the simple act of acknowledging your eating habits can make you more open to changing them.

• **Find and fix** your dietary downfalls (we all have 'em).

• **Learn the art** of eating out. Since we eat so many of our meals out of the house, learning to outsmart restaurant menus and navigate the minefield of fast-food dining is key.

In Part 2, you'll discover the 57 Magic foods and how to reap their blood sugar and weight-loss benefits. The Magic Meal Plans and Magic Recipes in Part 4 will be a great help, too, not to mention the Magic Meal Makeovers in Part 3. But before we take you there, let's get you ready to go.

# quiz How Magic is your diet?

Circle the number next to your answer for each question, then add up your score. Turn to page 62 to see how you did.

**1  If you were in my kitchen in the morning, you'd see me drinking:**

a. Coffee or tea, plain or with low-fat milk and/or a little sugar or sugar substitute — 1

b. Coffee or tea with full-fat cream and/or loads of sugar — 2

c. A soft drink — 3

**2  When I eat cereal for breakfast, I'm most likely to pick one like:**

a. Cornflakes, Rice Krispies, or Corn Chex — 3

b. Grape-Nuts or Cheerios — 2

c. All Bran, Bran Buds, or Muesli — 1

**3  When I drink juice, it's:**

a. A small glass of unsweetened juice such as orange or grapefruit — 1

b. A large glass of unsweetened juice such as orange or grapefruit — 2

c. A large glass of juice drink (5 to 30% juice) — 3

**4  When I drink milk (or pour it over my cereal), it's:**

a. Whole — 3

b. 2% — 2

c. 1% or fat-free — 1

**5  The bread on my counter right now is:**

a. 100% whole grain (wheat, rye, pumpernickel, sourdough) — 1

b. Made with white flour and some whole grain flour ("wheat" bread as opposed to "whole wheat" bread) — 2

c. White — 3

**6  Potatoes (including mashed potatoes, French fries, hash browns, etc.) are:**

a. The vegetables I eat most often — 3

b. On my plate two or three times a week — 2

c. On my plate once a week or less — 1

**7  Spinach, broccoli, and other dark green vegetables are:**

a. Strangers in my house — 3

b. Welcome as occasional visitors, if they keep quiet — 2

c. Practically family — 1

**8  When I make or buy a deli sandwich, I:**

a. Pile on the bologna, salami, and other full-fat meats — 3

b. Use roast beef — 2

c. Have low-fat meats like sliced turkey breast or lean ham — 1

**9  When I'm hungry in the afternoon, I grab:**

a. Some fruit, nuts, or low-fat yogurt — 1

b. Crackers and cheese or a cereal bar — 2

c. Chips or a candy bar — 3

**10** I eat nuts:

**a.** Rarely                                        3

**b.** By the bagful; can't get enough                2

**c.** By the small handful every day or two          1

**11** I eat at fast-food places:

**a.** At least twice a week                          3

**b.** Once a week or so                              2

**c.** Less than once a week                          1

**12** In my refrigerator, you're most likely to find:

**a.** Soft drinks or sports/energy drinks            3

**b.** Diet soft drinks                               2

**c.** Water or sparkling water                       1

**13** When I get pizza, I usually eat:

**a.** One or two slices with a side salad and a noncaloric drink    1

**b.** One or two slices, no salad, and a soft drink    2

**c.** Two or more slices plus a big soft drink and a side of garlic bread    3

**14** My favorite salad dressing is:

**a.** Something creamy or cheesy                     2

**b.** Olive oil and vinegar                          1

**c.** Who eats salad?                                3

**15** When I eat pasta, I:

**a.** Pile it high and top it with cheese sauce or meat sauce    3

**b.** Have a moderate amount paired with chicken, fish, or shellfish    1

**c.** Enjoy it as a side dish with some olive oil and grated cheese    1

**16** When I'm offered vegetarian bean chili for dinner, I think:

**a.** Looks good!                                    1

**b.** Okay, I guess, but I hope I'm not hungry later    2

**c.** Where's the beef?                              3

**17** When I eat beef for dinner, it's likely to be:

**a.** A large juicy steak, like T-bone or prime rib, or a big serving of pot roast swimming in gravy    3

**b.** A moderate serving of lean grilled beef, such as sirloin, with rice or potatoes    2

**c.** A small serving of lean beef that's grilled or mixed into a stir-fry    1

**18** Fish? I'll eat it:

**a.** Only if it's battered and deep-fried, if ever    3

**b.** Baked or broiled, a couple of times a week    1

**c.** Baked or broiled, every couple of weeks or so    2

**19** When I eat Chinese food, I eat this much rice:

**a.** About 1/2 cup                                  1

**b.** About 1 cup                                    2

**c.** Lots—as much as it takes to soak up all the sauce    3

**20** When it comes to dessert, I:

**a.** Live for it—usually a big slice of pie or cake or a bowl of full-fat ice cream    3

**b.** Eat it once in a while when I feel like indulging    1

**c.** Have fruit or a small bowl of reduced-fat ice cream or sorbet    1

## Your Score

**30 or under** You're generally eating the *Magic Foods* way—choosing low-GL carbs most of the time, keeping portions under control, limiting saturated fats, and getting some fruits and vegetables. Use the Magic food profiles, recipes, and meal plans in the rest of the book to help you further fine-tune your eating.

**31 to 40** Your diet could use some improvement. Pay particular attention to answers that were "3s"—these are your dietary downfalls. You do have some good things going for you in your diet, though, so build on them. Use the rest of this book to strengthen your healthy habits and retool your least healthy ones.

**41 or over** No blue ribbon for you—but that means you have your pick of small improvements to make. Look back over your answers and pick out some "3s" that you think you can edge into "2s" or "1s." You'll find lots of tips, tools, suggestions, and recipes in this book to help you improve your diet.

## Understanding Your Score

**1** Having a little sugar in your coffee isn't a big deal, but add 3 teaspoons, and you add nearly 50 calories and 12 grams of carbohydrate. Starting the day with a soft drink—an increasingly common habit—is a dietary downfall to be sure. One 16-ounce (473 ml) bottle of cola has the equivalent of 11 or 12 teaspoons of sugar and will push up your day's GL before you even get out the door.

**2** The (a.) cereal choices have the highest GLs, the (b.) choices are medium GL, and the (c.) cereals have the lowest GLs and are kindest to your blood sugar. If you like a higher-GL cereal, try mixing it with a lower-GL kind and/or pouring a smaller bowl. One cup is plenty.

**3** Orange juice is a healthy beverage, but it has a fair amount of sugar and calories, so don't drink it like water. Use small juice glasses for juice and save large glasses for water and low-calorie drinks only. Juice "drinks" are mostly sugar and water, so we suggest you avoid them altogether.

**4** Whole milk is a major source of saturated fat in our diets, and that's bad for your heart and insulin sensitivity. Drinking 2% milk is better, but this type still gets about a third of its calories from fat, much of it saturated. Fat-free (skim) and 1% are the best choices.

**5** When choosing bread, 100 percent whole grain varieties are best (and if they're made from coarsely ground flours with kernels and seeds, so much the better). Wheat breads that have some white flour are second choices, and white bread comes in last in terms of its effect on your blood sugar.

**6** Potatoes are a high-GL food; there's no getting around it. You don't need to ban them, but don't rely on them as a staple. Sweet potatoes, on the other hand, are a much better choice.

**7** You're not surprised, right? These dark green veggies are incredibly nutritious and have very little carbohydrate. Adding them to any dish or meal—a side of sautéed spinach, lightly steamed broccoli florets in a pasta salad—lowers the meal's overall GL per portion. So does adding nearly any other vegetable.

8 Sandwich meats are a main source of saturated fat in our diets. Lean meats, on the other hand, provide blood sugar–friendly protein without all the fat. Roast beef is in between—better than salami and bologna but fattier than turkey breast. Ask for your roast beef on rye or sourdough, and the sandwich is a step better already. Add mustard instead of mayo for the best blood sugar–lowering effect (it contains vinegar, a Magic food).

9 You can't go wrong with low-cal, high-fiber fruit. Low-fat yogurt, with its sugar-stabilizing protein, is another good choice if it's not overly sweetened. Crackers and cheese are okay, too, especially if the crackers are whole grain (with no trans fats), and you keep your portions in check. Potato or corn chips, though, have easily digested starches, and candy bars offer nothing much but fat and sugar.

10 Nuts are a Magic food thanks to their "good" fats and blood sugar–stabilizing protein. People who eat just a handful each day tend to have healthier hearts and may even have an easier time losing weight (nuts are that filling!). But eat too many, and the benefits will vanish.

11 If you eat at fast-food places often, chances are you're eating lots of fried foods, with too much saturated fat, and high-GL carbs in the bread and fries. Have fast-food meals a few times a month (or less), not a few times a week.

12 The GL of soft drinks isn't as sky-high as you might expect, but it's easy to down huge amounts. Remember, GL is related to portion size; double the amount you drink, and the GL doubles as well. Switching to water or sparkling water can have a dramatic effect on your calorie and sugar intake—and your waistline.

13 Pizza's another food that's okay in moderation, but more than a slice can really pile on the blood sugar–raising carbs and cheesy fat. When ordering, favor thinner crust and lots of veggies on top. Don't tip the scales by adding a big soft drink; have a small one or, better still, water, seltzer, or unsweetened iced tea.

14 A green salad topped with a vinegar-based dressing is perhaps the ideal Magic side dish. The vinegar even helps lower the GL of whatever you eat with your salad. Creamy dressings don't have the same effect, and they add a lot more calories, but even a salad with a little creamy dressing is better than no salad at all; try to limit dressing to a tablespoon or less.

15 Pasta's not bad for you; in fact, it's a Magic food. For a carb food, its GL is not very high, but it's still best eaten in moderation, as a base for lean protein or vegetables. Most cheese and meat sauces, though, are anything but low fat.

16 Beans are a high-protein, low-GL food, making them ideal for anyone concerned about heart health, weight, and blood sugar. Try to have a meatless main meal a few times a week.

17 Beef is a Magic food, but only when it's lean (and eaten in moderation). Even a "lean" hamburger has more saturated fat than the same amount of sirloin or chuck steak.

18 All fish is low in saturated fat, and the high-fat varieties have omega-3 fatty acids, which are good for your heart and even your blood sugar. Try to eat a couple of fish meals a week. Eating fish or seafood deep-fried erases all the benefits.

19 Rice has a surprising number of calories (about 200 per cup), and if you're eating white rice, a high GL. Stick with brown rice and keep your serving small.

20 Everyone should indulge in dessert once in a while, because eating well is not about depriving yourself. If you eat it every day, though, you're probably getting too many calories (unless your dessert is fruit or you're extremely good at controlling your portion sizes).

# Find—And Fix—Your Dietary Downfalls

All of us have dietary strengths and weaknesses, just as we have strengths and weaknesses in other areas of our lives. No one is perfect—and that's fine! But if you're like most people, there are a few things you're doing out of habit that are sabotaging your efforts to control your blood sugar and lose weight. If you change just one or two of them by setting your mind to it, you'll reap rewards in spades. First, though, you have to recognize them.

**PROBLEM** I like a big bowl of cereal in the morning.

**solution** Your first course of action is to make sure you're eating a low-GL cereal, such as Raisin Bran, All-Bran, or Bran Flakes, or at least a medium-GL type like Kellogg's Special K (see "How Cereals Rate" on page 85). If you're not used to these cereals, mix them with a bit of your usual cereal at first to make the transition easier. Second, pour less into the bowl and add something else to fill it up. You can top your cereal with fresh fruit, like chopped apples, strawberries, or blueberries. Adding a tablespoon of chopped nuts is an excellent strategy because nuts add protein and "good" fat, both of which help stabilize your blood sugar and keep you feeling full.

**PROBLEM** I don't eat breakfast until I get to work, and then there's not much to choose from except bagels or muffins.

**solution** Pack your breakfast in an insulated lunch bag the night before so you can grab it on the way out of the house. A fine breakfast is a piece of fruit, a plastic bag with a small handful of nuts, and 8 ounces (250 ml) of low-fat yogurt. Or make a batch of healthy bran muffins (see our recipe on page 197) over the weekend and grab one along with an orange. Another option: Keep a box of high-fiber, low-GL breakfast cereal (along with plastic spoons and bowls) at your desk, and bring the milk (in a Thermos), fruit, and nuts with you.

**PROBLEM** I like sweet drinks, not water.

**solution** That's okay. But think of these drinks, whether they're soft drinks, sweetened iced tea, or sugary fruit drinks, as a treat, like dessert. You wouldn't eat dessert more than once a day, so don't indulge in these drinks more often than that either. Wait until the afternoon and then get the smallest size you can find. In the meantime, cultivate another habit—sipping sparkling water. Some flavored varieties have few or no calories, and a good squeeze of lemon or lime juice makes plain sparkling water much more interesting and palatable. Buy seltzer or mineral water in bulk and make sure there's plenty at home and at the office. Changing this one habit can be a really effective way of improving your diet and even losing weight.

**PROBLEM** There's no place to get a healthy lunch near my office.

**solution** One strategy is to think through what changes would make it easier for you to bring lunch from home. If you're lucky, your office has a refrigerator, a microwave, or even a toaster oven. If so, get into the habit of making more of whatever you're having for dinner, then pack up the leftovers for lunch the next day. If there's no fridge, pack your lunch in a small insulated lunch bag with an ice pack. It will stay cold through lunchtime. On days when you don't pack your lunch, check out page 71 for our tips on eating better at fast-food places.

**PROBLEM** I like pizza. Is that so bad?

**solution** The devil is in the details. The thicker the crust—especially Sicilian—the higher the GL of the meal. If you add pepperoni, you really sabotage yourself with extra calories and saturated fat, which contributes to insulin resistance. So think healthier pizza: thin crust with veggies on top. Go for whole wheat crust if it's available. Stick with one or two slices. Add a salad with vinaigrette dressing so you get enough food to feel full; the vinegar in the dressing will also help lower the GL of the meal. And make the soft drink a small one or, better yet, have sparkling water.

**PROBLEM** When I get salad from the salad bar, I usually load it with cheese, croutons, and creamy dressing. Is it still good for me?

**solution** You might as well eat a hamburger with a side of lettuce. Full-fat cheeses and creamy dressings are high in saturated fat, which is bad for insulin sensitivity. They and the croutons (which are fried) are also loaded with calories. Don't abandon salads, just look for ways to keep them interesting and healthy. Add toasted sunflower seeds for crunch (and healthy fat) or a few black olives for richness (and again, "good" fat). Add hot peppers, if you like them, for kick. Throw on some chickpeas for addi-

tional texture. Top it all off with a vinegar-based dressing; experiment to find a tasty one you like, such as mustard vinaigrette for extra flavor.

**PROBLEM** I am starving at about 3:00 in the afternoon, and I eat whatever junk food is in sight.

**solution** If you eat Magic foods for breakfast and lunch, this won't happen. And that's good, because research shows that when they're really hungry, people can eat as much as twice as much food as they normally would. Snacking itself isn't bad at all, though, so keep healthy snacks on hand (think carrot sticks, apples, low-fat yogurt, a few whole grain crackers and peanut butter, or a handful of peanuts or almonds) to keep the sailing smooth between lunch and dinner.

**PROBLEM** I eat carbs when I'm stressed or anxious.

**solution** A lot of people reach for carbs when they're stressed. (The scientific jury is out as to whether carbs actually help calm you down. The effect may simply be due to a sense of comfort from a familiar food.) There's no quick solution here. The key is to figure out ways to cope other than eating. Practice deep breathing or give yourself a "timeout" by taking a 10-minute stroll, after which the craving should have passed. One of the best ways to deal with anxiety in general is to exercise; even a brisk 20-minute walk can lift your mood and calm you down. Studies show that people who exercise regularly have lower responses to stress than people who don't. You can also practice prevention at the supermarket: Avoid buying simple carbohydrates so they aren't within reach when you want them.

**PROBLEM** I know portion sizes are important, but it's so easy to finish what's on my plate.

**solution** Use a smaller plate! Really. Manufacturers are actually making many plates and bowls larger because we eat so much bigger portions than we used to. Fight the trend by serving dinner on a lunch plate. Serve juice in real juice glasses—they're much smaller than regular glasses. Instead of using a big bowl for cereal, try a smaller dessert bowl. And always spoon out your dinner onto individual plates rather than leaving bowls or platters on the table within easy reach.

**PROBLEM** I'd like to eat more beans, but I don't know much about cooking them.

**solution** You don't have to make bean dishes from scratch. Canned beans can be no-fuss additions to something you're already making. Making a salad? Rinse some canned chickpeas and toss them on top. Add canned kidney beans to nearly any vegetable soup. For a quick bean side dish, drain a can of white beans, put them into a microwavable bowl, and add some olive oil, grated Parmesan, and fresh pepper. Microwave for a minute or two, then mash for a delicious, high-protein, low-GL dish.

**PROBLEM** When I eat small portions at dinner, I'm still hungry.

**solution** First, make sure your dinner contains protein and "good fat," not just carbs. That way, it will keep you full longer (plus, you're less likely to overeat broiled chicken breast than buttery mashed potatoes). Second, try to eat a little slower so your stomach has more time to send the message to your brain that you're full. Take plenty of time between bites for conversation or sips of water. If these don't do the trick, start the meal with clear soup or a salad, both of which will occupy a lot of space in your stomach and help you put down your fork sooner. And remember: It's okay to leave the dinner table a tiny bit hungry. You'll feel fuller as your food digests.

**PROBLEM** I'd like to snack on fruit, but I just don't think of it.

**solution** Put it in front of your face, literally. Studies show that people eat more fruit when it's in a bowl on the counter rather than tucked away in the refrigerator. Lots of fruits stay fresh on the counter,  such as apples, pears, plums, nectarines, and bananas. When you buy fruit, wash it as soon as you come home, then put it in a bowl. If you keep fruit in the fridge—such as grapes, which taste great cold—make sure it's on the top shelf where it's easy to grab. Like melon? Cut it into slices or cubes and refrigerate it in an airtight container so it's ready to eat come snack time.

**PROBLEM** My pitfall is late-night desserts.

**solution** Try to have your dessert earlier. If you normally eat it at 10:00 p.m., aim for 8:30, and then brush your teeth so you're not tempted to eat again. Another strategy: Avoid bringing home the kinds of desserts that you most tend to overeat; most people won't leave the house at night just to get dessert. Finally, train yourself to enjoy healthier desserts, such as a bowl of berries with a dollop of low-fat ice cream or light whipped cream or a container of light pre-portioned pudding, and you won't have to worry as much.

# The Art of Eating Out

If most restaurants offered menus full of Magic fare like lean grilled meats, whole grain side dishes, and fruit-based desserts, it would be a snap to eat out the Magic way. But they don't. Nearly all of the most common carbohydrate-rich foods on menus reflect those in the typical Western diet. In other words, they are high-GL foods. And at most restaurants, from fast-food joints to the fanciest white-tablecloth establishments, the food is floating in fat and stuffed with extra calories. Add to that the amazingly large portions that we have grown to expect for our dining dollars, and eating out seems impossible to do well.

It can be done, though, and learning to do it is a survival skill. That's because we eat out—or have takeout meals—so often now that it's a staple of our lives. Fifty years ago, about one out of four meals was prepared outside the home; today, it's closer to one in two.

The first step is to accept how commonly you eat meals you haven't made yourself, then plan to order better.

## BE CAREFUL WHERE YOU EAT

Make the challenge of eating out easier by being smart about what kinds of restaurants you patronize. Avoid the temptation of all-you-can-eat places, or buffet-style restaurants, where portions are hard to control. Avoid places known for enormous portions, like most steak houses. And you probably won't find a lot of Magic foods on the menu at eateries that specialize in deep-frying an entire breaded onion. Enjoy a meal at one of these on your birthday, sure, but don't do it on a regular basis.

## MAKE FRIENDS WITH THE WAITPERSON

Once you're in the right kind of restaurant, get ready to get friendly with the waitperson. Ask them to hold the breadbasket so you're not tempted to fill up on usually high-GL carbs while waiting for your meal to arrive. Inquire about how a dish you're considering is prepared (Is it swimming in butter? Are the vegetables present in only token amounts?) and find out how big the portions are.

## ORDER CREATIVELY

When you order, be bold: Order soup, salad, and an appetizer (not fried) for your meal rather than an entrée. Split an entrée and share a side order of vegetables to get more veggies into your meal—and fewer calories. If a main dish comes with a potato, ask if you can get an extra vegetable instead. (Especially if you're a regular customer, you're likely to get your way.) If you plan to order dessert, plan to share it, too. The best situation is when you get to know a restaurant's regular fare, including how big the portions are, and use that knowledge to outsmart the menu.

## Eating Out
# Chinese

The traditional Chinese diet is a healthy one, with lots of vegetables, stir-fries with small chunks of meat or fish, and soy foods. But that's not evident in the typical fare in a Chinese restaurant here, where the meal is likely to be heavy on greasy meats and swimming in sauces with lots and lots of calories. Even the vegetables are usually in a fatty sauce.

Do you have to give up Chinese takeout? Of course not; that would be almost unthinkable. But to get a Magic meal, you do have to order carefully.

### just say NO

Crispy noodles

Egg rolls

Fried wontons

Fried rice

Pan-fried noodles

Lo mein

Crispy beef or chicken

Sweet-and-sour pork, chicken, and other meat dishes

Szechuan spicy fish

General Tso's chicken

Kung pao chicken

Spicy eggplant

## YOUR GAME PLAN

1. **Ask for brown rice.** Most restaurants give you the option. Remember, white rice is a blood sugar disaster waiting to happen. And don't eat the whole bowl or container of rice. Spoon a half cup onto your plate and leave the rest. Or do as a Chinese native would: Put a small amount in a small bowl and hold the bowl up, using your chopsticks (or fork) to eat a little rice in between bites of your main dish. Or be bold and don't eat any rice at all.

2. **Start your meal with wonton, egg drop, or hot-and-sour soup.** This will take the edge off your hunger without a lot of calories (avoid soups with coconut milk). If you want a ravioli-type appetizer, order steamed vegetable dumplings, but nothing fried.

3. **When it comes to entrées, order from the "health" menu.** Here is where you'll find steamed chicken and vegetables with sauce on the side and similar low-fat choices. Another good choice is moo goo gai pan (chicken with mushrooms). If you like stir-fries, ask the waitperson to have yours prepared with less oil and more veggies, and get the sauce on the side.

4. **Make sure you order plenty of vegetables.** If you really want to make the meal healthier, order a plate of steamed vegetables and add them to other dishes. Or ask for sautéed vegetables or Szechuan-style string beans.

5. **Take advantage of the bean curd (tofu).** Include a heart-healthy, low-GL dish like bean curd with sautéed Chinese mixed vegetables (ask for sautéed bean curd, not deep-fried).

6. **Plan to take home leftovers.** Portions are often large. Think of about a cup of a dish (without rice) as a serving.

## Eating Out
# Italian

A single slice of pizza with vegetables is a fine choice, especially if it's made with a whole wheat and/or thin crust. A cup of pasta with marinara sauce is all right, too. The problem is, few of us stop there.

Ironically, southern Italian food, prepared the traditional way, is among the healthiest in the world. Unfortunately, Italian restaurants are often parlors for the presentation of huge mounds of overcooked pasta and pizza. And even before these arrive, you'll have ample opportunity to eat bread. So unless you want to overload on carbs and send your blood sugar for a wild post-meal ride, tread carefully.

## YOUR GAME PLAN

1. Ask the waitperson not to bring the breadbasket. Instead, order minestrone or another broth-based soup to fill up on while you await your entrée. Pasta e fagioli, another Italian classic, is a delicious bean/pasta soup that's also a good starter.

2. If you want pasta, order a dish from the appetizer section of the menu, or share. That's the traditional way—a small first course of pasta followed by simple grilled meat, poultry, or fish and a side of sautéed greens. As for pasta sauces, opt for those based on tomatoes (marinara), vegetables, white wine, and garlic—not cream. Watch out: Pasta primavera is often made with lots of cream.

3. If it's on the menu, order simple grilled beef, veal, pork, chicken, fish, or shellfish. Add a side order of sautéed spinach or broccoli rabe (a slightly bitter Italian version of broccoli). Finish with a mixed green salad with vinaigrette dressing.

4. For dessert, ask for fresh berries or fruit ice, if it's available, or a small plate of cookies to share. Stay away from the custards and cheesecake, the cannoli, and the tiramisu.

## Eating Out
# Mexican

Ordering from a fast-food Mexican place is about as big as a blood sugar challenge can get. Portions are generally huge, the tortillas used for burritos are larger than your head and filled with a cup or more of white rice (blood sugar enemy # 1), and the entrées tend to be loaded with cheese—and we don't mean the Magic low-fat variety. Thread your way around these potholes, and you can arrive at a delicious, moderate-GL meal.

### just say NO

Tortilla chips

Nachos

Chimichangas

Quesadillas

Enchiladas (beef, cheese, or any other kind)

Chiles rellenos

Refried beans

Anything "grande"

## YOUR GAME PLAN

1. **Ask the waitperson to take away the tortilla chips.** The Mexican equivalent of a big breadbasket is either a bowl of chips with salsa or nacho chips covered with cheese. Just say no.

2. **Order a healthy starter instead.** Look for ceviches (marinated raw fish or seafood); guacamole, which is full of "good" fats (ask for soft tortillas instead of deep-fried chips to dip, and don't overeat them); gazpacho, a spicy cold vegetable soup; black bean soup; and tortilla soup (chicken in broth with vegetables and thin fried tortilla chips). Ask for extra salsa for the table and eat it with a spoon rather than on chips.

3. **For an entrée, look to fajitas.** These are made with lean beef (or chicken or shrimp) grilled with onions and peppers. Other good choices are grilled chicken or fish dishes.

4. **Order tacos or burritos without high-fat sour cream.** Ask for extra salsa instead. Hard tacos are fried, so you're better off with soft tacos; soft tortillas are even better. A small tortilla is the equivalent of a slice of bread.

If you're not eating rice, two or three soft tacos are fine, but stick to one or two if you are having rice. If you're getting a burrito, ask for no rice and more beans.

5. **As a side dish, go for rice and beans instead of Mexican rice.** Thanks to the beans, this dish has a lower GL than rice alone. But check first to be sure the beans aren't refried. Refried beans are loaded with fat.

6. **Have dessert at home.** Desserts at Mexican restaurants, such as flan and fried ice cream, are usually high in calories and fat, so skip them and eat something healthier elsewhere.

Eating Out

# Fast Food

An occasional visit to a fast-food joint never killed anyone. Burgers and fries are still the staples on these menus, but the restaurants are now offering a greater selection of healthier fare. True, you'll have trouble locating a decent vegetable, but you can keep the fat and calorie damage under control by ordering grilled sandwiches, salads, and even vegetarian burgers, chili, soup, and low-fat dairy desserts. Aim to make your meals "fast" ones less than once a week.

### just say NO

French fries

Chicken nuggets

Fried fish or chicken sandwiches

Onion rings

Special sauce

Bacon

Double burgers

Cheeseburgers

## YOUR GAME PLAN

1. Opt for simple grilled fare, if you can find it. If there's a grilled chicken sandwich and the chicken isn't breaded, that's a good start. Wendy's Ultimate Chicken Grill (360 calories) is a good choice, as is McDonald's Chicken McGrill.

2. A simple hamburger isn't bad either—if you order the smallest one. At 280 calories, Wendy's Jr. Hamburger is a low-cal burger. (By contrast, a Burger King Double Whopper with Cheese has 1,060 calories.) Another good option is a vegetarian burger. Burger King regularly offers vegetarian burgers (the BK Veggie; 380 calories), and McDonald's has them at some locations (the McVeggie; 350 calories).

3. Order à la carte. A meal that includes fries and a big soft drink is often cheaper, but it's no nutritional bargain. Skip the soft drink and ask for water—or orange juice, hot tea, coffee, or low-fat milk—instead. If it's a special treat, get the fries but buy the smallest size.

4. Take advantage of the salads. Just skip the cheese, bacon bits, and other add-ons. Ask for vinaigrette dressing. Try a salad as an entrée. Good choices include Burger King's Fire-Grilled Chicken (with vinaigrette) and Wendy's Mandarin Chicken Salad (with Oriental sesame dressing).

5. Have yogurt. At Wendy's, you can get fresh fruit with yogurt (220 calories); McDonald's offers Fruit 'n' Yogurt Parfait (160 calories).

THE MAGIC FOODS APPROACH IN ACTION | 71

## A (Scary) Trip to the Mall

Be prepared: The mall is a very dangerous place—for your nutritional safety. Before you leave, you'll get hungry, but like a fly in a spider's web, you're caught in a matrix of sticky choices that are nearly all disastrous.

If you succumb to a Classic Cinnabon, for example, you'll take in 730 calories, nearly all of them in the form of high-GL starches, sugar, and saturated fat. Go for the Cinnabon Caramel Pecanbon, and you get 1,100 calories—more than half the amount most people need in an entire day!

Or maybe Dunkin' Donuts is nearby. Grab a croissant (330 calories) and wash it down with a Coffee Coolata with cream (350), and you're up to 680 calories. And you haven't even had a meal, just a snack!

Maybe you're hungrier. If you're eyeing up Chick-fil-A, watch out: A Chicken Deluxe Sandwich with medium waffle fries and a large iced tea will cost you 950 calories.

Can you escape without catastrophe? Perhaps, if you keep your wits about you.

If there's a Subway, for instance, you can have a 6-inch (15 cm) roast beef sandwich on whole wheat bread for only 290 calories, with very little saturated fat and only a modest amount of carbohydrate (45 grams). You can get a similar low-fat, low-cal sandwich made with ham, oven-roasted chicken breast, turkey breast, or club style. Get it with minestrone soup for only 90 more calories. Wash it down with a diet soft drink or water, and you've eaten a real, satisfying meal for only 380 calories.

On the other hand, if you want only a snack, and you're smart, you'll have one with you. A handful of nuts is easy to throw into a resealable plastic bag. Baby carrots are similarly easy to bag and transport. And the old snack standby, an apple, always works well.

Now, throw away the apple core, put on your coat, get on the escalator, and walk out of the mall. No one will get hurt.

## A Hidden Hazard: Coffee Drinks

It's easy to drink yourself into a bad place. And we're not talking about alcohol, just big "coffee" drinks. We're highlighting Starbucks here, but it's the same story at Dunkin' Donuts and other establishments that use coffee as a vehicle for cream, chocolate, caramel, and sugar.

Consider the Double Chocolate Chip Frappucino Blended Crème with whipped cream, Venti size (24 ounces/710 milliliters). It has 86 grams of sugar. Since 10 grams of table sugar—about 2 1/2 teaspoons—has a GL of 6, you could estimate that the sugar in this drink would provide a GL of about 52. Since any food with a GL over 20 is high GL, this is *very* high. But that sweet beverage also contributes a whopping 25 grams of fat, more than half of it saturated—the kind that not only clogs arteries but also contributes to insulin resistance. That drink has more fat and saturated fat than you'd get in a McDonald's Quarter Pounder with Cheese.

A Mocha Frappucino Blended Coffee might be a little better, but a Venti size still packs 530 calories, 18 grams of fat, and 69 grams of sugar (the equivalent of about 17 teaspoons). Consider as an alternative a cappuccino made with fat-free milk. Even a huge Venti has only 130 calories and about 16 grams of sugar (about 4 teaspoons' worth, with a GL of 10).

Of course, freshly brewed black coffee has almost no calories at all. Consider a tall black coffee from Starbucks with 2 teaspoons of sugar. It has fewer than 40 calories. You'd have to drink more than 18 of them to get the same number of calories as in the Frappucino Blended Crème. Its GL is about 5. Even if you add 2 tablespoons of 2% milk, it has only 57 calories.

If you prefer a cold drink, ask for plain iced coffee (with fat-free milk if you like) and add your own sugar.

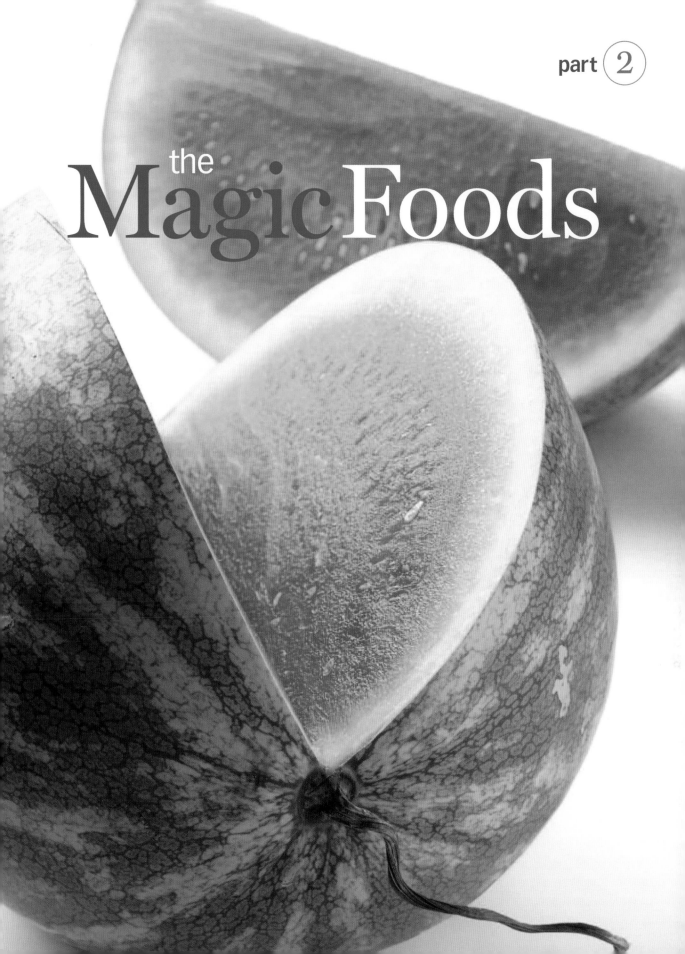

# the Magic Foods

# apples

**GL** LOW | Can eating an apple a day really help keep the doctor away? It can certainly help you control your blood sugar and gain all the benefits that come with that control. In fact, researchers have discovered that women who eat at least one apple a day are 28 percent less likely to develop type 2 diabetes than those who don't eat apples. That's probably because apples, from tart Granny Smiths to sweet, juicy Pink Ladies, are loaded with soluble fiber—number one for blunting blood sugar swings. A medium apple dishes up an impressive 4 grams of fiber, mostly pectin, which is also known for its ability to lower cholesterol.

Looking to trim your tummy? (Remember, belly fat is bad for blood sugar.) Try eating three small apples a day. A study from the State University of Rio de Janeiro found that doing so as part of a reduced-calorie diet helped women not only lose more weight but also lower their blood sugar more than women who ate another food instead of apples.

To press every bit of benefit from apples, opt for whole, unpeeled fruit. For apples with a lower GL, look for Braeburns, which have more acid and less sugar than Golden Delicious. Next on the glycemic scale is unsweetened applesauce, which offers many of the same health benefits. But steer clear of apple juice; it's not much better than apple-flavored liquid sugar.

## Health Bonus

Apples aren't particularly rich in vitamins or minerals, but that doesn't mean they're not good for you. In fact, they're loaded with antioxidant compounds called flavonoids, believed to reduce the risk of cancer and heart disease. One study found that eating a small apple with the skin provided total antioxidant and anti-cancer activity equal to 1,500 milligrams of vitamin C.

## Menu Magic

- Snack on half an apple with a smear of peanut butter (another Magic food).
- Add thinly sliced apples to sandwiches for a bit of tang and crunch.
- Mix chopped apples with low-fat yogurt and wheat germ (two other Magic foods) for a healthy mid-morning snack.
- Doctor up jarred salsa by adding chopped apples, cucumbers, onions, jalapeño peppers, and lime juice.
- Put together an apple-cabbage skillet dinner with chopped apples, shredded cabbage, low-fat turkey sausage, chopped onions, cider vinegar, and fresh parsley.
- Make applesauce by cubing apples and simmering them in a small amount of water until desirably mushy. Add a sprinkling of cinnamon, a Magic spice.

## Smart Substitutions

*Instead of raisins:* Try sliced apples on your oatmeal or other cereal. Unlike apples, raisins have concentrated sugars that raise blood sugar more quickly than apples do.

*Instead of oil:* Replace three-quarters of the butter or oil called for in cookie, cake, and brownie recipes with unsweetened applesauce.

### RELATED recipes

# avocado

**GL** VERY LOW

Unlike virtually all other fruits (yes, avocados are fruits), these rich, creamy treats are loaded with fat—a whopping 25 to 30 grams each. Since fat has no impact on blood sugar, avocados are great additions to a low-GL diet if you eat them in moderation.

But, you may wonder, what about all that fat? There is a saving grace: Most of it is monounsaturated fat, the same heart-healthy kind found in olive oil. Research suggests that diets rich in this type of fat may help keep blood sugar in check. That's the main reason for secret number 5 of Magic eating, Favor Good Fats. Add some avocado to a sandwich or anything else with bread or carbs, and the fat will slow digestion of the meal, thus making it easier on your blood sugar.

Unlike the saturated fats in butter and meat, monounsaturated fat won't increase insulin resistance, a condition that makes blood sugar control more difficult. In fact, the good fat in avocados (as well as olive oil and nuts) may actually *reverse* insulin resistance, helping your body steady its blood sugar levels. Avocados also contain more soluble fiber (which stabilizes blood sugar and lowers cholesterol) and protein than any other fruit.

Of course, with fat come calories, so you don't want to start eating avocados with total abandon—though you probably wouldn't anyway, since a little avocado goes a long way.

## Health Bonus

Avocados are rich in sterols, compounds shown to lower cholesterol. They're also packed with vitamins and minerals, including vitamin E, magnesium, vitamin C, folate, and zinc. Ounce for ounce, they provide more potassium than bananas!

## Cooks Tips

To choose just the right avocado, try this: Hold the avocado in your hand and press it gently, then roll it to the other side and press again. If it gives just a

## PERFECT portions: 1/5th avocado

Cut an avocado into five pieces and have one piece for 55 calories. If that sounds high to you, consider how it stacks up against a tablespoon of mayonnaise (100 calories), butter (also 100 calories), or salad dressing (about 75 calories). The avocado has fewer calories and offers a lot more nutrition.

bit but pressure doesn't leave a permanent dent (an indication that it's too ripe), it's ready to eat.

## Menu Magic

- Guacamole is the classic avocado dish. Add some curry for an Indian flair; hot bean sauce or oriental chili paste for an Asian influence; or basil, sun-dried tomatoes, Parmesan cheese, and pine nuts for a taste of Italy.

- Mash some avocado and use as a spread on sandwiches (made with whole grain bread, of course), bagels, or English muffins to lower the GL of your breakfast or lunch.

- Add chunks of avocado to a side salad to lower the GL of the meal. Adding it to salads also increases your body's ability to absorb the good-for-you carotenoids, such as beta-carotene, in salad greens.

## Smart Substitutions

*Instead of cheese in your sandwich:* Add a slice of avocado. You'll swap good fats for bad ones.

*Instead of cheese as a snack:* Have a slice of ripe avocado drizzled with lemon juice.

### RELATED recipes

Spinach, Grapefruit and Avocado Salad with Poppy Seed Dressing *216*

Turkey and Bean Chili with Avocado Salsa *243*

# barley

**GL** LOW

If you've only encountered barley in mushroom-barley soup, get ready to make friends with this underappreciated cereal grain. Whether pearled, hulled, or quick cooking, it can help transform your diet into a Magic one. In fact, think of barley as your new white rice.

Unlike white rice, which has a sky-high GL, barley's is low, thanks to its significant stash of soluble fiber. In fact, eating barley instead of white rice slashes the effect on your blood sugar by almost 70 percent. Add it to soups, use it instead of Arborio rice (the worst rice offender of all) in risotto, and serve it as a nutty, flavorful side dish. The possibilities are endless.

Because its insoluble fiber slows the rate at which food leaves the stomach, barley also helps you feel full on fewer calories.

## Health Bonus

Because it contains the same kind of cholesterol-lowering fiber found in oats, barley has FDA-approved bragging rights for its ability to lower cholesterol and cut the risk of heart disease.

## Menu Magic

While barley is a natural for soups, think outside the stockpot. Broaden your barley horizons and experiment.

**PERFECT portion : 1/2 cup**

This is a good amount for a side dish. For main dishes you can have 3/4 cup and still keep the GL in the "low" category.

- Instead of rice pilaf, make barley pilaf to serve with any main dish.
- Add barley to casseroles and use it in place of rice in rice salads.
- Serve barley and diced apples with rosemary baked chicken.
- Add cooked, chilled barley to a bean salad for a fantastic lunch.
- Try corn and barley relish. Add canned or frozen corn to cooked barley along with olive oil; wine vinegar; chopped fresh basil; salt; pepper; and chopped tomatoes, bell peppers, and onions.

### RELATED recipes

Barley Risotto with Asparagus and Lemon *262*
Barley Salad with Snow Peas and Lemon Dressing *211*
Bean and Barley Soup *222*
Black Bean and Barley Salad *213*
Mushroom-Barley Pilaf *264*

---

**BARLEY glossary** Like oats, barley comes in different varieties determined by how the grain is processed. All are beneficial to blood sugar.

**Hulled barley (barley groats):** Only the outer hull of the grain is removed; the bran is left intact. This is the least processed, most nutritious type.

**Pot or Scotch barley:** This is more processed than hulled barley but retains some of the bran layer.

**Pearled barley:** This is much more processed, with the outer hull and bran removed. Because the soluble fiber runs all the way through the grain, however, this type is still a smart choice.

**Quick-cooking barley:** Similar to pearled barley in taste and nutrition, this is presteamed, so it takes only about 10 minutes to cook compared to an hour for other types.

**Barley flour:** This provides more than three times the fiber of refined white flour. For baking, combine it with wheat flour; otherwise, it won't rise.

**Barley flakes:** Made from steam-rolled and dried barley, these are cooked for hot cereal.

whole wheat
pasta

oats

Don't blame grains—embrace them! The Magic grains have a moderate glycemic load and are too good for you to pass up.

- barley
- bran
- brown rice
- bulgur
- oats
- pasta
- pumpernickel bread
- rye bread
- sourdough bread
- wheatberries
- wheat germ
- whole wheat bread

magic grains

whole wheat bread

barley

# beans

**GL** LOW

Surely you remember the old childhood rhyme that begins "Beans, beans, they're good for your heart ... " Well, beans *are* good for your heart. But these slow-acting foods, rich in complex carbohydrates, are also fantastic for your blood sugar and are surely one of the foods most deserving of special attention in your Magic diet.

All beans, canned or dried, from black to white and chickpeas to cannellini, can tame both insulin and blood sugar levels thanks to their high soluble fiber content. In a recent study, men and women who ate a meal that included about 6 ounces (170 g) of chickpeas had 40 percent lower blood sugar an hour after eating than those who ate an equal amount of white bread with jam.

The soluble fiber in beans slows down digestion, leading to a slow, steady blood sugar rise rather than a spike. Beans also pack loads of protein, which doesn't raise blood sugar and actually helps your body process the carbohydrates in a meal more efficiently. Are they the perfect food for people with diabetes? Perhaps. Just stick with 1/2 cup or so per meal, since beans do contain carbohydrates.

If you're trying to lose weight, eat beans! Not only are they incredibly filling, they also pack a heap of nutrition in a relatively low-calorie package. Better still, some of the starch in beans is a type called resistant starch that the body can't even digest, so the calories don't count.

Beans are also full of folate, a B vitamin that may help reduce some of the nasty consequences of diabetes by helping to keep arteries clean.

Dietary guidelines recommend eating at least 3 cups of beans a week, but most of us lag far behind: We don't average even 1 cup a week. We would have to eat almost triple our current intake to meet the recommendation.

## Health Bonus

Looking for antioxidants? Look no further. A recent study ranked beans among the top ten foods richest in these health protectors. What's more, the same soluble fiber in beans that helps stabilize blood sugar also helps lower cholesterol.

## Perfect Pairings

Beans and rice is a classic dish, and for good reason, since together they make a complete protein (alone, each lacks certain amino acids, the building blocks of

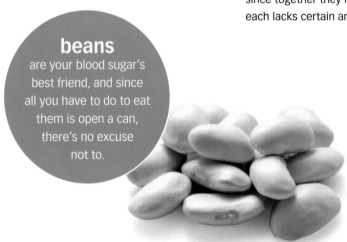

**beans** are your blood sugar's best friend, and since all you have to do to eat them is open a can, there's no excuse not to.

protein). While white rice has a high GL, combining it with beans—and therefore eating less rice—makes the GL of the dish much lower. To lower the GL of a pasta meal, use less pasta and top it with beans.

## Cooks Tips

The only black mark for beans is the sodium content of canned beans. Cut it in half by rinsing them in cold water before using.

Chickpeas can be ground into flour, allowing you to use less white flour and therefore lower the GL of baked goods. Bake some whole wheat bread with chickpea flour, and your blood sugar will be substantially lower a half hour after eating it than if you ate regular whole wheat bread, studies show.

### Silencing the Musical Fruit

Beans have the dubious distinction of being the "musical fruit" (translation: They give you gas). That's because they're rich in a specific type of carbohydrate that you can't digest but that provides fodder for the bacteria that live in your intestinal tract. Gas is the by-product. It's a big reason why people shy away from beans, but there's no need to do without this blood sugar fixer-upper.

You can "degas" beans by soaking them. Short on time? Boil the beans in water for 2 minutes, then remove from the heat and let stand for 2 to 4 hours with the lid on. Or, if you have the luxury of planning ahead, soak them for at least 12 hours. After either method, drain, then rinse twice and cover with fresh cold water before cooking.

Another degassing option: Take Beano with meals containing beans. It's a natural food enzyme that helps digest the gas-producing compounds in beans and other foods.

**PERFECT portions:** 1/2 cup

This amount provides 105 to 147 calories and keeps the GL low.

## Menu Magic

- Serve bean dip or hummus with a whole wheat pita cut into wedges.
- Mash beans or chickpeas to make a low-GL spread and serve on coarse-ground whole grain bread.
- Use drained and rinsed canned beans as the basis for easy weeknight bean soups.
- Add canned kidney beans (or any other kind) to green salads.
- Cook up a big pot of black bean chili on the weekend and freeze the leftovers.
- Mix mango, red pepper, onion, and black beans for a zesty summer salad. Add some cilantro if you like.

## RELATED recipes

Bean and Barley Soup *222*

Black Bean and Barley Salad *213*

Black Bean and Sweet Potato Burritos *263*

Black Bean Spread with Mexican Flavors *206*

Dahl with Spinach *261*

Hearty Split Pea Soup with Rye Croutons 223

Lentil and Bean Chili *262*

Mediterranean Split Pea Spread *205*

Tuna and Cannellini Salad with Lemon *213*

Turkey and Bean Chili with Avocado Salsa *243*

Warm Artichoke and Bean Dip *204*

Whole Wheat Pasta with Sausage, Beans and Greens *254*

# beef

**GL** VERY LOW

Beef for dinner? You bet! Beef is an important source of protein, and as long as you choose lean cuts and eat moderate portions (no giant T-bones that give the waiter a workout), there's no reason it can't be part of a Magic diet. In fact, here's how important protein is to your blood sugar: A study at the University of Minnesota tested two different diets, one high in protein and one with only half as much. The fat content was the same in both diets. In the group that followed the high-protein diet (which was also lower in carbs), blood sugar levels were reduced by as much as if the participants had taken pills prescribed to lower blood sugar.

Your leanest choices are the "skinny six": eye of round, top round, sirloin, bottom round, top loin, and tenderloin. The not-so-skinny cuts to trim from your diet include rib eye, prime rib, T-bone, and most ground beef, which are all high in saturated fat. (To get the leanest ground beef for hamburgers or meat loaf, look for "extra lean," or 93 percent to 95 percent lean, whether it's ground beef, ground round, or ground sirloin.) Saturated fat not only clogs your arteries, it can also contribute to insulin resistance, which makes it harder for your body to use insulin to get blood sugar out of the bloodstream and into cells.

Lean beef isn't just good for your blood sugar, it's even good for your waistline. Dieters tend to lose muscle along with fat, which slows their metabolisms, since muscle tissue burns more calories than fat tissue does. Eating protein helps you hang on to that muscle mass—and keep your metabolism burning on "high."

We're not advocating a diet super-high in protein or super-low in carbs, which simply isn't healthy. (If you haven't already, read "Why Radical Low-Carb Diets Aren't the Answer," starting on page 34.) Aim to keep your protein intake at 20 to 30 percent of the calories you eat.

## Health Bonus

Protein isn't the only selling point. Beef is also one of the best sources of zinc, a mineral that people often come up short on, especially if they're counting calories, and vitamin $B_{12}$, which you can get only from eating animal foods such as eggs, milk, and of course, beef. Another beef bonus: Its fat is rich in conjugated linoleic acid, or CLA, a fatty acid that helps lower blood sugar.

### Love Me Tender

While lean cuts of beef are better for you, they're also not as tender as fattier cuts (the fat is what makes a knife cut through a prime rib like butter). But there are ways to turn up the tenderness of healthier cuts.

⊛ Pound and flatten the meat into thinner, more tender slices.

⊛ Use the juice from a fresh pineapple as a marinade. It contains a powerful enzyme that breaks down the meat, tenderizing it. Canned pineapple juice won't work; the enzymes are destroyed during processing.

⊛ Use a marinade that contains vinegar, wine, or citrus juice. The acid softens the tissues of meat, making it more tender and tastier.

⊛ Cook tenderized beef either quickly at a high temperature or for an extended period with moist heat at a low to medium temperature.

## Cooks Tips

Want to beef up the health benefits of beef? If you can find it, you may want to opt for grass-fed beef, which can have as much as 60 percent more heart-healthy omega-3 fatty acids and about twice as much CLA as regular beef. But be prepared to pay: Grass-fed beef can cost at least twice as much.

## Menu Magic

- Throw together fajitas made with flank steak, bell peppers, and onions for a quick weeknight meal.

- Toss hot grilled beef with cold, crisp lettuce; lime juice; and chopped onion for a refreshingly delicious Asian-inspired salad.

- When company comes, serve up a nice (and lean) beef tenderloin.

- Stir-fry strips of beef with lots of veggies for an easy way to have your beef and get your vegetables, too.

- Cook up three-bean chili with a small amount of extra-lean ground beef.

- Make Asian kebabs with beef marinated in soy sauce, sesame oil, crushed garlic, and ginger. Serve over brown rice.

- Create healthier meat loaf by combining finely chopped spinach and onions and grated carrots with lean ground beef. Use oats as a binder.

- Make any cut of beef a taste standout by marinating it in balsamic vinegar, olive oil, basil, Dijon mustard, and garlic.

### RELATED recipes

**Beef and Veggie Meat Loaf** *230*
**Flank Steak with Balsamic Sauce** *228*
**Greek Pasta and Beef Casserole** *230*
**Orange Beef Stir-Fry with Broccoli and Red Pepper** *226*
**Slow-Cooker Beef and Vegetable Stew** *228*

**Lean beef** is good for your blood sugar and even your waistline, so don't cross it off your shopping list.

# berries

**GL** VERY LOW

Berries, from ruby red strawberries to midnight-blue blueberries, may be candy for your taste buds, but they're Magic for your blood sugar. Their sweetness is deceptive. Fructose, the natural sugar found in most fruits, is sweeter than what's in your sugar bowl (sucrose), so it takes much less (with fewer calories) to get that sweet taste. And fructose is friendlier to blood sugar, causing a much slower rise than table sugar does.

Berries are full of fiber and red-blue natural plant compounds called anthocyanins that may help keep your blood sugar in check. Scientists believe anthocyanins, also found in cherries, may help lower blood sugar by boosting insulin production.

Opt for fresh or frozen berries over berry juices. While the juices are packed with the same phytonutrients as whole berries, they are concentrated sources of carbs, and they lack an important ingredient for blood sugar control—fiber.

What about that jar of jam or jelly in your fridge? Spread lightly. Even those whose labels say they're 100 percent natural fruit spread contain either added sugar or added fruit juice and have higher GLs than whole fresh fruit. Still, a tablespoon is fine if you spread it on whole wheat toast or a whole wheat English muffin.

## Health Bonus

Berries, especially blueberries, have a well-earned reputation for being especially rich in powerful disease-fighting antioxidants. Studies show that if you make berries a daily indulgence, they can help keep your eyes healthy, reduce your risk of heart disease and cancer, and work to keep your brain and memory in tiptop shape.

Strawberries are a surprisingly good source of heart-healthy vitamin C, giving even oranges a run for their money; a cup of strawberry halves provides as much C as a cup of orange sections. And studies show that people who eat a serving of strawberries a day tend to have lower blood pressure and higher blood levels of the B vitamin folate, important for keeping arteries clear.

Eating cranberries can help fend off urinary tract infections. Experts say that about 1 1/2 ounces (45 g) of dried cranberries a day could do the trick. Researchers have discovered that blueberries contain some of the same infection-fighting compounds as cranberries.

## Cooks Tips

Berries are nutrition powerhouses, but they're also fragile fruits. Choose berries that are plump and free of bruises or mold. The skin of blueberries should be smooth and not shriveled. The hazy white coating you see on blueberries is a natural protective coating, so don't try to wash it off. Look for blackberries and raspberries that aren't leaking (if the small bumps that make up a berry burst, the juice inside leaks out, causing quicker spoilage).

Store berries in the fridge and rinse them just before serving; otherwise, they'll go bad faster.

Since strawberries have been named by the Environmental Working Group as one of the "dirty dozen" fruits and vegetables most likely to contain pesticide residues, buy organic when you can.

To get berry benefits year round, buy berries when they're in season and freeze them. Here are a few pointers.

- Blueberries and strawberries freeze the best. Raspberries and blackberries are more delicate, and freezing can change their texture.
- Wash the berries in cold water and let them dry completely on a paper towel or in a colander.

- Spread the dry berries out on a sheet of wax paper on a baking sheet and place in the freezer.
- Once they are completely frozen, pack them in a tightly sealed freezer container and put them back in the freezer right away.

## Menu Magic

Berries can complement countless dishes, adding eye appeal as well as sweetness and flavor.

- Top your waffles, pancakes, and cereal with berries.
- Add berries to muffin batter.
- Stir fresh or frozen blueberries into plain yogurt for a satisfying snack.
- Be adventurous and make wild blueberry salsa (wild blueberries are smaller, so they work better) with diced onion, jalapeño pepper, red bell pepper, cilantro, and lemon juice.
- Use whole strawberries as edible garnishes at breakfast, lunch, or dinner.
- Drizzle a tablespoon of chocolate syrup over fresh strawberries for a decadent but healthy dessert.
- Spoon a generous amount of fresh berries over a smallish serving of frozen yogurt or ice cream.
- Sprinkle fresh berries over tossed green salads.
- Add dried cranberries to green salads or grain side dishes.
- Make a very berry smoothie with yogurt, mixed berries (fresh or frozen), vanilla extract, and orange juice.

### RELATED recipes

Berry-Flaxseed Smoothie *208*

Blueberry-Oatmeal Muffins *198*

Cantaloupe and Blueberry Compote with Green Tea and Lime *276*

Cherry-Raspberry Crumble *287*

Chocolate-Raspberry Cheesecake *284*

Instant Strawberry Frozen Yogurt *277*

Lemony Blueberry Cheesecake Bars *279*

Mixed Berry-Almond Gratin *288*

Mixed Berry and Stone Fruit Soup *276*

Multi-Grain Pancakes or Waffles *192*

Peach-Raspberry Crumble *287*

Pear-Berry Clafouti *283*

Rhubarb-Blackberry Crumble *286*

**berries** are full of fiber, which keeps blood sugar low, and antioxidants, which benefit every cell in your body.

# bran

**GL** LOW

When you eat grains—and of course, they should be a regular part of your diet—you can't do better than bran. In fact, a bowl of bran cereal has just one-third the GL of a bowl of cornflakes. (Check out "How Cereals Rate" at right.) That means your blood sugar will go up only a third as much, so it doesn't have far to fall. (Remember, it's those precipitous drops that cause trouble and make you hungry again.)

There's really no better way to get one of the three daily servings of whole grains we recommend than starting your day with bran cereal. Top it with berries, and you've really hit your Magic eating stride.

Think of bran as the heavy "overcoat" worn by kernels of whole grain oats, wheat, or rice. It contains the highest concentration of fiber of any part of the grain (12 grams per 1/2 cup for wheat and rice bran; 7 grams per 1/2 cup for oat bran). As you know, fiber helps you feel fuller on fewer calories, smoothing the way for weight loss.

Bran also helps tame those wild blood sugar surges after meals. When researchers gave obese children either a sugar solution or a sugar solution plus 15 grams (about 4 tablespoons) of wheat bran, the kids' blood sugar levels were much lower when they ate the bran. If you add bran to your diet regularly, you could really lower your blood sugar over the long term—by as much as 22 percent. At least that's the drop experienced by people in a study who ate rice bran for two months as part of a heart-healthy diet.

Oat bran is high in soluble fiber, which gives it extra power over blood sugar. Adding oat bran to the mix—meaning pancake, muffin, or cookie mix—can significantly change the food's effect on your blood sugar. Researchers found that for each gram of beta-glucan, the type of soluble fiber found in oat bran, added to snack bars, the Glycemic Index of the bar dropped by 4 points. A lower GI translates into a lower GL—which means a milder blood sugar response after you gobble down the goody. It takes only 1/3 cup of oat bran to provide 1.5 grams of beta-glucan.

As you can tell, we're big on bran!

## Health Bonus

Oat bran can bring down high cholesterol and reduce the risk of heart disease, and it has an FDA-approved health claim to prove it. In one study, men who consumed the most wheat bran (about 9 grams per day) were 30 percent less likely to develop heart disease than those who consumed the least (not quite 2 grams per day).

Rice bran can also lower cholesterol, and early research in animals suggests it may help tame high blood pressure as well. The natural oils in rice bran may be the Magic ingredient. Rice bran is also gluten-free, a real plus for people who have a sensitivity to gluten.

Wheat bran may help reduce the risk of colon and breast cancer. And of course, bran helps keep you regular.

## Cooks Tips

Because bran contains oils that can become rancid, be sure to store it in the refrigerator or freezer once it's been opened. Many bran cereals, on the other hand, contain preservatives that will keep them fresh for several months in the pantry.

### don't fall for it

Bran muffins may appear to be health food, but they're usually anything but. Most store-bought muffins are loaded with sugar, fat, and calories. Make your own for a much healthier treat (see the Apple-Bran Muffins recipe on page 197).

## HOW cereals RATE

Some cereals are "fast acting" and send blood sugar on a rollercoaster ride, while others are digested slowly—more at the speed of an old-fashioned merry-go-round. Bran is among the slowest-acting cereals of all.

| Cereal | Serving (equal to 30 g) | Glycemic Load |
|---|---|---|
| Quaker Oat Bran | 1/16 cup | 3 |
| Kellogg's Bran Buds | 1/3 cup | 7 |
| Kellogg's All-Bran | 1/2 cup | 9 |
| Kellogg's Raisin Bran | 1 cup | 12 |
| Kellogg's Bran Flakes | 1 cup | 13 |
| Kellogg's Special K | 1 cup | 14 |
| General Mills Cheerios | 1 cup | 15 |
| Nabisco Cream of Wheat | 1 cup | 17 |
| Kellogg's Corn Flakes | 1 cup | 24 |
| Kellogg's Crispix | 1 cup | 22 |
| Kellogg's Rice Krispies | 3/4 cup | 22 |
| Nabisco Instant Cream of Wheat | 1 cup | 22 |

**PERFECT portions:** 1/2 cup

This much bran cereal should fill you up. Use less if you sprinkle it over yogurt.

## Menu Magic

- Make meat loaf more Magic by using oat bran or another bran as a binder in place of bread. It will help blunt the effect of the mashed potatoes you eat with it by lowering your blood sugar response to the entire meal.

- Sprinkle bran flakes on casseroles.

- Use bran in muffin recipes in place of half the flour for muffins that are high in fiber and loaded with nutrients. If you don't have bran flour on hand, try using bran cereal. Some brands have muffin recipes right on the box. Add fruit and nuts for truly Magic muffins.

- Start your day with plain bran cereal, hot or cold (look for Quaker and other brands). It's one of the lowest-GL cereals you can choose.

- Make pancakes or waffles with rice flour and rice bran or try adding different types of bran and experimenting with the taste and texture. Top with fresh blueberries to squeeze in a serving of fruit.

## Smart Substitution

*Instead of Cream of Wheat:* Have a bowl of cooked bran cereal topped with dried cranberries or fresh strawberries.

### RELATED recipes
**Apple-Bran Muffins** *197*
**Fudge Brownies** *280*

# broccoli

**GL**
VERY LOW

Because it's big on volume and small on calories, broccoli is a great way to bulk up carb dishes (think pasta, casseroles, and baked potatoes) to lower their GL.

Not only does broccoli have very little impact on your blood sugar, it's one of the best food sources of chromium, a mineral required for insulin to function normally (remember, insulin helps the body use up blood sugar so there's less in the bloodstream). One cup of broccoli provides almost half of your daily chromium requirement. Fiber, at a hearty 4 grams per stalk, is also part of broccoli's "benefits package."

Broccoli also packs a wallop of vitamin C. One cup contains more than 100 percent of the RDA for this vitamin. If you're fighting diabetes—or even if you already have it—that's important. According to a British population study, people with the highest blood levels of vitamin C were less likely to have elevated levels of glycated hemoglobin, a long-term indicator of high blood sugar. The researchers concluded, "Dietary measures to increase plasma vitamin C may be an important public health strategy for reducing the prevalence of diabetes." Even if vitamin C can't protect you from diabetes (the jury is still out), it and other antioxidants can certainly lower your risk of diabetes-related complications such as eye and nerve damage.

## Health Bonus

Broccoli is known for its cancer-fighting compounds. Numerous studies over the past 20 years have found that people who eat plenty of broccoli have a significantly lower risk of several cancers, including breast, colon, cervical, lung, prostate, and bladder cancer. Broccoli's also a good source of calcium, which may help lower high blood pressure, common in people with diabetes.

## Cooks Tips

Don't overcook broccoli; it will turn pale and mushy and lose some of its nutrients.

---

**PERFECT portions: 1/2 cup**

The GL of broccoli is based on a 1/2-cup serving, but feel free to eat as much as you want.

## Menu Magic

- For creamy soup without the cream, puree cooked broccoli, cauliflower, and onion with salt and white pepper. Add low-fat milk for a creamier texture.

- Add chopped broccoli florets to omelets, vegetable lasagna, and pizza.

- For a super-low-GL meal, make a beef and broccoli stir-fry and serve over a modest portion of brown rice.

- Whip up a broccoli salad to tote on your next picnic. Mix broccoli florets, sliced carrots, sliced green olives, diced pimientos, and chopped walnuts and marinate in Italian dressing.

- Top steamed broccoli with a spoonful of low-fat sour cream and some slivered almonds for a healthy side dish.

- Dip raw broccoli in light ranch or Italian dressing as a snack or an addition to lunch.

## RELATED recipes

Broccoli and Cheese Omelet *194*
Broccoli with Lemon Vinaigrette *272*
Orange Beef Stir-Fry with Broccoli and Red Pepper *226*
Whole Wheat Pizza with Broccoli and Olives *259*

### Hate Broccoli? Blame It on Your Genes

Does the taste of broccoli on your tongue make you recoil in disgust? You may be able to blame your genes. Researchers have discovered a gene that makes some people hypersensitive to the bitter-tasting compounds in broccoli, Brussels sprouts, and cabbage.

# brown rice

Brown rice doesn't have the wonderfully low GL of some other grains, like barley or oats. Nevertheless, it's a far better choice for your blood sugar than most white rice. So, if rice is on the menu, better make it brown.

As a nutrient-packed, fiber-rich whole grain, brown rice has many of the good qualities you expect in a Magic food. Not only does it boast six times the fiber of white rice, it's packed with vitamins, minerals, and natural plant compounds made by nature to protect

**PERFECT portions:** 1/2 cup

Stick with one serving, or 1/2 cup, per meal, since rice is, after all, a high-carb food.

your health. And, as a whole grain, brown rice is part of the formula for lowering your risk of diabetes and heart disease. Remember, we want you to aim to eat three servings a day of whole grains, which protect against metabolic syndrome, diabetes, heart disease, stroke, and cancer. A serving of brown rice is 1/2 cup.

*(continued)*

---

## RICE glossary

Who knew rice could be so complicated? Here's a rundown of rice terms to help get you through the rice maze.

**Brown rice:** Still has the bran and the germ of the whole rice kernel, so it contains all the nutrition of a whole grain. Has a longer cooking time and a higher fiber content. Has a nutty flavor and a hearty texture.

**Converted rice:** The rice is steamed before it's husked, allowing the individual grains to absorb more nutrients. Takes about the same amount of time to cook as white rice, but less time than brown rice.

**Wild rice:** Not a rice at all, but the seeds of a marsh grass. It's high in protein and fiber and several B vitamins. Has a pungent, earthy flavor.

**Basmati rice:** A long-grain, aromatic white rice grown in the Himalayas. It cooks up dry and fluffy. You can get brown or white basmati rice. The GL of brown basmati is lower, closer to that of brown rice.

**Long-grain white rice:** The most common rice used in cooking. The nutritious bran and germ have been processed out, taking fiber and natural plant compounds with them. As with most refined products, some nutrients, such as iron, thiamin, niacin, and folate have been added back. Has a bland flavor.

**Long-grain quick-cooking rice:** The rice is completely cooked and dehydrated, so cooking time is short, usually 10 to 15 minutes. Comes as white or brown rice.

**Sticky rice:** Also called glutinous rice, though it doesn't contain gluten, this is a short-grain, white, refined rice that sticks together. Though it's sometimes called "sweet rice," it has a bland flavor like most white rice.

**Arborio rice:** A plump, refined, short-grain white rice that absorbs water without developing a mushy texture. Used in risotto and noted more for its ability to absorb flavors.

**Jasmine rice:** A long-grain white rice that has a subtle flower-like aroma.

# brown rice continued

Regular brown rice takes about 35 minutes to cook. When time is of the essence, don't opt for instant rice, white or brown, which has been partially cooked and dehydrated and has a high GL. You'd do better to opt for converted white rice, which has a GL similar to that of brown rice and many of the nutrients, too. While brown rice should always be your number one rice choice (more nutrients and fiber), converted white rice is the next best thing.

All rice starts off as brown rice. Only when it's been refined and the bran and germ have been removed is white rice born. Different types of rice vary in their GL depending on the type of starch they naturally contain (see Rice Rankings). Three rices to avoid: jasmine, Arborio (the kind used in risotto), and "sticky rice."

## Health Bonus

Brown rice offers more than just fiber. It's rich in the bone-building mineral magnesium, the immune-boosting antioxidant selenium, and manganese, a mineral important for keeping up the body's natural defenses.

## Cooks Tips

Because brown rice contains some fat naturally found in the whole grain, it won't stay fresh as long as white rice. You can store uncooked brown rice in the cupboard for up to 6 months. Put it in the refrigerator to make it last longer.

## Menu Magic

✪ Substitute brown rice for white rice in casseroles, stir-fries, and side dishes to lower the GL of a meal while adding a chewy texture and nutty flavor.

### RELATED recipes

## rice RANKINGS

There's much more to rice than just white or brown. And different varieties vary as much in their effect on your blood sugar as they do in flavor. Take a look.

| Rice | Glycemic Load per 2/3 cup (150 g) |
|---|---|
| **Medium** | |
| Converted white rice | 16 |
| Brown rice | 18 |
| Wild rice | 18 |
| Cajun style rice mix | 19 |
| Long and wild rice blend | 20 |
| Mexican style rice mix | 22 |
| **High** | |
| Basmati rice | 23 |
| Long grain white rice | 23 |
| Long grain quick cooking | 27 |
| **Very High** | |
| Sticky rice (used in sushi rolls) | 31 |
| Arborio risotto rice | 36 |
| Jasmine rice | 46 |

# brussels sprouts

**GL**
VERY LOW

Like most vegetables, these mini-cabbages have a very low GL, which means they're kind to your blood sugar. But Brussels sprouts also have something special: soluble fiber (2 grams in 1/2 cup). This stuff forms a gel in your stomach that acts as a barrier between food and the enzymes that break it down, making your meal "slow acting" instead of "fast acting" when it comes to digestion. And that goes for everything in the meal— even the roll. Remember, where blood sugar is concerned, a slow rise is better.

One study found that women who ate cruciferous vegetables, including Brussels sprouts, most often reduced their risk of developing diabetes by two-thirds compared to those who ate cruciferous veggies least often. So get your fill!

Another surprising bonus: Almost one-third of the calories in Brussels sprouts come from protein, meaning that even though they seem substantial, these veggies are blessedly low in carbs.

If you have diabetes or any other risk factor for heart disease, take note: Brussels sprouts are a top source of vitamin C (50 milligrams per 1/2 cup), a must-have nutrient for keeping arteries healthy and fending off complications of diabetes. A large European study found that adults with the highest blood levels of vitamin C had only half the risk of dying from cardiovascular disease compared to those with the lowest levels.

## Health Bonus

Like their cousins cabbage and broccoli, Brussels sprouts are powerful anticancer foods. They're also rich in lutein and zeaxanthin, members of the carotenoid family that are celebrated for their ability to keep your eyesight sharp as you age. And sprouts are an underappreciated source of bone-building vitamin K, with six times the recommended daily amount.

### PERFECT **portions**: 1/2 cup

A serving is 1/2 cup, but there's no reason not to eat more.

## Cooks Tips

Like cabbage, Brussels sprouts can really stink up your kitchen. Cooking time equals odor intensity, so keep it short (steaming is a good option). Store leftovers in a well-sealed container, or else you'll smell the consequences when you open the fridge.

## Menu Magic

Brussels sprouts are one of those all-or-nothing foods; either you love 'em or you hate 'em. But before you decide once and for all, give these Brussels sprout dishes a try.

- Steam sprouts, then sauté them in olive oil along with any or all of the following: crushed mustard seed, cumin, fennel seed, cayenne pepper, finely chopped ginger, fresh lime juice, and salt. Top with slivered almonds.

- Get two Magic foods in one dish by combining baby carrots and halved Brussels sprouts. Sauté them in olive oil (a third Magic food), then add chicken broth and simmer. Add some lemon juice (another!) and dill just before they're done.

- Pair the strong taste of Brussels sprouts or other cruciferous vegetables with a sweet-tasting side dish such as applesauce or sweet potatoes.

- To make Brussels sprouts even more blood sugar-friendly, add vinegar. Marinate cooked sprouts overnight in vinegar (try tarragon vinegar), crushed garlic, minced onion, salt, and a bit of honey.

### RELATED **recipe**
Sautéed Brussels Sprouts with Red Pepper
and Caraway Seeds *273*

# bulgur

If you're following the Seven Secrets of Magic Eating, you're trying to get three servings of whole grains a day. For chewy texture and a slightly nutty taste, try bulgur as a deliciously filling side dish or hot cereal. It can even be used to make stuffing. Best of all, it cooks quickly.

Bulgur ranks right up there with whole wheat bread, wheatberries, and bran—all Magic foods, and all forms of the same nutritious wheat grain. That's right, bulgur isn't an individual type of grain. It's wheat grain that's been partially cooked by boiling or steaming, then dried and cracked.

Eating more whole grains has been shown to cut diabetes risk by 35 percent in men and women and reduce heart disease risk by 25 percent in women and 18 percent in men. Just six weeks on a whole grain diet can markedly improve insulin sensitivity, according to one study.

## Health Bonus

As with all whole grain foods, eating more translates into lower risk not only of diabetes and heart disease but also of certain cancers. In a Swedish study of more than 61,000 women, researchers found that those who ate at least 4 1/2 servings of whole grains a day had a 23 percent lower risk of developing colon cancer compared to women who ate fewer than 1 1/2 servings a day. The lignans in bulgur may also help protect against breast cancer.

## Cooks Tips

You'll find bulgur in different textures. Coarse bulgur is used for pilaf and rice dishes, medium is used as breakfast cereal, and fine is used for tabbouleh (a Middle Eastern salad made with bulgur, chopped parsley, cucumbers, tomatoes, olive oil, and lemon juice). The finer the grain, the quicker bulgur cooks up.

---

**PERFECT portions: 1/2 cup**

A typical serving size is 1/2 cup, but you can have as much as 3/4 cup of cooked bulgur and the GL will still be in the medium range.

## Menu Magic

◉ Try bulgur pilaf as a side dish. There are a million different recipes, some including dried fruit and some with vegetables and/or herbs. Grab a good cookbook and take your pick. You can also enjoy bulgur in cold salads.

◉ Throw together some tabbouleh as an excellent, portable summertime lunch salad or side dish. Toss in chopped vegetables from your garden, such as tomatoes and cucumbers, and add some goat or feta cheese or chicken for extra protein.

◉ Cook up hot bulgur cereal in salted water as you would oatmeal. Top with fresh fruit or with chopped walnuts, dried cranberries, cinnamon, and a drizzle of honey. Some manufacturers make bulgur cereals with extra ingredients, such as soy, which adds extra protein.

◉ Stuff zucchini with bulgur and extra-lean ground beef or pork.

## Smart Substitutions

*Instead of rice:* Use cooked bulgur in stir-fries.

*Instead of Cream of Wheat:* Have bulgur as your hot cereal in the morning (Cream of Wheat has a relatively high GL).

**RELATED recipe**
**Bulgur with Ginger and Orange** *264*

# cabbage

**GL** VERY LOW

For centuries, Russian peasants sustained themselves on this leafy veggie. But even if your fridge is full of other foods, you should still consider eating cabbage. It's very low in calories (just 16 calories per 1/2 cup cooked) and high in fiber. Together, these two attributes spell weight loss, which should benefit your blood sugar. Add to that the fact that cabbage is way low on the GL scale, and you've got a Magic winner. And eating cabbage doesn't mean spooning up pale stew; if you prepare it right, cabbage can be a culinary delight.

This veggie doesn't just help you lose weight. Cabbage (especially the red variety) is also a surprisingly excellent source of vitamin C, which some experts believe may reduce the risk of developing diabetes. Red cabbage offers another bonus: It's rich in natural pigments called anthocyanins, which new research suggests may help boost insulin production and lower blood sugar levels.

Finally, cabbage is often prepared with vinegar, which can help lower the GL of your whole meal.

## Health Bonus

Cabbage contains sulphoraphane, which has potent anticancer properties. One study of women found that those who ate the most cabbage and its cruciferous cousins, like broccoli and Brussels sprouts, had a 45 percent lower breast cancer risk than women who ate the least.

Cabbage may also help guard against lung cancer. Fermented cabbage, a.k.a. sauerkraut, may have even higher levels of anticancer compounds, a result of the fermentation process. Just beware of sauerkraut's high sodium content; rinse it before heating.

## Cooks Tips

Overcook cabbage, and you'll regret it when the smell lingers. Overcooking also destroys cabbage's stores of vitamin C, which can't stand the heat. Steam cabbage until limp, stir-fry it quickly, or chop it raw for salads and slaws. Older cabbage or cabbage that's been in the fridge for a while may have a stronger smell. To minimize the odor, cook the cabbage quickly in an uncovered pan with as little water as possible. Try adding a tablespoon of vinegar to the cooking water to further cut the odor.

## Menu Magic

- Enjoy cabbage in coleslaw.
- Add sliced or chopped cabbage to soups and stews.
- Place sautéed cabbage underneath a small serving of steak to add gourmet appeal.
- Braise red cabbage with chopped apples, walnuts, and red wine.
- Sauté cabbage and onions to serve as a side dish.
- Use shredded cabbage in place of lettuce on sandwiches and burgers.
- Combine cooked shredded cabbage with low-fat sour cream and caraway seed, then heat and serve as a side dish.
- Wrap thick fish fillets in cabbage leaves and steam over seasoned broth.

## RELATED recipes

Asian Noodle Hot Pot *225*
No-Mayonnaise Creamy Coleslaw *216*
Pork Chop and Cabbage Skillet Dinner *232*

Brussels sprouts

cabbage

tomatoes

carrots

broccoli

peas

eggplant

With low or very low glycemic loads, vegetables are one food group that won't play havoc with your blood sugar—and will help you fight diabetes and weight gain. We've chosen these veggies as Magic foods because of their impressive nutritional profile, and in the case of eggplant, the ability to stand in for meat.

✤ broccoli

✤ Brussels sprouts

✤ cabbage

✤ carrots

✤ cauliflower

✤ eggplant

✤ onion

✤ peas

✤ spinach

✤ tomato

magic
vegetables

# carrots

**GL**
**VERY LOW**

Carrots perfectly illustrate the difference between the glycemic index (GI) and the glycemic load (GL). When the GI first made waves among health enthusiasts, carrots got a bad rap for raising blood sugar. That's because the type of sugar they contain is transformed into blood sugar very rapidly—almost as fast as table sugar. But since the amount of sugar is low, carrots are still on the menu.

Thank goodness they are, because they're one of the richest sources of beta-carotene, which is linked to a lower risk of diabetes. One study found that people with the highest blood levels of beta-carotene had 32 percent lower insulin levels (suggesting better blood sugar control) than those with the lowest beta-carotene levels. Like most vegetables, carrots are also a good source of beneficial fiber.

## Health Bonus

Carrots won't help you throw away your reading glasses, but they will help protect against two sight-robbing conditions, macular degeneration and cataracts. They're also rich in soluble fiber, which helps lower cholesterol. One study found that volunteers who ate about a cup of carrots a day had an average 11 percent reduction in their cholesterol after three weeks.

## Cooks Tips

Cut off the green carrot tops before storing, or they'll pull moisture from the carrots and make them wither.

### don't fall for it

"Raw foods" proponents would have you believe that all foods are most healthful in their uncooked state. Not true. In the case of carrots, you get different benefits depending on whether they're raw or cooked. During cooking, the carrot's cell walls break down, releasing the beta-carotene inside. Raw carrots, on the other hand, contain more vitamin C.

---

**PERFECT portions:** 1/2 cup

A serving is 1/2 cup of cooked carrots or 1 cup raw. The GL of cooked is slightly higher.

## Menu Magic

- Add grated carrots to sandwiches. For a decidedly different sandwich spread, mix finely grated carrots with low-fat whipped cream cheese and add chopped green olives and grated onions.

- Munch on baby carrots and hummus as a snack or with lunch.

- Mix up spicy carrot soup by pureeing cooked carrots and adding them to sautéed onions and garlic along with vegetable broth and either soy milk or fat-free yogurt. Include chopped celery, salt, white pepper, and curry powder if you like.

- For a salad with Middle Eastern flair, combine cooked sliced carrots, olive oil, chopped parsley, minced garlic, fresh lemon juice, and salt. The lemon juice reduces the GL of the dish even more.

- Cook baby carrots with rosemary and thyme, olive oil, chopped onions, and black pepper. Squeeze the juice of orange wedges over the top.

### RELATED recipes

# cauliflower

**VERY LOW**

Not many vegetables are as filling and low in calories as cauliflower. While it's an acquired taste for some, cauliflower is perfect for your Magic diet if you like it, most obviously because it has so few calories, so much fiber, and so little carbohydrate. But we also like it because, when cooked the right way, it can substitute for mashed potatoes! It even stands in for rice.

Cauliflower's loaded with vitamin C—1 cup raw supplies 75 percent of what you need for the day. That makes it an ideal food for helping protect cells against damage from high blood sugar.

One caveat: If cauliflower is drowned in fatty cheese sauce, it's no longer a Magic food.

## Health Bonus

Cauliflower, like its cousins broccoli, cabbage, and Brussels sprouts, is rich in anticancer compounds. A review of 80 studies found that people who ate the largest amounts of these foods had the lowest risk of all types of cancer, particularly lung, stomach, colon, and rectal cancers. In a test-tube study, juice extracted from cauliflower blocked growth of breast cancer cells.

## Cooks Tips

Cook cauliflower in an uncovered pan to avoid trapping its strong odor. Add a couple of tablespoons of lemon juice to preserve its color. Overcooking not only intensifies the aroma, it also destroys much of the vitamin C.

If you're not a fan of cauliflower, try broccoflower, a milder hybrid of broccoli and cauliflower.

## Menu Magic

- Instead of mashed potatoes, try this tasty cauliflower puree. Boil a head of cauliflower cut into florets, one diced peeled potato, and six peeled garlic cloves until tender. Drain and puree (in batches) in a food processor and thin with enough warm milk to make it velvety. Drizzle olive oil on top and season with salt and pepper.

- Serve cauliflower raw or lightly steamed with

**PERFECT portions: 1/2 cup**

A serving of cauliflower, 1/2 cup cooked, provides a slim 17 calories and 2.5 grams of fiber. Not a bad deal at all.

seasoned yogurt dip.

- Combine cauliflower with broccoli in quiches, omelets, and casseroles.

- Toss florets with olive oil and garlic and roast in the oven.

- Bake a whole head of cauliflower to serve with dinner. Place a trimmed and rinsed head in a steamer, cover, and cook until firm but tender. Place in a baking dish and coat with a mixture of whole wheat bread crumbs, olive oil, garlic powder, salt, dried oregano, and minced garlic. Sprinkle a bit of Parmesan cheese on top and bake for 10 to 15 minutes at 350°F (176°C).

- Stir-fry cauliflower and broccoli florets with water chestnuts and season with a dash of soy sauce and sesame oil.

- Make a cauliflower salad by combining florets with tarragon vinegar, Dijon mustard, salt, white pepper, and olive oil. Cover and marinate overnight.

## Smart Substitution

*Instead of rice:* Shred cauliflower in a food processor until the texture is similar to rice. Lightly steam it and use in recipes that call for cooked rice.

### RELATED recipes
Cauliflower and Spinach Casserole 270
Spiced Cauliflower with Peas 272

# cheese

**GL** VERY LOW

With virtually zero carbs and loads of protein, cheese is a "better blood sugar" food for sure, because it won't budge the blood sugar needle even a bit, and it will make you feel plenty full. Cheese is also an excellent source of calcium, and studies show that getting plenty of calcium from food may help prevent insulin resistance, a harbinger of diabetes. According to a recent study, women who get plenty of calcium from dairy products also have a significantly lower risk of developing metabolic syndrome, which is linked to both diabetes and heart disease.

That doesn't mean you can load up on all the mac 'n' cheese you want, though. It's packed not only with calories but also with cheese's big "design flaw"—saturated fat, the kind that clogs arteries and reduces your body's sensitivity to insulin. That's why it pays to choose, whenever possible, lower-fat cheeses, such as low-fat cottage cheese, low-fat string cheese, part-skim mozzarella, skim ricotta, farmer cheese, and soft goat cheese. Otherwise, the drawbacks of cheese could easily outweigh its benefits. Soft cheeses have less fat per ounce (30 g) than hard cheeses (usually about 6 or 7 grams instead of 8 or 9).

When you do use a hard cheese like cheddar, you'll want to eat less of it and/or choose a low-fat version (see "The Art of Using Low-Fat Cheese" on the opposite page). You probably won't want to snack on low-fat cheddar, though, so give another cheese a try for nibbling. We suggest goat cheese sprinkled with herbs and drizzled with lemon juice. The acidic juice offers an added benefit, since the acid has the power to lower blood sugar. Another way to cut cheese calories is to choose a strong-flavored type like Parmesan, Romano, feta, or Muenster because a little goes a long way, and you can use less.

Cheese wouldn't be so bad if we didn't tend to use so much of it, as in lasagna or pizza that's downright gooey with the stuff—but that's easy to remedy! When making lasagna, you can use the usual amount of ricotta (part skim) and Parmesan but only half the mozzarella (part skim). Add a little extra spaghetti

## CHEDDAR & BETTER cheese

| Cheese 1 oz (30 g) except where noted | Calories | Fat (g) | Calcium (mg) |
|---|---|---|---|
| Blue | 100 | 8 | 175 |
| Brie | 95 | 8 | 52 |
| Camembert | 85 | 7 | 110 |
| Cheddar | 114 | 10 | 205 |
| Cottage cheese, 1% (1 cup) | 164 | 3 | 138 |
| Feta | 74 | 6 | 140 |
| Goat, soft | 76 | 6 | 40 |
| Gruyére | 117 | 9 | 287 |
| Limburger | 93 | 8 | 141 |
| Muenster | 105 | 9 | 204 |
| Mozzarella, part skim | 72 | 5 | 183 |
| Neufchâtel | 74 | 7 | 22 |
| Parmesan, grated | 129 | 9 | 390 |
| Romano | 110 | 8 | 302 |
| Swiss | 107 | 8 | 273 |

sauce to keep the lasagna moist. For pizza, you can ask for half the cheese at any pizzeria.

## Health Bonus

If you think milk is good for you, consider this: It takes about 10 pounds (4.5 kg) of milk to create a single pound (450 g) of cheese, making it a concentrated source of all the good stuff in milk, including phosphorus, zinc, vitamin A, riboflavin, vitamin $B_{12}$, and calcium. Probably because of their calcium content, low-fat dairy foods can also help bring down high blood pressure. (If you're a cottage cheese fan, though, note that it's one type of cheese that's *not* high in calcium.)

Cheese can even help prevent cavities, especially if you eat it after meals or as a between-meal snack.

## Cooks Tips

To make cheese last longer in the fridge, wrap it tightly in plastic wrap or aluminum foil to prevent it from drying out and change the wrapping each time you use the cheese to keep mold from taking hold.

## Menu Magic

- ✿ Serve cheese and fruit as an appetizer or a snack or even dessert. Mix and match flavors and textures. Try cheddar with sliced apples, Brie with pears, shaved Parmesan with Asian pears, or cottage cheese with peaches.

- ✿ Pack string cheese in your briefcase or purse for a low-fat, high-protein hunger tamer.

- ✿ Add feta or goat cheese to omelets.

- ✿ Create a salad with shredded Swiss, diced seedless grapes, chopped pecans, and chopped fresh basil. Serve with whole wheat crackers.

- ✿ Make an easy toaster-oven pizza by topping a whole wheat pita with tomato sauce, part-skim mozzarella, and a vegetable of your choice and cooking until the cheese melts.

### PERFECT portions: 1 ounce (30 g)

A serving of cheese is a scant 1 ounce (30 g). For hard cheese, that's about the size of two board-game die. Cheese calorie counts range from a low of about 72 per serving for part-skim mozzarella to a high of about 130 per serving for Parmesan.

### RELATED recipes

All-New Chicken Cordon Bleu 235

Cauliflower and Spinach Casserole 270

Cherry Tomatoes Filled with Pesto Cream Cheese 200

Chocolate-Raspberry Cheesecake 284

Greek Lentil Salad 217

Greek Pasta and Beef Casserole 230

Lemony Blueberry Cheesecake Bars 279

Macaroni and Cheese with Spinach 255

Mediterranean Salad with Edamame 215

Mushroom and Herb Pizza 258

Penne with Asparagus, Ricotta and Lemon 252

Penne with Tomato and Eggplant Sauce 256

Quick Spinach and Sausage Lasagna 253

Shrimp and Orzo Casserole 251

Spinach and Goat Cheese Omelet 194

Zucchini-Basil Frittata 193

## The Art of Using Low-Fat Cheese

At their worst, low-fat cheeses taste pretty much like cardboard. But used smartly, they're perfectly good stand-ins for their full-fat brethren.

- ✿ Fat-free cheeses are best used as is (uncooked) for sandwiches and salads. They can be difficult to shred, so consider buying them shredded.

- ✿ Don't melt low-fat cheeses under the broiler or in a toaster oven. They tend to toughen and get rubbery under direct heat. They do work, however, in casseroles and heated sandwiches and burgers.

- ✿ To melt low-fat cheeses for sauces, use low heat and stir slowly in one direction. Cook for about 25 percent longer than you would to melt full-fat cheese.

# cherries

**GL** VERY LOW

Remember secret number 3 of Magic eating, Eat More Fruits and Vegetables? These foods from the produce aisle are full of disease-fighting plant compounds, and they barely budge your blood sugar thanks to their very low GL. Cherries may be an especially good choice. Besides plenty of sugar-lowering soluble fiber, they contain red pigments that may increase your body's insulin output, which ultimately lowers your blood sugar. And they're low in calories to boot.

When you get a snack attack, reach for a handful of cherries instead of higher-GL foods like crackers or pretzels. At dessert time, pile them on a half portion of ice cream, and your bowl will look just as full but with far fewer calories.

Sorry, though, maraschino cherries don't cut it. These so-called cherries have been bleached, processed, and injected with sugar and red dye, taking all the magic out of a once-healthy food. Also skip cherry juice, which is usually sweetened and lacks the fiber of whole cherries.

## Health Bonus

Cherries pack a real antioxidant punch, rivaling even oranges. Their stash of vitamin C and other antioxidants helps fend off heart disease, cancer, and many complications of diabetes. One study found that the antioxidant compounds in cherries help protect brain cells, while other plant compounds can put a dent in your cholesterol.

The type of soluble fiber cherries contain, called pectin, is also great at lowering cholesterol.

## Cooks Tips

If chewing around the cherry pit and spitting it out is a little too messy for your taste, check into buying a cherry pitter. Some can pit olives as well. Instead of serve and spit, you'll pit and serve!

**PERFECT portions: 1/2 cup**

The GL of cherries is based on 1/2 cup's worth, but since the GL and the calorie count are so very low, feel free to eat more.

Caution: One bad cherry in a bag can truly spoil the whole bunch. Sort your cherries and pick out the bad ones before putting them in the fridge.

## Menu Magic

- Add finely chopped cherries to ground meat; you'll cut the fat, boost the nutrition, and add unexpected zip to meat loaf and burgers.

- Add frozen tart cherries to your next smoothie.

- Add chopped fresh cherries to low-fat yogurt for a fantastic midday snack.

## Smart Substitution

*Instead of hot fudge with ice cream:* Add cherries to your frozen treat.

### RELATED recipes

Cherry-Almond Gratin *288*
Cherry Clafouti *283*

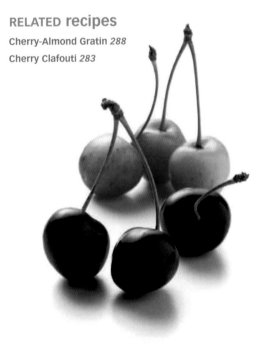

# chicken AND TURKEY

**GL**
VERY LOW

"A chicken in every pot" was a great political slogan back in the days of the Depression. It's also a good approach to Magic eating. Because chicken is full of all-important protein, low in fat, incredibly versatile, and cooks up fast, we consider it the ultimate convenience food.

Remember, protein foods don't raise blood sugar a bit. And chicken has a leg up (pun intended) on beef in the fat and calorie departments. A 3-ounce (85-g) serving of skinless chicken breast has 95 percent less saturated fat—the stuff that hampers insulin sensitivity—than an equal serving of beef tenderloin. It also has 40 percent fewer calories. (As you know, a wide waistline contributes to insulin resistance, which makes blood sugar control difficult.)

Because protein foods like chicken take a while to digest, they slow the digestion of the whole meal, including the carbs it contains (like the mashed potatoes on the plate with your roasted chicken breast and the bread holding your turkey sandwich fillings), making for a slower rise in blood sugar. Getting enough protein also helps keep you full longer, which in turn helps with weight loss. The plan: Serve up chicken as a main dish as often as you like, but also use it to add protein to salads and pasta.

Enjoy your chicken grilled, baked, sautéed, or broiled, but skip the fried chicken, or you'll be eating more fat than chicken. One extra-crispy fast-food chicken breast, for example, can contain close to half of a day's total recommended fat intake (28 grams), including 8 grams of saturated fat and 4.5 grams of trans fat—a virtual heart attack in a bucket. If you want the taste of fried chicken, try our Oven-Fried Chicken recipe on page 238.

What about turkey? If you serve it only at Thanksgiving, it's time to invite the big bird in more

---

**PERFECT portions: 3 ounces (85 g)**

A serving of chicken is 3 ounces (85 g) if you eat it twice a day or 6 ounces (170 g) if you eat it once a day. For easy portion control, try chicken breast tenders, small strips of skinless chicken breast perfect for stir-frying. Typically, two or three tenders equal about a 3-ounce (85-g) serving. Bulk up your stir-fry with plenty of vegetables—and serve it over brown rice, of course.

---

often. Turkey breast is actually lower in fat and cholesterol and higher in protein than chicken breast. Adding ground turkey is a great way to use less ground beef when making meat loaf, meatballs, and chili and thus lower the fat. Be sure to look for ground turkey *breast,* though; regular ground turkey is much higher in fat.

## Health Bonus

Chicken is a good source of the antioxidant mineral selenium. Low levels of selenium in the blood have been linked with poor blood sugar control and complications in people with diabetes, and selenium may offer some protection against the cell damage caused when blood sugar is out of control.

Chicken is also a good source of B vitamins, which play a role in preventing and treating many diseases, including asthma and nerve damage. They also support the immune system.

Got a cold? Homemade chicken soup really can help. Researchers have discovered that it can boost levels of immune cells that lessen inflammation, possibly cutting short a cold.

## Cooks Tips

To keep chicken moist, cook it with the skin on, then remove it before serving.

*(continued)*

# chicken AND TURKEY continued

## Menu Magic

A boneless chicken breast is like a blank canvas. Get as creative as you like! The possibilities are endless, but here are a few easy suggestions.

- ✪ Marinate your chicken in three other Magic foods— olive oil, lemon or lime juice, and minced garlic—to make it tasty and tender. Add chopped green chiles to take it up a notch. Marinate for at least 2 hours, then grill or sauté.

- ✪ Sauté sliced chicken tenders in olive oil and garlic and add to pizza.

- ✪ Keep grilled chicken breast or turkey slices from the deli in the fridge so you can throw them over salad greens for an easy, high-protein lunch.

- ✪ Stir-fry or sauté your chicken and add any of these other Magic foods: curry powder (its Magic ingredient is turmeric); broccoli; peaches; apples; almonds, peanuts, or cashews; sesame seeds; spinach; tomatoes; onions; and garlic.

- ✪ Whip up a tasty bowl of chicken fried rice with cooked brown rice, chicken breast strips, egg, sliced scallions, chopped red bell pepper, soy sauce, ground ginger, and crushed garlic. Quickly stir-fry in canola oil.

- ✪ Make a light version of chicken salad by using half low-fat mayo and half fat-free yogurt. Add scallions, dill, mustard, and lemon juice for extra flavor. Serve over fresh crunchy lettuce.

## Smart Substitutions

*Instead of beef meatballs:* Make yours turkey meatballs, and you'll get great taste with fewer calories and less saturated fat.

*Instead of beef chili:* Try turkey chili.

## RELATED recipes

**All-New Chicken Cordon Bleu** *235*

**Chicken Breasts with Peaches and Ginger** *234*

**Chicken Pot Pie with a Whole Grain Biscuit Crust** *236*

**Chicken Sauté with Apple** *235*

**Grilled Chicken Salad with Oranges** *210*

**Honey-Mustard Turkey Burgers** *240*

**Oven-Fried Chicken** *238*

**Peanut Chicken Soup** *224*

**Roasted Moroccan Chicken Thighs with Squash and Pearl Onions** *238*

**Turkey and Bean Chili with Avocado Salsa** *243*

**Turkey Meatballs** *242*

**Turkey Shepherd's Pie with Sweet Potato Topping** *241*

**Turkey-Noodle Casserole with Spinach** *239*

**Whole Wheat Noodles with Peanut Sauce and Chicken** *214*

**Whole Wheat Pasta with Sausage, Beans and Greens** *254*

Lean protein foods like **chicken** are at the crux of Magic eating, because they balance out the carbs in a meal and also make weight loss easier.

# cinnamon

**GL** VERY LOW

When you think of cinnamon, you might conjure up images of hot apple pie or warm-from-the-oven oatmeal cookies. And of course, there wouldn't be cinnamon toast without it. You'd probably never imagine, though, that cinnamon has health benefits. In fact, researchers recently discovered that this warming spice can actually help lower your blood sugar. Some of the natural compounds in cinnamon have the ability to mimic insulin, helping glucose get into cells, where it can be used for energy, and significantly lowering blood sugar in the process.

One study involving 60 men and women found that taking as little as 1/4 to 1/2 teaspoon of cinnamon a day lowered blood sugar by 18 to 29 percent. It also reduced bad LDL cholesterol by 7 to 27 percent in people with diabetes.

You probably also wouldn't guess that cinnamon is a good source of fiber (although actually, it's not so surprising when you consider that it comes from the bark of the cinnamon tree). Two teaspoons provides 2.5 grams of fiber—more than 1/2 cup of raw cabbage or bell peppers or two dried apricot halves.

Cinnamon also contains the mineral manganese, which may help improve the way your body uses blood sugar. Just 2 teaspoons can set you up with more than one-third of the manganese you need for the day.

## Health Bonus

The natural chemicals in cinnamon can help prevent blood platelets from clumping together and forming dangerous clots that can trigger a heart attack. And studies show that a mere whiff of cinnamon can boost brain activity and improve concentration.

## Menu Magic

There are more ways than you can imagine to sprinkle cinnamon into your diet.

- Add cinnamon to applesauce as the apples are cooking or use it to spice up baked apples.

**PERFECT portions: 1/2 teaspoon**

Just 1/2 teaspoon a day can benefit your health. If you like cinnamon, go ahead and eat a couple of teaspoons a day, but don't go overboard. Cinnamon contains natural compounds that can be toxic in high doses.

- Shake it on whole grain toast or whole grain English muffins.

- Add a half teaspoon or so of cinnamon to ground coffee before starting the pot. You can also add it to tea or drink chai, which contains cinnamon and other spices.

- Mix it into hot cereals, especially oatmeal.

- Sprinkle a little cinnamon on top of ice cream or frozen yogurt or add it to plain yogurt along with a little honey.

- Mix some with low-fat cream cheese for a tasty bread spread.

- Flavor winter squash or sweet potatoes with cinnamon.

### RELATED recipes

Apple-Bran Muffins *197*
Apple-Cranberry Crumble *286*
Blueberry-Oatmeal Muffins *198*
Chai *208*
Chocolate-Raspberry Cheesecake *284*
Fudge Brownies *280*
Greek Pasta and Beef Casserole *230*
Moroccan Spiced Carrots *274*
Multi-Grain Pancakes or Waffles *192*
Oatmeal with Apple and Flaxseeds *193*
Pumpkin Custards *278*
Spice-Crusted Pork Tenderloin with Peach Salsa *233*
Turkey Meatballs *242*
Upside-Down Nectarine Muffins *199*
Wheatberry Salad with Dried Apricots and Mint *266*

# citrus fruits

**GL** VERY LOW | Orange you in the mood for a sweet snack? (Sorry, we couldn't resist.) Whether you grab an orange, a tangerine, or half a grapefruit, citrus fruits have an amazing ability to help steady your blood sugar.

First, they're packed with pectin, a type of soluble fiber that helps keep blood sugar—and cholesterol—low. Pectin, like most types of fiber, also leaves you feeling full longer, taming the temptation to overeat at your next meal. How high in soluble fiber are these fruits? Out of the 20 most-eaten fruits and vegetables, oranges and grapefruit come out on top.

Citrus fruits are naturally low in calories (80 for an orange, 41 for half a grapefruit, and 45 for a tangerine). And speaking of calories, it seems we may have misjudged the much-maligned Grapefruit Diet. Apparently, grapefruit really can help you lose weight. A study at the Scripps Clinic in San Diego looked at 100 obese people and found that those who ate half a grapefruit or drank grapefruit juice before each meal lost an average of 3.3 to 3.6 pounds (1.5 to 1.6 kg) over 12 weeks compared to a loss of only 0.5 pound (225 g) by the people who didn't have the fruit. Grapefruit probably works by reducing insulin spikes after meals. (The smaller the spike in insulin, the better your body is able to process sugar.) Obviously,

eating grapefruit before a meal also dampens your appetite so you eat less of the higher-calorie main dish.

Citrus fruits are most renowned for their vitamin C, an antioxidant that can help fight heart disease and complications of diabetes, such as nerve damage and damage to the retina of the eye. You'll get more than a whole day's vitamin C requirement in a single orange; half a grapefruit will give you 78 percent.

Now, a few words about fruit juice. First, while it's a whole lot more nutritious than soda, you'll need to pour yourself a small glass. Four to 6 ounces (125 to 180 ml) is appropriate—that's why they make juice glasses. Without the fiber found in the whole fruit, fruit juice packs a lot more calories, and it has a greater effect on your blood sugar. The GL of a whole orange, for example, is very low at 5. The GL of 4 ounces (125 ml) of O.J., however, is a much higher 12—and most of us drink more than that.

Don't think that orange juice with pulp contains more fiber; it doesn't. Fresh-squeezed juice, however,

> You know **oranges** are loaded with vitamin C, but they also offer antioxidants called flavonoids that guard against heart disease.

may be higher in fiber than high-pulp O.J., since the fruit's membranes go into the juice.

If you choose grapefruit juice, check the label to be sure you're buying an unsweetened brand. Sound too bitter? Stick with red or pink grapefruit juice for a naturally sweeter taste.

## Health Bonus

Because citrus fruits can help lower your cholesterol, they deserve a starring role in your diet. You'll get some cancer protection, too, for your effort. Research shows that compounds in citrus fruits can help prevent cancerous changes from occurring in colon cells, and pink and red grapefruits contain lycopene, which studies show may help reduce the risk of developing breast and prostate cancer.

## Cooks Tips

Do you shun grapefruit because it's a pain to eat? Make it easy on yourself and buy a grapefruit knife or a special tool for citrus sectioning. This gizmo looks like a cross between salad scissors and a pizza cutter and lets you remove sections or leave them in place (it works for oranges, too.) A good old grapefruit spoon, the kind with serrated edges, is handy to have, too.

At the store, don't judge an orange by its color. That bright hue that looks so appealing may be due to dye rather than ripeness. Instead, look for fruit that's firm and heavy for its size.

## Menu Magic

- Start breakfast with half a grapefruit.
- Add grapefruit or orange sections to green salads.
- Garnish your dinner plate with orange sections— and eat them.

### Grapefruit and Meds May Not Mix

If you take prescription medication, watch your grapefruit intake or discuss it with your doctor. Researchers have found that the natural compounds in grapefruit can interfere with the action of some prescription drugs, making them either stronger or weaker than they're supposed to be. A case in point: Grapefruit and grapefruit juice can increase the action of statins, cholesterol-lowering drugs commonly prescribed for people with diabetes. The result? An increased risk of developing toxic side effects from the medication.

- Whip up an orange smoothie with peeled, seeded oranges; low-fat plain yogurt; frozen strawberries; and vanilla. Blend and pour.

### RELATED recipes

Grilled Chicken Salad with Oranges 210

Orange and Pomegranate Compote 278

Pink Grapefruit Brulée 277

Spinach, Grapefruit and Avocado Salad with Poppy Seed Dressing 216

# coffee

**GL**
VERY LOW

Health experts have gone 'round and 'round on the coffee issue—is it bad for you or good for you? Our answer: In moderation, coffee, especially decaf, may have beneficial effects on your blood sugar. A study from Finland, which boasts the highest coffee consumption in the world, found that the risk of developing type 2 diabetes went down as coffee consumption went up; the biggest benefits were to people who drank a whopping six cups a day (although we don't recommend that you follow suit). And a recent study from the Harvard School of Public Health found that among more than 88,000 women, drinking just one cup of coffee a day (caffeinated or decaffeinated) was associated with a 13 percent lower risk of developing type 2 diabetes compared with non–coffee drinkers; drinking two to three cups a day was associated with a 32 percent lower risk.

Coffee contains a long list of natural plant compounds, including polyphenol antioxidants called chlorogenic acids, that may contribute to its beneficial effect on blood sugar.

That said, *caffeine* does tend to cause blood sugar to spike, not to mention giving you the jitters. One clinical study found that among nine people who drank a single large cup of caffeinated coffee after an overnight fast, blood sugar was significantly higher for half an hour afterward than it was after drinking a sugar solution; not so after drinking decaffeinated coffee. The answer: Switch to decaf.

Coffee's not only our morning wakeup call, it's also the number one source of antioxidants in our diets, outpacing even cranberries and red grapes, according to a recent study. Mind you, cranberries, grapes, and other fruits and vegetables are much higher in antioxidants than coffee is, but we don't consume them the way we do coffee—too bad for us.

## Health Bonus

Several studies show that the antioxidants in coffee offer protection against disease of the liver and colon and Parkinson's disease. And a recent Canadian study found that as coffee drinking increased, the risk of developing Alzheimer's disease decreased.

## Menu Magic

A cup of coffee with your breakfast or after dinner, especially if it's decaf, is a good alternative to soda and may even reduce your craving for a sugary doughnut or dessert if you add a little flavor twist. Here are but a few.

- Make your own version of Irish coffee by adding a tablespoon each of orange juice and lemon juice. (Remember, lemon juice, which is acidic, lowers the effect of a food or drink on your blood sugar.) Top with a spoonful of whipped cream.

- Create a delicious grog by adding cloves, nutmeg, cinnamon, grated lemon, and orange peel to coffee. Stir in fat-free half-and-half and lightly sweeten.

- Make Mexican mocha with coffee, chocolate syrup, cinnamon, and nutmeg.

- Mix strong coffee and sugar-free hot chocolate. Add a dash of cinnamon and grated orange peel.

**RELATED recipe**
Iced Coffee Frappé *209*

# eggplant

**GL** VERY LOW

Aside from eggplant Parmesan, which contains more fat than two large servings of fast-food French fries, eggplant dishes aren't exactly regulars on most of our tables, but they should be. Voluminous and almost meaty in texture, eggplant is a great addition to pasta because it lets you use less pasta, lowering the GL of the meal, and still fill your plate. It's also a fabulous filling for lasagna in place of meat, reducing calories and saturated fat.

When it's not deep fried (eggplant acts like a sponge, soaking up four times as much fat as French fried potatoes), it's low in calories (it's almost 95 percent water) and carbs. Because its spongy flesh is also a good source of soluble fiber, eggplant makes the list of foods that can help lower both your blood sugar and your cholesterol.

## Health Bonus

While it's not a powerhouse of vitamins and minerals, eggplant is one of the richest plant sources of antioxidants you can find in the supermarket, ranking right up there with spinach and sweet potatoes.

## Cooks Tips

Eggplants come in an unexpected variety of sizes, shapes, and colors. Look for a type called Black Magic; it has nearly three times the antioxidants found in other eggplants.

**PERFECT portions: 1/2 cup**

Since eggplant has very few calories and a very low GL, feel free to eat more than this, especially if you don't add a lot of oil.

To limit the amount of oil eggplant soaks up, salt eggplant slices and lay them out on a cooling or cookie rack over the sink for at least 15 minutes. Turn the slices, salt the other side, and leave for at least 15 minutes more. Rinse off the excess salt, pat the slices dry, and you're ready to go.

## Menu Magic

- As an appetizer, whip up blood sugar–friendly baba ghanoush, a Middle Eastern dish made with pureed roasted eggplant, minced garlic, tahini (sesame paste), lemon juice, and olive oil. Serve it with a whole wheat pita or whole wheat crackers. It's also good as a sandwich spread.

- For dinner, make ratatouille, a hearty vegetable dish featuring eggplant and many other Magic foods, including onions, garlic, tomatoes, and olive oil.

- Sauté eggplant with onion and garlic and use it to replace some of the ground beef in beef dishes to cut fat and calories and add an antioxidant boost.

- Substitute eggplant and mushrooms for ground beef the next time you make lasagna.

- For a quick, easy side dish, grill small Japanese eggplants brushed with olive oil, minced garlic, and salt and pepper. There's nothing quite as good as grilled eggplant.

### RELATED recipes

Caponata *202*

Grilled Eggplant Sandwiches with
    Red Pepper-Walnut Sauce *220*

Penne with Tomato and Eggplant Sauce *256*

# eggs

## GL
VERY LOW

If there's one food that's developed an undeserved reputation over the years for being bad for your health, it's eggs. Let's reveal the realities.

Eggs are an excellent, inexpensive source of high-quality protein—so high, in fact, that egg protein is the gold standard nutritionists use to rank all other proteins. What makes the protein in eggs so superior? It contains all of the essential amino acids (the ones your body can't make on its own) in just the right proportions.

Because they're all protein and fat, eggs have no impact on your blood sugar, making them a much better breakfast choice than, say, a stack of white-flour pancakes. And like all protein foods, they may help control your appetite by keeping you full longer. One study found that women who ate two eggs with toast at breakfast felt less hungry before lunch and ate significantly fewer calories during the rest of the day than those who ate a bagel and cream cheese that provided the same number of calories.

Now, about eggs and cholesterol. Yes, it's true, eggs have a lot of it—about 213 milligrams—all in the yolk. It's also true that if you have diabetes, your heart health should be a top priority. But dozens of studies have found

Scrambled, poached, or hard boiled, **eggs** keep your blood sugar steady and provide many of the vitamins and minerals you need.

**PERFECT portions: 1 to 2 eggs**

A large egg serves up about 75 calories and 5 grams of fat, less than 2 grams of it saturated. The fat and cholesterol are all in the yolk. You can enjoy a two-egg omelet with a piece of whole grain toast, and your breakfast will still be reasonably low in calories as long as you don't load it up with butter and cheese. Studies find that even two eggs a day have no effect on cholesterol in most people. Replace one of the eggs with two egg whites if you like.

that it's saturated fat, not cholesterol, that has the greatest effect on blood cholesterol, so eating eggs in moderation is just fine. For people with elevated cholesterol or those who are especially sensitive to the cholesterol in foods (for some people, cholesterol levels do rise after eating a cholesterol-rich meal), experts recommend eating no more than three or four egg yolks a week. Egg whites, which contain no cholesterol, don't count.

## Health Bonus

Egg yolks are one of the few foods naturally rich in vitamin D, a much-needed vitamin that few of us get enough of. Vitamin D helps the body absorb calcium and has recently been linked with lower risks of various cancers to boot. Eggs are also a surprisingly good source of bone-building vitamin K. Plus, they're loaded with lutein (the chickens get it from their feed), which helps protect against macular degeneration, a leading cause of blindness in older folks.

Eggs also contain choline, a compound that animal studies suggest could help improve your memory as you age. Some studies found that giving extra choline to

*(continued on page 108)*

soy

eggs

Lean protein sources make the grade because they benefit blood sugar without clogging arteries.

❖ beans        ❖ milk

❖ beef         ❖ nuts

❖ cheese       ❖ peanut butter

❖ chicken      ❖ pork

❖ eggs         ❖ shellfish

❖ fish         ❖ soy

❖ lamb         ❖ yogurt

❖ lentils

magic proteins

fish

beans

pregnant rats created better-functioning brain cells in their babies.

## Cooks Tips

If you have an egg tray in your refrigerator door, ignore it. Eggs stay fresh best if you keep them in their original container, pointed ends down. Don't buy eggs sold at room temperature at the store. Eggs age more in a single day at room temperature than they do in a week when stored in the fridge.

You know that eating raw or undercooked eggs carries a risk of salmonella poisoning. The risk is lower than you might think (about 1 in 20,000 eggs carries the gut-wrenching bacteria), but it's not worth taking a chance. You have two options: Eat only thoroughly cooked eggs (that means no eggs "over easy" and no Caesar salad made with raw eggs) or buy pasteurized eggs, which have been warmed enough to kill any salmonella bacteria but not enough to cook the egg.

## Menu Magic

Like the chickens they come from, eggs are one of nature's most versatile foods. And they're not just for breakfast.

- Keep hard-boiled eggs in the fridge for a perfect protein-rich snack.

- For lunch, have an egg salad sandwich (made with low-fat mayonnaise) on whole wheat bread. Add chopped pickles to lower the glycemic effect of the bread. Or sprinkle on some turmeric, another Magic food (also good on scrambled eggs).

- Serve a frittata for dinner (think of it as Italian egg pie). We provide one recipe on page 193, but you can add almost anything to your frittata, such as lean ham, diced tomato, spinach, and goat cheese. Use 1 to 2 cups of filling for every four or five eggs.

- Prepare deviled eggs with low-fat mayonnaise, chopped pickles, chili powder or paprika, and mustard powder.

- Grill some French toast for breakfast. Dip whole wheat bread in a mixture of egg, cinnamon (another Magic food), vanilla, and milk, then spray the skillet with oil, add the bread, and cook. The protein and fat in the egg will help blunt the blood sugar impact of the bread.

- Pickle some eggs in vinegar, another Magic food. You get the benefit of high protein plus the blood sugar–lowering power of vinegar.

### RELATED recipes

**Lemony Blueberry Cheesecake Bars** *279*
**Pumpkin Custards** *278*
**Spinach and Goat Cheese Omelet** *194*
**Zucchini-Basil Frittata** *193*

## Designer Eggs: Worth the Price?

Environmental and ethical issues of chicken housing and feeding aside, eggs vary little in nutrition from one brand to the next, with two exceptions. One is eggs fortified with heart-smart omega-3 fatty acids. Usually, this is accomplished by adding flaxseed to the chickens' feed. Each egg typically provides 150 to 200 milligrams of omega-3s—a small fraction of the amount you'd get from eating a piece of fish, but some is better than none. The other exception is reduced-cholesterol eggs, which contain 25 percent less cholesterol than regular eggs. These eggs are usually produced by feeding the chickens a vegetarian diet high in canola oil.

# fenugreek

## GL
**VERY LOW**

This penetrating, pungent spice is not only a standout ingredient in strong, flavorful dishes like Indian curries, it's also proven to help tame blood sugar. In fact, fenugreek supplements are sold for that reason. Here's why fenugreek works: New research suggests it has an uncanny knack for mimicking insulin, which brings down blood sugar.

The yellowish brown seeds, which smell like celery but taste more bitter, also pack a soluble-fiber punch, and you know by now that this type of fiber helps lower blood sugar. One study in animals even suggested that fenugreek could help prevent weight gain, in part by preventing the absorption of fat calories—a definite plus for lowering your diabetes risk. All that makes fenugreek seeds a sweet deal.

Fenugreek leaves are often used in traditional Indian dishes. While they're packed with healthy plant compounds, they haven't been studied as much as the seeds for their ability to lower blood sugar.

## Health Bonus

With 1 gram of fiber in only 1/2 teaspoon, fenugreek seeds are a fabulous source of cholesterol-lowering soluble fiber. Plus, the natural antioxidant compounds they contain may help counteract some of the damaging effects of diabetes.

## Cooks Tips

For milder flavor, roast fenugreek seeds before grinding them (a coffee bean or spice grinder works well) for recipes. Don't overcook them, or they'll turn bitter.

## Menu Magic

Because of fenugreek's strong, some might say peculiar, flavor, the spice won't work with all your favorite recipes. But there are some dishes in which its flavor is a natural.

- Add ground seed to bread dough to make a spicy loaf.

- Sprinkle ground seed into eggs along with coriander, garlic, cardamom, and cumin for a taste of India in your omelet.

- Stir seeds into lentil dishes. Dahl is an Indian lentil or split-pea dish that wouldn't be complete without fenugreek among the ingredients.

- Find a favorite curry recipe; fenugreek is a common ingredient, either in the curry or in Indian spice mixes.

- Use a combination of fenugreek, cinnamon, ginger, and cumin as a spice rub for chicken. You could also add turmeric, another Magic food, or celery seeds. Store the mixture in a tightly closed container in a dark, cool place.

- Make an after-dinner tisane (a tea that requires straining) using 1/2 teaspoon fenugreek seeds. Steep for 5 to 10 minutes in freshly boiled water, then strain and drink.

### RELATED recipes

Curried Butternut Squash Puree *269*
Dahl with Spinach *261*

# fish

**GL**
VERY LOW

The Greenland Inuit eat an incredibly high-fat diet with few vegetables, yet their rate of heart disease is stunningly low. Chalk it up to all the fatty fish they eat: The staple food in their diet is fish rich in omega-3 fatty acids. You've probably heard by now that omega-3s fend off heart disease—something that could be right around the corner if your blood sugar is stuck in overdrive. It's no wonder fish makes our list of Magic foods.

A study at the Harvard School of Public Health found that women with diabetes who ate fish just once a week had a 40 percent lower risk of dying from heart disease than did women with diabetes who ate fish less than once a month.

## FISHING FOR
# Omega-3s

Some fish are richer in heart-healthy omega-3 fatty acids. See for yourself.

| Fish | Omega-3s g per 3 oz (85-g) serving |
|------|-----------------------------------|
| Herring | 1.71-1.81 |
| Salmon, Atlantic farmed | 1.09-1.83 |
| Sardines | 0.98-1.70 |
| Mackerel | 0.34-1.57 |
| Salmon, Chinook | 1.48 |
| Salmon, Pacific farmed | 1.04-1.43 |
| Trout, rainbow, farmed | 0.98 |
| Trout, rainbow, wild | 0.84 |
| Tuna, white, canned in water | 0.73 |
| Salmon, chum or sockeye | 0.68 |
| Flounder/sole | 0.42 |
| Tuna, light, canned in water | 0.26 |

*Source: Circulation, November 19, 2002.*

But omega-3s do more than protect your heart. They also quell inflammation in the body, a major contributor to numerous chronic diseases of aging, including insulin resistance and diabetes. It may even play a role in brain diseases such as Alzheimer's as well as certain cancers.

Of course, fish is also a protein food, and protein foods have virtually no impact on blood sugar. We suggest that you aim to eat fish for dinner once or twice a week when you might otherwise have chicken or beef. Make it baked, broiled, pan-fried, stewed, or grilled. Just don't make it fast food or deep fried, like fish and chips or a fish sandwich. Loaded with bad-for-you fats, this fare just isn't the same kettle of fish. One study found eating fried fish and fish sandwiches offered no heart benefits at all.

All fish contain some omega-3s, but fatty types such as albacore tuna, salmon, mackerel, lake trout, herring, and sardines are richest in them (see "Fishing for Omega-3s" at left).

## Health Bonus

While the strongest proof of the health benefits of fish points to the heart, there's also plenty of research showing that food with fins can cut the risk of prostate cancer and help maintain brain power as you age. There's also evidence that fatty fish may help defend against depression.

## Cooks Tips

One of the keys to successful fish dishes is buying the freshest fish possible. Here's what to look for.

**For whole fish**

- Shop at a busy fish counter. Lots of customers mean lots of turnover and fresher fish.

- The fish's eyes should be clear, not cloudy.

- The inside of the gills should be bright red, not grayish or even pink.

- It shouldn't smell bad. Fish should have a moist, almost musky smell like a cucumber or melon's.

## Safer Salmon

Salmon and other fatty fish, such as tuna and swordfish, have a tendency to store environmental pollutants like mercury by absorbing them into their fat tissue. Experts have debated whether the benefits of eating these fish outweigh the risks and whether wild or farmed fish is the best way to go.

A recent analysis involving a handful of researchers from different institutions came to this bottom line: Whenever you can, choose wild Pacific salmon instead of farmed salmon, which is typically higher in several chemical contaminants. If you really prefer farmed salmon, which has higher levels of omega-3s and is usually cheaper, opt for farmed salmon from Chile. It's the healthiest and safest by far. Canned salmon happens to come from wild varieties, making it a safe choice.

**For fish fillets**

☻ They should be moist and firm.

☻ If there are gaps or separations in the flesh, it's not fresh.

☻ They shouldn't smell fishy.

Fresh fish will keep in the fridge for a day or two, but cook it as soon as possible or freeze it for up to six months.

Don't bypass frozen fillets. Vacuum-packed sole, cod, or salmon fillets are the next best thing to fresh.

## Menu Magic

Fish makes a perfect weeknight meal because it's done before you know it.

☻ Fire up the grill; almost any type of fish tastes fabulous grilled, especially salmon. Brush it with a little olive oil to keep it from sticking. Throw some zucchini strips on the grill, too, and you have a blood

**PERFECT portions:** 3 ounces (85 g)

If you are having fish as your main meal of the day, a serving of up to 6 ounces (170 g) is acceptable.

sugar–friendly meal. (Add a side of whole grains such as a bulgur dish.)

☻ Wrap trout in foil with lemon slices, dill, thyme, salt, and pepper and bake. Serve over quinoa.

☻ Squeeze fresh lemon juice over fish seasoned with rosemary and sautéed on the stove. Serve with brown rice pilaf.

☻ Stuff a tomato with tuna salad made with low-fat mayonnaise or plain yogurt, hard-boiled eggs, chopped apples, celery, and onion. Serve with whole wheat crackers.

☻ If you're a fan of sardines, try this: Sauté some onion and garlic in olive oil, then add sardines canned in tomato sauce. When thoroughly heated, pour the mixture over whole wheat pasta and toss. Top with lemon juice and grated Parmesan.

☻ Pickled herring is another acquired taste, but it may be worth acquiring—check out its extraordinarily high omega-3 content in the chart on the facing page. As an appetizer, try pickled herring on small squares of whole grain rye toast, sprinkled with chopped parsley and hot paprika.

## RELATED recipes

Mustard-Glazed Salmon with Lentils *247*
Salmon Sandwiches with Wasabi Mayonnaise *220*
Salmon with Lemon and Dill Sauce *248*
Seared Fish Steaks with Tomato-Olive Sauce *246*
Smoked Salmon Canapés *203*
Sole Florentine *247*
Tuna and Cannellini Salad with Lemon *213*
Tuna and Carrot Salad on Rye *222*
Warm Salmon Salad with Olive Toasts *249*

# flaxseed

## GL
VERY LOW

Teeny-tiny, shiny brown flaxseeds are a godsend to your blood sugar as well as your heart, so if you haven't tried them yet, it's time for a trip to the store. Buy ground flaxseed or grind it yourself in a food processor or coffee grinder. If you don't see it in your supermarket, look in a natural foods store. Using flaxseed may be a mystery to you now, but it's simple once you know how. It has a pleasant, nutty flavor.

Flaxseed is rich in both protein and fiber (more than 2 grams per tablespoon of ground seeds). It's also a good source of magnesium, a mineral that's key to good blood sugar control, because it helps cells use insulin. Several large studies have found that the risk of developing type 2 diabetes skyrockets when magnesium intake is low, so get your fill. Even if you already have diabetes, getting plenty of magnesium can help.

Don't eat enough fish? Load up on flaxseed. It's rich in alpha linolenic acid (ALA), which the body uses to make the same type of omega-3 fatty acids you get from fish. Like fish, flaxseed keeps your heart healthy by lowering cholesterol, keeping your heart pumping normally,

and preventing dangerous blood clots from forming. Also like fish, it guards against inflammation in the body, which is linked to many age-related disorders, including insulin resistance and diabetes.

## Health Bonus

Because flaxseed protects against inflammation, it also helps guard against inflammatory conditions such as rheumatoid arthritis, asthma, Crohn's disease, eczema, and psoriasis.

The omega-3 fats in flaxseed help prevent and even help treat breast cancer, thanks to hormone-like plant compounds called lignans. In the body, these convert to compounds that are similar to the body's own estrogen but have much weaker activity. By occupying estrogen receptors on cells, they block the effects of natural estrogen and thus may provide protection against hormone-fueled cancers such as breast cancer. Flaxseed has several hundred times more lignans than any other plant food.

Like fish, flaxseed may also offer protection from Alzheimer's and depression.

Constipated? Flaxseed should do the trick. (Eat too much, and you'll quickly discover the laxative effects.)

Especially if you don't eat fish, make a point to add heart-smart, cancer-fighting **flaxseed** to your diet.

## Cooks Tips

The lignans in flaxseed are much better absorbed by the body if the seeds are eaten ground or crushed. (Whole seeds, on the other hand, tend to pass right through your body undigested.) But because of its high fat content, flaxseed will spoil if you grind it but don't use it right away. The solution: Buy whole seeds in bulk and grind them only as you need them. Whole seeds will last up to a year stored at room temperature. If you buy ground flaxseed, keep it in the fridge.

## Menu Magic

You can easily make ground flaxseed part of almost any meal.

- Sprinkle on hot or cold cereal.
- Add to meat loaf, meatballs, burgers, and casseroles.
- Stir into yogurt or add to granola or trail mix.

### What about Flaxseed Oil?

Flaxseed oil provides the omega-3 fatty acids that flaxseed does, but not the fiber or lignans. If heart health is your main concern, you may want to consider taking either flaxseed oil or fish oil daily to get more "good fats" into your diet. Because flax thins the blood, talk to your doctor before taking it if you're on aspirin therapy or taking blood-thinning medication. Dosages range from 1 teaspoon to 1 tablespoon once or twice a day.

The oil goes rancid easily, so keep it refrigerated. You can use it in salad dressings, add it to steamed vegetables after cooking, or sprinkle it over grain dishes, but don't cook with it, since heat destroys its nutrients.

### PERFECT portions: 1 to 2 tablespoons

A tablespoon or two a day, ground and blended into other foods, could do wonders for your blood sugar control and overall good health. You can also mix 1 or 2 tablespoons of ground flaxseed into a glass of water and drink it.

- Add a tablespoon or two to doughs and batters for pancakes, waffles, muffins, and breads. Just keep an eye on baked goods in the oven; the flaxseed could make them brown quicker than usual.
- Use as a topping for ice cream or frozen yogurt.
- Add to smoothies.
- Use to replace one-fourth of the flour in muffin or pancake batter.
- Add to cooked fruit desserts like baked apples or blueberry compote.
- Sprinkle in your favorite sandwich filling, such as tuna or chicken salad.
- Add to cream cheese or sprinkle on a soft cheese and enjoy with some whole grain crackers for a blood sugar–friendly snack.

### RELATED recipes

Berry-Flaxseed Smoothie *208*
Brown Rice Pilaf with Flaxseeds, Lime and Cilantro *265*
Brown Rice Pilaf with Toasted Flaxseed *265*
Oatmeal with Apple and Flaxseeds *193*
Whole Wheat Flaxseed Bread *196*

# garlic

**GL** VERY LOW

You probably know garlic is good for your cholesterol. And if you like garlic, you wouldn't even think of making your favorite recipes without it—which is a good thing because this pungent herb may also be good for your blood sugar.

According to early research with animals, garlic may increase insulin secretion, which would lower blood sugar, and improve insulin sensitivity, in effect helping to reverse diabetes. Since supplements show no blood sugar benefits, enjoy garlic the old-fashioned, tasty way. A recent animal study found that high doses of raw garlic significantly reduced blood sugar levels.

"The stinking rose" offers other health benefits as well. Study after study shows it can help keep cholesterol under control by lowering "bad" cholesterol (LDL) and pumping up "good" (HDL). In an analysis of five trials in which participants received either garlic supplements or placebos, the authors concluded that you could lower your total cholesterol by about 9 percent with the equivalent of 1 1/2 to 3 cloves of garlic daily for two to six months. Garlic also thins the blood, making it less likely to form artery-clogging clots.

## Health Bonus

A diet rich in garlic could mean a lower risk of several types of cancer, including cancer of the stomach and colon. Garlic also has the ability to bring down high blood pressure.

## Cooks Tips

Unless you enjoy chopping, buy a garlic press. Keep your garlic in a cool, dark place, either in a plain old cup in your cabinet or in a fancier garlic keeper—the kind made of terra cotta or pottery with a lid to keep light out and holes in the sides to let air in. Don't keep it in the fridge, or it will sprout quickly.

To peel garlic with minimal hassle, bang the side of the clove with the side of a large knife. The peel will practically slip off at that point.

## PERFECT portions: all you can eat

The more, the better.

## Menu Magic

- Add sautéed garlic to just about any chicken, fish, beef, or tofu dish.

- Use roasted garlic as a spread for bread instead of butter or add it to mashed potatoes or pasta. To roast, break the heads into cloves but don't peel them. Spread them on a baking sheet, drizzle with a bit of olive oil, sprinkle with salt, and bake at 375°F (190°C), shaking the pan occasionally, until tender, about 30 minutes. Then simply squeeze the cloves out of their skins.

- Add minced garlic to rice or other grain dishes before cooking.

- Add minced garlic to vinaigrette dressing.

- Sauté vegetables such as spinach or mushrooms in olive oil and garlic.

- Make a garlic/mustard marinade for beef by mixing spicy mustard, olive oil, balsamic vinegar, black pepper, and chopped garlic (lots of it). Add the beef to the marinade and refrigerate for at least 2 hours.

- If you're grilling, feel free to add the whole garlic bulb to the grill. Turn it so all sides are exposed to the heat. It's ready to eat when the skin is dark brown and peels easily.

## RELATED recipes

**Asian Peanut Dip** *204*
**Bean and Barley Soup** *222*
**Broccoli with Lemon Vinaigrette** *272*
**Caponata** *202*
**Cherry Tomatoes Filled with Pesto Cream Cheese** *200*
**Mediterranean Split Pea Spread** *205*
**Penne with Tomato and Eggplant Sauce** *256*
**Shrimp and Orzo Casserole** *251*
**Spiced Cauliflower with Peas** *272*
**Spring Vegetable Stir-Fry with Tofu** *260*

# jerusalem artichokes

**GL**
VERY LOW

This Magic food, also known as the sunchoke, is unusual in more ways than one. Not only does it have no connection with Jerusalem or artichokes (it's actually related to the sunflower), it looks more like a small gnarly potato than an artichoke, and it grows underground. But the similarity with potatoes ends there. Decidedly unlike potatoes, Jerusalem artichokes (which are crunchy and slightly sweet) have an amazingly beneficial effect on your blood sugar. That's because the starches they contain, called fructans (specifically types of fructans called inulin and oligofructose), aren't readily digested the way typical carbs are. In fact, they're barely digested at all.

Because these starches can't be broken down by enzymes in the small intestine, they travel to the large intestine (colon), where they are digested by intestinal bacteria and eventually excreted. In the end, they supply less than 40 percent as many calories as regular carbohydrates.

Along with being a low-GL food, Jerusalem artichokes may have another advantage. Foods that contain inulin, as 'chokes do, may help smooth out blood sugar and insulin levels after a meal. Preliminary studies are investigating whether higher doses of inulin may also increase fullness and help cut calorie intake.

## Health Bonus

Jerusalem artichokes may help improve the health of your colon. The fructans they contain act as prebiotics, meaning that they provide fodder for beneficial bacteria in the intestinal tract. Fructans also help increase the amount of water and bacteria in the stool, helping to relieve constipation.

Looking to boost your heart health? Jerusalem artichokes can help there, too. The same indigestible carbs that help smooth out blood sugar and relieve constipation may signal the liver to produce fewer triglycerides and fatty acids that can clog your arteries.

**PERFECT portions: 1/2 cup**

A half cup contains only 57 calories and few blood sugar–raising carbs.

## Cooks Tips

Jerusalem artichokes are in season between about October and April, although some stores carry them year-round. Look for firm 'chokes with a smooth, unblemished surface, and avoid those that feel soft, look dried out, or have sprouts. Scrub them well with a vegetable brush to get rid of grit and dirt (remember, they grow underground). Peeling is optional. You can drizzle on a little lemon juice or vinegar to help retain their white color.

A note of caution: Start with small servings; inulin can cause flatulence.

## Menu Magic

- Boil and mash a Jerusalem artichoke just like a potato, or if you prefer, add to regular mashed potatoes to decrease the GL.
- Toss thin raw slices into salads.
- Slice a 'choke and use in place of water chestnuts in stir-fries.
- Steam cubes or slices on the stove or in the microwave, then drizzle with olive oil and lemon juice.
- Grate into a vegetable slaw.
- Slice and serve a sunchoke with dip, along with other crudités.

## Smart Substitutions

*Instead of grated potatoes:* Use grated in potato pancake recipes.

*Instead of pureed potatoes:* Use as a thickener in soups.

### RELATED recipe

Jerusalem Artichoke Pancakes *268*

# lamb

**GL** VERY LOW

Lamb may very well have been the first meat eaten by humans. Today, in some parts of the world, people eat lamb as we eat beef—as a staple food. If you choose the right cuts, lamb is a Magic source of protein, just as beef is.

The leg—the classic spring roast—is the leanest of all, especially if you buy the shank as opposed to the butt, a.k.a. sirloin. (Actually, the foreshank is even slightly leaner but must be tenderized, usually by cooking in liquid for hours.) Loin chops are a bit fattier, and the shoulder is a bit fattier still. The ribs (rack of lamb) are the fattiest, along with ground lamb. If you want lean ground lamb, you'll have to ask the butcher to grind it for you from one of the leaner cuts.

Fortunately, lamb isn't marbled the way beef is; most of the fat is on the outside and is easily trimmed.

## Health Bonus

Like beef, lamb is rich in B vitamins, iron, and zinc. Zinc is essential for a healthy immune system. A shortfall of iron can sap anyone's energy and concentration. As for the B vitamins, they help improve cholesterol ratios and lower levels of homocysteine, an amino acid linked with increased risk of heart attack, stroke, and Alzheimer's disease.

## Cooks Tips

Lamb is meat from sheep less than a year old, so it's generally moist and tender. Get the most for your money by purchasing fine-textured, pink meat with a minimum of firm white fat. Always trim visible fat from fresh lamb and remove any pieces of fell, a papery membrane that covers surface fat. Meat from sheep more than a year old is called mutton and has a stronger taste. It tends to be leaner, though less tender, than lamb. To keep it tender, allow enough time to cook it slowly over medium heat.

**PERFECT portions: 3 ounces (85 g)**

If this is your main meat for the day, a serving of up to 6 ounces (170 g) is appropriate.

## Menu Magic

Lamb stew, lamb chops, lamb curry, leg of lamb… there are so many different, delicious ways to enjoy this Magic food.

- Make a big pot of lamb stew on the weekend and freeze the leftovers or enjoy them during the week. Include plenty of vegetables, such as carrots, squash, onions, peas, and sweet potatoes.

- Make some lamb kebabs by alternating chunks of uncooked lamb and vegetables such as zucchini, tomatoes, and onions on skewers. Grill and serve over whole wheat couscous.

- Braise lamb shanks slowly (2 to 3 hours) in a combination of red wine, minced garlic, and rosemary for a tender entrée. You'll want to brown the shanks before braising.

- Serve roasted or grilled lamb with a dollop of mint yogurt sauce made with low-fat plain yogurt, chopped mint leaves, minced garlic, and a dash of cayenne pepper.

- Use chopped leftover lamb to add protein to tabbouleh, or add it to bulgur cooked in chicken broth, sautéed celery and onions, and slivered almonds. Season with cinnamon, another Magic food.

### RELATED recipes
Lamb Stew with Spring Vegetables *229*
Mustard-Crusted Lamb Chops *232*

# lemons

**GL** VERY LOW

When life hands you lemons, eat 'em! That's right, get ready to pucker up, because lemon juice helps lower blood sugar, thanks to its incredible acidity (just thinking about lemons starts your salivary glands gushing). Because of that acidity (see Chapter 2 in Part 1 to brush up on the acid effect), even a little lemon juice can lower the GL of any meal. Lime juice should have a similar effect.

## Health Bonus

Four tablespoons of lemon juice will give you almost half the vitamin C you need for the day. Remember, antioxidants like vitamin C make cholesterol less likely to stick to your artery walls. Lemons are also packed with a natural disease-preventing compound called limonene that may help lower cholesterol and is even being studied for its potentially potent anti-cancer powers.

The citric acid in lemon juice also helps stave off kidney stones by reducing the excretion of calcium in the urine. Lemon rind is rich in a compound called rutin, which strengthens the walls of veins and capillaries, potentially reducing the pain and severity of varicose veins.

## Cooks Tips

Looking for a juicy lemon? Give it a squeeze. The softer the lemon, the thinner the skin and the juicier the fruit is. To maximize juice output, bring lemons to room temperature and roll them firmly back and forth on the counter a few times with the palm of your hand before cutting.

## Menu Magic

- Use lemon juice in salad dressings.
- Serve plenty of lemon slices alongside fish, which wouldn't be the same without them.

**PERFECT portions:** 1 to 2 tablespoons

If the effects of lemon juice are anything like those of vinegar—and we think they are—1 to 2 tablespoons should be enough to lower the blood sugar impact of a meal by as much as 30 percent.

- Add it to tuna the next time you make yourself a tuna sandwich.
- Spritz your water or seltzer with lemon juice to add flavor (possibly encouraging you to drink more water) and lessen the blood sugar impact of whatever you're eating.
- Think lemon chicken!
- Use lemon juice in marinades for meat or poultry. Combine lemon juice, balsamic vinegar, olive oil, fresh rosemary, and minced garlic, then add the meat and refrigerate overnight, if possible.
- Squeeze fresh lemon juice on vegetables, pasta, soups, rice, and stews. It will add so much flavor, you'll be able to cut back on salt.

## RELATED recipes

Barley Risotto with Asparagus and Lemon *262*
Barley Salad with Snow Peas and Lemon Dressing *211*
Black Bean Spread with Mexican Flavors *206*
Broccoli with Lemon Vinaigrette *272*
Cantaloupe and Blueberry Compote with Green Tea and Lime *276*
Greek Lentil Salad *217*
Grilled Chicken Salad with Oranges *210*
Lemony Blueberry Cheesecake Bars *279*
Mediterranean Split Pea Spread *205*
Penne with Asparagus, Ricotta and Lemon *252*
Roasted Moroccan Chicken Thighs with Squash and Pearl Onions *238*
Smoked Salmon Canapés *203*
Tuna and Cannellini Salad with Lemon *213*
Whole Wheat Noodles with Peanut Sauce *214*

# lentils

**GL** VERY LOW Lentils are the perfect slow-acting food, with an ideal mix of slow-digesting protein and complex carbohydrates. And since they cook quickly—no presoaking required—there's little excuse not to use them in soups, salads, and main dishes even on weeknights. If you add them to rice dishes, you'll be able to use less rice and significantly lower the GL of the dish.

Their secret weapon against blood sugar spikes is soluble fiber, and plenty of it. A cup of cooked lentils carries a whopping 16 grams of fiber, most of it the soluble type. Of course, soluble fiber is also the stuff that lowers cholesterol. It's little wonder that lentils are a staple in the Mediterranean diet, famous for protecting the heart.

Lentils are also a good source of protein (18 grams per cup, cooked), which makes them wonderfully filling and weight-loss friendly.

## Health Bonus

One recent study found that women who included lentils or beans in their diets at least twice a week had a 25 percent lower risk of breast cancer compared to women who ate them less than once a month. Lentils are also unusually rich in folacin, a B vitamin proven to lower blood levels of homocysteine, an amino acid linked with an increased risk of heart disease and dementia. The fiber in lentils also helps keep you regular.

## Cooks Tips

Stored in a cool, dry, dark place, lentils will keep for up to six months. Hang on to them any longer, and they'll dry out. Don't mix new lentils with older ones, since the older ones will take longer to cook.

---

**PERFECT portions: 1/2 cup**

Since the GL is very low, and lentils are among the most nutritious plant foods around, you can enjoy a bit more.

## Menu Magic

- Add cooked lentils to green salads or pasta dishes.

- Mash cooked lentils and blend with fresh salsa or with garlic, yogurt, and lemon juice for an easy and terrifically healthy dip or spread.

- Cook a pot—or open a can—of lentil soup. Interesting options include red lentil and tomato soup, lentil-barley soup, lentil and Swiss chard soup with lemon (chock full of Magic foods!), and chicken and lentil stew.

- Make lentils a main dish by cooking them with smoked turkey sausage, onion, tomatoes, and herbs.

- Reinvent rice by adding lentils. Cook and season a variety of colored lentils and serve over brown or converted rice.

### RELATED recipes

**Curried Red Lentil Soup** 224
**Dahl with Spinach** 261
**Greek Lentil Salad** 217
**Lentil and Bean Chili** 262
**Mustard-Glazed Salmon with Lentils** 247

# melons

**PERFECT portions:** 1 cup cubed

Since melons are mostly water, feel free to have a bit more.

**GL** VERY LOW | Despite their mouthwatering sweetness, melons are surprisingly blood sugar friendly, making them perfect with breakfast, as snacks, or in fruit salads and even salsas. Yes, the sugar they contain is quickly converted to glucose, or blood sugar, but melons are mostly water (as much as 90 percent), so they don't have as much sugar as you'd think. Because of their water content, melons are also remarkably low in calories.

Watermelon perfectly illustrates the difference between the glycemic index (GI) and the glycemic load (GL). Because the sugar it contains is fast acting, it has a sky-high GI—but since you get very little sugar when you eat a serving of watermelon, its GL is low.

The vitamin C in melons (cantaloupes are the real C standouts) makes them top-notch for preventing some of the damage high blood sugar can cause to cells as well as to arteries and blood vessels. And melons' potassium helps guard against high blood pressure, a real risk of diabetes. As one of the richest sources of lycopene (a natural compound that's close kin to beta-carotene), it may also help keep heart disease at bay, which is important since heart disease risk runs high for people with diabetes.

## Health Bonus

Lycopene-rich foods such as watermelon may offer protection against certain kinds of cancer, including prostate, breast, endometrial, lung, and colon cancers. The strongest evidence has been regarding prostate cancer. One study of 47,000 men found that those who ate two to four servings of tomatoes (another lycopene-rich food) a week had a 26 percent reduced risk of prostate cancer compared to those who ate none.

Remember Mom's admonition to eat your carrots for good eyesight? It's the beta-carotene in carrots that makes them good for your eyes, and cantaloupe is rich in this nutrient, too.

## Cooks Tips

If only melons came with tags indicating how ripe they were, you'd never pick a bad one again. They don't, but you can use these clues.

**Watermelon:** Thump it to see if it's ripe. If it sounds a bit hollow, it should be ready. You can also shake it to see if the seeds are loose, an indication of ripeness.

**Cantaloupe:** If it smells too sweet and musky, it's past its prime. Unlike watermelon, cantaloupe will continue to ripen at room temperature, so if you buy one that's not quite ripe, keep it on the counter until it's ready.

**Honeydew:** Look for a smooth outer peel and softness at the stem end of the melon (press it with your thumb).

Be sure to rinse melons well before you cut them. Since melons are grown on vines that lie on the ground, they come in contact with all kinds of bacteria

*(continued)*

from dirt, water, and animals. When you slice through the peel, you could move that bacteria from the outside to the inside on the knife.

For convenience, consider buying a melon baller. These come in various sizes and make it easy to serve melon as an appetizing snack or dessert. They're also good for coring pears and apples.

## Bitter Melon—More Like Medicine

Bitter melon, also part of the melon clan, is anything but sweet. As its name implies, this light green vegetable (yes, all melons are vegetables), which looks more like a cucumber with warts than a melon, has a very bitter taste due to a high concentration of quinine. Animal research shows that the natural compounds in bitter melon can lower blood sugar levels as much as some prescription drugs, possibly by boosting insulin secretion, improving the ability of cells to absorb glucose, blocking the absorption of sugar in the intestine, and hindering the release of glucose from the liver.

One of the largest studies of bitter melon in people with type 2 diabetes lasted only two days, but it showed significant drops in blood sugar for 100 participants within hours after they drank a liquid containing suspended pulp from the melon. A number of smaller but longer trials have had similar results.

Most people who try bitter melon use supplements, but if you want to eat the melon itself (it's very much an acquired taste), cut the white fibrous seed core in half and remove the seeds. Don't eat them! The red seed covering can be toxic. Blanching the melon before cooking will help reduce the bitter flavor. It can then be used in soups or stir-fries.

## Menu Magic

- ✿ Make melons part of any fruit salad. Use a scooped-out watermelon shell to serve the salad at a picnic.
- ✿ Try a salad with watermelon chunks and feta cheese, topped with fresh mint leaves and, if you like, some toasted pumpkin seeds or toasted pine nuts.
- ✿ Make a refreshing watermelon slush by mixing cubed watermelon and ice in the blender. Add a bit of honey at the end.
- ✿ Garnish plates with a slice of watermelon— and eat it!
- ✿ Serve honeydew with vanilla ice cream.
- ✿ Mix small melon cubes with chicken or seafood salad.
- ✿ Make watermelon salsa by blending watermelon, sweet onions, black beans, jalapeños, chopped cilantro, minced garlic, and salt.
- ✿ Keep melon cubes or balls in the fridge for handy, refreshing snacks.
- ✿ Blend cantaloupe, orange juice, lime juice, and cinnamon for a cold soup appetizer.
- ✿ Make a melon smoothie with cantaloupe, honeydew, lime juice, and a little honey.
- ✿ Place chunks or balls of several different types of melon on skewers for a fun, colorful appetizer. Add grapes between the melon pieces if you like.
- ✿ Eat thinly sliced cantaloupe or honeydew on top of Swiss cheese for a colorful snack.

## RELATED recipe

Cantaloupe and Blueberry Compote
with Green Tea and Lime *276*

# milk

**GL** VERY LOW

There's something rather mysterious about milk in relation to blood sugar. It moves the needle only a smidge, which isn't surprising since it's fairly low in carbohydrates and rich in protein (a perfect combination for steadying blood sugar). But researchers think there's some natural component in milk that may help directly protect against insulin resistance, a forerunner of type 2 diabetes.

Two Harvard studies found that people who made dairy foods part of their daily diets were 21 percent less likely to develop insulin resistance and 9 percent less likely to develop type 2 diabetes for each daily serving of dairy they had. Pretty impressive! (Apparently not everyone has gotten the word, though: Some Web sites actually tell you that milk *causes* diabetes.)

Choose fat-free milk over whole or even 2 percent, which still has a fair amount of saturated fat, the kind that increases insulin resistance and clogs arteries.

## Health Bonus

Milk is, of course, rich in calcium and vitamin D, both important for shoring up bone. Fat-free milk actually has more calcium than whole, and it's also virtually the only good source of vitamin D you're likely to find in your kitchen. D is a "don't miss" vitamin: Experts are realizing not only that our needs for it are higher than previously thought—and our blood levels woefully

### don't fall for it

Almost everyone has seen the commercials advertising dairy foods as an aid in losing weight. The trouble is, the results of studies on dairy and weight loss have been inconsistent, with the latest showing that people who eat a lot of calcium-rich dairy foods don't in fact have an easier time losing weight. There's no harm in getting more fat-free milk into your diet; just don't bank on dairy foods to solve your poundage problems.

### PERFECT **portions**: 1 cup

Three 8-ounce (250-milliliter) servings a day of low-fat milk or other dairy products, such as yogurt, may help tame insulin resistance and also provide much of the calcium you need.

low—but also that it may play a key role in preventing certain cancers if we get enough.

Low-fat dairy foods such as fat-free milk are also a cornerstone of the doctor-recommended DASH diet proven to help control high blood pressure.

## Cooks Tips

If you're not a fan of fat-free milk because it's too thin, try ultra-pasteurized fat-free milk, also called UHT (ultra-high temperature). Brands include Parmalat. It tends to have a creamier texture than regular fat-free milk but no more fat or calories.

## Menu Magic

- Pretend you're a kid again and drink a cold glass of fat-free milk with lunch or dinner.

- Make yourself a banana-strawberry smoothie with frozen strawberries, a frozen banana, fat-free milk, and a dash of vanilla extract.

- Create "cream" of carrot or tomato soup using fat-free milk. Thicken it with a small amount of flour.

- Enjoy a soothing cup of chai once in a while instead of coffee.

### RELATED **recipes**

**Cauliflower and Spinach Casserole** *270*

**Chai** *208*

**Cherry Clafouti** *283*

**Greek Pasta and Beef Casserole** *230*

**Macaroni and Cheese with Spinach** *255*

**Oatmeal with Apples and Flaxseeds** *193*

**Sole Florentine** *247*

# nuts

**GL** VERY LOW

There's a good reason that people put nuts in trail mix to take with them when they're hiking. Nuts provide sustained energy because, thanks to their mix of fat and protein, they're a "slow-burning" food. For the same reason, they're friendly to your blood sugar. In fact, Harvard researchers discovered that women who regularly ate nuts (about a handful five times a week) were 20 percent less likely to develop type 2 diabetes than those who didn't eat them as often.

Yes, nuts are high in fat—but it's mostly "good" fat. Remember secret number 5 of Magic eating, Favor Good Fats? Good fat may reduce insulin resistance, and in the case of most nuts, 85 percent of their fat is this kind.

Good fats, of course, also improve heart health, even boosting levels of "good" HDL cholesterol. In studies, people who ate as few as 5 ounces (150 g) of nuts a week as part of an overall heart-healthy diet lowered their risk of developing heart disease by 35 percent compared to those who ate nuts less than once a month. (This doesn't apply to macadamia nuts, though, because of their high saturated fat content.) In fact, one study found that a diet that includes unsaturated fats from almonds and walnuts may have 10 percent more cholesterol-lowering power than a traditional cholesterol-lowering diet.

If you eat nuts frequently, you may also be damping down chronic inflammation in your body, which can help reduce your risk of both diabetes and heart disease. And the protein in most nuts is unusually rich in the amino acid arginine, which may help relax blood vessels, making a heart attack less likely.

Some nuts, including peanuts, walnuts, and almonds, also contain plant sterols, which have been shown to lower cholesterol, and a natural compound called resveratrol, the same one found in red wine and shown to lower heart disease risk. Like fish, walnuts are a good source of omega-3 fats, another shot in the arm against heart disease.

Peanuts aren't technically nuts at all, but legumes. Unlike nuts that grow on trees, they grow underground, but for health, they rank right up there with all the aboveground nuts (also see the peanut butter entry on page 136).

## HOW MANY nuts IN A SERVING?

| Nut | Serving Size 1 oz (30 g) |
|---|---|
| Almonds | 20-24 |
| Brazil nuts | 9 or 10 |
| Cashews | 16-18 |
| Hazelnuts | 18-20 |
| Peanuts | 40 |
| Pine nuts | 150-157 |
| Pistachios | 45-47 |
| Walnuts | 8-11 halves |

## Health Bonus

Nuts provide a hard-to-find nutrient—vitamin E, an important antioxidant that may help fight prostate and lung cancers. Brazil nuts are selenium superstars, providing a whopping 200 times more of the mineral than any other nut. Selenium has been linked to prevention of both cancer and heart disease. Almonds provide bone-building calcium. Hazelnuts and cashews boast the most copper, a much-needed nutrient for people with diabetes.

## Cooks Tips

To squirrel away nuts, store them in an airtight container in the fridge for up to six months; in the freezer, they'll last for up to a year.

Roasting nuts brings out their flavor. Preheat the oven to 300°F (150°C). Place 1/2 cup of shelled nuts on a baking sheet in a single layer and roast for 7 to 10 minutes. Check near the end of the roasting time to make sure they don't burn.

## Menu Magic

Pick a dish, almost any dish—adding nuts can make it a real standout in terms of both taste and nutrition. Here are but a few simple suggestions to take your recipes to the next level.

- Stir chopped walnuts or pecans into rice dishes.
- Add pistachios to chicken salad.
- Mix pine nuts or chopped walnuts into pasta dishes along with olive oil, basil, and sun-dried tomatoes.
- Create your own trail mix for snacking with dried fruit, high-fiber cereal, and your favorite nuts.
- Top off pumpkin, squash, or tomato soup with chopped roasted nuts.
- Sprinkle your favorite chopped nuts and some dried cranberries on green salads.
- For better-tasting waffles, pancakes, and muffins, add chopped nuts to the batter.

**PERFECT portions: 1 ounce (30 g)**

Nuts are high in calories, so a serving is small. Because nuts come in all shapes and sizes, the number that equals a serving varies quite a bit (see "How Many Nuts in a Serving?" on opposite page). Macadamia nuts contain a whopping 1,000 calories per cup, so indulge sparingly.

- For a single-serving, low-GL snack in place of chips or crackers, place 1 ounce (30 g) of nuts in a self-sealing bag to carry with you.
- Sprinkle pecans into unsweetened applesauce.
- Stir nuts into stir-fry dishes.

## Smart Substitution

*Instead of white flour:* Use ground nuts to replace some of the white stuff called for in a crust or cake batter.

## RELATED recipes

Apple-Bran Muffin *197*

Asian Peanut Dip *204*

Bulgur with Ginger and Orange *264*

Caponata *202*

Cherry-Almond Gratin *288*

Cherry Tomatoes Filled with Pesto Cream Cheese *200*

Chocolate-Raspberry Cheesecake *284*

Fudge Brownies *280*

Grilled Chicken Salad with Oranges *210*

Maple-Walnut Roasted Apples *282*

Oatmeal-Peanut Butter Trail Bars *207*

Quinoa with Chiles and Cilantro *266*

Spiced Almonds *203*

Spinach with Pine Nuts and Currants *274*

Upside-Down Nectarine Muffins *199*

Wheatberry Salad with Dried Apricots and Mint *266*

Whole Wheat Noodles with Peanut Sauce and Chicken *214*

# oats

**GL MEDIUM**

A steaming bowl of oatmeal—sprinkled with Magic cinnamon, of course—is more than comfort food. Studies show that oats can reduce postmeal blood sugar and insulin levels in people with and without diabetes.

Soluble fiber is the reason oatmeal is top-notch for steady blood sugar. This type of fiber turns into a gel in your stomach, slowing the digestive process and blunting the rise in blood sugar that normally goes with it. Oats are also an excellent source of the mineral manganese, which plays a role in blood sugar metabolism.

Dozens of studies have concluded that eating oatmeal five or six times a week can reduce your risk of developing type 2 diabetes by as much as 39 percent. And, since oatmeal's a whole grain, starting your day with a bowl will take you one step closer to living the second secret of Magic eating, Make Three of Your Carb Servings Whole Grains.

Oats also fight heart disease, as it says right on the oatmeal box. This has been proven beyond a shadow of a doubt in more than 40 studies over 30 years of research. It's largely because of the special type of soluble fiber, called beta-glucan, in oatmeal.

One more benefit of this flaky food: It fills you up and keeps you full. In one study, people who ate oatmeal for breakfast consumed one-third fewer calories at lunch than those who ate a sugared flaked cereal. (The bran of the oat is just as good for your blood sugar as flakes, so be sure to read the bran entry on page 84.)

## Health Bonus

The soluble fiber called beta-glucan not only helps tame blood sugar and cholesterol, it may also help boost your immune system's ability to fight off infection, as well as reduce high blood pressure. Oats are also a good source of natural plant compounds that may help reduce the risk of breast cancer by mimicking estrogen and preventing the natural hormone from triggering the growth of cancer cells. And they're packed with powerful disease-fighting antioxidants called polyphenols and saponins.

---

## OATS glossary
*While all oats have the power to tame your blood sugar, there are differences in taste and texture among types.*

**Oat groats:** Oats that have been cleaned, toasted, hulled, and cleaned again. These are the most minimally processed of all the oat varieties and must be soaked and cooked for a long time.

**Steel-cut oats:** Whole grain groats that have been cut into two or three pieces using steel disks. These take 30 to 45 minutes to cook and have a hearty oat flavor and a chewier texture than rolled oats.

**Rolled (old–fashioned) oats:** Oats that have been steamed, rolled, resteamed, and toasted. They take about 15 minutes to cook.

**Instant oats:** These are prepared the same way as rolled oats but cut into smaller pieces so they cook faster. No actual cooking is required; just pour boiling water over them and stir.

**Oat flour:** Flour made by grinding groats and separating out the bran. It is gluten free.

**Oat bran:** This is made by grinding oat groats and separating the bran from the flour. It's higher in insoluble fiber than whole oats and can be prepared as a hot cereal like oatmeal.

## Are Some Oats Better than Others?

Some oats have been processed more or less than others. On the "less" end of the scale are steel-cut oats (see "Oats Glossary" on the facing page). The GL of less processed oats is about 20 percent lower than that of more processed forms, but even instant oats are a good source of fiber and have a moderate GL. Shop carefully for instant oatmeal, though; most brands have added sugar—as much as 4 teaspoons per packet. Generally, only "regular" (unflavored) instant oatmeal is sugar free.

## Cooks Tips

Don't substitute instant oats in a recipe that calls for quick-cooking or old-fashioned oats. The texture is different, and instant oats usually have other flavors added.

## Menu Magic

- Grind oats in the blender and use them to coat fish and chicken.

- Make a batch of oat bran muffins and keep them on hand for tasty breakfast treats.

- Next time you make pancakes or waffles, replace up to one-third of the flour in the batter with oatmeal ground to a fine powder in the blender.

- Bake up a tray of oatmeal cookies (using whole wheat flour in place of one-third of the white flour) and include Magic cinnamon, of course!

- Make fresh oat biscuits.

- Use oat flour as a thickener for stews and soups.

**PERFECT portions:** 1/2 cup, cooked

Oats are slow-acting carbs that are good for your blood sugar—if you keep the portion size reasonable. Eat more than a cup, and the GL moves into the high range. Fill up the rest of your bowl with fresh fruit and a sprinkling of nuts.

- For dessert, serve oat-rich fruit crisps and cobblers. Just watch the butter content. It's better to use a good-for-you brand of margarine such as Smart Balance instead.

## Smart Substitutions

*Instead of sugary cereal:* Have steel-cut or old-fashioned oatmeal with raisins and walnuts for a hearty and filling breakfast.

*Instead of bread crumbs:* Use oats in meat loaf and meatballs.

*Instead of wheat flour:* Substitute oat flour for a third of the wheat flour in baked goods.

### RELATED recipes

Apple-Cranberry Crumble *286*
Blueberry-Oatmeal Muffins *198*
Multi-Grain Pancakes or Waffles *192*
Oatmeal-Peanut Butter Trail Bars *207*
Oatmeal with Apples and Flaxseeds *193*
Turkey Meatballs *242*

# olive oil

**GL**
VERY LOW

It's a wonder olive oil isn't more expensive, because in the world of Magic eating, it's liquid gold.

Remember secret number 5 of Magic eating, Favor Good Fats? Well, olive oil is the flagship of the good-fats fleet. In fact, we recommend using olive or canola oil (when you need a neutral-tasting oil) most of the time instead of other oils.

Good fats like those in olive oil work miracles for your blood sugar—and your health in general. Unlike butter, these unsaturated fats don't increase insulin resistance and may even help *reverse* it, helping your body steady its blood sugar.

Olive oil also "spikeproofs" your meals by slowing digestion so carbs take longer to break down into blood sugar. Simply tossing your salad with olive oil and vinegar will help blunt the blood sugar impact of whatever else you're eating (see page 159 to find out why the vinegar's also important).

One recent Australian study found that when six men were given either olive oil, water, or a mixture of water and oil before a high-carb meal, it took almost three times as long for their stomachs to begin emptying—significantly delaying the subsequent rise in blood sugar—when they had the olive oil. You may also remember from the first chapter that meals that raise blood sugar quickly result in feeling hungrier before the next meal. Slower rises in blood sugar equal feeling full longer, which in turn equals weight loss!

As for heart health, eating generous amounts of olive oil is one of the main reasons that people who follow the Mediterranean diet have less heart disease and far fewer heart attacks. One study found that when 28 men and women added 2 tablespoons of extra-virgin olive oil a day to their usual diets for six weeks, they experienced a 12 percent drop in total cholesterol and a 16 percent drop in LDL ("bad") cholesterol. Numerous studies over the years have shown that olive oil not only lowers LDL but also raises HDL, the good kind. The oil is also rich in antioxidants called phenols, which help protect artery walls from cholesterol buildup.

## Olives: Magic Fruits

Olive oil, of course, comes from olives, the mother lode of good-for-you fats. So consider olives a Magic food, too. For true olive taste, buy fresh ones from the deli section, not canned. (Once you get used to them, you'll never go back to canned.) If you use quality, flavorful olives, a little will go a long way.

Like olive oil, olives pack a lot of calories (about 6 per medium black olive), so try to use them in place of other fats in your diet, not in addition to them.

## Health Bonus

Olive oil contains an anti-inflammatory component so strong that researchers liken it to aspirin. This may be another reason that people who follow the Mediterranean diet have such low rates of heart disease, which is linked to inflammation. So, by the way, is type 2 diabetes, not to mention other chronic diseases like Alzheimer's.

In contrast, a diet heavy in corn, safflower, and sunflower oils can actually promote inflammation in the body, which can damage arteries and lead to heart disease and other health problems. We recommend against using any of these types as your main cooking oil.

Olive oil also contains natural compounds called lignans, which may reduce the risk of cancers of the colon, breast, prostate, pancreas, and endometrium.

## Cooks Tips

Olive oil isn't like wine; it doesn't improve with age. In fact, it can become rancid. Store it in a tightly sealed dark container in a cool place. If your oil turns cloudy, it's time to throw it away and buy a new bottle.

## Menu Magic

Great cooks use olive oil in just about everything. Use it whenever you can in place of other vegetable oils, margarine, or butter. Here are a few suggestions.

- Serve a dish of good olive oil with cracked black pepper for dipping fresh bread (whole grain, of course!).

- Instead of using butter on bread or mashed potatoes, try olive oil mixed with roasted garlic (see the garlic entry for tips on roasting).

- Use it as a base for marinades for beef, chicken, fish, or pork.

- Add it to pasta, chopped tomatoes, crumbled feta cheese, chopped fresh basil, and capers for a fast and oh-so-simple supper.

- Use it to replace the smoked meats and sausage typically used to flavor bean and pea soups.

- In recipes that call for butter or margarine, use 3/4 teaspoon olive oil in place of 1 teaspoon butter or margarine.

- Dice olives into sauces, especially tomato-based types.

- Top your pizza with olives along with other vegetables of your choice.

- Add olives to green salads, pasta salads, and tuna sandwiches.

## RELATED recipes

# onions

Don't cry for onions—embrace them! They may be synonymous with tears and onion breath, but they're essential to cooks everywhere for their unique flavor. They're also good for you. It's true that these underground globes don't offer a whole lot of nutrients, but what they have in bulk are powerful sulfur-containing compounds, which are responsible for their pungent odor—and many of their health benefits.

According to several studies, onions may help bring down high blood sugar in diabetic animals. In one Egyptian study of diabetic rats, onion juice reduced blood sugar levels by an amazing 70 percent. One of few published studies in humans, from India, dates back some 30 years, but it found that people with diabetes who ate 2 ounces (60 g) of onions a day experienced a significant drop in blood sugar levels.

Researchers credit these effects to the sulfur compounds in onions as well as their flavonoids. These powerful antioxidant compounds also help fight some of the side effects of high blood sugar, not to mention heart disease.

Onions even seem to boost HDL, the "good" cholesterol. One study found that people who ate the most onions, along with other foods rich in flavonoids, had a 20 percent lower risk of heart disease. Thanks to their sulfur compounds, onions, like aspirin, also help prevent dangerous blood clots. And they're known to help lower high blood pressure.

Finally, onions are one of the richest food sources of chromium, a trace mineral that improves the body's ability to respond to insulin.

## Health Bonus

Onions' sulfur compounds and flavonoids may help fend off several forms of cancer. One Chinese study found that men who ate at least 1 tablespoon of chopped onions and other related vegetables (garlic, scallions, chives, and leeks) a day had about half the risk of developing prostate cancer compared to men who ate less than 1/4 tablespoon of these veggies daily. There's also a link between a high intake of flavonoids and reduced risk of lung cancer.

Evidence suggests that onions may help preserve bone and prevent osteoporosis. And because the sulfur compounds are strongly anti-inflammatory, onions may also help relieve the pain and swelling of arthritis.

The green tops of scallions, or spring onions, are rich in vitamin C and beta-carotene.

## Cooks Tips

The more tears they cause, the more health benefits onions have. To stem the flood while you're chopping, try chilling onions for about a half hour before cutting, and slice them from the top, leaving the root end intact; it has the strongest concentration of eye-burning compounds.

Be sure to wash onions well before chopping, especially if you're going to eat them raw. Onions grow underground and can harbor nasty bacteria. Store onions in a cool, dry place, not in the fridge, and not near potatoes. Potatoes give off moisture and a gas that causes onions to spoil faster.

### Antioxidant-Rich Onions

To reap the most benefit from onions, choose varieties with the most antioxidants. Here they're ranked from highest to lowest (we've included shallots, which are related to onions). If you don't recognize some of the names, don't worry. Just know that sweeter or milder-tasting onions have fewer antioxidants than their more pungent counterparts.

1. Shallots
2. Western yellow
3. Northern red
4. Empire sweet
5. Western white
6. Imperial Valley sweet
7. Vidalia

## Menu Magic

Like garlic, onions can be added to just about anything. Here are just a few suggestions.

- Add onions to almost any stew or stir-fry.

- To get a bit of raw onion into your diet, combine chopped onions, tomatoes, avocado, and jalapeño peppers for a blood sugar–friendly chip dip. Finish with a splash of lime juice.

- Sauté chopped onions in olive oil and add to corn, potatoes, or peas.

- Add chopped scallions to rice dishes.

- Add sliced onions to green salads.

- Use chopped onions to add crunch to any sandwich salad, such as chicken, tuna, or egg salad.

- Make fruit chutney with peaches, mangos, pears, apples, or apricots and plenty of chopped onion. Serve with meals as a condiment that won't upset your blood sugar balance.

- Roast some onions to serve as a savory side dish. Cut the root and top from a large onion. Place root side down on a foil-covered baking sheet and bake for about an hour at 400°F (200°C). When it's done, remove it from the oven and make a deep criss-cross cut in the top. Season with flavored vinegar, herbs, sea salt, coarse-ground pepper, and olive oil.

- Enjoy French onion soup, but go easy on the bread and cheese topping. Try adding a few whole grain croutons instead.

- Use caramelized onions to add wonderful flavor to any vegetable and pasta dish. To caramelize an onion, thinly slice onion, then heat 1 tablespoon olive oil in a heavy skillet over medium heat. Add onion and cook, covered, 10 minutes, stirring often. Remove cover and cook for 10 more minutes, stirring occasionally.

### RELATED recipes

Curried Butternut Squash Puree *269*

Curried Red Lentil Soup *224*

Greek Pasta and Beef Casserole *230*

Hearty Split Pea Soup with Rye Croutons *223*

Jerusalem Artichoke Pancakes *268*

Lamb Stew with Spring Vegetables *229*

Orange Beef Stir-Fry with Broccoli and Red Pepper *226*

Pork Chop and Cabbage Skillet Dinner *232*

Pork Stew with Latin Flavors *229*

Roasted Moroccan Chicken Thighs with Squash and Pearl Onions *238*

Sautéed Brussels Sprouts with Red Pepper and Caraway Seeds *273*

Slow-Cooker Beef and Vegetable Stew *228*

Spiced Cauliflower with Peas *272*

Spinach with Pine Nuts and Currants *274*

Spring Vegetable Stir-Fry with Tofu *260*

Turkey and Bean Chili with Avocado Salsa *243*

Zucchini-Basil Frittata *193*

# pasta

You might think there's nothing worse for your blood sugar than a bowl of pasta. Surprisingly, you'd be wrong. As it turns out, pasta has only a moderate effect on blood sugar levels. (The Italian bread you may eat with your pasta, however, is a different story.)

Yes, pasta is high in carbs. But the type of wheat it's made from (durum wheat) appears to be digested more slowly than similar white flours used to make bread. You can also thank the special protein structure of the dough for pasta's moderate GL. It's a protein "latticework" that traps the starch molecules so it takes more time for your stomach's digestive enzymes to get to them and turn them into blood sugar. (Want to know more? You'll need a degree in food chemistry.) The more thoroughly you cook pasta, though, the easier it is for your body to break it down, so if you like your pasta al dente, or slightly firm the way Europeans eat it, all the better.

Choose whole wheat pasta instead of regular old white pasta, and you'll have a serving or two of whole grain—and about three times as much fiber per serving. Remember, you're aiming to make three of your daily carbohydrate servings whole grains, which will lower your risk of diabetes.

Pasta is pretty much as good—or as bad—for you as what you eat with it. Pile on vegetables like tomatoes and spinach or steamed broccoli, add a little olive oil and garlic, and you've got a terrific low-GL meal. Drown your pasta in cream sauce, and you might as well eat cheesecake.

If you're watching your cholesterol, you might go a little easy with egg noodles. It's no secret that they're made with eggs, and since eggs contain cholesterol, so do the noodles. (As we pointed out in the egg entry on page 106, though, dietary cholesterol isn't the main contributor to high cholesterol levels.) Another option? Eggless "egg" noodles.

## Health Bonus

All white pasta is enriched with iron and B vitamins (pasta that's 100 percent whole grain is not). Pasta also contains some protein, although it's not a "complete" protein source, meaning that it's missing some of the amino acids that make up a complete protein. You can easily remedy this by sprinkling a little grated cheese on your pasta.

**pasta** is actually smart for your blood sugar if you choose the whole grain kind and keep your portions moderate.

## Cooks Tips

Yes, pasta *can* last longer than some marriages, up to three years. Store it in a closed pasta canister so you can easily toss it into boiling water on short notice.

After you've cooked your pasta (taste it; it should be firm when you bite it), drain it immediately or it will keep cooking.

## Menu Magic

Pasta has to be one of the most versatile foods ever invented. All you need to do is pick your pasta; for toppings, the sky's the limit. Think herbs, sautéed vegetables, beans, chicken, perhaps a bit of olive oil, and a sprinkling of Parmesan cheese. If you include garlic and onions, you could get as many as six Magic foods on one plate!

- Grab a bag of frozen vegetables, cook them, and toss them with hot pasta, some olive oil, sautéed garlic, and a bit of cheese for a healthy dinner in no time flat.

- Cook any vegetable you like and puree it in the blender. Serve on hot pasta and top with herbs and spices of your choice.

- Top pasta with meatballs made with ground turkey breast or extra-lean ground beef and some no-sugar-added tomato sauce. Serve with a nice big green salad.

- Add pine nuts or chopped walnuts to your pasta dish. Remember, nuts and seeds are Magic, too.

- Add beans, chickpeas, or lentils to a modest portion of pasta to fill up your plate and lower the GL of the meal. You'll also get more protein.

## Smart Substitution

*Instead of mashed potatoes:* Make pasta with olive oil and zucchini as a side dish with dinner.

### PERFECT portions: 1/2 to 1 cup

Serve 1 cup of pasta as a main dish or 1/2 cup as a side dish to keep the GL within the medium range.

### RELATED recipes

Asian Noodle Hot Pot *225*

Garden Pasta Salad *215*

Greek Pasta and Beef Casserole *230*

Macaroni and Cheese with Spinach *255*

Penne with Asparagus, Ricotta and Lemon *252*

Penne with Tomato and Eggplant Sauce *256*

Quick Spinach and Sausage Lasagna *253*

Shrimp and Orzo Casserole *251*

Turkey-Noodle Casserole with Spinach *239*

Whole Wheat Noodles with Peanut Sauce and Chicken *214*

Whole Wheat Pasta with Sausage, Beans and Greens *254*

### Powered-Up Pasta

For pasta that's even friendlier to your blood sugar, go with one of the many new high-fiber, high-protein options that have popped up on supermarket shelves. Some are multigrain pastas, made from grains such as oats, spelt, and barley in addition to durum wheat. Since these are higher in soluble fiber, they have less impact on your blood sugar than regular or even whole wheat pasta. Some contain flaxseed as a source of heart-healthy omega-3 fatty acids. Some have added protein—40 or 50 percent more than regular pasta—from sources like soy flour, milk solids, or egg whites. This also makes them more blood sugar friendly. One brand with many of these bells and whistles is Barilla Plus.

cherries

lemon

watermelon

peaches, apricots,
plums

apples

blueberries

oranges

Despite their sweetness, most fruits have a low glycemic load and fit in perfectly with a Magic diet. Lemons even directly lower blood sugar.

❖ apples

❖ berries

❖ cherries

❖ citrus fruits

❖ lemons

❖ melons

❖ peaches, apricots, plums

magic fruits

# peaches, apricots, plums

**GL** **VERY LOW**

Apricots, peaches, and plums … oh my! Like apples, citrus fruits, and berries, these stone fruits (so named because of the stone-like seed inside) make perfect low-calorie snacks or sweet additions to entrées and desserts. Chalk up their low GLs to their high water content and their stash of blood sugar–taming, cholesterol-busting soluble fiber.

Peaches boast the most fiber of the three. Apricots, which are close cousins to peaches, are richest in beta-carotene, linked with protection from heart disease and cancer. Plums are chock-full of several disease-fighting antioxidants, and dried plums outrank more than 20 other popular fruits and vegetables in antioxidant power, which is important for staving off heart disease and preventing damage caused by high blood sugar.

Fruit you bite into wins hands-down over fruit you spoon from a can. A peach contains only 35 calories, whereas a cup of peaches canned in heavy syrup has 190. If you buy canned, go for peaches packed in their own juice (110 calories per cup).

You may as well cross peach and apricot nectars or fruit juice blends off your grocery list. They usually contain a lot of added sugar or high-fructose corn syrup and little or no fiber—a devastating combo

**stone fruits** make delectable snacks that just happen to benefit your blood sugar thanks to their stash of soluble fiber.

## What's in a Name?

You may have seen fruits called pluots in the store. What the heck are they? A pluot looks much like a plum, but it's a cross between a plum and a plumcot. And what's a *plumcot*? A cross between an apricot and a plum. What about the plum sauce in some Chinese foods? It's not really made from plums at all. It's made from Umeboshi plums—a type of Japanese apricot!

Finally, you may have noticed that you don't see or hear the word *prune* as much these days. That's because of a major multimillion-dollar marketing effort to rename prunes *dried plums* in an effort to boost sales.

that could send your blood sugar through the roof. If you like nectars, dilute them with an equal amount of seltzer for a fizzy and still-sweet beverage. (Our Peachy Iced Tea on page 209 calls for 2 cups of peach nectar but serves eight people and has only 52 calories per cup. It's our way of weaning you off sugary fruit drinks.)

## Health Bonus

Stone fruits contain compounds that may help keep those baby blues (or browns or greens) crystal clear and free of cataracts. And study after study has pronounced that people who eat more fruits and vegetables are healthier all around, with less diabetes, heart disease, cancer, and obesity. Stone fruits also offer potassium, a mineral that helps defend against high blood pressure and stroke. And we would be remiss not to mention the unique intestinal benefits of dried plums (or prune juice)—consume them, and you will go, end of story.

## Cooks Tips

Apricots are delicious raw, but when they're cooked, their beta-carotene and soluble fiber are made more available to the body. For a savory accompaniment to grilled meat or poultry, pit and quarter fresh apricots and gently sauté them in olive oil with a touch of minced garlic.

## Menu Magic

- Top off whole grain pancakes and waffles with peach slices.
- Give chicken dishes or stews a taste of the Middle East by adding diced dried apricots or plums.
- Poach plums in red wine and sprinkle with grated lemon zest for a healthy dessert.
- Sprinkle cinnamon and nutmeg on sliced peaches and use them to top low-fat ice cream or yogurt.
- Sauté sliced, peeled peaches in a small amount of good-for-you margarine like Smart Balance (and some ginger, if you like) and serve alone or as a dessert topper.
- Blend up a peach smoothie with low-fat vanilla yogurt, diced peaches, frozen strawberries, and vanilla.

### don't fall for it

Have you sworn off dried fruit because you've heard it will send your blood sugar skyrocketing? Better rethink that decision. While the glycemic index (GI) of dried fruit is high, the glycemic load (GL), which takes serving size into account, is low. FYI: A serving of dried fruit is about 2 ounces (60 g), not a whole package.

### PERFECT portions: 1 peach or plum

Because apricots are smaller, consider two of them a serving.

- Add diced peaches to chicken salad for a sweet twist.
- Add chopped dried plums to poultry stuffing.
- Top off oatmeal with sliced peaches, dried plums, or diced apricots.
- Add chopped dried apricots to cold cereal.
- Dip dried apricots in dark chocolate for a decadent but still relatively healthy treat (but remember to keep portions small!).
- Add chopped apricots to wild rice before cooking.
- Create your own trail mix with nuts, pieces of bran cereal, and chopped dried apricots.
- Make plum sauce by blending juice-packed plums with cinnamon and spices. Pour over grilled chicken breast or pork tenderloin.

## Smart Substitution

*Instead of cream cheese and jelly:* Spread bread with Neufchâtel (reduced-fat cream cheese) and top with thin slices of ripe plums.

### RELATED recipes

Chicken Breasts with Peaches and Ginger *234*
Mixed Berry and Stone Fruit Soup *276*
Orange-Glazed Roasted Plums *282*
Peachy Iced Tea *209*
Plum-Walnut Crumble *287*
Spice-Crusted Pork Tenderloin with Peach Salsa *233*
Upside-Down Nectarine Muffins *199*

# peanut butter

**GL** *VERY LOW*

Think peanut butter is just for kids? Well, perhaps the classic PB&J (peanut butter and jelly on sticky white bread that melts in your mouth) is best left as part of childhood, but don't throw out the baby with the bathwater. Peanut butter is actually a smart addition to a Magic diet, and it makes perfect sense since peanuts are a Magic food, too.

Peanut butter packs a one-two punch against blood sugar spikes: protein and "good" (unsaturated) fat. In fact, the famed Nurses' Health Study found that women who ate peanut butter at least five times a week were as much as 30 percent less likely to develop diabetes.

On a related note, you may have heard of the peanut butter diet. Crazy? Maybe not. It seems that peanut butter sticks to your ribs as well as the roof of your mouth, thanks to its winning combo of good fat, protein, and fiber. A study at Purdue University found that eating it can dampen appetite for up to 2 hours longer than a low-fiber, high-carb snack. (Try our Oatmeal–Peanut Butter Trail Bars as the perfect between-meal stomach satisfier.)

## The Good News Spreads

Peanut butter doesn't stand alone when it comes to health benefits. Other nut butters, such as almond, walnut, and pistachio butters, are healthy choices, too. (Cashew and macadamia nut butters are higher in saturated fat.) Seed butters, including sunflower seed and pumpkin seed butter, fit the better-blood-sugar bill as well. Check out health food supermarkets and online stores for some of the more unusual varieties.

Like nuts, peanut butter is also a potent protector of the heart. Its good fat helps to tame high cholesterol—after all, it's the same type of fat found in olive oil. One study found that diets that got most of their monounsaturated fat from peanut butter provided almost the same reduction in heart disease risk as diets that got most of their monounsaturated fats from olive oil.

Like the peanuts it comes from, peanut butter is rich in plant compounds called sterols, one of the top proven cholesterol busters. (In fact, sterols are added to some cholesterol-lowering margarines.) Plus, it has a gram of fiber per tablespoon. You really couldn't pack many more benefits into something you can spoon out of a jar.

Watch what brand you buy, though. Many are sweetened with corn syrup or sugar—1/2 teaspoon per 2 tablespoons of peanut butter. We don't quite understand why, since ground peanuts taste great on their own. Natural and organic brands generally have no added sugar and less sodium than regular brands.

## Health Bonus

The stash of sterols in peanut butter not only helps control cholesterol, it may also help fend off colon, prostate, and breast cancers. Peanut butter is also a rich source of the heart-healthy antioxidant compound resveratrol, the one for which red wine is most famous. Natural brands of the spread contain even more resveratrol than other types of peanut butter.

Eating peanut butter (or nuts) several times a week is a proven way to keep high blood pressure under control. And peanut butter ranks right up there with most nuts for its stash of vitamin E, important for a healthy immune system.

Peanut butter as a bone builder? Yep. It's one of the top sources of the bone-building mineral boron. Finally, eat peanut butter and/or nuts at least five times a week, and you could lower your risk of developing gallstones, according to one study.

## Cooks Tips

Some natural peanut butters need to be refrigerated after you open them (check the label). If the oil separates, let the jar come to room temperature, then stir it up. Most national brands, however, can be sealed tightly and stored in the pantry.

## Menu Magic

☻ Spread peanut butter on whole grain waffles or pancakes for breakfast.

☻ Make a peanut butter and banana sandwich on whole grain bread for a pack-and-go lunch. Or smear half a banana with some peanut butter as a snack.

☻ For a nibble that won't make your blood sugar go haywire, spread peanut butter on whole grain crackers or triangles of toasted whole wheat pita bread.

☻ For an even lower-GL snack that will stave off hunger longer, spread peanut butter on apple slices, celery sticks, or carrots.

☻ Be adventurous and try different types of nut butters with different types of fruit and vegetables. Almond butter on sliced pears (Anjou, Bartlett, or Asian) is a delicious combination.

### PERFECT portions: 1 tablespoon

Peanut butter won't raise your blood sugar, but it does contain almost 100 calories per tablespoon. When you're spreading bread, a cracker, or a bagel, be sure you practice portion control and stick with that amount.

## Smart Substitution

*Instead of jam:* Spread peanut butter on your whole grain toast or bagel. You'll get more calories but also more hunger-satisfying protein and less sugar.

### RELATED recipes

Asian Peanut Dip *204*
Oatmeal–Peanut Butter Trail Bars *207*
Peanut Chicken Soup *224*
Whole Wheat Noodles with Peanut Sauce
 and Chicken *214*

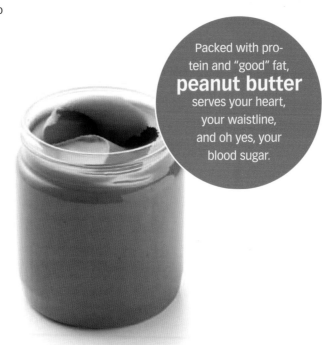

Packed with protein and "good" fat, **peanut butter** serves your heart, your waistline, and oh yes, your blood sugar.

# peas

## GL
**VERY LOW**

Want a high-protein food that's low in calories? Eat peas! That's right, peas.

Since they're on the starchy side as far as vegetables go, peas seem like a bad idea for blood sugar. But if you passed up peas, it would be a mistake.

You may not realize it, but peas are a super source of protein, one reason they leave blood sugar unscathed. A half cup contains an impressive 4 grams of protein and only 60 calories. Peas also have a low GL thanks in part to their stash of soluble fiber, the kind that lowers blood sugar. At almost 4.5 grams of total fiber per 1/2 cup (about a third of which is soluble), a small side of peas will help get you to the recommended 25 grams of fiber per day.

For heart protection, you can't beat these green legumes. The type of soluble fiber they contain, pectin, is top-notch for lowering cholesterol. Peas also pack potassium, which helps lower high blood pressure, and they fork over quite a bit of the B vitamin folate, which experts think may play a role in keeping arteries clear—extra-important for people with diabetes.

## Health Bonus

Green peas are an outstanding source of lutein and zeaxanthin; they contain even more than some supplements. These members of the carotene family lower the risk of cataracts and macular degeneration, the leading cause of blindness in older adults.

## Cooks Tips

Frozen peas are handy, but avoid canned peas, which usually contain added sodium and have much less flavor. Steer clear of frozen peas swimming in cheese or cream sauce. They'll overload you with calories before you can say, "Pass the peas, please."

Cook peas in as little water as possible, just until tender, to retain their nutrients. Use a steamer for the best results.

Peas are firmly in the very low GL category, so don't be too concerned about eating a little more than half a cup.

## Menu Magic

☻ Serve up a classic peas-and-carrots side dish.

☻ Add peas to any soup with noodles or other grain products in it. Peas are a complete protein when combined with grains.

☻ Top off salads with peas.

☻ Make peas part of just about any stew or casserole.

☻ Mix up a cold green pea salad for your next picnic. Recipes abound. One version uses frozen early peas, chopped pimientos, chopped scallions, a small amount of low-fat sour cream, chopped apple, lemon juice, salt, and pepper. Another combines peas with toasted almonds, scallions, feta cheese, low-fat mayonnaise, and balsamic vinegar.

☻ Toss peas in with pasta or noodles.

☻ Snack on snow peas or sugar snaps. The pods give you even more fiber, although the peas contain less protein than more mature, out-of-the-pod types.

## RELATED recipes

**Barley Salad with Snow Peas and Lemon Dressing** *211*

**Chicken Pot Pie with a Whole Grain Biscuit Crust** *236*

**Spiced Cauliflower with Peas** *272*

# pork

**GL**
VERY LOW

You can't eat like a pig and stay healthy, but you can *eat pig,* a.k.a. pork. Like other protein foods, pork won't bump up your blood sugar a bit. And the leanest cuts, such as tenderloin, are almost as low in fat as chicken! That's why advertisers dubbed pork "the other white meat," even though it is in fact red meat.

Over the past 20 years, changes in feeding and breeding practices have produced much leaner cuts of pork, making them appropriate in a Magic diet. Less fat means fewer calories, which means less excess weight and better blood sugar control.

## Health Bonus

Like all other animal foods, including beef and eggs, pork is a good source of vitamins $B_6$ and $B_{12}$, which help keep homocysteine in check. High levels of this amino acid raise the risk of heart disease and dementia. Pork is also a standout for riboflavin (vitamin $B_2$), important for metabolizing carbohydrates and for producing red blood cells.

## Cooks Tips

To keep pork as lean as possible, trim off any excess fat before you cook. One of the biggest mistakes made with pork is overcooking it. That's a recipe for a tough, dried-out dish. To keep lean cuts moist during roasting and to bring the GL of the meal even lower, try using a marinade that contains vinegar, wine, or citrus juice. The acid from the marinade will soften the meat, making it juicier and tastier.

Years ago, people worried about getting trichinosis, caused by intestinal parasites, from pork. Today, because of changes in the way animals are fed and raised, it's much less of a concern. And as was the case all along, cooking pork properly—to an internal temperature of 160°F (71°C)—will kill any trichina parasites that may be present.

**PERFECT portions:** 3 ounces (85 g)

If this is your only meat of the day, up to 6 ounces (170 g) is appropriate. Be sure to choose a lean cut.

## Menu Magic

Think of using pork just as you would beef or chicken, and the possibilities are endless.

- Use pork strips or cubes in stir-fries along with plenty of vegetables (try a frozen stir-fry mix).

- Try pork tenderloin on the grill.

- Create hearty pork and wild rice soup with cubed pork loin, white beans, chickpeas, cooked wild rice, chopped onion, chicken broth, olive oil, cumin, chopped parsley, and coriander.

- Make pork and black bean chili with cubed pork, black beans, chopped red bell peppers, diced tomatoes, chunky salsa, minced garlic, chopped onion, and chili powder. Cook in a slow cooker for 7 hours.

- Throw a lean pork chop on the grill along with sliced summer squash and halved tomatoes.

- Use extra-lean ground pork, labeled 97% lean, in place of regular or even extra-lean ground beef for meat loaf, meatballs, or burgers. You may have to go to a health food supermarket to get such lean pork, or order it online, but it's worth the effort since it's significantly lower in fat than pork labeled "lean" (and often lower than ground pork whose label says "extra lean" but doesn't include a number).

- Use pork in kebabs, along with cherry tomatoes and pieces of onion and yellow bell pepper.

### RELATED recipes
Pork Chop and Cabbage Skillet Dinner *232*
Spice-Crusted Pork Tenderloin with Peach Salsa *233*

# pumpernickel bread

**GL**
LOW

Pumpernickel bread combines the benefits of two other Magic foods: rye bread and sourdough bread. That's because traditional pumpernickel is made with coarsely ground rye flour (and perhaps some wheat flour) and is fermented with sourdough starter. The acetic acid from the starter (see the sourdough entry on page 147) and the soluble fiber in rye (see the rye entry on page 141) keep the GL of the bread low—much lower than that of white or even whole wheat bread.

A serving is about the size of a small slice. Obviously, you'll need two servings to make a sandwich.

One Canadian study found that pumpernickel bread had four to eight times as much resistant starch as breads made with wheat or barley. Resistant starch benefits blood sugar because it doesn't digest easily. Like dietary fiber, it travels right past the stomach and small intestine and settles in the colon, where it's broken down by bacteria and eventually expelled.

Not all store-bought pumpernickels have the same benefits as traditional German pumpernickel, though. Many get their dark color from molasses, not from whole rye kernels and a special baking process that takes many hours. These types usually contain more wheat flour than rye, and some are made using yeast instead of sourdough starter. Your best bet is to shop at a place that sells "artisan" breads. Such bakeries tend to use more traditional pumpernickel recipes. If the bread feels heavy for its size, it's probably the real thing. Commercial brands, if you can find them, include Mestemacher (imported from Germany) and Rubschlager, which makes cocktail rye breads.

## Health Bonus

As with rye bread, pumpernickel loads you up with lignans, the naturally occurring plant compounds that may help reduce the risk of breast and prostate cancers.

## Cooks Tips

If you buy traditional pumpernickel bread from the bakery or make it yourself, it's preservative free, so you'll need to store it in a plastic bag and use it within a few days.

## Menu Magic

❃ For appetizers, top small squares of pumpernickel bread with cream cheese, sliced onion, and tomato.

❃ Serve strong-flavored sandwich fillings, such as aged cheese, on pumpernickel.

❃ Mustard goes well with pumpernickel, so spread this Magic food (actually, the vinegar in mustard is the Magic ingredient) on your next ham and Swiss sandwich on pumpernickel.

❃ Serve a slice of pumpernickel as a hearty, satisfying accompaniment to soup or chili instead of crackers.

## RELATED recipes

**Salmon Sandwiches with Wasabi Mayonnaise** *220*
**Smoked Salmon Canapés** *203*

# rye bread

**GL** LOW

Why rye? Because research shows that unlike white bread, which is one of the worst foods for your blood sugar, whole grain rye bread (or whole grain rye crackers or cereal) can help smooth out blood sugar swings and actually reduce the risk of developing type 2 diabetes. Rye bread is even superior to whole wheat bread when it comes to blood sugar control.

In one study, on days when women ate whole-rye bread, their blood sugar levels were 10 percent lower than on days when they didn't eat it. Another study found that eating rye bread reduced the release of insulin compared to eating refined wheat bread, meaning that less insulin was needed to keep blood sugar in check. That's a good thing, because when the body regularly churns out a lot of insulin, the risk of insulin resistance goes up (and so does the risk of diabetes).

A third study found that men who ate whole grain rye bread, crackers, and cereal (they got 18 grams of fiber a day from rye) for four weeks saw a drop in blood sugar of up to 19 percent compared to their levels at the start of the study.

What's so special about rye? The structure and size of the starch particles in the bread certainly play a role. Another explanation: Rye contains about three times as much soluble fiber as wheat—also a plus for lowering high cholesterol.

There's one major caveat. By "rye" bread, we mean bread made from whole rye flour. Most of the rye breads you find in stores is made with a combination of refined rye and wheat flour, so they don't have the same fiber content or health benefits. Get out the magnifying glass if you have to and look for "whole grain rye flour" at the top of the ingredients list. Real rye bread is heavy and dense and bears little resemblance to white sandwich bread.

## Health Bonus

Rye is loaded with lignans, plant compounds that may help reduce the risk of breast and prostate cancers. And researchers have found that some of the unique plant compounds in whole grain rye are helpful for intestinal health. One study from Finland (the Finns love their rye) found that people who ate 4 1/2 slices of whole grain rye bread a day had 26 percent lower levels of compounds linked to colon cancer.

## Cooks Tips

If you feel a baking spree coming on, and you want to make your own whole grain rye bread, check out your local health food store or shop online for mail-order whole grain rye flour.

## Menu Magic

- Serve your favorite sandwich fixins' on whole grain rye bread.

- When you reach for cheese and crackers, make the crackers whole grain rye. Classic brands are Ryvita and Wasa.

- Try whole grain rye rolls at dinner instead of white rolls, if you can find (or make) them.

- For something different at breakfast, try a multi-whole grain hot cereal that contains rye. Look in a natural foods store for the widest selection.

### RELATED recipes

Hearty Split Pea Soup with Rye Croutons *223*
Smoked Salmon Canapés *203*
Tuna and Carrot Sandwich on Rye *222*

# seeds

GL
**VERY LOW**

Send in the seeds! Like nuts, they are emerging as nutritional superstars. Packed with protein, "good" fat, and fiber, they're just what the doctor ordered for steadying your blood sugar, whether you add them to dishes or eat them as snacks.

Although seeds are indeed high in fat—about 12 to 14 grams per ounce (30 g)—almost all of that fat is the heart-healthy monounsaturated and polyunsaturated kinds. Another plus? Seeds also pack plenty of protein, to the tune of 4 to 9 grams per ounce (30 g). For that same ounce you'll also get 2 to 10 grams of fiber (pumpkin seeds have the most).

Break open that package of pumpkin or sunflower seeds, and sprinkle on those sesame seeds. When you do, you may also lower your cholesterol. Seeds are rich in the natural plant compounds called sterols, which are proven cholesterol busters. (Sterols derived from other sources are even added to some cholesterol-lowering margarines.)

One recent study found that when people with high levels of "bad" LDL cholesterol ate about 1.5 ounces (40 g) of sesame seeds a day for four weeks as part of an already heart-healthy diet, their LDL levels dropped by almost 10 percent more than when they followed the same diet without sesame seeds. Not surprisingly, their LDL levels went back up after they stopped eating the sesame seeds.

Researchers in another study tested 27 varieties of nuts and seeds and found that sesame seeds had the highest sterol content. Sunflower seeds also ranked high in sterols.

## Health Bonus

By weight, both pumpkin and sesame seeds have more iron than liver does! And a single ounce of sesame seeds has almost as much calcium as a glass of milk. Sunflower seeds serve up selenium, a mineral that's been linked to a lower risk of both heart disease and cancer. Most seeds are also real vitamin E finds. Sunflower seeds, for example, provide most of the

---

**PERFECT portions:** 1 to 2 tablespoons

Seeds are high in calories, so don't go overboard. A 1/4-cup serving of sunflower seeds, for example, contains 210 calories. For snacks, stick with a handful of pumpkin seeds or a palmful of sunflower seeds. A tablespoonful will do if you're topping off a salad or sprinkling seeds on veggies.

---

day's needs for E, a nutrient that helps protect against everything from cataracts to cancer. Seeds are also good sources of immune-boosting zinc.

Pumpkin seeds are a traditional kitchen-cabinet treatment for prostate enlargement, and research suggests there may be good reason. Their zinc, vitamin E, selenium, and sterol content probably all help toward this end. The nutrients in seeds may even protect against prostate cancers.

## Smart Substitution

*Instead of chips:* When you crave a crunchy, salty snack, reach for a handful of seeds (or nuts). Your blood sugar and your arteries will thank you.

*(continued on page 144)*

### How to Perfectly Roast Seeds

You can make your own roasted seeds once you've eaten your fill of squash, pumpkin, or watermelon. Here's how.

Separate the seeds from the flesh and strings, wash them well, and let them dry. Then mix them in a bowl with a small amount of vegetable oil and salt. Spread them in a single layer on an ungreased baking sheet and sprinkle on some seasonings (take your pick of cumin, celery salt, cinnamon, paprika, or chili powder). Place the baking sheet in an oven preheated to 300°F (150°C) for about 45 minutes, shaking and stirring the seeds occasionally to prevent burning.

olive oil

The "good" fats in these foods are essential to Magic eating. They steady blood sugar and may even boost insulin sensitivity.

- avocados
- olive oil
- flaxseeds
- peanut butter
- nuts
- seeds

magic fats

alnuts

avocado

peanut butter

# seeds continued

## Cooks Tips

Seeds can go rancid if you store them too long. To keep them fresh for several months, store them in an airtight container away from heat.

A note of caution: Although peanut allergies are better known, reactions to sesame seeds are among the fastest-growing allergies. They are still relatively rare, but if you notice a rash, swelling, or trouble breathing after eating the seeds, you may be allergic.

## Menu Magic

- Add seeds to steamed or sautéed vegetables.
- Sprinkle sesame seeds over brown rice.
- Coat thin fish fillets or chicken cutlets with a mixture of crushed sunflower and pumpkin seeds, then pan fry.
- Chop pumpkin or sunflower seeds and add to hot or cold cereal.
- Add toasted sesame seeds to ground meat for meatballs. They add crunch as well as boosting the nutrition quota of your meal.
- Toss some sesame seeds into bread dough or muffin or pancake batter. You can also add them to piecrusts.
- Spread tahini (ground sesame paste) on toasted whole grain bread.

- Top off your favorite salad greens with pumpkin seeds.
- Add sunflower seed kernels to tuna salad.
- Blend sunflower seeds into scrambled eggs or a vegetable omelet.
- Sprinkle your favorite seeds on top of tomato, carrot, or squash soup.
- Add sesame seeds to fruit salad for crunch.

## RELATED recipes

No-Mayonnaise Creamy Coleslaw *216*

Oven-Fried Chicken *238*

Quinoa with Chiles and Cilantro *266*

Salmon Sandwiches with Wasabi Mayonnaise *220*

Sautéed Brussels Sprouts with Red Pepper and Caraway Seeds *273*

Sautéed Spinach with Ginger and Soy Sauce *275*

Spinach, Grapefruit and Avocado Salad with Poppy Seed Dressing *216*

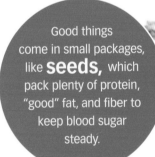

Good things come in small packages, like **seeds,** which pack plenty of protein, "good" fat, and fiber to keep blood sugar steady.

# shellfish

**GL** *VERY LOW*

When it comes to Magic eating, the underwater world is your oyster. It's not just food with fins that benefit your blood sugar; shrimp, lobster, and their crabby and clammy cohorts all count, too. They're rich in protein and low in calories, making them Magic foods indeed.

Shrimp and lobster are almost completely devoid of saturated fat, and they're good sources of omega-3 fatty acids. These are the same heart-smart fats found in fatty fish and renowned for their ability to reduce the risk of heart disease, a goal that's at the top of the list for anyone with diabetes. It's true these crustaceans are relatively high in cholesterol, but as we explained in the eggs entry (page 106), it's saturated fat, more than dietary cholesterol, that raises levels of cholesterol in the body. An average serving of shellfish has about one-third the cholesterol found in one egg, so moderate consumption generally isn't a problem. In fact, shellfish helps protect against heart disease.

Lobster, the upper crust of the crustacean world, happens to be a particularly rich source of a little-known mineral called vanadium, which some studies suggest may enhance insulin's effect in the body, helping to keep an anchor on blood sugar. (In human studies at Harvard's Joslin Diabetes Center, vanadium improved insulin sensitivity and lowered cholesterol, too. In another study, at Temple University in Philadelphia, vanadium supplements were shown to lower blood sugar.)

Despite how rich it tastes, lobster is one of the lowest-fat shellfish as long as you don't plunge it into a pool of melted butter. It's lower in fat than beef, pork, and even chicken.

## Health Bonus

Most shellfish are rich in copper and zinc, both important for your immune system to function at its peak. They also pack an astounding amount of vitamin $B_{12}$, which may help ward off depression, heart disease, and even Alzheimer's. And they're super sources of selenium, an anti-cancer mineral.

> **PERFECT portions: 3 ounces (85 g)**
>
> If this is your main meal of the day, up to 6 ounces (170 g) is an appropriate serving.

Clams are stuffed (pun intended) with sterols, the cholesterol-lowering compounds we've mentioned elsewhere.

## Cooks Tips

Clams, oysters, mussels, and scallops should be alive when you buy them. That means the shells will be tightly closed or should close when you tap them. You can store them in the fridge in a container covered loosely with a damp cloth, but don't store them in water. The shells will open during cooking (discard any that don't). Steam for 4 to 9 minutes or boil for 3 to 5 minutes after the shells open.

Eating shellfish raw (think oysters on the half shell) or less than well done is risky business. They may harbor bacteria, viruses, and parasites, all of which are killed by cooking.

Many large supermarkets now carry large bags of frozen shrimp, so stock your freezer. Thaw them according to package directions, and you have the makings of a fast, high-protein meal. Think shrimp stir-fry.

## Menu Magic

Keep it simple. Too often, shellfish are topped off with butter or creamy sauce or dipped in bread crumbs and fried. A generous squeeze of lemon juice (another Magic food) will usually suffice, especially if you don't overcook the shellfish; overcooking makes them dry.

- Serve boiled shrimp with cocktail sauce as a health-smart party appetizer.

- Use shrimp in stir-fries instead of chicken or beef. Add them in the last 5 minutes to avoid overcooking.

- Add cooked shrimp, clams, or mussels to your favorite pasta sauce.

*(continued)*

# shellfish continued

- Chop some cooked shrimp and sprinkle over a green salad to add low-fat protein. Use a lemony dressing.

- Make crab salad by mixing lump crabmeat (canned is fine) with vinaigrette dressing. Serve over greens.

- Top pizza with minced cooked clams.

- Toss some shrimp, scallops if you have them, and even fish chunks with olive oil and lemon juice, skewer them, pop them on the grill, and you're ready to eat in 5 minutes.

- Place a cooked medium shrimp, some small chunks of avocado and tomato, and a bit of salsa onto a lettuce leaf. Roll it up and eat!

- Put together shrimp tacos by combining shrimp, lettuce, tomato, a bit of shredded cheese, and green salsa in a corn taco shell.

- Order steamed clams as an appetizer.

- Instead of creamy, high-fat clam sauce like you'd get at a restaurant, make linguini with clams using canned clams (minced), garlic, olive oil, chopped hot peppers, and chopped tomatoes.

### RELATED recipes
Shrimp and Orzo Casserole *251*
Shrimp and Scallop Stew *250*

# Shellfish BY THE NUMBERS

Because shellfish are virtually devoid of carbohydrates, their GL is virtually zero. All shellfish are low in saturated fat, but different types offer slightly different nutritional advantages, as you'll see below.

| Shellfish 3 1/2 oz (100 g) | Calories | Protein (g) | Total Fat (g) | Cholesterol (mg) | Vitamins and Minerals |
|---|---|---|---|---|---|
| Clams | 74 | 12.77 | 0.97 | 34 | Excellent source of iron and potassium. |
| Crab, Alaska King | 84 | 18.29 | .60 | 42 | Good source of zinc. |
| Crab, Blue | 87 | 18.06 | 1.08 | 78 | Good source of zinc and calcium. |
| Crab, Dungeness | 86 | 17.41 | .97 | 59 | Good source of zinc and potassium. |
| Lobster | 112 | 20.6 | 1.51 | 70 | Excellent source of vitamin $B_{12}$ Good source of zinc. |
| Mussels (steamed) | 86 | 11.9 | 2.24 | 28 | Good source of iron. |
| Oysters Pacific Eastern farmed Eastern wild | 81 59 68 | 9.45 5.22 7.05 | 2.30 1.55 2.46 | 50 25 53 | Excellent source of zinc. Good source of iron and selenium. |
| Scallops | 88 | 16.79 | .76 | 33 | Good source of vitamin $B_{12}$. |
| Shrimp | 106 | 20.31 | 1.73 | 152 | Fair source of various vitamins and minerals and omega-3 fatty acids. |

# sourdough bread

GL LOW

This is one bread that won't hit a sour note when it comes to your blood sugar. Even though it's made from white flour (typically a no-no for Magic eating), sourdough bread has a relatively mild effect on blood sugar compared to other white breads.

Sourdough is an ancient bread with thousands of years of bread-making history behind it. It has a distinctive taste, the result of lactic acid produced by bacteria used to ferment the dough. A sourdough "starter" is made from a combination of yeast and bacteria growing in a paste of flour and water. Some is used for making a loaf, and the rest is saved to grow and use for future baking.

It's the acid produced by the bacterial culture that makes a poor blood sugar choice into a better one. One small Swedish study involving 12 healthy people found that when the volunteers ate a breakfast that included bread with added lactic acid in an amount found in sourdough bread, the rise in their blood sugar was 27 percent less after 1 1/2 hours than it was when they ate the same breakfast but with a bread made with a combination of whole grain flour and processed white flour.

## Health Bonus

One study using sourdough bread made with specific strains of bacteria found that it could reduce gluten intolerance in people sensitive to wheat gluten. While that doesn't mean that people diagnosed with gluten intolerance can eat sourdough bread with impunity, it does suggest that the bread is more easily digested than other breads made with wheat flour.

---

**PERFECT portions: 1 ounce (30 g)**

A serving is about the size of one small slice, depending on the brand. Eat two slices, as you would in a sandwich, and the bread becomes a medium-GL food—still reasonable.

## Cooks Tips

You can either make your own sourdough bread using a sourdough starter or buy a loaf at the local bakery. Note that all rye breads made with whole grain rye are by nature sourdough. (For bread to rise, yeast reacts with the gluten in the wheat. Rye doesn't contain enough gluten to rise with yeast, so sourdough starter is used to get the same effect.)

Some breads are called sour breads because they have sour flavoring agents added. While it's possible they could have a beneficial effect on blood sugar (say, if the souring agent is vinegar), they haven't been studied as sourdough bread has.

## Menu Magic

Sourdough bread has a distinctive tart taste, but you can use it whenever you might use regular bread. Try it for sandwiches and hamburgers, as a crunchy accompaniment to al dente spaghetti and sauce, or to go with soup.

### RELATED recipe

Grilled Eggplant Sandwiches
with Red Pepper–Walnut Sauce *220*

# soy foods

**GL** VERY LOW

Congratulations! If you've turned to this entry, it probably means you've already discovered soy foods and want to know more about their health benefits, or you have an open mind and are willing to try them. That's good for you—because so is soy.

For starters, soy has more protein, by volume, than beef and almost none of the saturated fat. Right off the bat, this earns it a secure spot on the list of Magic foods. Soybeans have an extraordinarily low GL of 1, which makes foods made from them, such as tofu, tempeh, miso, edamame, and roasted soy nuts (see "Soy Glossary" below) excellent additions to your Magic diet.

Studies suggest that soy may have special power to help lower blood sugar, beyond its low glycemic load. In a recent study on meal-replacement drinks that involved overweight people, those using soy-based drinks lost slightly more weight than those using milk-based drinks, and they also saw their blood sugar levels drop (the milk group didn't).

This result may be thanks to the type of protein in soy. When Swedish researchers fed study subjects meals containing protein from fish (cod), milk (cottage cheese), and soy, they discovered that the soy-protein meal was the friendliest to blood sugar.

Like many other foods, soybeans are best enjoyed in their most unadulterated forms. Products like soy protein bars and flavored soy milk often contain way too much added sugar or fat to be worth eating. Some flavored soy milks, for instance, are sweetened with as much as 6 teaspoons of sugar per 8 ounces (250 ml).

## Health Bonus

Soy is smart for your heart. It seems its cholesterol-lowering powers aren't quite as strong as we once thought, but soy is still good for overall heart health thanks to its "good" fats, its fiber, and its cholesterol-lowering plant sterols.

Eating soy can also help reduce the risk of a serious diabetes complication: kidney disease. In a small study of people with type 2 diabetes and kidney disease, those who were given about one-third of their protein intake as soy protein saw their urinary albumin excretion (UAE) drop by 9.5 percent, a sure sign that their kidneys were functioning better. In another study, the participants' kidneys were better able to filter blood when they followed a soy-based diet for eight weeks.

---

## soy glossary   Soy is a bean, but out of that bean comes many different products.

**Edamame:** Fresh green soybeans, available shelled or in the pod. You can eat them raw, but most people prefer them steamed with a bit of salt. You don't eat the pods.

**Mature soybeans:** You can buy these canned. Just rinse them before adding to casseroles, soups, or chili.

**Soy nuts:** Roasted mature soybeans, usually eaten as a snack.

**Tofu:** As one manufacturer put it, tofu is to the soybean as cheese is to milk. Cheese is made when milk separates into curds and whey.

Soybeans produce soy milk, which can also be separated into curds and whey; tofu is the bean curd. It comes in different textures, with silken tofu being the very softest and extra-firm the firmest.

**Tempeh:** Made from fermented soybeans and formed into a chewy cake, tempeh is used as a meat substitute in recipes.

**Miso:** Fermented soybean paste, used as a seasoning or soup base.

**Soy milk:** The creamy liquid that's pressed out of soaked, cooked soybeans.

Population studies suggest soy can lower the risk of several kinds of cancer, including prostate, breast, and endometrial cancers, and ease menopausal discomforts, all likely due to soy's estrogen-like compounds, called isoflavones. More research is needed before any specific recommendations on soy intake can be made.

## Cooks Tips

Keep tofu and tempeh refrigerated and use them within two or three days of opening them. Opened tofu should be stored in water that is changed daily. Miso will last in the refrigerator for several months. Fresh edamame should be eaten within a day or two. Roasted soy nuts can be kept in a cool, dry place for up to six months.

## Menu Magic

Soy products are a mystery to many people, but once you get to know them, you'll find they're easy to use and quite handy.

### Edamame

- Steam edamame in their pods, then shell them. Add the beans to grain or vegetable salads.
- Keep a bag of frozen edamame in the freezer and steam some for a high-protein Magic snack.

### Soy nuts

- Snack on these out of hand or sprinkle them into stir-fries. They have less fat and more fiber than true nuts (but they're still high in calories, so watch portion sizes).

### Soy burgers

- Crumble and add to pasta sauces in place of meat.

### Silken tofu

- Stir into low-fat sour cream for vegetable dip.
- Replace all or some of the cream in cream soups with silken tofu.
- Blend silken tofu with banana and peaches and a touch of honey to make a protein-rich smoothie.

### Tofu

- Use diced tofu to replace some of the cheese in lasagna or macaroni and cheese.
- Marinate tofu in low-sugar barbecue sauce and cook it on the grill.
- Mash it with cottage cheese and seasonings to use as a spread on whole grain rye crackers.
- Use extra-firm tofu instead of beef in stews.
- For Asian stir-fry dishes, use extra-firm tofu with red bell pepper strips, carrot strips, and snow peas.
- Make a tofu salad with cubes of firm tofu stir-fried in canola oil. Add to Romaine lettuce, corn, sliced avocado, sliced tomatoes, and chopped cilantro. Top with roasted pumpkin seeds and squeeze lime juice on top.
- Create a tofu curry with stir-fried tofu, red bell pepper strips, chickpeas, vegetable oil, curry powder (it contains turmeric, a Magic spice), and sesame seeds. Serve over brown or converted rice.

### Soy milk

- If you like soy milk, use it in place of regular milk in smoothies, on cereal, and in recipes. Buy the low-fat, unsweetened variety.

### RELATED recipes

Asian Noodle Hot Pot 225
Asian Peanut Dip 204
Cherry-Almond Gratin 288
Chocolate-Raspberry Cheesecake 284
Mediterranean Salad with Edamame 215
Pumpkin Custards 278
Spring Vegetable Stir-Fry with Tofu 260
Whole Wheat Noodles with Peanut Sauce and Chicken 214

# spinach AND OTHER DARK GREENS

**GL** VERY LOW

If everyone ate more spinach, we'd all have less diabetes, not to mention diseases like heart disease and cancer. No, spinach doesn't have any special power to lower your blood sugar, other than some soluble fiber and the fact that it's a vegetable, so that like almost all vegetables, it has little impact on your blood sugar. But the more fruits and vegetables you eat, the lower your risk of being overweight and of developing diabetes. It's that simple (remember secret number 3 of Magic eating, Eat More Fruits and Vegetables). Spinach is so all-around good for you, with so many nutrients and so few calories, it's a must for a Magic diet.

Despite what Popeye may have thought, spinach is not a very good source of iron. That's because the iron it contains isn't absorbed very well by the body. But it's loaded with other nutrients that can help stave off or treat just about every health concern, especially if you have diabetes or any of the risk factors for it.

Because spinach contains lots of potassium and magnesium, it (and other dark greens) can help keep blood pressure in check. Thanks to its store of carotenoids, it's one of the most antioxidant-rich vegetables on Earth. These antioxidants are powerful weapons against diabetes-related complications, including heart disease and nerve damage, not to mention cancer.

Speaking of antioxidants, spinach is a surprisingly good source of vitamin C. Two cups of raw leaves (enough for a nice-size salad) provides 28 percent of a day's allowance while dishing out only 14 calories. With such a small calorie count, spinach can help lower the overall calories of any dish you add it to.

## Health Bonus

Popeye probably never got cancer. Several studies have found that people who eat a lot of green, leafy vegetables, including spinach, have a lower risk of developing cancer than people who eat little of the leafy stuff.

Researchers have identified at least a dozen antioxidant compounds in spinach that may have anti-cancer activity. Lutein and beta-carotene are two at the top of the list. Known as carotenoids, they've been linked time and again with a reduced risk of several kinds of cancer, including colon and prostate cancers, lower risk of heart disease, and better eye health.

Spinach for your eyes? That's right. Spinach and its kin—kale, collards, turnip greens, and Romaine lettuce—are some of the richest sources of lutein, which research shows may help protect against cataracts and age-related macular degeneration, two conditions most likely to rob you of your sight as you age.

Another fact to bone up on: A single serving of spinach offers a full day's supply of vitamin K, which

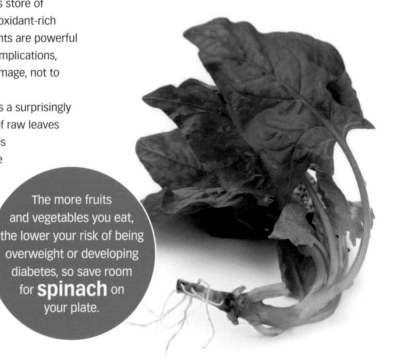

The more fruits and vegetables you eat, the lower your risk of being overweight or developing diabetes, so save room for **spinach** on your plate.

researchers now know is needed for a strong skeleton. Too many "senior moments"? Eat more spinach. Studies carried out by the USDA found that feeding middle-aged rats a spinach extract prevented some of the loss of long-term memory and learning ability that rats normally experience. Researchers chalk it up to the stash of antioxidant compounds in spinach.

## Cooks Tips

Wash fresh spinach thoroughly with cold water—twice. In addition to washing off any bacteria that may be lurking in the leaves, you want to get rid of the dirt that can make spinach gritty. (It does, after all, grow on the ground, and it does best in sandy soil.) If you buy bagged greens to save time, it's still a good idea to rinse them well before eating. Remove the stems, at least the larger, thicker ones, before cooking.

## Menu Magic

Look for any and every opportunity to "go green," from good old spinach salad to these ideas.

- For a super-nutritious side dish, sauté spinach (Swiss chard or kale works well, too) and sliced onions in olive oil. Sprinkle with sesame seeds, another Magic food.

- Stir steamed spinach into mashed potatoes so you get less potato and a lower GL with every bite. Top with sliced scallions.

- Top pizza with spinach.

- Steam spinach, then puree with parsley and lemon juice and use as a sauce for chicken or pasta.

- Make spinach pesto. Puree raw spinach with almonds, garlic, olive oil, and a bit of Parmesan cheese, then toss with whole grain pasta and chickpeas.

- "Beef" up lasagna with spinach instead of meat.

- Serve spinach with garlic and olive oil over pasta cooked al dente. Sprinkle with sesame seeds.

- For a quick soup, puree steamed spinach with garlic and low-fat plain yogurt.

## RELATED recipes

# sweet potatoes

**GL MEDIUM**

These sweet-tasting super-spuds hold a real surprise. Eat a baked sweet potato instead of a baked white potato, and your blood sugar will rise about 30 percent less! Compared to regular potatoes, a.k.a. blood sugar bombs, sweets rank relatively low on the GL scale. And the fact that they're packed with nutrients and disease-fighting fiber (almost 40 percent of which is soluble fiber, the kind that helps lower blood sugar and cholesterol) makes them a sweet deal indeed.

Sweet potatoes are extraordinarily rich in carotenoids, orange and yellow pigments that play a role in helping the body respond to insulin. And as unlikely as it may seem, coffee (another Magic food) and sweet potatoes have something in common: They're both rich in the natural plant compound chlorogenic acid, which may help reduce insulin resistance.

You may not think of vitamin C when you think of sweet potatoes, but they're actually an excellent source. That's important when you're battling high blood sugar, because the vitamin's antioxidant powers may help keep arteries from being damaged. Vitamin C may also help fight heart disease and complications of diabetes, such as nerve and eye damage.

Like so many other good-for-us foods, sweet potatoes are one of those staples that we like to gum up with gooey ingredients that essentially turn it into candy; think maple syrup, brown sugar, butter, and even marshmallows. If this is the only way you've ever enjoyed sweet potatoes, give some of our menu suggestions a try. Steer clear of canned sweets, which are usually packed in sugary syrup.

## Health Bonus

A recent study found that among almost 2,000 men studied, those whose diets were richest in beta-carotene and vitamin C—two nutrients plentiful in sweet potatoes—were more likely to survive prostate cancer than those whose diets contained little of the two nutrients.

The famous Nurses' Health Study at Harvard Medical School found that women who ate lots of foods rich in beta-carotene, such as sweet potatoes, reduced their risk of breast cancer by as much as 25 percent.

Eating sweet potatoes is a smart move for you if you have high blood pressure. That's because they're rich in potassium, a mineral known for bringing pressure down. You'll get more potassium from a sweet potato than you will from a banana!

## Cooks Tips

Choose sweet potatoes that are heavy for their size, with intact peels (no decay). If you're going to cook them whole, buy potatoes that are similar in size so the cooking time will be the same. Peel or scrub thoroughly before cooking. They'll keep for a month if you keep them cool but not cold (don't put them in the fridge).

## Yam I Am?

Is there a difference between sweet potatoes and yams? You bet. What you see in the supermarket is most likely one of two popular varieties of sweet potato. One has orange flesh and is moist and sweet; the other is yellow fleshed, drier, and not as sweet. Unless you're shopping at a market that specializes in ethnic foods, you're unlikely to find yams, which are native to Central America. Considerably larger than sweet potatoes, they have ivory-colored flesh and aren't particularly sweet.

## Menu Magic

Don't relegate sweet potatoes to candy-like dishes served only at Thanksgiving and Christmas. These spuds have a lot to offer all year round.

- Bake a sweet potato just as you would a white potato and serve alongside your favorite protein dish (beef, chicken, fish, pork, or lamb).

- If you're hooked on regular mashed potatoes, try using half regular potatoes and half sweets.

- For a Magic food trifecta, top mashed sweet potatoes with trans fat–free margarine, then season with cinnamon and sprinkle with chopped pecans.

- Grill sweet potato slices to serve with pork loin chops.

- Place sweet potato slices on top of your next casserole. Cover with foil to keep them moist and bake as usual.

- Add sweet potato cubes to soups and stews 30 to 45 minutes before the dish is done.

- Cube cooked sweet potatoes and use in stir-fries.

- Make roasted sweet potatoes seasoned with thyme for a savory side dish. Combine olive oil, minced garlic, thyme, salt, and coarsely ground black pepper in a bowl. Arrange peeled, sliced sweet potatoes in a single layer on a baking sheet and brush with the mixture. Bake at 425ºF (220ºC) until tender and slightly brown.

**sweet potatoes** raise blood sugar about 30 percent less than white potatoes do, thanks to their soluble fiber and plant compounds that help cells use insulin.

---

**PERFECT portions: 1 medium**

A medium sweet potato (5 ounces/140 g) is big enough to satisfy your appetite without tipping the blood sugar scales.

### RELATED recipes

**Black Bean and Sweet Potato Burritos** *263*
**Mashed Sweet Potatoes with Ginger and Orange** *267*
**Peanut Chicken Soup** *224*
**Sweet Potato Oven Fries** *268*
**Turkey Shepherd's Pie with Sweet Potato Topping** *241*

# tea

**GL** *VERY LOW*

Fire up the kettle, because after reading this entry, you'll be ready for a nice hot cup of tea. Laboratory studies show that tea can boost insulin activity more than 15-fold! The research, carried out by the USDA, found that all types of tea—green, black, and oolong—have the ability to enhance insulin activity, which of course means lower blood sugar. Almost all of that power comes from the naturally occurring antioxidant compound EGCG (epigallocatechin gallate) in tea.

Skip the milk, though. Adding milk may decrease this insulin-activating power by as much as 90 percent. It's not that milk is bad for you, it's just that it binds with the EGCG, making it unavailable to the body.

Drinking tea could even benefit people already being treated for diabetes. In a Taiwanese study of 20 people with type 2 diabetes, all of whom were taking glucose-lowering medication, drinking a lot of oolong tea—about six 8-ounce (250-ml) glasses a day was linked with a 29 percent drop in blood sugar. Most of us won't want to drink that much (tea has a diuretic effect), but even a cup or two should benefit you.

Some research suggests that tea may even speed up the body's metabolism and help control weight, which by itself could help lower your risk of insulin resistance and type 2 diabetes. In a group of 10 healthy men, a green tea extract that provided the active compounds found in about 2 cups of green tea increased the number of calories burned in a 24-hour period by 4 percent as compared to when no extract was taken. Another study found that people who drank tea at

## don't fall for it

Rumor has it that only green tea packs a big enough antioxidant punch to make a difference in your health. Not so. Tea is one of the most researched drinks around, and studies have found that while the exact types and amounts of antioxidant compounds vary from one tea type to the next, all types pack a healthy dose of these natural compounds.

## PERFECT portions: unlimited

Tea has zero carbs and virtually no calories, so you can have several cups a day as long as you don't add sugar. If you're sensitive to caffeine, stick with one cup in the morning.

least once a week for more than 10 years had almost 20 percent lower body fat than people who seldom drank tea, even after taking into account other lifestyle factors such as diet and exercise.

Want to make tea even better for your blood sugar? Brew a cup of chai, which combines tea with spices such as cinnamon, another Magic food. Watch out for the chai lattes you get at baristas like Starbucks, though. They're usually made with premixed liquids that include milk and are generously sweetened. Ask for a chai tea bag instead, and don't add anything (or just one packet of sugar, if you must).

If you're used to sweetening your tea, try black teas—not herbal teas—that taste better plain, such as ginger-peach or mint tea. By the way, a cup of tea has about half the caffeine of a cup of coffee.

## Health Bonus

Tea outranks even the best vegetables in terms of antioxidant wallop. Remember that antioxidants protect against everything from cancer to stroke to heart disease.

In a controlled study, 15 men and women who drank five 6-ounce (180-ml) cups of black tea a day for three weeks experienced an 11 percent drop in "bad" LDL cholesterol and a 6.5 percent drop in total cholesterol. Again, that's a lot of tea, but it's likely that drinking even a cup or two a day offers some benefits. In another study, more moderate tea drinkers had a 28 percent lower death rate after heart attacks than people who didn't drink tea.

*(continued on page 156)*

tea

garlic

Amazingly, something as simple as a cup of tea or a sprinkling of cinnamon can help keep your blood sugar in check.

- cinnamon
- coffee
- fenugreek
- garlic
- tea
- turmeric

magic herbs
& spices

cinnamon

turmeric

# tea continued

## Cooks Tips

You'll need to store tea properly if you want to keep the same subtle flavors that helped you make it your choice in the first place. Always store tea, whether ground leaves or tea bags, in an airtight container away from light, moisture, and strong odors, which can be absorbed by the leaves.

## Menu Magic

While drinking a cup of hot tea is the obvious way to consume this Magic food, tea is actually a more versatile plant than you might imagine.

- Grind oolong tea leaves in a pepper mill and blend them with freshly ground white pepper to sprinkle on chicken or pork.

- Tea also works wonders in a marinade; just add ground leaves to the mixture.

- Add tea leaves to chicken broth or stock for a dish with an Asian nuance.

### RELATED recipes

Cantaloupe and Blueberry Compote with
  Green Tea and Lime *276*

Chai *208*

Peachy Iced Tea *209*

---

## TEA glossary
True tea comes from the Camellia sinensis plant. Varieties are listed below. Herbal teas don't offer the same blood-sugar benefits.

**White tea:** It's picked and harvested before the leaf buds, which are covered with white fuzz, have opened. It's the least processed of the teas and has about half the amount of caffeine of black tea (about 15 milligrams per cup).

**Green tea:** The leaves are picked, then dried, steamed, or pan fried to keep enzymes in the tea from changing some of the antioxidant compounds and turning the tea dark.

**Oolong tea:** The leaves are dried for a longer time than for green tea, allowing the enzymes to work longer. Oolong is halfway between green and black tea in terms of processing.

**Black tea:** The leaves are processed longer to oxidize more of the compounds and produce a darker tea. Black tea contains the most caffeine (about 40 milligrams per cup).

**Chai:** This isn't a result of processing but rather is tea (usually black) that's combined with spices such as cardamom, cinnamon, cloves, and pepper.

# tomatoes

**GL** *VERY LOW*

I say "tom-*ay*-to," you say "tom-*ah*-to," but what really matters is how many you eat. No matter how you slice it, tomatoes are terrific for your blood sugar. These juicy fruits are incredibly low in calories (just 22 per tomato) and carbs (less than 5 grams each). What's more, they're rich in vitamin C, which helps protect the body from blood sugar damage, and lycopene, a member of the carotenoid family along with beta-carotene.

Lycopene may have special power against diabetes. Researchers from the Centers for Disease Control and Prevention looked at 1,665 men and women with and without diabetes and found that those with impaired glucose tolerance (essentially, prediabetes) had blood levels of lycopene that were 6 percent lower than those of healthy people. Levels averaged 17 percent lower in people with newly diagnosed diabetes. Two other studies found similar connections.

## Health Bonus

A Harvard study found that men who ate tomatoes and tomato products such as tomato sauce and tomato paste at least twice a week lowered their risk of prostate cancer by 24 to 36 percent.

Studies also suggest that eating tomatoes may reduce your risk of osteoporosis and asthma and may improve circulation and reduce inflammation.

## Cooks Tips

Store tomatoes on the counter; never keep them in the fridge. It ruins the texture and flavor.

## Menu Magic

The possibilities are virtually endless. Serve tomatoes raw, and you get the full vitamin C punch (heat destroys the vitamin); serve them cooked with a little oil, and you get the maximum lycopene dose (the oil helps the body absorb lycopene). Canned tomatoes, tomato sauce, and tomato paste all count, too. Ketchup isn't a good choice since it contains sugar, and while tomato juice is rich in lycopene, it's loaded with salt.

**PERFECT portions: 1 medium**

One juicy sliced tomato is a satisfying serving, but because tomatoes are so low in calories and carbs, feel free to have more.

- Include tomato wedges or grape tomatoes in green and pasta salads.

- Add tomato slices to your sandwiches.

- Whip up fresh tomato salsa using any recipe.

- Marinate peeled tomatoes in a mixture of olive oil, lemon juice, minced garlic, salt, pepper, and oregano and serve as an appetizer or side dish.

- Serve sliced tomatoes with low-fat mozzarella, balsamic vinegar, and olive oil as a snack or appetizer.

- Make a tomato pizza on a whole wheat pita. Brush the pita with olive oil and top with sliced tomatoes and onions. Sprinkle with basil and grated Parmesan cheese and bake.

- Come summertime, enjoy refreshing gazpacho.

## RELATED recipes

Bean and Barley Soup *222*
Caponata *202*
Cherry Tomatoes Filled with Pesto Cream Cheese *200*
Dahl with Spinach *261*
Garden Pasta Salad *215*
Greek Pasta and Beef Casserole *230*
Lentil and Bean Chili *262*
Mediterranean Salad with Edamame *215*
Penne with Tomato and Eggplant Sauce *256*
Quick Spinach and Sausage Lasagna *253*
Seared Fish Steaks with Tomato-Olive Sauce *246*
Shrimp and Orzo Casserole *251*
Slow-Cooker Beef and Vegetable Stew *228*
Spiced Cauliflower with Peas *272*
Tuna and Cannellini Salad with Lemon *213*
Turkey and Bean Chili with Avocado Salsa *243*
Whole Wheat Pasta with Sausage,
   Beans and Greens *254*

# turmeric

**GL** VERY LOW

Turmeric, the spice that gives mustard its bright yellow color and curried dishes their warm glow, may help tame wild blood sugar. That's because turmeric root, a relative of ginger, is one of Earth's most concentrated sources of curcumin, an antioxidant compound that's been shown to help prevent blood sugar surges, at least in diabetic animals. (Cumin is another source of curcumin.) While turmeric the spice has not been well studied, researchers have set their sights on extracts containing curcumin, the active ingredient. One study in lab rats, for example, found that 10 milligrams of a turmeric extract lowered blood sugar levels by 37 percent within 3 hours and by 55 percent after 6 hours.

Exactly how curcumin works isn't known, but researchers point to a number of different possibilities. The main one: It may act directly on the pancreas to stimulate the release of insulin.

Curcumin also has very powerful antioxidant effects that could help stave off heart disease as well as damage related to high blood sugar, including kidney disease, nerve damage, and retinopathy (eye damage).

## Health Bonus

Turmeric has a long history as a folk medicine in India and other countries for treating stomach ailments, inflammation, arthritis, and sprains. It's also being studied as an anti-cancer spice. Population studies find dramatically reduced rates of colon cancer in people whose diets are rich in curcumin. And in test tube studies, curcumin has caused the death of cervical cancer cells and blocked harmful cell changes.

Most recently, researchers have begun to look at whether curcumin may help prevent Alzheimer's. In India, where turmeric is practically ubiquitous in food, there is a very low incidence of the disease. In animal studies, curcumin decreased the formation of amyloid, the stuff that makes up the brain deposits characteristic of people with Alzheimer's. While the findings are promising, curcumin has not yet been studied for the treatment or prevention of Alzheimer's in humans.

## PERFECT portions: 1/8 to 1/4 teaspoon

Most of the studies with turmeric have used curcumin extracts derived from turmeric, so it's hard to know exactly how much is beneficial. The best advice? Use turmeric whenever you can. It adds deep color and richness to dishes you won't get from anything else.

## Cooks Tips

Be careful to keep turmeric contained when you use it, because it will stain almost anything—your fingernails, plastic cups and utensils, and even some kitchen countertops.

## Menu Magic

- Purchase bright yellow curry powder; it's likely to contain the most turmeric. Or add extra turmeric to your favorite brand of curry powder.
- Use yellow mustard on burgers and when cooking. Its color comes from turmeric.
- Add turmeric to rice instead of saffron in paella and Spanish rice.
- Include up to a teaspoon of turmeric in your favorite pea soup recipe.
- Add turmeric to stews and casseroles.
- A touch of turmeric works very well in lentil dishes.

### RELATED recipes
Curried Butternut Squash Puree *269*
Spiced Cauliflower with Peas *272*

# vinegar

## GL
**VERY LOW**

Fans of folk medicine swear by vinegar to treat just about anything that could ail a person, from sunburns to stomachaches to dull hair. But there's one truly effective use for vinegar that most people don't know about. It turns out that simply adding a high-acid food like vinegar to your meals can reduce the blood sugar effect of the entire meal—by 19 to 55 percent!

In one small Italian study, when five people consumed 1 gram of acetic acid (the equivalent of 1 1/3 tablespoons of vinegar) and olive oil (sounds suspiciously like a vinaigrette salad dressing!), followed by 50 grams of carbohydrates from white bread (the amount in about four small slices), their blood sugar went up 31 percent less than when they ate just the bread.

In another study, this one from Arizona State University, when healthy people consumed about 4 teaspoons of cider vinegar before eating a high-GI meal (a bagel, butter, and orange juice), their blood sugar rose an average of 55 percent less after an hour than when they drank water sweetened with saccharin before the meal. And in another study by the same researchers, people with insulin resistance who consumed vinegar before a bagel meal had a 34 percent increase, on average, in insulin sensitivity—which of course translates to better blood sugar control.

Yet another study, this one from Japan, found that when vinegar was part of a meal, it reduced the glycemic index of white rice by an impressive 20 to 40 percent.

One reason for the dramatic findings: The acid in vinegar slows the rate at which food leaves your stomach, also slowing the transformation of a meal's carbohydrates into blood sugar. Animal studies also suggest the acid may help increase the storage of glycogen (the form in which blood sugar is stored for future energy needs) in the liver and skeletal muscles, getting it out of the bloodstream.

## Health Bonus

Some of the same research that shows vinegar can lower blood sugar also shows that it can make you feel more satisfied after a meal—a boon to anyone trying to

Research suggests that making this much vinegar part of a meal can significantly lower your blood sugar response to the meal.

lose weight. Vinegar also fights bacteria and fungi, which is why it's used in some homemade preparations for swimmer's ear.

## Cooks Tips

Don't limit yourself to plain ol' distilled vinegar. Try red or white wine vinegar, rice vinegar, or apple cider vinegar. Or buy or make flavor-infused vinegars such as tarragon, raspberry, strawberry, and so on. See "Pump Up the Flavor" on page 160 to learn how to make your own flavored vinegar.

## Menu Magic

- Start dinner with a spinach salad dressed with balsamic vinegar and oil.

- Add red wine vinegar to lentil soup.

- Mix up Asian coleslaw with shredded red cabbage and carrots, mung bean sprouts, chopped bok choy, olive oil, rice vinegar, sesame seed oil, chopped cilantro, and toasted sesame seeds.

- Marinate sliced beets in balsamic vinegar, rosemary, crushed garlic, and herbes de Provence for about 20 minutes. Place the beets and marinade in a foil packet, seal tightly, and grill until tender.

- Make a balsamic vinegar glaze for grilled salmon. In a saucepan, boil balsamic vinegar, red wine, and a bit of honey until thick. Serve over the salmon.

*(continued)*

# vinegar continued

- Marinate chicken in cider vinegar and canola oil before baking or grilling.

- Serve soy-glazed chicken. In a skillet, sauté chopped garlic and shallots in olive oil, then add chopped tomato, distilled vinegar, soy sauce, honey, salt, and pepper. Stir well. Add cooked chicken breast and cook over medium-high heat, turning occasionally, until the vinegar mixture has thickened into a glaze.

- Pickle some carrots. In a medium saucepan, mix 1 cup distilled white vinegar, 2 tablespoons sugar, 1 teaspoon salt, pepper to taste, and 2/3 cup water. Bring to a boil, then remove from the heat and let cool slightly. Dice eight large carrots, place in sterile containers, and cover with the vinegar solution. Seal and refrigerate for 12 hours or overnight.

- For dessert, serve sliced strawberries splashed with balsamic vinegar and sprinkled with a few pinches of sugar.

## RELATED recipes

## Pump Up the Flavor

Here are basic instructions for making your own flavor-infused vinegar.

**1.** Use clean glass jars or bottles that are free of cracks or nicks and can be sealed with corks, screw-on caps, or two-piece canning lids.

**2.** Choose your flavoring and vinegar. White vinegar has a sharp, acidic taste and is good for delicately flavored herbs. Apple cider vinegar is milder and blends well with fruit. Wine and champagne vinegars work well with delicate herbs and lighter-flavored fruits. Red wine vinegar has a bolder flavor and complements spices and strong herbs like rosemary.

**3.** In a saucepan, heat the vinegar to just below the boiling point (at least 190° to 195°F/88° to 90°C).

**4.** Place three or four sprigs of fresh herbs, 3 tablespoons of dried herbs, 1 to 2 cups of fruits or vegetables, or the peel of one lemon or orange per pint of vinegar to be flavored into the jar. For some herbs, you may want to "bruise" the leaves or sprigs to release the flavors.

**5.** Pour the hot vinegar over the flavoring ingredient in the jar. Seal the jar and let stand undisturbed in a cool, dark place for three to four weeks.

**6.** Strain the vinegar through damp cheesecloth or a coffee filter until it's no longer cloudy, then pour it into a clean, dry glass jar.

Store all flavored vinegars in a cool, dark place in a tightly closed glass jar—not on your countertop in the sun. (If you keep it there for decoration, don't consume it.) Flavored vinegars will keep for three months in cool storage and for six to eight months in the fridge. Plain, unflavored distilled vinegar will keep indefinitely.

# wheatberries

**GL**
MEDIUM

In case you haven't noticed, we've been preaching the merits of whole grain foods in this book. (Remember secret number 2 of Magic eating, Make Three of Your Carb Servings Whole Grains?) Well, you can't get any more "whole grain" than wheatberries, which are, simply put, the entire grain (or "fruit") of the wheat plant, minus the hull. If you've read the bran and wheat germ entries, you know how good those are for your blood sugar and your health in general. Wheatberries offer both in one package.

As we said earlier, people who eat at least three daily servings of whole grain foods, like wheatberries, are much less likely to develop type 2 diabetes.

It's no wonder. According to a British study, eating wheatberries resulted in significantly lower levels of blood sugar and insulin than eating the same amount of carbs from flour. A Swedish study had similar results when healthy volunteers ate either white bread or coarse wheat bread made with wheatberries.

If you've shopped for prepared salads lately, you may have noticed some made with wheatberries. The berries have a nice, firm texture that requires some chewing, so they keep you from wolfing down your food. They're also more filling than other wheat products containing the same amount of carbohydrates, according to findings from Australia.

## Health Bonus

Large-scale studies have shown that eating whole grain foods lowers the risk not only of diabetes but also of heart disease, stroke, and several types of cancer.

Wheatberries supply minerals and other compounds that are lost when the grains are milled into white flour. Their germ portion is a rich source of cholesterol-lowering sterols.

## Cooks Tips

Since wheatberries take so long to cook (an hour or more, depending on whether you soak them first), you may want to cook extra, then store the surplus in a

There's no better way to get a whole grain into your diet.

covered container in the refrigerator for up to two days or in the freezer for up to six months. With cooked wheatberries on hand, it's easy to add them to salads, soups, pilafs, pancakes, muffins, and breads.

## Menu Magic

Wheatberries are most often enjoyed in wheatberry salads featuring anything from cranberries and nuts to avocados and tomatoes. They can be served as side dishes or main dishes, warm or chilled. Here are a few other ideas for using cooked wheatberries.

- Combine wheatberries with avocado cubes and cherry tomatoes and toss with a vinaigrette.

- Mix them with grilled bell peppers, place on a bed of lettuce, and top with a vinaigrette.

- For a flavorful side dish, combine wheatberries with raisins, sliced almonds, chopped scallions, and curry powder.

- Use as a hot or cold breakfast cereal, plain or with milk or soy milk and topped with a bit of brown sugar and a dash of cinnamon.

- Fold wheatberries into bread dough or pancake batter.

- Combine them with cooked lentils and season to taste.

- Use them in Italian soups along with beans. They offer a nice textural contrast to the soft, creamy beans.

### RELATED recipe
**Wheatberry Salad with Dried Apricots and Mint** *266*

# wheat germ

**GL** VERY LOW

You may wonder how any food whose name includes the word *germ* can be good for you, but don't let the name throw you. Wheat germ is another example of good things that come in small packages.

The germ (think of it as the grain's embryo) is the nutritional heart of the wheat kernel. Besides complex carbohydrates, it's packed with protein and sugar-stabilizing, hunger-fighting "good-for-you" fats as well as fiber, vitamins, and minerals, including zinc, selenium, and magnesium, which help the body manage blood sugar.

Magnesium is a potential diabetes fighter. Harvard researchers tallied the magnesium intakes of more than 127,000 men and women with no initial history of diabetes. After 18 years of follow-up in women and 12 years in men, they found that people whose diets provided the most magnesium were about 34 percent less likely to develop type 2 diabetes than those whose diets provided the least.

## Health Bonus

Vitamin E is wheat germ's crowning glory. E is a powerful antioxidant that thwarts cell damage from free radicals, the rogue molecules that are suspected of playing a role in chronic conditions such as heart disease, cataracts, and Alzheimer's disease.

Like magnesium, diets rich in E may help stave off diabetes. As part of the Insulin Resistance and Atherosclerosis Study, University of South Carolina researchers measured the levels of E in the blood of nearly 900 people without diabetes for five years. They found that among people who didn't take vitamin E supplements, those with the highest blood levels of E were 88 percent less likely to develop type 2 diabetes than those with the lowest levels.

The "good" fat in wheat germ, along with its cholesterol-lowering plant sterols, can also help lower harmful (LDL) cholesterol.

**PERFECT portions: 2 tablespoons**

Wheat germ has a very low GL thanks to its fat and protein, but it does have calories (55 in 2 tablespoons), so portion size is important.

## Cooks Tips

Buy plain toasted wheat germ and steer clear of sweetened varieties. Once the jar has been opened, store it in the refrigerator to prevent the wheat germ from going rancid.

## Menu Magic

Wheat germ's crunchy texture and nutty flavor make it perfect for a variety of uses.

- Add nutty crunch to steamed vegetables and green salads with a sprinkling of wheat germ.
- Sprinkle it on oatmeal or cold cereal.
- Top low-fat yogurt with berries and wheat germ.
- When coating chicken or fish, skip the bread crumbs in favor of a mixture of wheat germ, grated Parmesan cheese, and dried parsley.
- Add wheat germ to smoothies made with low-fat plain yogurt and fruit.
- Substitute wheat germ for some of the meat in your favorite meat loaf or meatball recipe.
- Add wheat germ to muffins, pancakes, casseroles, pizza dough, and savory piecrusts.

### RELATED recipes

**Macaroni and Cheese with Spinach** *255*
**Multi-Grain Pancakes or Waffles** *192*

# whole wheat BREAD AND FLOUR

## GL MEDIUM

Let's face it, bread isn't exactly a banner food for better blood sugar. So why eat it? If it's whole grain bread, here's all the reason you should need: People who eat more whole grains have a much lower risk of diabetes.

Whole grains also help improve the body's sensitivity to insulin, the hormone that manages blood sugar. In one study of 978 men and women, the higher their intake of whole grains, the greater their insulin sensitivity, which translates into better blood-sugar control.

There's another reason to eat whole grains: your heart. Countless studies have confirmed that people who eat a lot of whole grain foods cut their heart disease risk by anywhere from 15 to 30 percent compared with people who go "white" all the way (or avoid grains altogether). Chalk up whole wheat bread's heart benefits to its antioxidants, fiber, and cholesterol-reducing plant sterols.

Want to lose weight? Switch to whole wheat. The famous Nurses' Health Study from the Harvard School of Public Health looked at more than 74,000 women and found that those who ate the most whole grains were a whopping 49 percent less likely to gain weight over a 12-year period than those who ate the least. Why? Whole grains are filling, in large part because of their hefty fiber content (remember, fiber contains no calories, because it can't be digested). And of course, they're gentler on your blood sugar than their refined-grain counterparts. Steadier blood sugar means steadier weight.

Blood sugar aside, whole wheat bread has the edge over white bread in every other conceivable way. It contains the germ of wheat, where most of the nutrients are located (you may not know that whole wheat bread is a terrific source of antioxidants!). The germ is stripped out to make white bread, as is the bran, where most of the fiber is found. Just about all that's left in white bread is the starchy endosperm.

Want to make sure the good stuff is still in your bread? You'll have to become a label reader. See "The Whole Truth about Whole Wheat" on page 164 to learn exactly what to look for.

See "The Whole Truth about Whole Wheat" on page 164

### PERFECT portions: 1 slice

One small slice of whole wheat bread provides about 70 calories. But watch out: Some heftier slices have as many as 110 calories each.

## Health Bonus

Whole grains have surprising power to prevent certain cancers, including breast cancer and other hormone-related cancers, such as uterine and ovarian cancers, and gastrointestinal cancers, such as stomach and colorectal cancers. In fact, according to various studies, you can cut your overall risk of cancer by as much as 40 percent by eating plenty of whole grains. According to the American Institute for Cancer Research, for instance, when data from 40 recent studies on whole grains and cancer risk were combined and analyzed, the risk of cancer was reduced by 34 percent on average in people who ate a lot of whole grains compared to those who ate very little.

How can whole grain bread help prevent cancer? That depends on the cancer, but the ingredients at work probably include fiber, flavonoids (special types of antioxidants), and lignans, estrogen-like compounds found in the bran and germ layers of the grain.

Probably thanks to their fiber, whole grains also help prevent constipation as well as an intestinal disorder called diverticulitis.

## Cooks Tips

Since whole wheat flour contains more fat (it's the beneficial type) than white flour does, it's more perishable. Store it in an airtight container in the refrigerator or freezer.

You can usually replace up to half the white flour called for in recipes with whole wheat flour. But when making delicate baked goods like biscuits, opt for whole wheat pastry flour. It contains less gluten-forming protein than regular whole wheat flour and helps ensure a tender result.

*(continued)*

# whole wheat BREAD AND FLOUR continued

## Menu Magic

◉ Use whole wheat bread instead of refined white bread for sandwiches (when you're not using rye, pumpernickel, or sourdough, which are all Magic foods, too).

◉ Look for whole wheat hamburger buns.

◉ Make your pizza with whole wheat dough (see our recipe on page 258).

◉ If you're using croutons for soups or salads, make them whole wheat. The same goes for bread crumbs in cooking and baking. To make croutons, cube two slices of whole wheat bread (2 cups) and toss with 2 teaspoons olive oil, then spread in a small baking pan and bake at 350°F (175°C) until crisp, 15 to 25 minutes.

◉ Use whole wheat pitas as the base for quick, healthy lunches. Stuff with carrots and tuna or other good-for-you fixin's, such as chickpeas, tomatoes, arugula, and so on, or top with grilled vegetables, tomato sauce, and a bit of cheese for a fast pizza.

◉ If you enjoy baking bread and would like to make loaves with 100 percent whole wheat flour, add wheat gluten (vital gluten, found in the bulk section of natural foods stores) at a ratio of 1 tablespoon gluten to 2 cups flour. This helps compensate for the additional bran and germ in the whole wheat, which does not contain gluten.

## RELATED recipes

Apple-Bran Muffins *197*

Chicken Pot Pie with a Whole Grain Biscuit Crust *236*

Fudge Brownies *280*

Honey-Mustard Turkey Burgers *240*

Lemony Blueberry Cheesecake Bars *279*

Oven-Fried Chicken *238*

Quick Whole Wheat Pizza Dough *258*

Whole Wheat Flaxseed Bread *196*

## The Whole Truth about Whole Wheat

Buying whole wheat bread is trickier than it may seem. There are dozens of "wheat breads" on the shelves, but guess what? Most of them are white bread. You see, all flour comes from wheat, so any old bread can be called wheat bread, even if it's made with refined white flour. Some "wheat" breads may contain a bit of whole wheat flour, but usually not much.

The bottom line: It's not enough to look for the word *wheat* on *labels*. Instead, look for the word *whole,* preferably in the very first ingredient, to make sure the bread you buy is truly made from whole grain. That goes for any bread labeled "multigrain" as well—if the word *whole* isn't at the top of the list, pass it up.

You may have seen new breads on the market called whole grain white breads. Even though they're whole wheat, they look like white bread because they're made from a special variety of wheat (albino wheat) that's lighter in color, plus a host of "dough conditioners" that keep the bread soft like white bread. These breads are more processed than regular whole wheat breads because the whole grains are pulverized into tiny bits by special machinery to make the bread smooth. We don't know what effect this has on the bread's GL, but it certainly doesn't help it.

# yogurt

Like milk, yogurt has a naturally low GL (after all, yogurt is nothing more than fermented milk). The unidentified natural component in milk that experts think may help prevent insulin resistance is there in yogurt, too. Since it's fermented by bacteria, yogurt also contains acids, and you've already read that acids can help lower blood sugar.

You can drink your yogurt in a smoothie or eat it with fresh fruit. Another reason we like yogurt: It's a perfectly acceptable lower-fat substitute for some or all of the mayonnaise in creamy salads and the sour cream in baked goods, soups, and chip dips.

Compared to milk, yogurt is usually better tolerated by people who are lactose intolerant. Even though yogurt contains lactose, or milk sugar, the bacterial cultures used to make it produce the lactase enzyme required for proper digestion.

When it comes to yogurt types, low fat and fat free are of course your best choices. Skip "fruit on the bottom" brands, which are usually loaded with added sugar. You can always add your own fresh fruit.

## PERFECT portions: 1 cup plain

This amount will give you a low glycemic load and a good deal of calcium.

## Health Bonus

You can count yogurt in as a calcium-rich bone builder. It provides the same 300 milligrams per 8 ounces (250 ml) as milk. And it counts as a dairy food in the famously healthy DASH diet, proven to help control high blood pressure.

Yogurt contains "good" bacteria, the kind that offer numerous health benefits, including boosting the immune system, alleviating diarrhea caused by some infections or treatment with antibiotics, relieving constipation, and even reducing the risk of developing colon cancer. Some people like to eat yogurt whenever they're taking antibiotics to replace the beneficial bacteria in the gut that the drugs obliterate.

As far as yogurt's immune benefits go, more than 70 percent of the body's natural immune defenses are located in the digestive tract. Building up the population of good bacteria there may help boost production of important immune system compounds, making you more resistant to viruses.

There's also evidence that women who regularly eat yogurt with live *Lactobacillus acidophilus* cultures get fewer yeast infections.

*(continued)*

### don't fall for it

Frozen yogurt may seem like the next best thing to regular yogurt, but it's not. First, almost all frozen yogurt is sweetened and flavored. While there are several low-fat and fat-free options, they're typically high in sugar. In addition, levels of beneficial bacteria vary greatly. Some brands are heat treated after the bacterial cultures are added, rendering the bacteria useless to your health. In others, the bacteria are added to an ice cream–like mixture after the fact.

# yogurt continued

Only yogurts labeled "contains live, active cultures" have bacteria that are still active (unless they were pasteurized after the bacterial cultures were added, which destroys the bacteria; these yogurts should be labeled "heat-treated after culturing").

## Cooks Tips

To get the most bacterial benefit from yogurt, use it by the expiration date on the carton. The "friendly" bacteria begin dying when the yogurt is no longer fresh. Cooking destroys the beneficial bacteria, but even cooked yogurt is a low-GL food.

Cooking with yogurt on top of the stove can be tricky since it usually curdles when boiled. When adding it to hot dishes, stabilize it first by mixing in 1 teaspoon of cornstarch per cup of yogurt. Add it toward the end of the cooking time.

## Menu Magic

- Substitute yogurt for sour cream in baked goods.

- Make your favorite chip or vegetable dip using low-fat plain yogurt instead of sour cream.

- Replace half the mayonnaise in creamy salad dressings with yogurt.

- Use yogurt as a restaurant-worthy garnish for pureed vegetable soups, such as a squash or carrot soup. First, thin the yogurt with low-fat milk to make it the same consistency as the soup. Drop dollops of the mixture into the soup, then draw the tip of a knife or toothpick through it to create swirls.

- Use a dollop on chili instead of sour cream.

- Make cool, creamy fruit soup with low-fat plain yogurt, sliced peaches, strawberries, orange juice, and honey. Process in the blender, then garnish with fresh mint leaves.

- Serve a cucumber salad made with grated cucumbers and carrots, diced onion, chopped dill, low-fat plain yogurt, and salt and pepper to taste.

- Top sliced fruit with yogurt or create a beautiful breakfast parfait. In a tall, chilled parfait glass, layer low-fat plain yogurt with fresh blueberries and oat and nut granola.

- Dip Granny Smith apples into yogurt for a refreshing snack.

- Make a refreshing yogurt cooler (*ayran,* a traditional Turkish beverage) by combining equal parts yogurt and cold water and a pinch of salt in a blender. Serve over crushed ice.

- To make yogurt creamier and richer tasting, make yogurt "cheese." Spoon yogurt into a cheesecloth-lined sieve, set over a bowl, and refrigerate for at least 6 hours or overnight. Discard the liquid (whey) that has accumulated in the bowl. Use the "cheese" as a substitute for cream cheese or sour cream. Stir in chopped fresh herbs, scallions, and garlic to make a delicious low-fat herbed cheese spread.

## RELATED recipes

Berry-Flaxseed Smoothie *208*
Dahl with Spinach *261*
Garden Pasta Salad *215*
Instant Strawberry Frozen Yogurt *277*
Mixed Berry and Stone Fruit Soup *276*
No-Mayonnaise Creamy Coleslaw *216*
Oatmeal with Apples and Flaxseeds *193*
Orange-Glazed Roasted Plums *282*

# Meal Makeovers

# BREAKFAST makeovers

If your idea of breakfast is a bagel, a bowl of cornflakes, or a pile of pancakes or waffles, help is here.

Nothing sabotages your daily efforts to follow the Magic eating plan like a high-GL breakfast—the kind most of us eat. Breakfast is usually the most carbohydrate-filled meal of the day and thus the one that raises your blood sugar the most dramatically. That doesn't mean you should cut out the carbs, though. Just switching to "slower-acting" carbs, and eating less of them, will do the trick. You'll also want to find ways to add some protein to your plate.

## Our top five BREAKFAST GUIDELINES:

**1** Limit carbohydrates to one serving. Have one slice of bread instead of two, eat half a bagel (or a mini-bagel) instead of a whole one, and pour only 3/4 to 1 cup cold cereal instead of a huge bowlful (stick to 1/2 to 3/4 cup for hot cereal).

**2** Choose lower-GL cereals. These usually include whole grain cereals with at least 5 grams of fiber per serving (see "How Cereals Rate" in the bran entry on page 85). Bran cereals such as All Bran, Bran Buds, and 100% Bran are good choices, along with high-fiber, high-protein cereals such as Kashi GoLean and oat cereals such as Barbara's Shredded Oats.

**3** Totally avoid "white" carbs. This means no Pop-Tarts, white toast with jelly, or muffins made with white flour.

**4** Replace some carbohydrate calories with fruit and a high-protein food. Have some orange slices with your eggs, sprinkle nuts and berries on cereal, or enjoy grapefruit along with a bagel or toast spread with peanut butter. This will not only make the meal more filling, it will also lower its effect on your blood sugar.

**5** Use small glasses for juice. Fruit juice is fine for you—in moderation. Drink too much, and it quickly becomes a high-GL (and high-calorie) food.

In many ways, breakfast really is the most important meal of the day. If you start the day with a Magic breakfast, you're more likely to stay off the blood sugar rollercoaster—and eat less—all day long.

## Typical Breakfast

3 4-inch (10-cm) white flour waffles with
3 tablespoons maple syrup

2 slices regular bacon

8 ounces (250 ml) orange juice

1 cup coffee

**Total GL: 105**
**Total calories: 597**

MAKE IT A
**Magic**
meal

# Magic BREAKFAST

1 4-inch (10-cm) Multigrain Waffle
(recipe on page 192) with 1 tablespoon maple syrup

2 large eggs, scrambled

2 slices Canadian back bacon

1/2 medium grapefruit

1 cup coffee or tea

## THE FIXES

⊕ Substituted fiber-rich whole grain
waffles for the white flour waffles
to lower the GL.

⊕ Decreased the number of waffles
from three to one.

⊕ Added protein-rich eggs to replace
the waffle calories.

⊕ Decreased the amount of maple syrup
for fewer calories and a lower GL.

⊕ Substituted Canadian back bacon
for regular bacon. It's much lower
in saturated fat—which, you'll recall,
contributes to insulin resistance.

⊕ Replaced the orange juice with half
a grapefruit. Remember, whole fruit
has more fiber and a lower GL than
fruit juice.

**Total GL: 15**
**Total calories: 337**

**BETTER still:** Substitute a slice of rye
toast for the waffle.

BREAKFAST | 169

## Typical Breakfast

1 toasted large plain bagel with 2 tablespoons jam or jelly

12 ounces (341 ml) French vanilla coffee beverage

**Total GL: 46**
**Total calories: 612**

**MAKE IT A Magic meal**

# Magic BREAKFAST

1/2 toasted large whole wheat bagel with 1 tablespoon peanut butter

1 medium apple

1 cup coffee or tea

## THE FIXES

⊚ Substituted a whole grain bagel for the white flour bagel for more fiber and a lower GL.

⊚ Cut the bagel portion in half to limit carbs.

⊚ Added peanut butter as a filling source of protein and "good" fat to add back calories without increasing the GL.

⊚ Replaced the high-calorie, high-GL coffee beverage with plain coffee or tea.

**Total GL: 17**
**Total calories: 275**

## 3

**Typical Breakfast**

2 cups cornflakes with 1 cup 2% milk

1 cup coffee or tea

**Total GL: 49**
**Total calories: 321**

**MAKE IT A**
**Magic**
**meal**

# Magic BREAKFAST

3/4 cup Grape-Nuts Flakes with:
  1/2 cup fat-free milk
  1/2 cup strawberries
  1/2 ounce (14 g) slivered almonds

1 cup coffee or tea

## THE FIXES

◎ Switched the high-GL cereal for a lower-GL cereal.

◎ Decreased the cereal serving to further cut the GL.

◎ Cut calories and fat by switching from 2% milk to fat-free milk.

◎ Added fruit and nuts to the cereal to make up for the smaller portion. The fruit provides extra vitamins and phytochemicals, and the nuts, with their healthy fats, slow the digestion of the meal for a slower rise in blood sugar.

**Total GL: 19**
**Total calories: 258**

**BETTER still:** Go for All Bran cereal instead of Grape-Nuts Flakes.

# LUNCH**makeovers**

Lunch can be a tough meal because we often grab it on the go, and healthy fare can be harder to find when you're not at home. Regardless of where you eat lunch, though, you can make choices that will be gentler on your blood sugar.

## **Our top six** LUNCH GUIDELINES:

**1** Make your lunch at home. You'll have all the control you need over what you eat. If you do have to grab something from a fast-food place, we give some examples of smarter ordering.

**2** Switch your sandwich bread to whole grain. Choose rye or pumpernickel for the lowest possible GL. Whole wheat is also a good choice. If you do choose white bread, make it sourdough; its acids make its GL lower than that of other white breads.

**3** Ask for mustard instead of mayo. Mustard might as well be a Magic food because of its vinegar and turmeric content. Mayonnaise…well, it isn't.

**4** Favor fruit. Lunch is a great time to get one or more of your fruit servings for the day.

**5** Select a smart salad. Make sure it contains plenty of protein in the form of eggs, chicken, tuna, beans, tofu, or low-fat cheese. And choose a Magic vinegar-based dressing, not a creamy one.

**6** Skip the soda. It has a sky-high GL unless you order diet soda or stick to 8 ounces (250 ml)—less than one can. Opt for mineral water or unsweetened iced tea instead. If you prefer juice, look for one that's 100% juice and unsweetened (most are anything but, crammed with sugar in the form of high-fructose corn syrup), and either stick to 6 ounces (180 ml) or less or dilute it with seltzer.

Finally, don't forget to have a snack between lunch and dinner to keep your blood sugar on an even keel. See our snack makeovers starting page 178.

### Typical Lunch

2 slices white bread with 2 slices roasted turkey, 2 slices processed cheese, 1 tablespoon mayonnaise

1 medium banana

3 or 4 graham crackers

16 ounces (495 ml) apple juice

**Total GL: 59
Total calories: 891**

LUNCH MAKEOVERS  LUNCH MAKEOVERS

**MAKE IT A
Magic
meal**

# Magic LUNCH

2 slices whole grain bread with:
  2 slices roasted turkey
  1 slice processed cheese
  Lettuce
  2 slices tomato
  1 tablespoon mustard

12 sweet cherries

1 ounce (30 g) dark chocolate–covered almonds

6 ounces (180 ml) unsweetened grapefruit juice

## THE FIXES

- Swapped white bread for whole grain to boost fiber and lower the GL.

- Cut approximately 60 calories by switching from mayo to mustard.

- Exchanged the apple juice for grapefruit juice, which has a lower GL, and cut the quantity to reduce calories and further lower the GL.

- Switched the banana for cherries. All stone fruits have lower GLs than bananas do.

- Included dark chocolate–covered almonds instead of graham crackers. The almonds offer protein, "good" fats, vitamins, and fiber, while the crackers don't provide much nutrition and add significantly to the meal's GL.

**Total GL: 17
Total calories: 452**

**Typical Lunch**

McDonald's Big Mac

Large order of French fries

32 ounces (730 ml) soda

**Total GL: 109**
**Total calories: 1,427**

2

# **Magic** LUNCH

McDonald's Quarter Pounder

6 ounces (180 ml) Berries and Yogurt or Yogurt Parfait

Bottled water

## THE FIXES

- Switched to the Quarter Pounder, which has less bread and more meat than the Big Mac. Ordered it without cheese to keep calories in check.

- Avoided French fries, a.k.a. blood sugar bombs, and ordered Berries and Yogurt (or Yogurt Parfait) instead for fewer calories, less fat, and more nutrition.

**Total GL: 10**
**Total calories: 550**

**BETTER still:** A single hamburger and a side salad with vinaigrette dressing.

**3**

Typical Lunch

2 slices regular cheese pizza

32 ounces (730 ml) soda

Total GL: 86
Total calories: 580

MAKE IT A
**Magic**
meal

# Magic LUNCH

1 slice whole wheat pizza with cheese and vegetables

1 cup side salad with:
Lettuce, tomato, and cucumber
1 tablespoon oil and vinegar dressing

1 medium peach

20 ounces (495 ml) unsweetened iced tea

## THE FIXES

⊕ Cut carbs, fat, and calories by limiting pizza to one slice.

⊕ Boosted fiber by switching to whole wheat crust and adding vegetables.

⊕ Made up for the slice you're not eating by adding a salad and a piece of fruit, both nutritious, low-GL foods.

Total GL: 14
Total calories: 333

**BETTER still:** Make your own pizza at home by topping a whole grain pita with 2 tablespoons tomato sauce, 2 ounces (60 g) part-skim mozzarella, and plenty of veggies.

## Typical Lunch

1 large burrito made with a 13-inch (33-cm) white flour tortilla and 1 cup white rice, 2 ounces (60 g) beef filling 1 ounce (30 g) cheddar cheese, 2 tablespoons salsa

1.5 ounces (45 g) tortilla chips

1/4 cup salsa

32 ounces (730 ml) soda

**Total GL: 120**
**Total calories: 1,422**

MAKE IT A
**Magic**
meal

# Magic LUNCH

1 small burrito made with a 6-inch (15-cm) whole wheat tortilla and:
  1/2 cup black beans
  1.5 ounces (42 g) roasted chicken
  Plenty of lettuce, tomato, and salsa
  1/2 ounce (15 g) cheddar cheese

1/2 mango

Bottled water

## THE FIXES

- Cut carbs and lowered the GL by switching from an overgrown white flour tortilla to a more reasonably sized whole wheat tortilla.

- Lowered the GL significantly and added fiber by eliminating the white rice and including black beans instead.

- Added fruit instead of tortilla chips. Chips are an "empty-calorie" food, whereas fruit is packed with fiber and vitamins, not to mention having a low GL.

**Total GL: 22**
**Total calories: 519**

**BETTER still:** A grilled chicken or steak salad, if it's on the menu (no taco shell). If it's not, ask for a "naked burrito"—burrito filling without the tortilla.

### Typical Lunch

1 large white sub roll with 4 slices salami,
4 slices prosciutto, 2 slices provolone cheese,
1 tablespoon mayonnaise

2-ounce (60-g) bag potato chips

1 large chocolate chip cookie

32 ounces (730 ml) soda

**Total GL: 150**
**Total calories: 1,972**

MAKE IT A
**Magic**
meal

## Magic LUNCH

1/2 whole grain sub roll with:
  2 slices lean roast beef
  1 slice provolone cheese
  Oil and vinegar
  Lettuce, tomato, cucumber,
    onion, and olives

1 medium apple

4 ounces (125 ml) "light" chocolate
  pudding

Mineral water with lemon

### THE FIXES

- Switched to a whole grain roll, which has more fiber, and cut it in half to cut carbs.

- Substituted leaner meat for meats high in saturated fat, reduced the quantity of meat, and "beefed up" the sandwich with a generous helping of veggies.

- Replaced the chips with fruit for much less fat and more nutrients.

- Cut saturated fat and calories by replacing the cookie with light pudding, which also provides some calcium.

**Total GL: 38**
**Total calories: 588**

**BETTER still:** Enjoy a chef's salad with rolled cold cuts, cheese, and veggies.

# SNACK**makeovers**

It's 3:00 p.m., and your energy is dipping, as are your eyelids. You're thinking about raiding the vending machine, and your resolve is weakening. The good news: Snacking is good for you because going too long without eating sets you up for a huge blood sugar dip that could wreck your Magic eating for the rest of the day. The bad news: Most of the snacks in the vending machine are rotten choices.

## Our top three SNACKING GUIDELINES:

**1** Pack your snack with your lunch. It's easy enough to grab some carrot or celery sticks, some grapes or grape tomatoes, a container of yogurt, or some nuts and stick them in your "lunchbox."

**2** Stay away from chips and go easy on pretzels, which are not much more than white flour, with barely any protein to balance it out.

**3** Seek out protein. Peanut butter, nuts, yogurt, and even a hard-boiled egg are good snack sources.

MAKE IT A
**Magic** snack

2 ounces (60 g)
pretzels

Total GL: 33
Total calories: 216

3/4 ounce (20 g) pretzels
1/2 green apple with 1 tablespoon peanut butter

Total GL: 14
Total calories: 208

## THE FIXES

- Decreased the number of pretzels by more than half to limit refined carbs.

- Beefed up the snack with a filling piece of fruit and some peanut butter for blood sugar "staying power." This snack will help you stay full longer than if you ate just the pretzels.

MAKE IT A
**Magic** snack

1 berry cereal bar

Total GL: 26
Total calories: 140

14 ounces (125 ml) low-fat mixed-berry yogurt
topped with 2 tablespoons All Bran cereal

Total GL: 9
Total calories: 148

## THE FIXES

- Substituted yogurt for the cereal bar to slash the GL. Because these bars contain cereal, we often assume they're good for us, but they're often lower in fiber and higher in sugar than their cereal counterparts.

- Added All Bran cereal on top for crunch and a bit of whole grain.

15 plain salted crackers
3 ounces (85 g) cheddar cheese
Total GL: 22
Total calories: 624

6 whole wheat crackers
1 ounce (30 g) Swiss cheese, 1 small pear
Total GL: 13
Total calories: 299

## THE FIXES

◉ Switched to whole wheat crackers and cut the portion by more than half to decrease the GL.

◉ Limited the cheese to decrease saturated fat. Cheese is indeed a Magic food, but you need to eat it in moderation.

◉ Added a piece of fruit to add back some calories. Because of its fiber and water, the pear will fill you up more than the crackers.

1 chocolate chip
granola bar
Total GL: 14
Total calories: 163

1 cup light popcorn mixed with
10 peanuts and 1 tablespoon
semisweet chocolate chips
Total GL: 8
Total calories: 160

## THE FIXES

◉ Swapped the granola bar, filled with added sugar, for popcorn (a whole grain, high-fiber food) to lower the GL.

◉ Added peanuts for a sugar-stabilizing dose of protein and "good" fats that will help you stay fuller longer.

◉ Threw in some chocolate chips to satisfy your sweet tooth.

14 jelly beans
Total GL: 27
Total calories: 150

15 dry-roasted peanuts
Total GL: 1
Total calories: 84

## THE FIX

◉ Slashed the GL to almost nothing by substituting peanuts, which are satisfying and full of protein, fiber, and healthy fat, for jelly beans, full of nothing but blood sugar–raising sugar.

# DINNER**makeovers**

The most chaotic time in most households is dinnertime. You're tired, the family is hungry, and you just want to get something on the table fast. The good news is that you can make your dinner more Magic without spending any extra time making the meal.

## Our top five DINNER GUIDELINES:

**1** Limit yourself to one or two servings of carbohydrates. One serving would be 1/2 cup of pasta, potatoes, rice, or stuffing; two servings would be 1 cup.

**2** Fill the hole on your plate with veggies. Here's your best shot at meeting your vegetable quota for the day. Even if you're having a salad on the side, put at least 1/2 cup of veggies, such as sautéed carrots or green beans, on your plate. Rely on frozen veggies and prewashed, bagged salad greens if you're short on time.

**3** Leave the bread at the store. Bread isn't bad for you, but if you had a sandwich for lunch, that's probably all the bread you need for the day. Adding bread to dinner means you may not eat other, healthier foods; almost always adds butter to your meal; and certainly increases the GL.

**4** Keep your protein lean. Think turkey meatballs instead of beef, flank steak instead of ground beef, and chicken without the skin instead of fried chicken. Tofu, beans, fish, and shrimp are also good protein sources.

**5** Stick with water as your beverage of choice. Or, if you like milk, have a glass of fat-free. Wine is fine occasionally if your doctor okays it, but soda and juice add calories and GL without adding much (or any) nutrition. Most of us don't drink enough water throughout the day and come home feeling wilted. Drink a cold glassful at dinner to rehydrate.

Dish the food onto plates instead of placing a serving dish on the table for everyone to dig into. You're likely to eat less. A final tip: After dinner (or dessert, if you have it), close up the kitchen. For many people, late-night eating is a prime reason for eating too many calories in a day.

# 1

## Typical Dinner

7 ounces (200 g) grilled "select" sirloin steak

1 medium baked potato with 1 tablespoon butter

1 cup salad with 1 tablespoon ranch dressing

1 slice French bread with 1 tablespoon butter

4 ounces (125 ml) red wine

**Total GL: 64**
**Total calories: 1,003**

**MAKE IT A**
**Magic**
**meal**

## Magic DINNER

7 ounces (200 g) grilled "select" sir-loin steak

1/2 baked medium sweet potato with:
    1/2 tablespoon good-for-you margarine
    Cinnamon
    Nutmeg

1/2 cup steamed broccoli

2 cups mixed greens salad with:
    Roasted red and yellow bell peppers
    2 tablespoons oil and vinegar dressing

4 ounces (125 ml) red wine

### THE FIXES

- Replaced the white potato with half a sweet potato to dramatically decrease the GL. Eat the skin for added fiber.

- Doubled the salad size. Salad is filling and full of low-GL nutrition.

- Changed the ranch dressing to oil and vinegar to decrease unhealthy saturated fat and provide extra acidity, which lowers the meal's GL.

- Replaced the bread with broccoli to add vitamins and fiber and lower the GL.

**Total GL: 12**
**Total calories: 481**

## Typical Dinner

2 cups cooked regular spaghetti with
1 cup tomato sauce, 3.5 ounces (100 g) beef meatballs

2 small slices Italian bread with 1 tablespoon butter

1 cup salad with
Cucumber, tomato, 1 tablespoon blue cheese dressing

8 ounces (250 ml) soda

Total GL: 62
Total calories: 1,170

# Magic DINNER

1 cup cooked whole wheat spaghetti
   with:
   1/2 cup tomato sauce
   3.5 ounces (100 g) turkey meatballs
      (made with 90% fat-free
      ground turkey)

2 cups salad with:
   Tomato, cucumber, olives,
      and red onion
   2 tablespoons oil and vinegar dressing

8 ounces (250 ml) unsweetened iced tea

## THE FIXES

⊙ Cut the spaghetti portion in half and
switched to whole wheat spaghetti
to add fiber and lower the GL.

⊙ Eliminated the bread and doubled
the size of the salad (just as filling as
bread), thus swapping empty calories
for fiber and vitamins and lowering
the GL.

⊙ Topped the salad with oil and vinegar
dressing instead of blue cheese to cut
saturated fat and add a dose of sugar-
lowering acid from the vinegar.

Total GL: 14
Total calories: 550

**BETTER still:** Choose a pasta like
Barilla Plus, which contains extra protein,
fiber, and omega-3 fatty acids.

## 3

### Typical Dinner

1 4-ounce (125-g) pork chop

1 1/2 cups cooked fettucine with 1 tablespoon butter, 1 tablespoon Parmesan cheese, 1 tablespoon parsley

1 white dinner roll with 1 tablespoon butter

12 ounces (341 ml) beer

**Total GL: 33**
**Total calories: 627**

**MAKE IT A**
# Magic
**meal**

## Magic DINNER

1 4-ounce (125-g) pork chop

1/2 cup Bulgur with Ginger and Orange (recipe on page 264)

Sautéed Spinach with Ginger and Soy Sauce (recipe on page 275)

12 ounces (341 ml) light beer

### THE FIXES

◉ Swapped the fettucine for a better carbohydrate choice, bulgur. Pasta's not bad for you, but bulgur has more fiber and a lower GL.

◉ Eliminated the white roll, which adds nothing but GL to the meal.

◉ Added sautéed spinach to replace the roll. Spinach is loaded with fiber and nutrients and has a very low GL (and far fewer calories).

◉ Changed the regular beer to light beer to reduce carbs and calories.

**Total GL: 17**
**Total calories: 665**

**Typical Dinner**

1 1/2 cups takeout beef and broccoli stir-fry

1 cup white rice

8 ounces (250 ml) soda

**Total GL: 49**
**Total calories: 1,223**

# Magic DINNER

1 cup unshelled edamame

1 1/2 cups Orange Beef Stir-Fry with
   Broccoli and Red Pepper
   (recipe on page 226)

1/2 cup brown rice

Black or green tea

## THE FIXES

⊛ Made the stir-fry at home using leaner
   beef, less oil, and more vegetables.
   The result: fewer calories and less
   saturated fat, which clogs arteries
   and hampers insulin sensitivity.

⊛ Substituted brown rice for white and
   cut the portion in half to dramatically
   decrease the meal's GL.

⊛ Started the meal with edamame
   (steamed green soybeans) to fill you
   up on a low-GL, fiber- and protein-rich
   food so you won't miss the rest of the
   rice. Edamame also slows eating
   because it takes time to get the beans
   out of their shells.

⊛ Replaced high-GL soda with no-GL
   green tea.

**Total GL: 14**
**Total calories: 612**

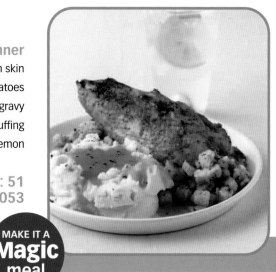

## Typical Dinner

1 roasted chicken breast with skin
1 cup mashed potatoes
1/2 cup gravy
1 cup stuffing
Mineral water with lemon

**Total GL: 51**
**Total calories: 1,053**

MAKE IT A
**Magic**
meal

## Magic DINNER

1 roasted chicken breast without skin

1/3 cup gravy

1 cup apple-walnut stuffing

3/4 cup Moroccan Spiced Carrots
(recipe on page 274)

Mineral water with lemon

### THE FIXES

- Eliminated the chicken skin, a significant source of saturated fat (which hampers insulin sensitivity) and calories.

- Cut out the un-Magic mashed potatoes and replaced them with carrots to increase fiber and vitamins and substantially lower the GL of the meal.

- Added apples and walnuts to the stuffing to decrease the GL (more apples and walnuts mean less bread) and add some "good" fat from the nuts to further lower the GL.

**Total GL: 28**
**Total calories: 760**

# DESSERT**makeovers**

Everyone likes dessert—but nowhere else do the evils of white flour, sugar, and saturated fat converge in such a perfect storm, making your blood sugar surge. In terms of glycemic load and extra calories, most desserts are the last thing you need. But that doesn't mean dessert in general is off-limits. When the cake comes around, don't say no; instead, say, "I'll take half a piece please, with lots of berries on top."

## Our top four DESSERT GUIDELINES:

**1** Think fruit, fruit, fruit. It's sweet and refreshing and easily transformed into an almost endless variety of attractive, easy-to-make desserts (for proof, check out the dessert recipes in Part 4).

**2** Watch portion sizes. The truth is, you can eat whatever you like if the portion is small enough. Use a small plate, such as a saucer, or a child-size cereal bowl for ice cream to help make smaller portions look more substantial. Or, to make your dessert fill up a big plate or bowl, add fruit such as pineapple, blueberries, or banana.

**3** Hunt for whole grains. Most baked goods are made with white flour, but they don't have to be. In fact, many of our dessert recipes in Part 4 cut down the amount of white flour in favor of blood sugar–friendly oats, whole wheat flour, and so on.

**4** Go low fat. Whether it's the ice cream you buy or the cream cheese you put in your cheesecake, make it reduced fat to avoid the nasty saturated fats that hamper your body's ability to handle blood sugar.

Finally, think of dessert as a treat—not a daily habit. Indulge twice a week to keep your sweet tooth happy. The rest of the week, top off dinner with an evening stroll instead.

**1**

Total GL: 29
Total calories: 363

DESSERT MAKEOVERS   DESSERT MAKEOVERS

MAKE IT A
**Magic**
dessert

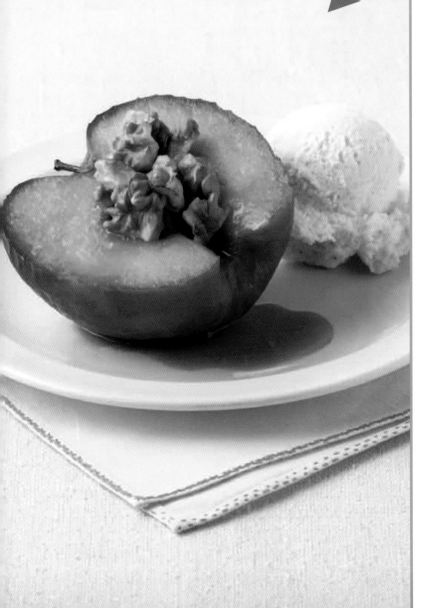

# Magic DESSERT

1 Maple-Walnut Roasted Apple
  with ice cream (recipe on page 282)

## THE FIXES

- Kept the apple but got rid of the piecrust and the extra sugar used for the filling. Both of these ingredients are responsible for increasing the GL of this dessert (plus, the piecrust is high in calories and full of saturated fat).

- Added walnuts for protein and "good" fat to help fill you up and further lower the dessert's GL.

- Cut the ice cream down to one small scoop and switched to reduced-fat ice cream to lower the saturated fat.

Total GL: 17
Total calories: 207

Typical Dessert
1 cup vanilla ice cream with
1/3 cup hot fudge sauce

Total GL: 39
Total calories: 329

MAKE IT A
**Magic**
dessert

# **Magic** DESSERT

1/2 cup vanilla ice cream with:
   1/2 cup strawberries
   5 toasted walnut halves

## THE FIXES

- Decreased the portion of ice cream since it has a lot of sugar and a high GL, not to mention saturated fat, which hampers insulin sensitivity.

- Scrapped the sugar-laden hot fudge, along with its glycemic load.

- Added walnuts and strawberries to fill up the bowl and provide fiber, nutrients, and healthy fats (from the walnuts) to help improve insulin sensitivity.

Total GL: 12
Total calories: 224

# 3

**Typical Dessert**

1 large piece chocolate cake
with frosting

Total GL: 23
Total calories: 439

DESSERT MAKEOVERS  DESSERT MAKEOVERS

**MAKE IT A**
**Magic**
**dessert**

## Magic DESSERT

1 small piece unfrosted chocolate cake
dusted with confectioner's sugar

1/2 cup mixed blueberries and
raspberries

### THE FIXES

- Decreased the portion size of the cake to cut refined carbohydrates and therefore the GL.

- Eliminated the frosting, which has a high GL.

- Added berries to increase the nutritional value of the dessert and make the smaller portion of cake more satisfying.

Total GL: 12
Total calories: 309

Typical Dessert
1 large chocolate chip cookie

Total GL: 19
Total calories: 196

# **Magic** DESSERT

1 Oatmeal–Peanut Butter Trail Bar
(recipe on page 207)

## THE FIX

⚙ Swapped the cookie, made with the triple evils of sugar, butter, and white flour, for an even more delicious trail bar made with whole grains (full of fiber) and peanut butter (full of protein and "good" fat) to lower the GL and keep you fuller longer. The bar also provides extra nutrition from dried fruit.

Total GL: 13
Total calories: 175

# Magic Recipes
## and meal plans

# BREAKFASTS

## Multi-Grain Pancakes or Waffles

**8** Serves

**Preparation time: 20 minutes**

**Cooking time: 15 to 20 minutes**

Most pancakes are anything but Magic, but here the weekend treats have been entirely re-imagined. We've slashed the white flour and added whole wheat flour and oats, plus an unexpected dash of sugar-lowering cinnamon. Wheat germ provides healthy fats, extra fiber, and deliciously nutty flavor. *See photo on page 195.*

2 cups low-fat buttermilk (see Tip, page 198)

1/2 cup old-fashioned rolled **oats**

2/3 cup **whole wheat flour**

2/3 cup all-purpose flour

1/4 cup toasted **wheat germ**

1 1/2 teaspoons baking powder

1/2 teaspoon baking soda

1/4 teaspoon salt

1 teaspoon **cinnamon**

2 large **eggs**

1/4 cup firmly packed brown sugar

1 tablespoon canola oil

2 teaspoons vanilla extract

1 cup maple syrup, warmed

1 1/2 cups sliced **strawberries** or **blueberries**

1. Mix the buttermilk and oats in a small bowl. Let stand for 15 minutes.

2. Whisk the whole wheat flour, all-purpose flour, wheat germ, baking powder, baking soda, salt, and cinnamon in a large bowl.

3. Whisk the eggs, sugar, oil, and vanilla in a medium bowl. Add the buttermilk mixture. Add this mixture to the flour mixture and mix with a rubber spatula just until flour mixture is moistened.

4. **To cook the pancakes:** Coat a large nonstick skillet with cooking spray. Heat over medium heat. Spoon about 1/4 cup batter for each pancake into the skillet and cook until bottoms are golden and small bubbles start to form on top, about 3 minutes. Flip the pancakes and cook until browned and cooked through, 1 to 2 minutes. (Adjust the heat as necessary for even browning.) Keep the pancakes warm in a 200°F (90°C) oven while you finish cooking the remaining batter.

**To cook the waffles:** Coat a waffle iron with cooking spray. Heat the iron. Spoon in enough of the batter to cover three-quarters of the surface, close the iron, and cook until the waffles are crisp and golden brown, 4 to 5 minutes. Keep the waffles warm in a 200°F (90°C) oven while you finish cooking the remaining batter.

5. Top with maple syrup and strawberries (or blueberries). One serving is 2 pancakes or waffles. Wrap any leftover pancakes or waffles individually in plastic wrap and refrigerate for up to 2 days or freeze for up to 1 month. Reheat in a toaster or toaster oven.

Per serving: 292 calories, 8 g protein, 60 g carbohydrates, 3 g fiber, 3 g total fat, 1 g saturated fat, 56 mg cholesterol, 331 mg sodium.

# Oatmeal with Apple and Flaxseeds

**4** Serves | **Preparation time: 5 minutes**
**Cooking time: 10 minutes**

What better way to start your day than with a comforting bowl of steaming oatmeal? This simple breakfast packs not one or two but *six* Magic foods to steady your blood sugar and keep you full till lunch.

2 cups low-fat (1%) **milk** or vanilla **soy milk**

3/4 cup old-fashioned rolled **oats** (*not* quick oats)

1 medium **apple,** peeled, cored and chopped

1/3 cup dried cranberries or raisins

1/2 teaspoon **cinnamon**

1/4 cup whole **flaxseeds,** ground (see Tip, page 197) or 1/3 cup flaxseed meal

1/4 cup nonfat plain or vanilla **yogurt**

1/4 cup maple syrup, warmed, or 2 tablespoons brown sugar

1. Combine the milk, rolled oats, apple, dried cranberries (or raisins), and cinnamon in a heavy medium saucepan. Bring to a simmer over medium-high heat, stirring almost constantly.

2. Reduce the heat to medium-low and cook, stirring often, until creamy and thickened, 3 to 5 minutes.

3. Stir in the flaxseeds. Spoon the cereal into individual bowls and top each serving with a dollop of yogurt and a drizzle of maple syrup. One serving is 2/3 cup. Leftovers will keep, covered, in the refrigerator for up to 2 days. Reheat in the microwave.

**Per serving:** 282 calories, 10 g protein, 47 g carbohydrates, 6 g fiber, 7 g total fat, 1 g saturated fat, 8 mg cholesterol, 84 mg sodium.

# Zucchini-Basil Frittata

**2** Serves | **Preparation time: 15 minutes**
**Cooking time: 8 to 12 minutes**

Eggs are one of our favorite Magic foods because they're an inexpensive and remarkably complete source of protein, which doesn't budge blood sugar a bit. This frittata (an Italian-style flat omelet) includes zucchini to help you get more veggies into your diet.

1 tablespoon **olive oil,** divided

1/2 cup thinly sliced **onion** (1 small)

1 1/2 cups shredded **zucchini** (1 small)

2 **garlic** cloves, minced

4 large **eggs**

1/2 teaspoon hot red pepper sauce, such as Tabasco

1/8 teaspoon salt, or to taste

Freshly ground black pepper to taste

1/2 cup grated Parmesan **cheese**

1/3 cup chopped fresh basil

1. Heat 2 teaspoons oil in a 10-inch (25-centimeter) nonstick broiler-proof skillet over medium heat. Add onion and cook, stirring often, until softened, 1 1/2 to 2 minutes. Add zucchini and garlic; cook, stirring often, until zucchini is tender and most of the moisture has evaporated, 2 to 3 minutes. Transfer to a plate and let cool slightly. Rinse and dry the skillet.

2. Blend the eggs, hot sauce, salt, and pepper briskly with a fork in a medium bowl. Stir in the zucchini mixture, Parmesan, and basil.

3. Preheat the broiler. Brush the remaining 1 teaspoon oil over the skillet. Heat over medium-low heat. Pour in the egg mixture. Cook, lifting edges with a heat-resistant rubber spatula and tilting the skillet to allow the uncooked egg to flow underneath from time to time, until the bottom is golden, 3 to 4 minutes.

**4.** Place the skillet under the broiler and cook until the top is firm to touch and set, 2 to 4 minutes. Slide the frittata onto a plate and cut into wedges.

Per serving: 219 calories, 17 g protein, 9 g carbohydrates, 2 g fiber, 13 g total fat, 4 g saturated fat, 18 mg cholesterol, 580 mg sodium.

# Spinach and Goat Cheese Omelet

| 1 | |
|---|---|
| Serves | **Preparation time: 10 minutes** |
| | **Cooking time: 2 minutes** |

A French-style, folded omelet is one of the fastest protein-rich meals you can make. It is also an excellent strategy for healthy solo dining. Omelet filling options are limitless. Try the variations below or improvise with leftover cooked vegetables or ingredients at hand. *See photo on next page.*

2 cups baby **spinach**, rinsed

2 tablespoons crumbled goat **cheese** or feta cheese

1 tablespoon chopped **scallion**

1 large **egg**

2 large **egg** whites

1/4 teaspoon hot red pepper sauce, such as Tabasco

Pinch of salt

Pinch of freshly ground black pepper

1 teaspoon **olive oil**

**1.** Bring about 1 inch (2.5 centimeters) of water to a boil in a large saucepan. Drop in spinach and cook just until wilted, about 30 seconds. Drain, press out liquid and chop coarsely. (Alternatively, place spinach in a microwave-safe bowl, cover with vented plastic wrap, and microwave on high for 1 to 2 minutes.) Place the spinach in a small bowl. Stir in the cheese and scallion.

**2.** Blend egg, egg whites, hot sauce, salt, and pepper briskly with a fork in a medium bowl. Heat oil in a 7- to 10-inch (18- to 25-centimeter) nonstick skillet over medium-high heat until hot. Tilt the skillet to swirl oil over surface. Pour in egg mixture. Immediately stir egg mixture with heat-resistant rubber spatula or fork for a few seconds. Then use spatula to push cooked portions at edges toward the center, tilting the skillet to allow uncooked egg mixture to fill in areas around edges. Sprinkle spinach mixture over the omelet. Continue to cook until almost set, and the bottom is golden. The entire cooking process should take about 1 minute.

**3.** Use a spatula to fold one-third of the omelet over the filling. Tip the skillet and, using spatula as a guide, slide the omelet onto a plate so that it lands, folded in thirds, seam-side down.

Per serving: 235 calories, 20 g protein, 4 g carbohydrates, 1 g fiber, 15 g total fat, 6 g saturated fat, 228 mg cholesterol, 471 mg sodium.

VARIATIONS
## Mushroom Omelet

Omit the spinach, goat cheese, and scallion. In Step 1, heat 1 teaspoon oil in a medium nonstick skillet over medium-high heat. Add 1/2 cup sliced mushrooms. Cook, stirring often, until browned, 3 to 4 minutes. Stir in 1 tablespoon parsley and a pinch of salt and pepper. In Step 2, sprinkle the mushroom mixture over the omelet.

## Broccoli and Cheese Omelet

Substitute 2 tablespoons chopped cooked broccoli and 2 tablespoons shredded Swiss or cheddar cheese for the spinach, goat cheese, and scallion in the filling.

**Spinach and Goat Cheese Omelet** *page 194*
spinach • cheese • scallion • egg • olive oil

**Blueberry-Oatmeal Muffins** *page 198*
whole wheat flour • cinnamon • oats • egg
• berries

**Multi-Grain Pancakes or Waffles** *page 192*
oats • whole wheat flour • wheat germ • cinnamon
• egg • berries

**Whole Wheat Flaxseed Bread** *page 196*
whole wheat flour • flaxseed • milk • olive oil

# BREADS AND MUFFINS

## Whole Wheat Flaxseed Bread

**1 Loaf**

**Preparation time: 20 minutes**

**Rising/baking time (for food processor method): about 3 hours**

Many of the healthy-sounding multi-grain and wheat breads on the shelves actually contain only a tiny proportion of whole grain. An enjoyable way to make sure you're getting at least 50 percent whole wheat flour in a loaf is to make your own. Flaxseed is a Magic addition to this bread; it increases the amount of blood sugar–lowering soluble fiber and contributes a delightful nutty taste. Note: Since bread machines come in both a 1-pound/450-gram (2 cup) and a 1 1/2-pound/700-gram (3-cup) capacity, we offer proportions to suit either. *See photo on page 195.*

### 1-POUND (450-GRAM) LOAF (8 SLICES)

1 1/3 cups **whole wheat flour**

2/3 cup bread flour or all-purpose flour

3 tablespoons whole **flaxseed,** ground (see Tip, opposite page), or 1/4 cup flaxseed meal

2 tablespoons nonfat dry **milk**

1 1/2 teaspoons bread machine yeast

3/4 teaspoon salt

3/4 cup water, at room temperature

1 tablespoon molasses or honey

1 tablespoon **olive oil**

### 1 1/2-POUND (700-GRAM) LOAF (12 SLICES)

2 cups **whole wheat flour**

1 cup bread flour or all-purpose flour

1/4 cup whole **flaxseed,** ground (see Tip, opposite page), or 1/3 cup flaxseed meal

3 tablespoons nonfat dry **milk**

2 teaspoons bread machine yeast

1 teaspoon salt

1 cup plus 2 tablespoons water, at room temperature

2 tablespoons molasses or honey

1 tablespoon **olive oil**

### TOPPING FOR FOOD PROCESSOR/OVEN METHOD

1 **egg** white, lightly beaten with 1 tablespoon water

1 tablespoon whole **flaxseed**

**To mix the dough and bake the bread in a bread machine:** Place all of the ingredients in a bread machine pan in the order recommended by the manufacturer (do not place the yeast in direct contact with the liquids and salt). Select the whole wheat or basic cycle and medium crust, then press start. Once the dough is mixed, check the consistency; it should be smooth yet soft to the touch. Adjust if necessary by adding flour 1 tablespoon at a time or water 1 teaspoon at a time. When the bread has finished the baking cycle, transfer it to a rack to cool.

**To mix the dough in a food processor and bake the bread in the oven:**

**1.** In a food processor fitted with a metal chopping blade, combine the whole wheat flour, bread (or all-purpose) flour, ground flaxseed (or flaxseed meal), dry milk, yeast, and salt and pulse several times to blend. In a measuring cup, stir together the water, molasses (or honey), and oil until the molasses is fully dissolved; set aside. With the motor running, slowly pour enough of the liquid through the feeder tube to make a smooth dough that pulls away from the sides of the workbowl. The consistency should be smooth yet soft to the touch; adjust if necessary by adding flour 1 tablespoon at a time or water 1 teaspoon at a time. Process for 1 minute to knead. Transfer the dough to a bowl coated with cooking spray and turn to coat. Cover with plastic wrap and let rise at room temperature until doubled in bulk, 1 1/2 to 1 3/4 hours.

2. Coat a baking sheet with cooking spray. When the dough has doubled, turn it out onto a lightly floured surface. Punch it down and shape into a round or oval loaf (or make 2 small loaves). Place the loaf on the baking sheet. Coat a sheet of plastic wrap with cooking spray and cover the loaf with it. Let rise until almost doubled in bulk, about 1 hour.

3. Meanwhile, place a small metal baking pan on the bottom oven rack. Preheat the oven to 400°F (200°C).

4. When the loaf has risen, brush it with the egg white mixture and sprinkle with the whole flaxseed. Pour 1 cup water into the baking pan in the oven to create steam. Use a serrated knife to score four 1/4-inch (5-millimeter)-deep slashes in the loaf. Bake until the bread is golden and sounds hollow when tapped, 20 to 30 minutes. Transfer to a wire rack to cool. One serving is 1 slice.

**Per serving:** 155 calories, 5 g protein, 27 g carbohydrates, 3 g fiber, 4 g total fat, 1 g saturated fat, 0 mg cholesterol, 229 mg sodium.

Tip: To grind flaxseeds, use a spice mill (such as a clean coffee grinder) or a blender to grind it into coarse meal. Flaxseeds must be ground in order for your body to reap the nutritional benefits.

# Apple-Bran Muffins

**12 muffins** | Preparation time: 20 minutes
| Baking time: 20 minutes

Bran muffins never tasted so good or boasted so many Magic ingredients. Applesauce keeps these low-fat, fiber-rich treats moist and tender. If you bake a batch on the weekend, you can wrap the leftovers individually in plastic wrap and freeze them so you can enjoy wholesome, homemade muffins on busy weekday mornings.

2 large **eggs**

1/2 cup packed light brown sugar

1 cup unsweetened **applesauce**

3/4 cup low-fat buttermilk (see Tip, next page)

1 cup unprocessed **wheat bran**

3 tablespoons canola oil

1 teaspoon vanilla extract

1 cup **whole wheat flour**

3/4 cup all-purpose flour

1 1/2 teaspoons baking powder

1/2 teaspoon baking soda

1/4 teaspoon salt

2 teaspoons ground **cinnamon**

1/4 teaspoon ground nutmeg

1 cup chopped peeled **apple** (1 medium)

1/3 cup chopped **walnuts**

1. Preheat the oven to 400°F (200°C). Coat 12 standard-size muffin cups (2 3/4 x 1 1/4-inch/ 7 x 3-centimeter) with cooking spray.

2. In a medium bowl, whisk the eggs and brown sugar until smooth. Add the applesauce, buttermilk, bran, oil, and vanilla and whisk until blended.

3. In a large bowl, whisk together the whole wheat flour, all-purpose flour, baking powder, baking soda, salt, cinnamon, and nutmeg. Add the egg mixture and mix with a rubber spatula

just until the dry ingredients are moistened. Fold in the apple. Spoon the batter into the muffin cups and sprinkle with the walnuts.

4. Bake until the tops of the muffins spring back when touched lightly, 18 to 22 minutes. Let cool in the pan on a rack for 5 minutes, then loosen the edges of the muffins and turn out onto a wire rack. Let cool slightly before serving. One serving is 1 muffin.

**Per serving**: 194 calories, 5 g protein, 31 g carbohydrates, 4 g fiber, 7 g total fat, 1 g saturated fat, 36 mg cholesterol, 194 mg sodium.

Tip: To thaw a frozen muffin, remove the plastic wrap, wrap in a paper towel, and microwave on defrost (20% power) for 1 to 2 minutes. To thaw in the oven, wrap in foil and bake at 300°F (150°C) for 25 to 35 minutes.

# Blueberry-Oatmeal Muffins

**12** muffins | **Preparation time: 25 minutes**
| **Baking time: 20 minutes**

Pairing rolled oats—filled with blood sugar–lowering soluble fiber—with antioxidant-rich blueberries makes for a Magic breakfast, especially when you add cinnamon, as we have. Maple syrup provides subtle sweetness; it complements the blueberries and lets the fruity flavor shine through—and it has a lower GL than table sugar. *See photo on page 195.*

3/4 cup plus 2 tablespoons whole wheat flour

3/4 cup all-purpose flour

1 1/2 teaspoons baking powder

1/2 teaspoon baking soda

1/4 teaspoon salt

1 teaspoon ground cinnamon

1 cup plus 2 tablespoons old-fashioned rolled oats

1 large egg

2 large egg whites

1/2 cup maple syrup

3/4 cup low-fat buttermilk (see Tip)

3 tablespoons canola oil

2 teaspoons grated orange zest

1 tablespoon orange juice

1 teaspoon vanilla extract

1 1/2 cups fresh blueberries, rinsed and patted dry

1. Preheat the oven to 400°F (200°C). Coat 12 standard-size (2 3/4 x 1 1/4-inch/7 x 3-centimeter) muffin cups with cooking spray or insert paper liners.

2. In a large bowl, whisk together the whole wheat flour, all-purpose flour, baking powder, baking soda, salt, and cinnamon. Stir in 1 cup rolled oats.

3. In a medium bowl, whisk the egg, egg white, and syrup until smooth. Add the buttermilk, oil, orange zest, orange juice, and vanilla and whisk until blended. Add to the flour mixture and mix with a rubber spatula just until the dry ingredients are moistened. Fold in the blueberries. Spoon the batter into the muffin cups, filling them almost to the top. Sprinkle the tops with the remaining 2 tablespoons rolled oats.

4. Bake until the muffins are lightly browned and the tops spring back when touched lightly, 18 to 22 minutes. Loosen the edges of the muffins, turn out onto a wire rack, and let cool slightly before serving. One serving is 1 muffin.

**Per serving**: 180 calories, 5 g protein, 30 g carbohydrates, 3 g fiber, 5 g total fat, 0 g saturated fat, 18 mg cholesterol, 190 mg sodium.

Tip: If you don't have buttermilk on hand, make your own "sour milk" by mixing 1 tablespoon lemon juice or vinegar with enough low-fat milk or plain soy milk to measure 1 cup. Alternatively, blend equal proportions of fat-free plain yogurt and low-fat milk. Shelf-stable buttermilk powder is another option; substitute according to package directions, but for added calcium and body, replace liquid with low-fat milk instead of water.

# Upside-Down Nectarine Muffins

**12** muffins

Preparation time: 25 minutes

Baking time: 20 minutes

There is nothing ordinary about these muffins. A bit like individual upside-down cakes, they boast an irresistible caramelized fruit topping. They're tasty treats indeed—with the Magic benefits of whole grains, stone fruit, nuts, and cinnamon.

## TOPPING

2 tablespoons packed light brown sugar

1/4 cup **walnuts,** chopped

12 ounces (340 grams) **nectarines** (about 3 medium), pitted and cut into 1/4-inch (5-millimeter)-thick wedges

## MUFFINS

1 cup **whole wheat flour**

1 cup all-purpose flour

1 1/2 teaspoons baking powder

1/2 teaspoon baking soda

1/4 teaspoon salt

1 1/2 teaspoons ground **cinnamon**

1/2 teaspoon ground nutmeg

2 large **eggs**

1/2 cup packed light brown sugar

1 cup low-fat buttermilk (see Tip, page 198)

3 tablespoons canola oil

1 teaspoon vanilla extract

1. Preheat the oven to 400°F (200°C). Coat 12 standard-size (2 3/4 x 1 1/4-inch/7 x 3-centimeter) muffin cups with cooking spray.

2. **To make the topping:** Sprinkle about 1/2 teaspoon brown sugar into each muffin cup and pat into an even layer, then sprinkle about 1 teaspoon walnuts into each cup. Arrange 3 or 4 nectarine slices, slightly overlapping, over the walnuts and brown sugar. Cover and set aside. Coarsely chop the remaining nectarines (you should have about 3/4 cup); set aside.

3. **To make the muffins:** In a large bowl, whisk together the whole wheat flour, all-purpose flour, baking powder, baking soda, salt, cinnamon, and nutmeg.

4. In a medium bowl, whisk the eggs and brown sugar until smooth. Whisk in the buttermilk, oil, and vanilla. Add to the flour mixture and mix with a rubber spatula just until the dry ingredients are moistened, then fold in the reserved nectarines. Spoon the batter into the muffin cups (they will seem quite full; the nectarine wedges will collapse during baking).

5. Bake until the muffins are lightly browned and the tops spring back when touched lightly, 18 to 22 minutes. Immediately loosen the edges and carefully turn the muffins out onto a wire rack. Replace any stray nectarine slices and spoon on any walnut pieces remaining in the muffin cups. Let cool slightly before serving. One serving is 1 muffin.

**Per serving:** 202 calories, 5 g protein, 32 g carbohydrates, 2 g fiber, 6 g total fat, 1 g saturated fat, 41 g cholesterol, 153 mg sodium.

---

**VARIATION**

Substitute 12 ounces (340 grams) plums or apricots for the nectarines.

# SNACKS, APPETIZERS, AND BEVERAGES

## Cherry Tomatoes Filled with Pesto Cream Cheese

**16** | Preparation time: 35 minutes
Serves | Cooking time: 0 minutes

Pesto and tomatoes are one of those time-honored combinations that taste better every time you try it. In this recipe, pesto is thickened with low-fat cream cheese to make a filling that bursts with the flavor of summer. Stuffed into cherry tomatoes, it makes an exceptionally attractive appetizer that is not at all hard to prepare. You can make the pesto cream cheese filling ahead of time (refrigerate it, covered, for up to 2 days), but wait until shortly before serving to stuff the tomatoes. *See photo on page 201.*

3 cups fresh basil leaves, washed and dried

1/3 cup plus 2 tablespoons pine **nuts,**
    toasted (see Tip)

2 medium **garlic** cloves, minced

1/2 teaspoon salt, or to taste

Freshly ground pepper to taste

1 tablespoon extra-virgin **olive oil**

1 package (8 ounces/250 grams) reduced-fat
    cream **cheese** (Neufchâtel), cut into chunks

2 pints (4 cups) cherry **tomatoes,**
    washed and dried

1. Combine the basil, 1/3 cup pine nuts, garlic, salt, and pepper in a food processor. Process until pine nuts are ground. With motor running, drizzle in olive oil. Add cream cheese and pulse until smooth and creamy.

2. Shortly before serving, make an X on the rounded side (opposite stem) of each cherry tomato with a serrated or sharp paring knife. Scoop out the seeds with a grapefruit spoon or your fingertips, taking care to keep the tomatoes intact.

3. Scrape the cream cheese filling into a pastry bag fitted with a star tip or small plastic food bag with a 1/2-inch (1-centimeter) hole snipped in one corner. Pipe a rosette of filling into each cherry tomato cavity. Garnish the cherry tomatoes with the remaining pine nuts. One serving equals 3 filled cherry tomatoes.

**Per serving:** 70 calories, 2 g protein, 2 g carbohydrates, 0 g fiber, 6 g total fat, 2 g saturated fat, 8 mg cholesterol, 116 mg sodium.

**Tip:** Toast pine nuts in a small dry skillet over medium-low heat, stirring constantly, until light golden and fragrant, 2 to 3 minutes. Transfer to a small bowl and let cool.

# Caponata

**12** Serves | Preparation time: 25 minutes
| Cooking time: 30 to 35 minutes

Caponata is terrific for entertaining because you can make it ahead of time. In fact, it gets better as it sits. Serve it in an attractive bowl, surrounded by whole grain crackers or toasted whole wheat baguette slices. You can also use it to perk up a sandwich filling or enliven a tomato-based pasta sauce. Made with plenty of vegetables and well flavored with olive oil—a "good fat" that may help reverse insulin resistance—this is a Magic way to begin a meal.

3 tablespoons **olive oil**

1 pound (450 grams) **eggplant,** cut into 1/2-inch (1 centimeter) cubes (6 cups)

1 cup chopped **onion** (1 small)

1 cup finely diced celery (4 stalks)

4 **garlic** cloves, minced

1/8 teaspoon crushed red pepper

1 can (14 1/2 ounces/398 milliliters) diced **tomatoes** (undrained)

1/4 cup sun-dried **tomatoes** (*not* oil-packed), finely chopped

3 tablespoons red-wine **vinegar**

8 cracked green **olives,** pitted and chopped (1/3 cup)

2 tablespoons drained capers, rinsed

1 tablespoon sugar

3 tablespoons currants

1/4 cup pine **nuts,** toasted (see Tip, page 256)

3 tablespoons chopped fresh parsley

1. Heat 1 tablespoon of oil in large nonstick skillet over medium-high heat. Add half of the eggplant and cook, stirring and turning eggplant, until browned and tender, 4 to 6 minutes. Transfer to a plate and set aside. Add 1 tablespoon oil to the skillet and repeat with the remaining eggplant. Set aside.

2. Add the remaining 1 tablespoon oil to the skillet. Add the onion and celery. Cook, stirring often until softened, 3 to 5 minutes. Add the garlic and red pepper. Cook, stirring, for 30 seconds. Add the diced tomatoes, sun-dried tomatoes, vinegar, olives, capers, sugar, and reserved eggplant. Bring to a simmer. Reduce heat to medium-low, cover skillet, and cook, stirring occasionally, until mixture has a chunky jam-like consistency, about 15 minutes. Add the currants and cook, covered, for 1 minute. Remove from heat. Stir in pine nuts and parsley. Let cool before serving. One serving is 2 1/2 tablespoons.

**Per serving:** 96 calories, 2 g protein, 10 g carbohydrates, 3 g fiber, 6 g total fat, 1 g saturated fat, 0 mg cholesterol, 182 mg sodium.

# Marinated Olives

**8** Serves | Preparation time: 5 minutes
| Cooking time: 2 minutes

Full of "good fats," these highly savory nuggets are a perfect appetizer for better blood sugar.

2 teaspoons **olive oil**

2 **garlic** cloves

4 (2 x 1/2-inch/5 x 1-centimeter) strips orange peel

1 1/2 teaspoons fennel seeds

2 cups rinsed kalamata **olives**

2 tablespoons orange juice

1. Heat olive oil in medium skillet over low heat until warm. Add garlic, orange peel and fennel seeds. Cook, stirring, until fragrant, 30 to 60 seconds. Add olives. Cook, stirring, until warmed through but not hot, about 1 minute.

2. Remove from heat. Stir in the orange juice. Cover and let stand at room temperature for 1 hour. Serve at room temperature. One serving is 2 tablespoons. Refrigerate leftovers.

**Per serving:** 93 calories, 1 g protein, 3 g carbohydrates, 0 g fiber, 9 g total fat, 1 g saturated fat, 0 mg cholesterol, 509 mg sodium.

# Smoked Salmon Canapés

## 12
**Serves**

| Preparation time: 15 minutes |
| Baking time: 15 minutes |

Party fare doesn't have to be a minefield of fatty foods and fast-acting carbohydrates. These elegant hors d'oeuvres offer a delectable bite of smoked salmon (a good source of protein and omega-3s), moistened with a light, lemony vinaigrette. Low-GL rye bread toasts make an excellent platform for the smoked salmon topping. Both the topping and toasts can be made early in the day. Refrigerate the topping, covered, for up to 8 hours. Store the toasts in an airtight container at room temperature. *See photo on page 201.*

24 slices cocktail **rye bread**

2 tablespoons **lemon** juice

2 tablespoons brewed black **tea** or vodka

1 tablespoon extra-virgin **olive oil**

2 teaspoons Dijon mustard

Freshly ground pepper to taste

8 ounces (250 grams) sliced smoked **salmon,** finely chopped (1 1/3 cups)

1/4 cup finely diced red **onion**

3 tablespoons chopped fresh dill, plus sprigs for garnish

2 tablespoons drained capers, rinsed and coarsely chopped

1. Preheat the oven to 325°F (160°C). Coat a baking sheet with nonstick spray. Arrange the cocktail rye bread slices in a single layer on the baking sheet. Spray the tops of slices lightly with nonstick spray. Bake the slices just until crisp, 12 to 15 minutes.

2. Whisk the lemon juice, tea (or vodka), oil, mustard, and pepper in a medium bowl. Add the smoked salmon, onion, dill, and capers. Toss to mix well.

3. Shortly before serving, mound about 1 tablespoon of topping on each slice of toast. Garnish each with a dill sprig. One serving is 2 canapés.

**Per serving:** 84 calories, 5 g protein, 9 g carbohydrates, 1 g fiber, 3 g total fat, 0 g saturated fat, 4 mg cholesterol, 311 mg sodium.

# Spiced Almonds

## 8
**Serves**

| Preparation time: 5 minutes |
| Cooking time: 25 to 30 minutes |

Warm spices turn plain almonds into irresistible nibbles. And thanks to almonds' protein and "good fat," these are blood sugar–smart.

1 cup unpeeled whole **almonds**

1 teaspoon **olive oil**

3/4 teaspoon ground cumin

1/4 teaspoon salt

1/8 teaspoon cayenne pepper

1. Toss the almonds with olive oil, cumin, salt, and cayenne in a pie plate or shallow baking dish.

2. Bake at 350°F (180°C), stirring occasionally, until fragrant, 25 to 30 minutes. Let cool. One serving is 2 tablespoons. Almonds will keep, enclosed in an airtight container, for up to 1 week.

**Per serving:** 112 calories, 4 g protein, 4 g carbohydrates, 2 g fiber, 10 g total fat, 1 g saturated fat, 0 mg cholesterol, 73 mg sodium.

# Warm Artichoke and Bean Dip

| **8** | Preparation time: 10 minutes |
|---|---|
| Serves | Baking time: 20 to 25 minutes |

Beans are the Magic ingredient in this lower-fat, higher-fiber version of a classic cheesy artichoke dip. It makes an appealing holiday appetizer and is an excellent choice for year-round entertaining as well. Try it with Whole Wheat Pita Crisps (page 207) or low-fat, whole grain crackers, such as Wasa, Kavli, or Ryvita. *See photo on page 201.*

1 can (19 or 15 ounces/540 or 398 milliliters) cannellini (white kidney) **beans,** drained and rinsed

1 can (14 ounces/398 milliliters) artichoke hearts, drained and rinsed

3 **garlic** cloves, minced

1 tablespoon reduced-fat mayonnaise

Pinch of cayenne pepper

Freshly ground pepper to taste

2/3 cup plus 2 tablespoons grated Parmesan **cheese**

1/4 cup chopped fresh parsley

1 teaspoon freshly grated lemon zest

1. Preheat the oven to 400°F (200°C). Coat a 2- to 3-cup baking dish with nonstick spray.

2. Place the beans, artichoke hearts, garlic, mayonnaise, cayenne, and black pepper in a food processor. Process until almost smooth, stopping to scrape down the sides of the workbowl once or twice. Transfer to a medium bowl. Stir in 2/3 cup of the Parmesan, parsley, and lemon zest. Scrape into the baking dish and smooth with a spatula. Sprinkle with the remaining 2 tablespoons Parmesan.

3. Bake the dip, uncovered, until heated through, 20 to 25 minutes. One serving is 1/4 cup.

**Per serving:** 116 calories, 7 g protein, 16 g carbohydrates, 5 g fiber, 3 g total fat, 2 g saturated fat, 7 mg cholesterol, 517 mg sodium.

**Tip:** Canned beans are high in sodium, but you can reduce the sodium by about 40 percent just by draining them. A 30-second rinse reduces sodium by another 3 percent. In our nutrition analyses we've assumed you've drained and rinsed the beans.

# Asian Peanut Dip

| **8** | Preparation time: 10 minutes |
|---|---|
| Serves | Cooking time: 0 minutes |

Tofu stretches the peanut butter in this spicy dip, reducing calories and giving it a velvety consistency. Serve with crudités or as a spread for grown-up peanut butter sandwiches, made with whole wheat bread, grated carrots, sliced cucumbers, and lettuce. The dip also can be used as a dressing for an Asian noodle salad.

1/2 cup natural-style **peanut butter**

1/3 cup low-fat, firm silken **tofu**

3 tablespoons firmly packed light brown sugar

2 tablespoons reduced-sodium soy sauce

2 tablespoons **lime** juice

1/2 to 3/4 teaspoon crushed red pepper

2 **garlic** cloves, crushed

Place all of the ingredients in a food processor and process until smooth and creamy, stopping once or twice to scrape down sides of the workbowl. One serving is 2 tablespoons. The dip will keep, covered, in the refrigerator for up to 2 days.

**Per serving:** 120 calories, 5 g protein, 10 g carbohydrates, 1 g fiber, 7 g total fat, 2 g saturated fat, 0 mg cholesterol, 216 mg sodium.

# Mediterranean Split Pea Spread

**16** | Preparation time: 10 minutes
Serves | Cooking time: 50 minutes

This Greek appetizer illustrates how the traditional Mediterranean diet can be healthy, and at the same time, delicious. The base of the spread is simply yellow split peas—boasting slow-acting complex carbohydrates. When seasoned with cumin, garlic, lemon juice, and fruity olive oil, they are transformed into a mouth-watering appetizer. Enjoy this spread as an opener to a leisurely meal, accompanied by Whole Wheat Pita Crisps (see page 207), whole grain crackers, olives, and feta cheese. It also makes a delicious sandwich filling.

2 1/4 cups water

3/4 cup dried yellow split **peas** or chana dahl, sorted and rinsed

6 **garlic** cloves, crushed

1/8 teaspoon crushed red pepper

3 tablespoons **lemon** juice

3 tablespoons extra-virgin **olive oil,** divided

1 1/2 teaspoons ground cumin

3/4 teaspoon salt, or to taste

2 tablespoons finely diced red **onion**

2 tablespoons coarsely chopped fresh dill

1. Combine the water, split peas (or chana dahl), garlic, and red pepper in a heavy medium saucepan. Bring to a boil. Reduce the heat to low, partially cover, and simmer, stirring occasionally, until the split peas are tender and most of the liquid has been absorbed, 40 to 50 minutes. (Add more water during cooking, if necessary. If the mixture seems too soupy at the end of cooking, simmer, uncovered, stirring constantly, for a few minutes, or until mixture has consistency of *very* thick split pea soup.) Let cool slightly.

2. Transfer the split pea mixture to a food processor. Add the lemon juice, 2 tablespoons of the olive oil, cumin, and salt. Process until smooth. To serve, spread the puree in a shallow serving dish. Drizzle with the remaining 1 tablespoon oil. Sprinkle with the red onion and dill. One serving is 2 tablespoons. The spread will keep, covered, in the refrigerator for up to 4 days.

**Per serving:** 58 calories, 2 g protein, 7 g carbohydrates, 1 g fiber, 3 g total fat, 0 g saturated fat, 0 mg cholesterol, 112 mg sodium.

# White Bean Spread with Italian Flavors

**12** | Preparation time: 10 minutes
Serves | Cooking time: 0 minutes

A snap to make and wonderfully flavorful, this could be the perfect spread.

1 can (19 or 15 ounces/540 or 398 milliliters) cannellini **beans,** drained and rinsed

2 tablespoons extra-virgin **olive oil**

2 tablespoons **lemon** juice

1 **garlic** clove, minced

Pinch of cayenne pepper

Pinch of salt

Freshly ground pepper

1 1/2 teaspoons chopped fresh rosemary

1. Combine cannellini beans, olive oil, lemon juice, garlic, cayenne pepper, salt, and ground pepper to taste in a food processor. Pulse into a chunky puree. Transfer to a medium bowl and stir in rosemary. One serving is 2 tablespoons.

**Per serving:** 55 calories, 2 g protein, 6 g carbohydrates, 2 g fiber, 3 g total fat, 0 g saturated fat, 0 mg cholesterol, 66 mg sodium.

# Chickpea Spread with Indian Flavors

**12** Serves

**Preparation time:** 10 minutes

**Cooking time:** 1 minute

This spread has a bit of a kick, offset nicely by the cool yogurt.

2 tablespoons canola oil

2 jalapeño peppers, seeded and minced

1 tablespoon minced fresh ginger

2 garlic cloves, minced

2 teaspoons ground cumin

1 teaspoon ground coriander

1 can (19 or 15 ounces/540 or 398 milliliters) chickpeas, drained and rinsed

1/3 cup nonfat plain yogurt

2 tablespoons lime juice

1/8 teaspoon salt

Freshly ground pepper to taste

2 tablespoons chopped fresh cilantro (or parsley)

1. Heat canola oil in a small skillet over medium-high heat. Add jalapeño peppers, ginger and garlic. Cook, stirring, until fragrant, about 30 seconds. Stir in cumin and coriander. Remove from heat and transfer to a food processor.

2. Add chickpeas, yogurt, lime juice, salt, and pepper to taste. Process until smooth. Transfer to a medium bowl and stir in cilantro (or parsley). One serving is 2 1/3 tablespoons.

**Per serving:** 65 calories, 2 g protein, 7 g carbohydrates, 2 g fiber, 3 g total fat, 0 g saturated fat, 0 mg cholesterol, 108 mg sodium.

# Black Bean Spread with Mexican Flavors

**12** Serves

**Preparation time:** 10 minutes

**Cooking time:** 0 minutes

Fiber-rich canned beans provide the base for an easy spread that makes a satisfying snack to serve with crudités, whole grain crackers, Whole Wheat Pita Crisps (recipe next page) or Baked Tortilla Chips (recipe next page). It can also be used as a sandwich filling—spread on sourdough or whole wheat bread and top with grated carrots, sliced cucumber, tomatoes, and lettuce.

1 can (19 or 15 ounces/540 or 398 milliliters) black beans, drained and rinsed

2 tablespoons lime juice

1 tablespoon extra-virgin olive oil

1 garlic clove, minced

1 teaspoon ground cumin

1/4 teaspoon hot red pepper sauce, such as Tabasco

Pinch of salt

Freshly ground pepper to taste

2 tablespoons chopped fresh cilantro or parsley

1. Combine the black beans, lime juice, oil, garlic, cumin, hot sauce, salt, and pepper in a food processor. Process until smooth, stopping to scrape down the sides of the workbowl once or twice. Transfer to a medium bowl and stir in cilantro (or parsley). One serving is 2 tablespoons. The spread will keep, covered, in the refrigerator for up to 4 days.

**Per serving:** 36 calories, 2 g protein, 7 g carbohydrates, 2 g fiber, 2 g total fat, 0 g saturated fat, 0 mg cholesterol, 162 mg sodium

# Baked Tortilla Crisps

**8** Serves | **Preparation time: 2 minutes**
| **Cooking time: 10 to 15 minutes**

These are a smart alternative to store-bought corn chips, which are much higher in fat and sodium.

1 package (9 ounces/297 grams) white corn tortillas (12 tortillas)

1/4 teaspoon salt

1. Stack tortillas and cut into 4 wedges. Spread wedges in a single layer on 2 baking sheets. Spray lightly with nonstick spray. Sprinkle with salt. Bake at 400°F (200°C) until light golden and crisp, 10 to 15 minutes. One serving is 6 crisps.

**Per serving:** 98 calories, 3 g protein, 20 g carbohydrates, 4 g fiber, 1 g total fat, 0 g saturated fat, 0 mg cholesterol, 411 mg sodium.

# Whole Wheat Pita Crisps

**8** Serves | **Preparation time: 3 minutes**
| **Cooking time: 8 to 10 minutes**

Here is a healthy whole grain dipper for any of the spreads here.

4 whole wheat pita breads

1. Cut each pita bread into 4 triangles. Separate each triangle into 2 halves at the fold. Arrange, rough side up, on a baking sheet. Spritz lightly with olive oil nonstick spray. Bake at 425°F (220°C) until crisp, 8 to 10 minutes. One serving is 4 crisps.

**Per serving:** 60 calories, 2 g protein, 12 g carbohydrates, 2 g fiber, 1 g total fat, 0 g saturated fat, 0 mg cholesterol, 120 mg sodium.

# Oatmeal-Peanut Butter Trail Bars

**24** Bars | **Preparation time: 25 minutes**
| **Baking time: 20 to 25 minutes**

When you bake your own "energy" bars, you can be assured that they include whole grains like rolled oats and whole wheat flour and healthy fats like canola oil, peanut butter, and walnuts. Peanut butter stands in for butter in these treats, reducing the saturated fat and boosting protein. These bars make ideal snacks—tuck one into your pocket when you head out the door.

1/2 cup whole wheat flour

1 teaspoon cinnamon

1/2 teaspoon baking soda

1/8 teaspoon salt

1/2 cup natural-style smooth peanut butter (see Ingredient Note, next page)

1/2 cup firmly packed brown sugar

1/3 cup honey

1 large egg

2 large egg whites (see Tip, next page)

2 tablespoons canola oil

2 teaspoons vanilla extract

2 cups old-fashioned rolled oats

1 cup dried cranberries (or raisins)

1/2 cup coarsely chopped walnuts or almonds (2 ounces/60 grams)

1/2 cup bittersweet or semisweet chocolate chips

1. Preheat the oven to 350°F (180°C). Coat a 9 x 13-inch (23 x 33-centimeter) baking pan with nonstick spray.

2. Whisk the flour, cinnamon, baking soda, and salt in a medium bowl. Beat the peanut butter, sugar, and honey in a large mixing bowl with an electric mixer until blended. Blend egg and egg whites with a fork in a small bowl. Add to the peanut butter mixture, along with oil and vanilla.

Beat until smooth. Add reserved flour mixture and mix with a rubber spatula. Mix in oats, dried cranberries (or raisins), walnuts (or almonds), and chocolate chips. Scrape batter into the prepared baking dish. Use a piece of plastic wrap to spread batter into an even layer.

3. Bake the bars until lightly browned and firm to the touch, 20 to 25 minutes. Let cool completely in the pan on a rack before cutting into 24 bars. One serving is one 2 x 2-inch (5 x 5-centimeter) bar.

Per serving: 175 calories, 4 g protein, 24 g carbohydrates, 2 g fiber, 8 g total fat, 1 g saturated fat, 9 mg cholesterol, 68 mg sodium.

Ingredient Note: If you must avoid peanut butter because of an allergy, you can substitute soy nut butter or sunflower seed butter (for tips on adapting recipes to sunflower seed butter, visit www.sunbutter.com). You can replace the nuts with unsalted roasted pepitas (pumpkin seeds) and/or sunflower seeds (look for unsalted seeds in the bulk bins of natural foods stores).

Tip: To avoid wasting the egg yolks, use reconstituted dried egg whites, such as Just Whites, which are available in the baking or natural foods sections of large supermarkets.

# Chai

2 | Serves

Preparation time: 2 minutes

Cooking time: 10 minutes

Chai, a milky spiced tea beverage that originated in India, is suddenly everywhere. It's easy to brew your own blend of this warming drink, and it's a good way to get some milk into your diet. This homemade version has a fraction of the calories and fat grams of coffee bar varieties—and it's much easier on your wallet.

1 1/2 cups water

1/4 teaspoon cinnamon

1/4 teaspoon ground cloves

1/4 teaspoon ground ginger

3 black tea bags

2/3 cup low-fat (1%) milk or vanilla soy milk

2 teaspoons honey, divided, or to taste

1. Combine the water, cinnamon, cloves, and ginger in a small saucepan. Bring to a simmer. Reduce heat to low, cover, and simmer for 5 minutes. Add the milk (or soy milk) and heat until steaming but not boiling. Remove from heat. Add the tea bags, cover, and let steep for 3 to 4 minutes. Pour the chai into 2 mugs and sweeten with honey, if desired. One serving is 1 cup.

Per serving: 63 calories, 3 g protein, 11 g carbohydrates, 0 g fiber, 1 g total fat, 1 g saturated fat, 3 mg cholesterol, 49 mg sodium.

# Berry-Flaxseed Smoothie

2 | Serves

Preparation time: 5 minutes

Cooking time: 0 minutes

A smoothie is a smart way to start your day, especially when it includes this tasty mix of Magic foods. Flaxseeds may seem like an unusual addition, but they blend in seamlessly and make this breakfast drink an excellent source of fiber. See photo on page 201.

2 tablespoons whole flaxseeds

1/2 cup orange juice

1/2 cup nonfat vanilla yogurt

1 cup unsweetened frozen mixed berries or blueberries

1 small banana, sliced

1. Place the flaxseeds in dry blender, cover, and blend until ground into a fine powder. Add the orange juice, yogurt, mixed berries (or blueberries), and banana. Cover and blend until smooth and creamy. One serving is 1 cup.

Per serving: 200 calories, 5 g protein, 36 g carbohydrates, 7 g fiber, 5 g total fat, 0 g saturated fat, 1 mg cholesterol, 33 mg sodium.

# Peachy Iced Tea

**8** Serves | **Preparation time: 5 minutes**
| **Cooking time: 2 minutes**

To help wean you off soft drinks and sugary juice drinks made with high-fructose corn syrup, we've invented this delightfully refreshing iced tea enhanced with the sweet perfume of peach nectar. When buying the peach nectar or juice, look for a no-sugar-added variety, usually available in the natural foods section of supermarkets.

7 black or green **tea** bags

6 cups boiling water

2 cups no-sugar-added peach nectar or juice

2 cups sliced **peaches** (2 medium)

Ice cubes

Mint sprigs (optional)

**1.** Steep the tea bags in boiling water for 5 minutes. Remove the tea bags. Combine the brewed tea and nectar in a large pitcher. Stir in the peaches. Refrigerate until chilled, at least 3 hours or overnight. Serve over ice and garnish with mint sprigs, if desired. One serving is 1 cup.

**Per serving:** 52 calories, 0 g protein, 13 g carbohydrates, 1 g fiber, 0 g total fat, 0 g saturated fat, 0 mg cholesterol, 9 mg sodium.

---

**VARIATION Berry Iced Tea**

Substitute blackberry or blueberry juice for the peach nectar and fresh blackberries for the peaches.

---

# Iced Coffee Frappé

**1** Serves | **Preparation time: 5 minutes**
| **Cooking time: 0 minutes**

Coffee bar drinks may seem innocent enough, but they are often outrageously high in calories, especially if you opt for the typical oversize portion. It is very easy to make your own frothy coffee-flavored drink. Our recipe has less than half the calories of a Starbucks Frappuccino.

2 teaspoons instant **coffee**

1 teaspoon sugar, or to taste

2 ice cubes

1/4 cup cold water

1/3 cup chilled vanilla **soy milk** or low-fat (1%) **milk**

Pinch of **cinnamon**

**1.** Combine the instant coffee, sugar, ice cubes, and water in a cocktail shaker or wide-mouth jar with tight-fitting lid (about 24-ounce/700-milliliter capacity). Secure lid and shake vigorously until frothy, about 30 seconds. Pour into a tall glass. Add the soy milk (or milk) and stir to mix. Sprinkle with cinnamon and serve with a straw. One serving is 2/3 cup.

**Per serving:** 70 calories, 3 g protein, 12 g carbohydrates, 0 g fiber, 1 g total fat, 0 g saturated fat, 0 mg cholesterol, 47 mg sodium.

# SALADS, SANDWICHES, AND SOUPS

## Grilled Chicken Salad with Oranges

**4** Serves

| Preparation time: | 25 minutes |
|---|---|
| Marinating time: | 20 minutes |
| Cooking time: | 10 to 15 minutes |

Slices of grilled chicken transform a fruity, Mediterranean salad into a satisfying hot-weather dinner that's packed with flavor—and Magic foods. Note: When marinating meat, fish, and poultry, remember to set aside a few tablespoons of the marinade for basting. Do not contaminate cooked food with marinade that has been in contact with raw meat. *See photo on page 218.*

1/3 cup orange juice

2 tablespoons lemon juice

3 tablespoons extra-virgin olive oil

1 tablespoon Dijon mustard

2 garlic cloves, minced

1/4 teaspoon salt, or to taste

Freshly ground pepper to taste

1 pound (450 grams) boneless skinless chicken breasts, trimmed

1/4 cup pistachios, or slivered almonds toasted

8 cups (5 ounces/140 grams) mesclun salad mix, rinsed and dried

1/2 cup thinly sliced red onion

2 medium oranges, peeled, quartered, and sliced

1. Place the orange juice, lemon juice, oil, mustard, garlic, salt, and pepper in a small bowl or jar with a tight-fitting lid; whisk or shake to blend. Reserve 1/3 cup of this dressing for the salad and 3 tablespoons for basting.

2. Place the remaining dressing in a shallow glass dish or a resealable plastic bag. Add the chicken and turn to coat. Cover or seal and marinate in the refrigerator for at least 20 minutes or up to 2 hours.

3. Preheat the grill to medium. Lightly oil grill rack by rubbing it with a piece of crumpled, oil-soaked paper towel (use tongs to hold paper towel). Remove chicken from marinade and discard marinade. Grill the chicken 4 to 6 inches (10 to 15 centimeters) from the heat source, basting the cooked sides with dressing reserved for basting, until no longer pink in the center and an instant-read thermometer inserted in the thickest part registers 170°F (75°C), 4 to 6 minutes per side. Transfer to a cutting board and let stand for 5 minutes.

4. Meanwhile, toast the almonds (or pistachios) in a small dry skillet over medium-low heat, stirring constantly, until light golden, 2 to 3 minutes. Transfer to a bowl and let cool.

5. Place the salad mix and onion in a large bowl. Toss with the dressing reserved for the salad. Divide the salad among 4 plates. Slice the chicken and distribute over the salads. Scatter orange slices over top and sprinkle with pistachios (or almonds).

**Per serving:** 331 calories, 30 g protein, 18 g carbohydrates, 5 g fiber, 16 g total fat, 3 g saturated fat, 68 mg cholesterol, 290 mg sodium.

# Barley Salad with Snow Peas and Lemon Dressing

**8**
Serves

Preparation time: 30 minutes

Cooking time: 40 to 45 minutes

As this delightful, colorful salad attests, sugar-lowering barley isn't just for soups. Peas add even more sugar-busting, cholesterol-bashing soluble fiber. What's more, the refreshing lemon dressing helps slow down your body's conversion of carbohydrates into blood sugar. To turn this into a main-course salad, just add some diced cooked chicken, salmon, or firm baked tofu.

## DRESSING

2 teaspoons freshly grated lemon zest

1/4 cup fresh **lemon** juice

1/4 cup finely chopped **shallot**

1 **garlic** clove, minced

1/2 teaspoon salt, or to taste

Freshly ground pepper to taste

1/3 cup extra-virgin **olive oil**

## SALAD

1 cup pearled **barley,** rinsed (see Tip)

2 1/2 cups water

1/4 teaspoon salt, or to taste

1 1/2 cups (6 ounces/170 grams) snow **peas** or sugar snap peas

1 medium red bell pepper, seeded and diced

1 cup grated **carrots** (3–4 medium)

1/4 cup chopped fresh parsley

1/4 cup snipped fresh chives

**1.** **To make the dressing:** Whisk the lemon zest, lemon juice, shallot, garlic, 1/2 teaspoon salt, and pepper in a medium bowl. Gradually whisk in the oil.

**2.** **To make the salad:** Place the barley, water, and 1/4 teaspoon salt in a large saucepan and bring to a simmer over medium-high heat. Reduce the heat to low and cook, covered, until the barley is tender and most of the liquid has been absorbed, 40 to 45 minutes. Transfer to a large bowl and let cool, fluffing with a fork occasionally to prevent sticking.

**3.** Meanwhile, remove the stem ends and strings from peas. Cut in half on the diagonal. Cook the peas in a large saucepan of lightly salted water or steam them until just tender, about 2 minutes. Drain and rinse with cold running water.

**4.** Add the peas, bell pepper, carrots, parsley, and chives to the barley. Drizzle the dressing over the salad and toss to coat well. One serving is 3/4 cup. To make ahead, prepare the dressing and salad and refrigerate in separate covered containers for up to 1 day. Toss the salad with dressing shortly before serving.

**Per serving:** 202 calories, 4 g protein, 25 g carbohydrates, 5 g fiber, 10 g total fat, 1 g saturated fat, 0 mg cholesterol, 234 mg sodium.

**Tip:** To save time, you can substitute quick-cooking barley. In Step 2, use 1 1/2 cups quick-cooking barley, 2 1/2 cups water, and 1/4 teaspoon salt. Bring to a simmer and cook, covered, for 10 to 12 minutes.

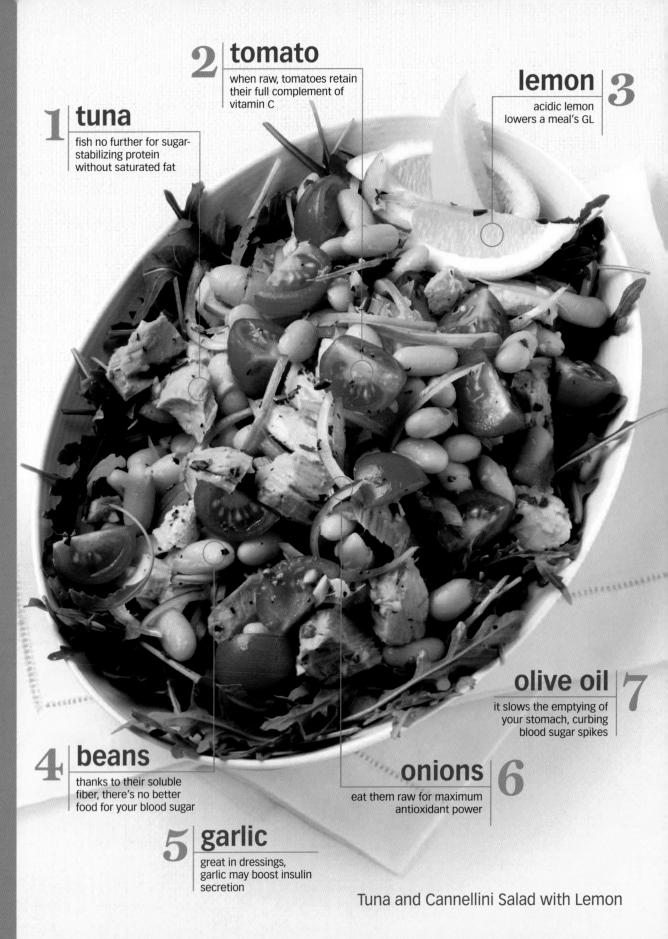

**2 tomato**
when raw, tomatoes retain their full complement of vitamin C

**1 tuna**
fish no further for sugar-stabilizing protein without saturated fat

**lemon 3**
acidic lemon lowers a meal's GL

**olive oil 7**
it slows the emptying of your stomach, curbing blood sugar spikes

**4 beans**
thanks to their soluble fiber, there's no better food for your blood sugar

**onions 6**
eat them raw for maximum antioxidant power

**5 garlic**
great in dressings, garlic may boost insulin secretion

Tuna and Cannellini Salad with Lemon

# Tuna and Cannellini Salad with Lemon

**4** Serves | **Preparation time: 25 minutes**
| **Cooking time: 0 minutes**

Tuna and beans are a classic combo as well as a practical and nutritious one. If you keep canned tuna and canned beans on hand, you can put this recipe together from pantry staples—just add fresh greens and cherry tomatoes. This version is distinguished by a seasoning of lemon zest and rosemary. It is perfect for a special lunch, picnic, or dinner on a steamy evening.

## LEMON-GARLIC DRESSING

3 tablespoons lemon juice

1 garlic clove, minced

1/4 teaspoon salt, or to taste

1/8 teaspoon crushed red pepper

1/4 cup extra-virgin olive oil

Freshly ground pepper to taste

## SALAD

1 can (19 or 15 ounces/540 or 398 milliliters) cannellini beans, drained and rinsed

1 can (6 ounces/170 grams) water-packed chunk light tuna, drained and flaked

1/3 cup finely diced red onion

2 teaspoons chopped fresh rosemary

1 1/2 teaspoons freshly grated lemon zest

6 cups arugula, washed, dried, and torn into bite-size pieces

1 cup cherry tomatoes, quartered

1. **To make the dressing:** Combine the lemon juice, garlic, salt, and crushed red pepper in a small bowl. Gradually whisk in the oil. Season with pepper.

2. **To make the salad:** Combine the beans, tuna, onion, rosemary, and lemon zest in a medium bowl. Add 1/4 cup of the lemon-garlic dressing (save remaining dressing for the arugula). Toss to coat well. (The tuna-bean salad will keep, covered, in the refrigerator for up to 1 day.)

3. Just before serving, place the arugula in a large bowl. Add the reserved lemon-garlic dressing and toss to coat well. Divide the arugula mixture among 4 plates. Top with tuna-bean salad and garnish with cherry tomatoes. One serving is 2/3 cup tuna-bean salad and 1 1/2 cups arugula.

**Per serving:** 305 calories, 18 g protein, 25 g carbohydrates, 7 g fiber, 15 g total fat, 2 g saturated fat, 26 mg cholesterol, 500 mg sodium.

# Black Bean and Barley Salad

**6** Serves | **Preparation time: 25 minutes**
| **Cooking time: 10 minutes**

With an all-star Magic foods lineup of barley, beans, vinegar, and citrus, this hearty salad is a real winner. It's great for picnics and barbecues and is an excellent accompaniment for grilled chicken, pork, or fish. *See photo on page 219.*

1 1/4 cups reduced-sodium chicken broth or vegetable broth

3/4 cup quick-cooking barley

1/4 cup cider vinegar

1/4 cup orange juice

1/4 cup extra-virgin olive oil

1 1/2 teaspoons ground cumin

1 teaspoon dried oregano

1 garlic clove, minced

1/4 teaspoon salt, or to taste

Freshly ground pepper to taste

1 can (15 1/2 or 19 ounces/398 or 540 milliliters) black beans, drained and rinsed

1 large red or yellow bell pepper, seeded and diced

2/3 cup chopped scallions, trimmed (1 bunch)

1/2 cup coarsely chopped fresh cilantro

Lime wedges

**1.** Combine the broth and barley in a medium saucepan and bring to a simmer. Cover and reduce heat to low. Simmer until the barley is tender and most of the liquid has been absorbed, about 10 minutes. Transfer the barley to a large bowl. Fluff with a fork and let cool.

**2.** Meanwhile, combine the vinegar, orange juice, oil, cumin, oregano, garlic, salt, and pepper in a jar with tight-fitting lid or small bowl. Shake or whisk to blend.

**3.** Add the beans, bell pepper, scallions, and cilantro to the barley. Drizzle with the dressing and toss to coat well. Garnish with lime wedges. One serving is 3/4 cup. The salad will keep, covered, in the refrigerator for up to 1 day.

**Per serving:** 230 calories, 7 g protein, 29 g carbohydrates, 7 g fiber, 11 g total fat, 2 g saturated fat, 0 mg cholesterol, 410 mg sodium.

# Whole Wheat Noodles with Peanut Sauce and Chicken

**8** Serves | Preparation time: 35 minutes
Cooking time: 8 to 10 minutes

This dish will be a big hit at your next potluck. Nutty-tasting whole wheat spaghetti complements the peanut sauce. Tofu stretches the peanut butter in the recipe, helping to keep calories in check and giving the sauce a velvety consistency. For a vegetarian version, substitute diced, baked, seasoned tofu for the chicken. If you are making the salad ahead, it is best to prepare all the components and toss the salad with the dressing shortly before serving.

DRESSING

1/2 cup natural-style **peanut butter**

1/3 cup low-fat firm silken **tofu**

1/4 cup reduced-sodium soy sauce

3 tablespoons **lime** juice

3 **garlic** cloves, minced

2 tablespoons firmly packed light brown sugar

3/4 teaspoon crushed red pepper

SALAD

12 ounces (340 grams) **whole wheat spaghetti**

2 teaspoons toasted sesame oil

2 1/2 cups shredded cooked skinless **chicken** breast

1 cup grated **carrots** (2–4 medium)

1 cup finely diced red bell pepper (1 small)

3/4 cup grated seedless (English) cucumber (1/4 medium)

1/3 cup coarsely chopped fresh cilantro leaves

1/4 cup chopped **scallions**

3 tablespoons unsalted dry-roasted **peanuts,** chopped

**Lime** wedges

**1.** Bring a large pot of lightly salted water to a boil for cooking the spaghetti.

**2. To make the dressing:** Combine all of the dressing ingredients in a food processor. Process until smooth and creamy, stopping once or twice to scrape down sides of workbowl. Set aside.

**3. To make the salad:** Cook the spaghetti in the boiling water, stirring often, until al dente (just tender), 6 to 9 minutes, or according to package directions. Drain and rinse with cold running water. Transfer to a large bowl. Drizzle with the oil and toss to coat.

**4.** Add the chicken, carrots, and bell pepper to the spaghetti. Add the peanut dressing and toss to coat. Sprinkle with the cucumber, cilantro, scallions, and peanuts. Serve with the lime wedges. One serving is 1 1/4 cups.

**Per serving:** 364 calories, 22 g protein, 43 g carbohydrates, 8 g fiber, 13 g total fat, 2 g saturated fat, 28 g cholesterol, 560 mg sodium.

# Mediterranean Salad with Edamame

**8** **Serves** | **Preparation time: 25 minutes** | **Cooking time: 4 minutes**

Torn leaves of fragrant herbs and delicate, protein-rich edamame beans distinguish this variation of a classic Greek salad. Edamame are immature soybeans. You can find them in the freezer section or the natural foods section of supermarkets or in natural foods stores. *See photo on page 218.*

1 cup frozen shelled **edamame** beans

1/3 cup extra-virgin **olive oil**

3 tablespoons **lemon** juice

2 **garlic** cloves, minced

1/4 teaspoon salt, or to taste

1/4 teaspoon sugar

Freshly ground pepper to taste

2 cups shredded romaine lettuce (1/2 small head)

2 cups cherry **tomatoes,** halved, or 2 medium tomatoes, cored, cut into 2- by 1-inch (5- by 2.5-centimeter) wedges

1 cup sliced English cucumber

2/3 cup chopped **scallions**

1/2 cup pitted kalamata **olives,** halved

1/2 cup fresh mint leaves, washed, dried, and torn into 1/2-inch (1-centimeter) pieces

1/2 cup fresh flat-leaf parsley leaves, washed, dried, and torn into 1/2-inch (1-centimeter) pieces

1 cup crumbled feta **cheese**

**1.** Bring a large saucepan of lightly salted water to a boil. Add the edamame beans and cook, covered, over medium heat until tender, 3 to 4 minutes. Drain and rinse with cold running water.

**2.** Combine the oil, lemon juice, garlic, salt, sugar, and pepper in a screw-top jar with a tight-fitting lid. Shake to blend.

**3.** Combine the lettuce, tomatoes, cucumber, scallions, olives, mint, parsley, and cooked edamame beans in a large bowl. Just before serving, drizzle the lemon dressing over salad and toss to coat well. Sprinkle each serving with feta. One serving is 1 1/4 cups.

**Per serving:** 220 calories, 7 g protein, 10 g carbohydrates, 3 g fiber, 17 g total fat, 5 g saturated fat, 15 mg cholesterol, 500 mg sodium.

# Garden Pasta Salad

**6** **Serves** | **Preparation time: 30 minutes** | **Cooking time: 8 to 10 minutes**

Pasta salads are perfect for potlucks, picnics, and back-yard barbecues. This version has been upgraded with whole wheat pasta and a generous quantity of colorful vegetables. Reduced-fat mayonnaise, blended with low-fat yogurt, makes a creamy dressing that has a fraction of the saturated fat and calories of typical mayonnaise dressings. If you'd like to make this salad more substantial, toss in canned tuna, cooked chicken, or chickpeas. *See photo on page 218.*

2 cups (6 ounces/170 grams) whole wheat rotini or fusilli **pasta**

1/3 cup reduced-fat mayonnaise

1/3 cup low-fat plain **yogurt**

2 tablespoons extra-virgin **olive oil**

1 tablespoon red-wine **vinegar** or **lemon juice**

1 **garlic** clove, minced

1/8 teaspoon salt, or to taste

Freshly ground pepper to taste

1 cup cherry or grape **tomatoes**, halved

1 cup diced yellow or red bell pepper (1 small)

1 cup grated **carrots** (2–4 medium)

1/2 cup chopped **scallions** (4 medium)

1/2 cup chopped pitted kalamata **olives**

1/3 cup slivered fresh basil

1. Bring a large pot of lightly salted water to a boil. Cook pasta, stirring often, until firm-tender, 8 to 10 minutes, or according to package directions. Drain and refresh under cold running water.

2. Whisk mayonnaise, yogurt, oil, vinegar, garlic, salt, and pepper in a large bowl until smooth. Add the pasta and toss to coat. Add the tomatoes, bell pepper, carrots, scallions, olives, and basil. Toss to coat well. One serving size is 1 cup. The salad will keep, covered, in the refrigerator for up to 1 day.

**Per serving:** 205 calories, 6 g protein, 29 g carbohydrates, 4 g fiber, 9 g total fat, 2 g saturated fat, 1 mg cholesterol, 291 mg sodium.

# No-Mayonnaise Creamy Coleslaw

**6**
Serves

| Preparation time: 20 minutes
| Cooking time: 0 minutes

You can't have a picnic without coleslaw, but the traditional version is drowned in a fatty, overly sweet dressing. Our version uses yogurt enriched with olive oil (a good fat) instead of mayonnaise. If you have red cabbage on hand, use a mix of red and green cabbage for extra color and to take advantage of the red variety's anthocyanins, pigments that may help boost insulin production and lower blood sugar. To save time, you can use 5 cups packaged coleslaw mix. *See photo on page 219.*

1/3 cup nonfat plain **yogurt**

4 teaspoons Dijon mustard

4 teaspoons apple cider **vinegar**

4 teaspoons extra-virgin **olive oil**

1 1/2 teaspoons sugar

1/2 teaspoon caraway **seeds** or celery seeds

1/4 teaspoon salt

1/4 teaspoon freshly ground pepper

4 cups shredded green **cabbage** (1/2 medium)

1 cup grated **carrots** (2–4 medium)

1. Whisk the yogurt, mustard, vinegar, oil, sugar, caraway seeds, salt, and pepper in a small bowl until smooth.

2. Combine the cabbage and carrots in a large bowl. Add the dressing and toss to coat well. One serving is 3/4 cup. The coleslaw will keep, covered, in the refrigerator for up to 1 day.

**Per serving:** 63 calories, 2 g protein, 7 g carbohydrates, 2 g fiber, 4 g total fat, 1 g saturated fat, 0 mg cholesterol, 141 mg sodium.

# Spinach, Grapefruit, and Avocado Salad with Poppy Seed Dressing

**4**
Serves

| Preparation time: 30 minutes
| Cooking time: 0 minutes

Consider this salad a trifecta of Magic foods. Juicy, tart grapefruit makes a delicious contrast to buttery avocado and crisp spinach. Serve it as an impressive starter salad or add cooked shrimp and/or scallops and enjoy it as a refreshing warm-weather main dish. You can prepare recipe through Step 2 up to 2 days ahead. Cover and refrigerate the grapefruit segments and dressing separately.

2 pink **grapefruit**

1 tablespoon white-wine **vinegar** or rice vinegar

1/4 cup finely chopped **shallot** (1 large)

2 teaspoons poppy **seeds**

1 teaspoon honey

1 teaspoon Dijon mustard

3 tablespoons extra-virgin **olive oil**

1/2 teaspoon salt, or to taste

Freshly ground pepper to taste

8 cups (6 ounces/170 grams) baby **spinach,** rinsed and dried

1 cup sliced radishes (1 bunch)

2 Haas **avocados,** peeled, pitted, and sliced

**1.** Place a sieve over a medium bowl. Using a sharp knife, remove the skin and white pith from the grapefruit. Working over the sieve, cut the grapefruit segments from their surrounding membrane, letting the segments collect in the sieve and the juices collect in the bowl. When you have removed all of the segments, squeeze the membrane to extract as much juice as possible.

**2.** Place 1/4 cup of the grapefruit juice (reserve the remainder for another use) in a small bowl or a jar with a tight-fitting lid. Add the vinegar, shallot, poppy seeds, honey, mustard, oil, salt, and pepper. Whisk or shake to blend.

**3.** Just before serving, place the spinach and radishes in a large bowl. Toss with half of the grapefruit juice dressing. Divide the salad among 4 plates. Strew the avocado slices and grapefruit segments over salads and drizzle with the remaining dressing. One serving is 2 cups.

**Per serving:** 326 calories, 4 g protein, 29 g carbohydrates, 10 g fiber, 25 g total fat, 3 g saturated fat, 0 mg cholesterol, 416 mg sodium.

# Greek Lentil Salad

**6**
Serves

| Preparation time: 20 minutes |
| Cooking time: 25 to 30 minutes |

Prized for their vegetable protein, soluble fiber, and high folate content, lentils are an essential Magic Foods pantry staple. And there is no need to wait for chilly soup weather to prepare lentils. They are also delicious in summer salads like this one. Feel free to substitute two cans (15 ounces/398 milliliters) of lentils (drained and rinsed) for the dried lentils.

1 cup dried green or brown **lentils** (see Ingredient Note), rinsed

1 teaspoon salt, divided

3 tablespoons **lemon** juice

2 tablespoons extra-virgin **olive oil**

1 **garlic** clove, minced

Freshly ground pepper to taste

1 cup chopped **scallions** (1 bunch)

1 cup (12 ounces) roasted red peppers from a jar, rinsed and diced

1/2 cup (2 ounces/60 grams) crumbled feta **cheese**

1/3 cup chopped fresh dill

6 cups trimmed arugula or watercress, washed, dried, and torn

**1.** Place the lentils in a large saucepan and cover with water. Bring to simmer. Reduce heat to medium-low, partially cover, and simmer for 15 minutes. Add 1/2 teaspoon of salt and cook until lentils are tender but not broken down, 10 to 15 minutes longer. Drain and let cool slightly.

**2.** Whisk the lemon juice, oil, garlic, the remaining 1/2 teaspoon salt, and the pepper in a large bowl. Add the warm lentils and toss gently to mix. Add the scallions, roasted red peppers, feta, and dill. Toss again. To serve, mound lentil mixture on a bed of arugula. One serving is 3/4 cup.

**Per serving:** 160 calories, 10 g protein, 13 g carbohydrates, 10 g fiber, 7 g total fat, 2 g saturated fat, 5 mg cholesterol, 700 mg sodium.

**Ingredient Note:** Common brown lentils are fine for this recipe, but small green lentils from France (often known as Le Puy lentils) are preferred for salads because they retain their shape and have an appealing chewy texture. Total cooking time is about 20 minutes for green lentils and 25 to 30 minutes for brown lentils.

Grilled Chicken Salad with Oranges *page 210*
lemon • olive oil • garlic • chicken • pistachios • onion • orange

Salmon Sandwiches with Wasabi Mayonnaise *page 220*
vinegar • salmon • scallion • seeds • pumpernickel bread

Garden Pasta Salad *page 215*
pasta • yogurt • olive oil • vinegar • garlic • tomato • carrot • scallion • olives

Mediterranean Salad with Edamame *page 215*
edamame • olive oil • lemon • garlic • tomato • scallion • olives • cheese

**No-Mayonnaise Creamy Coleslaw** *page 216*
yogurt • vinegar • olive oil • seeds • cabbage
• carrot

**Black Bean and Barley Salad** *page 213*
barley • vinegar • olive oil • garlic • beans
• scallion • lime

**Tuna and Carrot Sandwich on Rye** *page 222*
carrot • lemon • olive oil • scallion
• tuna • rye or pumpernickel bread

**Curried Red Lentil Soup** *page 224*
onions • garlic • lentils • tomato • cinnamon
• lemon • yogurt • scallion

# Salmon Sandwiches with Wasabi Mayonnaise

**4** Serves | **Preparation time: 20 minutes**
| **Cooking time: 0 minutes**

When you get tired of tuna sandwiches, try this recipe, which takes its inspiration from the sushi bar. Canned salmon is an essential pantry staple and a great way to get the benefits of wild salmon without paying the premium prices for fresh wild salmon. *See photo on page 218.*

6 tablespoons reduced-fat mayonnaise, divided

2 tablespoons rice **vinegar**

1 tablespoon grated fresh ginger

1 1/2 teaspoons wasabi powder
(see Ingredient Note)

1 teaspoon mirin (see Ingredient Note)

1 can (7.5 ounces/213 grams) **salmon,**
drained and flaked

2 tablespoons chopped **scallions**

1 tablespoon sesame **seeds,** toasted (see Tip)

8 slices **pumpernickel** bread

1 cup thinly sliced cucumber

1 cup trimmed watercress sprigs,
rinsed and dried

1. Whisk 3 tablespoons of the mayonnaise, the rice vinegar, ginger, wasabi powder, and mirin in a medium bowl. Add the salmon, scallions, and sesame seeds. Mix well.

2. Spread the remaining 3 tablespoons mayonnaise over 1 side of each bread slice. Divide the salmon mixture among 4 of the bread slices, spreading evenly. Top with cucumber and watercress. Set the remaining bread slices on top. Cut the sandwiches in half. One serving is 2 sandwich halves.

**Per serving:** 314 calories, 18 g protein, 36 g carbohydrates, 5 g fiber, 12 g total fat, 2 g saturated fat, 34 mg cholesterol, 860 mg sodium.

**Tip:** Toast the sesame seeds in a small dry skillet, stirring constantly, until light golden and fragrant, 2 to 3 minutes.

**Ingredient Notes:**
• Wasabi, the pungent sushi condiment, is made from the stem of a semi-aquatic member of the cabbage family. Add water to the powder to make the paste that accompanies sushi. Large supermarkets stock wasabi powder in the Asian foods section or with the sushi.

• Also known as rice wine, mirin is a sweet wine made from glutinous rice. It has a low alcohol content, and you can find it in the Asian foods section of most supermarkets.

# Grilled Eggplant Sandwiches with Red Pepper-Walnut Sauce

**4** Serves | **Preparation time: 30 minutes**
| **Cooking time: 0 minutes**

When it comes to sandwiches, think beyond the deli counter. This sophisticated and delicious combination pairs beautifully with low-GL sourdough breads and makes a special picnic sandwich. If you toast the bread and serve it right away, the sandwich makes a refreshing hot-weather supper. For panini (Italian-style grilled sandwiches), spritz the outside of the bread with non-stick spray and grill the sandwiches in a panini grill or contact grill.

3/4 cup Red Pepper-Walnut Sauce (recipe on opposite page)

2 medium-large baby **eggplants,** cut crosswise into 3/8-inch (1-centimeter)-thick slices

1/4 teaspoon salt, or to taste

Freshly ground pepper to taste

8 small slices **sourdough bread,**
    toasted, if desired

4 ounces (125 grams) creamy goat **cheese,**
    cut into 3/8-inch (1-centimeter)-thick slices

3/4 cup arugula leaves, washed and dried

1. Make the Red Pepper-Walnut Sauce.

2. Preheat the grill or broiler.

3. Spritz both sides of the eggplant slices
with the cooking spray and season with salt
and pepper. Lightly oil the grill or broiler rack
by rubbing it with a piece of oil-soaked paper
towel (use tongs to hold the paper towel when
working over a hot grill). Grill or broil the
eggplant until very tender and browned,
4 to 6 minutes per side.

4. Spread about 1 1/2 tablespoons of the Red
Pepper-Walnut sauce over one side of each
bread slice. Layer the eggplant slices and goat
cheese slices on four slices of bread. Top with
the arugula. Set the remaining bread slices on
the sandwiches. Cut the sandwiches in half. One
serving is 2 sandwich halves. The sandwiches
will keep, wrapped in plastic wrap or foil, in the
refrigerator or a cooler packed with ice packs for
up to 2 days.

**Per serving:** 349 calories, 14 g protein, 44 g carbohydrates,
6 g fiber, 13 g total fat, 5 g saturated fat, 13 mg cholesterol,
910 mg sodium.

**Tip:** Place a fine-meshed vegetable grill rack over
the grill grate to prevent the eggplant slices from
falling through.

# Red Pepper-Walnut Sauce

**4**
Serves

| Preparation time: 10 minutes |
| Cooking time: 0 minutes |

In addition to perking up sandwich fillings, this intensely
flavored sauce also makes an excellent appetizer spread
to serve with whole grain crackers or toasted Whole
Wheat Pita Crisps (page 207).

1/4 cup **walnuts**

1 tablespoon fine dry unseasoned bread crumbs

1 **garlic** clove, minced (1/2 teaspoon)

1 teaspoon ground cumin

1/8 teaspoon crushed red pepper

1/8 teaspoon salt, or to taste

1 jar (7 ounces/200 milliliters) roasted red peppers,
    drained and rinsed

1 tablespoon **lemon** juice

1. Combine the walnuts, bread crumbs, garlic,
cumin, crushed red pepper and salt in a food
processor; process until the walnuts are ground.
Add the roasted red peppers and lemon juice;
process until smooth. One serving is 3 tablespoons. The spread will keep, covered, in the
refrigerator for up to 4 days. Makes 3/4 cup.

**Per serving:** 76 calories, 2 g protein, 6 g carbohydrates, 1 g fiber,
5 g total fat, 1 g saturated fat, 0 mg cholesterol, 268 mg sodium.

# Tuna and Carrot Sandwich on Rye

**2** Serves | **Preparation time:** 15 minutes | **Cooking time:** 0 minutes

Adding more omega-3–rich seafood to your diet can be as simple as packing a tuna sandwich for lunch. This one is boosted by a lemony grated carrot salad, adding crunch and appeal while squeezing some vegetable into your sandwich. We've put it on rye bread, which can actually help *lower* your blood sugar. *See photo on page 219.*

2/3 cup shredded **carrot** (1 medium)

2 teaspoons **lemon** juice

2 teaspoons extra-virgin **olive oil**

1 tablespoon chopped **scallion**

1 tablespoon chopped fresh dill or parsley

1/8 teaspoon salt, or to taste

1 can (3 ounces/85 grams) water-packed chunk light **tuna,** drained and flaked

1/4 cup finely chopped celery

2 tablespoons reduced-fat mayonnaise, divided

4 slices **rye** or **pumpernickel bread**

4 lettuce leaves, rinsed and dried

1. Combine the carrot, lemon juice, oil, scallion, dill (or parsley), and salt in a small bowl. Toss with a fork to mix.

2. Mix the tuna, celery, and 1 tablespoon of the mayonnaise in a small bowl. Spread the remaining 1 tablespoon mayonnaise over the bread slices. Spread half of the tuna mixture over two of the bread slices. Top with the carrot salad and lettuce. Set remaining bread slices over filling. Cut each sandwich in half. One serving equals 2 sandwich halves. The sandwiches will keep, well wrapped, in the refrigerator or a cooler packed with ice packs for up to 1 day.

*Per serving:* 303 calories, 17 g protein, 38 g carbohydrates, 5 g fiber, 9 g total fat, 2 g saturated fat, 13 mg cholesterol, 758 mg sodium.

# Bean and Barley Soup

**8** Serves | **Preparation time:** 30 minutes | **Cooking time:** 40 minutes

A soothing soup is one of the most nourishing and practical meals possible. And a chunky soup like this one that focuses on low-GL carbohydrates, such as barley and beans, and Magic veggies like carrots and spinach, provides maximum satisfaction for just a few calories. Infusing canned low-sodium broth with garlic and herbs freshens the flavor and makes it taste as good as homemade.

7 cups reduced-sodium chicken broth or vegetable broth

6 **garlic** cloves, peeled and crushed

2 sprigs fresh rosemary (4 1/2 inches/ 10 centimeters long)

1/4 teaspoon crushed red pepper

1 can (19 or 15 ounces/540 or 398 milliliters) dark red kidney **beans,** drained and rinsed

2 teaspoons **olive oil**

1 cup chopped **onion** (1 medium)

1 cup diced peeled **carrots** (3–4 medium)

1/4 cup diced celery (1 stalk)

1 can (14 1/2 ounces/398 milliliters) diced **tomatoes**

1 cup quick-cooking **barley**

10 cups baby **spinach,** washed

Freshly ground black pepper to taste

1/2 cup grated Parmesan **cheese**

1. Bring the broth to a boil in a large saucepan. Add the garlic, rosemary, and crushed red pepper. Partially cover the saucepan and simmer over medium-low heat for 15 minutes to intensify flavor. Strain the broth through a sieve into a large bowl. Discard the solids.

2. Mash 1 cup of the kidney beans in a small bowl with a fork. Set the whole and mashed

beans aside. Heat the oil in a 4- to 6-quart (4- to 6-liter) soup pot over medium heat. Add the onion, carrots, and celery. Cook, stirring often, until softened, 3 to 4 minutes. Pour in the infused broth. Add the tomatoes, barley, and reserved mashed and whole beans. Bring to a simmer, stirring occasionally. Reduce heat to medium-low, cover, and cook at a lively simmer until the barley is almost tender, about 15 minutes.

3. Stir in the spinach. Cover and cook until the spinach has wilted and the barley is tender, 3 to 5 minutes. Season with ground pepper. Top each serving with 1 tablespoon Parmesan cheese. One serving is 1 1/3 cups. The soup will keep, covered, in the refrigerator for up to 2 days.

Per serving: 197 calories, 12 g protein, 30 g carbohydrates, 7 g fiber, 4 g total fat, 1 g saturated fat, 4 mg cholesterol, 757 mg sodium.

# Hearty Split Pea Soup with Rye Croutons

4 | **Preparation time: 15 minutes**
Serves | **Cooking time: 1 hour**

An old-fashioned split pea soup is back on the menu for Magic eating. Split peas, which are a good source of plant protein and fiber, are amazingly filling. This soup is wonderful for a supper and handy to tote to the office for lunch—it will easily sustain you until your afternoon snack. The rye bread croutons are a cinch to make and give the soup a final flourish. They're a far healthier alternative to store-bought croutons, which are typically made with white flour and often contain trans fat.

4 teaspoons **olive oil,** divided

1/2 cup diced Canadian back bacon, diced (2 ounces/60 grams or 4 slices)

1 cup chopped **onion** (1 medium)

1 cup chopped **carrots** (2–4 medium)

5 1/4 cups reduced-sodium chicken broth

1 cup green split **peas,** sorted and rinsed

1 teaspoon dried summer savory or thyme

1/8 teaspoon cayenne pepper

1 bay leaf

1 1/2 cups cubed **rye bread** (2 slices)

1. Heat 2 teaspoons of the oil in a 4- to 6-cup soup pot over medium heat. Add the bacon, onion, and carrots. Cook, stirring often, until softened and lightly browned, 3 to 5 minutes. Add the broth, split peas, savory (or thyme), cayenne, and bay leaf. Bring to a simmer. Reduce the heat to medium-low, cover, and cook until the split peas have broken down and thickened the soup, about 1 hour.

2. Meanwhile, preheat the oven to 350°F (180°C). Toss the bread cubes with the remaining 2 teaspoons oil in a medium bowl. Spread in a small baking pan and bake until crisp, 15 to 20 minutes.

3. When the soup is ready, discard the bay leaf. Garnish each serving with rye croutons. One serving is 1 cup. The soup will keep, covered, in the refrigerator, for up to 2 days

Per serving: 298 calories, 18 g protein, 44 g carbohydrates, 2 g fiber, 6 g total fat, 1 g saturated fat, 7 mg cholesterol, 298 mg sodium.

# Curried Red Lentil Soup

**8** Serves | Preparation time: 15 minutes
| Cooking time: 25 minutes

You may think of lentils as something to store in the back of your pantry until a day when you have lots of time to wait for them to cook. But lentils, especially the red variety (sold in natural foods stores), are surprisingly convenient. They require no presoaking and cook up quickly—red lentils in just 20 minutes and brown lentils in about 30 minutes. *See photo on page 219.*

2 teaspoons canola oil

2 cups chopped **onions** (2 medium)

4 **garlic** cloves, minced

4–5 teaspoons curry powder

1 1/2 cups red **lentils,** rinsed and picked over

6 cups reduced-sodium chicken broth or vegetable broth

3/4 cup water

2 tablespoons **tomato** paste

1/4 teaspoon **cinnamon**

2 tablespoons **lemon** juice

1/4 teaspoon salt, or to taste

Freshly ground pepper to taste

1/2 cup nonfat plain **yogurt**

1/4 cup chopped **scallion** greens

1. Heat the oil in a 4- to 6-quart (4- to 6-liter) soup pot over medium heat. Add the onion and cook, stirring frequently, until softened, 2 to 3 minutes. Add the garlic and curry powder. Cook, stirring, for 30 seconds. Add the lentils and stir to coat. Add the broth, water, tomato paste, and cinnamon. Bring to a simmer, reduce heat to low, cover, and simmer until the lentils are very tender, about 20 minutes.

2. In batches, transfer the soup to a food processor or blender and puree. (Use caution when blending hot liquids.) Return the puree to the soup pot and heat through. Season with lemon juice, salt, and pepper. Garnish each serving with a dollop of yogurt and a sprinkling of scallion greens. One serving is 1 cup. The soup will keep, covered, in the refrigerator for up to 2 days.

**Per serving:** 187 calories, 14 g protein, 29 g carbohydrates, 12 g fiber, 2 g total fat, 1 g saturated fat, 4 mg cholesterol, 199 mg sodium.

# Peanut Chicken Soup

**8** Serves | Preparation time: 20 minutes
| Cooking time: 25 minutes

If you think peanut butter is just for sandwiches, think again. The secret ingredient in this soup (based on a traditional African recipe), it contributes exceptionally rich flavor and body—without saturated fat. It also boosts the protein content of this simple but surprising recipe.

2 teaspoons canola oil

1 cup chopped **onion** (1 medium)

3 **garlic** cloves, minced

1 tablespoon curry powder

2 cans (14 ounces/398 milliliters each) reduced-sodium chicken broth

1 can (14 ounces/398 milliliters) diced **tomatoes**

1 small **sweet potato,** peeled and cut into 1/2-inch (1-centimeter) pieces (2 cups)

1 pound (450 grams) boneless skinless **chicken** breasts, trimmed and cut into 1/2-inch (1-centimeter) pieces

1/3 cup natural-style **peanut butter**

1/3 cup chopped fresh cilantro

2 tablespoons **lime** juice

Dash of hot pepper sauce, such as Tabasco

1. Heat the oil in a 4- to 6-quart (4- to 6-liter) Dutch oven or soup pot over medium-high heat. Add the onion and cook, stirring often, until softened, 2 to 3 minutes. Add the garlic and curry

powder; cook, stirring, until fragrant, about 20 seconds. Add the broth, tomatoes, and sweet potato and bring to a simmer. Reduce heat to medium-low, cover, and simmer for 10 minutes.

2. Add the chicken, cover, and simmer until the sweet potatoes are tender and the chicken is cooked through, about 10 minutes. Add the peanut butter and stir until blended into the soup. Stir in the cilantro, lime juice, and hot sauce. One serving is 1 cup. The soup will keep, covered, in the refrigerator for up to 2 days.

**Per serving:** 175 calories, 14 g protein, 14 g carbohydrates, 3 g fiber, 7 g total fat, 1 g saturated fat, 21 mg cholesterol, 406 mg sodium.

# Asian Noodle Hot Pot

4 Serves | Preparation time: 15 minutes
Cooking time: 30 minutes

Serving noodles in a fragrant, spicy broth is a good way to ensure an appropriate portion size. Canned broth is the base, but this soup is infused with ginger and garlic to give it a characteristic Asian flavor. Rounding out the broth and noodles are several key Magic foods: cabbage, carrots, tofu, and vinegar. You can substitute diced cooked chicken for the tofu, if you prefer.

5 1/4 cups reduced-sodium chicken broth or vegetable broth

3 slices (1/4 inch/5 millimeters thick) peeled fresh ginger

2 garlic cloves, crushed and peeled

1/4 teaspoon crushed red pepper

2 teaspoons canola oil

4 ounces (125 grams) fresh shiitake mushrooms, stems removed, wiped clean, and sliced

3 cups sliced napa cabbage (1/2 medium) or green cabbage (1/2 medium) (see Ingredient Note)

8 ounces (225 grams) firm regular tofu, drained, patted dry, cut into 3/4-inch (2.5-centimeter) cubes

1 cup shredded carrots (2–4 medium)

2 teaspoons reduced-sodium soy sauce

2 teaspoons rice vinegar

1 teaspoon toasted sesame oil

4 ounces (125 grams) whole wheat linguine or spaghetti

1/4 cup chopped scallions (2 medium)

1. Bring a large pot of lightly salted water to a boil.

2. Bring the broth to a simmer in a large saucepan. Add the ginger, garlic, and red pepper. Partially cover and simmer over medium-low heat for 15 minutes to intensify flavor. Strain the broth through a sieve into another large saucepan and discard the solids.

3. Heat the oil in large nonstick skillet over medium-high heat. Add the mushrooms and cook, stirring often, until tender, 3 to 5 minutes. Add the cabbage and cook, stirring often, until almost tender, 2 to 3 minutes. Add to the infused broth in the saucepan. Simmer, partially covered, over medium-low heat until cabbage is tender, about 5 minutes. Add the tofu and carrots and heat through. Stir in the soy sauce, vinegar, and sesame oil.

4. Meanwhile, cook the linguine (or spaghetti) in the boiling water until al dente (just tender), 6 to 9 minutes, or according to package directions. Drain the linguine and divide among 4 large soup bowls. Ladle the soup over the noodles and garnish each serving with scallions. One serving is 1 1/2 cups.

**Per serving:** 246 calories, 16 g protein, 32 g carbohydrates, 6 g fiber, 8 g total fat, 1 g saturated fat, 0 mg cholesterol, 917 mg sodium.

**Ingredient Note:** Napa, also known as Chinese cabbage, is a pale green, long, oval-shaped cabbage. Its flavor is more delicate than that of regular green cabbage.

# BEEF, LAMB, AND PORK

## Orange Beef Stir-Fry with Broccoli and Red Pepper

**4**
**Serves**

| Preparation time: 30 minutes |
| Cooking time: 8 minutes |

Recipes for beef and broccoli stir-fries may be common-place, but this one stands out. Stir-frying orange zest with fresh ginger gives the sauce extraordinary fragrance and satisfying flavor. This dish provides a generous quantity of vegetables balanced with lean protein, providing excellent nutritional value for the calories. For convenience, you can substitute 4 cups frozen broccoli florets for fresh and 2 1/2 cups frozen pepper stir-fry mix for the fresh bell pepper and onion. *See photo on opposite page.*

1/2 cup orange juice

2 tablespoons reduced-sodium soy sauce

1 tablespoon oyster-flavored sauce

1 tablespoon rice **vinegar**

1 1/2 teaspoons chile-garlic sauce or hot red pepper sauce

1 1/2 teaspoons cornstarch

1 tablespoon vegetable oil

12 ounces (340 grams) flank **steak,** trimmed, halved lengthwise, and cut into 1/4-inch (5-millimeter)-thick slices

1 tablespoon minced fresh ginger

2 teaspoons freshly grated orange zest (see Tip)

3 **garlic** cloves, minced

1 cup sliced **onion** (1 medium)

1 pound (450 grams) **broccoli** crowns, cut into 1-inch (2.5-centimeter) florets (4 cups)

1 red or yellow bell pepper, cut into 2- x 1/4-inch (5-centimeter x 5-millimeter) slivers (1 1/2 cups)

**1.** In a small bowl, whisk together the orange juice, soy sauce, oyster-flavored sauce, vinegar, chile-garlic sauce (or hot sauce) and cornstarch; set aside.

**2.** Heat 1 teaspoon oil in a large nonstick skillet or stir-fry pan over high heat. Add half of the steak and cook, without stirring or turning, until browned on the underside, about 1 minute. Stir and turn the slices, then cook just until browned on the other side, about 30 seconds. Transfer to a plate. Add another 1 teaspoon oil, repeat with the remaining steak, and transfer to the plate.

**3.** Add the remaining 1 teaspoon oil to the skillet, then add the ginger, orange zest, and garlic and stir-fry until fragrant, 10 to 20 seconds. Add the onion and stir-fry for 1 minute. Add the broccoli and bell pepper and stir-fry for 30 seconds. Add 1/4 cup water, cover, and cook just until crisp-tender, about 1 1/2 minutes. Push the vegetables to the outside of the pan. Stir the reserved sauce, pour into the center of the pan, and cook, stirring, until glossy and thickened, about 1 minute. Stir the vegetables into the sauce, return the steak to the skillet, and turn to coat. One serving is 1 1/2 cups.

Per serving: 247 calories, 25 g protein, 17 g carbohydrates, 3 g fiber, 9 g total fat, 3 g saturated fat, 34 mg cholesterol, 655 mg sodium.

**Tip:** A zester is the easiest way to remove zest from oranges and lemons. If you don't have one, use a vegetable peeler and mince the peels. Or cover a grater with plastic wrap and use the side made for grating hard cheese.

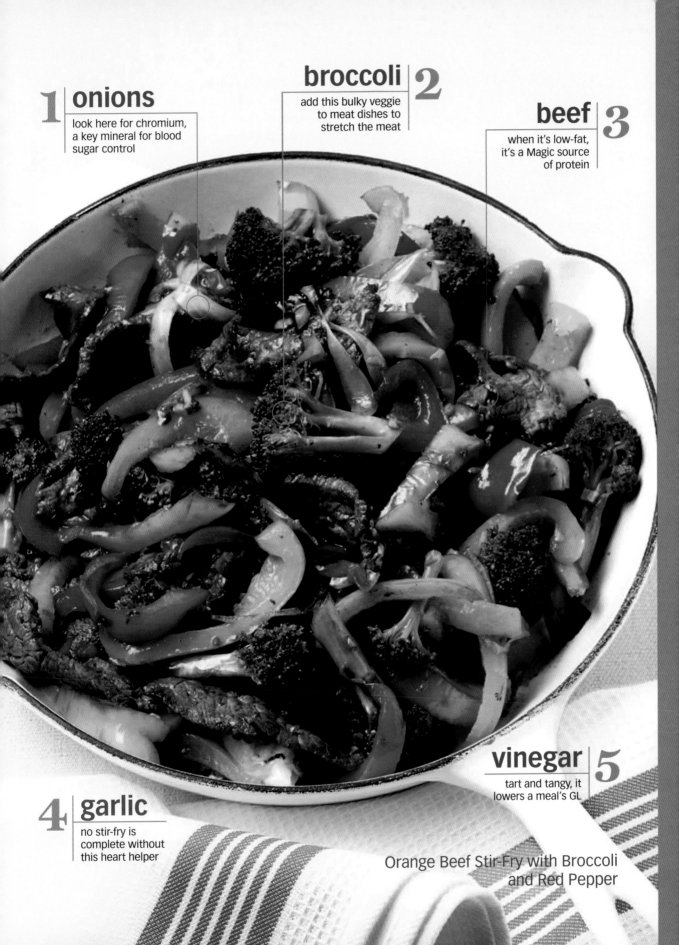

**1 | onions**
look here for chromium, a key mineral for blood sugar control

**broccoli | 2**
add this bulky veggie to meat dishes to stretch the meat

**beef | 3**
when it's low-fat, it's a Magic source of protein

**4 | garlic**
no stir-fry is complete without this heart helper

**vinegar | 5**
tart and tangy, it lowers a meal's GL

Orange Beef Stir-Fry with Broccoli and Red Pepper

# Flank Steak with Balsamic Sauce

**6**
Serves

| Preparation time: 20 minutes |
| --- |
| Marinating time: 2 hours |
| Cooking time: 12 to 14 minutes |

One of the leaner beef cuts, flank steak is an excellent choice when you're craving a steak dinner. It is economical, has lots of flavor, and becomes nice and tender when marinated. Since you slice the steak before serving, it's easy to control portion sizes. In this recipe, the zesty marinade is transformed into a rich-tasting sauce. We use a ridged grill pan or skillet, but you can also cook the steak on an outdoor grill or broil it. *See photo on page 245.*

1/3 cup orange juice or port

1/4 cup balsamic **vinegar**

1 teaspoon Worcestershire sauce

1 tablespoon chopped fresh thyme or 1 teaspoon dried thyme

2 **garlic** cloves, minced

1/2 teaspoon salt, or to taste

Freshly ground black pepper to taste

1 1/2 pounds (700 grams) **flank steak**, trimmed

2 tablespoons finely chopped **shallot** (1 large)

1 teaspoon **olive oil**

2 teaspoons unsalted butter

**1.** In a small bowl, whisk together the orange juice (or port), vinegar, Worcestershire sauce, thyme, garlic, salt, and pepper. Place the steak in a shallow glass dish, pour on the orange juice mixture, and turn to coat. Cover and refrigerate for at least 2 hours or up to 8 hours, turning several times.

**2.** Remove the steak from the marinade and pour the marinade into a small saucepan. Add the shallots and set aside. Brush a ridged grill pan or heavy skillet with oil and place over medium-high heat. Add the steak to the pan and,

depending on thickness, cook for 6 to 7 minutes per side for medium-rare, or until it reaches the desired doneness. Transfer to a cutting board and let stand for 5 minutes.

**3.** Meanwhile, bring the marinade to a boil over medium-high heat and cook until reduced to 1/3 cup, 3 to 5 minutes. Remove from the heat, add the butter, and whisk until melted.

**4.** Slice the steak thinly across the grain. Add any accumulated juices on the cutting board to the sauce and serve the sauce with the steak. One serving is 3 ounces (85 grams) steak and 1 tablespoon sauce. Leftover steak will keep, covered, in the refrigerator for up to 2 days.

**Per serving:** 196 calories, 25 g protein, 4 g carbohydrates, 0 g fiber, 8 g total fat, 3 g saturated fat, 41 mg cholesterol, 269 mg sodium.

# Slow-Cooker Beef and Vegetable Stew

**8**
Serves

| Preparation time: 30 minutes |
| --- |
| Cooking time: 15 minutes on the stovetop, then 4 to 4 1/2 hours in the slow cooker on high or 7 to 8 hours on low |

The trick to making a healthful, hearty meat stew is to include lots of vegetables and make a generous amount of full-bodied, low-fat gravy. You can't whip up this stew on a busy evening, so plan to make it on the weekend. It keeps well and tastes even better the next day.

1 1/2 pounds (700 grams) cubed boneless **beef** chuck (1 1/2-inch/4-centimeter cubes), trimmed

1/2 teaspoon freshly ground black pepper

1/4 teaspoon salt, or to taste

1 tablespoon **olive oil**

1 medium **onion,** chopped (1 cup)

2 tablespoons all-purpose flour

4 **garlic** cloves, minced

1 cup dry red wine

1 can (14 1/2 ounces/398 milliliters) diced **tomatoes,** undrained

3/4 cup reduced-sodium chicken broth

1 teaspoon Worcestershire sauce

1 1/2 teaspoons dried thyme

2 bay leaves

2 cups peeled baby **carrots**
(10 ounces/280 grams), rinsed

2 medium white turnips, peeled and cut into
bite-size chunks (2 cups)

1 1/2 cups frozen pearl **onions** (6 ounces/170 grams)

1/4 cup chopped fresh parsley

1. Pat the beef dry with paper towels and sprinkle with the pepper and salt. Heat 2 teaspoons oil in a large nonstick skillet over medium-high heat. Add half of the beef and cook, turning with tongs occasionally, until browned, 3 to 5 minutes, then transfer to a plate. Repeat with the remaining beef and transfer to the plate.

2. Add the remaining 1 teaspoon oil to the skillet. Add the chopped onion and cook, stirring frequently, until softened and lightly browned, 1 to 2 minutes. Add the flour and garlic and cook, stirring, for 30 seconds to 1 minute. Add the wine and bring to a boil, stirring to scrape up any browned bits from the skillet. Add the tomatoes and mash with a potato masher. Stir in the broth, Worcestershire sauce, thyme, and bay leaves and bring to a simmer.

3. Place the beef in 4-quart (4-liter) slow cooker and spoon on half of the tomato mixture. Place the carrots and turnips on top of the sauce, then top with the remaining tomato mixture. Cover and cook until the beef and vegetables are very tender, 4 to 4 1/2 hours on high or 7 to 8 hours on low.

4. Shortly before the stew is ready, cook the pearl onions according to package directions, then add to the stew. Discard the bay leaves and sprinkle with the parsley. One serving is 1 cup.

**Per serving:** 235 calories, 21 g protein, 14 g carbohydrates, 3 g fiber, 8 g total fat, 3 g saturated fat, 42 mg cholesterol, 371 mg sodium.

VARIATIONS

## Lamb Stew with Spring Vegetables

In Step 1, substitute 1 1/2 pounds (700 grams) cubed boneless lamb leg meat, trimmed, for the beef. In Step 2, substitute 1 cup dry white wine for the red wine and 2 tablespoons chopped fresh rosemary for the thyme. In Step 3, omit the turnips. In Step 4, cook 1 1/2 cups frozen pearl onions and 1 1/2 cups frozen peas separately according to package directions, then add to the stew.

## Pork Stew with Latin Flavors

In Step 1, substitute 1 1/2 pounds (700 grams) cubed boneless pork (choose a leg cut, also called fresh ham, rather than shoulder, which is higher in fat), trimmed, for the beef. In Step 2, substitute 1 cup lager beer for the wine and 1 can (14 1/2 ounces/398 milliliters) mild green chile–seasoned tomatoes for the diced tomatoes. Substitute 1 1/2 teaspoons ground cumin and 3/4 teaspoon dried oregano for the thyme and bay leaves. In Step 3, omit the carrots and turnips; instead use 1 medium sweet potato, peeled and cut into 1- by 3/4-inch (2.5- by 2-centimeter) chunks. In Step 4, cook 1 1/2 cups frozen pearl onions and 1 1/2 cups frozen corn niblets according to package directions, then add to the stew. Substitute 1/4 cup chopped fresh cilantro for the parsley. Serve with lime wedges and hot sauce.

# Beef and Veggie Meat Loaf

**8** Serves | **Preparation time: 20 minutes**
**Baking time: 1 hour, 5 minutes to 1 hour, 20 minutes**

An old-fashioned favorite gets a new lease on life with this Magic meat loaf makeover. We stretched the ground beef with grated carrots and zucchini, reducing the saturated fat, boosting the vegetable quota, and adding moisture. Whole grain rolled oats play the role of filler and help keep the meat loaf tender. If you're running late and can't wait for the meat loaf to bake, divide the meat mixture among 8 muffin cups coated with cooking spray and bake for about 30 minutes.

1 pound (450 grams) 93–95% extra-lean ground **beef** (ground round)

3/4 cup old-fashioned rolled **oats**

1 cup chopped **onion** (1 medium)

1 cup shredded **carrots** (2–4 medium)

1 cup shredded **zucchini** (1 small)

1 large **egg,** lightly beaten

2 large **egg** whites, lightly beaten

2 tablespoons ketchup

1 tablespoon Worcestershire sauce

2 teaspoons Dijon mustard

1 teaspoon dried thyme

3/4 teaspoon salt

1/2 teaspoon freshly ground black pepper

1. Preheat the oven to 350°F (180°C). Line an 8 x 4- or 9 x 5-inch (20 x 10- or 23 x 12-centimeter) loaf pan with foil, leaving a 1-inch (2.5-centimeter) overhang along the two long sides. Coat the foil with cooking spray.

2. In a large bowl, combine the beef, oats, onion, carrots, zucchini, egg, egg whites, 1 tablespoon ketchup, Worcestershire sauce, mustard, thyme, salt, and pepper and mix well. Transfer to the pan and press into a loaf. Spread the remaining 1 tablespoon ketchup over the top.

3. Place the pan on a baking sheet and bake for 1 hour. Drain off the fat, then bake until firm and an instant-read thermometer inserted in the center registers 165°F (75°C), 5 to 20 minutes, depending on the depth of the pan you're using. Drain off the fat and let the meat loaf stand for 5 minutes. Use the foil overhang to lift it out and transfer to a cutting board, then slice. One serving is 4 ounces (125 grams). Leftover meat loaf will keep, covered, in the refrigerator for up to 2 days.

**Per serving:** 165 calories, 19 g protein, 11 g carbohydrates, 2 g fiber, 5 g total fat, 2 g saturated fat, 68 mg cholesterol, 380 mg sodium.

# Greek Pasta and Beef Casserole

**8** Serves | **Preparation time: 50 minutes**
**Baking time: 40 to 50 minutes**

Known as pastitsio, this hearty Greek casserole serves up layers of creamy noodles separated by cinnamon-scented meat sauce. Like its Italian cousin, lasagna, it's an ideal make-ahead meal (assemble it through Step 5, then cover and refrigerate for up to 2 days). While there are several parts to this lightened version, none is difficult to make, and you can break up the workload by preparing the meat sauce a day ahead (it's also delicious on its own, tossed with whole wheat pasta).

## MEAT SAUCE

12 ounces (340 grams) 93–95% lean ground **beef** (ground round)

2 teaspoons **olive oil**

2 cups chopped **onion** (1 large)

3 **garlic** cloves, minced

1 1/2 teaspoons dried oregano

1 teaspoon ground **cinnamon**

1/2 teaspoon sugar

1/4 teaspoon salt, or to taste

1/2 cup dry white wine or reduced-sodium
   chicken broth

1 can (14 1/2 ounces/398 milliliters) no-salt-added
   diced **tomatoes,** with liquid

1/4 cup **tomato** paste

1/4 cup chopped fresh parsley

Freshly ground black pepper to taste


MACARONI AND CHEESE SAUCE

2 1/2 cups 1% **milk**

1/3 cup all-purpose flour

1 large **egg**

2 large **egg** whites

1 cup fat-free cottage **cheese**

1 cup grated Swiss **cheese**
   (3 ounces/85 grams)

1/4 teaspoon ground nutmeg

1/4 teaspoon salt, or to taste

Freshly ground black pepper to taste

8 ounces (250 grams) **whole wheat elbow
   macaroni** (2 cups) (see Ingredient Note)

1/4 cup grated Parmesan **cheese**
   (1/2 ounce/15 grams)


1. Preheat the oven to 400°F (200°C). Coat a
9 x 13-inch (23 x 35-centimeter) baking dish with
cooking spray. Bring a large pot of water to a boil.

2. **To make the meat sauce:** Cook the beef in
a medium nonstick skillet over medium-high
heat, crumbling with a wooden spoon, until
browned, 3 to 4 minutes. Drain in a colander
set over a bowl.

3. Heat the oil in a Dutch oven over medium
heat. Add the onion and cook, stirring frequently,
until softened, 3 to 4 minutes. Add the garlic,
oregano, cinnamon, sugar, and salt and cook,
stirring, for 30 seconds. Add the wine (or broth)
and bring to a simmer. Add the tomatoes and

mash with a potato masher. Return to a simmer
and stir in the tomato paste and beef. Reduce the
heat to medium-low, partially cover, and simmer,
stirring occasionally, for 20 minutes. Stir in the
parsley and pepper.

4. **To make the macaroni and cheese sauce:**
In a small bowl, whisk 1/2 cup milk and the flour
until smooth. Heat the remaining 2 cups milk
in a medium saucepan over medium heat until
steaming. Add the flour mixture and cook,
whisking constantly, until the sauce bubbles and
thickens, 3 to 4 minutes. Remove from the heat.
In a small bowl, blend the egg and egg whites
with a fork, then gradually whisk into the sauce.
Stir in the cottage cheese, Swiss cheese, nutmeg,
salt, and pepper.

5. Add the macaroni to the boiling water and
cook for 4 1/2 minutes, then drain and rinse
under cold running water (the macaroni will
continue to cook during baking). Transfer to a
large bowl, add the cheese sauce, and toss to
coat. Spread half of the pasta mixture in the
baking dish, then spread the meat sauce on top.
Top with the remaining pasta mixture and
sprinkle with the cheese.

6. Bake, uncovered, until the top is golden and
the casserole is bubbling, 40 to 50 minutes. Let
stand for 5 minutes before serving. One serving
is 1/8 of the casserole (about 1 1/4 cups).
Leftovers will keep, covered, in the refrigerator
for up to 2 days.

**Per serving:** 390 calories, 31 g protein, 40 g carbohydrates,
4 g fiber, 11 g total fat, 5 g saturated fat, 85 mg cholesterol,
440 mg sodium.

**Ingredient Note:** Look for Barilla Plus elbow
macaroni, which is higher in fiber, protein, and
omega-3 fatty acids than regular pasta.

# Mustard-Crusted Lamb Chops

**4** Serves

| | |
|---|---|
| **Preparation time:** 15 minutes | |
| **Marinating time:** 30 minutes | |
| **Cooking time:** 10 minutes | |

A full-flavored marinade of grainy mustard, rosemary, and garlic brings out the best in delicate lamb chops and forms an appealing crust during grilling. You can also use the marinade for lamb kebabs or increase the proportions for a grilled or roasted leg of lamb.

3 tablespoons coarse-grain mustard

2 tablespoons chopped fresh rosemary

2 tablespoons red-wine **vinegar**

1 tablespoon extra-virgin **olive oil**

1/2 teaspoon Worcestershire sauce

4 **garlic** cloves, minced

1/4 teaspoon salt

Freshly ground black pepper to taste

8 loin **lamb** chops (3 ounces/85 grams each), trimmed

1. In a shallow glass dish, whisk the mustard, rosemary, vinegar, oil, Worcestershire sauce, garlic, salt, and pepper until blended. Add the lamb chops and turn to coat well. Cover and refrigerate for at least 30 minutes or up to 4 hours.

2. Preheat the grill or broiler.

3. Lightly oil the grill or broiler rack by rubbing a piece of oil-soaked paper towel over the surface. Grill or broil the lamb chops for 4 to 5 minutes per side for medium-rare, or until they reach the desired doneness. One serving is 2 chops (about 3 ounces/85 grams boneless meat total).

**Per serving:** 247 calories, 19 g protein, 1 g carbohydrates, 0 g fiber, 18 g total fat, 7 g saturated fat, 70 mg cholesterol, 355 mg sodium.

# Pork Chop and Cabbage Skillet Dinner

**4** Serves

| | |
|---|---|
| **Preparation time:** 20 minutes | |
| **Cooking time:** 20 minutes | |

A pork chop dinner usually involves an oversize portion of fatty meat. But if you use thin-cut boneless chops (about 1/2 inch/1 centimeter thick), you can ensure an appropriate portion size and get the protein benefits of lean meat. Teamed with low-calorie cabbage, the chops make a hearty dinner in just minutes. To trim the preparation time, use the food processor slicing disk to slice the onion, carrot, and cabbage or substitute 5 1/2 cups prepared coleslaw mix for the cabbage and carrots. *See photo on page 245.*

1 teaspoon dried thyme

1/4 teaspoon salt

1/4 teaspoon freshly ground black pepper, plus more to taste

1 pound (450 grams) thin-cut boneless **pork** chops, trimmed

1 tablespoon canola oil

1 cup sliced **onion** (1 medium)

5 cups shredded green **cabbage** (1/2 medium head)

1/2 cup sliced **carrots** (2 medium)

1 can (14 ounces/284 milliliters) reduced-sodium chicken broth (1 3/4 cups)

2 teaspoons coarse-grain mustard

1 teaspoon apple cider **vinegar**

1. In a small bowl, combine the thyme, salt, and pepper. Rub the mixture over the pork chops. Heat 2 teaspoons oil in a large nonstick skillet over medium heat. Add the chops and cook until browned and just cooked through, 2 to 3 minutes per side. Transfer to a plate, cover loosely with foil, and keep warm.

**2.** Add the remaining 1 teaspoon oil to the skillet. Add the onion and cook over medium heat, stirring frequently, until softened, 1 to 2 minutes. Add the cabbage and carrots and cook, stirring, until the cabbage is wilted, about 2 minutes. Add the broth and 3/4 cup water and bring to a simmer. Cover and cook until the cabbage is tender, 10 to 15 minutes. Stir in the mustard and vinegar and season with pepper. Serve the pork chops over the cabbage mixture. One serving is 3 ounces (85 grams) pork and 3/4 cup vegetables.

Per serving: 224 calories, 24 g protein, 9 g carbohydrates, 3 g fiber, 10 g total fat, 2 g saturated fat, 57 mg cholesterol, 564 mg sodium.

# Spice-Crusted Pork Tenderloin with Peach Salsa

**4** | Preparation time: 35 minutes
Serves | Cooking time: 20–25 minutes

Peaches, one of the sweet Magic foods, are not just for desserts. Try them in this lively salsa, which sets off lean pork tenderloin beautifully. If you prefer to roast the pork, brown the tenderloin in 1 teaspoon vegetable oil in a skillet for 2 to 4 minutes, then transfer to a baking sheet and roast in a 400°F (200°C) oven for 15 to 20 minutes.

SALSA

1 cup diced peeled **peach** (1 large)
 (see Tip on page 234)

1/2 cup diced red bell pepper (1/2 small)

1/4 cup chopped **scallions** (2 medium)

2 tablespoons minced seeded jalapeño chile pepper
 (1 medium)

2 tablespoons **lime** juice

1 tablespoon chopped fresh cilantro

Pinch of salt

PORK

2 teaspoons ground cumin

1 teaspoon brown sugar

1 teaspoon paprika

1/2 teaspoon ground **cinnamon**

1/2 teaspoon ground ginger

1/2 teaspoon salt, or to taste

1/4 teaspoon freshly ground black pepper

1 teaspoon canola oil

1 pound (450 grams) **pork** tenderloin, trimmed

**1.** Preheat the grill.

**2. To make the salsa:** In a medium bowl, combine the peach, bell pepper, scallions, jalapeño pepper, lime juice, cilantro, and salt and toss to mix well.

**3. To make the pork:** In a small bowl, combine the cumin, brown sugar, paprika, cinnamon, ginger, salt, and pepper. Add the oil and mix well. Rub the spice paste over the pork.

**4.** Lightly oil the grill rack by rubbing it with a piece of oil-soaked paper towel. Grill the pork, covered, over medium heat, turning occasionally, until it reaches an internal temperature of 155°F (65°C), 20 to 25 minutes. Transfer to a cutting board and let stand for 5 minutes. Cut into slices 1/2 inch (1 centimeter) thick. One serving is 3 ounces (85 grams) pork (about 4 slices) and 1/3 cup salsa.

Per serving: 178 calories, 25 g protein, 7 g carbohydrates, 2 g fiber, 6 g total fat, 1 g saturated fat, 74 mg cholesterol, 388 mg sodium.

Ingredient Note: When working with chile peppers, wear rubber or latex gloves to protect your hands from the irritating oils. Keep your hands away from your eyes.

# POULTRY

## Chicken Breasts with Peaches and Ginger

**4**
Serves

Preparation time: 25 minutes

Cooking time: 10 to 12 minutes

Squeezing more fruit into your diet has never been simpler or more delicious. Here, sweet peaches, accented with fresh ginger, dress up a simple chicken sauté. The vinegar in the sauce balances the flavors and helps lower your blood sugar response to the meal. In winter, you can substitute 1 cup frozen peaches for the fresh peach. *See photo on page 244.*

1 bunch **scallions,** trimmed

1 pound (450 grams) boneless skinless **chicken** breast halves, trimmed

1/4 teaspoon salt, or to taste

Freshly ground black pepper to taste

2 teaspoons canola oil

3 tablespoons apple cider **vinegar**

2 tablespoons sugar

1/2 cup no-sugar-added peach juice or nectar, or apple juice

2 tablespoons grated fresh ginger

1 1/4 cups reduced-sodium chicken broth

1 large **peach,** peeled (see Tip) and sliced (1/2-inch/1-centimeter wedges)

2 teaspoons cornstarch

2 teaspoons water

1. Chop the scallions, reserving all of the white portions and 1/4 cup of the green portions separately.

2. If the chicken pieces are large, cut them in half lengthwise so that you have at least 4 pieces. Place the chicken between 2 pieces of plastic wrap and pound with a rolling pin or meat mallet into a 1/2-inch (1-centimeter) thickness. Season with the salt and pepper.

3. Heat the oil in a large nonstick skillet over medium-high heat. Add the chicken and cook until browned and no longer pink in the center, 3 to 3 1/2 minutes per side. Transfer to a plate.

4. Add the vinegar and sugar to the skillet. Stir to dissolve the sugar. Cook, swirling the skillet, until the syrup turns dark amber, 30 to 60 seconds. Add the scallion whites, peach juice, and ginger. Bring to a boil, stirring to scrape up any caramelized bits in the skillet. Cook for 1 minute. Add the broth and peaches. Return to a boil. Cook, turning the peaches from time to time, until tender, 2 to 4 minutes. Mix the cornstarch and water. Add to sauce. Cook, stirring, until slightly thickened, about 30 seconds. Reduce the heat to low and return the chicken and any accumulated juices to the skillet. Simmer gently until the chicken is heated through, about 1 minute. Garnish with the reserved scallion greens.

**Per serving:** 223 calories, 28 g protein, 17 g carbohydrates, 1 g fiber, 4 g total fat, 1 g saturated fat, 67 mg cholesterol, 275 mg sodium.

Tips:

• To peel peaches, dip them in boiling water for 20 to 30 seconds to loosen skins. Remove with a slotted spoon and let cool slightly. Slip off skins with a paring knife.

• Pounding the chicken breasts to make them thinner ensures quick, even cooking. And, by cutting super-size chicken breasts in half and then pounding them, you can ensure appropriate portion sizes. If you purchase thin-cut chicken breasts, you can skip this step.

### VARIATION

Substitute 1 large nectarine or 2 plums for the peach. There's no need to peel either of these fruits.

# Chicken Sauté with Apple

**4 Serves** | **Preparation time: 20 minutes**
| **Cooking time: 15 minutes**

This simple chicken sauté features delectable morsels of boneless chicken and a generous amount of luxurious sauce that tastes deceptively rich, thanks to tart, fresh apples and a small amount of reduced-fat sour cream.

1 pound (450 grams) **chicken** tenders, trimmed, or 1 pound (450 grams) boneless skinless chicken breasts, trimmed and cut into 1/2-inch (1-centimeter)-thick slices

1/8 teaspoon salt, or to taste

Freshly ground pepper to taste

1 teaspoon **olive oil**

1 medium **apple,** peeled, cored, and sliced (prepare just before cooking)

1/4 cup finely chopped **shallot** (1 large)

3/4 teaspoon dried thyme

1/2 cup apple cider or apple juice

1 1/4 cups reduced-sodium chicken broth

1 1/2 teaspoons cornstarch

2 teaspoons water

1/4 cup reduced-fat sour cream

2 teaspoons coarse-grain mustard

1 tablespoon chopped fresh parsley or chives

1. Season the chicken with salt and pepper. Heat 2 teaspoons of the oil in a large nonstick skillet over medium-high heat. Add the chicken and cook, turning from time to time, until browned and no longer pink in the center, 5 to 6 minutes. Transfer to a plate, cover loosely with foil, and keep warm. (Do not wash the skillet.)

2. Add the remaining 1 teaspoon of oil to the skillet. Add the apple, shallot, and thyme. Cook, stirring often, until apple is lightly browned, 2 to 3 minutes. Add the apple cider (or apple juice) and bring to a boil, stirring to scrape up any browned bits. Cook for 1 1/2 minutes. Add the broth and return to a boil. Cook for 3 minutes.

3. Mix the cornstarch and water in a small bowl. Add to the sauce and cook, stirring, until slightly thickened. Reduce heat to low. Add the sour cream and mustard. Whisk until smooth. Return the chicken and any accumulated juices to the skillet and simmer just until heated through, about 1 minute. Garnish with parsley (or chives). One serving is 1 cup.

**Per serving:** 322 calories, 20 g protein, 31 g carbohydrates, 2 g fiber, 13 g total fat, 4 g saturated fat, 52 mg cholesterol, 706 mg sodium.

# All-New Chicken Cordon Bleu

**4 Serves** | **Preparation time: 25 minutes**
| **Cooking time: 22 minutes**

Crispy chicken breasts with a surprise nugget of cheesy filling are a family favorite. This version trims fat and calories by avoiding deep-frying. Instead, the chicken is browned on one side in a skillet and then finished in a hot oven, producing a crisp crust, without all the fat and fuss. If you would like to get things ready ahead of time, prepare the recipe through Step 4. Cover and refrigerate for up to 8 hours.

1/4 cup shredded Swiss, Monterey Jack, or part-skim mozzarella **cheese**

2 tablespoons chopped boiled or baked lean deli ham

1 tablespoon low-fat mayonnaise

2 teaspoons Dijon mustard

1/8 teaspoon freshly ground pepper

4 boneless skinless **chicken** breast halves (1 to 1 1/2 pounds/450 to 700 grams total), trimmed

1/2 cup Italian-style dry bread crumbs

1 large **egg** white

2 teaspoons **olive oil**

1. Preheat the oven to 400°F (200°C). Coat a baking sheet with nonstick spray.

2. Mix the cheese, ham, mayonnaise, mustard, and pepper in a small bowl.

3. Using a small sharp knife, make a horizontal slit along the thinner, long edge of a chicken breast half, cutting nearly through to the opposite side. Open up the breast and place about 1 tablespoon of the cheese mixture in the center. Close the breast over the filling and press the edges firmly together to seal. Repeat with the remaining chicken breast halves and cheese mixture.

4. Place the bread crumbs in a shallow glass dish. Lightly beat the egg white with a fork in a medium bowl. Holding each stuffed chicken breast together, dip them in the egg white, then dredge in the bread crumbs. (Discard any leftover bread crumbs.)

5. Heat the oil in a large nonstick skillet over medium-high heat. Add the chicken breasts and cook until browned on one side, about 2 minutes. Using tongs, place chicken breasts, browned side up, on the baking sheet.

6. Bake the chicken until no longer pink in the center, about 20 minutes. An instant-read thermometer inserted in the center should register 170°F (75°C). One serving is 1 stuffed chicken breast half.

**Per serving**: 260 calories, 32 g protein, 11 g carbohydrates, 1 g fiber, 9 g total fat, 3 g saturated fat, 76 mg cholesterol, 607 mg sodium.

---

**VARIATION** Chicken Breasts Stuffed with Pesto

In Step 2, substitute 2 tablespoons reduced-fat cream cheese and 1 tablespoon prepared basil pesto for the Swiss cheese, ham, mayonnaise, and mustard. Blend the cream cheese, pesto, and pepper together in a small bowl with a fork.

# Chicken Pot Pie with a Whole Grain Biscuit Crust

**5** Serves | Preparation time: 1 hour
Baking time: 30 to 40 minutes

Everyone loves chicken pot pie, but it's a killer when it comes to calories. We've topped ours with a tender, low-fat crust and included a generous serving of vegetables bathed in a light but still-creamy sauce. Bake this whenever you have cooked poultry or a store-bought rotisserie chicken on hand. If you are cooking for a crowd, double the recipe and use a 9 x 13-inch (23 x 33-centimeter) baking dish. To trim preparation time, purchase cleaned, sliced mushrooms and sliced carrots (fresh or frozen).

FILLING

2 teaspoons canola oil

3 cups sliced white mushrooms (8 ounces/250 grams)

1 1/4 cups sliced **carrots**

1/4 cup all-purpose flour

2 1/4 cups reduced-sodium chicken broth or turkey broth, divided

1/4 cup reduced-fat sour cream

1 1/2 teaspoons freshly grated lemon zest

1/8 teaspoon salt, or to taste

1/8 teaspoon freshly ground pepper

2 cups diced, cooked skinless **chicken** (11 ounces/325 grams)

1 1/4 cups frozen green **peas,** rinsed under cold water to thaw

CRUST

1 cup **whole wheat pastry flour** (see Ingredient Note)

1 teaspoon sugar

3/4 teaspoon baking powder

1/4 teaspoon baking soda

1/8 teaspoon salt

4 tablespoons (2 ounces/60 grams) cold, reduced-fat cream **cheese** (Neufchâtel), cut into small pieces

1 tablespoon cold unsalted butter, cut into small pieces

1 tablespoon canola oil

About 1/3 cup low-fat buttermilk

1 teaspoon low-fat (1%) **milk** for brushing

1. Preheat the oven to 400°F (200°C). Coat an 8-inch (20-centimeter) square (or similar 2-quart/2-liter) baking dish with cooking spray.

2. **To make the filling:** Heat the oil in a large nonstick skillet over medium-high heat. Add the mushrooms and cook, stirring or shaking the skillet from time to time, until browned and tender, 5 to 7 minutes. Steam the carrots until just tender, 3 to 5 minutes. Rinse with cold running water.

3. Whisk the all-purpose flour with 1/2 cup cold broth in a small bowl until smooth. Bring the remaining 1 3/4 cups broth to a simmer in a medium saucepan over medium-high heat. Gradually whisk in the flour mixture. Cook, whisking, until the sauce boils and thickens. Reduce the heat to low and simmer for 1 minute. Remove from the heat and whisk in the sour cream, lemon zest, salt, and pepper. Stir in the chicken, peas, mushrooms, and carrots. Scrape into the baking dish, spreading evenly.

4. **To make the crust:** Whisk the flour, sugar, baking powder, baking soda, and salt in a large bowl until blended. Using a pastry blender or 2 knives, cut in the cream cheese and butter until the mixture resembles coarse crumbs. Add the oil and toss with a fork to blend. With a fork, stir in just enough of the buttermilk until a soft, slightly sticky dough forms. Turn out onto a lightly floured surface and knead several times, just until smooth. Pat or roll the dough into a rough 9 x 7-inch (23 x 18-centimeter) rectangle, about 1/2 inch (1 centimeter) thick. With a sharp knife, cut the dough in half lengthwise, then cut each half into 5 triangles, trimming as needed. Arrange the biscuit triangles over the filling. Brush the tops with milk.

5. Bake the pie until the filling is bubbly and the biscuits are golden and firm, 30 to 40 minutes. One serving equals 1 cup filling and 2 biscuit triangles. You can prepare the filling ahead through Step 3. (Chill the sauce before mixing with the vegetables and chicken.) Cover and refrigerate for up to 1 day.

**Per serving:** 390 calories, 28 g protein, 43 g carbohydrates, 8 g fiber, 12 g total fat, 4 g saturated fat, 58 mg cholesterol, 706 mg sodium.

**Tip:** Cutting the biscuit dough into triangles, rather than the traditional circles, allows you to cover a square baking dish efficiently, minimizing waste.

**Ingredient Note:** Whole wheat pastry flour is lower in protein than regular whole wheat flour. Since it has less gluten-forming potential, it is an excellent choice for tender baked goods. You can find it in large supermarkets and natural foods stores.

## VARIATION Turkey Pot Pie with a Whole Grain Biscuit Crust

In Step 3, substitute diced skinless turkey breast for the chicken.

# Oven-Fried Chicken

**4** Serves

| Preparation time: 20 minutes |
| Marinating time: 30 minutes |
| Baking time: 40 to 50 minutes |

This simple chicken recipe, loaded with Magic extras like mustard (it contains vinegar, a Magic food) and sesame seeds, makes a great family meal. Marinating the chicken in buttermilk keeps it moist and succulent, and a light coating of whole wheat flour, sesame seeds, and spices replaces the fatty chicken skin and forms an appealing crust during baking.

1/2 cup buttermilk

1 tablespoon Dijon mustard

2 **garlic** cloves, minced

1 teaspoon hot red pepper sauce, such as Tabasco

2 1/2 –3 pounds (1.25 to 1.5 kilograms) bone-in **chicken** legs, skin removed, fat trimmed, thighs and drumsticks separated at the joint

1/2 cup **whole wheat flour**

2 tablespoons sesame **seeds**

1 1/2 teaspoons baking powder

1 1/2 teaspoons paprika

1 teaspoon dried thyme

Pinch of salt

Freshly ground pepper to taste

1. Whisk the buttermilk, mustard, garlic, and hot sauce in a shallow glass dish until well blended. Add the chicken and turn to coat. Cover and marinate in the refrigerator for at least 30 minutes or up to 8 hours.

2. Preheat the oven to 425°F (220°C). Line a baking sheet with aluminum foil. Set a wire rack on the baking sheet and coat it with non-stick spray.

3. Whisk the flour, sesame seeds, baking powder, paprika, thyme, salt, and pepper in a small bowl. Place the flour mixture in a paper bag or large plastic food bag. One at a time, place the chicken pieces in the bag and shake to coat. Shake off excess flour and place the chicken on the rack. (Discard any leftover flour mixture and marinade.) Spray the chicken pieces lightly with nonstick spray.

4. Bake the chicken until golden brown and no longer pink in the center, 40 to 50 minutes. An instant-read thermometer inserted in the center should register 180°F (85°C). One serving is 1 drumstick and 1 thigh.

**Per serving:** 227 calories, 34 g protein, 5 g carbohydrates, 1 g fiber, 7 g total fat, 2 g saturated fat, 130 mg cholesterol, 262 mg sodium.

# Roasted Moroccan Chicken Thighs with Squash and Pearl Onions

**4** Serves

| Preparation time: 25 minutes |
| Cooking time: 40 to 45 minutes |

Try this dinner from a roasting pan for a special meal that's easy to make and serve. Boneless skinless chicken thighs, which cook in the same time as the vegetables, are a convenient option for roasting. A flavorful spice rub gives them a faux skin, sealing in the juices and reducing the fat significantly.

1 pound (450 grams) peeled, seeded butternut squash, cut into 3/4-inch (2-centimeter) cubes (3 cups)

2 cups frozen pearl **onions,** rinsed in cold water to thaw

4 teaspoons **olive oil,** divided

1/2 teaspoon salt, divided

Freshly ground pepper to taste

2 teaspoons honey

2 teaspoons plus 1 tablespoon **lemon** juice, divided

2 teaspoons paprika

1/2 teaspoon ground cumin

1 pound (450 grams) boneless skinless **chicken** thighs, trimmed

12 fresh cilantro sprigs, plus 1/4 cup coarsely chopped cilantro

1 cup reduced-sodium chicken broth

1. Preheat the oven to 450°F (230°C). Coat a large roasting pan with nonstick spray.

2. Combine the squash, onions, 2 teaspoons oil, 1/4 teaspoon salt, and pepper in a large bowl. Toss to coat. Set aside.

3. Mix the remaining 2 teaspoons oil, the honey, and 2 teaspoons lemon juice in a small bowl until smooth. Add the paprika, cumin, remaining 1/4 teaspoon salt, and pepper. Rub this mixture over the chicken thighs.

4. Place the cilantro sprigs in the center of the roasting pan. Set the chicken thighs over the cilantro sprigs. Surround the chicken with the squash and onions. Bake, uncovered, until chicken is cooked through (an instant-read thermometer inserted in the center should register 180°F (85°C) and vegetables are tender, turning vegetables twice, 40 to 45 minutes. Transfer the chicken and vegetables to a platter or individual plates (leave cilantro sprigs in the roasting pan).

5. Add the chicken broth and remaining 1 tablespoon lemon juice to roasting pan and place over high heat. Bring to a simmer, stirring to scrape up any browned bits. Simmer for 1 minute. Strain the broth through a sieve into a medium bowl. Spoon pan sauce over chicken and vegetables. Sprinkle with chopped cilantro. One serving is 2 chicken thighs, 1 cup vegetables, and a few tablespoons pan sauce.

**Per serving:** 304 calories, 28 g protein, 27 g carbohydrates, 4 g fiber, 10 g total fat, 2 g saturated fat, 107 mg cholesterol, 447 mg sodium.

# Turkey-Noodle Casserole with Spinach

## 8
Serves

Preparation time: 40 minutes

Cooking/baking time: 50 to 60 minutes

Leftover turkey begs to be made into a creamy casserole. Ours is made with whole wheat pasta, a light, lemony sauce, and extra vegetables. This is an ideal dish to make ahead. Prepare the casserole through Step 3, cover and refrigerate for up to 2 days or freeze for up to 3 months (thaw before baking).

2 tablespoons plus 1 teaspoon **olive oil,** divided

1 medium **onion,** chopped

1/2 cup all-purpose flour

4 cups reduced-sodium chicken broth, heated

1/2 cup reduced-fat sour cream

2 teaspoons freshly grated lemon zest

1 tablespoon **lemon** juice

1/4 teaspoon salt, or to taste

Freshly ground pepper to taste

8 ounces (250 grams) whole wheat **pasta,** such as rotini or fusilli

2 cups sliced **carrots** (4 medium)

1 bag (12 ounces/300 grams) baby **spinach,** rinsed

3 cups diced cooked skinless **turkey** or **chicken** (12 ounces/340 grams)

1/2 cup grated Parmesan **cheese**

1/4 cup fine dry plain bread crumbs

1. Bring a large pot of lightly salted water to a boil. Preheat the oven to 400°F (200°C). Coat a 9 x 13-inch (23 x 33-centimeter) baking dish with nonstick spray.

2. Heat 2 tablespoons of the oil in a large saucepan over medium heat. Add the onion and cook, stirring often, until softened, 2 to 3 minutes. Add the flour and cook, stirring, for 30 to 60 seconds. Remove from the heat. Add the hot broth and whisk to blend. Place the saucepan

over medium-high heat and bring the sauce to a simmer, whisking constantly. Reduce the heat to low and simmer, whisking occasionally, until slightly thickened, about 5 minutes. Remove from the heat and whisk in the sour cream, lemon zest, lemon juice, salt, and pepper.

3. Add the pasta and carrots to the boiling water and cook for 5 minutes. Add the spinach and stir until wilted, 30 to 60 seconds. Drain the pasta and vegetables. Refresh under cold running water. (The pasta will seem quite firm but will continue to cook during baking.) Transfer the pasta mixture to a large bowl. Add the sauce and turkey. Toss to coat well. Scrape the mixture into the prepared baking dish, spreading evenly. Sprinkle with the Parmesan. Mix the bread crumbs and remaining 1 teaspoon oil in a small bowl and sprinkle over the casserole.

4. Bake the casserole, uncovered, until it is bubbly and the topping is lightly browned, 35 to 45 minutes. One serving is 1 1/3 cups.

Per serving: 333 calories, 23 g protein, 32 g carbohydrates, 6 g fiber, 9 g total fat, 3 g saturated fat, 42 mg cholesterol, 378 mg sodium.

# Honey-Mustard Turkey Burgers

4 Serves | Preparation time: 20 minutes
Cooking time: 10 to 12 minutes

Next time you're hankering for a burger, try this turkey burger. A little low-fat mayonnaise helps keep the patties moist, while mustard and honey perk up the flavor. When shopping for ground turkey, check labels. Regular ground turkey, made from breast and leg meat (and often skin), is almost as high in calories and fat as extra-lean ground beef. Ground turkey breast, on the other hand, is truly lean.

1/4 cup coarse-grain mustard

2 tablespoons honey

1 1/2 teaspoons Worcestershire sauce

1 pound (450 grams) lean ground **turkey** breast

1 tablespoon low-fat mayonnaise

1 **garlic** clove, minced

1/2 teaspoon salt, or to taste

1/4 teaspoon freshly ground pepper

4 **whole wheat hamburger rolls,** split

Optional garnishes: lettuce leaves, sliced tomato, sliced red or sweet onion, ketchup, reduced-fat mayonnaise

1. Stir the mustard, honey, and Worcestershire sauce together in a medium bowl. Reserve 2 tablespoons of this mixture to use as glaze. Add the ground turkey, mayonnaise, garlic, salt, and pepper to the mustard mixture remaining in the bowl. Mix with a potato masher. Divide the mixture into 4 portions, then form each one into a 1/2-inch (1-centimeter)-thick patty.

2. Preheat the grill to medium-high.

3. Lightly oil the grill rack by rubbing the surface with a piece of oil-soaked paper towel. Grill the patties for 4 minutes. Turn the patties over and brush the cooked sides with the reserved glaze. Cook for 4 minutes. Turn the patties over and brush again with the glaze. Cook until the juices run clear and an instant-read thermometer inserted in the center registers 165°F (70°C), 2 to 4 minutes longer. Just before the patties are cooked, place the rolls, cut side down, on the grill until lightly toasted, 30 to 60 seconds. Place a patty on each roll and garnish as desired. One serving is 1 patty and 1 roll.

Per serving (without garnishes): 331 calories, 28 g protein, 33 g carbohydrates, 2 g fiber, 11 g total fat, 3 g saturated fat, 65 mg cholesterol, 952 mg sodium.

# Turkey Shepherd's Pie with Sweet Potato Topping

**6** Serves

Preparation time: 45 minutes

Baking time: 35 to 40 minutes

A Magic version of an old-fashioned favorite, this shepherd's pie uses lean ground turkey instead of ground beef and sweet potatoes in place of white potatoes in the topping. The taste is reminiscent of a Thanksgiving dinner, but you can enjoy this easy-to-make pie throughout the year. To make it ahead, prepare through Step 4, cover and refrigerate for up to 2 days, then continue with the recipe.

## FILLING

1 1/4 pounds (600 grams) lean ground **turkey** breast

2 teaspoons **olive oil** or canola oil

1 cup chopped **onion** (1 medium)

1 cup chopped **carrots** (2–4 medium)

2 **garlic** cloves, minced

1 teaspoon dried thyme

1/3 cup all-purpose flour

2 1/4 cups reduced-sodium chicken broth

1 teaspoon Worcestershire sauce

1 cup frozen green **peas,** rinsed under cold water to thaw

Freshly ground pepper to taste

## TOPPING

2 medium-large **sweet potatoes,** peeled and cut into chunks

1/2 cup low-fat (1%) **milk**

1/2 teaspoon freshly grated lemon zest

3/4 teaspoon salt, or to taste

Freshly ground pepper to taste

**1.** Preheat the oven to 400°F (200°C). Coat an 11 x 7-inch (28 x 18-centimeter) or 9 x 13-inch (23 x 33-centimeter) baking dish with cooking spray.

**2. To make the filling:** Cook the turkey in a large nonstick skillet over medium-high heat, crumbling with a wooden spoon, until no longer pink, 4 to 5 minutes. Transfer to a plate.

**3.** Add 2 teaspoons oil to the skillet. Add the onion and carrots; cook over medium-high heat, stirring often, until softened, 2 to 4 minutes. Add the garlic and thyme; cook, stirring, for 30 seconds. Sprinkle in the flour and stir to coat well. Gradually stir in the broth and bring to a simmer, stirring. Return the turkey to the skillet and reduce the heat to medium. Partially cover and simmer, stirring occasionally, until the carrots are tender, about 10 minutes. Stir in the peas and Worcestershire sauce. Season with pepper. Transfer the turkey mixture to the baking dish.

**4. To prepare the topping:** Place the sweet potatoes in a large saucepan. Add enough lightly salted water to cover and bring to a simmer. Reduce the heat to medium, cover, and simmer until the sweet potatoes are tender, 10 to 15 minutes. Drain and return the sweet potatoes to the saucepan. Mash with a potato masher or portable electric mixer. Gradually stir or beat in the milk. Season with lemon zest, salt, and pepper. Spoon the sweet potato mixture over the turkey filling. Use the back of a spoon to cover the filling and make decorative swirls.

**5.** Bake the pie, uncovered, until the filling is bubbling and the topping is heated through, 35 to 40 minutes. One serving is 3/4 cup filling and 1/2 cup topping.

**Per serving:** 317 calories, 31 g protein, 43 g carbohydrates, 7 g fiber, 3 g total fat, 0 g saturated fat, 39 mg cholesterol, 656 mg sodium.

# Turkey Meatballs

**8 Serves**

Preparation time: 40 minutes

Cooking time: 40 to 50 minutes

Made with lean ground turkey breast, these tender meatballs provide protein without the baggage of saturated fat. The Magic cinnamon seasoning in the meatballs adds a delightful accent to the tomato sauce. Spaghetti and meatballs is a crowd-pleaser, ideal for serving a hungry crowd. But even if you are cooking for one or two, make a batch of meatballs and sauce and freeze it in portion-size containers. Serve over whole wheat spaghetti, allowing 2 ounces (60 grams) uncooked pasta per person, or use in sandwiches.

## SAUCE

2 teaspoons **olive oil**

4 **garlic** cloves, cut into thin slivers

1/2 teaspoon dried oregano

1/8 teaspoon crushed red pepper

3 cans (14 ounces/398 milliliters each) diced **tomatoes**

2 cans (8 ounces/213 milliliters each) no-salt-added **tomato** sauce

## MEATBALLS

1 pound (450 grams) lean ground **turkey** breast

1 cup fresh whole wheat bread crumbs (see Tip)

1 cup finely chopped **onion** (1 medium)

1 large **egg,** lightly beaten

1/3 cup grated Parmesan **cheese**

3/4 teaspoon salt, or to taste

1/2 teaspoon **cinnamon**

1/4 teaspoon freshly ground pepper

2 teaspoons **olive oil,** divided

2 tablespoons chopped fresh parsley

1. **To make the sauce:** Heat the oil in a Dutch oven over medium-low heat. Add the garlic, oregano, and red pepper. Cook, stirring, until softened but not browned, 1 to 2 minutes. Add the diced tomatoes and mash with a potato masher. Add the tomato sauce and bring to a simmer over medium-high heat. Reduce heat to medium-low, cover, and simmer while you prepare the meatballs.

2. **To make the meatballs:** Mix the ground turkey, bread crumbs, onion, egg, cheese, salt, cinnamon, and pepper thoroughly in a large bowl. Form into 1/2-inch (1-centimeter) meatballs.

3. Heat 1 teaspoon of the oil in a large nonstick skillet over medium-high heat. Add half of the meatballs and cook, turning occasionally, until browned on all sides. Transfer to a plate. Repeat with the remaining 1 teaspoon oil and meatballs. Add the browned meatballs to the simmering tomato sauce and simmer, covered, for 20 minutes. Uncover and simmer, stirring occasionally, until the meatballs are cooked through and the sauce has thickened slightly, 20 to 40 minutes longer. Sprinkle with parsley. One serving is 3 or 4 meatballs and 1 cup sauce. The meatballs and sauce will keep, covered, in the refrigerator for up to 2 days or in the freezer in an airtight container for up to 3 months (thaw in the refrigerator). Reheat on the stovetop or in the microwave.

**Per serving:** 184 calories, 19 g protein, 15 g carbohydrates, 3 g fiber, 5 g total fat, 1 g saturated fat, 52 mg cholesterol, 703 mg sodium.

**Tip:** To make fresh bread crumbs, tear fresh bread into pieces and place in a food processor or blender. Pulse until broken down into fine crumbs. Two slices of bread make 1 cup of crumbs.

# Turkey and Bean Chili with Avocado Salsa

**8** Serves

Preparation time: 35 minutes

Cooking time: 1 hour, 10 minutes

Beans, with their wallop of sugar-lowering soluble fiber, should be on your menu weekly, and this full-flavored chili's a great way to enjoy them. We lightened up the typical chili by using turkey instead of beef and gave it a Magic boost with avocado salsa, full of good fat. Offer a selection of garnishes, such as chopped scallions, lime wedges, hot sauce, reduced-fat sour cream, and grated low-fat cheese, so your family and guests can personalize their chili bowls. *See photo on page 244.*

## CHILI

12 ounces (340 grams) lean ground **turkey** breast

1/4 cup chili powder

1 tablespoon ground cumin

1 1/2 teaspoons dried oregano

2 teaspoons canola oil

2 cups chopped **onion** (1 large)

4 **garlic** cloves, minced

2 cans (4 1/2 ounces/127 milliliters each) chopped green chiles

1 can (28 ounces/796 milliliters) diced **tomatoes** (undrained)

1 can (14 ounces/398 milliliters) reduced-sodium chicken broth

1 can (19 ounces/540 milliliters) black **beans,** drained and rinsed

1 can (19 ounces/540 milliliters) red kidney **beans,** drained and rinsed

## AVOCADO SALSA

2 medium Hass **avocados,** diced

2/3 cup diced, seeded fresh **tomato** (1 medium plum tomato)

1/4 cup finely diced white or red **onion**

2 tablespoons minced seeded jalapeño pepper (1 small)

2 tablespoons chopped fresh cilantro

2 tablespoons **lime** juice

1/4 teaspoon salt, or to taste

1. Cook the ground turkey with the chili powder, cumin, and oregano in a large nonstick skillet over medium-high heat, breaking up the meat and mixing in spices with a wooden spoon, until browned, 4 to 5 minutes. Remove from the heat and set aside.

2. Heat the oil in a Dutch oven over medium heat. Add the onion and cook, stirring often, until softened, 3 to 5 minutes. Add the garlic and green chiles. Cook, stirring, until fragrant, 1 to 2 minutes. Add the tomatoes, broth, and browned ground turkey. Bring to a simmer. Reduce heat to low. Cover and simmer, stirring occasionally, for 45 minutes.

3. Stir in the black beans and kidney beans. Return to a simmer. Cover and simmer over low heat until flavors have blended, 15 to 20 minutes.

4. **To make the Avocado Salsa:** combine the avocado, tomato, onion, jalapeño, cilantro, lime juice, and salt in a medium bowl. Toss gently to mix.

5. Spoon 2 tablespoons of salsa on each serving of chili. One serving of chili is 1 1/4 cups chili and 2 tablespoons salsa. The chili will keep, covered, in the refrigerator for up to 2 days or in the freezer in an airtight container for up to 3 months.

**Per serving:** 327 calories, 23 g protein, 38 g carbohydrates, 12 g fiber, 11 g total fat, 1 g saturated fat, 17 mg cholesterol, 748 mg sodium.

Shrimp and Orzo Casserole *page 251*
olive oil • garlic • tomato • pasta • shrimp • cheese

Seared Fish Steaks with Tomato-Olive Sauce *page 246*
*Broccoli with Lemon Vinaigrette page 272*
lime • olive oil • halibut • onion • garlic • tomato • olive

Turkey and Bean Chili with Avocado Salsa *page 243*
turkey • onion • garlic • tomato • beans • avocado • lime

Chicken Breasts with Peaches and Ginger *page 234*
*Brown Rice Pilaf with Toasted Flaxseeds page 265*
scallion • chicken • vinegar • peach

Flank Steak with Balsamic Sauce *page 228*
*Moroccan Spiced Carrots page 274*
vinegar • garlic • steak • shallot • olive oil

Macaroni and Cheese with Spinach *page 255*
milk • cheese • spinach • pasta • wheat germ

Pork Chop and Cabbage Skillet Dinner *page 232*
pork • onion • cabbage • carrot • vinegar

Mushroom and Herb Pizza *page 258*
whole wheat flour • olive oil • garlic • cheese
• onion • tomato

# FISH AND SEAFOOD

## Seared Fish Steaks with Tomato-Olive Sauce

**4** Serves

| | |
|---|---|
| **Preparation time: 25 minutes** | |
| **Marinating time: 10 to 20 minutes** | |
| **Cooking/baking time: 10 to 12 minutes** | |

Firm fish like swordfish and halibut benefit from this easy two-step technique of first browning the steaks on one side and then finishing cooking in the oven (cooking the fish entirely in the skillet can make the outside tough and requires more fat). The spicy tomato sauce sets off the succulent fish steaks beautifully. *See photo on page 244.*

1 tablespoon **lime** juice

4 teaspoons **olive oil,** divided

1/8 teaspoon salt, or to taste

Freshly ground pepper to taste

4 1-inch (2.5-centimeter) thick **halibut** steaks (4 ounces/125 grams each) or **swordfish** steaks (6 ounces/170 grams each)

1/2 cup chopped **onion**

1 **garlic** clove, minced

1/2 teaspoon ground cumin

Pinch of crushed red pepper

1 can (10 ounces/398 milliliters) diced **tomatoes** with green chiles

1/3 cup water

1 tablespoon chopped pitted green **olives**

2 teaspoons drained capers, rinsed

**Lime** wedges

1. Preheat the oven to 425°F (220°C). Coat a baking sheet with nonstick spray.

2. Mix the lime juice, 1 teaspoon oil, salt, and pepper in a shallow glass dish. Add the fish steaks and turn to coat. Cover and marinate in the refrigerator for 10 to 20 minutes.

3. Meanwhile, heat 2 teaspoons oil in a medium saucepan over medium heat. Add the onion and cook, stirring often, until softened, 3 to 4 minutes. Add the garlic, cumin, and red pepper. Cook, stirring, for 30 seconds. Add the tomatoes and water. Bring to a simmer. Cook over medium heat, stirring occasionally, until thickened, about 10 minutes.

4. While sauce is simmering, cook the fish. Heat the remaining 1 teaspoon oil in a large nonstick skillet over medium-high heat. Add the fish and cook until browned on one side, 2 to 3 minutes. Transfer the fish to the baking sheet, browned side up. Bake until the fish is opaque in the center, 8 to 10 minutes.

5. Stir the olives and capers into the tomato sauce. Season with black pepper. Top each fish steak with sauce and serve with lime wedges. One serving is 1 fish steak and 1/4 cup sauce.

Per serving: 198 calories, 22 g protein, 6 g carbohydrates, 1 g fiber, 10 g total fat, 2 g saturated fat, 41 mg cholesterol, 551 mg sodium.

Tip: The tomato-olive sauce (Steps 2 and 5) is also delicious over grilled boneless skinless chicken breasts.

# Sole Florentine

**4** | Preparation time: 30 minutes
Serves | Cooking/baking time: 40 to 45 minutes

The term Florentine simply means "with spinach"—the perfect partner for a delicate fish like sole or haddock. The cheesy sauce in this recipe not only enhances the fish and spinach, it also provides calcium, vitamin D, and extra protein.

1 teaspoon freshly grated lemon zest

1 3/4 cups low-fat (1%) milk, divided

3 tablespoons all-purpose flour

1/2 cup grated Parmesan cheese, divided

1/4 teaspoon salt, or to taste

Freshly ground pepper to taste

Pinch of cayenne pepper

1 1/2 packages (10 ounces/300 grams each) frozen spinach

1 pound (450 grams) sole, haddock, flounder, or orange roughy fillets

2 teaspoons lemon juice

3 tablespoons Italian-style bread crumbs

1 teaspoon olive oil

1. Preheat the oven to 425°F (220°C). Coat an 8 x 11 1/2-inch (20 x 30-centimeter) baking dish (or similar 2-quart/2-liter capacity dish) with nonstick spray. Sprinkle the baking dish with lemon zest.

2. Whisk 1/4 cup of the cold milk and the flour in a small bowl until smooth. Heat the remaining 1 1/2 cups milk in a heavy medium saucepan over medium heat until steaming. Add the flour mixture and cook, whisking constantly, until the sauce bubbles and thickens, 2 to 3 minutes. Remove from the heat. Stir in 1/4 cup Parmesan, salt, pepper, and cayenne.

3. Meanwhile, cook the spinach according to package directions. Drain and refresh under cold running water. Press out excess moisture.

4. Spread the spinach over the bottom of the baking dish. Arrange the fish fillets, slightly overlapping, over the spinach. Sprinkle with the lemon juice. Spoon the cheese sauce evenly over the fish. Sprinkle the remaining 1/4 cup Parmesan over the sauce. Mix the bread crumbs and oil in a small bowl and sprinkle over the sauce.

5. Bake until golden and bubbly and the fish flakes when poked with a small sharp knife, 30 to 35 minutes.

Per serving: 278 calories, 35 g protein, 19 g carbohydrates, 4 g fiber, 8 g total fat, 3 g saturated fat, 70 mg cholesterol, 661 mg sodium.

# Mustard-Glazed Salmon with Lentils

**4** | Preparation time: 10 minutes
Serves | Cooking time: 12 to 15 minutes

It doesn't get much easier than this: canned lentil soup (drained so it has the consistency of braised lentils), topped with roasted salmon. This delightful pairing of two Magic foods is actually a French bistro classic, which translates seamlessly into healthy home cooking.

2 cans (19 ounces/540 milliliters each) lentil soup

1 pound (450 grams) salmon fillet, cut into 4 portions

Freshly ground pepper to taste

3 tablespoons coarse-grain or Dijon mustard

2 teaspoons olive oil

2/3 cup scallions, trimmed and chopped (1 bunch)

1/2 teaspoon dried thyme

1 tablespoon lemon juice

Lemon wedges

1. Preheat the oven to 450°F (230°C). Line a small baking pan with aluminum foil and coat it with nonstick spray.

2. Place the lentil soup in a sieve set over a bowl. Set aside to drain for several minutes.

3. Place the salmon, skin side down, in the baking pan. Season with pepper and spread with the mustard. Bake the salmon until opaque in the center, 12 to 15 minutes.

4. Meanwhile, heat the oil in a medium saucepan over medium heat. Add the scallions and cook, stirring, until softened, 1 to 2 minutes. Add the drained lentil soup and thyme. Heat through. Stir in the lemon juice. Spoon the lentils onto plates and top each serving with a piece of salmon. Garnish with lemon wedges. One serving is 3 ounces (85 grams) salmon and 2/3 cup lentils.

**Per serving**: 330 calories, 34 g protein, 28 g carbohydrates, 9 g fiber, 10 g total fat, 1 g saturated fat, 59 mg cholesterol, 981 mg sodium.

Tip: To cook salmon in the microwave, place in a microwave-safe dish, cover with wax paper, and microwave on high for 5 to 7 minutes.

# Salmon with Lemon and Dill Sauce

4 Serves | **Preparation time: 20 minutes**

**Baking time: 15 to 20 minutes**

Salmon is your best source of omega 3 fatty acids, which can actually *improve* insulin sensitivity, benefiting your blood sugar. Here is a foolproof way to prepare it. Baking salmon with a small amount of liquid and shallots produces exceptionally moist and succulent results. The creamy sauce, a lighter, much easier version of Hollandaise, is made with low-fat mayonnaise and brightened with fresh herbs and lemon.

SALMON

1 pound (450 grams) center-cut salmon fillet (about 1 1/4 inches/3 centimeters thick), cut into 4 portions

2 tablespoons dry white wine or water

2 tablespoons finely chopped shallots (1 medium)

1/4 teaspoon salt, or to taste

Freshly ground pepper to taste

Lemon wedges

SAUCE

1/4 cup reduced-fat mayonnaise

1/4 cup low-fat (1%) milk

2 tablespoons chopped fresh dill

1 teaspoon freshly grated lemon zest

1 tablespoon lemon juice

2 teaspoons Dijon mustard

1. Preheat the oven to 425°F (220°C). Coat a shallow baking dish, such as a 9-inch (23-centimeter) glass pie plate, with nonstick spray. Place the salmon pieces, skin side down, in the dish. Sprinkle with wine (or water), then sprinkle with shallots and season with salt and pepper. Cover with aluminum foil and bake until the salmon is opaque in center, 15 to 20 minutes.

**2.** **To make the sauce:** Place the mayonnaise in a small saucepan. Gradually whisk in the milk. Set the saucepan over medium-low heat and cook, whisking constantly, until mixture is smooth and heated through but not bubbling, about 2 minutes. Remove from the heat and stir in dill, lemon zest and juice, mustard, and pepper. Keep warm.

**3.** Divide the salmon among 4 plates. Pour the liquid remaining in the baking dish into the sauce and stir to mix. Spoon the sauce over the salmon and serve with lemon wedges. One serving is 3 ounces (85 grams) salmon and 2 tablespoons sauce.

Per serving: 250 calories, 23 g protein, 4 g carbohydrates, 0 g fiber, 14 g total fat, 3 g saturated fat, 68 mg cholesterol, 384 mg sodium.

# Warm Salmon Salad with Olive Toasts

**4** Serves

Preparation time: 25 minutes
Cooking time: 5 minutes

Chunks of pink salmon contrast beautifully with dark, leafy greens in this satisfying but light main-course salad, perfect for a warm summer evening. The olive oil dressing is sharpened with fresh lemon juice, which gives the salad an appealing kick and also dampens your blood sugar response to the meal. Crisp toasts, spread with appetite-teasing black olive spread, round out the salad. This is an excellent opportunity to enjoy the rye or pumpernickel bread that is recommended for Magic eating.

2 tablespoons plus 2 teaspoons extra-virgin **olive oil**

1 tablespoon plus 1/4 cup **lemon** juice

1/2 teaspoon Dijon mustard

1 **garlic** clove, minced

1/4 teaspoon salt, divided

Freshly ground pepper to taste

8 cups (5 ounces/140 grams) mesclun salad mix, rinsed and dried

4 slices **rye** or **pumpernickel bread**

1 pound (450 grams) **salmon** fillet, skin removed, cut into 1 1/4-inch (3-centimeter) chunks

1/2 cup finely chopped red **onion**

4 teaspoons drained capers, rinsed

2 tablespoons black **olive** spread (*olivada*) or tape-nade or finely chopped pitted kalamata olives

**1.** Combine 2 tablespoons of the oil, 1 table-spoon lemon juice, mustard, garlic, 1/8 teaspoon salt, and pepper in a small bowl or jar with a tight-fitting lid. Whisk or shake to blend. Place the salad mix in a large bowl. Drizzle with the lemon dressing and toss to coat well. Divide the salad among 4 plates. Toast the bread slices.

**2.** Season the salmon with the remaining 1/8 teaspoon salt and pepper. Heat 2 teaspoons of the oil in a large nonstick skillet over medium-high heat. Add the salmon and cook, turning several times, until browned, 3 to 4 minutes. Add the remaining 1/4 cup lemon juice, onion, and capers. Cook, shaking the skillet, until salmon is opaque in the center, 30 to 60 seconds. Spoon the salmon, onion, capers, and pan juices over the salads. Cut each slice of toast in half and spread with the olive paste (or chopped olives). Garnish each salad with 2 olive toasts. One serving is 2 cups of salad, 3 ounces (85 grams) salmon, and 1 slice of bread.

Per serving: 347 calories, 22 g protein, 9 g carbohydrates, 2 g fiber, 25 g total fat, 5 g saturated fat, 62 mg cholesterol, 399 mg sodium.

## VARIATION Warm Tuna Salad with Olive Toasts

In Step 2, substitute fresh tuna for the salmon.

# Shrimp and Scallop Stew

**4** | **Preparation time: 25 minutes**
Serves | **Cooking time: 15 minutes**

If you think seafood cookery is all about deep-frying, think again. This simple but elegant stew demonstrates how poaching keeps seafood moist and provides a flavorful base for the sauce. Cooking fish in wine is a method preferred by French chefs, but it is also a good idea for home cooks everywhere because the acids in the wine have blood sugar–control benefits. Although butter is at the top of The Magic Foods Pyramid, just a little goes a long way here in delivering a delicious finish.

2 teaspoons **olive oil**

1 cup sliced **leek** (1 large; white and light green part only)

1/2 cup dry white wine

3/4 cup reduced-sodium chicken broth

8 ounces (250 grams) medium **shrimp** (61/70 count), peeled and deveined

8 ounces (250 grams) **sea scallops,** halved (See Ingredient Note)

4 teaspoons butter, cut into small pieces

2 teaspoons freshly grated lemon zest

1/8 teaspoon salt, or to taste

Freshly ground black pepper to taste

Pinch of cayenne pepper

2 tablespoons coarsely chopped fresh tarragon or snipped fresh chives

1. Heat the oil in a deep sauté pan or Dutch oven over medium-low heat. Add the leek and cook until tender but not browned, 4 to 6 minutes. (Add 1 tablespoon water, if necessary, to prevent scorching.) Add the wine and broth. Bring to a simmer. Add the shrimp and scallops, cover, and simmer over medium-low heat until shrimp are pink and scallops are opaque in the center, 4 to 5 minutes.

2. Transfer the shrimp and scallops to a warm bowl with a slotted spoon. Cover and keep warm. Increase the heat under the pan to medium-high. Boil the cooking liquid for 2 to 3 minutes to intensify flavor. Remove from the heat. Add the butter, whisking until melted and incorporated into the sauce. Whisk in the lemon zest, salt, black pepper, and cayenne. Spoon the sauce over the shrimp and scallops and garnish with the tarragon (or chives). One serving is 1 cup.

**Per serving:** 205 calories, 23 g protein, 6 g carbohydrates, 1 g fiber, 7 g total fat, 3 g saturated fat, 140 mg cholesterol, 323 mg sodium.

**Ingredient Note:** Fish counters sell two types of scallops. Sea scallops are the largest and the most commonly available. Bay scallops are considerably smaller—about the diameter of a quarter. For the best quality (you'll need access to a good fishmonger), seek out "dry-pack" scallops. These have not been treated with phosphates, which are often added to improve appearance and extend shelf life, or soaked in water. "Dry-pack" scallops have a better texture and shrink less when they are cooked than "wet-pack" scallops. Scallops should be used within a day or two of purchase.

# Shrimp and Orzo Casserole

**6** **Serves** | **Preparation time: 20 minutes**
**Baking time: 20 to 25 minutes**

This easy recipe for heart-healthy shrimp is prepared Greek-style, with tomatoes, orzo pasta cooked just until al dente, and tangy reduced-fat feta cheese. Convenient canned artichokes are a surprisingly good source of fiber. *See photo on page 244.*

2 teaspoons **olive oil**

2 **garlic** cloves, minced

1/2 teaspoon dried oregano

Pinch of crushed red pepper

1 can (14 1/2 ounces/398 milliliters) diced **tomatoes** (undrained)

1 can (14 1/2 ounces/398 milliliters) reduced-sodium chicken broth

1 cup (6 ounces/170 grams) orzo **pasta** (See Ingredient Note)

1 can (14 ounces/398 milliliters) artichoke hearts, drained, rinsed, and quartered

1 teaspoon freshly grated lemon zest

Freshly ground pepper to taste

1 pound (450 grams) cooked medium **shrimp**, tails removed (see Tip)

2 tablespoons chopped fresh parsley

1 cup (3 ounces/85 grams) crumbled reduced-fat feta **cheese**

1. Preheat the oven to 425°F (220°C). Coat an 8 x 11 1/2-inch (20 x 30-centimeter) baking dish (2-quart/2-liter capacity) with cooking spray.

2. Heat the oil in a large saucepan over medium heat. Add the garlic, oregano, and red pepper. Cook, stirring, until fragrant but not colored, 30 to 60 seconds. Add the tomatoes and mash with a potato masher. Add the broth and bring to a simmer. Stir in the orzo, artichoke hearts, lemon zest, and pepper. Transfer to the baking dish. Cover tightly with aluminum foil.

3. Bake the casserole for 15 minutes. Stir the ingredients in the casserole, then stir in the shrimp. Sprinkle with the parsley, then the feta. Bake, uncovered, until the orzo is firm-tender and the feta starts to melt, 5 to 10 minutes longer. One serving is 1 cup.

Per serving: 273 calories, 27 g protein, 33 g carbohydrates, 6 g fiber, 4 g total fat, 2 g saturated fat, 154 mg cholesterol, 544 mg sodium.

**Tip:** To cook shrimp, place in a large saucepan of lightly salted boiling water. Cook until shrimp turn pink, 2 to 3 minutes, then drain. You can also use frozen cooked shrimp. Thaw before using.

**Ingredient Note:** If possible, use whole wheat orzo for extra fiber and whole grain goodness. It's not yet widely available in stores, but it is available online at sites such as amazon.com.

# PASTA AND PIZZA

## Penne with Asparagus, Ricotta and Lemon

| **4** | Preparation time: 15 minutes |
|---|---|
| Serves | Cooking time: 8 to 10 minutes |

Bulking up a pasta dish with vegetables can be as easy as tossing veggies into the boiling water along with the pasta. Just watch the timing. In most cases, add the vegetables midway through cooking. This super-simple pasta dish, highlighting asparagus, lemon, and herbs and finished with a ricotta sauce, is perfect for a light spring supper.

1/2 cup reduced-fat ricotta **cheese**

1/2 cup freshly grated Parmesan **cheese**, divided

2 tablespoons chopped fresh parsley

2 teaspoons freshly grated lemon zest

2 teaspoons **lemon** juice

1/2 teaspoon salt, or to taste

Freshly ground pepper to taste

2 cups (8 ounces/250 grams) **whole wheat penne**

1 pound (450 grams) asparagus, stem ends snapped off, cut into 1 1/2-inch (4-centimeter) lengths (2 cups)

**1.** Bring a large pot of lightly salted water to a boil for cooking the penne.

**2.** Stir the ricotta, 1/4 cup of the Parmesan, parsley, lemon zest, lemon juice, salt, and pepper in small bowl until smooth.

**3.** Add the penne to the boiling water and cook, stirring occasionally, for 4 minutes. Add the asparagus and cook until the penne is al dente (just tender) and the asparagus is tender, 4 to 6 minutes longer. Reserve 1/3 cup of the pasta cooking water. Drain the pasta and asparagus and place in a large bowl.

**4.** Add 1/3 cup of the reserved pasta cooking water to the ricotta mixture, whisking until smooth. Toss the pasta with the ricotta sauce. Pass the remaining Parmesan separately. One serving is 1 1/2 cups.

**Per serving:** 306 calories, 15 g protein, 49 g carbohydrates, 7 g fiber, 6 g total fat, 2 g saturated fat, 16 mg cholesterol, 482 mg sodium.

### VARIATION Penne with Spinach, Ricotta, and Lemon

In Step 3, omit the asparagus; cook the penne for 8 to 12 minutes. While the penne is cooking, cook one 10-ounce (300-gram) package frozen spinach according to package directions. In Step 4, toss the penne with the ricotta sauce and spinach.

# Quick Spinach and Sausage Lasagna

**6** **Serves** | **Preparation time: 30 minutes**
**Cooking/baking time: 1 hour**

You can't beat lasagna for crowd-pleasing appeal and make-ahead convenience. We've given our favorite lasagna a healthier spin by lightening up the meat and cheese layers and bulking up the spinach layer. Oven-ready noodles speed up preparation time. You can assemble the recipe in advance through Step 4, cover, and refrigerate for up to 2 days or freeze for up to 3 months (thaw in the refrigerator before baking).

1 link (4 ounces/125 grams) hot Italian turkey sausage, casing removed

1 jar (26 ounces/700 milliliters) **marinara sauce** (3 cups)

1 teaspoon dried oregano

1/4 teaspoon crushed red pepper

1 1/2 packages (10 ounces/300 grams each) frozen **spinach**

1 large **egg**

1 container (15 ounces/475 grams) reduced-fat ricotta **cheese**

1/2 cup grated Parmesan **cheese,** divided

1/8 teaspoon ground nutmeg

Freshly ground pepper to taste

12 oven-ready lasagna noodles (see Tip)

1 1/3 cups shredded part-skim mozzarella **cheese**

1. Preheat the oven to 400°F (200°C). Coat a 9 x 13-inch (23 x 33-centimeter) baking dish with nonstick spray.

2. Cook the sausage in a small nonstick skillet over medium heat, crumbling with a wooden spoon, until browned, 2 to 4 minutes. Blot the sausage with paper towel. Transfer to a medium bowl. Stir in the marinara sauce, oregano, and red pepper.

3. Cook the spinach according to package directions. Drain and refresh under cold running water. Drain the spinach well and press out moisture. Whisk the egg and ricotta in a medium bowl until smooth. Add the spinach, 1/4 cup of the Parmesan, the nutmeg, and the black pepper. Mix well.

4. Place 3 of the lasagna noodles in a deep dish or bowl and cover with warm water. Let soak while you assemble the lasagna. Spread about 3/4 cup of the marinara sauce mixture in the baking dish. Place 3 of the remaining unsoaked noodles crosswise over the sauce. Spread about 1 1/3 cups of the spinach mixture over the noodles. Spoon 1/2 cup marinara sauce over the spinach mixture. Sprinkle with 1/3 cup mozzarella. Add another layer of unsoaked noodles and repeat layering with spinach mixture and marinara sauce and mozzarella 2 more times. Lift the soaked noodles from the water, shake off excess, and arrange over lasagna. Spread the remaining marinara sauce evenly over the final layer of noodles.

5. Cover the lasagna with aluminum foil and bake for 35 minutes. Sprinkle with the remaining 1/4 cup Parmesan and 1/3 cup mozzarella. Bake, uncovered, until noodles are tender and lasagna is bubbly, about 15 minutes longer. Let stand for 5 minutes before serving. One serving is one 4 1/2 x 3 1/2-inch (11 x 9-centimeter) piece.

**Per serving:** 400 calories, 24 g protein, 34 g carbohydrates, 5 g fiber, 19 g total fat, 8 g saturated fat, 82 mg cholesterol, 986 mg sodium.

**Tip:** Oven-ready lasagna noodles eliminate the step of boiling the noodles. However, even when the top layer of oven-ready noodles is thoroughly covered with sauce, it never seems to tenderize properly. To remedy this problem, soak the 3 noodles for the top layer in warm water before assembling the lasagna.

# Whole Wheat Pasta with Sausage, Beans and Greens

**6**
Serves

Preparation time: 25 minutes

Cooking time: 20 to 25minutes

A small amount of lean turkey sausage goes a long way in imparting a full flavor to this quick pasta sauce. We've boosted the fiber with cannellini beans and the vegetable content with vibrant Swiss chard, which cooks conveniently in the pasta water.

1 link (4 ounces/125 grams) hot Italian turkey sausage, casing removed

1 teaspoon **olive oil**

3/4 cup chopped **onion** (1 small)

3 **garlic** cloves, minced

1 can (15 ounces/398 milliliters) no-salt-added diced **tomatoes**

1 can (8 ounces/213 milliliters) no-salt-added tomato sauce

1 can (19 or 15 ounces/540 or 398 milliliters) cannellini **beans,** drained and rinsed

1/4 cup water

Freshly ground pepper to taste

4 cups (12 ounces/340 grams) whole wheat **pasta,** fusilli, penne, or rigatoni

1 bunch (1 pound/450 grams) **Swiss chard,** stems trimmed (see Tip), leaves washed, and torn into bite-size pieces

6 tablespoons grated Parmesan **cheese**

1. Bring a large pot of lightly salted water to a boil for cooking pasta. Cook the sausage in a large nonstick skillet over medium heat, crumbling the sausage with a wooden spoon, until browned, 3 to 5 minutes. Transfer the sausage to a paper towel–lined plate to drain.

2. Add the oil to the skillet. Add the onion and cook over medium heat, stirring often, until softened, 1 to 2 minutes. Add the garlic and cook, stirring, for 10 to 20 seconds. Add the diced tomatoes and mash with a wooden spoon. Add the tomato sauce, beans, water, and browned sausage. Bring to a simmer. Cook, uncovered, at a lively simmer over medium-low heat, stirring occasionally, until flavors have blended, 10 to 15 minutes. Season with pepper.

3. Meanwhile, add the pasta to the boiling water and cook for 5 minutes. Add the Swiss chard and stir to immerse. Cook until the pasta is just tender and the chard has wilted, 3 to 5 minutes longer. Drain well and transfer to a large bowl. Toss with the tomato sauce. Sprinkle each serving with Parmesan cheese. One serving is 1 1/3 cups pasta and sauce and 1 tablespoon cheese.

**Per serving:** 390 calories, 19 g protein, 65 g carbohydrates, 11 g fiber, 6 g total fat, 1 g saturated fat, 22 mg cholesterol, 409 mg sodium.

Tips

• The celery-like stems of Swiss chard are edible and have a pleasant, mild taste. Cut them into bite-size pieces and steam or boil until tender, 6 to 8 minutes.

• Leftovers? Transform them into a pasta gratin. Spread the leftovers in a shallow baking dish coated with cooking spray. Moisten with a little water and top with grated Parmesan and bread crumbs. Bake, uncovered, at 425°F (220°C) until the top is golden and crusty, 25 to 30 minutes.

# Macaroni and Cheese with Spinach

**6** | **Preparation time: 15 minutes**
Serves | **Cooking/baking time: 45 to 55 minutes**

A crusty casserole of mac and cheese is pure comfort food—and it can be a Magic food as well. We've improved the dish with your blood sugar in mind by using whole wheat pasta, a lightened cheese sauce, a surprise layer of spinach, and a topping of wheat germ. You can assemble the recipe through Step 5 in advance, cover, and refrigerate for up to 2 days or freeze for up to 3 months (thaw in the refrigerator before baking). *See photo on page 245.*

1 3/4 cups low-fat (1%) **milk,** divided

3 tablespoons all-purpose flour

2 cups (6 ounces/170 grams) grated extra-sharp cheddar **cheese**

1 cup 1% low-fat cottage **cheese**

1/8 teaspoon ground nutmeg

1/2 teaspoon salt, or to taste

Freshly ground pepper to taste

1 package (10 ounces/300 grams) frozen **spinach** or 4 cups individually quick-frozen spinach

2 cups (8 ounces/250 grams) **whole wheat macaroni**

1/4 cup toasted **wheat germ**

1. Preheat the oven to 400°F (200°C). Coat an 8-inch (20-centimeter) square baking dish (2-quart/2-liter capacity) with nonstick spray. Bring a large pot of lightly salted water to a boil for cooking the macaroni.

2. Whisk 1/4 cup of the cold milk with the flour in a small bowl until smooth. Set aside. Heat the remaining 1 1/2 cups milk in a heavy medium saucepan over medium heat until steaming. Add the flour mixture and cook, whisking constantly, until the sauce boils and thickens, 2 to 3 minutes. Remove from the heat. Add the cheddar cheese,

stirring until melted. Stir in the cottage cheese, nutmeg, salt, and pepper.

3. Cook the spinach according to package directions. Drain, refresh under cold water, and press out excess moisture.

4. Cook the macaroni, stirring often, in the boiling water until not quite tender, 4 to 5 minutes. (The macaroni will continue to cook during baking.) Drain, rinse with cold running water, then drain again.

5. Mix the macaroni with the cheese sauce in a large bowl. Spread half of the macaroni mixture in the baking dish. Spoon the spinach on top. Spread the remaining macaroni mixture over the spinach layer. Sprinkle with wheat germ.

6. Bake the casserole until bubbly and golden, 35 to 45 minutes. One serving is 1 1/3 cups.

**Per serving:** 357 calories, 22 g protein, 40 g carbohydrates, 6 g fiber, 12 g total fat, 7 g saturated fat, 35 mg cholesterol, 606 mg sodium.

## VARIATION Southwestern Macaroni and Cheese and Peppers

In Step 1, substitute a mixture of 1 cup shredded pepper Jack cheese and 1 cup shredded extra-sharp cheddar cheese for the 2 cups cheddar. Omit the nutmeg. Add 4 1/2 ounces (125 milliliters) canned chopped mild green chiles, 1/3 cup chopped fresh cilantro, and a dash of cayenne pepper to the cheese sauce. In Step 3, omit the spinach. Instead, sauté 2 cups frozen pepper stir-fry vegetables in 1 teaspoon olive oil until tender, 3 to 4 minutes. In Step 5, spread the pepper mixture over bottom macaroni layer.

# Penne with Tomato and Eggplant Sauce

## 6 Serves

**Preparation time: 20 minutes**

**Cooking time: 25 minutes**

Whole wheat pasta has come a long way in recent years. Supermarkets now stock a wide array of shapes. The nutty taste of the whole wheat pasta pairs well with assertive flavors like this full-flavored tomato sauce, which has a rich, meaty taste thanks to the Magic eggplant, an excellent meat substitute.

4 teaspoons **olive oil,** divided

1 large (8 ounces/250 grams) baby **eggplant,** cut into 3/4-inch (2-centimeter) cubes (3 cups)

1 cup chopped **onion** (1 medium)

4 **garlic** cloves, minced

1/8 teaspoon crushed red pepper

1 can (28 ounces/796 milliliters) diced **tomatoes**

3 tablespoons chopped fresh parsley or basil, divided

1/8 teaspoon salt, or to taste

Freshly ground pepper to taste

4 cups (12 ounces/340 grams) whole wheat **pasta,** such as penne or rigatoni (see Tip)

3/4 cup crumbled reduced-fat feta **cheese**

6 tablespoons pine **nuts,** toasted (see Tip)

1. Bring a large pot of lightly salted water to a boil for cooking the pasta.

2. Heat 2 teaspoons of the oil in a large nonstick skillet over medium-high heat. Add the eggplant and cook, turning from time to time, until browned and tender, 5 to 7 minutes. Transfer to a plate.

3. Reduce the heat to medium and add the remaining 2 teaspoons oil to the skillet. Add onion and cook, stirring often, until softened, 2 to 3 minutes. Add the garlic and red pepper. Cook, stirring, until fragrant, about 30 seconds. Add the tomatoes and mash with a potato masher. Bring to a simmer. Add the eggplant. Simmer, uncovered, over medium-low heat until the flavors have developed and the sauce has thickened, 15 to 20 minutes. (Add a little water if the sauce thickens too quickly.) Stir in 2 tablespoons of the parsley. Season with salt and pepper.

4. Meanwhile, cook the pasta in the boiling water until al dente (just tender), 8 to 10 minutes, or according to package directions. Drain and add to the sauce in the skillet. Toss to coat well. Sprinkle each serving with feta, pine nuts, and some of the remaining parsley (or basil). One serving is 1 1/3 cups pasta and sauce, 2 tablespoons feta, and 1 tablespoon pine nuts.

**Per serving:** 390 calories, 15 g protein, 57 g carbohydrates, 8 g fiber, 13 g total fat, 2 g saturated fat, 8 mg cholesterol, 556 mg sodium.

### Tips

• Toast the pine nuts in a small dry skillet over medium-low heat, stirring constantly, until golden and fragrant, 1 to 3 minutes.

• Test the pasta often toward the end of cooking, so you will be sure to catch it when it has just become tender or "al dente." When pasta is overcooked, not only does it lose its appeal, it has a higher GL.

**2** **tomato**
their lycopene may have special power against diabetes

**3** **pine nuts**
their "good" fats help slow the digestion of your dinner

**pasta** **4**
whole wheat has three times the fiber per serving

**1** **cheese**
reduced-fat feta provides calcium, which may help boost your sensitivity to insulin

**olive oil** **8**
this liquid gold helps "spike-proof" your meals

**eggplant** **7**
adding bulky veggies like eggplant to pasta lowers the GL of the dish

**onions** **6**
indispensable onions may lower high blood sugar

**5** **garlic**
it helps keep blood clots and cholesterol in check

Penne with Tomato and Eggplant Sauce

# Quick Whole Wheat Pizza Dough

**1 pizza**

| | |
|---|---|
| **Preparation time:** 10 minutes | |
| **Rising time:** 10 to 20 minutes | |

**Makes 12 ounces (340 grams) pizza dough, enough for one 12-inch (30-centimeter) pizza**

A food processor mixes and kneads this "better blood sugar" pizza dough in just minutes. You can also make this dough in a bread machine; use bread-machine yeast and room temperature water. Place the ingredients in your bread machine in the order recommended by the manufacturer and select the manual setting.

3/4 cup **whole wheat flour**

3/4 cup all-purpose flour

2 teaspoons quick-rising yeast (see Ingredient Note)

3/4 teaspoon salt

1/4 teaspoon sugar

1/2–2/3 cup hot water (120–130°F/50–55°C)

2 teaspoons **olive oil**

1. Combine the whole wheat flour, all-purpose flour, yeast, salt, and sugar in a food processor. Pulse to mix. Combine the hot water and oil in a measuring cup. With the motor running, gradually pour the hot liquid through food processor feed tube. Process until dough forms a ball, then process 1 minute to knead. The dough should be quite soft. If it seems dry, add 1 to 2 tablespoons warm water. If too sticky, add 1 to 2 tablespoons flour.

2. Transfer the dough to a lightly floured surface. Spray a sheet of plastic wrap with nonstick spray and place it, sprayed side down, over the dough. Let the dough rest for 10 to 20 minutes before rolling.

**Ingredient Note:** Quick-rising yeast is a special variety of yeast that can be mixed directly with dry ingredients, works with hotter liquids than regular yeast, and requires only a 10-minute rest rather than the standard 1 1/2-hour rising time. Fleischmann's RapidRise yeast is the most common brand. You can find it in the refrigerated dairy case.

# Mushroom and Herb Pizza

**Serves 4**

| | |
|---|---|
| **Preparation time:** 30 minutes | |
| **Cooking/baking time:** 20 minutes | |

Yes, pizza, can be part of your Magic Foods eating plan, especially when you make your own with a thin whole grain crust, topped with lots of vegetables and a moderate amount of cheese. Using our Quick Whole Wheat Pizza Dough, you can bake your own wholesome pizza in about the same time it takes for delivery pizza to arrive at your door. We offer two toppings, one with meaty-tasting mushrooms and a variation with broccoli and olives. *See photo on page 245.*

12 ounces (340 grams) Quick Whole Wheat Pizza Dough or purchased whole wheat pizza dough

Cornmeal for dusting

1 tablespoon **olive oil,** divided

3 cups (8 ounces/250 grams) baby bella or cremini mushrooms, stem ends trimmed, wiped clean, and sliced

2 **garlic** cloves, minced

Pinch of salt

Freshly ground pepper to taste

2 tablespoons chopped fresh parsley

2/3 cup prepared **marinara sauce**

2 tablespoons chopped fresh marjoram or oregano

1/8 teaspoon crushed red pepper

1 cup shredded part-skim mozzarella cheese

1/2 cup diced red onion

1/4 cup grated Parmesan cheese

1. Prepare the Quick Whole Wheat Pizza Dough, if using.

2. Place a baking stone or inverted baking sheet on lowest rack of oven. Preheat the oven to 500°F (260°C) or highest setting. Coat a 12 1/2-inch (32-centimeter) pizza pan with nonstick spray. Dust with the cornmeal.

3. Heat 2 teaspoons of the oil in a large non-stick skillet over medium-high heat. Add the mushrooms and cook, stirring or shaking the skillet from time to time, until tender and lightly browned, 3 to 4 minutes. Add the garlic and cook, stirring, for 30 seconds longer. Remove from the heat and stir in parsley, salt, and pepper.

4. Mix the marinara sauce, marjoram (or oregano), and red pepper in a small bowl.

5. On a lightly floured surface, roll the dough into a 13-inch (33-centimeter) circle. Transfer to the pizza pan. Turn the edges under to make a slight rim around the outside edge. Brush the remaining 1 teaspoon oil over the rim. Spread the marinara sauce over the crust, leaving a 1/2-inch (1-centimeter) border. Sprinkle the mozzarella over the sauce. Scatter the mushrooms over the mozzarella. Sprinkle with the onion. Top with the Parmesan cheese.

6. Place the pizza pan on heated baking stone (or baking sheet) and bake until the bottom crust is crisp and golden, 10 to 14 minutes. One serving is 1/4 of a 12-inch (30-centimeter) pizza.

**Per serving**: 368 calories, 18 g protein, 45 g carbohydrates, 6 g fiber, 14 g total fat, 5 g saturated fat, 22 mg cholesterol, 916 mg sodium.

## VARIATION Whole Wheat Pizza with Broccoli and Olives

In Step 3, steam 2 cups broccoli florets (3/4-inch/2-centimeter pieces) until crisp-tender, 2 to 3 minutes. In Step 4, mix 2/3 cup prepared marinara sauce with 1 teaspoon dried oregano and 1/8 teaspoon crushed red pepper. In Step 5, spread the marinara sauce over the crust. Sprinkle 1 cup shredded part-skim mozzarella cheese over the sauce. Scatter the broccoli, 1/2 cup diced red onion, and 1/4 cup coarsely chopped, pitted kalamata olives over top. Spritz the top lightly with olive oil nonstick spray. Bake the pizza as directed in Step 6.

# MEATLESS MAIN DISHES

## Spring Vegetable Stir-Fry with Tofu

**4** Serves

| | |
|---|---|
| **Preparation time:** 25 minutes | |
| **Marinating time:** 10 minutes | |
| **Cooking time:** 10 minutes | |

This colorful stir-fry celebrates spring with seasonal asparagus and sweet onions. It is a protein-rich vegetarian dish, thanks to the tofu. And with its zesty sauce, it will appeal even to resolute meat lovers. You can vary the recipe by using snow peas instead of asparagus and red bell pepper rather than carrots. Substitute sliced boneless chicken breast for the tofu, if you like—just be sure that it is cooked through when you brown it in Step 2.

1 package (14 to16 ounces/400 to 425 grams) extra-firm water-packed **tofu,** drained

1/2 cup orange juice

2 tablespoons reduced-sodium soy sauce

1 tablespoon oyster-flavored sauce (see Ingredient Note)

1 tablespoon medium-dry sherry, rice wine, or nonalcoholic white wine

1 1/2 teaspoons chile-garlic sauce (see Ingredient Note)

1 teaspoon sugar

1 1/2 teaspoons cornstarch

1 tablespoon vegetable oil, divided

1 tablespoon grated fresh ginger

2 teaspoons freshly grated orange zest

3 **garlic** cloves, minced

1 cup thinly sliced sweet **onion,** such as Vidalia or Walla Walla (1 small)

1 pound (450 grams) asparagus, stem ends snapped off, cut into 1 1/4-inch (3-centimeter) lengths (2 cups)

1 cup baby **carrots,** quartered lengthwise

1/4 cup water

1. Pat the tofu dry and cut into 3/4-inch (2-centimeter) pieces. Whisk the orange juice, soy sauce, oyster-flavored sauce, sherry (or wine), chile-garlic sauce, and sugar in a medium bowl. Add the tofu and toss gently to coat. Marinate for about 10 minutes, turning from time to time, while you prepare the vegetables.

2. When you are ready to cook, drain the tofu, reserving the marinade in a medium bowl. Add the cornstarch to the reserved marinade and whisk until smooth. Reserve for the sauce. Heat 2 teaspoons of the oil in nonstick skillet or stir-fry pan over high heat. Add the tofu and cook, turning from time to time, until browned and crusty, 3 to 5 minutes. Transfer to a plate.

3. Add the remaining 1 teaspoon oil to the skillet. Add the ginger, orange zest, and garlic. Stir-fry until fragrant, 10 to 20 seconds. Add the onion and stir-fry for 1 minute. Add the asparagus and carrots. Stir-fry for 30 seconds. Add the water, cover, and cook just until vegetables are crisp-tender, about 2 minutes. Push vegetables to the outside perimeter of the skillet. Stir the reserved sauce and add it to the center of the skillet. Cook, stirring the sauce, until it becomes glossy and thickens, about 1 minute. Stir the vegetables into the sauce and return the tofu to the skillet. Stir to coat. One serving is 1 1/3 cups.

**Per serving:** 263 calories, 19 g protein, 23 g carbohydrates, 6 g fiber, 12 g total fat, 2 g saturated fat, 0 mg cholesterol, 454 mg sodium.

**Ingredient Note:** Oyster-flavored sauce and chile-garlic sauce can be found in the Asian foods section of large supermarkets.

# Dahl with Spinach

**6** | **Preparation time: 20 minutes**
Serves | **Cooking time: 45 to 50 minutes**

Dahl turns up frequently in Indian cooking and it is one of those confusing terms that refer to both a preparation and an ingredient. As an ingredient, dahl encompasses a wide variety of dried pulses (legumes), including lentils and split peas, all of which are valuable sources of soluble fiber and vegetable protein. The preparation is a dish like this one, made with seasoned stewed pulses. We've squeezed three Magic seasonings—turmeric, fenugreek, and garlic—into this spicy stew.

## DAHL

1 cup yellow **split peas** or chana dahl
 (see Ingredient Note), sorted and rinsed

3 cups water

1/2 teaspoon **turmeric**

1 tablespoon canola oil

1 teaspoon cumin **seeds**

1 cup chopped **onion** (1 medium)

1 tablespoon grated fresh ginger or 1/2 teaspoon
 ground ginger

3 **garlic** cloves, minced

1 teaspoon ground **fenugreek** (optional)

1/4 teaspoon cayenne pepper

1 can (14 1/2 ounces/398 milliliters) diced
 **tomatoes** (undrained)

1 package (10 ounces/300 grams) frozen
 cut-leaf **spinach**

1/2 teaspoon salt, or to taste

## RAITA

1 cup low-fat plain **yogurt**

4 teaspoons **lime** juice

1 teaspoon ground cumin

1/8 teaspoon salt, or to taste

1. **To make the dahl:** Combine the split peas (or chana dahl), water, and turmeric in a large saucepan. Bring to a simmer. Partially cover, reduce heat to medium-low, and cook until the split peas are tender, 40 to 45 minutes.

2. Meanwhile, heat the oil in a large nonstick skillet over medium heat. Add the cumin seeds and cook, stirring, until fragrant, 10 to 20 seconds. Add the onion and cook, stirring often, until softened, 2 to 3 minutes. Add the ginger, garlic, fenugreek, if using, and cayenne. Cook, stirring, until fragrant, 20 to 30 seconds. Add the tomatoes and cook until most of the liquid has evaporated, 5 to 10 minutes.

3. Cook the spinach according to package directions. Drain, pressing out excess moisture.

4. When the split peas are tender, stir them (and any remaining cooking liquid) into the tomato mixture, along with the spinach. Cook for 2 to 3 minutes to blend the flavors. Season with salt.

5. **To make the raita:** Mix all the raita ingredients in a small bowl. Serve the dahl with raita. One serving is 3/4 cup dahl and 2 1/2 tablespoons raita. Leftover dahl will keep, covered, in the refrigerator for up to 2 days. Reheat on the stovetop or in the microwave, adding a little additional water, if necessary.

**Per serving:** 199 calories, 12 g protein, 33 g carbohydrates, 12 g fiber, 4 g total fat, 0 g saturated fat, 0 mg cholesterol, 412 mg sodium.

**Ingredient Note:** Chana dahl are split chickpeas. You can find them in Indian markets and some supermarkets.

# Barley Risotto with Asparagus and Lemon

**4** | **Preparation time: 20 minutes**
Serves | **Cooking time: 20 minutes**

A creamy risotto is traditionally made with arborio rice, which falls in the top (undesirable) tier of the Magic Foods Carb Pyramid (see page 43). We've created this blood sugar-friendly version, which swaps nutty tasting whole grain barley for the white rice. Since risotto requires almost constant stirring, quick-cooking barley is a more practical choice then pearl barley.

2 cans (14 1/2 ounces/284 milliliters) vegetable broth or reduced-sodium chicken broth (3 1/2 cups)

3/4 cup water

1 pound (450 grams) asparagus, stem ends snapped off, cut into 1-inch (2.5-centimeter) lengths (2 cups)

1 tablespoon olive oil

1/2 cup chopped scallions

1 cup quick-cooking barley

1/2 cup grated Parmesan cheese

1/4 cup chopped fresh parsley or snipped chives

2 teaspoons freshly grated lemon zest

1 tablespoon lemon juice

Pinch of salt

Freshly ground pepper to taste

1. Combine the broth and water in a medium saucepan. Bring to a simmer over medium heat. Drop in the asparagus and cook, uncovered, until crisp-tender, 2 to 4 minutes. Transfer the asparagus to a plate with a slotted spoon and set aside. Reduce the heat to low and keep the broth at a bare simmer.

2. Heat the oil in a Dutch oven over medium heat. Add the scallions and cook, stirring, until softened, about 1 minute. Add the barley and cook, stirring, for 30 seconds. Add about 1 cup of the hot broth and cook, stirring, until most of the liquid has been absorbed, 1 to 1 1/2 minutes.

Continue to simmer and stir almost constantly, adding broth about 1/2 cup at a time and waiting until most of it has been absorbed before adding more, until barley is tender and risotto has creamy consistency, about 15 minutes.

3. Add the reserved asparagus and stir until heated through, about 1 minute. Remove the risotto from the heat. Stir in the Parmesan, parsley, lemon zest, lemon juice, salt, and pepper. One serving is 1 cup.

**Per serving:** 221 calories, 9 g protein, 7 g carbohydrates, 3 g fiber, 7 g total fat, 3 g saturated fat, 13 mg cholesterol, 319 mg sodium.

# Lentil and Bean Chili

**8** | **Preparation time: 20 minutes**
Serves | **Cooking time: 50 minutes**

Nothing takes the chill out of a winter evening like a bowl of steaming, spicy chili. The combination of lentils and beans produces a vegetarian version that is rich in soluble fiber and protein, both strong allies in the battle against blood sugar spikes. Garnish the chili with diced avocado, grated pepper Jack or cheddar cheese, chopped fresh cilantro, chopped scallions, and reduced-fat sour cream.

2 teaspoons olive oil

1 cup chopped onion (1 medium)

1 cup diced carrots (2–4 medium)

3 garlic cloves, minced

5 teaspoons chili powder

4 teaspoons ground cumin

1 teaspoon dried oregano

4 cups vegetable broth or reduced-sodium chicken broth

3/4 cup brown lentils, sorted and rinsed

2 cans (10 ounces/398 milliliters each) diced tomatoes with green chiles

2 cans (15 or 19 ounces/398 or 540 milliliters each) dark red kidney beans, drained and rinsed

Freshly ground pepper to taste

1. Heat the oil in a Dutch oven over medium heat. Add the onion and carrots. Cook, stirring often, until softened, 3 to 5 minutes. Add the garlic, chili powder, cumin, and oregano. Cook, stirring, until fragrant, 30 to 60 seconds. Add the broth and lentils. Bring to a simmer. Reduce the heat to medium-low, cover, and simmer for 25 minutes.

2. Add the tomatoes, beans, and pepper. Return to a simmer. Cook, covered, over medium-low heat until lentils are tender, 15 to 20 minutes longer. One serving is 1 cup. Leftovers will keep, covered, in the refrigerator for up to 2 days. Reheat on the stovetop or in the microwave.

Per serving: 199 calories, 12 g protein, 36 g carbohydrates, 12 g fiber, 3 g total fat, 0 g saturated fat, 0 mg cholesterol, 691 mg sodium.

# Black Bean and Sweet Potato Burritos

8 Serves | Preparation time: 25 minutes
Cooking time: 20 minutes

Sweet potatoes and fiber-rich beans are a Magic marriage in this flavor-packed vegetarian entrée. If you are cooking for just one or two, make up the sweet potato–bean filling (through Step 2) and store, covered, in the refrigerator for up to 2 days. For a quick pick up meal, just heat leftover filling and individual tortillas in the microwave (see Tip).

2 teaspoons canola oil

1 cup chopped onion (1 medium)

2 garlic cloves, minced

4 teaspoons ground cumin

1/2 teaspoon dried oregano

3/4 cup vegetable broth or reduced-sodium chicken broth

1 medium sweet potato, peeled and diced (3 cups)

1 can (14 1/2 ounces/398 milliliters) mild green chile-seasoned diced tomatoes (undrained)

1 can (15 1/2 ounces/398 milliliters) black beans, drained and rinsed

3/4 cup frozen corn

1/4 cup chopped fresh cilantro

1 tablespoon fresh lime juice

1/8 teaspoon freshly ground pepper

8 (8-inch/20-centimeter) whole wheat wraps or tortillas

1 cup shredded pepper Jack or Monterey Jack cheese

1/2 cup reduced-fat sour cream

1. Preheat the oven to 325°F (160°C).

2. Heat the oil in a large nonstick skillet over medium heat. Add the onion and cook, stirring often, until softened, 2 to 3 minutes. Add the garlic, cumin, and oregano. Cook, stirring, until fragrant, 10 to 20 seconds. Add the broth and sweet potato. Bring to a simmer. Cover and cook for 5 minutes. Add the tomatoes, beans, and corn. Return to a simmer. Cover and cook until the sweet potato is tender, 5 to 10 minutes longer. Mash about 1/4 of the vegetable mixture with a potato masher. Stir the mashed and unmashed portions together. Stir in the lime juice, cilantro, and pepper.

3. Meanwhile, enclose the wraps (or tortillas) in aluminum foil and heat in oven for 10 to 15 minutes.

4. To serve, spoon about 2/3 cup of the sweet potato filling down center of each tortilla. Sprinkle with about 2 tablespoons cheese. Fold in edges of wrap, then fold 1 side over filling and wrap up the burrito. Serve with sour cream for dipping. One serving is 1 wrap, 2/3 cup filling, 2 tablespoons shredded cheese, and 1 tablespoon sour cream.

Per serving: 262 calories, 14 g protein, 35 g carbohydrates, 15 g fiber, 10 g total fat, 4 g saturated fat, 21 g cholesterol, 784 mg sodium.

Tip: To heat individual wraps or flour tortillas in the microwave, place 1 wrap between 2 paper towels and microwave on high for 10 to 12 seconds.

# SIDE DISHES

## Bulgur with Ginger and Orange

**4** Serves | **Preparation time:** 15 minutes
**Cooking time:** 25 minutes

Instead of cooking a side of rice or potatoes (both high-GL foods) to go with your next chicken, beef, or pork dinner, reach for the bag of bulgur instead. Bulgur cooks in about the same time as white rice but offers the blood sugar benefits of a whole grain rich in soluble fiber.

2 **oranges,** scrubbed

2 teaspoons canola oil

2 tablespoons minced fresh ginger

2 **garlic** cloves minced

1 cup **bulgur,** rinsed

2 teaspoons firmly packed brown sugar

1/4 teaspoon salt, or to taste

2/3 cup chopped **scallions**

1 tablespoon reduced-sodium soy sauce

1/3 cup slivered **almonds,** toasted (see Tip)

1. Grate the orange peels to make 1 tablespoon zest. Juice the oranges and add enough water to measure 1 1/2 cups.

2. Heat the oil in a large, heavy saucepan over medium-high heat. Add the ginger and garlic. Cook, stirring, until fragrant, about 30 seconds. Add the bulgur and stir to coat. Add the diluted orange juice, sugar, and salt. Bring to a simmer. Reduce heat to low, cover, and simmer until the bulgur is tender and most of the liquid has been absorbed, 15 to 20 minutes.

3. Add scallions, soy sauce, and the reserved orange zest to the bulgur. Mix gently and fluff with a fork. Sprinkle with almonds. One serving is 3/4 cup. Leftovers will keep, covered, in the refrigerator for up to 2 days. Reheat in the microwave.

**Per serving:** 234 calories, 7 g protein, 38 g carbohydrates, 8 g fiber, 7 g total fat, 1 g saturated fat, 0 mg cholesterol, 295 mg sodium.

**Tip:** Toast almonds in a small dry skillet over medium-low heat, stirring constantly, until light golden and fragrant, 2 to 3 minutes. Transfer to a plate and let cool.

### VARIATION Bulgur with Carrot Juice and Sesame Seeds

Substitute carrot juice for the orange juice and toasted sesame seeds for almonds.

## Mushroom-Barley Pilaf

**6** Serves | **Preparation time:** 15 minutes
**Cooking time:** 10 to 15 minutes

Taking its inspiration from the classic barley-mushroom soup, this easy pilaf is an ideal side dish to accompany beef, pork, or chicken entrées. Finishing the pilaf with a splash of vinegar heightens the flavors while dampening the blood-sugar effects of your whole meal.

4 teaspoons **olive oil,** divided

1 cup chopped **onion** (1 medium)

1 cup quick-cooking **barley**

1 can (14 ounces/284 milliliters) reduced-sodium chicken broth or vegetable broth (1 3/4 cups)

8 ounces (250 grams) mushrooms, stem ends trimmed, caps wiped clean, sliced (3 cups)

1 medium red bell pepper, seeded and diced

1 **garlic** clove, minced

1/4 cup chopped fresh dill

1 tablespoon balsamic **vinegar** or **lemon** juice

Freshly ground pepper to taste

**1.** Heat 2 teaspoons of the oil in a large sauce-pan over medium heat. Add the onion and cook, stirring often, until softened, 2 to 3 minutes. Add the barley and cook, stirring, for 1 minute. Add the broth and bring to a simmer. Reduce the heat to low, cover, and simmer until the barley is tender and the liquid has been absorbed, 10 to 15 minutes.

**2.** Meanwhile, heat the remaining 2 teaspoons oil in a large nonstick skillet over medium-high heat. Add the mushrooms, bell pepper, and garlic. Cook, stirring often, until tender, 3 to 5 minutes. Add to the barley, along with dill, vinegar, and pepper. Stir gently to mix. One serving is 2/3 cup. The pilaf will keep, covered, in the refrigerator for up to 2 days. Reheat in the microwave.

Per serving: 128 calories, 5 g protein, 21 g carbohydrates, 3 g fiber, 4 g total fat, 1 g saturated fat, 1 mg cholesterol, 45 mg sodium.

# Brown Rice Pilaf with Toasted Flaxseeds

**6** Serves

**Preparation time: 10 minutes**

**Cooking time: 45 to 55 minutes**

Nutty flaxseeds give a simple rice pilaf a soluble-fiber boost to help lower blood sugar. If you don't have time to cook brown rice, substitute parboiled (converted) white rice; use 1/4 cup water and cook the pilaf for about 20 minutes. With its fresh lemon and parsley accent, this pilaf makes an excellent accompaniment to fish or chicken entrées.

2 teaspoons **olive oil**

1 cup chopped **onion** (1 medium)

1 cup long-grain brown rice

1 can (14 ounces/284 milliliters) reduced-sodium chicken broth or vegetable broth (1 3/4 cups)

3/4 cup water

1/4 cup whole **flaxseeds**

2 teaspoons freshly grated lemon zest

1 tablespoon **lemon** juice

1/4 cup chopped fresh parsley

Freshly ground pepper to taste

**1.** Heat the oil in a large, heavy saucepan over medium heat. Add the onion and cook, stirring often, until softened, 2 to 3 minutes. Add the rice and stir for 30 seconds. Add the broth and water and bring to a simmer. Reduce heat to low, cover, and simmer until the rice is tender and the liquid has been absorbed, 45 to 55 minutes.

**2.** Meanwhile, toast the flaxseeds in a small dry skillet over medium-low heat, stirring constantly, until fragrant and starting to pop, 2 to 3 minutes. Transfer to a small bowl and let cool. Place the flaxseeds in a spice grinder or blender and pulse several times until broken down but not ground.

**3.** When rice is ready, add the flaxseeds, lemon zest, lemon juice, parsley, and pepper. Fluff and mix gently with a fork. One serving is 1/2 cup. Leftovers will keep, covered, in the refrigerator for up to 2 days. Reheat in the microwave.

Per serving: 166 calories, 4 g protein, 27 g carbohydrates, 3 g fiber, 5 g total fat, 0 g saturated fat, 0 mg cholesterol, 166 mg sodium.

## VARIATION Brown Rice Pilaf with Flaxseeds, Lime, and Cilantro

Substitute 1 teaspoon lime zest for 2 teaspoons lemon zest, lime juice for lemon juice, and cilantro for parsley.

# Wheatberry Salad with Dried Apricots and Mint

**6**
Serves

**Preparation time: 25 minutes**

**Cooking time: 1 1/2 to1 3/4 hours**

You may have to plan ahead to purchase and cook the wheatberries, but you'll be rewarded with a great-tasting, whole grain salad that's truly blood sugar–friendly. Look for wheatberries in the bulk bins of natural foods markets and allow enough time to cook them—plan on about 1 1/2 hours for unsoaked berries. These chewy, nutty berries are lovely in salads. Here they are complemented by a spiced citrus vinaigrette, dried fruit, and nuts. Serve as a side dish with lamb or poultry.

3/4 cup hard **wheatberries** or spelt berries, rinsed (see Tip)

1/2 cup dried apricots, diced

1/4 cup extra-virgin **olive oil**

3 tablespoons orange juice

2 tablespoons **lemon** juice

1/2 teaspoon honey

1/2 teaspoon **cinnamon**

1 **garlic** clove, minced

1/2 teaspoon salt, or to taste

Freshly ground pepper to taste

1/2 cup chopped **scallions**

1/3 cup chopped fresh mint

1/3 cup slivered **almonds** or chopped peeled pistachios, toasted (see Tip)

**1.** Place the wheatberries in a large saucepan and cover generously with water. Bring to a simmer over medium-high heat. Reduce heat to medium-low, partially cover, and cook until the wheatberries are tender, 1 1/2 to 1 3/4 hours. (Add more water, if necessary.) Drain and rinse with cold running water.

**2.** Meanwhile, place the apricots in a small bowl. Cover with boiling water and let soak for 5 to 10 minutes. Drain.

**3.** Combine the oil, orange juice, lemon juice, honey, cinnamon, garlic, salt, and pepper in a medium bowl or a jar with a tight-fitting lid. Whisk or shake to blend.

**4.** Combine the cooked wheatberries, soaked dried apricots, scallions, and mint in a large bowl. Add the orange juice dressing and toss to coat well. Just before serving, sprinkle with nuts. One serving is 2/3 cup. The salad will keep, covered, in the refrigerator for up to 2 days.

**Per serving:** 262 calories, 6 g protein, 32 g carbohydrates, 5 g fiber, 13 g total fat, 2 g saturated fat, 0 mg cholesterol, 200 mg sodium.

**Tip:** If you soak the wheatberries for at least 8 hours or overnight in a large bowl of water, you can reduce cooking time to about 1 hour (cook the wheatberries in fresh water).

# Quinoa with Chiles and Cilantro

**6**
Serves

**Preparation time: 15 minutes**

**Cooking time: 30 minutes**

Quinoa, a delicately flavored whole grain that originated in South America, is higher in protein than any other grain. You can find it in natural foods stores or in the natural foods section of large supermarkets. The good news for busy cooks is that it takes no longer to cook than white rice. Accented with Latin flavors, this versatile side pairs well with seafood, poultry, or pork. *See photo on page 271.*

1 cup **quinoa**

2 teaspoons canola oil

1 cup chopped **onion** (1 medium)

1 can (4 ounces) chopped green chiles

2 **garlic** cloves, minced

1 3/4 cups reduced-sodium chicken broth or
   vegetable broth

3/4 cup coarsely chopped fresh cilantro

1/2 cup chopped **scallions**

1/4 cup **pepitas** (pumpkin seeds), toasted (see (Tip)

2 tablespoons **lime** juice

1/4 teaspoon salt, or to taste

1. Toast the quinoa in a large dry skillet over medium heat, stirring often, until it crackles and becomes aromatic, 3 to 5 minutes. Transfer to a fine sieve and rinse thoroughly.

2. Heat the oil in a large saucepan over medium heat. Add the onion and cook, stirring often, until softened, 2 to 3 minutes. Add the chiles and garlic. Cook, stirring, for 30 seconds. Add the broth and quinoa and bring to a simmer. Reduce the heat to low, cover, and cook until the quinoa is tender and most of the liquid has been absorbed, 20 to 25 minutes.

3. Add the cilantro, scallions, pepitas, lime juice, and salt to the quinoa. Mix gently and fluff with a fork. One serving is 2/3 cup.

**Per serving:** 182 calories, 7 g protein, 27 g carbohydrates, 4 g fiber, 6 g total fat, 1 g saturated fat, 0 mg cholesterol, 145 mg sodium.

**Tip:** Toast the pepitas in a small dry skillet over medium-low heat, stirring constantly, until fragrant, 3 to 5 minutes.

# Mashed Sweet Potatoes with Ginger and Orange

**6**
Serves

| Preparation time: 20 minutes |
| Cooking time: 12 to 15 minutes |

Like French fries, mashed potatoes are blood sugar nightmares—but not if they're made from sweet potatoes, one of our favorite Magic foods. In this dish, fresh citrus and ginger provide delicious accents. Reducing the orange juice enhances its natural sweetness, while just a touch of butter provides exceptional enrichment with a minimum of saturated fat. This puree makes a superb holiday side dish, but it is also easy enough for simple weeknight suppers. Try it with chicken, turkey, or pork tenderloin.

1 1/2 pounds (700 grams) **sweet potatoes**
   (2 medium-large), peeled and cut into
   1 1/2- to 2-inch (4- to 5-centimeter) chunks

1 1/4 cups fresh orange juice (4 oranges)

1 tablespoon grated fresh ginger

1 **garlic** clove, minced

2 teaspoons unsalted butter

1/4 teaspoon salt, or to taste

Freshly ground pepper to taste

1. Place the sweet potatoes in a large saucepan, add enough water to cover, and bring to a boil. Reduce heat to medium, cover, and simmer until the sweet potatoes are tender, 10 to 12 minutes.

2. Meanwhile, combine the orange juice, ginger, and garlic in a small saucepan and bring to a boil. Reduce the heat to medium and simmer, uncovered, until the juice is reduced to 3/4 cup, 5 to 8 minutes. Remove from the heat, add the butter, and stir until melted.

3. When the sweet potatoes are tender, drain them and return to the saucepan. Mash with a potato masher or portable electric mixer. Gradually add the reduced orange juice mixture,

stirring with wooden spoon or beating at low speed with the electric mixer. Season with the salt and pepper. One serving is 1/2 cup. Leftovers will keep, covered, in the refrigerator for up to 2 days. Reheat in the microwave.

**Per serving:** 116 calories, 2 g protein, 24 g carbohydrates, 3 g fiber, 2 g total fat, 1 g saturated fat, 3 mg cholesterol, 130 mg sodium.

# Sweet Potato Oven Fries

4 | Preparation time: 10 minutes
--- | ---
Serves | Cooking time: 25 to 30 minutes

French fries are one of the top 10 worst foods for blood sugar. But these fries, made in the oven with sweet potatoes, have a dramatically lower GL and more nutrition to boot. They're so tasty you might even prefer them to French fries. *See photo on page 271.*

2 medium **sweet potatoes** (12–16 ounces/340–450 grams), peeled

2 teaspoons **olive oil**

1/2 teaspoon paprika

1/4 teaspoon salt, or to taste

1/8 teaspoon freshly ground pepper

1. Preheat the oven to 450°F (230°C). Coat a baking sheet that has a rim or a large roasting pan with cooking spray.

2. Cut the sweet potatoes in half crosswise, then lengthwise into 1/2-inch (1-centimeter)-wide wedges. Place on the baking sheet. Toss with the oil, paprika, salt, and pepper.

3. Bake the sweet potatoes, turning wedges over several times, until golden brown and tender, 25 to 30 minutes. One serving is 1 cup.

**Per serving:** 100 calories, 2 g protein, 19 g carbohydrates, 3 g fiber, 2 g total fat, 0 g saturated fat, 0 mg cholesterol, 177 mg sodium.

# Jerusalem Artichoke Pancakes

4 | Preparation time: 20 minutes
--- | ---
Serves | Cooking/baking time: 25 minutes

Believe it or not, you can enjoy delicious "potato" pancakes without the potatoes! Here we've used Jerusalem artichokes, also called sunchokes. Not to be confused with leafy globe artichokes, these low-GL tubers are plenty starchy, slightly sweet, and perfect for these pancakes.

1 pound (450 grams) **Jerusalem artichokes** (sunchokes), peeled

1 medium **onion,** halved and peeled

1 large **egg**

3 tablespoons all-purpose flour

1/2 teaspoon salt, or to taste

Freshly ground pepper to taste

4 teaspoons vegetable oil, divided

1/2 cup low-fat plain **yogurt**

1. Preheat the oven to 425°F (220°C). Coat a large baking sheet with nonstick spray.

2. Grate the artichokes and onion in a food processor fitted with a grating disk or on a box grater. (You should have about 2 1/2 cups grated vegetables.)

3. Whisk the egg in a large bowl. Add the grated artichoke mixture, flour, salt, and pepper, and mix well with a fork.

4. Brush 2 teaspoons of the oil over a large non-stick skillet; heat over medium-high heat. Allowing a heaping tablespoon of the artichoke mixture per pancake, drop 4 pancakes into the skillet, spacing evenly. Flatten each pancake with the back of a spatula. Cook until golden, 1 1/2 to 2 1/2 minutes per side. Transfer the pancakes to the prepared baking sheet. Repeat 2 more times

with the remaining artichoke mixture and oil, using 1 teaspoon oil for each successive batch.

5. Place the baking sheet in the oven and bake until crisp and heated through, about 10 minutes. Serve with yogurt. One serving is 3 pancakes and 2 tablespoons yogurt.

**Per serving:** 167 calories, 5 g protein, 23 g carbohydrates, 2 g fiber, 6 g total fat, 1 g saturated fat, 55 mg cholesterol, 328 mg sodium.

Tip: Once grated, Jerusalem artichokes discolor quickly. Make up the batter and cook the pancakes right away.

Ingredient Note: Jerusalem artichokes are gnarly and look similar to ginger root. Choose smooth, unblemished tubers that are firm, not soft.

# Curried Butternut Squash Puree

4 | **Preparation time: 10 minutes**
Serves | **Cooking time: 30 to 35 minutes**

A departure from traditional sweet winter squash preparations, this recipe has an exotic flavor thanks to a simple seasoning of fenugreek seeds and turmeric, two Magic spices. Fenugreek seeds have a distinctive aroma reminiscent of curry.

1 tablespoon vegetable oil

2 medium **onions,** chopped (2 cups)

2 teaspoons ground **fenugreek** seeds
  (see Ingredient Note)

1/2 teaspoon **turmeric**

Pinch of cayenne pepper

4 cups cubed (1 1/2-inch/4-centimeter chunks)
  peeled butternut squash (20 ounces/575 grams)
  (see Ingredient Note)

1 cup water

1/2 teaspoon salt, or to taste

2 teaspoons **lemon** juice

1. Heat the oil in a Dutch oven over medium heat. Add the onions and cook, stirring often, until softened but not colored, 2 to 3 minutes. Add the fenugreek seeds, turmeric, and cayenne. Stir for a few seconds until fragrant. Add the squash, water, and salt. Stir to coat. Return to a simmer, then cook, covered, over medium-low heat until the squash is very tender, 25 to 30 minutes. (Add a little additional water, if necessary.)

2. Mash the squash coarsely with a potato masher. Stir in the lemon juice. One serving is 2/3 cup. Leftovers will keep, covered, in the refrigerator for up to 2 days. Reheat in the microwave.

**Per serving:** 129 calories, 2 g protein, 25 g carbohydrates, 4 g fiber, 4 g total fat, 1 g saturated fat, 0 mg cholesterol, 299 mg sodium.

Ingredient Note: Fenugreek can be found in the bulk bins of natural foods stores, at Indian grocers, and at Web sites, such as www.kalustyans.com or www.namaste.com. If using whole fenugreek seeds, grind them in a spice mill (a coffee grinder reserved for spices works well).

# Cauliflower and Spinach Casserole

**6** Serves

Preparation time: 20 minutes

Cooking/baking time: 50 minutes

This crispy-topped casserole will win over even fussy eaters who claim they don't like vegetables. It's great for special occasions and potlucks because it can be prepared in advance and baked just before serving. (Prepare through Step 4. Cover and refrigerate for up to 2 days.) Frozen vegetables can also be used. Substitute 1 1/2 packages (16 ounces/450 grams) frozen cauliflower and 1 package (10 ounces/300 grams) frozen spinach for fresh. *See photo on opposite page.*

3 tablespoons plain dry bread crumbs

1 teaspoon **olive oil**

1/4 teaspoon paprika

1 medium **cauliflower**
(about 2 1/2 pounds/1.25 kilograms),
cored and cut into 1 1/2-inch (4-centimeter)
florets (about 7 cups)

1 package (10 ounces/300 grams) fresh **spinach**
(12 cups), stems trimmed, washed

1 3/4 cups low-fat (1%) **milk,** divided

3 tablespoons all-purpose flour

1 1/3 cups grated extra-sharp cheddar **cheese**

1 1/2 teaspoons dry mustard

1/2 teaspoon salt, or to taste

Freshly ground pepper to taste

1. Preheat the oven to 425°F (220°C). Coat a 12 x 8-inch (30 x 20-centimeter) shallow baking dish (2 1/2-quart/2 1/2-liter capacity) with non-stick spray.

2. Mix the bread crumbs, oil, and paprika in a small bowl.

3. Cook the cauliflower, uncovered, in a large pot of lightly salted boiling water until tender, about 6 minutes. Stir in the spinach. Cook until the spinach has wilted, about 1 minute longer. Drain cauliflower and spinach. Rinse with cold water to stop further cooking. Drain the vegetables thoroughly and spread in the baking dish.

4. Whisk 1/4 cup of the cold milk with the flour in a small bowl until smooth. Heat the remaining 1 1/2 cups milk in a heavy medium saucepan over medium heat until steaming. Remove from the heat and whisk in the flour mixture. Return to medium heat and cook, whisking constantly, until the sauce bubbles and thickens, 2 to 3 minutes. Remove from the heat. Stir in the cheese, mustard, salt, and pepper. Pour the sauce over the vegetables, spreading evenly. Sprinkle with the reserved bread crumb mixture.

5. Bake the casserole, uncovered, until golden and bubbly, 30 to 35 minutes. One serving is 1 cup.

**Per serving:** 175 calories, 13 g protein, 14 g carbohydrates, 10 g fiber, 9 g total fat, 5 g saturated fat, 23 mg cholesterol, 519 mg sodium.

Sweet Potato Oven Fries *page 268*
sweet potato • olive oil

Sautéed Brussels Sprouts with Red Pepper
and Caraway Seeds *page 273*
Brussels sprouts • onion • seeds • vinegar

Caulilflower and Spinach Casserole *page 270*
olive oil • cauliflower • cheese

Quinoa with Chiles and Cilantro *page 266*
quinoa • onion • garlic • scallion • seeds • lime

# Spiced Cauliflower with Peas

**6**
Serves

Preparation time: 25 minutes

Cooking time: 15 minutes

This vegetable braise from India gets its golden hue from the spice turmeric, which boasts anti-inflammatory properties and is believed to have positive affects on blood sugar. The aromatic spice mixture transforms plain old cauliflower and peas into a star-attraction side dish to accompany chicken or dahl (stewed lentils). Since the complex flavors of the spice blend develop as the dish sits, it is a good candidate for making ahead.

1 tablespoon canola oil

1 teaspoon cumin seeds

2 medium **onions,** thinly sliced (2 cups)

2 jalapeño peppers, seeded, deveined, and minced

4 **garlic** cloves, minced

1 tablespoon grated fresh ginger

1 tablespoon ground coriander

1 teaspoon ground cumin

1/2 teaspoon **turmeric**

1 cup water

1 medium head **cauliflower,** cut into florets (7–8 cups)

3/4 teaspoon salt, or to taste

1 medium **tomato,** diced (1 cup)

1 cup frozen green **peas,** rinsed under cold water to thaw

1/3 cup chopped fresh cilantro

**Lime** wedges

1. Heat the oil in a Dutch oven over medium-high heat. Add the cumin seeds and cook, stirring, until they sizzle, 10 to 20 seconds. Add the onions, jalapeños, garlic, and ginger. Cook, stirring often, until softened, 2 to 3 minutes.

Add the coriander, ground cumin, and turmeric. Stir until fragrant, 10 to 20 seconds. Add the water, cauliflower, and salt. Stir to coat well. Cover and cook until the cauliflower is almost tender, about 8 minutes.

2. Stir in the tomato and peas. Cover and cook until the cauliflower is tender and the peas are heated through, 2 to 3 minutes. Sprinkle with the cilantro and serve with the lime wedges. One serving is 1 cup. Leftovers will keep, covered, in the refrigerator for up to 2 days. Reheat in the microwave.

**Per serving:** 85 calories, 4 g protein, 13 g carbohydrates, 4 g fiber, 3 g total fat, 0 g saturated fat, 0 mg cholesterol, 349 mg sodium.

# Broccoli with Lemon Vinaigrette

**4**
Serves

Preparation time: 10 minutes

Cooking time: 5 to 8 minutes

Heaping your plate with a generous portion of broccoli is an excellent strategy for Magic eating—but not if you drown it in butter or cheese sauce. Follow the example in this recipe and use a flavorful olive oil–lemon dressing to moisten steamed broccoli. For convenience, you can substitute one 16-ounce (450-gram) package frozen broccoli florets for fresh; cook according to the package directions.

1 teaspoon freshly grated **lemon** zest

2 tablespoons **lemon** juice

1 tablespoon extra-virgin **olive oil**

2 **garlic** cloves, minced

1/4 teaspoon salt, or to taste

1/8 teaspoon crushed red pepper

Freshly ground pepper to taste

1 large bunch (1 1/2 pounds/700 grams) **broccoli**

1. Whisk the lemon zest, lemon juice, oil, garlic, salt, red pepper, and black pepper in a large bowl.

2. Separate the broccoli florets and cut into 1-inch (2.5-centimeter) pieces. Trim about 3 inches (7.5 centimeters) from stems. Peel remaining portions of stems with a paring knife and cut into 1/2-inch (1-centimeter)-thick slices. Rinse the broccoli. Place in steamer basket over boiling water. Cover and steam until crisp-tender, 5 to 8 minutes. Add to the bowl with the lemon dressing and toss to coat well. (Serve right away. The lemon juice will cause the broccoli to discolor.) One serving is 1 cup.

**Per serving:** 85 calories, 5 g protein, 10 g carbohydrates, 5 g fiber, 4 g total fat, 1 g saturated fat, 0 mg cholesterol, 192 mg sodium.

# Sautéed Brussels Sprouts with Red Pepper and Caraway Seeds

4
Serves

| Preparation time: 15 minutes |
| Cooking time: 12 minutes |

Brussels sprouts are often enjoyed as part of a Thanksgiving feast but ignored during the rest of the year. That's a shame, because this hardy vegetable is loaded with Magic benefits. Sautéed with colorful red pepper, they make a superb side dish to accompany lean meat or poultry for a simple weeknight dinner. *See photo on page 271.*

3 cups (10 ounces/280 grams) **Brussels sprouts,** trimmed and cored

2 teaspoons canola oil

1 cup sliced **onion** (1 medium)

1 medium red bell pepper, cored, seeded, and cut into 2-inch (5-centimeter)-long slivers

1 1/2 teaspoons caraway **seeds**

1/2 cup reduced-sodium chicken broth or vegetable broth

3 tablespoons cider **vinegar**

1/4 teaspoon salt, or to taste

Freshly ground pepper to taste

1. Quarter Brussels sprouts with a sharp knife or shred in a food processor fitted with a slicing disk.

2. Heat the oil in a large nonstick skillet over medium-high heat. Add the onion and bell pepper. Cook, stirring often, until softened, 3 to 4 minutes. Add the caraway seeds and cook, stirring, for 30 seconds. Add the Brussels sprouts and cook, stirring, for 2 minutes. Add the broth, cover, and cook until the sprouts are crisp-tender, about 2 or 3 minutes. Stir in the vinegar, salt, and pepper. One serving is 3/4 cup.

**Per serving:** 75 calories, 3 g protein, 11 g carbohydrates, 4 g fiber, 3 g total fat, 0 g saturated fat, 0 mg cholesterol, 233 mg sodium.

# Moroccan Spiced Carrots

4 | **Preparation time: 10 minutes**
Serves | **Cooking time: 8 minutes**

It is hard to believe that humble carrots can be transformed into such a rich-tasting yet low-calorie dish. The secret is the Moroccan spice blend, which includes a subtle hint of Magic cinnamon. And of course, we've used olive oil instead of butter.

1 1/2 pounds (700 grams) **carrots** (8–10 medium), peeled and cut into 2 1/2 x 1/2-inch (6 x 1-centimeter) sticks (4 cups)

1 tablespoon extra-virgin **olive oil**

1 **garlic** clove, minced

3/4 teaspoon paprika

1/2 teaspoon ground cumin

1/8 teaspoon **cinnamon**

Pinch of cayenne pepper

3 tablespoons **lemon** juice

2 tablespoons chopped fresh parsley or cilantro

1/4 teaspoon salt, or to taste

1. Steam the carrots until crisp-tender, 4 to 6 minutes.

2. Heat the oil in a large nonstick skillet over medium-low heat. Add the garlic, paprika, cumin, cinnamon, and cayenne. Cook, stirring, until fragrant, 1 to 2 minutes. Add the carrots, lemon juice, parsley (or cilantro), and salt. Stir to coat the carrots with the spice mixture. One serving is 3/4 cup.

**Per serving:** 107 calories, 2 g protein, 18 g carbohydrates, 5 g fiber, 4 g total fat, 1 g saturated fat, 0 mg cholesterol, 265 mg sodium.

# Spinach with Pine Nuts and Currants

4 | **Preparation time: 10 minutes**
Serves | **Cooking time: 10 minutes**

Even if you haven't had time to shop for fresh produce or are too busy to rinse fresh greens, there is no excuse for not including a side of Magic spinach on your menu. Frozen spinach works beautifully in this adaptation of a traditional Spanish recipe. Note: Use the frozen cut-leaf spinach that is packed loose in a poly bag (rather than frozen in a block and packed in a box). It is easier to sauté and tastes more like fresh spinach.

1/3 cup dried currants or coarsely chopped dark raisins

Boiling water

2 teaspoons extra-virgin **olive oil**

1/4 cup pine **nuts**

1 cup finely chopped **onion** (1 medium)

1 **garlic** clove, minced

1 bag (16 ounces/450 grams) frozen cut-leaf **spinach**

1 tablespoon balsamic **vinegar**

1/2 teaspoon salt, or to taste

Freshly ground pepper to taste

1. Place the currants in a small bowl and pour in enough boiling water to cover. Let plump for 5 to 10 minutes. Drain, reserving the soaking liquid.

2. Heat the oil in a large nonstick skillet over medium-low heat. Add the pine nuts and cook, stirring, until light golden, 1 to 2 minutes. Transfer pine nuts to a small bowl and set aside. (Do not wash the skillet.)

3. Add the onion and garlic to the skillet. Cook, stirring, until softened and light golden, 2 to 3 minutes. Add the frozen spinach and 2 tablespoons of the reserved soaking liquid. Increase

heat to medium-high and cook, stirring, until heated through and no frozen bits remain, 3 to 5 minutes. Stir in the currants and pine nuts. Season with vinegar, salt, and pepper. One serving is 3/4 cup.

**Per serving:** 165 calories, 6 g protein, 19 g carbohydrates, 5 g fiber, 9 g total fat, 1 g saturated fat, 0 mg cholesterol, 434 mg sodium.

# Sautéed Spinach with Ginger and Soy Sauce

**2** Serves | **Preparation time: 10 minutes**
**Cooking time: 5 to 8 minutes**

You cannot have enough recipes for simple spinach side dishes in your repertoire. This one has an Asian flair and features aromatic toasted sesame oil, which is low in saturated fat and has an appealing nutty flavor. You can also use frozen spinach for this recipe. In Step 1, substitute one package (10 ounces/300 grams) frozen spinach for fresh; cook according to package directions.

1 package (10 ounces/300 grams) fresh **spinach** (12 cups), stems trimmed, washed

1 tablespoon reduced-sodium soy sauce

2 teaspoons rice **vinegar**

1 teaspoon toasted sesame oil

1/4 teaspoon firmly packed brown sugar

2 teaspoons canola oil

1 **garlic** clove, minced

1 1/2 teaspoons minced fresh ginger

Dash of crushed red pepper

1 tablespoon sesame **seeds,** toasted (see Tip)

1. With just the water clinging to the leaves after washing, cook the spinach in a large, wide pot over medium-high heat just until wilted, 3 to 5 minutes. Drain, refresh under cold running water, and press out excess moisture.

2. Mix the soy sauce, vinegar, sesame oil, and sugar in a small bowl. Heat the oil in a large nonstick skillet over medium-high heat. Add the garlic, ginger, and red pepper. Stir-fry until fragrant but not browned, about 10 seconds. Add the spinach and cook, stirring often, until heated, through 2 to 3 minutes. Stir in the soy sauce mixture and toss to coat well. Sprinkle with the sesame seeds. One serving is 3/4 cup.

**Per serving:** 119 calories, 4 g protein, 7 g carbohydrates, 3 g fiber, 10 g total fat, 2 g saturated fat, 0 mg cholesterol, 348 mg sodium.

**Tip:** To toast sesame seeds, heat a small heavy skillet over medium-low heat. Add sesame seeds and stir constantly for 2 to 3 minutes or until light golden and fragrant. Transfer to a small bowl and let cool.

# DESSERTS

## Cantaloupe and Blueberry Compote with Green Tea and Lime

6 Serves | **Preparation time: 10 minutes**
| **Cooking time: 0 minutes**

Cantaloupe and blueberries are a natural pairing of Magic foods. Here a tart lime seasoning and light green tea syrup give a distinctive and thoroughly refreshing finish to a low-calorie dessert or breakfast compote.

2 green **tea** bags

2/3 cup boiling water

2 tablespoons sugar

1 teaspoon grated lime zest

2 tablespoons **lime** juice

1/2 **cantaloupe,** cut into 1 1/2-inch (4-centimeter) cubes (3 cups)

2 cups **blueberries,** rinsed and dried

1. Place the tea bags in the boiling water and let steep for 3 to 4 minutes. Remove the tea bags. Add the sugar to the tea and stir until dissolved. Stir in the lime zest and lime juice. Let cool to room temperature.

2. Combine the cantaloupe and blueberries in a large bowl. Pour the green tea mixture over the fruit and toss to coat well. One serving is 2/3 cup. The compote will keep, covered, in the refrigerator for up to 2 days.

Per serving: 72 calories, 1 g protein, 18 g carbohydrates, 2 g fiber, 0 g total fat, 0 g saturated fat, 0 mg cholesterol, 13 mg sodium.

## Mixed Berry and Stone Fruit Soup

8 Serves | **Preparation time: 20 minutes**
| **Cooking time: 0 minutes**

Don't let the title mislead you—this "soup" is actually a cool, refreshing dessert. Made with some of our favorite Magic berries and stone fruits, it bursts with flavor but contains surprisingly few calories and no fat. Serve this pretty dessert with pride.

1/4 cup orange juice

1 tablespoon **lemon** juice

3 tablespoons sugar

2 medium **nectarines,** pitted and cut into 1 x 1/2-inch (2.5 x 1-centimeter) pieces (1 1/2 cups)

3 medium **plums,** pitted and cut into 1 x 1/2-inch (2.5 x 1-centimeter) pieces (1 1/2 cups)

1 cup fresh **blueberries,** rinsed

1 cup fresh **blackberries,** rinsed

2 tablespoons frozen orange juice concentrate

2 ice cubes, crushed (see Tip)

1/2 cup nonfat vanilla **yogurt**

Mint sprigs for garnish

1. Combine the orange juice, lemon juice, and sugar in a large bowl. Stir to dissolve the sugar. Gently stir in the nectarines, plums, blueberries, and blackberries. Transfer 3/4 cup of the fruit and juices to a blender. Add the frozen orange juice concentrate and ice cubes to the blender and blend until smooth. Scrape the puree into the bowl containing the remaining fruit. Stir gently to combine.

2. To serve, ladle the "soup" into dessert bowls and garnish each serving with a dollop of yogurt and a mint sprig. One serving is 1/2 cup.

Per serving: 88 calories, 2 g protein, 21 g carbohydrates, 2 g fiber, 0 g total fat, 0 g saturated fat, 0 mg cholesterol, 10 mg sodium.

## Tips

- This "soup" is best served chilled. The addition of frozen orange juice concentrate and ice cubes cools down the fruit puree base quickly, so you can serve it right away. But if you have time, cover and refrigerate the "soup" for at least 1 hour before serving.

- To crush ice cubes, place them in a resealable plastic bag, seal, and smash with a rolling pin or saucepan.

# Pink Grapefruit Brûlée

2 Serves | **Preparation time: 5 minutes**
| **Cooking time: 5 to 7 minutes**

Chilled fresh grapefruit is always a refreshing breakfast treat, but when it is caramelized with a cinnamon-scented honey drizzle and warmed, it becomes a simple and satisfying winter dessert or brunch dish.

1 pink **grapefruit**

2 teaspoons honey

Pinch of **cinnamon**

1. Preheat the broiler. Line a small baking sheet with aluminum foil (the caramelized drippings can be hard to clean up). Cut the grapefruit in half crosswise. Use a paring knife or grapefruit knife to separate the flesh from the rind and membrane. Drizzle 1 teaspoon honey over each grapefruit half and spread evenly. Sprinkle with cinnamon. Set the grapefruit halves on the baking sheet and broil until the grapefruit skin is lightly browned in places and the grapefruit is warmed through, 5 to 7 minutes. One serving is 1/2 grapefruit.

**Per serving:** 59 calories, 1 g protein, 15 g carbohydrates, 1 g fiber, 0 g total fat, 0 g saturated fat, 0 mg cholesterol, 0 mg sodium.

# Instant Strawberry Frozen Yogurt

6 Serves | **Preparation time: 5 minutes**
| **Cooking time: 0 minutes**

Homemade desserts don't come faster or easier than this one. Even if you don't own an ice cream maker, you can still enjoy frozen yogurt that is better tasting—and better for you—than anything you can buy. Start with unsweetened frozen fruit and use your food processor to whirl in yogurt for a low-calorie frozen treat in just minutes.

16 ounces (450 grams) unsweetened frozen **strawberries** (3 1/2 cups)

1/2 cup sugar

1/2 cup nonfat plain **yogurt**

1 tablespoon orange juice

1. Place the strawberries and sugar in a food processor. Pulse until coarsely chopped. Mix the yogurt and lemon juice in a measuring cup. With the motor running, gradually pour the yogurt mixture through feed tube. Process until smooth and creamy, stopping once or twice to scrape down the side of workbowl. Serve the frozen yogurt directly from the food processor workbowl or place in freezer for 30 minutes to harden before serving. One serving is 1/2 cup.

**Per serving:** 100 calories, 1 g protein, 25 g carbohydrates, 2 g fiber, 0 g total fat, 0 g saturated fat, 0 mg cholesterol, 13 mg sodium.

---

**VARIATION** Instant Peach Frozen Yogurt

Substitute unsweetened frozen peaches for the strawberries.

# Orange and Pomegranate Compote

### 4
Serves

**Preparation time:** 15 minutes

**Cooking time:** 0 minutes

The best strategy for making Magic desserts is to celebrate the fruits of the season. This simple but elegant compote brightens a winter meal with two seasonal favorites, oranges and pomegranates, and a splash of orange liqueur. Ruby-red pomegranate seeds, renowned for their antioxidant content and high in fiber, lend an exquisite, tart flavor and an appealing crunch.

2 tablespoons orange liqueur, such as Grand Marnier or Cointreau, or orange juice

1 tablespoon sugar

3 medium-large navel oranges

1/2 pomegranate

1. Stir the orange liqueur (or orange juice) and sugar together in a medium bowl. Peel the oranges, removing the white pith with a paring knife. Quarter the oranges and slice. Add the orange segments to the bowl with the orange liqueur. Toss to coat.

2. Scoop the seeds from the pomegranate half into a small bowl, discarding the membrane. Sprinkle the pomegranate seeds over the oranges. One serving is 3/4 cup. The compote will keep, covered, in the refrigerator for up to 2 days.

**Per serving:** 94 calories, 2 g protein, 23 g carbohydrates, 3 g fiber, 0 g total fat, 0 g saturated fat, 0 mg cholesterol, 1 mg sodium.

# Pumpkin Custards

### 6
Serves

**Preparation time:** 20 minutes

**Baking time:** 50 to 55 minutes

Think of these custards as the best part of a pumpkin pie and enjoy the fact that they are significantly lower in calories and much easier to make. A pumpkin filling is distinguished by its seasoning. This one has a generous amount of cinnamon, which not only makes it taste good, it helps with blood sugar control. Vanilla soy milk makes exceptionally rich-tasting, low-fat custards. If you don't have any on hand, substitute low-fat (1%) milk and increase the vanilla to 1 teaspoon. *See photo on page 281.*

2 large eggs

2 large egg whites

2/3 cup sugar

3/4 cup canned unseasoned pumpkin puree

1 1/2 teaspoons cinnamon

1/2 teaspoon ground nutmeg

1/4 teaspoon salt

1/2 teaspoon vanilla extract

1 1/2 cups vanilla soy milk

3 tablespoons whipped cream or low-calorie whipped topping

1. Preheat the oven to 325°F (160°C). Line a roasting pan with a folded kitchen towel (this prevents the custard cups from sliding around). Put a kettle of water on to boil for the water bath.

2. Whisk the eggs, egg whites, and sugar in a large bowl until smooth. Add the pumpkin puree, cinnamon, nutmeg, salt, and vanilla. Whisk until blended. Gently whisk in the soy milk.

3. Divide the mixture among six 6-ounce/ 180-milliliter (3/4-cup) custard cups. Skim foam from the surface of the custards. Set the custard cups on the towel in the roasting pan. Pour enough boiling water into the roasting pan to come halfway up sides of the custard cups. Place the roasting pan in the oven and bake, uncovered, until custards are set, 50 to 55 minutes. Transfer

the custard cups to a rack and let cool. Cover the custards and refrigerate until chilled, at least 1 hour. Just before serving, top each custard with a dollop of whipped cream (or whipped topping). One serving is 1 custard and 1/2 tablespoon whipped cream.

Per serving: 166 calories, 5 g protein, 28 g carbohydrates, 1 g fiber, 4 g total fat, 1 g saturated fat, 75 mg cholesterol, 165 mg sodium.

# Lemony Blueberry Cheesecake Bars

## 24 Bars

Preparation time: 25 minutes

Cooking time: 55 to 60 minutes

If you love cheesecake—and who doesn't?—you will certainly enjoy this wholesome bar cookie. We've used naturally sweet blueberries to stretch the creamy filling. We've also swapped out the traditional shortbread crust (made with white flour and a copious amount of butter) for a whole wheat crust, which contains more fiber and a fraction of the saturated fat. *See photo on page 281.*

### CRUST

1 1/2 cups **whole wheat pastry flour** (see Ingredient Note, page 280*)*

1/4 teaspoon baking powder

1/4 teaspoon baking soda

1/4 teaspoon salt

2 tablespoons unsalted butter, softened

2 tablespoons canola oil

1/2 cup sugar

1 large **egg,** lightly beaten

1 teaspoon vanilla extract

### CREAM CHEESE FILLING

12 ounces (340 grams) reduced-fat cream **cheese** (Neufchâtel)

1/2 cup sugar

1 tablespoon cornstarch

2 large **eggs,** lightly beaten

4 teaspoon freshly grated lemon zest

1 1/2 teaspoon vanilla extract

3 cups fresh or partially thawed frozen **blueberries**

1. Preheat the oven to 350°F (180°C). Coat a 9 x 13-inch (23 x 33-centimeter) baking dish with nonstick spray.

2. **To make the crust:** Whisk the flour, baking powder, baking soda, and salt in a medium bowl. Beat the butter, oil, and sugar with an electric mixer in a mixing bowl until smooth. Add the egg and vanilla. Beat until smooth. Add the dry ingredients and mix with a rubber spatula just until the dry ingredients are moistened. Transfer the dough to the prepared baking dish. Use a piece of plastic wrap to press it into an even layer.

3. Bake the crust, uncovered, until puffed and starting to brown around the edges, about 20 minutes.

4. **To make the cream cheese filling:** Blend the cream cheese, sugar, and cornstarch with an electric mixer or in a food processor until smooth and creamy. Add the eggs, lemon zest, and vanilla. Beat or process until smooth. Spread the blueberries over the crust. Pour the cream cheese batter over the blueberries, spreading evenly.

5. Bake the bars until the filling has set, 35 to 40 minutes. Let cool completely in the pan on a wire rack. Cut into 24 bars with a sharp knife that has been coated with nonstick spray. One serving is 1 bar. The bars will keep, covered, in the refrigerator for up to 4 days or in the freezer for up to 1 month.

Per serving: 140 calories, 3 g protein, 17 g carbohydrates, 1 g fiber, 6 g total fat, 3 g saturated fat, 40 mg cholesterol, 105 mg sodium.

# Fudge Brownies

## 24 Bars

**Preparation time:** 20 minutes

**Baking time:** 20 to 25 minutes

Nearly everyone has a craving for a chewy chocolate treat from time to time. Here is a way to indulge yourself with a whole grain brownie that contains much less saturated fat than traditional recipes. We've lowered the GL by replacing some of the flour with oat bran and seasoning the brownies with cinnamon, a delicious complement to the chocolate. *See photo on next page.*

3 ounces/85 grams (3 squares) unsweetened chocolate

2/3 cup **whole wheat pastry flour** (see Ingredient Note)

1/3 cup **oat** bran

1/2 teaspoon **cinnamon**

1/4 teaspoon salt

1/3 cup unsweetened cocoa powder

4 large **egg** whites (see Tip)

3 large **eggs**

1 1/3 cups firmly packed light brown sugar

3/4 cup unsweetened applesauce or Lighter Bake (see Ingredient Note)

1/4 cup canola oil

1 teaspoon vanilla extract

1/2 cup bittersweet or semisweet chocolate chips

1/3 cup chopped **pecans** or **walnuts**

1. Preheat the oven to 350°F (180°C). Coat a 9 x 13-inch (23 x 33-centimeter) baking dish with nonstick spray.

2. Melt the chocolate in a double boiler over barely simmering water or in the microwave.

3. Combine the flour, oat bran, cinnamon, and salt in a medium bowl. Sift in the cocoa. Whisk to blend the dry ingredients.

4. Beat the egg whites, eggs, and sugar in a large mixing bowl with an electric mixer or a whisk until smooth. Add the applesauce (or Lighter Bake), oil, and vanilla. Beat until blended. Add the melted chocolate and beat until blended. Add the flour mixture and mix at low speed just until dry ingredients are moistened. Stir in the chocolate chips. Scrape the batter into the prepared baking dish, spreading evenly. Sprinkle with the nuts.

5. Bake the brownies until the top springs back when touched lightly, 20 to 25 minutes. Let cool completely on a wire rack. Cut into 24 bars. One serving is one 2 x 2-inch (5 x 5-centimeter) square.

**Per serving:** 156 calories, 3 g protein, 22 g carbohydrates, 2 g fiber, 8 g total fat, 3 g saturated fat, 26 mg cholesterol, 48 mg sodium.

**Tip** To avoid wasting the extra egg yolks, use reconstituted dried egg whites, such as Just Whites, which can be found in the baking section of most supermarkets.

### Ingredient Notes

• Whole wheat pastry flour is lower in protein than regular whole wheat flour. Since it has less gluten-forming potential, it is an excellent choice for tender baked goods. You can find it in large supermarkets and natural foods stores.

• Lighter Bake is a product produced by Sunsweet Growers. It is made from prunes and apples and designed for use as a fat replacement in baking. You can find it in large supermarkets in the baking section or with the dried fruits.

**Lemony Blueberry Cheesecake Bars** *page 279*
whole wheat flour • egg • cheese • blueberries

**Orange-Glazed Roasted Plums** *page 282*
plum • almonds • yogurt

**Fudge Brownies** *page 280*
whole wheat flour • oats • cinnamon • egg
• pecans

**Pumpkin Custards** *page 278*
egg • cinnamon • soy milk

# Maple-Walnut Roasted Apples

**4**
Serves

| Preparation time: 15 minutes |
| Baking time: 30 to 40 minutes |

Eaten out of hand, crisp raw apples are one of the tastiest, healthiest snacks going, but when cooked they can also be the starting point for an easy low-calorie dessert. Our sophisticated yet simple baked apple features walnuts for a dose of protein and "good" fat and maple syrup instead of brown sugar. If possible, use Red Rome or Cortland apples, considered the best choice for baking because they retain their shape, as well as their tart flavor, during baking.

1/3 cup maple syrup

3 tablespoons apple cider or apple juice

2 teaspoons unsalted butter

2 large **apples,** halved

2 tablespoons chopped **walnuts**

1 cup reduced-fat ice cream or low-fat vanilla frozen yogurt

1. Preheat the oven to 400°F (200°C). Coat an 8-inch (20-centimeter) square baking dish with nonstick spray.

2. Combine the maple syrup, apple cider, and butter in a small saucepan. Bring to a simmer, stirring. Remove from the heat.

3. Wash and dry the apple halves (leave the skin on) and remove cores. Place the apples cut side up, in the baking dish. Pour the maple syrup mixture over apples. Cover with aluminum foil and bake for 20 minutes.

4. Baste the apples with the maple syrup mixture. Sprinkle with the walnuts. Return to the oven and bake, uncovered, until the apples are tender and glazed, 10 to 20 minutes, basting once or twice. Let cool slightly. Place an apple half on each dessert dish and drizzle with syrup. Serve with a scoop of vanilla ice cream (or frozen yogurt). One serving is 1 apple half, about 2 tablespoons syrup, and 1/4 cup ice cream.

*Per serving*: 207 calories, 2 g protein, 38 g carbohydrates, 2 g fiber, 6 g total fat, 2 g saturated fat, 10 mg cholesterol, 29 mg sodium.

# Orange-Glazed Roasted Plums

**4**
Serves

| Preparation time: 15 minutes |
| Baking time: 30 to 40 minutes |

Roasting brings out the natural sweetness in fruits and is a delicious way to prepare fiber-rich stone fruits. Here, an orange-scented syrup provides a delicate balance to the tart plums. Pluots, which are hybrids of plum and apricot, have become increasingly available and also work well in this recipe. *See photo on page 281.*

1 teaspoon grated orange zest or grated fresh ginger

1/4 cup fresh orange juice (1 orange)

3 tablespoons firmly packed brown sugar

2 teaspoons unsalted butter

4 medium **plums** or pluots (1–1 1/4 pounds/ 450–600 grams), halved and pitted

2 tablespoons slivered **almonds**

1/2 cup fat-free vanilla **yogurt**

1. Preheat the oven to 400°F (200°C). Coat an 8-inch (20-centimeter) square baking dish with nonstick spray.

2. Combine the orange zest (or ginger), orange juice, and brown sugar in a small saucepan. Bring to a simmer, stirring to dissolve the sugar. Remove from the heat, add butter, and stir until melted.

3. Place the plums, cut side up, in the baking dish. Pour the orange juice mixture over the

plums. Cover with aluminum foil and bake until the plums are almost tender, 20 to 25 minutes.

4. Baste the plums with the orange syrup and sprinkle with the almonds. Bake, uncovered, until the plums are tender and glazed, 10 to 15 minutes, basting once or twice. Serve the plums warm or chilled, drizzled with the syrup and accompanied by a dollop of yogurt. One serving is 2 plum halves, about 2 tablespoons syrup, and 2 tablespoons yogurt.

Per serving: 151 calories, 3 g protein, 28 g carbohydrates, 1 g fiber, 4 g total fat, 1 g saturated fat, 6 mg cholesterol, 25 mg sodium.

# Cherry Clafouti

**8**
Serves

| Preparation time: 25 minutes |
| Baking time: 35 to 40 minutes |

Cherries are one of our favorite low-GL foods, and it's hard to think of a more delicious way to enjoy them than in a clafouti. This rustic French dessert is a cross between a custard and a baked pancake. It's simple to make and ever-so-comforting. If you're using fresh cherries, use a cherry pitter to speed the pitting process. Or use frozen cherries, which are already pitted.

2 tablespoons plus 1/2 cup sugar, divided

1/2 cup all-purpose flour

2 large **eggs**

2 large **egg** whites (see Tip page 280)

1 cup low-fat (1%) **milk**

1 tablespoon unsalted butter, melted

1 teaspoon vanilla extract

1 pound/450 grams (3 cups) fresh or partially thawed frozen sweet **cherries,** such as Bing, pitted

Confectioners' sugar for dusting

1. Preheat the oven to 400°F (200°C). Coat a 9- or 9 1/2-inch (23- or 24-centimeter) pie pan with nonstick spray. Sprinkle with 1 tablespoon sugar and tilt to coat.

2. Place 1/2 cup sugar, the flour, eggs, egg whites, milk, butter, and vanilla in a food processor or blender. Process until smooth.

3. Spread the cherries in the pie pan. Pour the egg batter over the cherries. Sprinkle with the remaining 1 tablespoon sugar. Bake the clafouti until light brown and puffed, 35 to 40 minutes. Let cool slightly. (The clafouti will sink as it cools.) Dust with confectioners' sugar and serve warm. (Leftovers are also delicious chilled.)

Per serving: 176 calories, 5 g protein, 33 g carbohydrates, 1 g fiber, 3 g total fat, 2 g saturated fat, 59 mg cholesterol, 48 mg sodium.

## VARIATION Pear-Berry Clafouti

In Step 2, add 2 teaspoons grated lemon zest to the custard. In Step 3, substitute 2 sliced, peeled Anjou pears and 1 cup fresh or unsweetened frozen raspberries for the cherries.

# Chocolate-Raspberry Cheesecake

**12** Serves

| **Preparation time: 40 minutes** |
| **Baking time: 60 to 70 minutes** |

This rich-tasting, fudgy cheesecake plays on the delicious contrast of tart raspberries and dark chocolate to make a truly impressive dessert. No one will ever guess that it is relatively low in calories and saturated fat. The secret ingredient is silken tofu. It bakes up into a velvety cheesecake, and the protein it provides helps to offset the carbohydrates in the dessert.

## CRUST

1 1/4 cups chocolate wafer cookies
   (see Ingredient Note)

1/3 cup **walnuts**

4 teaspoons light brown sugar

1/8 teaspoon **cinnamon**

3 tablespoons canola oil

## FILLING

1 package (12 ounces/350 grams) reduced-fat
   firm silken **tofu**

1 package (8 ounces/250 grams) reduced-fat
   cream **cheese** (Neufchâtel)

3/4 cup firmly packed light brown sugar

1/2 cup granulated sugar

2/3 cup unsweetened cocoa powder

4 ounces (125 grams) bittersweet
   (*not* unsweetened) chocolate, melted
   (see Ingredient Note)

2 tablespoons cornstarch

2 teaspoons vanilla extract

3 large **eggs,** lightly beaten

1 1/2 cups fresh **raspberries**

## GARNISH

1 1/4 cups Raspberry Sauce (*recipe follows*)

2 cups fresh **raspberries**

1/4 cup chocolate shavings (see Tip)

Confectioners' sugar for dusting

1. Preheat the oven to 325°F (160°C). Coat a 9-inch (23-centimeter) springform pan with cooking spray. Wrap the outside of pan with a double thickness of foil to keep water out while cheesecake is baking.

2. **To make the crust:** Put the cookies, walnuts, 4 teaspoons brown sugar, and cinnamon in a food processor. Pulse until fine crumbs form. Add the oil and pulse until the crumbs are moistened. Transfer to the pan and use the bottom of a glass to press the crumb mixture over bottom and 1/2 inch (1 centimeter) up the sides. Bake the crust until firm to the touch, 10 to 15 minutes. Set aside to cool. (Rinse and dry the food processor workbowl.

3. **To make the filling:** Put the tofu in a food processor and process until smooth, stopping to scrape down sides of workbowl once or twice. Add the cream cheese, 3/4 cup brown sugar, granulated sugar, cocoa, chocolate, cornstarch, and vanilla. Process until well blended. Add the eggs and pulse just until mixed in.

4. Put a kettle of water on to boil for the water-bath. Rinse the raspberries and pat thoroughly dry. Scatter the raspberries over the bottom of the baked crust. Scrape the chocolate batter into the pan and spread evenly. Place the cheesecake in a shallow roasting pan and pour in enough boiling water to come 1/2 inch (1 centimeter) up sides of springform pan. Bake the cheesecake until set around edges but center still jiggles when pan is tapped, 50 to 55 minutes. Turn off the oven and prop oven door open with a wooden spoon. Let the cheesecake cool in oven for 1 hour.

**5.** Remove the foil and place the springform pan on a wire rack to cool completely. Cover with plastic wrap and refrigerate until chilled, at least 4 hours or up to 4 days.

**6. To prepare the garnish:** Make the Raspberry Sauce. Rinse 2 cups raspberries and pat thoroughly dry. Run a small, sharp knife between cheesecake and pan rim to loosen edges, then remove pan rim. Set the cheesecake on a serving platter and arrange raspberries over the top. Sprinkle with chocolate shavings and dust with confectioners' sugar. Serve with Raspberry Sauce. One serving is 1/12th of the cheesecake and 1 1/2 tablespoons Raspberry Sauce.

Per serving: 352 calories, 8 g protein, 52 g carbohydrates, 6 g fiber, 16 g total fat, 6 g saturated fat, 11 mg cholesterol, 138 mg sodium.

Tip: To make chocolate shavings, warm a chunk or piece of bittersweet chocolate at low power in the microwave for a few seconds, just until pliable but not melted. Use a vegetable peeler to shave off curls.

Ingredient Notes:

• It's worth going to the natural foods section or store to find chocolate wafers for the crust that don't contain hydrogenated oils.

• Seek out the best dark chocolate, preferably one with 70 percent cocoa content. Not only do these chocolates have the truest chocolate flavor, they are richest in antioxidants.

# Raspberry Sauce

**12** Serves | **Preparation time: 5 minutes**

**Makes 1 1/4 cups**

This elegant sauce is made by simply pureeing raspberries (frozen berries work just fine). Use it to dress up a compote of strawberries or mixed berries or as a topping for low-fat vanilla ice cream or yogurt. It does contain sugar, so keep your serving sizes small.

1 package (12 ounces/300 grams) frozen unsweetened **raspberries,** thawed

1/3 cup confectioners' sugar

1 tablespoon orange juice

**1.** Put the raspberries, sugar, and orange juice in a food processor. Process until pureed. Pass the puree through a fine sieve set over a medium bowl. Discard seeds. One serving is a generous 1 1/2 tablespoons.

Per serving: 25 calories, 0 g protein, 6 g carbohydrates, 0 fiber, 0 g total fat, 0 g saturated fat, 0 mg cholesterol, 0 mg sodium.

# Apple-Cranberry Crumble

8 Serves | **Preparation time: 20 minutes**
**Baking time: 40 to 55 minutes**

With its emphasis on whole grains and fruit, this could be the ideal Magic dessert. We've replaced the white flour in the typical recipe with whole wheat to make a 100 percent whole grain topping and substituted fruit juice concentrate and canola oil for much of the butter. This is an extremely versatile concept. The variations at right offer a special dessert for every season. Top off the crumble with a dollop of fat-free vanilla yogurt.

5 cups sliced peeled **apples** (4–5 medium)

1 cup fresh or frozen **cranberries**

1/3 cup granulated sugar

2/3 cup **whole wheat flour**

1/2 cup old-fashioned rolled **oats**

1/2 cup firmly packed light brown sugar

2 teaspoons **cinnamon**

Pinch of salt

1 tablespoon unsalted butter, cut into small pieces

1 tablespoon canola oil

3 tablespoons frozen apple juice concentrate

1 tablespoon chopped **walnuts**

1. Preheat the oven to 375°F (190°C). Coat an 8-inch (20-centimter) square baking dish (2-quart/2-liter capacity) with nonstick spray.

2. Combine the apples, cranberries, and granulated sugar in the baking dish. Toss to mix. Cover with aluminum foil and bake for 20 minutes (25 minutes, if using some frozen fruit).

3. Meanwhile, mix the flour, oats, brown sugar, cinnamon, and salt with a fork in a medium bowl. Add the butter and crumble with a pastry blender or your fingertips until well blended. Add the oil and stir to coat. Add the apple juice concentrate and stir and toss until the dry ingredients are moistened.

4. When the crumble has baked for 20 minutes, sprinkle the flour mixture evenly over the fruit. Sprinkle with the walnuts. Bake, uncovered, until the fruit is bubbly and tender and the topping is lightly browned, 20 to 30 minutes longer. Let cool for at least 10 minutes before serving warm or at room temperature. One serving is 1/2 cup.

**Per serving:** 241 calories, 3 g protein, 46 g carbohydrates, 4 g fiber, 6 g total fat, 1 g saturated fat, 4 mg cholesterol, 26 mg sodium.

# Rhubarb-Blackberry Crumble

8 Serves | **Preparation time: 20 minutes**
**Baking time: 40 to 55 minutes**

If you enjoy the tart taste of rhubarb, you'll adore this sweet and tangy springtime dessert.

5 cups diced (1/2-inch/1-centimeter pieces) rhubarb (1 1/2 pounds/700 grams before trimming)

1 cup **blackberries**

1/2 cup granulated sugar

1 tablespoon cornstarch

2/3 cup **whole wheat flour**

1/2 cup old-fashioned rolled **oats**

1/2 cup firmly packed light brown sugar

1 teaspoon **cinnamon**

Pinch of salt

1 tablespoon unsalted butter, cut into small pieces

1 tablespoon canola oil

3 tablespoons frozen orange juice concentrate

1 tablespoon chopped slivered **almonds**

1. Preheat the oven to 375°F (190°C). Coat an 8-inch (20-centimter) square baking dish (2-quart/2-liter capacity) with nonstick spray.

2. Combine the rhubarb, blackberries, granulated sugar and cornstarch in the baking dish. Toss to mix. Cover with aluminum foil and bake for 20 minutes.

3. Meanwhile, mix the flour, oats, brown sugar, cinnamon, and salt with a fork in a medium bowl. Add the butter and crumble with a pastry blender or your fingertips until well blended. Add the oil and stir to coat. Add the orange juice concentrate and stir and toss until the dry ingredients are moistened.

4. When the crumble has baked for 20 minutes, sprinkle the flour mixture evenly over the fruit. Sprinkle with the walnuts. Bake, uncovered, until the fruit is bubbly and tender and the topping is lightly browned, 20 to 30 minutes longer. Let cool for at least 10 minutes before serving warm or at room temperature. One serving is 1/2 cup.

**Per serving:** 227 calories, 4 g protein, 45 g carbohydrates, 4 g fiber, 4 g total fat, 1 g saturated fat, 4 mg cholesterol, 28 mg sodium.

VARIATIONS

## Peach-Raspberry Crumble

In Step 2, combine 5 cups sliced peeled peaches (2 pounds/1 kilogram), 1 cup raspberries, 2 tablespoons sugar, and 1 tablespoon lemon juice in the baking dish. Toss to mix.

In Step 3, reduce cinnamon to 1 teaspoon and substitute frozen orange juice concentrate for the apple juice concentrate.

In Step 4, substitute chopped slivered almonds for the walnuts.

## Cherry-Raspberry Crumble

In Step 2, combine 5 cups pitted sweet cherries, such as Bing, (1 1/2 pounds/ 700 grams), 1 cup raspberries, 1/3 cup sugar, 1 tablespoon cornstarch, and 1 tablespoon lemon juice in the baking dish. Toss to mix.

In Step 2, reduce the cinnamon to 1 teaspoon and substitute frozen orange juice concentrate for the apple juice concentrate. In Step 3, substitute chopped slivered almonds for the walnuts.

## Plum-Walnut Crumble

In Step 2, combine 6 cups sliced plums (2 pounds/1 kilogram), 1/3 cup sugar, 2 teaspoons freshly grated orange zest, and 1 tablespoon orange juice in the baking dish. Toss to mix.

In Step 3, reduce the cinnamon to 1 teaspoon.

# Cherry-Almond Gratin

**6** Serves

| Preparation time: 30 minutes |
| --- |
| Baking time: 30 to 40 minutes |

Fruit baked in a rich-tasting almond cream makes a homey yet special dessert. Tofu may seem like a surprising ingredient, but it makes a very successful and healthful substitute for butter in this almond cream.

1/3 cup slivered **almonds**

1/3 cup sugar

1 tablespoon all-purpose flour

Pinch of salt

1 large **egg**

1 large **egg** white

1/2 cup reduced-fat firm silken **tofu**

1 tablespoon unsalted butter, softened

1/4 teaspoon almond extract

3 cups fresh or partially thawed frozen sweet **cherries,** such as Bing, pitted

Confectioners' sugar for dusting

1. Preheat the oven to 375°F (190°C). Coat a 9 1/2-inch (24-centimeter) pie pan with nonstick spray.

2. Spread the almonds in a small baking dish. Toast in the oven until light golden and fragrant, 4 to 6 minutes. Let cool.

3. Combine the almonds, sugar, flour, and salt in a food processor. Process until the almonds are ground. Add the egg, egg white, tofu, butter, and almond extract. Process until smooth.

4. Spread the cherries in the pie pan. Scrape the tofu mixture evenly over the cherries. Bake the gratin until light golden and firm to the touch, 30 to 40 minutes. Let cool slightly. Dust with confectioners' sugar. Serve warm or at room temperature.

**Per serving:** 168 calories, 5 g protein, 26 g carbohydrates, 2 g fiber, 6 g total fat, 2 g saturated fat, 40 mg cholesterol, 28 g sodium.

VARIATIONS

## Mixed Berry-Almond Gratin

In Step 4, substitute 3 cups mixed berries, such as raspberries, blackberries, and blueberries (fresh or frozen and partially thawed) for the cherries.

## Pear and Dried Cranberry Gratin

In Step 4, substitute 3 sliced peeled firm pears, such as Anjou or Bosc, and 1/2 cup plumped dried cranberries (microwave with 2 tablespoons water on high for 1 minute) for the cherries.

# day
## MEAL PLANS

Incorporating a few Magic foods into your diet is easy as pie. But what does a whole day of Magic eating look like? How do you know if you're eating too many carbohydrates—or not enough? How do you know if you're eating too much *food?*

To help you put the *Magic Foods* approach to work on your plate, we designed week-long meal plans based on three different calorie goals. Each meal, snack, and dessert incorporates the Seven Secrets of Magic Eating, and each day features at least a dozen different Magic foods.

You'll see for yourself not only how much food you should be eating but also what a good breakdown of carbohydrates, protein, and fat looks like; what three daily servings of whole grains look like; and what five or more daily servings of fruits and vegetables look like.

How do you know which calorie target is right for you? (Remember, controlling portion sizes and calories is key to controlling your blood sugar.) If you're trying to lose some weight, simply multiply your current weight in pounds by 10 to get the number of calories you should be eating. For instance, if you currently weigh 180 pounds and want to shed some of them, 1,800 calories a day would be about right for you. (To convert kilograms to pounds, multiply by 2.2. To convert pounds back to kilograms, multiply by 0.453.)

Otherwise, consider the 1,400-calorie target appropriate for most smaller women or women trying to lose weight; the 1,800-calorie target for most larger women, average-size men, and larger men who want to lose weight; and the 2,200-calorie target for larger or highly active men.

We don't necessarily expect you to follow every day's meal plan to the letter (although if you want to, terrific!), but do try one or two days' worth to see what the *Magic Foods* approach is like—and how good it makes you feel.

# 1400

**calorie** MEAL PLAN

| | monday | tuesday | wednesday |
|---|---|---|---|
| **breakfast** | 2/3 cup Oatmeal with Apples and Flaxseeds *page 193*<br><br>Coffee or tea | 1 orange<br><br>1 cup low-fat fruit yogurt<br><br>Coffee or tea | 3/4 cup Raisin Bran cereal with 1/2 cup sliced strawberries and 1/2 cup fat-free milk<br><br>Coffee or tea |
| **lunch** | 1 cup Turkey and Bean Chili with Avocado Salsa *page 243*<br><br>1 sliced pear with 1/2 ounce (15 grams) sliced low-fat Swiss cheese<br><br>Unsweetened iced tea or mineral water | Turkey sandwich on whole grain bread with 3 slices turkey, 1 slice avocado, lettuce, tomato, and mustard<br><br>2 celery sticks (5 inches/13 centimeters) with 1 table-spoon peanut butter<br><br>1/2 apple<br><br>Water | 2 cups Grilled Chicken Salad with Oranges *page 210*<br><br>2-inch (5-centimeter) pumpernickel dinner roll<br><br>Water or mineral water |
| **snack** | 6 red bell pepper rings<br><br>2 tablespoons Asian Peanut Dip *page 204*<br><br>Water | 2 tablespoons White Bean Spread with Italian Flavors *page 205*<br><br>4 Whole Wheat Pita Crisps *page 207* | 2 tablespoons Mediterranean Split Pea Spread *page 205*<br><br>3 small melba toast crackers |
| **dinner** | 3/4 cup Chicken Sauté with Apple *page 235*<br><br>1/2 cup Mushroom-Barley Pilaf *page 264*<br><br>1 cup steamed green beans<br><br>Water with lemon | 1 2/3 cups Greek Pasta and Beef Casserole *page 230*<br><br>1 cup Broccoli with Lemon Vinaigrette *page 272*<br><br>Unsweetened iced tea or mineral water | 1 serving Mustard-Glazed Salmon with Lentils *page 247*<br><br>1/2 cup Brown Rice Pilaf with Toasted Flaxseeds *page 265*<br><br>6 steamed asparagus spears<br><br>Water or mineral water |
| **dessert** | | | 1 serving Pumpkin Custard *page 278* |
| **NUTRITIONAL INFORMATION** | Calories: 1402; Protein: 82 g; Carbohydrate: 185 g; Fat: 42 g; Fiber: 33 g<br><br>Percentage of calories from carbs: 53; protein: 23; fat: 27 | Calories: 1445; Protein: 88 g; Carbohydrate: 197 g; Fat: 43 g; Fiber: 27 g<br><br>Percentage of calories from carbs: 54; protein: 24; fat: 28 | Calories: 1429; Protein: 90 g; Carbohydrate: 180 g; Fat: 44 g; Fiber: 30 g<br><br>Percentage of calories from carbs: 50; protein: 25; fat: 28 |

| thursday | friday | saturday | sunday |
|---|---|---|---|
| 3/4 cup Kashi GoLean cereal with 1/2 cup fat-free milk<br><br>1 nectarine<br><br>1/2 cup orange juice | 3/4 cup hot oat bran with 1/2 cup blueberries and 1/2 cup fat-free milk<br><br>Coffee or tea | 2 Multi-Grain Pancakes with syrup and strawberries *page 192*<br><br>1/2 cup fat-free milk | Spinach and Goat Cheese Omelet *page 194*<br><br>2 cantaloupe wedges<br><br>Coffee or tea |
| Tuna and Carrot Sandwich on Rye *page 222*<br><br>8 Spiced Almonds *page 203*<br><br>1 peach<br><br>Unsweetened iced tea | Whole wheat wrap with 3 slices lean ham, 1 slice low-fat Muenster cheese, lettuce, and tomato<br><br>3/4 cup grapes<br><br>1 container (4 ounces/ 125 milliliters) low-fat fruit yogurt<br><br>Water with lemon | 1 1/2 cups Curried Red Lentil Soup *page 224*<br><br>1 tablespoon hummus<br><br>8 baby carrots<br><br>Water | 1 1/4 cups Whole Wheat Chicken and Noodles with Peanut Sauce *page 214*<br><br>2 fresh pineapple slices<br><br>Water with lemon |
| 1 Oatmeal–Peanut Butter Trail Bar *page 207* | 1 1/2 cups popcorn mixed with 7 peanuts and 1/2 tablespoon Smart Balance or Becel (in Canada) spread | 1 1/2 ounces (45 grams) semisoft goat cheese drizzled with lemon juice<br><br>1 Wasa Crispbread rye cracker | 4 whole wheat pretzel sticks<br><br>1 stick reduced-fat string cheese |
| 5 ounces (140 grams) Flank Steak with Balsamic Sauce *page 228*<br><br>3/4 cup brown rice<br><br>2 cups romaine lettuce salad with cherry toma-toes, cucumber, 1/4 cup chickpeas, and 1 table-spoon each olive oil and balsamic vinegar<br><br>Water | 1 1/2 cups Shrimp and Orzo Casserole *page 251*<br><br>1 cup green beans<br><br>2 cups baby spinach salad with tomato and cucumber and 1 table-spoon each olive oil and balsamic vinegar<br><br>Unsweetened iced tea or mineral water | 1 1/2 cups Slow-Cooker Beef and Vegetable Stew *page 228*<br><br>1/2 slice Whole Wheat Flaxseed Bread *page 196*<br><br>1 1/4 cups romaine lettuce salad with cherry toma-toes, cucumber, and 1/2 tablespoon each olive oil and vinegar<br><br>Water with lemon | 1 3/4 cups Spring Vegetable Stir-Fry with Tofu *page 260*<br><br>1/2 cup brown rice<br><br>Green tea |
| | | 3/4 cup Orange and Pomegranate Compote *page 278* | 1/2 cup Instant Strawberry Frozen Yogurt *page 277* |
| Calories: 1417; Protein: 83 g; Carbohydrate: 175 g; Fat: 50 g; Fiber: 28 g<br><br>Percentage of calories from carbs: 49; protein: 24; fat: 31 | Calories: 1399; Protein: 84 g; Carbohydrate: 172 g; Fat: 42 g; Fiber: 26 g<br><br>Percentage of calories from carbs: 49; protein: 24; fat: 27 | Calories: 1444; Protein: 81 g; Carbohydrate: 186 g; Fat: 41 g; Fiber: 35 g<br><br>Percentage of calories from carbs: 52; protein: 22; fat: 26 | Calories: 1401; Protein: 82 g; Carbohydrate: 169 g; Fat: 49 g; Fiber: 25 g<br><br>Percentage of calories from carbs: 48; protein: 23; fat: 32 |

# 1800
## calorie MEAL PLAN

| | monday | tuesday | wednesday |
|---|---|---|---|
| **breakfast** | 3/4 cup Oatmeal with Apples and Flaxseeds *page 193* with 4 slivered almonds<br><br>1/2 cup unsweetened grapefruit juice | 1 Blueberry Oatmeal Muffin *page 198*<br><br>1 orange<br><br>1/2 cup low-fat fruit yogurt<br><br>Coffee or tea | 3/4 cup Raisin Bran cereal with 1/2 cup sliced strawberries, 5 walnuts (chopped), and 1/2 cup fat-free milk<br><br>Coffee or tea |
| **lunch** | 1 1/4 cups Turkey and Bean Chili with Avocado Salsa *page 243*<br><br>1 sliced pear with 1/2 ounce (15 grams) sliced low-fat Swiss cheese<br><br>Unsweetened iced tea | Turkey sandwich on whole grain bread with 3 slices turkey, 1 slice avocado, lettuce, tomato, and mustard<br><br>2 celery sticks (5 inches/13 centimeters) with 2 tablespoons peanut butter<br><br>1 apple<br><br>Water | 2 1/2 cups Grilled Chicken Salad with Oranges *page 210*<br><br>2-inch (5-centimeter) pumpernickel dinner roll<br><br>Water |
| **snack** | 6 red bell pepper rings<br><br>3 tablespoons Asian Peanut Dip *page 204*<br><br>Water | 3 tablespoons White Bean Spread with Italian Flavors *page 205*<br><br>8 Whole Wheat Pita Crisps *page 207* | 2 tablespoons Mediterranean Split Pea Spread *page 205*<br><br>5 small melba toast crackers |
| **dinner** | 1 1/4 cups Chicken Sauté with Apple *page 235*<br><br>1/2 cup Mushroom-Barley Pilaf *page 264*<br><br>1 cup steamed green beans<br><br>Water with lemon | 2 cups Greek Pasta and Beef Casserole *page 230*<br><br>1 cup Broccoli with Lemon Vinaigrette *page 272*<br><br>Unsweetened iced tea | 1 1/2 servings Mustard-Glazed Salmon with Lentils (use 6 ounces/170 grams fish) *page 247*<br><br>1/2 cup Brown Rice Pilaf with Toasted Flaxseeds *page 265*<br><br>6 steamed asparagus spears<br><br>Water |
| **dessert** | | | 1 serving Pumpkin Custard *page 278* |
| **NUTRITIONAL INFORMATION** | Calories: 1814; Protein: 102 g; Carbohydrate: 233 g; Fat: 59 g; Fiber: 39 g<br><br>Percentage of calories from carbs: 51; protein: 23; fat: 29 | Calories: 1781; Protein: 103 g; Carbohydrate: 229 g; Fat: 60 g; Fiber: 34 g<br><br>Percentage of calories from carbs: 51; protein: 23; fat: 30 | Calories: 1804; Protein: 118 g; Carbohydrate: 209 g; Fat: 63 g; Fiber: 38 g<br><br>Percentage of calories from carbs: 46; protein: 26; fat: 31 |

| thursday | friday | saturday | sunday |
|---|---|---|---|
| 1 cup Kashi GoLean cereal with 1/2 cup fat-free milk<br><br>1 nectarine<br><br>1/2 cup orange juice | 3/4 cup hot oat bran with 1/2 cup blueberries, 4 pecans (chopped), and 1/2 cup fat-free milk<br><br>Coffee or tea | 2 Multi-Grain Pancakes with syrup and strawberries *page 192*<br><br>1/2 tablespoon Smart Balance or Becel (in Canada) spread<br><br>1/2 cup fat-free milk | 1 Spinach and Goat Cheese Omelet *page 194*<br><br>1/2 whole wheat English muffin<br><br>1/2 tablespoon Smart Balance or Becel (in Canada) spread<br><br>2 cantaloupe wedges<br><br>Coffee or tea |
| Tuna and Carrot Sandwich on Rye *page 222*<br><br>15 Spiced Almonds *page 203*<br><br>1 peach<br><br>Unsweetened iced tea | Whole wheat wrap with 3 slices lean ham, 1 slice low-fat Muenster cheese, lettuce, tomato, and mustard<br><br>1 cup grapes<br><br>1/2 cup low-fat fruit yogurt with 2 tablespoons ground flaxseeds<br><br>Water with lemon | 2 cups Curried Red Lentil Soup *page 224*<br><br>2 tablespoons hummus<br><br>8 baby carrots<br><br>Water | 1 2/3 cups Whole Wheat Chicken and Noodles with Peanut Sauce *page 214*<br><br>2 slices fresh pineapple<br><br>Water with lemon |
| 1 Oatmeal–Peanut Butter Trail Bar *page 207* | 2 cups popcorn mixed with 7 peanuts and 1 table-spoon Smart Balance or Becel (in Canada) spread | 1 1/2 ounces (45 grams) semisoft goat cheese drizzled with lemon juice<br><br>2 Wasa Crispbread rye crackers | 6 whole wheat pretzel sticks<br><br>2 ounces (60 grams) low-fat Colby cheese (2 1-inch/2.5-centimeter squares) |
| 6 ounces (170 grams) Flank Steak with Balsamic Sauce *page 228*<br><br>1 cup brown rice<br><br>2 cups romaine lettuce salad with cherry toma-toes, cucumber, 3/4 cup chickpeas, and 1 table-spoon each olive oil and vinegar<br><br>Water | 2 cups Shrimp and Orzo Casserole *page 251*<br><br>1 cup steamed green beans<br><br>2 cups baby spinach salad with tomato, cucumber, and 1 tablespoon each olive oil and balsamic vinegar<br><br>Unsweetened iced tea | 2 cups Slow-Cooker Beef and Vegetable Stew *page 228*<br><br>1 slice Whole Wheat Flaxseed Bread *page 196*<br><br>1 1/4 cups romaine lettuce salad with cherry toma-toes, cucumber, and 1/2 tablespoon each olive oil and vinegar<br><br>Water with lemon | 2 1/4 cups Spring Vegetable Stir-Fry with Tofu *page 260*<br><br>3/4 cup brown rice<br><br>Green tea |
| | | 3/4 cup Orange and Pomegranate Compote *page 278* | 1/2 cup Instant Strawberry Frozen Yogurt *page 277* |
| Calories: 1813; Protein: 101 g; Carbohydrate: 1237 g; Fat: 59 g; Fiber: 37 g<br><br>Percentage of calories from carbs: 52; protein: 22; fat: 29 | Calories: 1797; Protein: 103 g; Carbohydrate: 204 g; Fat: 65 g; Fiber: 36 g<br><br>Percentage of calories from carbs: 45; protein: 23; fat: 32 | Calories: 1828; Protein: 108 g; Carbohydrate: 222 g; Fat: 64 g; Fiber: 35 g<br><br>Percentage of calories from carbs: 48; protein: 24; fat: 31 | Calories: 1836; Protein: 103 g; Carbohydrate: 231 g; Fat: 55 g; Fiber: 47 g<br><br>Percentage of calories from carbs: 50; protein: 23; fat: 27 |

# 2200
## calorie MEAL PLAN

| | monday | tuesday | wednesday |
|---|---|---|---|
| **breakfast** | 3/4 cup Oatmeal with Apples and Flaxseeds *page 193* with 4 slivered almonds<br><br>1/2 cup unsweetened grapefruit juice<br><br>Coffee or tea | 1 Blueberry Oatmeal Muffin *page 198*<br><br>1 orange<br><br>1 cup low-fat fruit yogurt<br><br>Coffee or tea | 1 cup Raisin Bran cereal with 3/4 cup sliced strawberries, 7 walnuts (chopped), and 3/4 cup fat-free milk<br><br>Coffee or tea |
| **lunch** | 2 cups Turkey and Bean Chili with Avocado Salsa *page 243*<br><br>1 sliced pear with 4 (1/2 ounce/15 grams) slices low-fat Swiss cheese<br><br>Unsweetened iced tea | Turkey sandwich on whole grain bread with 3 slices turkey, 1 slice provolone cheese, 1 slice avocado, lettuce, tomato, and mustard<br><br>4 celery sticks (5 inches/13 centimeters) with 2 tablespoons peanut butter<br><br>1 apple<br><br>Water | 3 cups Grilled Chicken Salad with Oranges *page 210*<br><br>2-inch (5-centimeter) pumpernickel dinner roll<br><br>Water |
| **snack** | 6 red bell pepper rings<br><br>3 tablespoons Asian Peanut Dip *page 204*<br><br>Water | 4 tablespoons White Bean Spread with Italian Flavors *page 205*<br><br>8 Whole Wheat Pita Crisps *page 207*<br><br>1/4 cucumber, sliced | 3 tablespoons Mediterranean Split Pea Spread *page 205*<br><br>5 small melba toast crackers |
| **dinner** | 2 cups Chicken Sauté with Apple *page 235*<br><br>1/2 cup Mushroom-Barley Pilaf *page 264*<br><br>1 cup steamed green beans<br><br>Water with lemon | 2 1/2 cups Greek Pasta and Beef Casserole *page 230*<br><br>1 cup Broccoli with Lemon Vinaigrette *page 272*<br><br>Unsweetened iced tea | 8 ounces (250 grams) Mustard-Glazed Salmon with Lentils *page 247*<br><br>3/4 cup Brown Rice Pilaf with Toasted Flaxseeds *page 265*<br><br>8 steamed asparagus spears<br><br>Water |
| **dessert** | | | 1 serving Pumpkin Custard *page 278* |
| **NUTRITIONAL INFORMATION** | Calories: 2202; Protein: 123 g; Carbohydrate: 278 g; Fat: 74 g; Fiber: 47 g<br><br>Percentage of calories from carbs: 50; protein: 22; fat: 30 | Calories: 2196; Protein: 131 g; Carbohydrate: 272 g; Fat: 74 g; Fiber: 37 g<br><br>Percentage of calories from carbs: 49; protein: 24; fat: 30 | Calories: 2196; Protein: 149 g; Carbohydrate: 259 g; Fat: 72 g; Fiber: 47 g<br><br>Percentage of calories from carbs: 47; protein: 27; fat: 29 |

| thursday | friday | saturday | sunday |
|---|---|---|---|
| 1 1/4 cups Kashi GoLean cereal with 1/2 cup low-fat milk<br><br>1 nectarine<br><br>1/2 cup orange juice | 1 1/4 cups hot oat bran with 2/3 cup blueberries and 6 pecans (chopped)<br><br>3/4 cup fat-free milk<br><br>Coffee or tea | 2 Multi-Grain Pancakes with syrup and strawberries *page 192*<br><br>1 tablespoon Smart Balance or Becel (in Canada) spread<br><br>3/4 cup fat-free milk | 1 Spinach and Goat Cheese Omelet *page 194*<br><br>1/2 whole wheat English muffin<br><br>1/2 tablespoon Smart Balance or Becel (in Canada) spread<br><br>2 cantaloupe wedges<br><br>Coffee or tea |
| 2 Tuna and Carrot Sandwiches on Rye *page 222*<br><br>15 Spiced Almonds *page 203*<br><br>1 peach<br><br>Unsweetened iced tea | Whole wheat wrap with 3 slices lean ham, 2 slices low-fat Muenster cheese, lettuce, and tomato<br><br>1 1/2 cups grapes<br><br>1/2 cup low-fat fruit yogurt with 2 tablespoons ground flaxseeds<br><br>Water with lemon | 2 1/2 cups Curried Red Lentil Soup *page 224*<br><br>2 tablespoons hummus<br><br>8 baby carrots<br><br>Water | 1 2/3 cups Whole Wheat Chicken and Noodles with Peanut Sauce *page 214*<br><br>1/4 cup edamame<br><br>2 pineapple slices<br><br>Water with lemon |
| 1 Oatmeal–Peanut Butter Trail Bar *page 207* | 2 cups popcorn mixed with 7 peanuts and 1 tablespoon Smart Balance or Becel (in Canada) spread | 2 ounces (60 grams) semi-soft goat cheese drizzled with lemon juice<br><br>2 Wasa Crispbread rye crackers | 4 whole wheat pretzel sticks<br><br>1 stick reduced-fat string cheese |
| 6 ounces (170 grams) Flank Steak with Balsamic Sauce *page 228*<br><br>1 cup brown rice<br><br>2 cups salad with romaine lettuce, cherry tomatoes, cucumber, 1/2 cup chickpeas, and 1 tablespoon each olive oil and vinegar<br><br>Water | 2 1/4 cups Shrimp and Orzo Casserole *page 251*<br><br>1 cup steamed green beans<br><br>2 cups baby spinach salad with tomato, cucumber, and 1 tablespoon each olive oil and balsamic vinegar<br><br>Unsweetened iced tea | 2 1/2 cups Slow-Cooker Beef and Vegetable Stew *page 228*<br><br>1 slice Whole Wheat Flaxseed Bread *page 196*<br><br>2 1/2 cups salad with romaine lettuce, cherry tomatoes, cucumber, and 1 tablespoon each olive oil and vinegar<br><br>Water with lemon | 2 3/4 cups Spring Vegetable Stir-Fry with Tofu *page 260*<br><br>1 cup brown rice<br><br>Green tea |
| | | 3/4 cup Orange and Pomegranate Compote *page 278* | 3/4 cup Instant Strawberry Frozen Yogurt *page 277* |
| Calories: 2232; Protein: 121 g; Carbohydrate: 272 g; Fat: 73 g; Fiber: 44 g<br><br>Percentage of calories from carbs: 49; protein: 22; fat: 29 | Calories: 2177; Protein: 124 g; Carbohydrate: 248 g; Fat: 77 g; Fiber: 42 g<br><br>Percentage of calories from carbs: 46; protein: 23; fat: 32 | Calories: 2221; Protein: 126 g; Carbohydrate: 256 g; Fat: 75 g; Fiber: 55 g<br><br>Percentage of calories from carbs: 46; protein: 23; fat: 30 | Calories: 2201; Protein: 126 g; Carbohydrate: 275 g; Fat: 76 g; Fiber: 43 g<br><br>Percentage of calories from carbs: 50; protein: 23; fat: 31 |

# index

Page numbers in *italic* type indicate recipe titles. Page numbers in ***bold italic*** type indicate recipe photos.

# Food Cures

## Breakthrough Nutritional Prescriptions for Everything from Colds to Cancer

Marianne Wait, Editor

Reader's Digest

The Reader's Digest Association, Inc.
New York, NY | Montreal

# Chief Consultants

**Susan Allen, RD, CCN**
Private Practice
Past Chair, American Dietetic Association's
Nutrition in Complementary Care Practice
Group

**Mary M. Austin, MA, RD, CDE**
Private Practice
Past President, American Association of
Diabetes Educators

**William G. Christen, ScD, OD**
Associate Professor in Medicine
Harvard Medical School

**Karen Collins, MS, RD**
Nutrition Advisor
American Institute for Cancer Research

**Randy J. Horwitz, MD, PhD**
Medical Director, Program in Integrative
Medicine
University of Arizona, Tucson

**David L. Katz, MD, MPH**
Associate Clinical Professor
Public Health and Medicine
Yale University School of Medicine

**Ben Kligler, MD, MPH**
Associate Professor of Medicine (Family
Medicine)
Albert Einstein College of Medicine
Research Director
Continuum Center for Health and Healing

**Ashley Koff, RD**
Private Practice

**Victoria Maizes, MD**
Executive Director
Program in Integrative Medicine
University of Arizona

**Daniel Muller, MD, PhD**
Associate Professor of Medicine
(Rheumatology)
University of Wisconsin-Madison

**Jeri W. Nieves, PhD**
Associate Professor of Clinical Epidemiology
Columbia University

**David Perlmutter, MD**
Board-Certified Neurologist
Private Practice

**Rebecca Reeves, DrPH, RD**
Assistant Professor of Medicine
Baylor College of Medicine

**Steve L. Taylor, PhD**
Professor and Director
Food Allergy Research & Resource Program
Department of Food Science & Technology
University of Nebraska-Lincoln

**SPECIAL THANKS TO** Eugene Arnold, MD;
Neil Barnard, MD; Scott Berliner, RPh; Amy
Brown, PhD, RD; Laura Coleman, PhD, RD;
Tanya Edwards, MD; Evan Fleischman, ND;
Marc Greenstein, DO; Jon D. Kaiser, MD;
Penny Kris-Etherton, PhD; Jessica Leonard,
MD; Alan Magaziner, DO; Alexander
Mauskop, MD; Eva Obarzanek, PhD;
Alexandra J. Richardson, PhD; Michael
Rosenbaum, MD, MSc; Roseanne Schnoll,
PhD, RD, CDN; Suzanne Steinbaum, DO;
Bonnie Taub-Dix, MS, RD; Mark Toomey,
PhD; Jan Zimmerman, MS, RD.

# contents

**PART**

*two*

# Your Food Cures Arsenal  *352*

## Top 20 Healing Foods  354

## 10 Healing Herbs and Spices  374

## Where the Nutrients Are  378

PART

*three*

# Food Cures for Common Conditions 386

PART

*four*

# Healing Recipes 588

# Food, Wonderful Food

For those who follow news from the world of medical research, the past few years have been filled with intriguing announcements. All kinds of breakthrough healing medicines have been "discovered"—but many of them aren't pills. Instead, they're oatmeal for heart disease, salmon for asthma, peanuts for high cholesterol, and yogurt for eczema. Forget about wonder drugs; we're living in a time of wonder foods.

Of course, the concept of food as medicine is many thousands of years old. Hippocrates, considered the father of medicine, prescribed a veritable pharmacy of edibles, from bread soaked in wine to boiled fish. Yet somehow, over the past century, this message got lost. Until recently, few doctors ever recommended a food as a potential solution to a health problem. So what has changed?

Primarily, we have become far smarter about the underlying causes of common diseases. Researchers have discovered, for instance, that arthritis isn't a simple case of wear and tear but rather a destructive process spurred by molecules called free radicals. This knowledge opened the door to the next discovery: that getting more leafy greens and orange and yellow produce, rich in antioxidants that neutralize free radicals, helps stave off this crippling condition. We've also learned more about the healing powers of specific foods. We now know that pumpkin seeds improve symptoms of an enlarged prostate, that regularly eating yogurt effectively suppresses the bacteria that cause most ulcers, and that cabbage helps the stomach lining heal.

What else has changed? The medical community is finally taking the research to heart. Doctors are talking about nutrition and food solutions to everyday ailments more often than ever before. And what outstanding news this is! Who wouldn't rather eat a piece of dark chocolate than swallow a high-cost, potentially dangerous pill? Best of all, in contrast to most prescription drugs today, most healthy foods provide multiple benefits to your body. Our message: Food can be a source of both pleasure and healing. So take a few minutes now and turn to one of the health problems that concerns you, then follow our food and supplement prescriptions. Even better, try some of the healing recipes that we've included—they're as delicious as they are healthy! You'll see for yourself the very real power of food as medicine.

Neil Wertheimer
**Editor in Chief**
**Reader's Digest Health Books**

# The New Food Medicines

*An apple a day can keep the doctor away—and now researchers finally know why. Welcome to the new world of food as medicine, where nature's bounty has the power to ease, erase, and abolish many of the nagging health problems and major killers of our day.*

There's a new frontier in medicine. Researchers at the forefront say the key to a longer, healthier life is an idea that's radical—some old-school doctors still don't seem to get it—yet simple: Food can help heal what ails you. That is, adding the right foods to your diet, while leaving others off the menu, can bolster your body's defenses against disease, treat disease directly, and even slow the aging process.

The tools of this discipline aren't scalpels and scanners but rather serving spoons and spatulas. Nevertheless, it's strong medicine. The studies are piling up fast, and they're impossible to ignore: Choose wisely in your grocer's produce section, the data show, and you may spend less time in line at the pharmacy. Get to know your local fishmonger, and you may never meet a cardiologist. Start thinking about food in a novel way—as a form of therapeutic and preventive medicine—and you may need a lot less of the kind of medicine that gets itemized on insurance bills.

Maybe you already make occasional forays into this new frontier. Have you skipped the porterhouse steak and potato in favor of salmon and a green salad lately? Made breakfast toast with dense, chewy slices of whole-grain bread instead of the nutrient-challenged white variety? Snacked on a tangerine instead of a candy bar or finally switched to fat-free milk?

Taking simple measures such as these can have profound effects on your health and well-being—and not just because they spare your body from a lot of *un*healthy stuff, such as saturated fat and refined sugar, though that certainly is a good start. Exciting new studies have confirmed what some healers have believed for thousands of years: Many foods are packed with beneficial chemicals that can promote health and protect your body from the ravages of disease.

The idea of nutrition therapy goes all the way back to the beginning. "Let food be thy medicine and medicine be thy food," said Hippocrates, the ancient Greek who is widely regarded as the father of modern medicine. True to his word, Hippocrates prescribed a grocery list of edible cures, everything from bread soaked in wine to boiled fish. If those remedies don't exactly pique your appetite, don't worry. In the pages that follow, you'll learn about a cornucopia of foods that please the palate *and* contain remarkable medicinal qualities. Almonds and avocados. Strawberries and sweet potatoes. Fruity extra-virgin olive oil and delicacies from the sea.

You probably already know that these foods are good sources of vitamins, minerals, and nutrients. But you may not realize that fruits, vegetables, and other plant foods also contain thousands of newly discovered compounds, known as phytochemicals or phytonutrients, that scientists are still busy cataloging. These chemicals provide flavor and color, yet cutting-edge research suggests that many of them are also important—some scientists say essential—to your health. For instance, a cup of green tea contains 30 to 40 different catechins, which are chemicals that fight cancer, lower cholesterol, and may even help you drop a few pounds.

In short, the foods described in these pages are nutritional powerhouses bursting with compounds that have specific and well-defined health benefits. They have another advantage: You won't find many reports in the medical literature of broccoli overdoses, and the only way a banana can hurt you is if you slip on the peel—which isn't something you can say about those medicines you store in a cabinet over the bathroom sink.

Rare is the medication that doesn't have at least some potential for problems. Can you spell "Vioxx"? Maybe so, but you can no longer find it at your pharmacy; manufacturers were forced to pull the once-popular prescription

> Many foods are packed with beneficial chemicals that promote health and protect your body from the ravages of disease.

painkiller and several similar drugs off the market due to concerns that they damage the cardiovascular system. Some studies suggest that over-the-counter pain relievers, such as ibuprofen, slightly increase the risk of heart attacks, too. In fact, a report by the Institute of Medicine estimated that at least 1.5 million Americans become ill or die each year due to errors in prescribing, dispensing, and taking medications.

Changing your diet won't guarantee that you'll never need drugs or get sick, of course. But according to the Harvard School of Public Health, if all Americans ate the right foods—and exercised regularly and avoided tobacco—the number of heart attacks in the United States would drop by about 82 percent. Strokes would diminish by roughly 70 percent. Type 2 diabetes would practically disappear, and colon cancer rates would decrease by 70 percent. This book will teach you the steps that can put you on the right side of those numbers.

# Fat Gets a Facelift

The less fat you eat, the better—right? Not necessarily. Although fat was once the very face of dietary evil, recently it's gotten major facelift of sorts. It's no wonder we equate "fat" with "bad." A half century

ago, scientists made a discovery that made us think hard, almost for the first time, about our food and our health: People who live in countries where the diets are rich in saturated fat have far more heart attacks than people who eat less meat, dairy foods, and other sources of the stuff. Later research showed that eating saturated fat raises blood levels of cholesterol, causing this waxy substance to build up in the arteries and block blood flow to the heart.

Fat eventually became nutrition enemy number one. Remember the old USDA Food Guide Pyramid? Fats and oils (which are simply liquid fat) were lumped together with sweets in the tiny uppermost wedge of the pyramid, accompanied by the stern recommendation: USE SPARINGLY. Cookbooks loaded with fat-free recipes filled bookstore shelves. "Nonfat!" and "Fat-Free!" were stamped on food labels, often on products that never contained fat in the first place. Doctors-turned-authors, such as Dean Ornish, M.D., preached the virtues of very low fat diets.

These messages may have convinced you to make some very good, important changes, such as switching from whole milk to fat-free and stripping bacon from your diet. But they also led consumers to make some unfortunate choices, and we're not just talking about those tofu dogs you bought a few years back. One consequence of the anti-fat movement was that many people cut back on *all* fats—a trend that may have actually made us sicker, according to some prominent experts.

"There was no benefit, and there was likely some harm," says Walter Willett, M.D., of the Harvard School of Public Health.

## "Vitamin F"

Your body stores about 80 percent of the fat you consume. Ideally, you burn off most of this reserved energy by staying physically active. If not, the fat you eat becomes the fat you fear, the kind that makes your clothes too snug and imperils your health.

However, about 20 percent of the fat in your diet is not stored. Instead, your body puts it right to work, since an astonishing variety of tissues and biological processes require a daily infusion of fat. Without fat, your hair and skin would be dull and dry. More important, fat in the diet allows your body to absorb the so-called fat-soluble vitamins, including A, D, E, and K. Every cell in your body needs fat to build a healthy protective membrane. Fat also provides the raw materials that your body uses to produce chemicals that control blood pressure, prevent blood clots, and regulate the body's response to injury and infection. In fact, the stuff that gives many foods that familiar luscious texture is so important to human health that scientists in the 1920s briefly called certain forms of fat "vitamin F."

If you crave fudge or filet mignon with béarnaise sauce, blame evolution. Our ancestors developed a taste for fat as a way to be sure of packing on extra pounds to survive in times when food was scarce. A gram of fat has twice as many calories as an equal amount of carbohydrate or protein. No wonder survival food rations are often laden with fat.

Of course, few of us need extra calories today. And it's still as important as ever to cut back on saturated fat—think beef, butter, and cheese—a major culprit behind heart attacks, not to mention insulin resistance, the problem at the core of diabetes. But cutting out all the fat in your diet might not pay off as you'd expect. That's because experts have discovered that far from being deadly, daily doses of certain fats actually fight disease. Many scientists and nutrition experts now believe that these unsaturated fats—a.k.a. the "good" fats—inhibit everything from diabetes, depression, and dementia to cancer, joint pain, and yes, even heart disease.

Replacing some of the calories in your diet that come from saturated fat with calories from unsaturated fat (trading a hamburger for a salmon burger, for instance) may be even better for you than replacing them with carbohydrate calories. Studies show that swapping saturated fat in your diet for carbohydrate-rich foods, such as rice or pasta, has only a modest effect on heart disease risk. On the other hand, Harvard researchers studied the diets of 80,000 nurses for 14 years and determined that replacing just 5 percent of calories from saturated fat with an equal amount of good fat can reduce the risk of heart disease by 42 percent.

It's not just your heart that benefits from these fats, though. They also fight an impressive range of other diseases, as you'll read shortly. But first let's explain which fats we're talking about.

## Defining Good Fats

As anyone who has ever struggled to lose weight knows, the body is very good at making its own fat, which it stores most prominently on the hips, thighs, and midsection. That's because even if you eat nothing but rice cakes and carrot sticks, but you eat too many of them, your body converts the sugars in those foods that it doesn't burn as energy into triglycerides, the storage form of fat.

However, your body can't make some types of fatty acids—the building blocks of fat—that

> Far from being deadly, daily doses of certain fats actually fight disease.

are essential to health. That's why your diet must include the aptly named essential fatty acids, which come primarily from fish and plant oils and fall into the broader category of polyunsaturated fats. Meanwhile, you can live without eating monounsaturated fats, which form the other major category of unsaturated fat—but mounting research suggests that you may not live as long or as well as people who do enjoy plenty of these other good fats.

### Monounsaturated fats: Olive oil and beyond

You may have been surprised to learn a few years back that a bit player in your cupboard was in fact a nutritional marvel. Scientific trials, such as the Lyon Diet Heart Study, found that eating a so-called Mediterranean diet appears to protect the cardiovascular system more effectively than a typical low-fat one. The cornerstone of a traditional Mediterranean diet? It's olive oil, one of nature's richest sources of monounsaturated fat.

In fairness, some of the wonders of the olive may have been overhyped by the cooking oil industry. After all, the traditional Mediterranean diet also includes frequent servings of fruits and vegetables as well as plenty of fish. But it's hard to ignore the fact that people in the Lyon Diet Heart Study who ate a Mediterranean-type diet consumed plenty of fat, much of it in the form of monounsaturated fatty acids in olive oil, yet they had four times *fewer* heart attacks than people asked to eat a standard low-fat diet.

Olive oil isn't the only good source of monounsaturated fat that may already be in your kitchen. Its shelf mate, canola oil, is another. Nuts are packed with monos, too, so add peanut butter and peanut oil to the list. Need an excuse to eat avocados? The green flesh of these nubby-skinned fruits contains nearly as many grams of fat as a Big Mac, but the fat is mostly monounsaturated.

### Polyunsaturated fats: Go fish, go nuts

Remember the cod-liver oil of your grandparents' day? It used to be fashionable to joke

## Don't Spoil Your Oil

Olive oil and canola oil are excellent sources of healthy fats and antioxidants. But cooking oil is a fragile food that turns rancid and loses antioxidants in a hurry if it's not stored properly. Protect yours from these four influences to keep it fresh and nutritious.

**Light:** Oils spoil faster when kept in clear containers. Ceramic or tinted-glass bottles are better choices. A dark, dry cupboard is ideal for storing most cooking oils.

**Heat:** Make sure that cupboard isn't next to the stove. Storing oil in the refrigerator is another option if you live in a warm climate or don't plan to use it promptly. (Nut oils turn rancid quickly, so they must be refrigerated.) Some oils become thick and cloudy when chilled but reliquefy when raised to room temperature.

**Air:** Oxygen and oil don't mix, so make sure whatever container you choose has an airtight lid or cover.

**Age:** Even under the best conditions, cooking oils have a limited shelf life. Most taste best and retain more nutrients when used within one year of opening the original container.

about this favorite all-purpose remedy. But who's laughing now? Fish oil is the best source of omega-3 fatty acids, one of the two main types of polyunsaturated fat and probably the best-for-you fat around. In recent years, scientists have linked a boatload of new health benefits to consuming this form of fat, such as lower rates of heart disease and depression. (You'll read much more about the special benefits of omega-3s in a bit.)

You don't have to swallow cod-liver oil to get omega-3s, though. Eating seafood, especially cold-water fish, is your best option. The fat that protects all marine creatures from cold water, from arctic char to Atlantic salmon, is packed with omega-3s. Unlike with beef or pork, you want to go for the fattiest fish possible, such as salmon, since more oil means more healthful omega-3s. Albacore tuna is another good choice, as are Atlantic mackerel, lake trout, herring, and sardines. (But think twice before gulping cod-liver oil, even if you can stand the taste; the recommended doses may contain toxic levels of vitamins A and D.)

Fish-phobes, fear not: There are other ways to put these fats to work in your body. Fish-oil capsules are one option, though you should talk to your doctor before taking them because they can thin the blood. Walnuts, walnut oil, flaxseed, and flaxseed oil won't give you omega-3s exactly, but they do supply a type of fat called alpha-linolenic acid (ALA), which your body can turn into omega-3s.

Less famous—and perhaps less healthful—than the omega-3s are their cousins, the omega-6s, the kind of fat you get when you pour corn, sunflower, or safflower oil into your pan or eat packaged foods that contain soybean oil, which food processors use in a wide range of products. Margarine, usually made of vegetable oil, is another major source of omega-6s, Most of us consume far more of these fats than of omega-3s, and that may spell trouble, according to many experts. More on this shortly.

By the way, all fats and oils contain a blend of saturated, monounsaturated, and polyunsaturated fatty acids, along with smaller amounts of other elements. But any given fat or oil tends to have a higher concentration of one type. For example, 62 percent of the fat in butter is saturated, while 29 percent is monounsaturated and a trace is the polyunsaturated variety. By contrast, just 14 percent of the fat in olive oil is saturated, while 74 percent is monounsaturated and 8 percent is polyunsaturated.

## Better Fats, Better Health

Are you getting enough fat in your diet? Just a few years ago, the question would have sounded crazy, but many scientists and nutrition experts now believe that mono- and polyunsaturated fats have a critical role in any healthy eating plan. These versatile fats seem to offer a variety of benefits for the cardiovascular system; likewise, they fight an impressive range of diseases.

### Fish, Not Defibrillators

Each year, about a quarter of a million people in the United States with no prior history of cardiovascular disease die of sudden cardiac death, which occurs when the heart starts beating erratically. To battle this problem, health officials are encouraging people to learn how to use defibrillators, which shock the heart back to steady rhythm. But one study determined that even if every home and public place (such as airports and restaurants) in a community had defibrillators, only about 1 percent of sudden cardiac deaths would be prevented.

By contrast, raising blood levels of omega-3 fatty acids within a population would avert *eight times* as many deaths, according to an analysis in the *American Journal of Preventive Medicine*. To get the necessary level of protection, people would need to take fish-oil supplements, the authors of this study say. However, one study of 20,000 men found that simply eating fish once a week slashes the risk of sudden cardiac death in half. Another study found that dining on fish just once or twice per month provides similar protection against strokes. The American Heart Association recommends eating several servings of fish each week.

It's not just the polyunsaturated fats in fish that protect the cardiovascular system. The good fats in nuts, most of which contain a healthy dose of both kinds of unsaturated fat

## Anatomy of "Good" Fats

Chemical structure distinguishes good fats—the unsaturated ones—from saturated fats. The details get pretty technical but boil down to this: All fat molecules are made of carbon, hydrogen, and oxygen atoms. Saturated fats are full of hydrogen atoms, and monounsaturated fats are missing a pair, while polyunsaturated fats lack two or more pairs. These differences, among other chemical attributes, affect the appearance of a fat—and influence how it behaves inside your body. They're why saturated fats tend to be solid at room temperature, while unsaturated fats are easily converted to oils once they're liberated from the fish, nuts, seeds, and other foods they come from.

# THE HEALING POWERS OF
# nuts

Brazil nuts contain more selenium, an antioxidant trace mineral, than any other food.

Nuts are loaded with monounsaturated fats that benefit the heart, stabilize blood sugar, and help you lose weight.

Most nuts are significant sources of antioxidants.

An ounce of almonds has more fiber than a cup of strawberries.

Not a fish fan? Go nuts with walnuts, one of the best nonfish sources of omega-3 fatty acids.

Almonds are one of nature's best sources of vitamin E and are rich in calcium, too.

(mono and poly), also offer this benefit. Eating three servings of almonds, peanuts, pecans, or walnuts per week as part of an overall heart-healthy diet may decrease total cholesterol by up to 16 percent and LDL ("bad") cholesterol by up to 19 percent, according to a study published in the *Journal of Nutrition*. The fat in vegetable oil helps lower cholesterol, too. (The fat in fish has little effect on cholesterol, but it does lower levels of triglycerides, another blood fat linked to heart attacks, by up to 33 percent.)

### Add Oil, Hold the Sugar

Eating more nuts, olive oil, and other foods rich in monounsaturated fats may also help safeguard you from the threat of type 2 diabetes. For starters, filling up on these good fats means you'll have less room for fatty meat, whole milk, and other sources of saturated fat, which contributes to insulin resistance—and high blood sugar. Left unchecked, chronically elevated blood sugar can cause type 2 diabetes—yet another reason why trimming the saturated fat from your meals is a no-brainer.

Exchanging saturated fat for monounsaturated fat may be even better than exchanging it for carbs. This theory remains somewhat controversial, but research shows that diets high in monounsaturated fat control blood sugar just as effectively as the typical high-carb, low-fat diet many doctors recommend to prevent and control diabetes. In fact, some studies have shown them to be superior.

What's more, increasing your intake of monounsaturated fats appears to have other benefits you don't get from a high-carb diet, such as lowering levels of triglycerides. A study by Mexican researchers found that diabetes patients were able to lower their blood sugar while eating diets rich in olive oil and avocados. The study found that switching over to a high-carb diet worked, too. However, the patients' triglyceride levels dropped 20 percent while eating the high-mono diet, compared to just 7 percent when they followed the high-carb meal plan.

### Fighting Cancer, Mediterranean Style

The Lyon Diet Heart Study mentioned earlier grabbed headlines mostly for the apparent

## Inside Omega-3s: Alphabet Soup

The two major components of omega-3s are a mouthful to pronounce—docosahexaenoic acid and eicosapentaenoic acid—but you can call them DHA and EPA. You may have begun to notice these letters on products such as packages of eggs enriched with DHA. The FDA allows food manufacturers that add DHA or EPA to their products to state on labels that consuming these omega-3 fatty acids "may reduce the risk of coronary heart disease."

DHA, a fatty acid found in some eggs and in fish, may be one of the best nutrients for the brain.

cardiovascular benefits of the Mediterranean-style diet. But here's more good news: Those same study subjects, who ate plenty of fish and olive oil, cut their risk of cancer by 61 percent.

Although many questions remain about the link between diet and cancer, intriguing evidence suggests that healthy fats may protect against some forms of the disease. For example, studies in the 1990s showed that women who consume plenty of olive oil lower their risk of breast cancer by about 25 percent. More recently, a team of researchers at Northwestern University in Chicago discovered that oleic acid, the main form of monounsaturated fat in olive oil, reduces activity of a gene that causes an aggressive form of breast cancer by 46 percent. What's more, oleic acid appeared to increase the effectiveness of transluzumab (Herceptin), a drug used to treat breast cancer. A second study found that fish oil may offer similar benefits.

### Salmon, the Edible Antidepressant

If you ever travel to Iceland in the middle of January, don't count on seeing much of the sun: It rises at about 10 a.m. and disappears by 5 p.m. However, don't expect to find a bunch of gloomy natives, either. Icelanders have surprisingly low rates of seasonal affective disorder, the mood condition caused by low exposure to sunlight. Their secret to happiness? Some scientists think it's fish oil.

Consider this: The typical Icelander eats five times more seafood than do people in the United States or Canada. Several other studies have shown that rates of depression tend to be lower in countries where fish is frequently the main course. What's more, University of Pittsburgh researchers recently found that people who had the highest levels of omega-3 fatty acids in their blood were 53 percent less likely to report feeling mildly or moderately depressed.

No one is certain why fish oil may help fight the blues, although DHA may affect the formation of chemicals linked to depression. While there's no guarantee that eating more salmon and tuna will make you happy-go-lucky, some scientists are studying whether having low levels of omega-3s contributes to depression. One scientific trial found that people with bipolar depression who added fish-oil supplements to their medication regimen had milder symptoms and fewer relapses than similar patients given placebo supplements.

### Feed Your Memories Well

Think of fish oil as brain food. The body uses its DHA to build and repair the membranes that protect brain cells. DHA also seems to be necessary for brain cells to communicate with one another. Eating plenty of fish may even lower your risk of dementia, the gradual loss of mental ability that sometimes accompanies aging. For example, researchers at Chicago's Rush-Presbyterian-St. Luke's Medical Center found that people who ate fish just once a week reduced their risk of Alzheimer's disease by 60 percent. The same research group also found that diets high in saturated fat and trans fats (the kind in hydrogenated cooking oil used by restaurants and food processors) seem to increase the risk of dementia. "What appears to be healthy for preventing cardiovascular disease also appears to be helpful for preventing Alzheimer's disease," says lead scientist Martha Clare Morris, Ph.D.

Scientists have also linked a deficiency of omega-3s to other cognitive problems, including attention deficit hyperactivity disorder, or ADHD. Blood tests show that children who struggle with the impulsivity, tantrums, and learning difficulties associated with this condition tend to have unusually low levels of DHA. Preliminary research hints that correcting that deficiency may help kids with ADHD settle down and focus. For example, one study by researchers at McLean Hospital near Boston showed that dietary supplements containing salmon oil and other fatty acids (as well as vitamins and plant nutrients) controlled ADHD symptoms as well as Ritalin, the widely prescribed stimulant drug.

> Diets high in monounsaturated fat control blood sugar just as effectively as the typical high-carb, low-fat diet many doctors recommend.

# Nature's Advil:
## THE NEW SUPER-HEALERS

We've talked about the benefits of unsaturated fats, particularly the omega-3 fats in fish. But we haven't even touched on the biggest, most far-reaching benefits of omega-3s—and no doubt the most important

new breakthrough in our understanding of how our diets affect our health.

Here's a conundrum: About half of all heart attacks strike people who have normal cholesterol levels. Most cardiologists now agree that much of the "cholesterol gap" can be explained by a natural phenomenon gone awry: inflammation. In fact, inflammation has taken center stage as a major contributor to just about every chronic disease, from heart disease to diabetes to cancer. And fighting inflammation, as it turns out, is one of the jobs that omega-3s do best.

Inflammation plays a useful, even lifesaving role when it's acting as nature intended—to help an injury heal. Without it, a paper cut on your pinky finger could be fatal. That cut, or any other type of injury, from a scraped knee to a tongue burned by hot coffee, sets off a chain of events intended to limit the damage. First, the body increases blood flow to the injury site, delivering white blood cells that begin mopping up dead cells and bacteria, if any, to prevent infection. Other proteins arrive and seal off the area to stop germs and other harmful stuff from spreading to neighboring tissue. Inflamed skin feels warm to the touch because your body turns up the metabolic rate in the damaged tissue to speed the healing process. Even the pain and swelling that can accompany inflammation are beneficial, since the discomfort forces you to take it easy, which allows cells in the injured body part to repair and heal.

A scraped knee is one thing, but there's much more to inflammation than most of us—even

most experts—ever thought. Cardiologists now agree that inflammation triggers many heart attacks by causing artery-clogging plaques filled with cholesterol and other gunk to burst and form blood clots. In fact, studies show that having very high levels of inflammation-causing chemicals in the blood increases the risk of heart attack up to fourfold.

It's also increasingly clear that controlling inflammation with omega-3s can lower heart attack risk and also quiet the symptoms of some common conditions, such as rheumatoid arthritis. It may even offer protection against diseases as diverse and deadly as diabetes and cancer.

## A Case of "Global Warming"

When inflammation is short-lived, it's not a problem. But thanks in part to our modern-day lifestyles, including the foods we favor and the extra weight that many of us carry, our bodies are living in a state of chronic inflammation—a sort of biological "global warming." To a growing number of scientists from many fields, this chronic inflammation is a silent scourge that causes premature aging and disease.

Intriguingly, scientific evidence is emerging to suggest that inflammation is the link between apparently unrelated diseases. For instance, a study at Weill Medical College at Cornell University found that people with rheumatoid arthritis have a threefold increase in their risk of developing early signs of heart disease. People with lupus and the inflammatory skin disease psoriasis have an unusually high risk for heart attacks, too.

Chronic inflammation is silent; you can't feel it the way you can feel a sore thumb. That doesn't mean it can hide, however. Inflammation leaves behind a trail in the form of a marker called C-reactive protein, or CRP, which can be measured with a simple blood test. Some doctors use the CRP test to decide how aggressively to treat patients who have other risk factors for heart attacks and strokes, such as high cholesterol and obesity.

## Dousing the Flames with Fish Oil

If inflammation's so bad for you, you may wonder, why not control it by popping an ibuprofen tablet or two every day? Ibuprofen and other nonsteroidal anti-inflammatory drugs (NSAIDs), including aspirin, have a place in any medicine chest; nothing beats them for relieving an occasional headache or sore muscles after exercise. But using them too much can lead to gastrointestinal problems— and worse, in some cases. As you probably know, prescription drugs used to treat pain and inflammation, such as Vioxx, have been linked to heart trouble. However, according to recent studies, even over-the-counter NSAIDs such as ibuprofen may increase the risk of heart attacks, particularly in people who already have cardiovascular disease.

> Inflammation has taken center stage as a major contributor to just about every chronic disease, from heart disease to diabetes to cancer.

It's enough to make you padlock your pill box. Fortunately, you can help control inflammation and the destruction it can cause by eating more fish and other foods rich in omega-3 fatty acids, nature's own anti-inflammatories. Scientists first began to suspect there was something special about omega-3s when they noticed that heart disease is rare among people who eat a lot of seafood. And we do mean a lot—the original research involved Greenland Eskimos, who at the time survived largely on whale and seal meat.

However, scientists also discovered that these Eskimos rarely developed certain other diseases, including asthma, psoriasis, and rheumatoid arthritis. The common link? Out-of-control inflammation. Researchers eventually showed that omega-3 fatty acids appear to stifle inflammation in several ways. For one, they prevent the body from using other fatty acids needed to create prostaglandins and other hormone-like compounds that cause inflammation. They also block and reduce the number of hostile white blood cells the immune system dispatches to inflamed regions of the body. Consuming more omega-3s may be the key to quelling these and other common conditions.

### Heart disease

An idea that seemed kooky not so long ago has gained wide acceptance. Doctors now believe that persistent low levels of inflammation create an unstable environment in the arteries, causing clumps of cholesterol and other gunk to burst open and form heart-stopping clots. But cheer up: Help is as close as the fish counter or natural foods aisle at your supermarket. In one study, women who ate the most fish, flaxseed, and other foods rich in omega-3s had 29 percent less inflammation in their arteries (as indicated by levels of CRP) than women who consumed the least. Eating more fish appears not only to reduce inflammation but also to protect the heart in several other ways—by lowering levels of triglycerides and stabilizing heart rhythm, for example.

### Cancer

Many oncologists now believe that excessive inflammation causes or speeds up the growth of many types of cancer. According to one theory, inflammation increases the rate at which cells "turn over," which raises the odds that defective cells will emerge in their place, leading to the out-of-control cell growth that produces malignant tumors. In some cases, persistent inflammation from common infections may increase cancer risk. For example, it's well known that some types of the human papillomavirus can cause cervical cancer, while stomach cancer primarily strikes people who have been infected with *Helicobacter pylori*, the bacteria that cause ulcers. Other sources of chronic inflammation have been linked to malignancies, too. People plagued by inflammatory bowel diseases, for example, have an unusually high risk of colon cancer.

Scientists are still studying whether dampening inflammation by consuming more omega-3 fatty acids prevents cancer, but some tantalizing clues have emerged. For instance, high doses of fish oil block colon tumors from forming in lab animals, apparently by cooling inflammation. What's more, eating fish three times a week halved the risk of prostate cancer in one study of nearly 48,000 males, while a Swedish study found that men who never ate seafood had double or triple the risk for the disease.

### Asthma

Asthma rates are rising persistently, and some doctors believe our diets may be to blame. The wheezing and gasping brought on by an asthma attack occur because the bronchial tubes, which deliver air to the lungs, become inflamed. Inflammation causes the airways to narrow, which causes the asphyxiating symptoms. Recently, some scientists have speculated that the omega-6 fatty acids in many types of cooking oil and (in smaller amounts) in animal foods may be the culprits. (Read more on these fats starting on page 329.) Many Americans consume large amounts of omega-6s, which the body uses to produce chemicals that cause inflammation.

Since omega-3 fatty acids reduce inflammation, consuming more fish oil—and fewer foods that contain omega-6s—may help prevent asthma attacks, at least in theory. Some evidence supports this idea. For example, an Australian study found that children who ate fish regularly cut their asthma risk by 75 percent. A study by Dutch researchers found a 50 percent reduction in asthma rates among children who had the highest intake of fish and whole grains.

## Choosing Safe Seafood

In recent years, concerns about toxicity have threatened to sink fish's reputation as a healthy food. Seafood is one of nature's best sources of disease-fighting omega-3 fatty acids, but some varieties pack high levels of mercury and other toxins. Is eating fish really worth the risk?

Yes, say many leading health experts. In 2006, the *Journal of the American Medical Association* (*JAMA*) and the Institute of Medicine (which advises the federal government on health policy) published separate reports examining fish safety. The *JAMA* study determined that eating one or two servings of fish per week reduces the threat of a fatal heart attack by 36 percent and the overall risk of dying by 17 percent. The authors flatly state that "the benefits of fish intake exceed the potential risks."

The second report, though less conclusive, endorsed the following levels of fish consumption.

- *For children under 12 and women of childbearing age:* Two 3-ounce servings of fish per week is a reasonable goal, but stick to no more than 6 ounces of canned tuna or 12 ounces of any fish, total. Avoid varieties that have high levels of mercury (see below).

- *For all other adults:* Two 3-ounce servings per week is a reasonable goal. If you eat more, be sure to choose a variety of fish.

Other guidelines for selecting healthy seafood:

- Favor varieties with the highest concentration of omega-3 fatty acids. In order, the top 10 are salmon, Atlantic herring, anchovies, Atlantic mackerel, halibut, albacore tuna, mussels, oysters, trout, and sardines.

- Limit or avoid fish with high mercury content. Four types to skip are golden bass (also called tilefish), shark, swordfish, and king mackerel.

- Think twice before paying extra for "wild" fish. Many species are endangered, but ecological issues aside, wild fish may not be the healthiest choice. For instance, farmed salmon has significantly more omega-3 fatty acids than wild salmon does.

## Flax for Fish-Phobes?

If you want the benefits of omega-3 fatty acids and the convenience of a pill, fish-oil supplements may seem like the answer. But many people can't bear the side effects, which can include fishy-smelling breath, skin, and even urine. Freezing the capsules or switching brands may help, although another strategy might seem more appealing: taking flaxseed-oil supplements instead. After all, flax contains alpha-linolenic acid (ALA), which the body can convert to the two most important omega-3 fatty acids, EPA and DHA.

Unfortunately, this conversion isn't very efficient. It's thought that only a small percentage of the ALA you consume turns into EPA, and the amount that converts to DHA is even smaller.

While many studies suggest that fish-oil capsules can reduce the risk of heart attacks, the evidence to support using ALA supplements is far less convincing. However, flax oil is certainly better than nothing. One recent survey found that women who eat frequent servings of food that contains ALA cut their risk of sudden cardiac death by up to 40 percent. The American Heart Association recommends including plenty of ALA-rich foods, such as flaxseed and flaxseed oil, walnuts and walnut oil, canola oil, and tofu, in your diet.

### Diabetes

Most people who develop type 2 diabetes are overweight. Fat cells produce chemicals that contribute to insulin resistance, the hallmark of the disease. They also churn out proteins that cause inflammation. Several large studies, which included more than 50,000 subjects combined, found that women with the highest levels of chronic inflammation had a fourfold increase in their risk of type 2 diabetes.

Scientists aren't sure why, but inflammatory chemicals may interfere with the work of insulin, causing blood sugar to rise. Perhaps it's no coincidence that population studies show that fish lovers have unusually low rates of type 2 diabetes.

## Battling Autoimmune Diseases

Fish oil may also help relieve symptoms of some autoimmune disorders, such as rheumatoid arthritis. These are diseases in which the immune system mistakenly recognizes a perfectly healthy organ or other tissue, such as your thyroid or knee joints, as the enemy. In its confusion, it orders battalions of inflammatory chemicals to attack the healthy body part, leaving a wake of inflammation.

Autoimmune disorders include many common conditions, including type 1 diabetes (this occurs when the immune system mistakenly destroys insulin-producing beta cells in the pancreas) and thyroid disease. In lupus, the body attacks tendons, cartilage, and other connective tissue.

Consuming more omega-3 fatty acids won't necessarily prevent any of these diseases, but it may help relieve their symptoms in some cases. Think of eating fish for dinner or sprinkling flaxseed on your cereal as giving yourself a low dose of natural pain-relief medicine. Research into omega-3 fatty acids for treating autoimmune disorders has focused on fish-oil supplements, which appear to offer promise for treating two particular autoimmune conditions.

### Rheumatoid arthritis

Since the 1990s, an impressive number of studies has shown that fish oil prevents and treats rheumatoid arthritis (RA). Unlike the more common osteoarthritis, RA occurs when the immune system attacks joints in the fingers, wrists, toes, and other parts of the body, causing them to swell, ache, and feel weak. Patients with RA often rely on medications such as aspirin, ibuprofen, and other NSAIDs to ease their pain and stiffness.

Just as eating fish cuts your odds of having a heart attack, it also makes you less likely to develop RA. In fact, eating just two fish dinners per week may slash the risk of this joint disease by 50 percent, according to a University of Washington study. There have been at least 18 formal studies of people with RA who were asked to take daily fish-oil supplements (about 3.5 grams per day on average) to control their symptoms; all but one found at least some improvement. In one trial, patients who took fish-oil capsules reported less morning stiffness, pain, and tenderness after six months; many were able to stop taking NSAIDs altogether. Patients in a comparison group who took capsules containing corn oil experienced no improvement.

> Think of eating fish for dinner or sprinkling flaxseed on your cereal as giving yourself a low dose of natural pain-relief medicine.

### Inflammatory bowel disease

Persistent inflammation causes several common and maddening gastrointestinal conditions. These so-called inflammatory bowel diseases (IBDs) include Crohn's disease and ulcerative colitis. While Crohn's disease can produce inflammation anywhere in the GI tract, it usually strikes in the small intestine, resulting in abdominal pain, fever, diarrhea, and fatigue. Ulcerative colitis affects the colon and rectum.

It's painful, too, but also causes bloody diarrhea and urgent bowel movements; left untreated, long-term inflammation from colitis can increase the risk of colon cancer.

Some IBD patients require powerful anti-inflammatory medications called corticosteroids, which can prevent or treat flare-ups but may also cause unwanted side effects. While adding a few servings of fish to your weekly menu may not relieve these troublesome disorders, there is reason to believe that fish-oil supplements can help. In one study, Italian researchers asked a group of people with Crohn's disease who had gone into remission to take 2.7 grams of omega-3 fatty acids per day in the form of fish-oil capsules. A similar group of patients took placebo pills. After one year, the people taking high doses of omega-3s were twice as likely to still be in remission. A few other studies of fish oil and Crohn's disease offer hope, too, although overall, the results have been mixed.

The outlook is somewhat less clear for ulcerative colitis, but research hints that increasing your intake of omega-3 fatty acids may be worthwhile. In particular, studies suggest that people with moderate to severe colitis may be able to reduce their doses of corticosteroid medication if they supplement their diets with fish oil. In one small trial, nearly three-quarters of the subjects who took 4.2 grams of omega-3s per day in the form of fish oil either reduced or eliminated their use of medications.

# THE HEALING POWERS OF
# fish

Fish oils have emerged again and again as effective treatments for health conditions involving inflammation.

Good fats are a main reason people who eat plenty of fish have unusually low rates of type 2 diabetes.

DHA, one type of omega-3 fatty acid, cuts the risk of Alzheimer's. EPA eases skin conditions.

Ounce for ounce, a salmon steak has one fourth the saturated fat of beef steak.

Most fish contains about the same amount of protein as meat and provides iron and vitamin $B_{12}$, important for energy.

# A Cool Diet:
## MORE WAYS TO CHILL INFLAMMATION

You've started dreaming up new ways to cook salmon. When you toss a salad, you sprinkle on some chopped walnuts. You've even learned to love flaxseed. So far, so good, but adding omega-3 fatty acids to your

diet is just the first step you should take to turn down the heat in your body. To gain total control over the damaging effects of chronic inflammation, cutting back on or eliminating certain foods may be just as important.

Which foods spark flames? Relax—you don't have to give up *chiles rellenos* or any other tongue-searing dishes you may enjoy. The main inflammation inducers in most diets are less obvious—and more omnipresent. Some may be staples in your kitchen. Others you may not think much about unless you read the ingredient lists on labels. All coax your body's immune system into producing more inflammatory chemicals than it needs to defend itself, which could increase your risk of developing one of many debilitating chronic illnesses.

If the thought of avoiding certain foods leaves you feeling deprived, don't worry. In some cases, the inflammation-inducing culprits described below have healthful counterparts that will fit nicely into your diet. In other instances, food processors have begun to replace such ingredients with safer alternatives.

## Time for an Oil Change?

Omega-3 fatty acids may be nutritional superstars, but some nutritionists take a dimmer view of their fellow polyunsaturated fats—the omega-6 fatty acids, prominent in corn oil, sunflower oil, and safflower oil. However, they're not all bad by any means. After all, omega-6s aren't considered "essential" for

nothing—your body needs them for normal development and a strong immune system, among other roles. However, few of us need to worry about getting enough omega-6s, since deficiency of these fats is practically unheard of. Instead, some scientists say, our bodies suffer from an oversupply.

Consider this: Our cave-dwelling ancestors consumed a diet that included roughly equal amounts of omega-3 and omega-6 fatty acids. Today, the typical American consumes at least 10 times more omega-6s than omega-3s. Some experts, including Artemis Simopoulos, M.D., author of *The Omega Diet*, believe the ratio is even higher. "Our genes haven't changed in 10,000 years," says Dr. Simopoulos. "If you're on the standard American diet, we know you're not getting enough omega-3s. And we also know that you're getting an enormous amount of omega-6 fatty acids."

In fairness, some nutrition experts don't believe that the ratio of essential fatty acids we consume is making us sick. Says Harvard's Dr. Walter Willett, "It's amazing how strong that myth seems to have become. There's really no human evidence to support it and quite a bit to suggest that it's not true. The ratio is really irrelevant." For instance, population studies indicate that people who replace saturated fat with either monounsaturated or polyunsaturated fat (which includes omega-6s) reduce their risk of heart disease, he notes.

However, other nutritionists feel that cutting back on our high intake of omega-6s may be as important as increasing our woefully low consumption of omega-3s. The imbalance creates problems, explains Dr. Simopoulos, because the human body processes both of these fats with the same enzymes. When omega-6s outnumber omega-3s, there are fewer enzymes around to process omega-3s, robbing the body of an inflammation fighter. What's more, omega-6s provide the raw materials for the body to produce prostaglandins, which promote inflammation. (And that's not all: A high intake of omega-6s may increase the risk of blood clots and cause LDL cholesterol to become oxidized, making it more likely to clog arteries.)

The solution? Dr Simopoulos and others recommend banning corn oil from your kitchen, since it's brimming with omega-6 fatty acids. Sunflower and safflower oil contain even more. As part of an overall plan to limit inflammation, you may want to consider replacing these cooking oils with olive, canola, peanut, or flaxseed oil.

> Gram for gram, trans fats increase the risk of heart disease more than any other food ingredient.

## Trans Fats: "Metabolic Poison"

If there's still debate over corn oil, there is no argument among scientists over the threat posed by another form of cooking oil: hydrogenated oil, which is simply vegetable oil with added hydrogen. This molecular tweaking gives cooking oil a longer shelf life and other properties that make it ideal for use in packaged goods and fast foods. Unfortunately, hydrogenation also produces sinister compounds called trans fatty acids, which raise levels of LDL cholesterol and also seem to lower levels of HDL cholesterol. Gram for gram, trans fats increase the risk of heart disease more than any other food ingredient, according to a review in the *New England Journal of Medicine*. No wonder Dr. Willett calls them metabolic poison. Scientists now know that along with wreaking havoc on cholesterol, these fats increase the risk of a number of other diseases, including Alzheimer's, type 2 diabetes, and gallstones.

Eating trans fats may even cause greater weight gain than eating other fats, according to one provocative study.

One reason trans fats have such far-reaching effects on the body appears to be that they ignite inflammation. It's not clear why, but studies consistently show that eating foods that contain trans fats causes levels of inflammatory chemicals to soar. In one study, women who consumed the most foods containing trans fats had 73 percent more inflammation, as indicated by levels of CRP, than women who ate the least. By one estimate, cutting your intake of trans fats in half could lower inflammation enough to slash your risk of heart disease by 30 percent.

Need another reason to curb your enthusiasm for cookies, chips, fast-food french fries, and other empty-calorie treats? You've got it, since these foods are the leading sources of trans fats in most diets. Some brands of margarine contain trans fats, too. A number of manufacturers have reduced or eliminated hydrogenated oils in their products, although they are still widely used in restaurants and food processing. Diet guidelines from the USDA recommend reducing your intake of trans fats to less than 1 percent of your daily calories. That means if you eat a typical American diet, you're getting two or three times what you should. (Toting up your intake became easier to do in 2006, when the USDA began requiring manufacturers to list trans fat content on food labels.)

## Fighting Inflammation: New Reasons to Follow Old Rules

Along with reconsidering which cooking oil you use and steering clear of trans fats, you can snuff out inflammation in your body even further by adhering to some familiar advice. People who keep their weight down, avoid saturated fat, and eat plenty of fruits and vegetables live longer for many reasons. One of them, scientists now know, is that these steps help reduce inflammation. Following a bit of newer advice—choosing your carbohydrates wisely—seems to help, too.

## Watch Your Weight

Scientists now know that fat cells do more than simply add flab to your hips and thighs. They constantly churn out proteins that affect your health, including several that promote inflammation. One study of 16,000 adults found that obese males were twice as likely to have elevated levels of inflammation compared to normal-size men. Obese women were six times more likely than slender women to have high CRP levels. Many scientists now believe that inflammation is a key reason people who struggle with weight suffer disproportionately from heart disease and diabetes.

Fortunately, shedding pounds appears to lower inflammation. In one 2006 study, for example, women who lost an average of 13 pounds lowered their CRP levels by an impressive 41 percent.

## Give Up Hamburgers

You already know that the saturated fat in marbled meats and whole milk raises cholesterol, but it increases inflammation, too. That's because meat and dairy foods contain arachidonic acid, a type of omega-6 fatty acid that the body uses to form inflammatory proteins. (As we noted earlier, eating fish and other sources of omega-3 fatty acids blocks this process.) What's more, people who eat diets rich in saturated fat tend to pack on pounds in the midsection, giving them an apple-shaped silhouette. Studies in lab animals and humans suggest that this abdominal fat produces the most inflammation.

If you need to lose a few pounds, chalk up yet another reason to eat more fish and flax: Several studies show that circulating levels of chemicals that promote inflammation drop when overweight people consume omega-3 fatty acids.

## Listen to Mom

Your mother was right—again—when she told you to eat your vegetables. Could adding a side dish of carrots to a meal help dampen chronic inflammation? You bet.

## The Worst Trans Fat Offenders

The USDA recommends limiting your intake of trans fats to 1 percent of total calories, which works out to roughly 2 grams per day. That's less than the amount in a typical doughnut. Fortunately, many restaurants and food processors have caught on and have stopped using trans fats. But until these artery cloggers are banned outright, you still need to read labels and ask servers whether a meal has been prepared with trans fats to know how much you're consuming. According to an analysis by Harvard researchers published in the *New England Journal of Medicine*, the following restaurant and prepared foods tend to be the worst offenders (note that some fast-food restaurants are overhauling their french fry recipes, so fries may eventually lose their spot at the top of the list).

| FOOD | GRAMS OF TRANS FAT IN A TYPICAL SERVING |
|---|---|
| Fastfood french fries | 4.7–6.1 |
| Breaded fish burgers | 5.6 |
| Breaded chicken nuggets | 5.0 |
| Pie | 3.9 |
| Danish or sweet rolls | 3.3 |
| Pancakes | 3.1 |
| Frozen french fries | 2.8 |
| Doughnuts | 2.7 |
| Vegetable shortening | 2.7 |
| Crackers and enchiladas | 2.1 |
| Stick margarine | 0.9–2.5 |

# THE HEALING POWERS OF
## vegetables

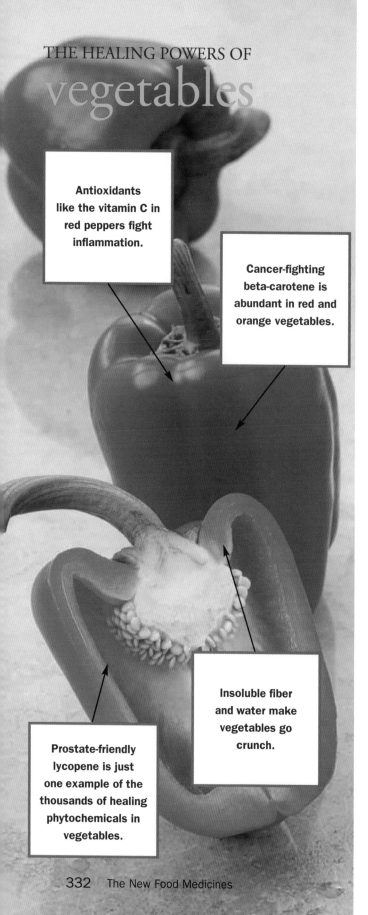

**Antioxidants like the vitamin C in red peppers fight inflammation.**

**Cancer-fighting beta-carotene is abundant in red and orange vegetables.**

**Insoluble fiber and water make vegetables go crunch.**

**Prostate-friendly lycopene is just one example of the thousands of healing phytochemicals in vegetables.**

Here's why: Produce is nature's most abundant source of antioxidants. As you'll learn later, these disease fighters neutralize the effects of naturally occurring molecules known as free radicals that attack and damage healthy cells. The body responds to this damage as it would to any injury: by producing inflammation. When fewer antioxidants are available to protect cells, that can mean more inflammation. A British study showed, for example, that men who consumed the least vitamin C had twice as much CRP in their blood as men who got plenty of this potent antioxidant.

The good news: In the first study of its kind, German researchers showed that men who increased their intake of fruit and vegetables from two servings a day to eight cut their CRP levels by one-third in just four weeks. Most of the inflammation-fighting punch, the team determined, came from fruit and vegetables rich in antioxidants called carotenoids, which include—what else?—carrots, as well as tomatoes and red bell peppers.

By the way, Mom was also right when she told you to brush your teeth. No matter what or how much you eat, be sure to brush after meals and floss regularly. Gum disease increases inflammation throughout the body and seems to raise the risk of heart disease and diabetes.

### Choose Your Carbs Carefully

In the pages to come, you'll learn what scientists have discovered in recent years about the complex—and controversial—role of carbohydrates in a healthy diet. For now, let's just say that in order to turn down the inflammation in your body, you may need to rethink your daily bread, among other carb choices.

Carbohydrates make up a vast and varied category of foods; some quell inflammation, while others make the problem worse. Learning to choose cooling carbs is easy once you get the hang of a few simple concepts that you'll read about next.

# Smart Carbs:
## FOODS FOR FIGHTING FLAB AND INSULIN RESISTANCE

Sometimes it seems like the carbohydrate story has taken more twists than a French braid. A generation ago, doctors concerned about rising rates of heart disease began advising patients to eat less fat—and more

carbohydrates. Waistlines bulged, and an epidemic of type 2 diabetes broke out.

Coincidence? Authors of the many low-carbohydrate diet books published in the 1990s didn't think so. These books blamed flabby thighs and bulging hips on carbohydrates, vilifying starches and sugars much the way many doctors demonized fat years earlier. Bad news about carbohydrates also began to turn up elsewhere in the library: namely in medical journals, as studies uncovered unusually high rates of diabetes, heart disease, and other conditions in people who eat carb-heavy diets.

The plot thickens, though, since carbohydrates are making a comeback—some carbs, that is. Thanks to important new research published in the past few years, it's now clear that carbohydrates share something in common with fats: Some are essential to a healthy diet, while others should be regarded as occasional treats.

Bashing *all* carbohydrates never made a lot of sense, given how many different varieties there are and how essential carbs are to human health. After all, soda pop and Skittles may be sources of carbohydrates, but so are snap peas and summer squash. What's more, carbohydrates provide ready fuel for your body, and they're the best source of energy for your brain cells.

Research shows that improving the quality of the carbs you eat can reap major benefits, and all it takes is making some simple exchanges on your daily menu. For instance, swapping

just one baked potato per week for a serving of brown rice could reduce your odds of developing type 2 diabetes by up to 30 percent, according to one study. (You'll learn shortly why white potatoes fall into the "occasional treat" category of carbs.) What's more, other research shows that you can dramatically slash your risk of heart disease and control your weight, too, if you learn to play your carbs right.

## Quality Control: Choosing Better Carbs

Most doctors now agree that eating the wrong kinds of carbohydrates has helped to make Americans sicker and fatter. For a while, low-carb diets (a.k.a. high-protein diets) were the professed answer, at least according to the authors of some bestselling books. But the typical high-protein diet recommended a dramatic reduction in all carbohydrates—including healthful fruits, vegetables, and grains—especially in the early stages. And they were loaded with saturated fat, which raises cholesterol. What's more, kicking "good" carbs off your plate strips your diet of powerful disease fighters.

### The Unrefined Truth about Whole Grains

When it comes to carb foods, white bread, sugary breakfast cereal, and other foods made from sugar and white flour remain the popular choices today. But overwhelming scientific evidence suggests that it's far healthier to go with the grain—the whole grain, that is.

Consider the irony: In the 17th century, milling techniques became sophisticated enough to turn coarse whole grains into the fine white flour needed to bake white bread, which became a coveted luxury. Dark bread became "peasant food." Little did the rich realize they were paying more for imperfection.

The milling and sifting needed to remove the bran (the outer layer) and germ (the portion that sprouts new plants) from whole grains also strips away nutrients, including B vitamins, trace minerals, and protein. Today food processors restore some lost vitamins and minerals, but not all. For instance, whole-grain bread (but not white bread) is a good source of magnesium, which your body needs to form enzymes that help burn glucose as energy. People with type 2 diabetes tend to have low levels of this important mineral.

Refining grains has another major downside: It removes a great deal of fiber. Whole grains are just one source of fiber, but most people don't eat anywhere close to the 20 to 35 grams of fiber per day that experts recommend. As you'll learn next, there have never been more reasons to fiber up.

### Fiber: Nature's Secret Non-Nutrient

Technically, fiber is not a nutrient since it doesn't dissolve in the digestive tract and never enters the bloodstream. But it's still indispensable, and we're not just talking about its ability to promote "regularity." Insoluble fiber (the rough stuff in whole-wheat bread and broccoli) acts like a sponge by mopping up water in the intestines, which helps make stools bulky and soft. Soluble fiber turns into a sticky gel in your intestines. This gel pulls cholesterol along with it as it moves through the body, preventing cholesterol from entering the bloodstream and clogging arteries. The gel also removes bile acid, a digestive juice that's made from cholesterol. If you've ever wondered how humdrum

> Most doctors now agree that eating the wrong kinds of carbohydrates has helped to make Americans sicker and fatter.

oat bran became so fashionable, here's your answer: It's a soluble-fiber powerhouse. Other good sources include peas and dried beans, barley, apples, oranges, and carrots.

Fiber has another benefit that makes it a valuable disease fighter: It passes slowly from the stomach into the intestines. That makes fiber a must if you're trying to lose weight, since it makes you feel full longer. It also means that most high-fiber meals enter the bloodstream gradually. This is one instance where inefficiency is a good thing, since the sugars and starches that are part of your meal convert to glucose slowly, without overwhelming your body's capacity to store carbs as fuel and raising your blood sugar.

### The Carbo-Rater: Using the Glycemic Index

One of the keys to choosing the best carbohydrates is knowing which ones raise blood sugar rapidly and which ones break down slowly. Avoiding the "fast-acting" carbs can help prevent diabetes and other devastating diseases. The reason: Chronically elevated blood sugar can damage organs and tissue throughout the body, leading to an alarming variety of health problems.

To identify how different carbohydrates affect blood sugar levels, researchers at the University of Toronto devised the glycemic index (GI) in the early 1980s. The GI is determined by measuring the effect of a food on people's blood sugar levels. Volunteers are fed whatever serving size of the food equals 50 grams of carbohydrate—to compare it against the effects of 50 grams of pure glucose—and then their blood sugar is measured. Glucose is assigned a GI value of 100. Jellybeans produce a rise in blood sugar that is 78 percent as high as the increase glucose produces. Jellybeans, then, have a GI value of 78. The closer to 100 a food is ranked, the more it increases blood sugar. (A few foods, such as Jasmine rice and even some baked potatoes, actually rank higher than pure glucose.) As a

Coarsely ground breads with kernels and seeds digest the slowest.

The bran and germ are the most nutritious parts of the grain—and the parts that are stripped out in making white flour.

Magnesium relaxes arteries, and B vitamins such as folate lower homocysteine, which is linked with heart disease.

Cereal fibers like those in whole-grain bread actually lower the risk of diabetes and even the risk of breast cancer.

Buyer beware! Most "wheat breads" are simply white bread. Look for the word *whole* in the first ingredient.

rule, a GI value under 55 is considered low, 56 to 69 is moderate, and 70 or more is high. That doesn't mean you can never eat another waffle (76) or bowl of white rice (72). But choosing lower-GI alternatives most of the time could help keep your blood sugar under control.

Critics have charged that the GI is too difficult for the average person to use, since most meals include not only carbohydrates but also fat and protein, which tend to blunt the rise of blood sugar. In other words, skeptics insist, you can look up the GI of a baked potato, but that number becomes irrelevant if you eat it with a steak or top the spud with butter and sour cream. However, in one recent study, researchers asked volunteers to eat 14 different typical meals (such as bagels and cream cheese with orange juice, for example), then measured the change in their blood sugar levels. They found that the GIs of the foods in each meal were about 90 percent accurate in predicting how much the volunteers' blood sugar levels changed, according to a study in the *American Journal of Clinical Nutrition*.

Some scientists and nutritionists prefer to use a fine-tuned version of the glycemic index known as the glycemic load (GL), which takes into account the amount of carbohydrate in a *typical* serving of the food instead of however much you'd need to eat to get to 50 grams. The GL turns some seemingly "unhealthy" foods (according to the GI) "healthy" again. For example, watermelon has a high GI (76) but a low GL (4). That's because you'd have to eat about 6 cups to consume 50 grams of carbohydrate, whereas a more typical serving is about 3/4 cup.

Using either the GI or the GL may help prevent blood sugar spikes and reduce your risk of type 2 diabetes and other conditions, studies show. But if keeping track of all those numbers makes you dizzy, following a few simple rules can also keep your blood sugar in shape.

**DON'T WORRY ABOUT FRUITS AND VEGETABLES (WITH A FEW EXCEPTIONS).** Most produce contains only modest amounts of carbohydrate per serving. What's more, much of the sugar in fruit is fructose, a form that doesn't cause blood sugar to rise.

**EAT FEWER ROOT VEGETABLES.** Here's the major exception to the first rule: Go easy on the potatoes, parsnips, and other starchy root vegetables. Starch contains more glucose than pure sugar, so it causes a rapid rise in blood sugar levels. These exceptions have their own exceptions, however: Carrots and sweet potatoes contain soluble fiber, which lowers their GI (see "Eat more fiber," below).

**CHOOSE YOUR OTHER STARCHES WISELY.** Face it, you're not going to give up bread, but you can select better varieties. Most white bread, for instance, has a high GI (an exception is sourdough, which has a high acid content and slows digestion). Look for hearty-looking whole-grain breads, not whole-wheat breads that essentially look like white bread (see "Whole Grain Doesn't Always Mean Low GI" on the opposite page). If you're choosing between rice and pasta, take the latter; its starch breaks down more gradually.

**EAT MORE FIBER.** Especially look for soluble fiber, which causes blood sugar to rise gradually by slowing digestion. That's why oats, barley, apples and some berries, and legumes tend to have low GI values.

**AVOID SUGARY FOODS.** The truth is, many types of soft drinks and candy have only a moderately high GI value, not the sky-high one you'd expect, since sugar digests more slowly than pure glucose. But this is one form of moderation you can do without, since sugary foods provide empty calories and little else.

## "Good" Carbs, Better Health

The science is unambiguous: Choosing better carbs not only crowds out empty-calorie, glucose-raising foods but also helps battle many of today's leading health threats. Here's what eating more high-fiber, low-GI foods will do for you.

### Lower your risk of diabetes

The so-called diabetes epidemic has made headlines, and for good reason. The number of cases of type 2 diabetes (the most common type) is exploding, and many more people are in line for developing the disease. At the core is a condition called insulin resistance. Most people don't know they have it—or that the "wrong" kinds of carbs contribute to it.

Insulin resistance occurs when the body stops responding to this critical hormone. Think of insulin as a kind of doorman. Normally, it triggers a reaction that allows glucose to pass through cell walls, where it is burned to produce energy or stored for later use. In some people, however, cells start to ignore insulin, which means the pancreas must manufacture more of it. Insulin resistance is "silent" because often the pancreas can keep up with demand by working overtime. Eventually, however, it may fail to keep up, resulting in type 2 diabetes.

Your genes, excess body fat, and lack of exercise cause insulin resistance, but eating the wrong kinds of carbohydrates seems to worsen the problem. In one study, British researchers asked a group of nondiabetic women to eat a high-GI diet for three weeks, while a second group ate low-GI foods. An analysis of their fat cells detected more insulin resistance in the women who ate the high-GI diet. It's hardly surprising, then, that several large population studies have shown that people who eat diets filled with low-fiber, high-GI carbohydrates appear to double their risk of type 2 diabetes.

The good news: You can reverse the threat of diabetes by up to 42 percent simply by trading in your white bread, white rice, and sugary breakfast cereal for hearty dark loaves, brown rice, and oatmeal, according to a Harvard study of nearly 43,000 men.

### Lower your risk of heart disease

Eating more whole grains could also lower your risk of heart attacks—by up to 29 percent, according to James W. Anderson, M.D., the University of Kentucky nutritionist whose research helped make oat bran a nutritional superstar in the 1980s. Dr. Anderson chalked up the benefits to oats' soluble fiber, which lowers cholesterol. But there's more going on than that. (In fact, one analysis published in the *American Journal of Clinical Nutrition* estimated that you'd have to eat three bowls of

## Whole Grain Doesn't Always Mean Low GI

There's no doubt that whole grains are good for us. But just because a whole-grain food like whole-wheat bread has a lot of fiber doesn't necessarily mean it has a low GI. The grains used may have been ground into fine flour, which, like white flour, is digested quickly. Whole-wheat bread is still a good choice, but you can make it even better by choosing coarse breads that have intact grains. (These breads may be labeled with phrases such as "stone ground.") Or you can opt for oat bread and hot oatmeal over whole-wheat bread and breakfast cereal to eliminate this concern. Oats contain soluble fiber, which slows digestion, resulting in a modest increase in blood sugar. You can also simply consult the glycemic index (www.glycemicindex.com) to determine if a whole-grain food makes the grade.

## Will More Protein Make You Lean?

As you rethink the kinds of carbohydrates you consume, you may also want to consider cutting back on sugars and starches altogether—and replacing them with protein. A growing body of research suggests that eating more protein, in the form of lean meat, poultry, seafood, eggs, and low-fat dairy foods, can safely promote weight loss and reduce your risk of heart disease.

For example, one 1999 study found that overweight men and women who followed a high-protein diet for six months lost about 8 pounds more, on average, than members of a similar group who ate a high-carbohydrate diet. One of protein's key benefits: It leaves you feeling full and satisfied longer than carbohydrates do, so you eat less. In fact, research shows that a high-protein meal helps curb appetite for up to a day. Most high-protein foods have low GIs, and they slow digestion, which reduces the overall effect a meal has on blood sugar and insulin.

Other studies suggest that you can shed pounds on any low-calorie diet, whether it's a high-carbohydrate or high-protein plan, and that most diets produce equal weight loss after a year or so. Yet high-protein diets may offer the fastest path to slimmer thighs and a taut belly, since they appear to burn flab more efficiently. Some trials comparing the two approaches show that high-protein diets produce up to 50 percent greater loss of stored fat. Increasing protein intake may also lower levels of dangerous blood fats called triglycerides.

Some doctors fear that consuming too much protein may damage kidneys and weaken bones. Recent diet studies don't support those concerns, though most have lasted only three to six months.

oatmeal a day to lower total cholesterol by only about 2 percent.)

Eating lower-GI carbs like oatmeal and whole-wheat pasta also keeps blood sugar levels in check, and there's little question that persistently high blood sugar increases the threat of heart attacks, perhaps by raising levels of destructive compounds called free radicals. These compounds "oxidize" cholesterol particles, making them more dangerous to your arteries. (You'll read more later about free radicals and how you can squelch them with the right foods.) One study of more than 3,300 subjects found that people with elevated blood sugar levels were nearly three times more likely to develop heart disease.

Glucose begins to build up in the blood as insulin resistance worsens. No one is sure why, but people who have insulin resistance also tend to have high blood pressure, elevated triglycerides (a type of blood fat linked to cardiovascular disease), and low levels of heart-friendly HDL cholesterol—a recipe for disaster. This cluster of problems, along with obesity, comes together in insulin resistance syndrome, also known as metabolic syndrome.

Again, the right diet—and the right carbs—can help. One recent study at the University of Maryland showed that every serving of whole grains that you add to your diet further decreases your odds for developing metabolic syndrome. Another study, by researchers at several hospitals in Boston, found that overweight people who adopted a low-GI diet had lower insulin levels, triglycerides, and blood pressure than other dieters given a low-fat meal plan. They had less inflammation, too, which is another benefit of high-quality carbs, as you'll see next.

### Curb Inflammation

When cholesterol assaults artery walls, the immune system responds the way it does to any injury—with inflammation. Choosing carbs rich in soluble fiber may help put the chill on that process by clearing out some of that cholesterol.

You can cool inflammation by filling up your menu with both types of fiber—soluble and insoluble—according to a recent study at the

University of Massachusetts Medical School. The researchers followed a group of more than 500 people for a little over a year, measuring their blood periodically for levels of CRP (the marker of inflammation we've mentioned before). They also asked the subjects to describe their diets. People who ate the most fiber—more than 20 grams per day, which is the minimum amount most experts recommend—had 63 percent less inflammation than others who ate low-fiber diets.

## Help you lose weight

Can eating bran cereal and brown rice lead to slimmer hips and thighs? Population studies have shown that people who get most of their carbs from the low end of the GI tend to weigh less than others who gravitate toward sugary or starchy foods. One reason appears to be that meals that include low-GI foods keep you full longer (probably by slowing digestion), which helps curb appetite later in the day.

In a recent study, researchers at the University of Sydney in Australia showed that people who ate low-GI diets were twice as likely to lose 5 percent of their body weight—and keep it off—as people who ate the conventional high-carb, low-fat diet that doctors have been recommending for years. If a 5 percent weight loss doesn't sound like much, consider this: If you're overweight and have even a hint of insulin resistance, that modest amount of slimming can reduce your risk of diabetes by 58 percent.

For some reason, low-GI diets seem to be particularly effective in women. Compared with female subjects who ate a typical high-carb, low-fat diet, women who filled up on low-GI foods lost 80 percent more body fat. They retained more muscle, too. The high-carb, low-GI plan had a bonus: Not only did dieters who adopted this menu keep the pounds off, but their LDL cholesterol dropped, too.

Navy beans are among nature's best sources of fiber, with more than 19 grams per cup of cooked beans.

Pintos and other beans are rich sources of folate, the B vitamin that guards against heart attacks and cognitive decline.

Legumes contain more protein than any other plant food. High in complex carbs and low in fat, they're a nearly perfect food.

Hearty enough to stand in for meat, red kidney beans have more than twice the iron of beef.

339

# The *New* Antioxidant Revolution

A glass of orange juice. A side dish of steamed broccoli. Corn on the cob. All of these are simple pleasures that you may enjoy now and then without even realizing that these and other common foods and

beverages are brimming with antioxidants, which are critical disease fighters.

Remember antioxidants? Back in the 1990s, pills packed with these vitamins, minerals, and other natural compounds were touted as medical wonders. Many books, including bestsellers such as *Dr. Kenneth H. Cooper's Antioxidant Revolution* and *The Antioxidant Miracle*, insisted that antioxidant supplements could dramatically slash the risk of heart attacks and cancer and even slow the aging process.

Fast-forward to today: Mounting research suggests that the preventive and healing powers of antioxidants may extend beyond heart disease and cancer to include a wide range of chronic, painful, and potentially devastating conditions. For example, doctors once believed that daily wear and tear on the joints caused osteoarthritis, the most common type of this degenerative condition. However, recent studies show that damage by free radicals—the villainous molecules antioxidants were born to battle—may speed up the onset of osteoarthritis by attacking the cells that form cartilage. Studies also show that certain antioxidant compounds can slash the risk of cataracts and macular degnereation.

What has changed since the first "antioxidant revolution"—besides our knowledge that antioxidants are even more important than we thought—is that high-dose antioxidant supplements *aren't* the answer anymore. The answer is food.

## In Sync: Antioxidants Work Better Together

There's no doubt about it: Many studies show that people who eat plenty of antioxidant-rich foods seem to lower their risk of heart attacks, cancer, and various chronic and debilitating diseases. This promising research led scientists to wonder whether high doses of these same antioxidants—extracted from food and packed into pills—would provide even greater disease protection.

Studies evaluating the benefit of antioxidant supplements have had mixed results. Take vitamin E, for example. Past research showed that people who consumed a lot of it from food had 30 to 40 percent fewer heart attacks than others whose diets included little. Yet several teams of scientists have compared large groups of people who took vitamin E supplements with others who took placebos. Most of these studies have found that people in both groups had the same risk of cardiovascular disease, raising doubts about whether vitamin E protects the heart.

There are several possible explanations for these disappointing results. For example, in some studies, people at risk for heart disease may have started taking the supplements too late for the pills to do much good. However, mounting research suggests that antioxidants simply work better as a team. That is, individual antioxidants such as vitamin E may be more potent when you toss them down the hatch with other antioxidants—the way they occur naturally in food.

"Antioxidants interact in a very dynamic inter-relationship," says nutrition scientist Jeffrey Blumberg, Ph.D., chief of antioxidant research at Tufts University in Boston. "It may be that for optimal health, we need to eat foods that have these complex mixtures of compounds." His research shows, for example, that vitamin E's antioxidant punch increases up to *300 percent* when the vitamin is combined in a test tube with certain flavonoids found in almonds.

That doesn't mean Dr. Blumberg and other scientists have given up on vitamin E pills or any other antioxidant supplements. In recent years, the National Institutes of Health has sponsored research on the use of antioxidant therapy to prevent or treat a long list of conditions. But the most powerful evidence on the books today suggests that eating foods rich in antioxidants is the best way to defend yourself against diseases that are caused or worsened by the daily assaults of free radicals.

For instance, drinking a cool glass of orange juice at least three times a week may help reduce the risk of Alzheimer's disease by up to 76 percent, thanks to its high content of antioxidants called polyphenols, according to a study by Vanderbilt University researchers. Meanwhile, a study in the *Archives of Ophthalmology* found that women who eat plenty of corn, squash, and other yellow vegetables—which are full of antioxidants called carotenoids that protect the eyes from free radicals—halved their risk of macular degeneration, which can cause blindness. And an Italian study recently found that a small daily dose of antioxidants from a surprising source—dark chocolate—lowered blood pressure better than most standard medications. How sweet is that?

## Free Radicals: Necessary Evils

Here's news that may leave you holding your breath: Oxygen is toxic. You can't live without it, of course, since every cell in your body requires oxygen to spark metabolism, or the production of energy. However, 1 to 3 percent of the oxygen you inhale never gets burned. Instead, it reacts with naturally occurring metal compounds in your body to produce renegade molecules called free radicals.

There are many different types of free radicals, but they all share one thing in common: Unlike normal molecules, they are missing a pair of electrons. This defect makes them dangerous, since they will attack anything in their path in order to replace their missing parts. Free radicals aren't entirely bad, though. In fact, your immune system produces them as part of your body's overall defense scheme, since free radicals kill bacteria and defuse viruses. However, in their quest for electrons, free radicals may also destroy healthy molecules, including proteins in cell membranes, fats, and even DNA.

In addition to the free radicals your body makes on purpose, exposure to certain triggers in the environment, including sunlight, air pollution, tobacco smoke, and radiation (from microwave ovens or computers, for example), can produce these unstable molecules. It's also clear that the hormones that flood your body when you feel emotionally stressed produce free radicals.

Your body tries to keep these oxygen-borne baddies under control, but when levels rise too high, you experience a condition scientists call oxidative stress. Everyone undergoes at least a little oxidative stress now and then, but living in a chronic state of overwhelming oxidative stress seems to contribute to a long list of diseases.

## Antioxidants to the Rescue

If free radicals are reckless marauders that disturb the peace in your body, antioxidants are the riot police. These various vitamins, minerals, and other natural compounds curb the chaos with generosity instead of brute force. An antioxidant neutralizes a free radical by first surrounding it, then giving it a pair of its own electrons, ending

> People who eat plenty of antioxidant-rich foods lower their risk of heart attacks, cancer, and various chronic diseases.

## Antioxidant Superstars

Could your diet use an infusion of antioxidants? The column on the left lists, in order, the food categories that offer the highest average antioxidant content. The column on the right lists the foods in each category with the highest concentration of antioxidants by weight.

Want to take a seasoned approach to better health? Cook with cloves, allspice, cinnamon, rosemary, and oregano, which are among the most concentrated antioxidant sources of all.

| ANTIOXIDANT SOURCE | BEST CHOICE |
| --- | --- |
| Berries | Blueberries |
| Nuts and seeds | Walnuts |
| Chocolate | Dark chocolate |
| Fruits | Pomegranates |
| Vegetables | Kale |
| Wine | Red varieties |
| Fruit juice | Grape |
| Coffee | Black, filtered |
| Tea | Green |
| Grains | Barley |

the destructive behavior. This gesture turns the antioxidant itself into a free radical since it's now missing a pair of electrons, but the new molecule is toothless and does no harm.

As we mentioned earlier, your body produces its own lineup of antioxidants. Many have names that sound as if they came straight out of a science fiction novel, such as superoxide dismutase and coenzyme Q10. These homegrown antioxidants are a talented lot; one, called lipoic acid, is particularly versatile, capable of recycling used-up antioxidants and thus restoring their effectiveness. But your body makes only a portion of the antioxidant force needed to keep free radicals from taking over. What's more, your naturally occurring levels of antioxidants decline with age. That's why it's critical to get reinforcements from antioxidant-rich foods and, in some cases, dietary supplements. Many dietary antioxidants have been well studied and have familiar names, like vitamin C. Others belong to an emerging class of compounds that scientists are just beginning to identify and understand. All belong in your diet.

### Vitamins and minerals

Your body can perform remarkable feats of chemistry, but it has limitations. While your inner chemist can build proteins from amino acids, for instance, it can't whip up many of the raw compounds needed to maintain daily functions and prevent disease. Instead, we rely on food for these critical compounds, known as vitamins and minerals. Not only is your body incapable of manufacturing its own vitamins and minerals, but it also has a limited capacity for storing them. That's why you must restock your inventory frequently by eating a well-balanced diet.

Most individual vitamins and minerals perform a lengthy list of chores. For instance, your body needs vitamin C to build a healthy immune system, brain cells, and bones, to name just a few of its roles. Vitamin E, meanwhile, is necessary for many tasks, such as forming red blood cells and muscle, lung, and nerve tissue. Both of these vitamins are powerful antioxidants, too. A healthy diet must also include a variety of minerals. One mineral, selenium, is needed to form certain enzymes that act as antioxidants.

# Antioxidant Vitamins and Minerals

Here's a snapshot of the four most common and powerful antioxidant vitamins and minerals in the diet.

| VITAMIN OR MINERAL | MAY HELP PREVENT OR TREAT | GOOD SOURCES |
|---|---|---|
| Beta-carotene | Some cancers | Carrots, squash, sweet potatoes, cantaloupe, peaches, apricots |
| Vitamin C | Some cancers, heart disease, arthritis | Citrus fruits, green bell peppers, broccoli, strawberries |
| Vitamin E | Heart disease, some cancers, Alzheimer's disease, cataracts | Olive and canola oil, nuts, seeds, whole grains, green leafy vegetables |
| Selenium | Lung, colon, and prostate cancer; arthritis, HIV | Brazil nuts, beef, fish, poultry, grains, vegetables (selenium content of the latter varies by region) |

*Source:* Office of Dietary Supplements

## Phytochemicals

You may be surprised to learn just how much you have in common with a tomato vine or blueberry bush. Just as your body makes antioxidants to fend off illness, plants produce chemicals that protect them against disease. Scientists have identified thousands of so-called phytochemicals (*phyto-* is Greek for "plant"). While they are not technically nutrients, many phytochemicals are now known to be critical for keeping your body up and running. "We may eventually discover that some of these phytochemicals are essential to human health," says antioxidant expert Dr. Blumberg.

Growing evidence shows that phytochemicals play a wide variety of roles in the body, such as preventing blood clots and slowing the spread of cancer cells. But perhaps the most attention has been focused on their potential as antioxidants. There are two main categories of phytochemicals that act as antioxidants.

**CAROTENOIDS:** Fruits and vegetables that are yellow, orange, or red tend to be good sources of these antioxidant plant chemicals. Think tomatoes, oranges, carrots, and pink grapefruit.

Some green vegetables, such as spinach and kale, are full of carotenoids, too. Everyone has heard of beta-carotene, which your body converts to vitamin A, but studies show that several carotenoids with less familiar names are critical to human health, too.

**FLAVONOIDS:** These blue, blue-red, and violet pigments are another important category of antioxidants (which technically belongs to a larger category called polyphenols) that may be particularly important in helping us fight diseases ranging from allergies to heart disease to cancer. One type of flavonoid, known as quercetin, appears to be particularly good for the cardiovascular system, since it prevents LDL cholesterol from being oxidized (making it less likely to stick to artery walls). Red and yellow onions, kale, broccoli, red grapes, and apples are all good sources of quercetin. Cocoa contains flavonoids called epicatechins, also thought to benefit the heart. These compounds, also found in tea, prevent blood clots, slow the oxidation of LDL cholesterol, improve blood vessel function, and even reduce inflammation.

# Antioxidant Phytochemicals

Scientists have identified many thousands of phytochemicals; there are more than 6,000 flavonoids alone. Here are some of the most important antioxidant phytochemicals.

| PHYTOCHEMICAL | MAY HELP PREVENT OR TREAT | GOOD SOURCES |
|---|---|---|
| Catechins | Heart disease, some cancers | Dark chocolate, tea, fruit, beans and other legumes |
| Lutein | Cataracts, macular degeneration, heart disease, some cancers | Spinach, broccoli, and other leafy green vegetables; brussels sprouts; artichokes |
| Lycopene | Prostate cancer; possibly osteoporosis and male infertility | Tomatoes (especially ketchup and other cooked tomato products), watermelon, pink grapefruit, red bell peppers |
| Proanthocyanidins | Heart disease, cancer | Tea, cocoa, berries, grapes, red wine |
| Quercetin | Heart disease, lung cancer, asthma, hay fever | Apples, onions, broccoli, cranberries, grapes |
| Resveratrol | Heart disease | Red wine, grapes, peanuts |
| Zeaxanthin | Cataracts, macular degeneration, some cancers | Leafy green vegetables, corn, tangerines, nectarines |

## Antioxidants in Action: The Benefits of Defusing Free Radicals

Free radicals don't sleep or take vacations. One expert quoted in *The Antioxidant Miracle* estimated that the DNA in every cell in the human body suffers about 10,000 "hits" from free radicals each day. It's not surprising then that the oxidative stress that can result when your antioxidant support isn't up to full strength can produce an array of debilitating conditions. However, if you choose your diet wisely and use supplements as necessary (always under your physician's guidance), antioxidants may do the following.

### Protect your heart

Even though studies haven't shown conclusively that antioxidant supplements prevent heart disease, there's no doubt that your diet must include frequent doses of antioxidants to keep LDL cholesterol, the "bad" stuff, from turning even worse. Oxidized cholesterol—that is, cholesterol that's been attacked by free radicals—is more likely to burrow into artery walls. Once cholesterol makes its way there, it's even more likely to become oxidized. When this happens, your immune system senses trouble and responds by sending white blood cells to the scene. These defender cells devour cholesterol, turning into frothy blobs called foam cells. As these fat-filled cells accumulate, they form raised patches called plaques, which narrow arteries. Plaques can erupt, blocking the artery and causing a heart attack.

People who eat plenty of antioxidant-rich fruit and vegetables have a low risk of heart disease, many studies have shown. Other good sources of heart-healthy antioxidants include tea and wine; both beverages contain high concentrations of flavonoids. Studies suggest that eating a diet high in flavonoids may lower the risk of heart disease by up to 65 percent.

Want to lower the workload for your body's homegrown crew of antioxidants? Eat fewer sweets and starches, which seem to raise levels of free radicals. A study by University of California researchers found that people whose diets included the most high-GI foods had the highest levels of oxidized cholesterol, the kind most likely to cause heart attacks.

## Protect your DNA

Free radicals can damage the DNA in healthy cells, which may alter their operating instructions and cause them to reproduce uncontrollably and form cancerous tumors. People who eat lots of fruits and vegetables have a low risk for some types of cancer. Lab studies show that phytochemicals stifle the growth of tumors in various ways, including by scavenging and demobilizing free radicals.

This news should have you seeing red—and orange and yellow—when you shop for vegetables, since carotenoids (which tend to have these pigments) may be one of the most potent types of antioxidants for fighting cancer. In particular, studies have revealed low rates of prostate cancer among men who consume a lot of tomatoes and cooked tomato products, which contain the carotenoid lycopene. One study found a 64 percent reduction in prostate cancer among men who consumed the most beta-carotene, a carotenoid that's found in carrots and other yellow or orange fruit and vegetables.

## Control diabetes complications

High blood sugar seems to speed up production of some unusually nasty free radicals. These destructive molecules probably cause many of the complications that make diabetes so frightening, such as blindness, nerve damage, and kidney failure.

Some promising signs suggest that antioxidants could alleviate some diabetes symptoms. For instance, European studies have shown that dietary supplements containing alpha-lipoic acid (found in spinach, broccoli, and beef) may relieve the pain and discomfort of

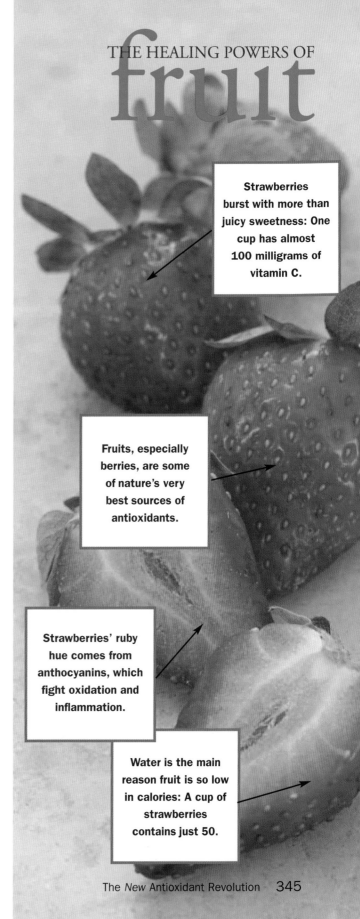

THE HEALING POWERS OF
# fruit

Strawberries burst with more than juicy sweetness: One cup has almost 100 milligrams of vitamin C.

Fruits, especially berries, are some of nature's very best sources of antioxidants.

Strawberries' ruby hue comes from anthocyanins, which fight oxidation and inflammation.

Water is the main reason fruit is so low in calories: A cup of strawberries contains just 50.

diabetic neuropathy. Scientists in India have shown that the antioxidant compound curcumin, which gives the spice turmeric its yellow color, slowed kidney damage in diabetic rats. The antioxidants resveratrol (found in red wine) and quercetin (apples and onions are good sources) had a similar effect.

Some phytochemicals may even offer protection against diabetes itself. In a Finnish study of more than 4,300 nondiabetic men and women whom researchers followed for 23 years, those who ate the most of a type of carotenoid found in citrus fruits, red bell peppers, papaya, cilantro, corn, and watermelon cut their risk of type 2 diabetes by 42 percent.

### Defend against dementia

Brain cells of people diagnosed with devastating cognitive conditions show evidence of damage by free radicals. What's more, free radicals seem to be one cause of the clumps of proteins in the brain, called amyloids, that are characteristic of Alzheimer's disease.

No one is sure how to prevent Alzheimer's, but eating more oranges and whole-grain bread could be a good start. Human studies offer clues that vitamins C and E may be your brain's best defense. Dutch researchers asked more than 5,000 people over age 55 about their diets, then followed them for six years. In the end, people who consumed the most vitamin C reduced their risk of Alzheimer's by 34 percent, while diets rich in vitamin E appeared to be even more protective, slashing the threat of dementia by nearly half.

It's less clear whether taking high doses of antioxidants will do an even better job of safeguarding the brain. One study published in the *New England Journal of Medicine* found that taking daily supplements containing 2,000 IU of vitamin E—or about 66 times more than you'll find in a multivitamin—appeared to slow the onset of Alzheimer's. However, other studies have failed to show that vitamin E pills protect the brain. (The Alzheimer's Association doesn't recommend the use of antioxidant supplements.)

### Save your sight

Tired jokes about rabbits not wearing eyeglasses aside, carrots are indeed good for your eye health (although they won't do anything to sharpen your eyesight). As anyone who tends a garden knows, rabbits eat many other plants besides carrots, and so should you. Here's why.

Carrots are loaded with beta-carotene, which the body converts to vitamin A—an essential nutrient for healthy eyes. But the latest research suggests that other antioxidant phytochemicals may also be critical for preserving vision. Take lutein, another carotenoid like beta-carotene, which is found in hefty amounts in spinach, kale, and collard greens. Retina cells at the back of the eyeball soak up lutein, apparently to ward off free radicals. When researchers analyzed the diets of more than 1,700 female volunteers in Iowa, Oregon, and Wisconsin, they found that women under 75 who ate plenty of foods rich in lutein and zeaxanthin, another carotenoid, appeared to halve their risk of macular degeneration, a leading cause of vision loss in older folks.

Consuming lots of foods filled with these antioxidants may help prevent cataracts, too. So eat your carrots, but don't skimp on the leafy greens, squash, corn, or peas, all of which are good sources of lutein and zeaxanthin, as are egg yolks, honeydew, and kiwifruit.

> Studies suggest that eating a diet high in flavonoids may lower the risk of heart disease by up to 65 percent.

# Busting the Crockery:
## FOOD MYTHS DEBUNKED

If you miss eggs, here's an invitation to get cracking again. And if you eat raw broccoli because you're afraid to steam away all the nutrients—and you *hate* raw broccoli—we've got some good news there, too.

Did you quit drinking coffee because you read somewhere that it causes cancer in lab rats? Too bad for lab rats; you should feel free to pick up a Starbucks card and savor some dark brew.

Over the years, myths and misconceptions have arisen about certain foods and scary diseases. To make matters worse, the allegedly evil dishes rarely turn out to be liver or lima beans. Instead, false and undeserved claims often end up tainting the reputations of favorite foods, some of which turn out to be good for you. One large study, for instance, found that women who drank up to four cups of coffee a day cut their risk of diabetes by 47 percent.

Here's the truth about some common—and stubborn—food falsehoods.

### MYTH: **Eggs are bad for you**

This is a classic instance of good intentions but scrambled science. For years, nutrition experts cautioned that eggs were unhealthy. After all, those gifts from the henhouse are one of the richest sources of cholesterol in the human diet. Since cholesterol plugs up arteries, eggs must raise the risk of heart attacks and strokes, right?

Wrong. Large studies suggest that this theory is full of feathers. For example, the famous Framingham Heart Study, which first showed that high blood cholesterol causes heart attacks, found no connection between eating eggs and cardiovascular disease. Another study, involving more than 117,000 men and women, failed to show an increased risk of heart attacks in people who ate up to one egg per day.

How could that be? It turns out that only about 25 percent of the cholesterol in your blood comes from food. The other 75 percent is manufactured by the liver, which produces lots of cholesterol when you eat cheeseburgers, doughnuts, and other sources of saturated fat—something eggs are *low* in. Eggs are also filled with plenty of useful nutrients that may offset any damage done by their cholesterol content, including unsaturated fat, folate and other B vitamins, and minerals. And if you shop around, you can find eggs that are enriched with healthful omega-3 fatty acids.

Eggs can fit into a balanced diet. In fact, even two eggs a day won't budge most people's cholesterol. Just keep in mind that each little orb contains about 200 milligrams of cholesterol. The American Heart Association recommends consuming no more than 300 milligrams of cholesterol per day, so plan on enjoying your omelet instead of—not alongside—the bacon and home fries.

By the way, eggs aren't the only high-cholesterol food that has been exonerated by nutritionists. In the 1990s, research showed that eating another delicacy that's notoriously high in cholesterol—shrimp—had barely any effect on cholesterol levels.

### MYTH: **Coffee causes cancer**

While we're on the topic of breakfast, coffee is another wrongly maligned staple of the morning meal. It's hard to say when doubts about this stimulating beverage first emerged, but it has been linked to cancer on several occasions over the past generation or so. In the late 1970s, for example, researchers reported that caffeine caused the growth of cysts in breast tissue. That finding raised concerns since women who frequently develop cysts often go on to have breast cancer. Then, in 1981, a Harvard study found an increase in pancreatic cancer among coffee drinkers.

However, other scientists later looked for links between coffee and these cancers, using superior research methods and studying larger groups of people. They found none. Likewise, major studies examining the risk of other cancers among coffee drinkers came up empty. In some cases, just the opposite appeared to be true. For instance, a review of 17 studies conducted from 1990 to 2003 found a 24 percent reduced risk of colon cancer among people who regularly sipped coffee (including decaffeinated brew) and tea.

Need another reason to raise your cup? Studies have also shown in recent years that drinking coffee appears to offer some protection against other conditions, including Parkinson's disease and type 2 diabetes (although in order to substantially lower your risk for the latter, you may need to imbibe a jitters-inducing six cups per day). Some people also worry that consuming too much caffeine will raise their blood pressure. While caffeine may cause your pressure to rise, a study of more than 155,000 women found that the coffee lovers among them did not have an increased risk of high blood pressure.

### MYTH: To protect your heart, drink red wine or don't bother filling your glass

It's called the French paradox: French men and women have far fewer heart attacks than Americans do, despite their fondness for some notably unhealthy lifestyle habits. (They smoke more cigarettes, for example. And don't forget—these people invented french fries.) Some scientists have speculated that their love of wine, especially red wine, at least partly explains their superior cardiovascular health. It seems logical, since red wine contains high levels of a phytochemical called resveratrol, which acts as an antioxidant and reduces

inflammation. (What's more, recent research offers intriguing clues that resveratrol may actually slow the aging process.)

As it turns out, though, it's the alcohol in red wine—and white wine and beer—that's responsible for most of its heart-related benefits. Large population studies suggest that most people enjoy at least some health benefits from sipping *any form* of alcohol in moderation. For example, the Harvard School of Public Health asked more than 38,000 men about their drinking habits, then checked up on them 12 years later. Men who had up to a drink or two per day were 37 percent less likely to have had heart attacks than men who rarely or never indulged.

Alcohol—no matter how you drink it—raises HDL ("good") cholesterol and seems to make blood less likely to clot. If you enjoy alcoholic beverages, most health authorities agree that having no more than a drink or two per day (one for women, two for men) may offer some benefits and probably can't hurt.

### MYTH: Fat-free and low-fat foods are always healthier than full-fat varieties

When it comes to dairy products and some other foods, such as meat, you can reliably adopt a simple rule: The less fat, the better. But that's not always the case with other foods. Take salad dressing. If you're trying to lose weight, switching from an oil-based dressing to a low-fat or fat-free dressing may make sense. But sparing yourself 100 calories or so (per 2 tablespoons) comes at a cost.

For starters, salad dressings made with healthy monounsaturated fats, such as olive or canola oil, may help prevent heart disease and other conditions. What's more, a recent study shows that you may be missing out on important disease protection by going oil-free. That's because without some fat in the meal, your digestive tract won't absorb many of the nutrients in a salad.

Researchers at the University of Iowa demonstrated this phenomenon by asking volunteer diners to eat three different salads. Each included romaine lettuce, spinach leaves, grated carrots, and cherry tomatoes. But the first was topped with fat-free Italian dressing, the second with reduced-fat dressing, and the third with conventional full-fat dressing. The researchers took blood samples from the volunteers after they ate each salad and measured levels of carotenoids, the important antioxidants we've talked so much about. After eating the salad with fat-free dressing, the volunteers absorbed just a tiny amount of carotenoids, including beta-carotene and lycopene. The reduced-fat dressing improved matters only slightly, while the volunteers' bodies absorbed an adequate amount of carotenoids after eating the salad with the full-fat dressing. There's no need to drown your greens in oil, however; 1 or 2 tablespoons will get the job done.

### MYTH: Raw fruits and vegetables are more nutritious than cooked ones

The idea sounds logical enough. Doesn't it make sense to eat fruits and vegetables in their natural state? Some "raw food" enthusiasts take this theory to the extreme, unwilling to eat so much as a pea pod if it's been boiled, steamed, or exposed to any form of heat.

However, the theory that cooking foods makes them less nutritious is a bit half-baked. Raw food advocates note that heat destroys enzymes in foods that make them more easily digested. While that's true, cooking also breaks down fiber, making it easier for your body to process. (Just imagine trying to chew, much less digest, a spear of raw asparagus.) Subsisting primarily on raw fruit and vegetables could even backfire if your goal is to get healthier. German researchers studied 201 men and women who adopted raw-food diets and found that their total cholesterol and triglyceride levels dropped. However, the raw-food diet also lowered their HDL cholesterol. Meanwhile, their levels of homocysteine (an amino acid linked to heart attacks and strokes) rose.

Scientists have discovered in recent years that cooking actually *boosts* levels of important compounds in some fruits and vegetables. For instance, ketchup contains five to six times more of the antioxidant lycopene than raw tomatoes do, making it much more useful against diseases such as prostate cancer.

## Raw Sugar: A Raw Deal?

Should you pay more for so-called raw sugar? Sure, if you like its taste and texture. But don't buy the hype suggesting that it's more nutritious or wholesome than plain old table sugar.

Most "raw" sugar sold in the United States is turbinado sugar, so named because it is partially refined in turbines, or centrifuges. While common white sugar crystals are stripped of molasses during processing, turbinado sugar retains some of this syrup, so it has a yellow-gold or tan color. Similar sweeteners include demerara and muscovado sugars.

While these sugars have unique taste and cooking properties, they are scarcely more healthful than other sweeteners. Unlike table sugar, they contain minerals, but only a trace. Nor do turbinado and related sugars offer any edge for dieters; like table sugar, they provide 15 calories per teaspoon.

What's more, using the term *raw* to advertise any sugar sold to consumers in the United States is misleading. Strictly speaking, *raw sugar* is the term used for the tan or brown granules produced when mills process sugarcane stalks. Raw sugar is then refined to make table sugar and other forms of the sweetener. You can't buy true raw sugar, since the FDA declares it unfit for human consumption—and you wouldn't want to, since it contains yeast, mold, bacteria, dirt, bug parts, and other undesirable stuff.

# THE HEALING POWERS OF
# olive oil

Dieters were once advised to shun salad dressing, but eating some fat makes a healthy diet easier to stick with.

Olive oil, especially extra-virgin oil, is considered "liquid gold" because of its antioxidants and its ability to tame inflammation.

Rosemary is a highly potent source of antioxidants, as are other spices such as oregano.

Dressing a salad with a bit of oil makes the nutrients in the veggies much easier for your body to absorb.

Monounsaturated fats like those in olive oil can dramatically slash the risk of heart attacks.

Vinegar, thanks to its acids, blunts postmeal spikes in blood sugar by 30 to 55 percent.

Heat does rob fresh produce of some nutrients, especially vitamins that dissolve in water. For example, cooking fruits and vegetables tends to reduce their levels of vitamin B$_6$, vitamin C, and folate in particular. But it increases the antioxidant levels of some vegetables, such as sweet corn and carrots. The bottom line: If you like raw produce, crunch away—but don't fear the vegetable steamer or stir-fry pan.

**MYTH: Frozen and canned fruits and vegetables are less nutritious than fresh ones**

Fresh fruits and vegetables *are* more nutritious than the frozen and canned variety—at the instant they are picked. However, the foods you find in the produce section have often had a long journey from the moment they were packed in crates, spending days or even weeks in transit from the farm or orchard. During shipping and storage, natural enzymes are released in fresh fruit and vegetables that cause them to lose nutrients.

By contrast, food processors quick-freeze fresh-picked produce, which preserves much of its vitamin and mineral content. "With some fruits and vegetables, you actually lock in a higher nutrient content by freezing," says Douglas Archer, Ph.D., a professor of food science at the University of Florida. A 1992 University of Illinois study found, for instance, that frozen beans retained twice as much vitamin C as fresh beans purchased in a grocery store. Contrary to common belief, canning does not deplete fruit and vegetables of significant amounts of nutrients either. While heat processing may reduce levels of some vitamins, certain canned foods—such as spinach and pumpkin—actually have higher levels of vitamin A than fresh versions.

But what about taste? You'll never mistake a frozen strawberry for a fresh one, but freezing technology has made huge leaps in recent years. "Frozen vegetables used to have both texture and taste problems," says Dr. Archer. "Now they're quite good and are even used by professional chefs."

**MYTH: Nuts are too fattening—eat them sparingly**

And deprive yourself of a nutritious and satisfying food? To be sure, nuts contain a lot of fat, but it's mostly the good kind. Dry-roasted peanuts, for example, have three to four times more heart-healthy monounsaturated fat than saturated fat. Recent research suggests that eating nuts as part of a healthy diet may even help you lose weight.

Researchers believe that the fat in nuts helps people feel full, and the protein may use up calories as it digests. What's more, a study by British researchers shows that high-protein foods help trigger the release of a hormone known to reduce hunger.

Nuts' high concentration of healthy fats makes them a guilt-free way to satisfy hunger without raising cholesterol or other blood fats. What's more, nuts are an excellent fiber source and provide a long list of nutrients, including vitamin E, magnesium, folate, and copper. It's no wonder people who include nuts in their diet tend to be so healthy. For instance, women who eat just 1 ounce of nuts most days of the week are 35 percent less likely to have heart attacks than those who avoid nuts, according to a Harvard study of more than 80,000 nurses. Prefer peanut butter sandwiches? Eat one five days a week (preferably on whole-grain bread), and you may lower your risk of type 2 diabetes by 21 percent.

# PART two

# Your Food Cures
## Arsenal

*Food heals! That's the happy message we shouted in Part One. Now*

*read on to learn which foods make our "top 20" list, plus our top*

*10 healing herbs and spices. Also discover which pantry staples are*

*treasure troves of specific vitamins, minerals, and other key nutrients*

*that show up again and again in our "food prescriptions" in Part Three.*

# Avocados

## What You're Eating

The reproductive part of the tree—and the fattiest fruit on Earth (even fattier than olives). Like olives, these odd-looking fruits, dubbed alligator pears for their shape and bumpy green skin, are an incredibly concentrated source of good-for-you monounsaturated fat. The dark-skinned, rough-textured California-grown variety (Hass) is fattier than the smooth-skinned, bright green Florida-grown variety. Avocados contain more soluble fiber and protein than any other fruit, and half a medium avocado provides more potassium than a banana.

## Healing Powers

Despite their fat, or actually because of it, avocados can lower your cholesterol. Researchers find that replacing just 5 percent of your calories from saturated fat (think butter or cheese) with monounsaturated fat—the kind in avocados—could slash the risk of heart attack by more than a third. An added benefit: Avocados are also high in beta-sitosterol, a plant sterol (also found in cholesterol-lowering margarines such as Benecol) that blocks the absorption of cholesterol from food, and the anti-cancer compound glutathione, a powerful antioxidant.

## Healthful Hint

Use avocados to replace other fat sources in your diet, not add to them.

## HOW MUCH IS ENOUGH

At about 227 calories per Hass avocado, a little goes a long way. Cut an avocado into five pieces and enjoy one piece for just 45 calories—half the calories of a tablespoon of mayonnaise and much more healthful.

## BUYING RIGHT

Hold a few fruits in the palm of your hand and choose one that seems heavy for its size. Store it on the kitchen counter until it's ripe or place it in a paper bag to hasten ripening. Hass avocados become very dark when ripe. To tell if the fruit is ready to eat, pull the stem off the end. If it comes off easily and the flesh of the fruit is green, the avocado is ripe.

## Three Clever Ideas

**1.** To prevent a cut avocado from turning brown in the refrigerator, remove the seed and spray the flesh with cooking spray, then wrap in plastic. Use within three days.

**2.** Mashed avocado makes a healthy replacement for condiments. Spread on sandwiches in lieu of mayo or add to hot baked potatoes instead of sour cream.

**3.** If avocados are ripening faster than you can eat them, mash them with 1/2 tablespoon lemon or lime juice per avocado. Place in an airtight container, cover, and freeze. Use within four months.

# Beans

## What You're Eating

We don't normally think of beans as seeds, but that's what they are. Dry beans (legumes) grow inside pods, just as green beans do. After they're picked and cleaned, beans are often polished to command a better price. Because they're the plant's seeds, or embryos, beans are loaded with nutrients, including folate and iron. They're also stuffed with protein, with a cup of cooked lentils providing nearly 18 grams—about as much as a serving of T-bone steak.

## Healing Powers

Beans are in fact good for your heart, thanks in large part to their soluble fiber, which soaks up cholesterol so the body can dispose of it before it can stick to artery walls. Studies find that diets high in soluble fiber can cut total cholesterol by 10 to 15 percent. The same soluble fiber, combined with beans' protein, makes beans beneficial to blood sugar. Their magnesium helps relax arteries, giving blood more room to flow and lowering blood pressure. Finally, a recent study ranked beans among the top antioxidant foods.

## Healthful Hint

Choose small red beans for truly astounding antioxidant power, followed by red kidney beans, then pinto beans. Beans contain more protein than any other plant food, but the protein is incomplete. Eating a grain such as rice at any time during the day will "complete" the protein. Rinse canned beans before using to remove some of the salt.

**KEY NUTRIENTS**

> Folate (a B vitamin)
> Vitamins A and C
> Protein
> Iron

**HOW MUCH IS ENOUGH**

1/2 cup a day.

**BUYING RIGHT**

If you're buying your beans in a bag rather than a can, note that older beans take longer to cook than fresh ones—ideally, they should be less than a year old. For freshness, purchase from a busy, reputable store.

## Three Clever Ideas

**1**. Store dry beans in a glass jar with a dried chile pepper, which will ward off pantry bugs. For a spicy dish, include the pepper; otherwise, discard it.

**2**. To prevent gas, change the soaking water several times when preparing beans. Never cook the beans in the soaking water. Or opt for canned beans, which contain less flatulence-causing substances, and rinse them first.

**3**. Snack on baked chickpeas! Toss about 2 cups drained and patted dry beans with one beaten egg white and a mix of spices such as cumin, chili powder, and cayenne pepper or cinnamon, ginger, and nutmeg. Bake, stirring occasionally, at 400°F until golden.

# Blueberries

## What You're Eating

A lot of antioxidants. These berries have more antioxidants—those magical molecules that can help prevent cancer, heart disease, eye disease, memory loss, and a host of other maladies—than 40 other common fruits and vegetables tested. Blueberries are also one of only three fruits native to North America (Concord grapes and cranberries are the other two) and are the only truly blue food in nature, not counting some blue-purple potatoes from remote corners of the globe, a few fruits that can almost pass as blue, and blue corn. Blueberries may be small, but 1/2 cup contains almost 2 grams of fiber, the same as a slice of whole-wheat bread.

## Healing Powers

The antioxidant plant pigments that make blueberries blue—flavonoids called anthocyanins—guard against heart disease, cancer, and age-related blindness and memory loss. Like their cranberry cousins, blueberries (and blueberry juice) are tops when it comes to preventing urinary tract infections, thanks to antioxidant epicatechins, which keep bacteria from sticking to bladder walls. Plus, the fiber in blueberries makes them powerful antidotes to constipation.

## Healthful Hint

If you like blueberry pancakes, sprinkle on the blueberries at the last minute. Cooking the berries destroys valuable vitamin C. To get even more antioxidant power from berries, seek out elderberries, black currants, and chokeberries, all of which tested even higher than blueberries in antioxidant activity.

### KEY NUTRIENTS

> Fiber

> Antioxidants

> Vitamin C

> Iron

### HOW MUCH IS ENOUGH

1/2 cup blueberries equals one fruit serving.

### BUYING RIGHT

Go for dry, plump berries full of fragrance and free of dents and bruises. They should have a silvery white coating called a bloom. If shriveled or lacking the bloom, they've been overhandled. Gently shake the container; fruit that doesn't move freely is overripe or damaged. Stains under the package also indicate overripe fruit. Wash just before serving.

## Three Clever Ideas

**1**. Don't discard the little plastic container the blueberries come in; it makes a perfect mini-colander. Use it to rinse the berries, then save the container for rinsing small amounts of other foods.

**2**. To dry these delicate berries, place in a salad spinner lined with paper towels and give a quick spin.

**3**. Add blueberries to your lemonade. Place a few berries in each section of an ice cube tray, fill with lemonade, and freeze. Plop three cubes in each glass of lemonade.

# Broccoli

## What You're Eating

Broccoli is a member of the cabbage family, which helps explain its anticancer powers (all cabbages are anticancer foods). Almost 90 percent water, it's nevertheless loaded with nutrients. One stalk has as much fiber as a healthy breakfast cereal and as much vitamin C as two Florida oranges. By the way, the leaves are edible.

## Healing Powers

Consider broccoli your number one cancer fighter, thanks to its sulfur compounds, such as sulforaphane, which you can smell as broccoli cooks. These compounds signal our genes to boost production of enzymes that detoxify potentially cancer-causing compounds. Eat more broccoli, and you could slash your risk of everything from breast and lung cancer to stomach and colon cancer by as much as half. Sulforaphane has also been found to kill the bacteria that cause ulcers. Broccoli's also a surprising nondairy source of calcium and potassium, making it good for your bones as well as your blood pressure. Its vitamin C and beta-carotene protect your eyes from cataracts and safeguard your brain cells from memory-robbing attacks by free radicals.

## Healthful Hint

Steam broccoli for 3 to 4 minutes until it's crisp-tender to free up more of its sulforaphane. Don't cook it in a lot of water, or the nutrients will leach into the water. Eat the florets, where much of the beta-carotene is stored, but if you like the stalks, eat them, too—they also contain plenty of nutrients.

### KEY NUTRIENTS

> Anticancer compounds (such as sulforaphane)
> Beta-carotene
> Calcium
> Fiber
> Folate (a B vitamin)
> Vitamin C

### HOW MUCH IS ENOUGH

1/2 cup cooked broccoli is one vegetable serving.

### BUYING RIGHT

Choose florets with a dark green, purple, or blue hue; they contain more beta-carotene and vitamin C than light green or yellow ones. Limp stalks or flowering buds are signs of poor quality.

## Three Clever Ideas

**1**. Don't discard the leaves from broccoli stalks; they contain more vitamin A than the florets. Chop and add to the broccoli or toss in green salads. Eat the stalks, too. Peel away the tough outer skin before chopping or shredding.

**2**. If your broccoli has gotten limp, cut 1/2 inch off the bottom of each stalk. Place the stalks in a glass of cold water and chill. It will be crisp again in a few hours.

**3**. Although lemon juice keeps cut fruit from turning brown, it has the opposite effect on broccoli (or any other vegetable with chlorophyll), turning it a dull gray. Season with lemon or lime juice only after it has cooled.

# Carrots

## What You're Eating

Bugs Bunny's favorite food—and the vegetable that gave the all-important group of phytochemicals called carotenoids their name. Real rabbits, though, are more likely to eat the leafy green tops of the vegetable than its bright orange root, so they miss out on beta-carotene, which gives carrots their color and holds the key to their significant health benefits. One large raw carrot provides almost all the vitamin A you need in a day; a cooked carrot supplies even more. While most of us see orange carrots at the store, they come in many varieties and colors, including purple.

## Healing Powers

Carrots won't prevent or correct nearsightedness, although they do help prevent night blindness, which is caused by a deficiency of vitamin A, as well as cataracts. Thanks to their soluble fiber, carrots also lower cholesterol. In one USDA study, eating 1 cup of carrots a day lowered cholesterol 11 percent after three weeks. Carotenoids like beta-carotene also protect against cancer, especially lung cancer.

## Healthful Hint

Cooked carrots contain more beta-carotene since cooking breaks down the cellular walls that encase this nutrient. To preserve carrots' natural sweet flavor and nutrients, cook them, covered, in as little liquid as possible, a technique known as sweating. To best absorb the beta-carotene, eat your carrots with a little fat (add a little trans fat–free margarine or sauté them in olive oil).

### KEY NUTRIENTS

> Beta-carotene
> Vitamins $B_6$ and C
> Fiber

## HOW MUCH IS ENOUGH

1/2 cup cooked carrots is one vegetable serving.

## BUYING RIGHT

Go for the darkest orange carrots because they have the most beta-carotene. To ensure freshness, check that the roots are firm and bright in color and the carrots aren't wilted or cracked. If you purchase carrots with tops, remove them before refrigerating, or they'll rob the carrots of moisture and vitamins.

## Three Clever Ideas

**1**. The fastest way to cut carrots into julienne strips is to start with packaged, peeled mini-carrots. They're the perfect size to simply slice lengthwise into quarters and then cut into 1/8-inch strips.

**2**. For a change of pace, sauté sliced carrots in broth for 2 minutes. Cover and cook until crisp-tender. Finish by tossing with a few tablespoons of orange marmalade.

**3**. Add fiber and sweetness to hash browns, meat loaf, sauces, or casseroles by stirring in grated carrots—a great way to eat more vegetables.

# Dark Chocolate

## What You're Eating

Good-for-you candy loaded with antioxidants. It's made from the roasted beans of the cacao tree, native to South America. Columbus "discovered" these beans, and the returning crew of his fourth voyage took them to Europe. Originally cocoa was consumed as a beverage made by combining the ground beans with water. Chocolate was first introduced in bar form about 1910. It's made mainly from cocoa solids and cocoa fat (a.k.a. cocoa butter) plus sugar. Milk chocolate also contains milk or milk powder. White chocolate (mostly sugar and cocoa butter) lacks the cocoa solids that provide the health benefits of its darker cousins. Chocolate's melting point is just below human body temperature—the reason it melts so nicely in your mouth.

## Healing Powers

Dark chocolate contains hefty amounts of disease-fighting flavonoids, antioxidants also found in red wine and many fruits and vegetables. In fact, it appears to have more flavonoids than any other food. Studies find its antioxidants can significantly improve blood pressure, prevent blood clots, slow the oxidation of LDL cholesterol (making it less likely to stick to artery walls), and reduce inflammation. Some research suggests that eating 1.5 ounces a day can cut heart attack risk by 10 percent. Eating dark chocolate can also lower insulin resistance, the main problem behind diabetes.

## Healthful Hint

For the most antioxidants, look for dark chocolate that contains at least 60 percent cocoa.

**KEY NUTRIENTS**

> Potassium
> Vitamins A, B$_1$ (thiamin), C, D, and E
> Iron
> Flavonoids

**HOW MUCH IS ENOUGH**

About 1.5 ounces is considered one serving.

**BUYING RIGHT**

Shop in a store with good turnover and look for bars with clean, neat packaging, a sign the chocolate is fresh. To store, wrap in foil, then in plastic wrap. Chocolate may develop a light coating or "bloom," but fear not; it won't affect flavor or texture.

## Three Clever Ideas

**1**. Grate 1/2 ounce dark chocolate into your coffee cup. Fill with hot coffee and steamed milk for a delicious mocha cappuccino.

**2**. The easy way to melt chocolate: put in a heatproof bowl, cover with a small plate, and place on your coffeemaker's heating plate. Turn it on, then stir the chocolate occasionally until melted.

**3**. Vanilla extract boosts the flavor of chocolate. Try doubling the amount called for in a recipe, adding as much as 1 tablespoon.

# Flaxseed

## What You're Eating

These seeds, also known as linseeds, come from the same plant that provides the fiber for linen. Flax is one of those plants in which every part is used: After the seeds are pressed to make the oil, the high-protein stuff left over is fed to horses to keep their coats shiny. It's just as healthy for humans, especially thanks to phytoestrogens called lignans. Flax is actually the richest source of these compounds ever discovered.

## Healing Powers

A tablespoon of ground flaxseed sprinkled over cereal or yogurt provides an easy 2.3 grams of fiber, often more than what's in the cereal itself! But flaxseed is most revered for its lignans. These act like estrogen in the body, blocking estrogen receptors on cells and contributing to reduced rates of certain hormone-related cancers, such as breast cancer. Flaxseed is also a fantastic source of alpha-linolenic acid (ALA), an essential fatty acid the body uses to make omega-3 fatty acids. ALA thins the blood and makes it less sticky, reducing the risk of heart attack and stroke. The little seeds also can lower cholesterol, thanks to their big stores of soluble fiber. Their anti-inflammatory power may also help keep various conditions, from acne to asthma, at bay.

## Healthful Hint

Make sure your flax is ground; otherwise, the seeds will come out the same way they went in (whole), and you won't reap any health benefits. Eat too much flaxseed, and you'll quickly discover its laxative effect.

### KEY NUTRIENTS

> Alpha-linolenic acid
> Fiber
> Vitamins $B_6$ and E
> Folate (a B vitamin)
> Magnesium
> Lignans (phytoestrogens)

### HOW MUCH IS ENOUGH

1 to 2 tablespoons ground flaxseed daily.

### BUYING RIGHT

Purchase ground flaxseed, often called flax meal, or grind your own in a clean coffee grinder. Choose vacuum-packed packages to ensure freshness. If you buy flaxseed oil, which turns rancid quickly, look for it in refrigerated dark bottles and buy only as much as you can use in a month.

## Three Clever Ideas

**1.** Use flaxseed oil in salad dressings, replacing at least half of olive oil with flaxseed oil. Don't cook flaxseed oil, or "good" fat will turn to "bad."

**2.** If you don't have a spare coffee grinder for flaxseed, here's a simple way to "grind" it. Place the seeds on a cutting board and surround them with a few drops of water (just enough to moisten and hold them in place), then chop with a chef's knife.

**3.** Out of eggs? In a blender, combine 1 tablespoon ground flaxseed with 3 tablespoons water and process for 1 minute, then let stand until viscous. Use for adhering crumbs to chicken or fish; as filler in meatballs; or in muffin or pancake batter.

# Garlic

## What You're Eating

An edible antibiotic. The French chemist Louis Pasteur was the first to demonstrate garlic's antiseptic properties, which were put to good use in World War I. Long before that, the Egyptians fed it to slaves while they built the pyramids. Garlic has been used in folk medicine for everything from constipation to leprosy. And garlic breath? Blame garlic's sulfur compounds, which are also responsible for most of its healing powers.

## Healing Powers

More health benefits have been ascribed to garlic than to just about any other food—and some of them even hold true. Garlic has antibacterial, antifungal, and antiviral properties; it even appears to banish some antibiotic-resistant bacteria, at least in test tubes. Most of its disease-fighting potential comes from its sulfur compounds, which act as antioxidants, providing many of its cardiovascular benefits. Garlic lowers cholesterol only modestly, but it also acts as a blood thinner, reducing the formation of blood clots and your risk of heart attack and stroke. Just six or more cloves a week can slash your risk of colorectal, stomach, and prostate cancer in half, compared to eating one clove a week or less. The sulfur compounds flush out carcinogens before they can damage cell DNA, and they force cancer cells that do develop to self-destruct.

## Healthful Hint

Garlic makes its healing chemical compounds only when the cloves are chopped, crushed, chewed, or otherwise assaulted, which triggers the breakdown of sulfur-containing compounds in the cells. Chop or crush your garlic, then let it stand for 10 minutes to fully release its healing potential.

### KEY NUTRIENTS

> Copper
> Iron
> Zinc
> Magnesium
> Germanium
> Selenium

### HOW MUCH IS ENOUGH

At least a clove a day.

### BUYING RIGHT

Garlic bulbs should be plump, with smooth, firm cloves. Store in an open container in a cool, well-ventilated place for up to two months; don't refrigerate. Cloves that have sprouted are fine to use, though they're less pungent. Mince the sprout and cook along with the garlic.

## Three Clever Ideas

**1**. For perfectly minced garlic, rub a clove over a fine grater or zester. Before using the grater again, run it through the dishwasher to remove all flavor.

**2**. For a small amount of garlic paste, place one clove on a cutting board and mash with a fork, occasionally changing the direction of the tines.

**3**. To reduce the pungency of garlic when adding it raw to vinaigrettes or dips, simmer peeled cloves in a little water for 2 minutes, then drain.

# Low-fat Milk

## What You're Drinking

The same thing mama cows feed their young—almost. In the United States, it's usually pasteurized and homogenized. Homogenization breaks up and disperses milk fat globules, making the liquid smoother; otherwise, the fat would rise to the top of the milk like oil lying on top of water. (Although milk is an excellent source of protein, it's 87 percent water.) Pasteurization destroys bacteria and disables certain natural enzymes. Until the 1950s, you could get your milk only one way—full fat, with 3.25 percent milk fat in 8 ounces. Today you can get milk with less than 0.5 percent fat (fat-free). Removing the fat also removes vitamins A and D, which are later added back.

## Healing Powers

If you left milk behind with your childhood, you're missing out on one of the best sources of calcium. Fat-free milk actually has more calcium than whole milk because calcium is found in milk solids, not milk fat. Milk is also fortified with vitamin D, making it one of the only dietary sources of this nutrient, which is emerging as an anticancer vitamin. Dairy products are excellent sources of potassium and magnesium, which naturally reduce blood pressure. A daily glass of milk can also reduce the risk of colorectal cancer by 15 percent.

## Healthful Hint

Skin forms on heated milk when water evaporates and calcium and protein combine. If you skim it off, you lose valuable nutrients. Heat milk in a covered pan to reduce evaporation.

### KEY NUTRIENTS

> Calcium
> Vitamins A, $B_2$ (riboflavin), $B_{12}$, and D (vitamins A and D are added)
> Phosphorus
> Zinc
> Magnesium

**HOW MUCH IS ENOUGH**
At least 8 ounces a day.

**BUYING RIGHT**
Always check the sell-by date and don't buy more than you'll use by then. And of course, choose fat-free or 1% milk to keep your fat intake down. Also keep a can of low-fat evaporated milk in your cupboard. It makes a great substitute for cream in recipes, and it's an even better source of calcium than regular milk.

## Three Clever Ideas

**1.** Dairy cuts the heat from spicy ingredients like chile peppers. If a dish comes out too spicy, remove it from the heat and stir in some milk. It will cut the spice and the acid as well.

**2.** For rich, creamy grains, such as oatmeal, rice, or barley, substitute milk for some or all of the cooking water.

**3.** Remember Creamsicles? Here's a way to get your milk and enjoy that flavor. In a blender, combine 3/4 cup milk, 3 tablespoons frozen orange juice concentrate, 1/4 teaspoon vanilla extract, and six ice cubes. Blend and enjoy.

# Nuts

## What You're Eating

Many of our top 20 foods, including avocados, beans, and flaxseed, have something in common, and it's no coincidence: They are the seeds or embryos of plants. Nuts are the embryos of various trees (peanuts, which don't grow on trees, aren't technically nuts but legumes). As such, they contain all the nutrients needed to grow a new plant. Americans eat about 600 million pounds of peanuts a year in addition to the more than 700 million pounds of peanut butter we spread, enough to cover the floor of the Grand Canyon.

## Healing Powers

Nuts are high in calories, but most of them come from healthy mono- and polyunsaturated fats, which are behind nuts' ability to slash cholesterol and heart attack risk (by as much as 39 percent) when eaten in place of animal fats. Walnuts in particular are rich in omega-3 fatty acids, the reason they're considered heart-smart snacks. Some nuts, including peanuts, walnuts, and almonds, also contain plant sterols, which lower cholesterol. Nuts are a "slow-burning" food; studies show they can even help people lose weight. Their nutritional benefits vary. One Brazil nut delivers a day's supply of selenium, pecans are especially rich in antioxidants, and 1 ounce of almonds provides nearly half your recommended daily quota of vitamin E. Just don't overdo: A cup of walnuts has more calories than a Big Mac.

## Healthful Hint

Eat your peanuts roasted, not raw or steamed. Roasting boosts levels of the antioxidant p-coumaric acid, believed to help prevent stomach cancer, by 22 percent.

**KEY NUTRIENTS**

- > Protein
- > Omega-3 fatty acids
- > Selenium
- > Vitamin E
- > Potassium
- > Calcium
- > Iron
- > Magnesium
- > Zinc

**HOW MUCH IS ENOUGH**
1 ounce at least five times a week.

**BUYING RIGHT**
When buying nuts in the shell, look for whole, clean shells without cracks or holes. Shelled nuts should be plump and firm. Since nuts contain fat, they will go rancid. Store them in the fridge for up to a month or freeze in a sealed container for a few months.

## Three Clever Ideas

**1**. Walnuts are, well, a tough nut to crack. Forgo struggling with a nutcracker to break the shells. Reach instead into your toolbox for a vise grip (or curved-jaw locking pliers) for perfectly shelled nuts every time.

**2**. Avoid the mess from chopping nuts by placing them in a zipper-seal plastic bag and crushing with a rolling pin. Why not do more than you need and freeze the rest in the bag?

**3**. Toast nuts to bring out their flavor. Preheat the oven to 300°F. Place 1/2 cup shelled nuts in a single layer on a baking sheet and roast for 7 to 10 minutes. Don't let them burn.

# Oats

## What You're Eating

Oats are the seeds of the plant—packing all the future potential of the cereal grain into their tiny forms. Historically, oats were viewed in some countries as inferior, to be used only as horse feed because they couldn't be made into bread. But they're one of the best sources of plant-based protein. In 1997, Quaker Foods hit pay dirt when the FDA allowed the company to make the first-ever food-specific health claim on its oatmeal products. That claim—that oats, as part of a healthy diet, could reduce the risk of heart disease—has stood the test of time.

## Healing Powers

Oats' cholesterol-lowering powers (and its blood pressure–lowering powers) come from beta-glucan, a type of soluble fiber. One cup a day of cooked oat bran, 1 1/2 cups of cooked oatmeal, or three packets of instant oatmeal provide enough beta-glucan to lower blood cholesterol by about 5 percent and heart attack risk by about 10 percent. Oats may reduce heart attack risk in other ways, too. They contain antioxidants, which help prevent "bad" cholesterol from being oxidized, making it less likely to stick to artery walls. The soluble fiber has another benefit: It forms a gel in the stomach that slows digestion (critical for heading off blood sugar spikes) and helps keep hunger under control.

## Healthful Hint

Buy the type of oatmeal you'll eat. It doesn't matter much if it's steel-cut or instant. Just watch out for added sugar in most "instant" brands.

**KEY NUTRIENTS**

- > Calcium
- > Iron
- > Manganese
- > Zinc
- > Vitamin E
- > B vitamins

### HOW MUCH IS ENOUGH

Aim for 10 grams of soluble fiber each day. Cooked oats contain 2 to 3 grams per serving.

### BUYING RIGHT

The most commonly used oats are rolled oats. Old-fashioned rolled oats are grains that have been steamed, rolled into flakes, and dried. Quick-cooking oats are cut into small pieces before rolling. Store oats in a tightly sealed container for up to six months.

## Three Clever Ideas

**1**. Add fiber to baked goods by replacing 1/2 cup of the regular flour called for with 1/2 cup oat flour. To make your own, finely grind quick-cooking or old-fashioned oats in a food processor or blender.

**2**. Toasting rolled oats boosts their flavor. Spread them in a single layer on a baking sheet and bake, stirring, at 350°F for 3 to 5 minutes or until fragrant.

**3**. Make your own flavored oatmeal "packets." In snack-size zipper-seal bags, combine 1/2 cup quick-cooking oatmeal, 2 tablespoons raisins, 1 tablespoon wheat germ, 1 teaspoon brown sugar, 1/4 teaspoon cinnamon, and a pinch of salt.

# Olive Oil

## What You're Eating

Press an olive, and you get one of the healthiest fats in the world. Yet olive oil accounts for just 3 percent of world oil consumption and for about 8 percent in the United States, or about 1/2 quart per person per year. Compare that to Mediterranean countries like Italy (3.5 gallons per person per year), Spain (4 gallons), and Greece (6.9 gallons). Given the amount of olive oil Greeks consume, it's not surprising that Greece devotes some 60 percent of its cultivated land to olive growing. Don't just pluck one off a tree, though. Raw olives are incredibly bitter until processed (which often involves soaking them in a lye solution). Extra virgin is considered the Rolls Royce of olive oils for its low acidity.

## Healing Powers

The main benefit of olive oil, and there are many, is that it lowers "bad" LDL cholesterol and raises "good" HDL cholesterol, thanks to its monounsaturated fats. Olive oil is also packed with antioxidants called phenols, which may protect artery walls from cholesterol buildup. Researchers even discovered recently that olive oil acts as an anti-inflammatory, which further protects your heart, and the rest of your body, too. Inflammation is strongly linked not only to heart disease but also to type 2 diabetes, Alzheimer's disease, and cancer.

## Healthful Hint

Look for "virgin," "extra-virgin," or "cold-pressed" oils. They are extracted by pressing alone. The solvents and heat used to produce "light" or "extra-light" oils destroy antioxidants. All olive oils have 120 calories per tablespoon.

**KEY NUTRIENTS**

> Vitamins E and K
> Monounsaturated fats
> Antioxidants

**HOW MUCH IS ENOUGH**
Up to 1 tablespoon a day.

**BUYING RIGHT**
Delicate extra-virgin olive oil is best used uncooked for salad dressings or dipping. Virgin olive oil is perfect for sautéing, so you'll want to keep both on hand.

## Three Clever Ideas

**1**. Best stored in the refrigerator, olive oil does solidify when chilled. A solution: Keep the bottle in the fridge, but fill a clean, pretty, dark wine bottle with 1 cup of oil. It'll always be there when you need it.

**2**. Using flavored oils saves you from having to add seasoning to dishes. Make your own by adding dried herbs and seasonings to a bottle of oil. Start with different combinations in small bottles until you find a favorite.

**3**. To prevent over-pouring, don't remove the safety seal from a new bottle. Instead, poke through the seal with the tip of a paring knife. To pour, squeeze or shake the oil into the pan or measuring spoon.

# Red Wine & Grape Juice

## What You're Drinking

The juice or, in the case of wine, the fermented juice, of grapes. Most wines are made from purple grapes. In making white wine, the grape skins are removed before they add color. The skins contain most of the antioxidants that contribute to wine's health benefits. Grape juice also contains many of the antioxidant compounds found in grape skins. Alcohol, a byproduct of fermentation, is toxic to all living things at various doses; the yeasts that excrete it cannot tolerate an environment that's more than 15 percent alcohol, which is why fermentation stops at about this concentration. In small doses, though, alcohol can be good for the body.

## Healing Powers

Most of the health benefits of wine come from the alcohol itself, which raises HDL cholesterol and lowers LDL cholesterol. Drinking one to two glasses a day of any type of alcohol dramatically reduces the risk of heart disease, death from heart disease, and premature death from any cause. Red wine does offer some added benefits from the plant compounds found in grape skins, such as flavonoids, which help prevent blood clots, and resveratrol, which helps lower cholesterol and has been shown to slow the growth of cancer cells. Wine consumption may also help keep dementia at bay. That said, alcohol promotes certain cancers, including breast cancer and colon cancer. If you have a family history of cancer, favor grape juice.

## Healthful Hint

Drink alcohol with meals instead of by itself for the greatest protection from heart attacks.

---

**KEY NUTRIENTS**

> Alcohol

> Antioxidants, especially flavonoids and phenols

**HOW MUCH IS ENOUGH**
One to two 4-ounce glasses of wine (one for women, two for men) or grape juice a day.

**BUYING RIGHT**
Whether for drinking or cooking, select wine you'll enjoy. Avoid cheap cooking wines loaded with sodium. One rule of thumb: If you wouldn't drink it, don't cook with it.

---

## Three Clever Ideas

**1**. Red wine can be served with many dishes. Fish, chicken, and eggs need lighter wines like Beaujolais or Pinot Noir. Denser foods with more fat—beef, lamb, and stews—can handle Shiraz, Cabernet, or Zinfandel.

**2**. When you have just a touch of wine left over, instead of discarding it, place it by tablespoons in an ice cube tray. When frozen, transfer to a zipper-seal plastic bag. Add to sauces as needed.

**3**. To remove a broken cork from a bottle, place a coffee filter over a carafe or measuring cup and pour the wine through the filter. The cork will come out, too. Serve from the carafe or pour back into the bottle.

# Salmon

## What You're Eating

A healthier alternative to steak and one of the best sources of omega-3 fatty acids, particularly EPA and DHA—nature's heart medicines. Much of the salmon you see in supermarkets is farmed; in fact, farmed salmon outnumbers wild 85 to 1. If you want wild salmon, choose Pacific salmon (more than 80 percent is wild caught). Most canned salmon in the United States is also wild caught. Farmed salmon is fed a diet with artificial coloring to turn the fish "salmon" colored. The fish don't eat the krill and other tiny shellfish that give wild salmon its naturally pink/red color.

## Healing Powers

The fat in salmon is like liquid gold when it comes to your blood vessels. Just two servings of salmon a week can reduce your risk of dying from cardiovascular disease by 17 percent and your risk of having a heart attack by 27 percent. And the benefits appear to go beyond the heart. A Swedish study that followed more than 6,000 men for 30 years found that those who ate moderate amounts of fatty fish slashed their risk of prostate cancer by a third. And researchers recently found that people who had the highest levels of omega-3 fatty acids in their blood were 53 percent less likely to report feeling mildly or moderately depressed.

## Healthful Hint

Farmed salmon has higher levels of contaminants than fresh, but researchers evaluating the risks/benefits of farmed over wild concluded that either is fine. (For more details, see page 325.) If you eat more than two 3-ounce servings of fish per week, be sure to choose a variety of fish, not just salmon.

**KEY NUTRIENTS**

> Omega-3 fatty acids
> Protein
> Vitamins A, B_3 (niacin), B_{12}, and D
> Zinc
> Magnesium

### HOW MUCH IS ENOUGH

Two 4- to 6-ounce servings a week.

### BUYING RIGHT

Fresh wild salmon, available from early summer to fall, should look moist and firm. It should smell sea-fresh, not overwhelmingly fishy. When fresh is out of season, go for frozen wild salmon fillets. Traditionally packed canned salmon offers many benefits, including increased calcium due to its tender edible bones. But since it's messy and time consuming to remove the skin and large bones, opt for ready-to-use boneless, skinless pink salmon sold in cans or pouches.

## Three Clever Ideas

**1.** For a fun appetizer, cut salmon fillets into 1-inch-thick strips and thread onto wooden skewers that have been soaked in water for 30 minutes. Brush with teriyaki sauce and grill just until opaque.

**2.** To easily remove pin bones from a salmon fillet, place the fish skin side down over a bowl. The bones will stick up, ready for removal with tweezers or pliers.

**3.** Transferring a large fillet from a baking sheet to a serving plate can be tricky. Slide a flexible cutting board under the cooked fish and gently move to the plate.

# Soy

## What You're Eating

One of the most nutritious plant foods and the only legume that provides complete protein. All soy foods—from miso to tofu to edamame (green soybeans)—come from soybeans. Tofu is made from pureed soybeans processed into a "cake"; miso, used in soup broths, is fermented soybean paste; soy sauce is a byproduct of miso production; and tempeh is fermented cooked soybeans. While soybeans are native to Southeast Asia, today 55 percent of soybean production occurs in the United States, most of it for oil.

## Healing Powers

Just a cup of boiled soybeans provides up to 6 grams of fiber—more than in a baked sweet potato. Volume for volume, soy contains more protein and iron than beef and more calcium than milk. But it's soy's phytoestrogens called isoflavones that take center stage. They may help cool off hot flashes, and there's some evidence they may block certain hormone-related cancers, including breast and prostate cancer. They're thought to help lower blood pressure and stave off bone loss. Soy foods may reduce your risk of heart disease, especially if you eat them in place of meat and full-fat dairy foods, which is easy to do since soy can mimic nearly any food product, from meat (think soy crumbles) to milk (soy milk) to nuts (soy nuts, which are roasted soybeans).

## Healthful Hint

Unprocessed soy foods like tofu, soy nuts, and soy milk retain more isoflavones than processed soy products like soy-based deli "meat" or soy "bacon."

### KEY NUTRIENTS

> B vitamins
> Protein
> Potassium
> Zinc
> Iron

## HOW MUCH IS ENOUGH

There's no official overall recommendation. Some experts recommend 25 grams of soy protein a day. Others just recommend replacing meat with soy whenever you can.

## BUYING RIGHT

Look for soy milk in the refrigerated section of your supermarket and buy a low-fat brand. It keeps for about a week after opening. Choose soy sauce that's labeled "naturally brewed" to avoid artificial flavoring and coloring. Edamame is most readily available frozen, both in and out of the shell. Look for fresh edamame in summer.

## Three Clever Ideas

**1**. Add soy flour to your baked goods by substituting it for one-third of the flour called for. It's best cooked at lower temperatures, so decrease the oven temperature by 25°F and check for doneness 5 to 10 minutes early.

**2**. Soy nuts make great snacks, especially if you buy them unsalted. Also toss them into salads instead of croutons.

**3**. Snack on edamame in the pods by slipping the beans out of the pod and into your mouth. To add flavor, partially steam the pods, then add to a hot skillet with a bit of oil and stir-fry until lightly browned. Sprinkle with salt.

# Spinach

## What You're Eating

One of the best sources of the B vitamin folate—a cancer fighter—and carotenoids such as lutein, which helps prevent macular degeneration, the leading cause of blindness in older adults. One thing you're not eating: a lot of iron. The myth that spinach is rich in iron (which made Popeye strong) surfaced back in 1870 when a researcher's misplaced decimal point in a publication gave spinach an iron content 10 times higher than reality. Reality is that a serving (1/2 cup) of raw spinach contains less than 1 milligram of iron. The calcium it contains isn't absorbed very well by your body, thanks to high concentrations of oxalic acid.

## Healing Powers

In addition to protecting your eyes from age-related macular degeneration, thanks to its carotenoids, spinach has high concentrations of vitamin K, which can help maintain bone density and prevent fractures. The green stuff is also a powerful source of potassium and magnesium as well as folate, all of which can keep blood pressure low, reducing the risk of stroke. Folate also appears to slash the risk of lung cancer in former smokers.

## Healthful Hint

To absorb more of the calcium from spinach, eat it with foods rich in vitamin C, such as red bell peppers or orange slices.

### KEY NUTRIENTS

> Beta-carotene
> Vitamins $B_2$ (riboflavin), $B_6$, C, and K
> Folate (a B vitamin)
> Potassium

### HOW MUCH IS ENOUGH

1 cup raw or 1/2 cup cooked spinach leaves is one vegetable serving.

### BUYING RIGHT

Choose crisp, bright green leaves and stems with no sign of yellowing, wilting, or bruising. For mild flavor and delicate texture, buy baby spinach. The best way to remove sand is to swish the spinach in a sink or bowl of water; as the leaves float, the sand sinks. Opting for prepackaged, prerinsed spinach eliminates this step, but even this spinach should be rinsed before using.

## Three Clever Ideas

**1**. A quick way to squeeze spinach dry is to place it in a single layer on a plate and top with an identical plate, then hold the plates together vertically over the sink and press them together.

**2**. Your teakettle will make preparing blanched spinach a breeze. Place clean, stemmed spinach in a metal colander in the sink and pour boiling water over it. Follow with cold water to stop the cooking.

**3**. Sneak some spinach into soups and stews by cutting it as you would an herb. To chiffonade, stack about 10 leaves on top of each other, roll them like a cigar, and slice crosswise into thin strips.

# Sweet Potatoes

## What You're Eating

A New World plant introduced to Europeans by Columbus and other explorers; not to be confused with white potatoes, to which they are unrelated. They are also unrelated to yams (starchy edible roots native to Africa and low in vitamins), although they are sometimes marketed as yams in North America. They derive their flavor from an enzyme that converts starches to sugars. Like other orange-yellow vegetables, they're an excellent source of beta-carotene, a precursor of vitamin A. Just one provides more than 100 percent of the RDA of vitamin A and more than a third of the RDA of vitamin C.

## Healing Powers

Sweet potatoes are a great source of the soluble fiber pectin, which soaks up cholesterol, and of insoluble fiber (mostly in the skin), which helps prevent constipation and hemorrhoids and may reduce the risk of stomach and colon cancer. Their high levels of beta-carotene protect against heart disease and many cancers, help keep skin healthy, and fuel a healthy immune system.

## Healthful Hint

Eat the skin of the sweet potato since that's where much of the fiber lies.

**KEY NUTRIENTS**

> Beta-carotene
> Vitamins $B_6$, C, and E
> Potassium
> Folate (a B vitamin)
> Iron

### HOW MUCH IS ENOUGH

One medium (5-ounce) sweet potato is one vegetable serving.

### BUYING RIGHT

Choose smooth, plump, dry sweet potatoes free of wrinkles, sprouts, or decay. Grab the ones with the darkest skin, as these also have bright orange flesh that offers the most nutrients. Store in a cool, dark place other than the refrigerator. Toss any that show the least sign of mold; once mold strikes, the entire potato will taste "off."

## Three Clever Ideas

**1**. Cooking sweet potatoes in lots of water, as for traditional mashed potatoes, will leach nutrients and flavor. Instead, simmer over low heat in a bit of broth and mash without draining.

**2**. Not just for the holidays, sweet potatoes are great in the summer. Grill skewers of sweet potato chunks brushed with a touch of olive oil and sprinkled with cinnamon or ginger. They cook fastest on metal skewers that get hot and cook the potato from the inside while the flame sears the outside.

**3**. A simple way to test baked sweet potatoes for doneness is to squeeze them with tongs. You'll feel whether the center is tender or needs a bit more cooking time.

# Tea

## What You're Drinking

The world's most popular nonalcoholic beverage and one of the most potent sources of antioxidants in nature (more potent than any fruit or vegetable). Whether you're drinking black tea, green tea, or something in between, you're drinking a beverage made from the leaves of the *Camellia sinensis* plant. In black tea, the leaves are crushed and allowed to "ferment" in the tea's own enzymes; green tea is not fermented. The finest leaves are plucked from the youngest shoots and unopened leaf buds. Tea contains antioxidants that belong to a group called flavonoids and is especially rich in catechins, which give it most of its health benefits.

## Healing Powers

Tea's antioxidants offer protection from heart disease, stroke, and cancer. They appear to protect against heart disease by slowing the breakdown of "bad" LDL cholesterol, preventing blood clots, and improving blood vessel function. People who drink a cup or two of tea a day have a 46 percent lower risk of developing narrowed arteries. The antioxidants also protect against the DNA damage that causes cells to turn cancerous. In cell studies, one of the most important catechins, called epigallocatechin gallate (EGCG), blocked an enzyme that cancer cells need to grow. While black tea may stain your teeth, tannins and fluoride protect against tooth decay.

## Healthful Hint

Brew black tea for at least 5 minutes to draw out the maximum amount of catechins. Drink most of your tea between meals since the tannins interfere with the absorption of iron from food.

### KEY NUTRIENTS

> Flavonoids (antioxidants), especially catechins
> Tannins
> Vitamin K (green tea only)

### HOW MUCH IS ENOUGH

Two to five cups daily.

### BUYING RIGHT

For the freshest tea, shop at a store that has a good turnover rate and buy only as much as you can use in a month. Tea is best stored in airtight dark glass containers in a cool, dry place since refrigerating or freezing can ruin its flavor. Choose green tea over black for less caffeine.

## Three Clever Ideas

**1.** The easiest way to remove tea bags from iced tea is to first tie the bags onto a skewer. Place the skewer over a pitcher with the tea bags hanging down, then add water. After the tea brews, simply lift out the skewer.

**2.** When boiling water to cook whole grains, add a green tea bag. Boil for 3 minutes, then remove the bag before adding the grains.

**3.** Sprinkle green or white tea leaves on salads or stir-fries or add to chicken- or fish-based soups or stews.

# Whole Wheat

## What You're Eating

Wheat in its "whole" form. That includes the bran, or outer husk of the plant, which is strong enough to protect the other two major parts of the plant—the germ and endosperm—from too much sunlight, water, and attacks from pests and diseases. The germ is the plant's embryo, which eventually becomes a new stalk of wheat. Many of the nutrients and much of the fiber in wheat are contained in the bran and germ—the parts that are removed when whole wheat is refined into white flour. That leaves the endosperm, which is mostly starch and protein.

## Healing Powers

Whole grains are a surprising source of antioxidants. The high fiber and B vitamin content of whole wheat plays a major role in the grain's ability to reduce the risk of death from cardio-vascular disease—and in fact from any cause. The fiber may also lower your risk of colon cancer. Whole grains such as whole wheat contain plant estrogens called lignans, which help lower estrogen levels and encourage cancer cells to self-destruct. On the whole (no pun intended), whole grains digest more slowly than refined grains do, so they don't raise blood sugar as quickly or dramatically. This keeps insulin levels low—a boon to both diabetes and cancer prevention.

## Healthful Hint

Make sure the word *whole*, as in "whole-wheat flour," is part of the first ingredient listed in any grain product to make sure you're getting the real thing. If you see "wheat flour," that's white flour.

### KEY NUTRIENTS

> Fiber

> Vitamins $B_2$ (riboflavin), $B_3$ (niacin), and other B vitamins

### HOW MUCH IS ENOUGH

At least three servings of a whole-wheat or whole-grain food a day to help boost your daily fiber intake. A serving is a slice of bread or an ounce of breakfast cereal.

### BUYING RIGHT

Since whole-wheat flour doesn't move as fast as white flour, be sure to purchase it from a store with good turnover. Whole-wheat flour contains some fat from the bran, so store it in a sealed container in the fridge for up to six months.

## Three Clever Ideas

**1.** For baking, use white whole-wheat or whole-grain (wheat) pastry flour. These types are more finely ground than whole-wheat flour and work better in baking.

**2.** Although whole-wheat bread is readily available, whole-wheat crumbs are not. Make your own by saving bread ends and any stale slices in the freezer in a zipper-seal plastic bag. Pulse in a food processor to form crumbs.

**3.** Create a delicious, healthy topping for baked casseroles or gratins by sprinkling with toasted wheat germ before baking.

# Yogurt

## What You're Eating

Pasteurized milk to which live bacteria cultures have been added for fermentation. Once the desired acidity is reached, the fermentation is stopped by cooling the yogurt. The bacteria cultures consume much of the lactose, or milk sugar, found in milk—which is why even people who are lactose intolerant can often eat yogurt with no problem—and release lactic acid, the stuff that makes yogurt tangy. Yogurt contains the same amount of fat as the milk it's made with. Some brands contain pectin or gelatin for added body.

## Healing Powers

Yogurt is a great source of bone-building calcium, but its real strength lies in live beneficial bacteria, known as probiotics, that keep down the growth of harmful bacteria in your gut. Too many "bad" bacteria can lead to gastrointestinal and other health problems. Eating more yogurt could help with inflammatory bowel disease, ulcers, urinary tract infections, and vaginal yeast infections, to name a few conditions. Getting plenty of "good" bacteria from yogurt is particularly important when you take antibiotics, which wipe out all bacteria, good and bad, in your gut. Probiotics also produce immunity-enhancing compounds and natural antibiotics that help reduce levels of nasty bacteria in the gut.

## Healthful Hint

Look on the label for *Lactobacillus acidophilus,* *Bifidobacterium bifidum,* and *Streptococcus thermophilus,* among other active cultures.

### KEY NUTRIENTS

> Protein
> Calcium
> Vitamin A
> B vitamins
> Zinc
> Phosphorus

**HOW MUCH IS ENOUGH**

1 cup a day of low-fat or fat-free yogurt with live cultures.

**BUYING RIGHT**

Choose low-fat yogurt that's not overly sweetened and look for "live bacteria" on the container. Also get the freshest yogurt you can find; the longer a product has been refrigerated and the more pasteurized it is, the fewer active bacteria it contains.

## Three Clever Ideas

**1**. Yogurt can break down during cooking, so if you're adding it to a hot dish, stir 1 tablespoon flour or cornstarch into 1 cup yogurt. Remove the pan from the heat and stir in the yogurt until creamy.

**2**. Most store-bought chocolate yogurt doesn't contain as many live, active cultures as plain yogurt. Make your own by stirring cocoa powder and a bit of sugar into fat-free or low-fat plain yogurt.

**3**. When coating pork, chicken, or fish with bread crumbs, replace the eggs used to moisten the meat with plain yogurt. Plan on using about 8 ounces of yogurt per pound of protein.

# 10 Healing Herbs AND Spices

Imagine garlic bread without the garlic, apple pie without the cinnamon, and lamb curry without the turmeric (the stuff that makes curry powder yellow).

There's no doubt that herbs and spices add distinctive flavors to our cooking. But little do most people know that the red, yellow, and brown powders they sprinkle on their food—not to mention the fresh herbs they cook with—also add significant health benefits. After all, herbs and spices come from plants, and many plants, as scientists are learning, contain a variety of healing substances—often found in high concentrations in the seeds, oils, and other plant parts that make up herbs and spices.

You may think of blueberries when you think of antioxidants, but you should also think of cloves. You know by now that fatty fish combats inflammation, but so does ginger. Certain herbs and spices—garlic and turmeric in particular—may even help us stave off cancer. And many are potent killers of bacteria and viruses.

Dozens of herbs and spices contain useful plant compounds, but the following 10 are healing standouts.

## Cayenne

That burning sensation in your mouth when you eat foods spiced with cayenne (red) pepper comes from capsaicin, the oily compound behind most of the health benefits of cayenne and its peppery cousins. Capsaicin is the active ingredient in many prescription and over-the-counter creams, ointments, and patches for arthritis and muscle pain. Over time, it short-circuits pain by depleting nerve cells of a chemical called substance P, which helps transfer pain signals along nerve endings to the brain. It's also used for treating shingles pain and diabetes-related nerve pain.

Cayenne's benefits don't end there, however. Sprinkle some onto your chicken soup to turbocharge that traditional cold remedy, since cayenne shrinks blood vessels in your nose and throat, relieving congestion. It's also a metabolism booster, speeding up your calorie-burning furnace for a couple of hours after eating. Cayenne is thought to act as an anti-inflammatory and antioxidant. Studies find that it also has some anticancer properties, and researchers are exploring its potential as a cancer treatment. Finally, in at least one study, published in the *American Journal of Clinical Nutrition*, researchers found that people with diabetes who ate a meal containing liberal amounts of chile pepper required less postmeal insulin to reduce their blood sugar, suggesting the spice may have antidiabetes benefits.

## Cinnamon

Cinnamon on toast or oatmeal is so tasty it's hard to believe the brown powder has any health benefits at all, but it's actually one of the most powerful healing spices. It's become most famous for its ability to improve blood sugar control in people with diabetes. Some of its natural compounds improve insulin function, significantly lowering blood sugar with as little as 1/4 to 1/2 teaspoon a day. The same amount could cut triglycerides and total cholesterol levels by 12 to 30 percent. The apple pie spice can even help prevent blood clots, making it especially heart smart.

Like many other spices, cinnamon has antibacterial and anti-inflammatory properties. It's been shown to conquer *E. coli,* among other types of bacteria. Researchers have even discovered recently that it's rich in antioxidants called polyphenols—another reason it's good for your heart. It's also high in fiber (after all, it comes from the bark of a tree) and can reduce heartburn in some people.

## Cloves

Cloves, an aromatic spice common in Indian cooking, contain an anti-inflammatory chemical called eugenol. In recent animal studies, this chemical inhibited COX-2, a protein that spurs inflammation (the same protein that so-called COX-2 inhibitor drugs such as Celebrex quash). Cloves also ranked very high in antioxidant properties in one study. The combination of anti-inflammatory and antioxidant properties spells heaps of health benefits, from boosting protection from heart disease to helping stave off cancer, as well as slowing the cartilage and bone damage caused by arthritis. Compounds in cloves, like those found in cinnamon, also appear to improve insulin function.

Have a toothache? Put a couple of whole cloves in your mouth. Let them soften a bit, then bite on them gently with good molars to release their oil. Then move them next to the painful tooth and keep them there for up to half an hour. Clove oil has a numbing effect in addition to bacteria-fighting powers. In test tubes, cloves also killed certain bacteria that were resistant to antibiotics.

## Coriander

Coriander seeds yield cilantro, also known as Chinese parsley, a staple herb in Mexican, Thai, Vietnamese, and Indian cooking. The seeds have been used for thousands of years as a digestive aid. Try making a strong tea from crushed seeds (strain before drinking). The herb can be helpful for some people with irritable bowel syndrome, as it calms intestinal spasms that can lead to diarrhea. Preliminary studies in animals support another traditional use for coriander— as an antianxiety herb. Its essential oil appears to fight bacteria, including *E. coli* and salmonella. It's also being studied for its potential cholesterol-reducing benefits and has been shown to lower cholesterol in animals.

Like many other herbs, this one acts as an antioxidant. According to one study, cilantro leaves provide the most antioxidant punch.

## Garlic

Smash a clove of garlic and take in the pungent fragrance. That famous odor comes from byproducts of allicin, the sulfur compound believed to be responsible for most of the herb's medicinal benefits. It's what gives garlic its "bite."

When eaten daily, garlic can help lower heart disease risk by as much as 76 percent. How? By moderately reducing cholesterol levels (by between 5 and 10 percent in some studies), by thinning the blood and thereby staving off dangerous clots, and by acting as an antioxidant. Garlic's sulfur compounds also appear to ward off cancer, especially stomach and colorectal cancer. The compounds flush out carcinogens before they can damage cell DNA, and they force cancer cells that do develop to self-destruct.

Strongly antibacterial and antifungal, garlic can help with yeast infections, some sinus infections, and the common cold. It can even repel ticks (as well as friends and family, if you eat enough).

## Ginger

This gnarled root has been a major player in Asian and Indian medicine for centuries, primarily as a digestive aid. Today researchers are most excited by ginger's ability to combat inflammation. Several studies have found that ginger (and turmeric) reduces pain and swelling in people with arthritis. It may work against migraines by blocking inflammatory substances called prostaglandins. And because it reduces inflammation, it may also play a role in preventing and slowing the growth of cancer.

Ginger's still good for the tummy, too. It works in the digestive tract, boosting digestive juices and neutralizing acids as well as reducing intestinal contractions. It's proven quite effective against nausea. In fact, at least one study found ginger to work just as well as Dramamine (dimenhydrinate) and other nausea-stopping drugs, with the added benefit that it doesn't make you sleepy. The trick is to take ginger (in tablet, powder, or natural form) *before* you think you may become nauseated, when it works best. It's also an effective, short-term treatment for morning sickness.

## Mustard

Mustard is made from the seeds of a plant in the cabbage family—a strongly anticancer group of plants. Indeed, mustard seeds contain compounds that studies suggest may inhibit the growth of cancer cells.

Mustard also packs enough heat to break up congestion, the reason it was traditionally used in chest plasters. Like cayenne pepper, it has the ability to deplete nerve cells of substance P, a chemical that transmits pain signals to the brain, when used externally. A mustard compress also brings more blood to the fingers of people with Raynaud's phenomenon, a circulatory problem that causes frigid fingers.

Mustard is also said to stimulate appetite by increasing the flow of saliva and digestive juices. A bit of mustard powder added to a footbath helps kill athlete's foot fungus. Don't eat too many mustard seeds or more than a teaspoon of mustard powder; the former has a strong laxative effect, while the latter can induce vomiting.

## Nutmeg

Like cloves, nutmeg contains eugenol, a compound that may benefit the heart. It was one of the key spices that give the Spice Islands their name, and some historians link its popularity in the spice trade to the hallucinatory effects that result from ingesting large amounts. The euphoria, which is due to nutmeg's active ingredient, myristicin, is described as similar to that caused by the drug ecstasy. Don't worry about your teens raiding your spice drawer for a quick high, however; it also packs some nasty side effects, and nutmeg poisoning is a very real risk.

Medically, nutmeg (the seed of an evergreen tree) and mace (the covering of the seed) have strong antibacterial properties. It's been found to kill a number of bacteria in the mouth that contribute to cavities. Myristicin has also been shown to inhibit an enzyme in the brain that contributes to Alzheimer's disease and to improve memory in mice, and researchers are currently studying its potential as an antidepressant.

## Sage

Perhaps it's no coincidence that "sage" describes a wise person; the herb is a known memory enhancer and has been shown in some lab studies to protect the brain against certain processes that lead to Alzheimer's disease. In at least one human study, a sage-oil concoction improved the mood of participants, increasing their alertness, calmness, and contentedness. In a British study, healthy young adults performed better on word recall tests after taking sage-oil capsules.

Like so many other herbs and spices, sage has anti-inflammatory and antioxidant properties as well as anticancer actions. One of its phytochemicals is thujone, best known as a chemical in the liquor absinthe that is said (falsely) to have hallucinatory effects. Today sage shows potential as a diabetes treatment. It appears to boost the action of insulin and reduce blood sugar. As a result, sage is sometimes called nature's metformin since it performs like the common antidiabetes drug. Some researchers have already suggested that sage supplements may help prevent type 2 diabetes.

## Turmeric

Turmeric, the spice that gives curry powder its yellow hue, is used in Indian medicine to stimulate the appetite and as a digestive aid. But lately it's grabbing some serious attention as a potentially powerful cancer fighter. The chemical responsible for turmeric's golden color, called curcumin, is considered a top anticancer agent, helping to quell the inflammation that contributes to tumor growth and working in much the same way as broccoli and cauliflower to clear carcinogens away before they can damage cellular DNA and to repair already damaged DNA. Lab studies show turmeric helps stop the growth and spread of cancer cells that do form. Research suggests that it may protect against colon cancer as well as melanoma, the deadliest form of skin cancer. Researchers at Rutgers University in New Jersey are investigating a combination of curcumin and phenethyl isothiocyanate (the anticancer compound in cruciferous vegetables) as a possible treatment for prostate cancer.

Studies have also linked turmeric to reduced inflammation in a number of conditions, including psoriasis. In animal studies, curcumin decreased the formation of amyloid, the stuff that makes up the brain deposits characteristic in people with Alzheimer's disease.

# WHERE THE Nutrients Are

Coming up in Part Three, you'll discover food prescriptions for 57 common ailments, which highlight foods rich in key nutrients and phytochemicals that science tells us can help treat what ails us or prevent new health problems. Look to the tables here to find more good food sources of these substances, such as macronutrients (like monounsaturated fats and omega-3 fatty acids), micronutrients (like vitamins and minerals), and phytochemicals (like beta-carotene and isoflavones). These are the compounds that put the healing power in nature's edible medicines. We've also included fiber here even though it's not technically a nutrient because it isn't absorbed by the body.

One of the units of measurements you'll see in these tables is "µg," which stands for micrograms (a microgram is 1/1,000 of a milligram). Another unit is IU, which stands for international units. Used for some vitamins—especially those that come in different forms—it indicates the amount of a vitamin needed to achieve a certain biological effect. To convert milligrams of vitamin E to IUs of alpha-tocopherol (the natural form of E), multiply the number of milligrams by 1.5 (or by 2.2 to convert to IUs of synthetic vitamin E). To convert IUs of vitamin E to milligrams of natural vitamin E, multiply the number of IUs by 0.67 (or by 0.45 for synthetic E).

Researchers haven't yet discovered all of food's healing compounds. A good rule of thumb, then: Eat more fruits and vegetables, add fish to your weekly menu, and choose whole grains over refined grains.

| NUTRIENT/PHYTOCHEMICAL | FOOD | AMOUNT |
|---|---|---|
| **Antioxidants** (measured by total antioxidant capacity) | Small red beans, dried (1/2 cup) | 13,727 |
| | Pinto beans, dried (1/2 cup) | 11,864 |
| | Blueberries, cultivated (1 cup) | 9,019 |
| | Cranberries (1 cup) | 8,983 |
| | Artichoke hearts (1 cup) | 7,904 |
| | Blackberries (1 cup) | 7,701 |
| | Raspberries (1 cup) | 6,058 |
| | Strawberries (1 cup) | 5,938 |
| | Apple, red delicious with peel | 5,900 |
| | Pecans (1 oz) | 5,095 |
| | Russet potato, cooked | 4,649 |
| | Walnuts (1 oz) | 3,846 |
| | Avocado, Hass | 3,344 |
| | Pear, green | 3,172 |
| | Cloves, ground (1 g) | 3,144 |
| | Hazelnuts (1 oz) | 2,739 |
| | Cinnamon (1 g) | 2,675 |
| | Raisins (1/2 cup) | 2,490 |
| | Blackeyed peas, dried (1/2 cup) | 2,258 |

| NUTRIENT/PHYTOCHEMICAL | FOOD | AMOUNT |
|---|---|---|
| | Oregano (1 g) | 2,001 |
| | Yellow bell pepper | 1,905 |
| | Turmeric (1 g) | 1,592 |
| | Almonds (1 oz) | 1,265 |
| | Sweet potato, cooked | 1,195 |
| | Baking chocolate (1 g) | 1,039 |
| Beta-carotene | Carrot juice, canned (1 cup) | 21,955 µg |
| | Pumpkin, canned (1 cup) | 17,003 µg |
| | Sweet potato, baked, with skin | 16,803 µg |
| | Spinach, frozen, cooked (1 cup) | 13,750 µg |
| | Carrots, boiled (1 cup) | 12,998 µg |
| | Collards, frozen, cooked (1 cup) | 11,591 µg |
| | Kale, frozen, cooked (1 cup) | 11,470 µg |
| | Turnip greens, frozen, cooked (1 cup) | 10,593 µg |
| | Carrots, raw (1 cup) | 9,114 µg |
| | Pumpkin pie (1 piece) | 7,366 µg |
| | Beet greens, cooked (1 cup) | 6,610 µg |
| | Winter squash, all varieties (1 cup) | 5,726 µg |
| | Cantaloupe (1 cup) | 3,232 µg |
| | Broccoli, cooked (1 cup) | 1,449 µg |
| Calcium | Wheat or white flour, enriched (1 cup) | 423 mg |
| | Collards, frozen, cooked (1 cup) | 357 mg |
| | Rhubarb, frozen, cooked (1 cup) | 348 mg |
| | Yogurt, fruit, low-fat (8 oz) | 345 mg |
| | Sardines, with bones (3 oz) | 325 mg |
| | Milk, fat-free (1 cup) | 306 mg |
| | Spinach, frozen, cooked (1 cup) | 291 mg |
| | Milk, 1% (1 cup) | 290 mg |
| | Soybeans, green, cooked (1 cup) | 261 mg |
| | Cheddar cheese (1 oz) | 204 mg |
| | White beans, canned (1 cup) | 191 mg |
| | Salmon, canned, with bones and liquid (3 oz) | 181 mg |
| | Soybeans, mature, cooked (1 cup) | 175 mg |
| Fiber | Navy beans, cooked (1 cup) | 19.1 g |
| | Kidney beans, canned (1 cup) | 16.4 g |
| | Split peas, cooked (1 cup) | 16.3 g |
| | Lentils, cooked, (1 cup) | 15.6 g |
| | Pinto beans, cooked (1 cup) | 15.4 g |
| | Black beans, cooked (1 cup) | 15.0 g |
| | Wheat flour, whole grain (1 cup) | 14.6 g |
| | Oat bran, raw (1 cup) | 14.5 g |

| NUTRIENT/PHYTOCHEMICAL | FOOD | AMOUNT |
|---|---|---|
| | Dates (1 cup) | 14.2 g |
| | Lima beans, cooked (1 cup) | 13.2 g |
| | Chickpeas, cooked (1 cup) | 12.5 g |
| | Raspberries, frozen, sweetened (1 cup) | 11.0 g |
| | Soybeans, mature, cooked (1 cup) | 10.3 g |
| | Cornmeal, whole grain, yellow (1 cup) | 8.9 g |
| | Green peas, frozen, cooked (1 cup) | 8.8 g |
| | Cereal, Kellogg's All-Bran (1/2 cup) | 8.8 g |
| | Bulgur, cooked (1 cup) | 8.2 g |
| | Mixed vegetables, frozen, cooked (1 cup) | 8.0 g |
| | Raspberries (1 cup) | 8.0 g |
| | Soybeans, green, cooked (1 cup) | 7.6 g |
| | Spinach, frozen, chopped, cooked (1 cup) | 7.0 g |
| | Brussels sprouts, frozen, cooked (1 cup) | 6.4 g |
| | Spaghetti, whole wheat, cooked (1 cup) | 6.3 g |
| | Pearled barley, cooked (1 cup) | 6.0 g |
| | Winter squash, cooked (1 cup) | 5.7 g |
| | Oat bran, cooked (1 cup) | 5.7 g |
| | Raisins (1 cup) | 5.4 g |
| | Pear | 5.1 g |
| | Sweet potato, cooked, with skin | 4.8 g |
| | Carrots, cooked (1 cup) | 4.7 g |
| | Potato, baked, with skin | 4.4 g |
| **Folate** (folic acid) | Cereal, Total, fortified whole grain (3/4 cup) | 807 µg |
| | White rice, long grain, enriched (1 cup) | 797 µg |
| | Cornmeal, degermed, yellow (1 cup) | 518 µg |
| | Turkey giblets, cooked (1 cup) | 486 µg |
| | Wheat flour, white, enriched (1 cup) | 395 µg |
| | Chicken giblets, cooked (1 cup) | 373 µg |
| | Lentils, cooked (1 cup) | 358 µg |
| | Cowpeas (blackeyed, crowder, southern) (1 cup) | 358 µg |
| | Pinto beans, cooked (1 cup) | 294 µg |
| | Chickpeas (1 cup) | 282 µg |
| | Okra, frozen, cooked (1 cup) | 269 µg |
| | Spinach, frozen, cooked (1 cup) | 263 µg |
| | Soybeans, green, cooked (1 cup) | 200 µg |
| | Broccoli, cooked (1 cup) | 168 µg |
| | Brussels sprouts, cooked (1 cup) | 157 µg |
| | Collard greens, cooked (1 cup) | 129 µg |
| | Papaya | 116 µg |
| | Orange juice, from concentrate (1 cup) | 110 µg |

| NUTRIENT/PHYTOCHEMICAL | FOOD | AMOUNT |
|---|---|---|
| **Iron** | Clams, canned (3 oz) | 23.77 mg |
| | Cereal, fortified whole grain (3/4 cup) | 22.35 mg |
| | Turkey giblets, cooked (1 cup) | 11.18 mg |
| | Flour, wheat or white, enriched (1 cup) | 10.03 mg |
| | Rice, white, long grain, enriched (1 cup) | 9.73 mg |
| | Soybeans, cooked (1 cup) | 8.84 mg |
| | Baked beans, canned, with pork and tomato sauce (1 cup) | 8.20 mg |
| | Beans, white, canned (1 cup) | 7.83 mg |
| | Lentils, cooked (1 cup) | 6.59 mg |
| | Cornmeal, enriched (1 cup) | 6.53 mg |
| | Spinach, cooked (1 cup) | 6.43 mg |
| | Oysters, raw (6 medium) | 5.50 mg |
| | Pumpkin seeds, roasted (1 oz) | 4.24 mg |
| | Potato, baked, with skin | 4.08 mg |
| | Turkey, dark meat, cooked (1 cup, 140 g) | 3.37 mg |
| | Beef, chuck blade roast, cooked (3 oz) | 3.13 mg |
| | Shrimp, cooked (3 oz) | 2.63 mg |
| | Beef, bottom round, cooked (3 oz) | 2.44 mg |
| | Beef, ground, 85% lean, cooked (3 oz) | 2.21 mg |
| | Beef, top sirloin, cooked (3 oz) | 1.59 mg |
| | Tuna, light, canned in water (3 oz) | 1.30 mg |
| **Isoflavones** (phytoestrogens) (100 grams for all weights) | Soy flour, full fat (3.5 oz) | 177.89 mg |
| | Soybeans, Korean, raw (3.5 oz) | 144.99 mg |
| | Soy flour, defatted (3.5 oz) | 131.19 mg |
| | Soybean flakes, full fat (3.5 oz) | 128.99 mg |
| | Soybeans, dry roasted (3.5 oz) | 128.35 mg |
| | Soy protein concentrate (3.5 oz) | 102.07 mg |
| | Soy protein isolate (3.5 oz) | 97.43 mg |
| | Miso soup mix, dry (3.5 oz) | 60.39 mg |
| | Natto (fermented soybeans), boiled (3.5 oz) | 58.93 mg |
| | Soybeans, boiled (3.5 oz) | 54.66 mg |
| | Soybean chips (3.5 oz) | 54.16 mg |
| | Tempeh, cooked (3.5 oz) | 53.00 mg |
| | Tofu (3.5 oz) | 23.61 mg |
| | Soy milk (3.5 oz) | 9.65 mg |
| | Soy cheese, mozzarella (3.5 oz) | 7.70 mg |
| | Split peas (3.5 oz) | 2.42 mg |
| **Lycopene** | Tomatoes, pureed, canned (1 cup) | 54,385 µg |
| | Pasta sauce, marinara, ready to serve (1 cup) | 42,998 µg |
| | Tomato sauce, canned (1 cup) | 37,122 µg |
| | Vegetable juice cocktail, canned (1 cup) | 23,377 µg |

| NUTRIENT/PHYTOCHEMICAL | FOOD | AMOUNT |
|---|---|---|
| | Tomato juice, canned (1 cup) | 21,960 µg |
| | Pasta with meatballs in tomato sauce, canned (1 cup) | 19,326 µg |
| | Tomato soup, canned (1 cup) | 13,322 µg |
| | Watermelon (1 wedge) | 12,962 µg |
| | Tomatoes, stewed, canned (1 cup) | 10,289 µg |
| | Vegetable soup, chunky, canned (1 cup) | 7,087 µg |
| | Tomatoes, whole, canned (1 cup) | 6,480 µg |
| | Beef noodle soup, canned (1 cup) | 5,017 µg |
| | Pink grapefruit (1/2) | 1,745 µg |
| | Red bell peppers (1 cup) | 549 µg |
| Magnesium | Buckwheat flour, whole groat (1 cup) | 301 mg |
| | Trail mix, with chocolate chips, salted nuts, and seeds (1 cup) | 235 mg |
| | Bulgur, dry (1 cup) | 230 mg |
| | Oat bran, raw (1 cup) | 221 mg |
| | Chocolate, semisweet (1 cup) | 193 mg |
| | Halibut, cooked (1/2 fillet) | 170 mg |
| | Wheat flour, whole grain (1 cup) | 166 mg |
| | Spinach, canned (1 cup) | 163 mg |
| | Barley, pearled, raw (1 cup) | 157 mg |
| | Spinach, cooked (1 cup) | 157 mg |
| | Cornmeal, whole grain (1 cup) | 155 mg |
| | Pumpkin seeds, roasted (1 oz) | 151 mg |
| | Navy beans, cooked (1 cup) | 107 mg |
| | Pinto beans, cooked (1 cup) | 94 mg |
| | Almonds (1 oz) | 78 mg |
| | Baking chocolate, unsweetened, liquid (1 oz) | 75 mg |
| Monounsaturated fatty acids | Macadamia nuts, dry roasted (1 oz, 10–12 nuts) | 16.800 g |
| | Hazelnuts (1 oz) | 12.940 g |
| | Pecans (1 oz, about 20 halves) | 11.570 g |
| | Olive oil (1 Tbsp) | 9.850 g |
| | Almonds (1 oz, about 24 nuts) | 9.116 g |
| | Canola oil (1 Tbsp) | 8.246 g |
| | Peanuts, oil roasted, salted (1 oz) | 7.353 g |
| | Cashew nuts, dry roasted, salted (1 oz, about 18 nuts) | 7.349 g |
| | Peanuts, dry roasted, salted (1 oz, about 28 nuts) | 6.985 g |
| | Peanut oil (1 Tbsp) | 6.237 g |
| | Pine nuts, dried (1 oz) | 5.320 g |
| | Peanut butter, chunky (1 Tbsp) | 3.930 g |
| | Peanut butter, smooth (1 Tbsp) | 3.794 g |
| | Avocado, Hass (1 oz) | 2.778 g |
| | Avocado, Florida (1 oz) | 1.563 g |

| Nutrient/Phytochemical | Food | Amount |
|---|---|---|
| **Omega-3 fatty acids** | Flaxseed oil (1 Tbsp) | 8.2 g |
| | Walnuts (1/4 cup) | 2.6 g |
| | Flaxseed (1 Tbsp) | 2.2 g |
| | Trout, lake, cooked (3.5 oz) | 2.0 g |
| | Herring, Pacific (3.5 oz) | 1.8 g |
| | Salmon, farmed, cooked (3.5 oz) | 1.8 g |
| | Anchovies, canned (3.5 oz) | 1.7 g |
| | Tuna, bluefin, cooked (3.5 oz) | 1.6 g |
| | Walnut oil (1 Tbsp) | 1.6 g |
| | Sablefish, cooked (3.5 oz) | 1.5 g |
| | Salmon, Chinook, cooked (3.5 oz) | 1.5 g |
| | Sardines, canned (3.5 oz) | 1.5 g |
| | Mackerel, Atlantic, cooked (3.5 oz) | 1.3 g |
| | Herring, pickled (3.5 oz) | 1.2 g |
| | Canola/rapeseed oil (1 Tbsp) | 1.0 g |
| | Swordfish, cooked (3.5 oz) | 0.7 g |
| **Potassium** | Beet greens, cooked (1 cup) | 1,309 mg |
| | White beans, canned (1 cup) | 1,189 mg |
| | Dates (1 cup) | 1,168 mg |
| | Tomatoes, pureed, canned (1 cup) | 1,098 mg |
| | Raisins (1 cup) | 1,086 mg |
| | Potato, baked, with skin | 1,081 mg |
| | Soybeans, cooked (1 cup) | 970 mg |
| | Lima beans, cooked (1 cup) | 955 mg |
| | Pasta sauce, marinara, ready to serve (1 cup) | 940 mg |
| | Halibut (1/2 fillet) | 916 mg |
| | Winter squash, all varieties, cooked (1 cup) | 896 mg |
| | Banana | 422 mg |
| **Selenium** | Brazil nuts (1 oz) | 543.5 µg |
| | Mixed nuts, roasted (1 oz) | 119.4 µg |
| | Chicken giblets, cooked (1 cup) | 86.4 µg |
| | Wheat flour, whole grain (1 cup) | 84.8 µg |
| | Tuna salad (1 cup) | 84.5 µg |
| | Pearled barley, raw (1 cup) | 75.4 µg |
| | Orange roughy, cooked (3 oz) | 75.1 µg |
| | Halibut, cooked (1/2 fillet) | 74.4 µg |
| | Flounder/sole, cooked (1 fillet) | 73.9 µg |
| | Rockfish, cooked (1 fillet) | 69.7 µg |
| | Tuna, light, canned (3 oz) | 68.3 µg |
| | Swordfish, cooked (1 piece) | 65.4 µg |
| | Haddock, cooked (1 fillet) | 60.8 µg |

| Nutrient/Phytochemical | Food | Amount |
|---|---|---|
| **Vitamin B$_6$** | Cereal, Kellogg's All-Bran (1/2 cup) | 3.60 mg |
| | Chickpeas (1 cup) | 1.10 mg |
| | Tuna, yellowfin, cooked (3 oz) | 0.88 mg |
| | Beef liver, cooked (3 oz) | 0.87 mg |
| | Turkey giblets, cooked (3 oz) | 0.84 mg |
| | Rice, white, long grain (1 cup) | 0.84 mg |
| | Potatoes, hash brown (1 cup) | 0.74 mg |
| | Chestnuts (1 cup) | 0.71 mg |
| | Buckwheat flour, whole groat (1 cup) | 0.70 mg |
| | Turkey meat, roasted (1 cup) | 0.64 mg |
| | Halibut, cooked (1/2 fillet) | 0.63 mg |
| | Bananas (1 cup) | 0.55 mg |
| | Dried plums, stewed (1 cup) | 0.54 mg |
| | Beef, top sirloin, cooked (3 oz) | 0.54 mg |
| **Vitamin B$_{12}$** | Clams, canned (3 oz) | 84.06 µg |
| | Beef liver, cooked (3 oz) | 70.66 µg |
| | Turkey giblets, cooked (1 cup) | 48.21 µg |
| | Oysters, raw (6) | 16.35 µg |
| | Chicken giblets, cooked (1 cup) | 13.69 µg |
| | Clam chowder, New England, canned, with milk (1 cup) | 10.24 µg |
| | King crab, Alaskan, steamed (3 oz) | 9.78 µg |
| | Salmon, sockeye, cooked (1/2 fillet) | 8.99 µg |
| | Sardines, canned, with bones (3 oz) | 7.60 µg |
| | Cereal, General Mills, whole grain (3/4 cup) | 6.42 µg |
| | Rainbow trout, farmed, cooked (3 oz) | 4.22 µg |
| **Vitamin C** | Red bell peppers (1 cup) | 293.7 mg |
| | Papaya | 187.9 mg |
| | Orange juice (1 cup) | 124.0 mg |
| | Green bell peppers (1 cup) | 119.8 mg |
| | Pineapple/grapefruit juice drink, canned (8 oz) | 115.0 mg |
| | Chile pepper, green | 109.1 mg |
| | Cranberry juice cocktail, bottled (8 oz) | 107.0 mg |
| | Broccoli, boiled (1 cup) | 101.2 mg |
| | Strawberries (1 cup) | 97.6 mg |
| | Orange juice, from concentrate (1 cup) | 96.9 mg |
| | Brussels sprouts, cooked (1 cup) | 96.7 mg |
| | Orange sections (1 cup) | 95.8 mg |
| | Kiwifruit | 70.5 mg |
| | Cantaloupe (1 cup) | 58.7 mg |
| | Pineapple (1 cup) | 56.1 mg |
| | Kale, cooked (1 cup) | 53.3 mg |

| Nutrient/Phytochemical | Food | Amount |
|---|---|---|
| **Vitamin D** | Salmon, cooked (3.5 oz) | 360 IU |
| | Tuna, canned in oil (3 oz) | 200 IU |
| | Milk, fortified (1 cup) | 98 IU |
| | Cereal, fortified (3/4–1 cup) | 40 IU |
| | Egg yolk | 20 IU |
| **Vitamin E** | Cereal, General Mills, whole grain (1 cup) | 13.50 mg |
| | Sunflower seeds (1/4 cup) | 8.35 mg |
| | Almonds (1 oz) | 7.33 mg |
| | Spinach, frozen, cooked (1 cup) | 6.73 mg |
| | Sunflower oil (1 Tbsp) | 5.59 mg |
| | Pasta sauce, marinara, ready to serve (1 cup) | 5.10 mg |
| | Tomato sauce, canned (1 cup) | 5.10 mg |
| | Safflower oil (1 Tbsp) | 4.64 mg |
| | Turnip greens, frozen, cooked (1 cup) | 4.36 mg |
| | Hazelnuts (1 oz) | 4.26 mg |
| | Spinach, cooked (1 cup) | 3.74 mg |
| | Soy milk (1 cup) | 3.31 mg |
| **Vitamin K** | Kale, frozen, cooked (1 cup) | 1,146.6 µg |
| | Collards, frozen, cooked (1 cup) | 1,059.4 µg |
| | Spinach, frozen, cooked (1 cup) | 1,027.3 µg |
| | Turnip greens, frozen, cooked (1 cup) | 851.0 µg |
| | Collards, cooked (1 cup) | 836.0 µg |
| | Beet greens, cooked (1 cup) | 697.0 µg |
| | Mustard greens, cooked (1 cup) | 419.3 µg |
| | Brussels sprouts, frozen, cooked (1 cup) | 299.9 µg |
| | Broccoli, cooked (1 cup) | 218.9 µg |
| | Onions, spring (1 cup) | 207.0 µg |
| | Lettuce, butterhead (1 cup) | 166.7 µg |
| | Parsley (10 sprigs) | 164.0 µg |
| **Zinc** | Oysters, raw (6) | 76.28 mg |
| | Oysters, breaded, fried (3 oz) | 74.06 mg |
| | Cereal, General Mills, whole grain (3/4 cup) | 17.46 mg |
| | Baked beans, canned, with pork and tomato sauce (1 cup) | 13.86 mg |
| | Beef, chuck blade roast, cooked (3 oz) | 8.73 mg |
| | Crab (3 oz) | 6.48 mg |
| | Lamb, cooked (3 oz) | 6.21 mg |
| | Chicken giblets, cooked (1 cup) | 6.13 mg |
| | Beef, ribs, cooked (3 oz) | 5.91 mg |
| | Duck, cooked (1/2) | 5.75 mg |
| | Ground beef, cooked (3 oz) | 5.36 mg |
| | Beef, bottom round, cooked (3 oz) | 5.02 mg |

# three

# Food Cures for
# Common Conditions

*Food cures go way beyond chicken soup for colds. Try fish for allergies, pomegranates for arthritis, and oatmeal for diabetes. Here are proven food solutions for 57 common conditions.*

# ACNE

If you think pizza and chocolate are the bad guys behind breakouts, think again. These days, acne is blamed mostly on heredity and hormones. During puberty, a surge in male hormones called androgens (women have them, too) stimulates an increase of sebum, responsible for keeping skin moist, and keratin, needed to make hair. When too much of either clogs a hair follicle, acne can result.

Eating a cheesy pizza probably won't make much difference to your skin, but what *will* make a difference—a positive one—is eating more fruits, vegetables, and other foods that help keep hormones in balance and fight inflammation.

## YOUR FOOD PRESCRIPTION

### Brazil nuts

These are rich in selenium, a powerful antioxidant that appears to help improve acne, probably by protecting cells from inflammatory damage and preserving skin's elasticity. Selenium works particularly well when it's accompanied by vitamins E and A, so eat your Brazil nuts with some almonds and perhaps some red bell peppers.

**Aim for:** One Brazil nut delivers a full day's supply. Other foods rich in selenium are meats, fish, poultry, onions, garlic, and whole grains.

### Oysters, beans, poultry, fish,
*and other foods rich in zinc*

No one knows exactly why, but getting enough zinc appears to help put the brakes on breakouts. It may be that zinc helps to control the release of male hormones that kick-start acne. Zinc also helps the body absorb vitamin A, another important nutrient for healthy skin.

**Aim for:** The recommended amount for men is 11 milligrams; for women, it's 8 milligrams. Three ounces of oysters has 30 milligrams of zinc, while 3 ounces of dark turkey meat has 4 milligrams.

**Helpful hint:** Vegetarians who avoid animal products altogether should consider consulting a nutritionist for advice on supplementing with zinc.

### Salmon, flaxseed,
*and other foods rich in omega-3 fatty acids*

Some dermatologists think that omega-3 fatty acids, which help keep inflammation at bay, may help keep acne under control. Fatty fish like salmon, sardines, and mackerel all boast omega-3 fatty acids, as do flaxseed and walnuts.

**Aim for:** At least two servings of fatty fish per week. You can also sprinkle salads with flaxseed oil, use ground flaxseed in baking and smoothies, and add toasted walnuts to casseroles and hot and cold cereals.

### Sweet potatoes, carrots, cantaloupe, bell peppers,
*and other foods rich in beta-carotene*

Beta-carotene (found in many orange-, yellow-, and red-hued fruits and vegetables) converts in the body to vitamin A, another of the nutrients that helps to enhance selenium's benefits to skin.

**Aim for:** At least 1/2 cup of red- or yellow-hued vegetables a day.

### Almonds, eggs, leafy greens,
*and other foods rich in vitamin E*

The antioxidant vitamin E helps skin heal from damage and scarring caused by acne. It's not easy to get a lot of E from a low-fat diet, but unrefined (minimally processed) vegetable oils, nuts, and whole grains are good sources.

Aim for: The recommended daily intake of vitamin E is 15 milligrams. One tablespoon of canola oil has 2 milligrams, and a 5-ounce sweet potato has 5 milligrams. Some physicians recommend 200 milligrams or more per day, which you'd need a supplement to get.

Helpful hint: Vitamin E is fat soluble, so eat it along with foods that contain a little fat. When you eat kale or spinach, for example, drizzle on a little olive oil.

## Fruits and vegetables

When scientists looked at the diets of teens in the Kitavan Islands of New Guinea and the Ache region of Paraguay—where not one case of acne was found—they took note: The diets were rich in fruits and vegetables like yams and greens and low in refined foods like white sugar and white flour, which can cause hormones to spike. When people from a similar gene pool moved to Western regions and began to eat refined foods, they began to experience acne.

Aim for: At least nine servings over the course of a day. A serving generally means one medium piece of fruit, 1 cup of raw produce, or 1/2 cup of cooked produce.

## Oranges, tomatoes, melons, *and other foods rich in vitamin C*

These juicy vitamin C bombs won't cure you of breakouts, but because the vitamin strengthens cell walls, it can help protect your skin from scarring that blemishes can cause. Bioflavonoids, which often come from a C source (such as the white rind inside citrus fruits), also act as natural anti-inflammatories that can enhance the healing action of vitamin C.

Aim for: Eat enough vitamin C–rich foods to total at least 250 and preferably 500 milligrams of C per day. A half cup of raw red bell pepper packs 163 milligrams of C, and 1 cup of strawberries has 85 milligrams.

## NUTRITIONAL SUPPLEMENTS

**A multivitamin/mineral.** Several nutrients, including vitamin E and selenium, are important for controlling acne. You'll find both in most multis. **DOSAGE:** One a day.

**Chromium.** Some dietitians recommend chromium supplements to acne patients. There is good evidence linking chromium to better insulin use and some evidence that acne is linked with poor insulin sensitivity. Because chromium may aggravate a low blood sugar condition, check with your doctor before taking supplements. **DOSAGE:** 200 micrograms per day.

## OFF THE MENU

**Iodized salt and other strong sources of iodine.** For unknown reasons, iodized salt can cause acne flare-ups. Watch the amount of sodium you take in from prepared and processed foods and how much iodized salt you add from the saltshaker. Consider using sea salt, which is lower in iodine. Also limit shrimp and shellfish, which are high in iodine.

**Refined foods.** If you're serious about stopping acne, scale back on the "white" foods in your diet—white bread, white flour, mashed potatoes, french fries, and anything made with lots of sugar. They cause blood sugar and insulin to spike, and scientists suspect that those insulin spikes may contribute to acne. Diets full of refined foods and low in fruits and vegetables also come up short on magnesium, a mineral that helps to balance acne-inducing hormones.

### FEATURED RECIPES

**Ultimate Spiced Nuts** *p. 592*
**Spinach Salad with Chickpeas** *p. 596*
**Tropical Fruit Salad** *p. 590*
**Citrus Chicken Salad** *p. 598*
**Sweet Potato Soup** *p. 601*
**Three-Bean Chili** *p. 610*
**Baked Chicken with Tomatoes** *p. 615*
**Salmon Cake Sandwiches** *p. 606*

# ALLERGIES

When the trees bud, the grasses sprout, or the ragweed blooms, you probably reach for allergy pills and a family-size box of tissues. But if you reach for foods like fish and onions, both before and during allergy season, you may find that your sneezing has decreased and your breathing is a whole lot easier.

How can foods possibly tame hay fever? When allergens—pollen, grasses, dust mites, or molds—find their way into your nose, your body goes into attack mode if it's hypersensitive, or allergic. Immune cells release histamines, the chemicals responsible for most of your allergy symptoms. These in turn kick-start inflammation that's intended to keep the allergens from traveling into the body. The inflammation makes sinuses and nasal passages swell and eyes itch. Histamines also stimulate the nasal passages to release fluids, resulting in a runny nose and itchy throat, and cause sneezing, another attempt to send the allergens packing. Many of the foods that may help reduce allergies work by reducing inflammation or calming the immune system.

## YOUR FOOD PRESCRIPTION

## Salmon and other fatty fish

Fatty fish like salmon, sardines, and mackerel should be your first line of dietary defense against allergies. That's because they contain generous amounts of omega-3 fatty acids, which help minimize inflammation, a direct cause of most allergy symptoms. Several studies suggest that kids who start eating fish early in life may even be less likely to have allergies later. Eating more fish helps balance out the ratio of omega-3s to omega-6s in the body, which seems to have several beneficial effects on the immune system that translate into fewer allergy symptoms.

One Australian study that analyzed nearly 500 eight-year-olds found that those who ate fish at least once a week were 80 percent less likely to have ryegrass pollen allergies, a common cause of hay fever, than those who rarely ate fish. A similar study in Norway compared the fish-eating habits of more than 2,500 four-year-olds and found that those who had eaten fish in their first year of life had a significantly lower risk of developing hay fever and asthma than those who had not.

Can't get your kids to eat fish? If they're at least three years old, have them eat 1 ounce of walnuts (or 14 walnut halves) a day. Flaxseed also contains omega-3s.

Grownups should dine on fin food more often, too. One German study involving 568 adults found that high content of omega-3 fatty acids in red blood cells or in the diet was associated with decreased risk of hay fever.

**Aim for:** One to two servings of fatty fish such as salmon, tuna, and mackerel per week. Look to fish-oil supplements if you want to get even more omega-3s. Start your children on a fish-rich diet early in life.

## Garlic

What isn't garlic good for? In the case of hay fever, the oh-so-smelly bulbs appear to work by supporting the immune system with their rich store of antioxidants. Researchers have identified a link between a higher intake of certain antioxidants and a lower incidence of hay fever.

**Aim for:** Use fresh garlic liberally as a seasoning. You can also cut a whole clove into several chunks and swallow them like pills for a daily dose. Your stomach acids will break them down and release antioxidants as the garlic travels through the colon.

## Onions

This humble bulb packs a hefty dose of quercetin, an antioxidant that can help reduce inflammation and may help prevent the release of histamine from immune cells called mast cells. Quercetin also helps improve the body's absorption of vitamin C, another antioxidant with immunity-boosting powers. Quercetin may even work to stabilize cell membranes so they're less reactive to allergens. Other good sources are apples with skin, berries, red grapes, and black tea.

**Aim for:** Sprinkle raw onions on salads, stews, burritos, and other foods whenever you can.

## Yogurt with live cultures
*and fermented milk*

The live beneficial bacteria found in yogurt and other fermented products like kefir help keep the flora and fauna in your gut—where many immune cells are located—healthy. Some experts believe that the Western diet no longer includes enough fermented foods to keep a balance of healthy bacteria in our gastrointestinal tracts and that the prevalence of allergies has risen in response. These foods stimulate the body to produce certain white blood cells and antibodies as well as various growth factors that are important for keeping the body from over-reacting to allergens.

A recent Italian study found that when volunteers who regularly had bouts of hay fever ate 2 cups of yogurt daily for four months, they had half the histamine levels in their blood and fewer hay fever symptoms than those who drank 2 cups of fat-free milk daily.

Pregnant women take note: When moms-to-be eat foods that contain probiotics, such as yogurt, on a regular basis, their babies have a lower risk of developing allergies as they grow up. Studies have indicated that probiotics are especially important for infants and children, whose immune systems are still developing.

**Aim for:** One or 2 cups of yogurt or other fermented milk products per day. Check the label for *lactobacillus, bifidobacterium* and *Bacillus clausii,* among other live, active cultures.

**Helpful hint:** If 2 cups of yogurt sounds like too much for you, vary your source of probiotics with kefir, a fermented milk product available in health food stores and many supermarkets. Substitute 1 cup of kefir for one serving of yogurt. Add it to milkshakes and fruit smoothies.

## Sweet potatoes, leafy greens, wheat germ, almonds,
*and other foods rich in vitamin E*

In one German study on the dietary habits of 1,700 adults with and without hay fever, those who ate foods rich in vitamin E (the equivalent of 10 to 13 milligrams per day) had a 30 percent lower incidence of hay fever than those who ate diets low in the vitamin.

**Aim for:** Lots of leafy greens, whole grains, nuts, and avocados. One cup of cooked spinach or 1 ounce of almonds provides 4 milligrams of vitamin E. A 5-ounce sweet potato provides 5 milligrams.

Can you make the switch from ice cream to frozen yogurt? You should! Many frozen yogurts have the same live cultures that make regular yogurt so helpful in battling allergies. And frozen yogurt usually has less fat and sugar than ice cream.

## Oregano, lemon balm, rosemary, *and other herbs*

All of these herbs, along with sage and marjoram, contain rosmarinic oil in their leaves. One Japanese study showed that this acid, an extract of the oil, has an anti-inflammatory effect that helps reduce the symptoms of seasonal allergies.

**Aim for:** Season your dishes liberally with fresh herbs to reap the most benefit. Make lemon balm tea, add chopped oregano and rosemary to pasta dishes, and use sage and marjoram on poultry and fish.

### FEATURED RECIPES

**Spinach Salad with Chickpeas** *p. 597*
**Sweet Potato Soup** *p. 601*
**Fish Tacos** *p. 611*
**Roasted Salmon with Sautéed Greens** *p. 613*
**Salmon Steaks with Peach Salsa** *p. 612*
**Tuna Kebabs** *p. 610*
**Almond Rice** *p. 626*
**Raspberry-Almond Muffins** *p. 628*

## NUTRITIONAL SUPPLEMENTS

**Omega-3 fatty acids.** If you don't like the smell or taste of seafood, you may still get hay fever relief by getting omega-3s in fish-oil supplements. **DOSAGE:** 1 to 3 grams a day. Check with your pharmacist to make sure you're buying high-quality capsules. Store them in the refrigerator.

**Flaxseed oil.** Flaxseed oil, an alternative to fish oil, provides substances that are converted to omega-3 fatty acids in the body. **DOSAGE:** 1 to 3 tablespoons per day.

**Probiotics.** If you can't manage to eat a lot of yogurt every day, consider probiotic supplements. Look for products that contain *lactobacillus, bifidobacterium* and *Bacillus clausii* in particular. **DOSAGE:** Take a one-billion count capsule with *lactobacillus* and *bifidobacterium* twice daily. Both live and heat-killed varieties appear to be effective.

**Vitamin C.** The jury is still out on the use of vitamin C to help prevent hay fever, with some studies concluding that 2 to 4 grams of C can reduce symptoms and others finding no such benefits. Because vitamin C is safe to take, it may be worth trying for a month or two to see if it works on your symptoms. **DOSAGE:** 1 to 3 grams per day in divided doses (for example, 1 gram in the morning, another in the afternoon, and another at bedtime). If you experience diarrhea, cut back.

**Quercetin and bromelain.** If you're not eating enough apple skins, berries, and onions to get a therapeutic dose of quercetin, which appears to inhibit the release of histamine, try a supplement. Look for one that also contains bromelain, an enzyme that comes from the pineapple plant and also helps keep inflammation under control. Early studies on both of these compounds have shown promise in the treatment of hay fever, but more research is needed. **DOSAGE:** Look for a combination supplement with 200 to 400 milligrams of quercetin and up to 125 milligrams of bromelain. You can also find these two in combination with vitamin C.

**Vitamin E.** One of the most powerful antioxidants known, vitamin E may help reduce inflammation that causes hay fever symptoms. **DOSAGE:** 200 IU per day with food. Because E is fat soluble, it's better absorbed when taken with a little fat, such as olive oil or cheese on a salad.

## OFF THE MENU

**Honey.** The honeybee harvests flower after flower for its pollen. This means that if you have allergies to any of the pollens used by the bee, you may react to the honey they went into. Before you abandon the food of the gods completely, though, experiment with pure flower honeys, produced when bees are confined to a single crop. If you react to clover honey, for example, you may not necessarily react to lavender honey.

**Fatty red meat.** Studies have shown a higher incidence of hay fever in people who consume significant amounts of arachidonic acid, an inflammatory component of fatty red meats and organ meats as well as shellfish.

**"Cross-reactive" fruits and vegetables.** Some people with hay fever experience similar symptoms when they eat certain fruits and vegetables, a phenomenon known as cross-reactivity. People with birch pollen allergies, for example, may notice that they get an itchy tongue when eating apples and stone fruits like peaches, cherries, and plums. People with ragweed allergies often react to melons. Although pollen allergies are seasonal, cross-reactive reactions may persist all year. Cooking the problematic fruits and vegetables often eliminates the allergic reaction.

**Red wine.** Some people with hay fever get headaches when they drink red wine because, along with beneficial tannins and flavonoids, the skins of red grapes contain bothersome histamines. Green grapes contain fewer histamines.

## Into the Mouths of Babes

Although there is no perfect formula for preventing allergies, studies have shown that infants who have been breastfed for at least six months (and preferably longer) have a lower incidence of allergies when they get older, especially if their mothers never had hay fever. Pediatricians also recommend that babies not eat solid foods until they're four months of age, dairy products until they're one year old, and eggs until the age of two.

One study suggests another way to help your baby avoid allergies. In the study, mothers-to-be with a family history of allergies took probiotic supplements for a few weeks prior to giving birth. The newborns continued to get probiotics for six months after birth, either through breast milk (the moms continued with their supplements) or in formula. The result: Babies who had probiotics in their diets were half as likely to develop eczema (a form of allergy itself, and a good predictor of future allergies) compared to those who didn't receive probiotics.

# ALZHEIMER'S DISEASE

Alzheimer's is perhaps the one disease that strikes even more fear in our hearts than cancer does. One in three people over the age of 80 will be its victim, and most of us sit back and hope we won't be one of them. But there *are* concrete steps you can take to lower your risk—by a lot, not just a little. In fact, a recent study at Columbia University showed that New York City residents who ate plenty of vegetables, legumes, fruits, cereals, fish, and monounsaturated fats such as those in olive oil—the staples of centuries-old diets in Greece and Italy—had a *40 percent lower* risk of Alzheimer's disease than those whose diets least resembled the Mediterranean diet.

While you're at it, also plan to finally keep your promise to exercise more (recent epidemiological studies have found that people who exercised three or more times a week were much less likely to develop Alzheimer's), and don't forget to challenge your mind (think crossword puzzles or learning to play a musical instrument).

Alzheimer's disease often begins with what appears to be simple forgetfulness, but it wreaks much more havoc over time, destroying speech, comprehension, and coordination and causing restlessness and dramatic mood swings. Autopsies on the brains of Alzheimer's patients have revealed thick clumps of a protein called amyloid as well as tangled bundles of nerve fibers known as neurofibrillary tangles. Inflammation also plays a role, although researchers aren't sure if it's a cause or an effect of the disease.

Some of the risk factors for heart disease and stroke, such as high blood pressure, high cholesterol, and low levels of folate, may also increase the risk of Alzheimer's.

The right diet can't guarantee that you will avoid Alzheimer's, but if it lowers your risk or delays the onset of the disease, isn't a weekly salmon dinner worth it? Other steps are as simple as starting your mornings with a cup of tea, cutting out those cheeseburgers, and putting more fruits and vegetables on your plate.

A final note: If you're carrying a lot more pounds than you should, here's a compelling reason to shed some of them. Research has found that people who were obese at midlife were much more likely to develop dementia and Alzheimer's disease later in life.

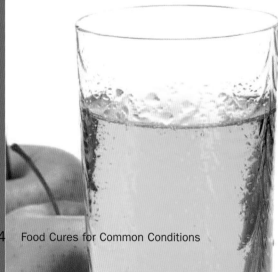

To help battle Alzheimer's, choose your drinks smartly. Have tea with your breakfast in the morning. During the day, switch from soda to natural fruit juices. Come evening, enjoy a glass of wine. All these beverages have been proven to lower the risk of the disease.

# Fatty fish, nuts, and olive oil

You may know these as staples of the famously heart-healthy Mediterranean diet, but recent evidence suggests they can lower the risk of Alzheimer's, too. Eating fatty fish such as salmon, herring, or white tuna once a week may slow cognitive decline by 10 percent. Omega-3 fatty acids, especially the type known as DHA, found in fatty fish appear to be the key. Since high levels of DHA are needed for normal brain development, that makes sense. In addition, omega-3 fatty acids of all varieties—including those found in walnuts, flaxseed, and olive oil—counter inflammation, which may contribute to protein buildup in the brain.

**Aim for:** At least one meal of fatty fish a week as well as several tablespoons of walnuts, olive oil, or flaxseed.

**Helpful hint:** Some fatty fish contain mercury, which can damage the brain. Children and women of childbearing age should avoid shark, swordfish, king mackerel, and tilefish because of high mercury levels. Canned white albacore tuna has more omega-3s than canned light tuna, but it also has slightly higher levels of mercury. Limit your intake to 6 ounces per week.

# Broccoli, strawberries, almonds,
*and other foods rich in vitamins C and E*

The brain is one of the most dynamic parts of the body, with neurons firing, cells growing, and webs of electrical and chemical activity masterminding bodily functions. But the by-product of all of these chemical reactions is free radicals, unstable molecules that damage cells, possibly contributing to amyloid plaques and speeding up mental decline.

Foods that contain antioxidants neutralize those free radicals, "mopping up" the "pollution" in your brain. Research on the dietary habits of large groups of people has found that eating plenty of foods rich in vitamin C (like red peppers, currants, broccoli, and strawberries) and

vitamin E (like kale, sweet potatoes, and almonds) may reduce the risk of developing Alzheimer's.

In a study conducted by researchers at the Rush Institute for Healthy Aging at Rush-Presbyterian-St. Luke's Medical Center in Chicago, people who consumed the most vitamin E from foods (averaging 11.4 IU) had a risk of Alzheimer's that was a whopping 67 percent lower than that of people who got the least (averaging 6.2 IU).

The effect of supplements is less clear, possibly because they tend to be taken in high-dose increments, unlike food that's eaten over a lifetime. Foods also contain all forms of vitamin E, whereas supplements typically contain only one type, alpha-tocopherol. The different forms of vitamin E neutralize different forms of free radicals.

**Aim for:** *Vitamin E:* 25 IU of vitamin E a day from foods such as 1 cup of cooked frozen spinach (10 IU), 1 ounce of almonds (11 IU), or 1 cup of tomato sauce (8 IU). *Vitamin C:* At least 130 milligrams a day from foods like 1 cup of papaya (87 milligrams), 1 cup of cooked broccoli (100 milligrams), or 1 cup of fresh orange juice (124 milligrams). A cup of chopped red bell peppers, with 312 milligrams, or two kiwifruits, with 150 milligrams, are also terrific choices.

# Tea, berries, pomegranate juice, apples, *and other foods and beverages high in flavonoids*

To defend themselves from solar radiation and hungry herbivores, plants have created an arsenal of protective chemicals called polyphenols. Flavonoids are among the toughest of these, and they also fall into the antioxidant category. Flavonoid-rich fruits include apples, blueberries, cranberries, and grapefruit. Vegetables that boast flavonoids include asparagus, brussels sprouts, cabbage, garlic, kale, kohlrabi, kidney and lima beans, onions, peas, and spinach. One study found that people who drank fruit and vegetable juices such as orange, apple, or tomato three times a week were less likely to develop

Alzheimer's disease. An animal study showed that pomegranate juice halved the risk of Alzheimer's disease in rats. Other studies have observed that the more flavonoids a person eats, the lower the likelihood of developing dementia.

**Aim for:** At least 15 milligrams of flavonoids daily. This shouldn't be difficult, since 1/4 cup of blueberries has 39 milligrams, a medium apple with skin has 13 milligrams, and 1 cup of grapefruit juice has 60 milligrams.

# Curry powder

Cooks in India and other countries use curry abundantly, and the incidence of Alzheimer's is lower in these places than in many Western nations. Curry could be one of the reasons. A prime ingredient in curry powder is turmeric, which contains curcumin (which gives curry its yellow color). In lab and animal studies, researchers have found that curcumin is a potent antioxidant, anti-inflammatory, and anti-amyloid compound. It binds to amyloid proteins

and prevents them from grouping together to form plaque, so it may be that curcumin offers a triple blow to Alzheimer's disease. Studies have shown that people who consumed the highest amounts of curried foods actually have better brain performance.

**Aim for:** There's no particular recommended dosage. The best advice? Add either curry powder or turmeric to as many dishes as you can. Purchase bright yellow curry powder, which is likely to contain the most turmeric. Or take one 400-milligram turmeric capsule a day.

**Helpful hint:** Include up to a teaspoon of turmeric in pea soup or add it to your favorite lentil dish.

# Spinach, fortified cereal,
*and other foods high in folate*

Doctors have known for years that deficiency of certain B vitamins, particularly folate, can make it difficult to perform some cognitive tasks. New evidence shows that even slightly low levels can have a similar effect because folate, along with vitamins $B_6$ and $B_{12}$, helps to keep homocysteine levels in check. This amino acid impairs brain function and can dramatically increase a person's risk of Alzheimer's disease (as well as heart disease). The good news is that folate from foods like dark leafy greens and dried beans may slow cognitive decline.

**Aim for:** The recommended daily amount of 400 micrograms. Many fortified breakfast cereals and breads provide this amount. Other good sources are cooked frozen spinach (100 micrograms per half cup), great Northern beans (90 micrograms per half cup), and orange juice (69 micrograms per 8 ounces).

# Wine

One French study showed that drinking three 4-ounce glasses of wine per day reduced the risk of Alzheimer's disease by a whopping 75 percent.

**Aim for:** Up to a glass a day for women and two for men.

## NUTRITIONAL SUPPLEMENTS

**DHA.** Some experts recommend taking this omega-3 supplement in order to get a high dose of the most active form of omega-3 fatty acids while avoiding mercury and other contaminants found in some fish. **DOSAGE:** Up to 400 milligrams of DHA daily. Check with your pharmacist to make sure you're buying high-quality capsules.

**Vitamins C and E.** The Nurses Health Study, which is tracking health data on thousands of women, has found that supplementing with C and E over the long term slowed cognitive decline. A study of some 4,000 elderly Utah residents found that supplementing with these two vitamins was associated with a 72 percent lower risk of Alzheimer's. Another study found that vitamin E supplements slowed the progress of the disease in people with moderate cases, but other studies have raised doubt about this. **DOSAGE:** *Vitamin C:* 500 milligrams daily. *Vitamin E:* 400 IU of d-alpha-tocopherol daily.

**Sage.** As its name suggests, sage has been used since ancient times to improve memory and sharpen the mind—and for good reason, as it turns out. Some human trials have found that the herb or its oil can indeed improve memory and cognitive function, and one four-month Iranian study found the extract improved cognitive function in Alzheimer's patients more than a placebo did.

More clinical research is under way. Sage appears to work by protecting acetylcholine, one of the chemical messengers in the brain that's critical to memory and that often drops in the brains of people with Alzheimer's. It may also have anti-inflammatory benefits that help slow the progress of the disease. **DOSAGE:** 25 to 50 microliters of *S. lavandulaefolia* (Spanish sage) oil or 300 to 600 milligrams of dried sage in supplement form. You can also steep 2 teaspoons of dried sage in boiling water for a strong cup of sage tea that provides the same dosage.

## OFF THE MENU

**Saturated fat, trans fat, and cholesterol.** Another reason to eat your chicken grilled instead of deep-fried: A diet high in these heart-wrecking fats is linked to a significant decline in cognitive function—as is a diet low in unsaturated fat (so trade that steak for a piece of salmon and that butter for olive oil or margarine made without trans fat). Trans fat is found in some margarines as well as highly processed foods such as packaged baked goods and "meals in a box." Avoid foods that list partially hydrogenated oils on the label.

**Sugar and refined grains.** They may look tempting, but those store-bought muffins in the cellophane wrap are a bad idea if you're worried about Alzheimer's disease. Diets rich in sugar and refined grains (like white flour) can contribute to the risk of type 2 diabetes, a condition that in turn quadruples the risk of Alzheimer's. One theory proposes that insulin resistance, at the core of type 2 diabetes, means that cells don't get the sugar they need to function properly, and brain cells may die as a result. Another theory suggests that an insulin imbalance may lead to additional protein clumping that gums up the pathways of the brain. If you already have diabetes, keep your blood sugar under strict control to help reduce the risk of Alzheimer's.

# ANEMIA

Imagine your body gasping for oxygen and pooping out like a car with a bad carburetor. That's pretty much what happens with anemia, either because there are too few red blood cells to carry enough oxygen through the body or because the blood cells lack sufficient hemoglobin, the protein that carries oxygen. Daily life becomes double the effort due to fatigue. Anemia can also lead to headaches, cold hands and feet, and pale skin (after all, it's blood that puts the blush into cheeks).

Most cases of anemia are caused by iron deficiency, often triggered by blood loss (think bleeding ulcers or heavy menstrual periods). Another type of anemia, called pernicious anemia, is caused by a deficiency of vitamin $B_{12}$, which is needed to make red blood cells. Older people are at risk for this because with age, the body's ability to absorb $B_{12}$ from food tends to diminish. Folic acid is also needed for red blood cell production, so if you don't get enough, you could develop "folic acid anemia." Alcoholics, smokers, people with certain digestive disorders, vegetarians, people over 50, and pregnant or nursing women are at highest risk for folic acid and pernicious anemia.

You may need a prescription from your doctor to correct anemia, but a robust and varied diet will help keep you out of the woods once it's under control.

## YOUR FOOD PRESCRIPTION

### Beef, fish, shellfish,
*and other foods rich in vitamin $B_{12}$*

When your diet supplies too little vitamin $B_{12}$, you run the risk of developing pernicious anemia. Vegetarians are particularly vulnerable because $B_{12}$ is most abundant in animal products like meat and fish; cheese and eggs also provide modest amounts. Many fortified cereals offer a generous dose. If you have signs of pernicious anemia, such as shortness of breath, fatigue, loss of appetite, rapid heart rate, and tingling and numbness in your hands and feet, see your doctor; you may need $B_{12}$ supplements.

**Aim for:** 2.4 micrograms of $B_{12}$ per day, the amount in 3 ounces of beef.

### Clams, red meat, chicken, shellfish, *and other iron-rich foods*

The body needs iron to make hemoglobin, the protein that enables red blood cells to carry oxygen. Red meat is a classic powerhouse of heme iron, the form we absorb best and that's found in animal foods. Liver is another source, but it's loaded with cholesterol. Like clams? The canned variety is one of the best sources of iron and an outstanding source of vitamin $B_{12}$.

Lentils, tofu, and raisins contain nonheme iron, which is less easily absorbed. To squeeze more iron from these foods, eat them with a food rich in heme iron or in vitamin C, which helps you soak up iron.

Also look to foods like oatmeal and cereal, usually fortified with iron, to "beef up" your diet.

**Aim for:** 18 milligrams of iron for women up to age 50; 8 milligrams for women 51 and older and adult men. This often won't be enough to correct anemia, but it should help you maintain good iron levels once the anemia is under control. You'll get 3.6 milligrams of iron from 3 ounces of beef tenderloin, 14 milligrams from six oysters, and as much as 22 milligrams from a serving of fortified cereal.

## Citrus fruits, peppers, broccoli,
### and other foods rich in vitamin C

Vitamin C helps the body absorb iron, so pair up half an orange and a cup of iron-fortified Cream of Wheat, or add some red peppers to your beef or chicken stir-fry. Vitamin C also helps counter the effects of phytates, substances in fiber-dense foods like wheat bran, wheat germ, nuts, barley, and oats that bind with iron. A study from Sweden showed that when vitamin C was consumed along with high-phytate foods, iron absorption increased significantly.

Aim for: At least a cup of C-rich foods per day.

## Lentils, beans,
### and other foods rich in folate

Folate, one of the B vitamins, helps red blood cells divide rapidly, replenishing the body's oxygen carriers. Some people may need oral or even intravenous treatment with folic acid supplements if they have trouble absorbing folate from food, but most people can benefit from getting more folate in their diets.

Aim for: 400 micrograms of folate per day. You'll get almost this much in a cup of cooked lentils, and more from a serving of fortified cereal.

### NUTRITIONAL SUPPLEMENTS

**Iron.** Dietary iron often may not be enough to correct a deficiency. For women who have particularly heavy menstrual bleeding, or anyone with a condition that causes blood loss, supplements may be in order. Have your doctor do a blood test first to confirm iron-deficiency anemia. **DOSAGE:** Take iron only under medical supervision, at the level the doctor recommends.

**Vitamin C.** To help the blood absorb iron, take your vitamin C and iron supplements at the same time. **DOSAGE:** 250 to 500 milligrams two or three times a day, taken with meals to enhance iron absorption from foods. Reduce the dose if diarrhea develops.

**Vitamin $B_{12}$.** Check with your doctor about what dosage you may need. **DOSAGE:** Doctors often recommend 1,000 micrograms of $B_{12}$ combined with 400 micrograms of folic acid, in a form that's placed under the tongue so it's absorbed through the mouth, twice a day.

**Folic acid.** The body absorbs the folic acid in supplements better than the folate in foods. But take heed: If you exceed the upper limit for folic acid (1,000 micrograms), you risk a vitamin $B_{12}$ deficiency. Take folic acid with $B_{12}$ because a high intake of one can mask a deficiency of the other. **DOSAGE:** 400 micrograms from food (check your cereal, since grain products in many countries are fortified with folic acid) and another 400 micrograms from supplements daily.

### OFF THE MENU

**Tea.** The tannins in tea bind with iron, blocking absorption. To avoid this problem, drink tea by itself rather than with meals.

**Spinach, nuts, berries, chocolate, wheat bran and germ, tea, and other foods high in oxalates.** Oxalates are compounds that bind with iron and calcium, making them hard to absorb. Don't cross these foods off your menu entirely, but if you have anemia, it's best to avoid them until your red blood count has returned to normal. Other foods high in oxalates are rhubarb, beets, tofu, tangerines, and baked beans.

### FEATURED RECIPES

**Shrimp and Grapefruit Salad** *p. 598*
**Lentil-Tomato Soup** *p. 603*
**Beef in Lettuce Wraps** *p. 606*
**Turkey Cutlets with Grapefruit Salsa** *p. 617*
**Barbecued Flank Steak** *p. 618*
**Beef and Broccoli Stew** *p. 620*

# ARTHRITIS

In *The Wizard of Oz*, the Tin Man kept a can of oil handy to keep his joints from freezing up. Believe it or not, getting the right kinds of oils from foods can actually help *your* joints, too, albeit in a much different way. Evidence is beginning to mount that certain foods high in anti-inflammatory compounds—especially the oils in fatty fish—help reduce the inflammation and pain of arthritis. It's not surprising, since both osteoarthritis (the most common type) and rheumatoid arthritis, or RA (an autoimmune condition in which inflammation is triggered by an immune system reaction) result in inflamed joint tissues for which anti-inflammatory medications are often prescribed.

Although doctors don't yet fully understand arthritis, it's clear that everyday wear and tear on cartilage is hardly the whole story. Researchers now know, for example, that free radicals—unstable molecules that attack healthy cells—increase inflammation and speed up the aging process, including the deterioration of joints and cartilage, a process best slowed in anyone, but especially in people with arthritis. It's an excellent reason to add more antioxidant-rich fruits, vegetables, and tea to your menu.

## YOUR FOOD PRESCRIPTION

### Salmon, mackerel, flaxseed,
*and other foods high in omega-3 fatty acids*

For years, researchers have noticed that people with arthritis who eat plenty of oily fish seem to have less inflammation and pain than those who don't eat as much fish. Now they have an explanation: It seems that like aspirin, the omega-3 fatty acids in fatty fish boost production of a recently discovered class of anti-inflammatory fats called resolvins. In one study, both omega-3s and aspirin boosted the production of resolvins, which in turn inhibit the activity of inflammatory cells. This is good news for people with osteoarthritis and particularly for those with RA, which can inflame organs as well as joints.

**Aim for:** Two to three 4-ounce servings of fish a week. If you don't like fish, aim for 1 to 2 tablespoons of ground flaxseed daily.

**Helpful hint:** Researchers have found that a diet plentiful in fish fights inflammation best when partnered with low doses of aspirin. However, check with your doctor before taking aspirin.

Even low doses can cause gastrointestinal bleeding in some people. But for many others, taking one low-dose aspirin per day will provide loads of health benefits.

### Leafy greens, peppers, broccoli,
*and other foods rich in antioxidants*

Need yet another reason to eat more fruits and veggies? Here it is: Colorful produce, rich in antioxidants that fight free radicals, helps protect your joints.

Researchers have suspected for some time that free radicals, those unstable molecules that attack healthy cells, play a role in causing arthritis. Now it's becoming clear how they wreak their havoc on joints. According to a recent Japanese study, free radicals sabotage cartilage's ability to maintain and repair itself. People with arthritis tend to have more than their fair share of free radicals and therefore should make an extra effort to get more antioxidants, especially vitamin C and beta-carotene, from foods.

In a large nine-year British study, researchers found that even a modest boost in intake of orange and yellow fruits and vegetables—as modest as adding a glass of orange juice a day—can lower the risk of RA. People who ate the most yellow/orange fruits and vegetables, full of antioxidants known as carotenoids, halved their risk of developing the disease. Think of carrots and sweet potatoes in addition to that morning glass of orange juice.

Vitamin C in citrus fruits like oranges and kiwifruit, and zeaxanthin, an antioxidant found in green leafy vegetables, lowered the risk, too. Those leafy greens (like spinach and turnip greens) also pack a fair amount of vitamin E, and some studies have shown that large doses of this vitamin from supplements may also relieve osteoarthritis pain, especially in combination with vitamin C (250 to 500 milligrams a day).

There's less research so far into the effectiveness of antioxidants for osteoarthritis, but researchers believe eating more fruits and vegetables is a smart move whatever form of arthritis you have. Although supplements are available for many antioxidants, the studies have focused on antioxidants in foods.

**Aim for:** Five to six servings of a range of vegetables and three to four servings of a variety of fruits per day.

**Helpful hint:** Certain arthritis medications, such as nonsteroidal anti-inflammatory drugs (NSAIDs), can cause constipation. Many fruits and vegetables are high in fiber, which can help relieve that side effect.

## Pomegranate juice

Knees ache? What about your hands or hips? Try some of this sour Persian fruit, which has both anti-inflammatory and antioxidant powers. It could actually protect your cartilage. When researchers at Case Western Reserve University in Cleveland put a pomegranate extract on tissue samples of cartilage damaged by osteoarthritis, something good happened: The juice lowered levels of an inflammatory chemical linked with overproduction of a certain enzyme. In normal amounts, this enzyme is essential for cartilage

replacement, but when too much is produced—as in osteoarthritis—cartilage wears away.

Of course, you won't be pouring pomegranate juice directly on your cartilage, but it's thought that joints do absorb the juice when you drink it, so it's reasonable to believe that it may help. Although pomegranate capsules are available, it's better to just drink the juice.

**Aim for:** 2 to 3 tablespoons of undiluted pomegranate juice per day.

**Helpful hint:** To cut the juice's bitterness, add 1 tablespoon to a glass of iced green tea—also high in antioxidants and anti-inflammatory compounds—and drink it two or three times daily.

## Pineapple

Bromelain, a protein-digesting enzyme in this tropical fruit, is surprisingly good at bringing down inflammation. It may be as effective for reducing osteoarthritis pain as some anti-inflammatory medications like ibuprofen, at least when it's taken in supplement form. Some studies of bromelain supplements suggest it may help reduce the pain of RA as well. Eat your pineapple between meals, not with them, or the enzymes will be used up digesting your food, and choose fresh or frozen pineapple, not canned pineapple or pineapple juice.

**Aim for:** Studies have found that effective doses range from 200 to 540 milligrams of bromelain a day. The amount in each serving of pineapple varies depending on the ripeness of the pineapple and its exposure to heat, but a cup a day is a good goal.

**Helpful hint:** Bromelain is a stomach soother, which is good to know if arthritis medications are irritating your tummy. If you develop mouth sores from NSAIDs or methotrexate, eat the pineapple dipped in honey, also a natural anti-inflammatory.

## Turmeric, ginger, cloves,
### *and other anti-inflammatory spices*

Researchers have discovered that many spices fight inflammation. Ginger and turmeric—a yellow spice that lends its color and taste to curries—contain a powerful compound called curcumin, which inhibits enzymes and proteins that promote inflammation. Several studies have found that ginger and turmeric specifically reduce pain and swelling in people with arthritis. Cloves contain an anti-inflammatory chemical called eugenol. In recent animal studies, eugenol inhibited COX-2, a protein that spurs inflammation—the same protein that COX-2 inhibitor drugs like celecoxib (Celebrex) quash. Cloves, turmeric, and ginger also contain antioxidants, important in slowing the cartilage and bone damage caused by arthritis.

**Aim for:** *Ginger:* 1 tablespoon of chopped fresh ginger or 1 teaspoon of powdered ginger daily. *Turmeric:* 300 to 400 milligrams three times a day, or about 1/2 teaspoon sprinkled on rice or vegetables daily. *Cloves:* 2 to 3 grams, or l to 1 1/2 teaspoons, a day.

**Helpful hint:** Ginger, known for soothing upset stomachs, is a great choice if arthritis medications stir up gastrointestinal problems.

### FEATURED RECIPES

**Tropical Fruit Salad** *p. 590*
**Spinach Salad with Chickpeas** *p. 597*
**Citrus Chicken Salad** *p. 598*
**Ginger Butternut Squash Soup** *p. 602*
**Tomato-Roasted Mackerel** *p. 612*
**Salmon Steaks with Peach Salsa** *p. 612*
**Pomegranate Ice** *p. 638*
**Mixed Berry Tart** *p. 639*

## Green tea, onions, berries, tomato juice, *and citrus fruits*

This motley crew is drawn together by one thing: quercetin. Laboratory and animal studies indicate that this chemical compound acts as a powerful anti-inflammatory and antioxidant. Early studies in animals suggest green tea may help prevent or ease symptoms of RA. And according to the Iowa Women's Health Study, women who drank more than three cups of tea a day were 60 percent less likely to develop RA than women who didn't drink any.

**Aim for:** The best bet is to drink three to four cups of tea (preferably green tea) daily and to eat a wide range of quercetin-containing foods each day.

**Helpful hint:** Include pineapple in your fruit salad. The bromelain in pineapple increases the body's absorption of quercetin, and its vitamin C increases quercetin's antioxidant activity.

### NUTRITIONAL SUPPLEMENTS

**Omega-3 fatty acids.** If you're not a big fish fan—and even if you are—supplementing with omega-3 fatty acids is something many doctors recommend. Supplements come in soft-gel capsules. Because omega-3s are sensitive to heat, light, and oxygen, store the supplements in the refrigerator. Also, choose a supplement that contains vitamin E, which will help keep the omega-3s from turning rancid. Burping fish oil after taking them means the oil is rancid. **DOSAGE:** 1 to 3 grams per day for general health and 3 to 6 grams for relief of morning stiffness and tenderness from RA. Don't take more than 9 grams per day, and if you bleed easily, you should check with your doctor before taking these supplements.

**Bromelain.** Bromelain is available in tablets or capsules. A wide range of doses has been studied and used safely. **DOSAGE:** 500 to 2,000 milligrams daily, divided into two doses.

**Ginger, turmeric, and cloves.** Unless you cook with them a lot, it can be hard to get therapeutic doses of these anti-inflammatory spices. Talk to your doctor about whether supplements of one of them might help you. Be aware, though, that ginger supplements may irritate the stomach. Ginger and cloves also thin the blood, so check with your doctor before taking them if you take blood-thinning medication. Stop taking any of the supplements if they upset your stomach or if you see no effect after 10 days.

**DOSAGE:** *Ginger:* 500 milligrams from capsules per day or 100 to 300 milligrams from an extract three times a day. *Turmeric:* 400 to 600 milligrams three times a day, always with food. *Cloves:* Although there is no established dose, a recent study found 2 to 3 grams a day effective for alleviating inflammation.

### OFF THE MENU

**Corn oil, fatty meats, full-fat dairy products, and trans fat.** Fish counters inflammation; other foods stoke it. The omega-6 fatty acids in vegetable oils like corn, safflower, and sunflower oils and the saturated fat in full-fat dairy products fan the flames by producing inflammatory versions of hormone-like substances called eicosanoids. Arachidonic acid, found in red meats, egg yolks, and organ meats, leads to the formation of eicosanoids, also whipping up inflammation. And definitely add anything made with partially hydrogenated oils, or trans fat, to your list of foods to avoid.

**Allergy triggers.** Several studies have linked dairy products, corn, and wheat to increased inflammation in people with arthritis. Researchers believe that some food proteins may trigger the production of antibodies in a small percentage of people. The protein and antibodies then partner up to irritate joints. Another theory is that the antibodies attack the lining of the joints directly. The safe way to test whether certain foods such as those above act as inflammation triggers is to consult with your doctor or a registered dietitian, who can put you on an elimination diet, then add back one food at a time and observe changes in your symptoms.

## Less Food, Less Burden

Excess weight is tough on joints. The foods most likely to layer on pounds also tend to rob you of energy (think sugar) and trigger inflammation (think saturated fats in meats, dairy products, and baked goods). The best way to lose weight is to cut out processed foods and sugar and eat fresh fruits and vegetables, whole grains, and lean proteins like fish.

These foods are not only healthier for you, they are far less dense with calories. And because they digest slower, they keep you fuller longer.

Just as important as switching to healthier, less calorie-dense foods is reducing portion sizes. Switch to smaller plates, put your fork down between bites, and take a sip of water after each bite, and you'll quickly find that you're perfectly content with your meal even though you've eaten less than you used to.

# ASTHMA

We'll never tell you to reach for food instead of an inhaler. That said, studies show that nutritional therapy may help you cut down on the number and intensity of your asthma attacks.

The idea that food can soothe asthma symptoms may seem shocking, but if you understand what causes those symptoms, it makes perfect sense. During an asthma attack, an allergen or irritant—perhaps a few grains of dust or pollen—sends the immune system into full-scale attack mode. The body unleashes a barrage of histamine and other chemicals that cause inflammation in the lining of the airways. Chronic inflammation actually leads to thickening of the bronchial tubes, which means your airways are narrowed even when you feel okay. To make matters worse, the bronchial tubes begin to churn out extra mucus, which gums up the works and makes it even harder for air to make its way through, so you're left gasping for oxygen.

Inflammation is the main culprit behind asthma symptoms—and the target of many asthma drugs—so foods that fight inflammation are the natural remedies, along with those that thin bronchial mucus. Getting plenty of certain nutrients from food has also been linked with a lower risk of *developing* asthma, which is important to know (and act on) if you have kids.

## YOUR FOOD PRESCRIPTION

## Onions

Regularly eating onions may help you experience fewer asthma attacks. That's because onions contain several compounds that combat inflammation. One is a type of flavonoid (a class of antioxidant) called quercetin. In test tube studies, quercetin has been shown to inhibit the release of inflammatory substances from mast cells, which are involved in allergic responses. This is also how some asthma drugs work. Onions also contain mustard oils (isothiocyanates) that seem to counter asthma-induced inflammation, at least in lab animals. Pungent foods such as onions, hot peppers, and spicy mustard also trigger the release of watery fluids that help thin the mucus your body produces. (Be aware, however, that in a small percentage of people with asthma, onions actually trigger attacks.)

Aim for: There's no set amount, so just aim to get more onions in your diet.

Helpful hint: You can extract the quercetin from onion skins (where it's highly concentrated) by adding a whole unpeeled onion to a pot of soup while it's simmering. The quercetin will leach into the broth. Just be sure to remove the peel before eating the soup.

## Coffee

Although it's no substitute for asthma medication, a strong cup or two of coffee, or even a cola, can help in a pinch because caffeine acts like theophylline, a drug that dilates the airways. Don't use coffee and a prescription theophylline drug at the same time, however.

Studies suggest that drinking coffee regularly may even help prevent asthma attacks, perhaps because the caffeine keeps the airways open. (If caffeine keeps you up at night, this is obviously not a good strategy for you.) Coffee also contains magnesium and antioxidants that may play a beneficial role.

Aim for: A cup or two as needed during an attack or a cup or two every day to help ward off attacks.

## Green tea

Like apples and onions, green tea contains quercetin, along with extraordinary amounts of another flavonoid called epigallocatechin.

Aim for: Get in the habit of drinking two cups a day, or less when your asthma isn't bothering you. Freshly brewed black tea also contains some quercetin.

Helpful hint: The taste of green tea may take some getting used to, although some people love it. To make sure it's not too bitter, use hot but not boiling water and don't let the tea steep for more than 2 minutes. Experiment with different brands to find one you like. Or try white tea, which is more fragrant and has a pleasant taste and even more antioxidants.

## Salmon, mackerel,
*and other foods rich in omega-3 fatty acids*

Omega-3 fatty acids, found in fatty fish and a few other foods, have the unique power to reduce inflammation in the body, including the airways. As with antioxidants, it appears that people who take in more omega-3s have a lower risk of developing asthma than people who consume less. Getting more of these nutrients may also help if you already have asthma.

Are you wondering whether taking fish-oil supplements may help tame asthma? So are researchers. Although there is some encouraging early research, large well-controlled clinical trials are needed.

Omega-3s are also found in walnuts and ground flaxseed, but only about 20 percent are converted to usable forms.

Aim for: At least 1 gram of omega-3s a day. You can get more than this amount by eating 4 ounces of salmon or mackerel.

Helpful hint: Like anchovies? Order them on your pizza; they're another great source of omega-3s.

## Apples and berries

An apple a day may not keep the doctor away, but eating enough apples may stave off that next asthma attack. Like onions, apples are rich in quercetin, but be sure to eat the skin, since that's where most of the quercetin is. (Applesauce has only about half the quercetin of apples with the skin.) Berries are also rich in this flavonoid.

The same British researchers who showed the benefits of selenium for asthma also found that people who ate five or more apples per week reduced their likelihood of having asthma by 40 percent.

Aim for: Eat as many as you like!

*food for thought . . .*

"A possible contributing factor to the increased incidence of asthma in Western societies may be the consumption of a pro-inflammatory diet."

— *Journal of Alternative and Complementary Medicine, December 2004*

# Foods rich in antioxidants,
## *especially vitamins C and E and selenium*

As the airways become inflamed during an asthma attack, the body produces molecules called free radicals, which make the inflammation worse. Antioxidants such as vitamins C and E and the mineral selenium neutralize these free radicals. They may help boost lung function in people with asthma, and they definitely lower the risk of developing asthma in the first place.

Studies show that people who develop asthma tend to consume less of these antioxidants than people who don't. In fact, British researchers found that people who consumed at least 55 micrograms of selenium a day were about *half* as likely to have asthma as those who consumed 30 micrograms or less.

Antioxidants also neutralize free radicals produced in response to ozone, an air pollutant and common asthma trigger. Studies suggest they may boost lung function in people who live in polluted areas, as many of us do, and are sensitive to ozone.

Getting a combination of different antioxidants—especially vitamins C and E and selenium—is best, since these nutrients work synergistically. Eating a variety of antioxidant-rich foods will also help ensure that you get plenty of magnesium (a mineral that helps relax the airways) and other beneficial nutrients.

Aim for: *Vitamin C:* 500 milligrams daily, the amount in a cup of raw red bell peppers plus a cup each of orange juice and cooked broccoli or brussels sprouts, spread throughout the day.

## FEATURED RECIPES

**Tropical Fruit Salad** *p. 590*
**Ultimate Spiced Nuts** *p. 592*
**Updated Waldorf Salad** *p. 594*
**Salmon Cake Sandwiches** *p. 606*
**Tomato-Roasted Mackerel** *p. 612*
**Salmon Steaks with Peach Salsa** *p. 612*
**Almond Rice** *p. 626*
**Brussels Sprouts with Caramelized Onions** *p. 623*
**Mixed Berry Tart** *p. 639*

*Vitamin E:* At least 80 milligrams daily. You won't be able to get this much from food, but get as much as you can from sources such as wheat germ, almonds, and sunflower seeds. *Selenium:* 55 micrograms daily, less than the amount in an ounce of mixed nuts, a single Brazil nut, or a piece of white fish.

**Helpful hint:** Kiwifruit contains more vitamin C than almost any other food. To eat a kiwi with minimal hassle, simply cut it in half, then spoon out the fruit. No peeling required!

## NUTRITIONAL SUPPLEMENTS

**Vitamin C, vitamin E, and selenium.** So far, the evidence is mixed as to whether antioxidant supplements help people with asthma. For ozone-induced airway constriction, however, there does seem to be a benefit from taking a combination of antioxidant supplements. **DOSAGE:** *Vitamin C:* 250 to 500 milligrams twice a day. *Vitamin E:* 80 milligrams of a product containing both natural tocopherols (d-alpha-tocopherol) and tocotrienols. If you can't find that, look for a product with mixed natural tocopherols and take 400 IU daily. Since vitamin E is fat soluble, it's best absorbed when taken with a meal containing some fat. *Selenium:* 200 micrograms once a day. Selenium and vitamin E facilitate each other's absorption, so take them together.

**Quercetin.** Besides drinking green tea and eating more apples, onions, berries, and citrus fruits, you might consider a quercetin supplement. In lab animals, extracts have been shown to have anti-inflammatory and bronchodilating effects. **DOSAGE:** 400 to 500 milligrams three times a day.

**Vitamin B$_6$.** One well-designed study showed this vitamin helped to improve peak flow rates (a measurement of breathing capacity) in a group of adults with severe asthma. In people with low blood levels of B$_6$, supplements may help decrease wheezing. **DOSAGE:** 50 to 100 milligrams a day.

**Magnesium.** Studies are under way to determine whether oral supplements of magnesium—often administered intravenously to asthma patients in the ER because it relaxes the airways—may help. The jury's still out on the benefits of taking supplements, but there's probably no harm in trying them in appropriate doses, although some forms of magnesium may cause diarrhea. **DOSAGE:** 200 to 400 milligrams of magnesium glycinate a day.

## OFF THE MENU

**Food triggers.** If you suspect your asthma attacks are brought on by certain foods, start keeping a detailed food diary in which you also note your asthma symptoms. Once you've identified a possible trigger, eliminate that food from your diet for two weeks and see if your asthma improves. If you dare to confirm your food trigger, reintroduce the food to see if your symptoms get worse again.

Common triggers include eggs; nuts; milk and other dairy products; sulfites (preservatives added to many foods, including dried fruit, instant soup and potato mixes, and red wine); and other food additives, such as aspartame (an artificial sweetener), benzoates, and yellow dye #5 (also called tartrazine).

**Most vegetable oils, foods with trans fat, fatty meats, and full-fat dairy foods.** Just as it's a good idea to eat plenty of foods that counter inflammation if you have asthma, it's also smart to cut down on foods that tend to promote it. Many experts believe these include corn, sunflower, and safflower oils as well as the many processed foods that contain them. Population studies show that people who consume a lot of polyunsaturated oils such as these have an increased risk of developing asthma, eczema, and allergies. Use olive or canola oil instead.

You'll also want to cut way back on trans fat, found in any food with partially hydrogenated oil listed on the label. These are a major source of omega-6 fatty acids, which help the body make arachidonic acid, a building block of prostaglandins and leukotrienes—the primary culprits in inflammation.

You might also consider cutting back on meat and full-fat dairy foods, since saturated fat is

## Preventing Asthma in Kids

Recent studies showed a clear link between a lower risk of asthma and the consumption of the antioxidants vitamin C, beta-carotene, and selenium. It appears that making sure your child gets plenty of these nutrients from foods like citrus fruits, carrots, squash, whole grains, and fish will significantly reduce her chances of developing asthma. If anyone in your house smokes, you should make doubly sure your kids get enough vitamin C. The research shows that kids who are regularly exposed to secondhand smoke have as much as a 40 percent lower asthma risk when they get enough C.

another major source of arachidonic acid. In one small study, 92 percent of asthma patients put on a vegan diet (no animal products, including dairy and eggs) experienced a significant decrease in symptoms after a year; 71 percent reported improvement after four months. All the participants were using long-term asthma medication such as cortisone at the start of the study. By the end, almost all were able to stop or drastically reduce their medication use.

# ATTENTION DEFICIT HYPERACTIVITY DISORDER

Attention deficit hyperactivity disorder (ADHD) is one of the most controversial health conditions of our day, one that's long on theories and unanswered questions and short on treatments. Although it's arguably the most prevalent behavioral condition diagnosed in children, ADHD is really more a grab bag of behaviors than a single, well-defined disease. Affecting three times as many boys as girls, ADHD can—but doesn't always—include hyperactivity, distractibility, tantrums, anxiety, blue moods, impulsive behavior, and learning disabilities. It's believed to be related to a host of contributing factors, including asthma, genetic predisposition, secondhand smoke exposure, early exposure to television, and not being breastfed, although its "cause" remains murky.

That said, what *is* becoming clear is that what children eat—and don't eat—is an enormous part of the ADHD equation. Much of the research points to a likely connection between ADHD behavior and food sensitivities/allergies, along with deficiencies of key nutrients critical for brain development and function.

Most researchers are reluctant to say definitively that a child's diet causes ADHD or that eliminating food allergy triggers or correcting nutritional imbalances might cure it. Even so, consider that the first impulse is to medicate unruly kids with stimulant drugs like methylphenidate (Ritalin). Despite the drug's ability to tame bad behavior in 7 out of 10 kids with ADHD, there are concerns that in relying on it, we're making a devil's bargain. Ritalin's chemical composition is similar to cocaine's, one reason it's become the recreational street drug of choice for many teens. And it comes with a laundry list of possible side effects, including appetite loss, stunted growth, sleep disruption, tics, and heart problems. Given all the red flags, tinkering with a child's diet may be the safer place to start.

## FEATURED RECIPES

**Buckwheat Pancakes with Fruit Sauce** *p. 590*
**Lentil-Tomato Soup** *p. 603*
**Beef in Lettuce Wraps** *p. 606*
**Salmon Cake Sandwiches** *p. 606*
**Mac 'n Cheese Primavera** *p. 608*
**Tuna Kebabs** *p. 610*
**Chicken-Barley Bake** *p. 616*

YOUR FOOD PRESCRIPTION

# A diet that emphasizes protein and complex carbohydrates

This is perhaps the most important change you can make to your child's diet. Shifting it away from foods rich in refined sugar and flours and instead filling Junior's plate with more protein and high-fiber complex carbohydrates may eliminate some ADHD symptoms simply by stabilizing blood sugar levels. While the brain relies on blood sugar as its main energy source, too much can actually disrupt proper brain function.

Here's what happens. Sugar and other refined carbohydrates ("white foods" like rice and potatoes as well as soft drinks and juices that readily break down into sugars) are digested very quickly. That sends blood sugar levels soaring. The body overcompensates by releasing large amounts of insulin to move the sugar out of the bloodstream, making blood sugar levels plummet. The brain really rebels when blood sugar levels get too low, and that's when we start to feel tired, irritable, unfocused, and unable to concentrate. Sounds a bit like ADHD, doesn't it? Eating meals high in fiber and protein, on the other hand, slows digestion and helps level out those wild blood sugar spikes and plunges. Our brains, sated with a more continuous source of energy, function better—and it's quite possible that that can lead to better behavior.

It may be especially important to start your child's day with a good breakfast. A Tufts University study found that kids who ate oatmeal—rich in complex carbohydrates that supply sustained energy as well as being a source of protein—for breakfast performed better an hour later on memory tests than kids who ate sugary cereal or no breakfast at all.

Aim for: Fill half your child's plate with brightly colored vegetables, a quarter with lean protein such as chicken, and a quarter with whole grains, such as barley or brown or wild rice. (Oatmeal and whole-wheat bread count as a whole grains, too.)

Helpful hint: One way to wean kids off sugary breakfast cereals is to mix a handful with a healthier high-fiber brand (with no more than 2 grams of sugar) to help kids get used to the new taste. Slowly reduce the amount of sugary cereal in the mix until you can eliminate it altogether.

# Lean beef, beans, lentils,
*and other iron-rich foods*

Iron is important for regulating dopamine, and low levels are associated with decreased attention, ability to focus, and mental activity. When French researchers looked at children with and without ADHD, they found that iron levels were markedly lower among those with ADHD. But even though a few very small studies suggest that supplements may help to reduce hyperactivity and improve behavior and scores on cognition tests, most health experts recommend getting iron from food, not supplements. Some iron supplements may be constipating, which can throw off digestion and absorption of other critical nutrients, and too much iron is dangerous.

Aim for: About 10 milligrams of iron daily.

Helpful hint: Beef is a super iron source (buy organic to avoid any chemicals that may aggravate ADHD symptoms). If you don't want all the fat and cholesterol, try almonds or pumpkin seeds. Just 1/4 cup of almonds and 2 tablespoons of pumpkin seeds can provide almost half of a child's daily iron needs.

# Salmon, flaxseed, *and other foods rich in omega-3 essential fatty acids*

A deficiency of omega-3s has been linked with a variety of developmental and psychiatric disorders, such as depression and autism, so it's not surprising that it's also associated with ADHD. Studies indicate that some people with ADHD have significantly lower blood levels of key essential fatty acids; other studies show that children with low blood levels of omega-3s have more learning and behavior problems than kids with higher levels. (One way to tell if your child is deficient is to look at his skin and hair; dry skin and hair are signatures of essential fatty acid deficiency. So are excessive thirst and urination.)

It's possible that kids with ADHD are low in omega-3s either because they don't get enough in their diets or because their bodies don't metabolize what they do get very effectively. That may also help explain why ADHD affects more boys than girls: When the diet is lacking in omega-3s, estrogen helps conserve these essential fats, while testosterone has the opposite effect.

How do the omega-3 fats factor into ADHD? One theory is that they influence neurotransmitters, including dopamine and serotonin. Low levels of omega-3s are associated with low levels of dopamine, particularly in the part of the brain that's responsible for "executive functions" like planning ahead, controlling impulses, and staying on task. Ritalin works by increasing dopamine. It's possible that increasing omega-3 levels could do likewise.

Another part of this grand jigsaw puzzle is that some researchers have noticed that certain aspects of ADHD look remarkably like aspects of early bipolar (manic-depressive) disorder, leading some to wonder if much of what's thought of as ADHD may actually be an underlying mood or anxiety disorder. Researchers are still trying to fit the puzzle pieces together, but those who study psychiatric disorders have already linked low levels of omega-3s with depression and schizophrenia. It's not a big stretch to consider that insufficient omega-3s may also be a factor for ADHD children who tend to be moody or anxious.

If you can get your child to eat fish, terrific, but don't overdo it, because fish can contain mercury and other toxins. While most experts agree that any dangers of eating fish are outweighed by the benefits, children and pregnant women should take extra care by choosing canned light tuna rather than canned white albacore or tuna steaks, for instance. (For more tips on Choosing Safe Seafood, see page 325.)

More kid-friendly omega-3 sources are sunflower seeds, pumpkin seeds, and flaxseed as well as raw refrigerated nut butters, such as those made from Brazil nuts, cashews, and sunflower seeds, and tahini, made from sesame seeds. (Avoid peanuts, which are a common allergen and a possible trigger for food sensitivity–related ADHD.) The body can convert the fats in these foods to the same kinds found in fish, but unfortunately, it doesn't do it very efficiently, so fish is still a preferred source.

**Aim for:** Two 3-ounce servings of fatty fish a week.

**Helpful hint:** Whole flaxseed stays fresh longer than ground seed. Keep it refrigerated and use a coffee or spice grinder to grind it as needed, then add to yogurt, cereal, egg salad, or the batter for baked goods. You can combine flaxseed oil with margarine to make a healthier spread by melting a stick of trans fat–free margarine, adding a few ounces of flaxseed oil, and then allowing it to solidify again.

## NUTRITIONAL SUPPLEMENTS
**Essential fatty acids, especially DHA.**
Children with ADHD tend to have low levels of omega-3 essential fatty acids. Does that mean that supplements can tame hyperactive kids and allow daydreamers to focus and concentrate? Given that studies of omega-3 supplements for depression have yielded some promising results, it's an intriguing possibility.

In one four-month, double-blind, placebo-controlled study of 50 children with ADHD at Purdue University, some of the kids were given a daily essential fatty acid supplement that contained a mixture of omega-3s along with a smattering of omega-6s; the rest were given an olive oil placebo. While the supplement didn't improve all of the symptoms associated with ADHD, it did improve parent-reported conduct problems and teacher-reported attention problems.

Most research now focuses on DHA as the omega-3 component most important for brain function. Fatty fish is the best source, but these days there is concern about high levels of brain-damaging pesticides and mercury in fish, which is why some health organizations recommend limiting fish consumption by children. Fortunately, supplements are now enriched with vegetarian-derived DHA made from marine algae. In fact, this is the source of DHA used to enrich infant formulas. **DOSAGE:** About 200 milligrams of DHA daily.

**Probiotics.** Food sensitivities and allergies are thought to be associated with ADHD behavior. Some nutritionally oriented physicians believe that when there's an overgrowth of harmful microorganisms, like bacteria or yeast, the lining of the intestines is damaged, allowing undigested food particles to leak into the bloodstream, where they can provoke an immune response or allergic reaction. Probiotic supplements, which contain billions of friendly bacteria like *lactobacillus* and *bifidobacterium,* keep these harmful microorganisms in check and therefore may help prevent these kinds of food sensitivities/allergies. There are hundreds of probiotic products on the shelves. Choose a refrigerated supplement that contains live cultures and delivers several billion live organisms per serving. **DOSAGE:** Follow the label directions for the product you choose.

**A multivitamin/mineral.** Researchers are studying the effects of individual nutrients, such as zinc, magnesium, and $B_6$, to treat ADHD, but because the data is still so speculative, parents may just want to stick with having their kids take a multivitamin/mineral supplement. Some very good double-blind, placebo-controlled studies suggest that when elementary school children are given a multi that meets even the most basic nutrient requirements, behavior and academic performance improve, particularly for kids who may have undetected nutrient deficiencies.

Researchers at California State University ran several trials with kids at two elementary schools in Phoenix. In one four-month study, 80 children were divided into two groups and given either a multi formulated at 50 percent of the recommended daily allowance or a

*food for thought . . .*

"For treating ADHD, nutrients are actually the most sensible place to start, rather than jumping straight for a drug [Ritalin] that really isn't as good as it's been cracked up to be."

— Alexandra Richardson, PhD, senior
research fellow at the University of
Oxford and author of *They Are What
You Feed Them* ▪

placebo. The vitamin takers had just under half the discipline problems compared to the placebo group. In another study with children at the same schools, the researchers gave the same type of multi to 245 children. This time they measured IQ. Although the supplements didn't produce dramatic increases in IQ for most of the children, among the students believed to eat a substandard diet, the gains were impressive, about 16 points. **DOSAGE:** Follow the label directions.

**Zinc.** It's not clear just how zinc factors into ADHD, but some association is likely because children with ADHD tend to be at least marginally deficient in the mineral. (An easy preliminary way to check your child's zinc status is to feel the skin on her arms. Little bumps on the outer arm are a hallmark of zinc deficiency, although your pediatrician should confirm low levels with a blood test.)

Whether zinc deficiency is a direct cause of ADHD or merely a marker of the condition is still unknown, but some research suggests a correlation between low zinc levels and difficulty paying attention. It's also not certain whether zinc supplements improve attention span, but some intriguing preliminary research suggests that it might. **DOSAGE:** In some of the studies on zinc in kids with ADHD, the levels used were high—as high as 150 milligrams. But one study showed that children who were taking Ritalin and also took 15 milligrams of zinc, the amount in a good multivitamin, improved more and faster than kids who didn't take zinc. Don't give or take more than the amount in a multivitamin except under a doctor's supervision. Too much zinc can suppress the immune system.

## OFF THE MENU

**Refined sugar, refined flours, and other simple carbohydrates.** It's a myth that sugar makes kids hyperactive. Nevertheless, you might think about helping your child cut back not only on sugary foods but also on other foods that tend to make blood sugar skyrocket, such as white rice and cereals with little fiber. In addition to affecting blood sugar, these highly processed foods are notoriously low in important vitamins and minerals (although cereal manufacturers add some of them back). Remember, steady blood sugar levels benefit the brain, whether a child has ADHD or not. But hyperactive children may have particular problems metabolizing sugar. It's worth noting that the hallmarks of low blood sugar include problems with attention and focus, moodiness, and frustration.

Nixing sugar also helps starve out the harmful fungi and bacteria in the digestive tract that thrive on sugary foods and contribute to food sensitivities/allergies and imbalanced immune function. It's interesting to note that overgrowth of harmful bacteria like clostridia has been linked to another childhood developmental condition, autism.

**Food dyes and additives.** Eliminating artificial colors, additives, preservatives, and any foods that may provoke an allergic response is the cornerstone of most nutritional therapy for ADHD. Some experts believe that two-thirds of children with ADHD may have undiagnosed food allergies that may be responsible for their symptoms—although this theory isn't universally accepted. Still, for those kids who may be vulnerable to such sensitivities/allergies, removing trigger foods and additives often improves ADHD symptoms. Elimination diets have varying rates of success, with behavior improving in 58 to 82 percent of children, depending on the study cited.

Because there are literally thousands of substances that could potentially worsen ADHD symptoms, instead of driving yourself and your child crazy, start with food colors (look for names like FD&C red, yellow, green, and blue on labels). Researchers from Columbia University and the New York State Psychiatric Institute analyzed 15 double-blind, placebo-controlled trials that involved 219 children who were fed a diet containing artificial food colors and then given a diet free of dyes. They found that the children's behavior on the dye-free diet was significantly better than when they ate foods loaded with artificial colors. The researchers compared the effect of the dye-free diet to about one-third to one-half of the effect that could be expected from ADHD medication.

Artificial colors show up in many products, like vitamins, medicines, and toothpaste, so be vigilant. You may also want to consider avoiding common additives, flavorings, and preservatives. (Look for names like BHA, BHT, TBHQ, sodium benzoate, benzoic acid, vanillin, acesulfame-K, aspartame, saccharin, and sucralose.)

**Food allergens.** Common food allergy triggers include wheat, dairy, eggs, oranges, chocolate, apples, peanuts, and soy. Start by eliminating them for several weeks, then slowly add them back one at a time and see if there's any change in your child's behavior. (It's best to try an elimination diet with the help of a registered dietitian.) Another way to find your child's trigger foods is to think about the ones he really craves. Does he drink gallons of milk? Gorge on bread or crackers? Gobble down chocolate? A favorite food, one that he eats or drinks all the time, may be the very one he's sensitive or allergic to. Try eliminating it and see if his behavior improves.

Because there's no prescribed "ADHD diet," it may take trial and error before you home in on what sets your child off.

**Caffeine.** In a recent study done at the Smell and Taste Treatment and Research Foundation in Chicago, when 20 first graders were given caffeinated cola, their scores on an ADHD rating scale were much higher than when they drank decaffeinated soda, even when researchers accounted for the drinks' sugar content.

## Can Breastfeeding Prevent ADHD?

We know that breastfed babies have much lower rates of all sorts of infections. They also appear to have lower rates of allergies and asthma. But can breastfeeding also protect against ADHD? A recent small study suggests that it's possible.

When Polish researchers looked at a group of 100 children ages 4 to 11—60 with ADHD symptoms and 40 without—they found that 60 percent of the ADHD kids had been breastfed for less than three months. Among the healthy children, just a third had been breastfed for that short a time. Although this is only one small study, researchers suspect that being weaned early may put some children at risk for ADHD, no doubt because breast milk is a superior source of the essential fatty acids needed for proper brain and eye development. The American Academy of Pediatrics recommends that babies be breastfed for at least 12 months. If you simply can't breastfeed—and for some women, it is a legitimate challenge either because they don't produce enough milk or because their babies have trouble latching on—look for formulas fortified with docosahexaenoic acid (DHA).

# BREAST CANCER

Although women are actually more likely to develop heart disease, it's breast cancer that strikes fear in their hearts. After lung cancer, it's the most commonly diagnosed cancer in women, yet for most women, preventing it is a big mystery.

To some extent, your risk is already determined—by your age; your family medical history; when you got your first period and entered menopause; whether you had children or took birth control pills or hormone replacement therapy; and whether you carry one of the breast cancer genes, BRCA1 or BRCA2 (only 5 to 10 percent of breast cancers are BRCA-related).

Even if the breast cancer odds aren't in your favor, you can give yourself an edge. Monthly breast self-exams and annual mammograms are key, of course, to finding lumps that could be tumors. And the right diet can help prevent them. Scientists are still working to pinpoint which foods guard against breast tumors, but we do know that eating more fruits, vegetables, whole grains, and lean protein while curbing saturated fat and trans fat covers you against a lot of diseases, including cancer.

This may be because fruits and vegetables contain certain phytochemicals that have been singled out as effective cancer fighters. It's also because produce-rich diets are naturally lower in calories and fat. That's important because the one thing we do know for sure about breast cancer is that gaining weight, especially later in life, substantially increases risk.

There's much about breast cancer we can't control, but what and how much we eat is something we can. Here's where to start.

## YOUR FOOD PRESCRIPTION

### Broccoli *and other cruciferous vegetables*

If you're going to eat more of just one vegetable, make it broccoli. Lab studies have found that a cancer-fighting compound in broccoli called sulforaphane stops breast cancer cells in their tracks and encourages them to self-destruct. Plus, another compound in broccoli, called indole-3-carbinol, appears to inhibit estrogen's power to promote the growth of breast cancer cells. Broccoli's anticancer powers have been shown in human studies, too. In one called the Western New York Diet Study, premenopausal women who ate the most broccoli had a 40 percent lower breast cancer risk than women who didn't eat as much.

A bonus: Cruciferous vegetables like broccoli, cauliflower, and brussels sprouts, which protect barbecue lovers from colon cancer, may also shield them from breast cancer. If you're a big fan of cookouts, you'll definitely want to steam some broccoli to go with those burgers and hot dogs.

Aim for: Four 1/2-cup servings a week of broccoli and other cruciferous veggies, which include cabbage, watercress, bok choy, turnip greens, mustard greens, and collard greens.

Helpful hint: If you're not a fan of straight broccoli, sneak it into other dishes. Try adding a half cup to pasta sauces, soups, pizza toppings, and even omelets. Steam, stir-fry, or microwave (in just a bit of water) it instead of boiling it. These three cooking methods best conserve vegetables' vitamins and protective compounds.

## Beans, leafy green vegetables,
*and other foods rich in folate*

Especially if you like to drink alcohol, even moderately, make sure you load your plate with plenty of these foods that supply folate, a B vitamin that alcohol depletes. It protects cells from the potentially carcinogenic effects of alcohol.

The foods listed above also contain plenty of fiber, which helps lower estrogen levels and in turn breast cancer risk. (Many breast cancer tumors feed on estrogen, so reducing it may prevent tumors from developing.)

**Aim for:** At least one of the five vegetable servings recommended each day should be from this group of foods.

**Helpful hint:** Spinach is one of the richest sources of folate. If you won't eat it alone, try layering it into lasagna or casseroles or sautéing it with olive oil, garlic, and sesame seeds to add other flavors.

## Whole grains

Whole grains are another good source of fiber, and when it comes to preventing breast cancer, you really can't get too much. Think of fiber as a type of flypaper, but instead of pesky insects, what you're trapping is estrogen. Estrogen continually cycles through the digestive tract and is reabsorbed into the bloodstream. Fiber grabs it so it won't be reabsorbed, thereby lowering your body's estrogen levels.

Whole-grain foods may also help in other ways. Because fiber slows carbohydrate metabolism, foods like high-fiber cereals and whole-wheat bread may indirectly protect against breast tumors by reducing blood sugar spikes, thereby keeping insulin levels low. Excess insulin is known to promote breast cancer growth.

In addition to their fiber, whole grains contain antioxidant phytochemicals called phenols, which can prevent and perhaps even repair damage to cells from dangerous molecules called free radicals. They also pack lignans, plant estrogens that lower natural estrogen levels in the body and actively slow the growth and spread of cancer cells.

Not all studies have demonstrated that fiber actively protects against breast cancer, but one in particular, the Canadian National Breast Cancer Screening Study, which examined nearly 57,000 women, found that those with fiber-rich diets had a 30 percent lower risk than those who ate smaller amounts.

**Aim for:** At least three servings of whole grains daily. One serving is 1/2 cup of whole-grain pasta or rice or a slice of whole-grain bread.

**Helpful hint:** Try mixing a cup of whole-grain cereal with 1/4 cup of dried fruit for a tasty snack that covers you for a serving of whole grains and a serving of fruit.

## Fatty fish

You already know that fatty fish like salmon and tuna protect against heart disease, but could they protect against breast cancer, too? Some lab studies show that the omega-3 fatty acids in these fish slow the growth of breast cancer cells. Studies in people have been less conclusive, but data from the Singapore Chinese Health Study gives us some reason to be hopeful. That study looked at breast cancer incidence among more than 35,000 women and found that compared to women who did not eat much fatty fish, those who ate about three servings a week lowered their breast cancer risk by 26 percent. One reason may be that the anti-inflammatory fats in these fish help reduce the low-grade inflammation that's thought to spur tumor growth.

Researchers are discovering that omega-3s seem to pack more punch when you also eat fewer omega-6 fats like those in corn, safflower, and sunflower oils, which tend to promote inflammation. Women in the Singapore study whose diets were high in omega-6s and low in omega-3s had an 87 percent greater risk of breast cancer than those whose diets were low in both types of fat.

## The Soy Story

Does soy protect against breast cancer? That may depend on how old you are when you start eating it. Soy contains phytoestrogens, which are thought to lower the amount of estrogen circulating in your body and thus your breast cancer risk. But cancer specialists now believe that the reason Asian women have lower rates of breast cancer is that they grow up eating soy, unlike Western women who may start eating soy as adults.

The thought is that soy's phytochemicals may alter breast tissue as breasts are developing, making them more resistant to cancer-causing substances. Unfortunately, those phytochemicals may not protect women much once they reach adulthood.

That said, eating soy may still help, albeit indirectly. Eating tofu instead of, say, steak helps lower your calorie and saturated fat intake and maintain a healthy weight, all of which help reduce your overall risk of breast cancer. But there is one caveat: If you're taking tamoxifen or another anti-estrogen medication, such as an aromatase inhibitor that blocks estrogen, you shouldn't eat soy.

Even if omega-3s don't turn out to actively fight breast cancer, there are still good reasons to eat fish. If you have a salmon dinner in place of a steak dinner, you're cutting back on saturated fat, which, as you'll read later, is a good idea if you're worried about breast cancer.

**Aim for:** It's not clear how much fatty fish may protect against breast cancer. However, the American Heart Association recommends two servings (8 to 12 ounces total) of fatty fish each week to protect against heart disease.

## Milk and dairy foods

That milk mustache you've seen in so many ads may help prevent breast cancer—depending on your age. In the Nurses Health Study, which looked at more than 80,000 women, dairy foods seemed to have no effect for postmenopausal women, but premenopausal women who averaged two to three servings of low-fat or fat-free milk or dairy foods each day lowered their breast cancer risk by 28 to 32 percent compared to women who ate dairy just three times a month. Another study found that among more than 68,000 *postmenopausal* women, those who ate at least two servings of dairy foods a day lowered their breast cancer risk by 19 percent. Until we get more definitive data, eating low-fat dairy foods is worthwhile.

Why dairy? It's not entirely clear. The calcium may play a role, but researchers are also focusing on vitamin D. New research suggests that the type of vitamin D used to fortify milk (known as vitamin $D_3$) reduces breast density, considered a risk factor for breast cancer.

**Aim for:** Three servings of milk daily is the current recommendation. You may also want to take a D supplement, though. A cup of milk contains only about 100 IU of vitamin $D_3$, and recent research suggests that 1,000 IU daily is associated with up to a 35 percent lower risk of breast cancer. The Nurses Health Study found that premenopausal women who consumed more than 500 IU of vitamin D each day lowered their breast cancer risk by 28 percent.

# Extra-virgin olive oil

It's not just how *much* fat you eat but also what *type* of fat you eat that influences your breast cancer risk. While it's generally thought that eating too much fat increases risk, one can't help but notice that that's not always the case in Mediterranean countries, where fat intake is high but breast cancer incidence is low. The key, many researchers suspect, is that people in Mediterranean cultures consume monounsaturated fat like that in olive oil rather than saturated fat like that in butter, ice cream, and meat or even polyunsaturated fat like that in corn or safflower oil. Indeed, a study of women in the Canary Islands showed that those who used at least 2 teaspoons of olive oil daily lowered their risk of breast cancer by an amazing 73 percent.

Research in this area is still unfolding, but a few theories have emerged. One is that olive oil is simply a healthier type of fat and that eating it in place of unhealthy saturated fat and trans fat lowers risk. The other piece of the puzzle is that olive oil comes from olives, fruits that contain many of the therapeutic compounds, like phenols and lignans, that we already know fight cancer. (Phenols inhibit the formation of cancer-causing compounds. Lignans convert in the body to a weak estrogen-like compound that can displace the body's own, stronger estrogen from cells.) Researchers at Northwestern University have also discovered that the oleic acid in olive oil actively suppresses a gene associated with the development of a very aggressive form of breast cancer and even improves the effectiveness of the cancer drug transluzumab (Herceptin).

The caveat, of course, is that olive oil is high in calories, so use it sparingly—*instead of* other fats, not with them.

**Aim for:** 1 to 2 tablespoons a day.

**Helpful hint:** One reason olive oil may be so cancer protective is that it makes those veggies go down a little easier. Try sautéing vegetables in olive oil instead of butter or using olive oil in place of other vegetable oils in salad dressings.

# Flaxseed

These tiny seeds may turn out to offer big protection against breast cancer. Flaxseed (but not flaxseed oil) is even richer in lignans than olive oil and supplies alpha-linolenic acid, the plant form of omega-3 fatty acids, as well. Cell and animal studies as well as a preliminary study of 32 postmenopausal women with breast cancer suggest that flaxseed helps reduce tumor growth and spread. *Note:* Research is still under way to determine how flaxseed may interact with anti-estrogen medications such as tamoxifen or aromatase inhibitors, so if you're taking one of these breast cancer drugs, talk to your doctor before loading up on flaxseed. Also, pregnant and breastfeeding women shouldn't eat a lot of flax since there's no safety data for them.

**Aim for:** A tablespoon of ground flaxseed daily. Buy it ground or grind it yourself in a coffee grinder, blender, or food processor. Store ground flaxseed in an airtight container in the fridge.

**Helpful hint:** Add flaxseed to your meals by sprinkling it over cereal or salads, mixing it into yogurt or smoothies, or buying flaxseed-enriched grain products like breads and waffles.

## FEATURED RECIPES

**Edamame Hummus with Pita Crisps** *p. 592*
**Broccoli Salad** *p. 595*
**Coleslaw with Orange-Sesame Vinaigrette** *p. 596*
**Spinach Salad with Chickpeas** *p. 597*
**Tuna and White Bean Salad** *p. 599*
**Brown Rice Risotto** *p. 625*
**Chicken-Barley Bake** *p. 616*
**Tomato-Roasted Mackerel** *p. 612*

## NUTRITIONAL SUPPLEMENTS

**Vitamin D.** Some research suggests that taking 1,000 IU of vitamin D lowers breast cancer risk between 10 and 35 percent. Check the label on your supplement to ensure you're getting $D_3$ (listed as cholecalciferol), which is the more cancer-protective form. **DOSAGE:** 1,000 IU a day.

## OFF THE MENU

**Foods high in saturated fat and trans fat.**
Already linked with so many other diseases, like heart disease, saturated fat promotes inflammation in the body, which can stimulate tumor growth. While not all studies have definitively linked fat intake with breast cancer risk, at least one suggests that women who consume more than 35 grams of saturated fat a day have double the risk of breast cancer compared to women who limit their intake to only 10 grams a day.

There's also some suggestion that trans fat, found in many packaged baked goods, snack foods, and commercially fried foods, may be linked with higher breast cancer risk. When researchers took fat samples from the backsides of nearly 700 European women with and without breast cancer, they found that the women with the highest levels of trans fat stored in their bodies also had a 40 percent higher risk of breast cancer.

Researchers involved with the Women's Health Initiative Study, which followed more than 48,000 postmenopausal women, found that those who started the study with the highest-fat diets and then cut their fat intake to 24 percent of calories were able to lower their breast cancer risk by 15 to 20 percent.

That said, the jury's still out on whether reducing fat intake definitely lowers breast cancer risk. But since eating less saturated and trans fat helps with so many other conditions, it makes good sense either way.

**Sugary foods and refined carbohydrates.**
Some cancer experts are adding overconsumption of sugary foods and the starchy, refined carbohydrates that quickly become sugar in the body (think white bread, white rice, white potatoes, and foods like muffins and pancakes made with white flour) to the list of breast cancer risks. That's largely because when we overeat sugar, not only do we gain weight, we also increase two key factors that are known to raise estrogen levels and stimulate tumor growth: insulin and insulin-like growth factor-1. A study of more than 1,800 women in Mexico found that those who ate a lot of refined carbohydrates had double the breast cancer risk of women whose diets were more balanced.

**Alcohol.** Because alcohol raises estrogen levels, the same drink a day that is considered heart healthy can raise a woman's risk of breast cancer by 1 1/2 times. If you do drink, make sure you eat plenty of foods rich in folate, as mentioned earlier.

Health-conscious cooks know to have a second coffee grinder just for spices, herbs, and seeds. In particular, use it to grind flaxseed, considered by some to be the ultimate food for breast cancer prevention. For maximum freshness, grind flaxseed just before you add it to your dishes.

## Lose Weight, Lower Your Risk

There's one thing you can do that will surely help lower your risk of breast cancer: Maintain a healthy weight. Not only are heavy women more likely to develop breast cancer, they're also more likely to die from it. Data from the Nurses Health Study suggests that nonsmoking women who are overweight when they're diagnosed are almost twice as likely as slender women to die of breast cancer.

More body fat equals higher estrogen levels. And excess body fat, particularly around the belly, produces proteins called cytokines, which increase inflammation and cause the kind of cell damage that can lead to cancer. For that reason, "apple-shaped" premenopausal women have more than double the breast cancer risk of their "pear-shaped" counterparts. Being overweight also goes hand in hand with higher levels of the tumor-stimulating hormones insulin and insulin growth factor-1.

During pregnancy, it's important not to gain significantly more than the recommended 25 to 35 pounds and to lose that weight after giving birth. A Finnish study of more than 27,000 breast cancer patients found that gaining 40 pounds during pregnancy was associated with a 40 percent increase in breast cancer risk.

Gaining weight after menopause is also problematic. According to the Nurses Health Study, women who put on 22 pounds after menopause raised their breast cancer risk by 18 percent.

So cut calories—and get off the couch. Even apart from weight loss, exercise appears to influence hormones in a way that's protective against breast cancer.

# BREAST TENDERNESS

We wish we could report that eating a pint of ice cream will banish breast tenderness. It won't. But there are plenty of other dietary tweaks that may lessen the discomfort.

Most breast tenderness can be blamed on hormone fluctuations that precede menstruation. The breasts also respond to menstruation by absorbing extra fluid, which doesn't help. Another cause is fibrocystic breast disease, in which benign lumps form in the breast tissue and can become tender, especially close to and during menstruation. Stress, pregnancy, and medications like hormones can also cause breast pain. In rare cases, breast cancer (which usually doesn't involve pain) or noncancerous tumors can cause tenderness, so letting your doctor know about breast discomfort is a good idea.

Although Ben and Jerry's won't make it all better, there are some foods you can add to your diet that may help. Subtracting certain other foods may be even more important.

## YOUR FOOD PRESCRIPTION

### Oily fish, flaxseed,
#### and other foods high in omega-3 fatty acids

With each bite of grilled salmon, you get omega-3 fatty acids that help balance eicosanoids, hormone-like substances that help control inflammation, pain, and swelling. You also get resolvins, a recently discovered class of anti-inflammatory fats, which appear to ease inflammation much the same way aspirin does.

Flaxseed offers omega-3s as well as some fiber and lignans, plant estrogens that may reduce the risk of breast cancer. To get the most benefit from flaxseed, buy whole seeds and keep them refrigerated. Grind them as needed in a coffee or spice grinder.

**Aim for:** 1,000 milligrams of omega-3s a day, about the amount in 2 ounces of salmon or five walnut halves. If you're not a fish fan, aim to eat 2 tablespoons of ground flaxseed a day, added to breakfast cereal, oatmeal, smoothies, or yogurt.

**Helpful hint:** If you eat a lot of fatty fish or other foods high in omega-3s, you need more vitamin E than people whose diets are lower in omega-3s. Look to almonds, wheat germ, and spinach for this vitamin, which may itself help relieve breast pain, although the jury's still out.

### Soy foods

The estrogen-like plant chemicals in soy and flaxseed weakly mimic human estrogen and may help assuage breast tenderness. In a small, two-month British study of women ages 18 to 35, eating soy protein containing 68 milligrams of soy isoflavones every day (about the amount in two servings of soy foods) significantly reduced breast tenderness and swelling compared to a placebo.

One caveat: If you're taking tamoxifen or another anti-estrogen medication, such as an aromatase inhibitor, you shouldn't eat soy.

**Aim for:** About 68 milligrams of soy isoflavones daily, about the amount you'd get from a glass of soy milk and a half cup of tofu. It can't hurt to have one or two soy-based meals a week, snack on edamame (green soybeans), and pour soy milk instead of dairy milk.

## Whole grains, lentils, pears,
### and other foods high in fiber

One of the most important tweaks you can make to your diet to lessen breast pain is to eat more fiber. Fiber lowers estrogen levels, which helps minimize breast tenderness as well as other PMS symptoms.

Aim for: 25 to 35 grams of fiber a day. You can get there by eating a serving of bran cereal in the morning, a salad with 1/2 cup of cooked lentils at lunchtime, a pear as a snack, and a cup of winter squash with dinner.

## Water

One reason breasts may get sore around menstruation is that they absorb extra fluid. Ironically, drinking plenty of water every day can decrease water retention; the more you drink, the less fluid the body feels it must hold.

Aim for: Eight 8-ounce glasses a day.

### NUTRITIONAL SUPPLEMENTS

**Vitamin E.** Some studies have found that vitamin E is helpful in relieving breast pain; others have not. **DOSAGE:** 400 IU daily, the dose that appeared to relieve breast tenderness in several studies.

**Omega-3 fatty acids.** Omega-3s come in soft-gel fish-oil capsules or in liquid forms such as flaxseed oil (though flaxseed oil doesn't provide any of the fiber or lignans that ground flaxseed does). Choose a supplement that contains vitamin E, which will help prevent spoilage, and store it in the fridge. **DOSAGE:** 1 to 3 grams a day. Check with your doctor before taking omega-3s if you're also taking a blood thinner such as warfarin (Coumadin).

**Chasteberry extract.** Women have used chasteberries for thousands of years to tame menstrual problems. Over the past 50 years, more than 30 European trials have shown that the supplements improve menstrual symptoms, including breast tenderness. **DOSAGE:** Many of the studies used 4 milligrams per day.

**Vitamin B$_6$.** According to some studies, B$_6$ may help relieve PMS symptoms, including breast tenderness. **DOSAGE:** 50 to 100 milligrams daily.

### OFF THE MENU

**Saturated fat and most vegetable oils.** Put the coffee cake and corn oil away. The saturated fat in butter and fatty meats promotes inflammation, and many experts believe that so do the omega-6 fatty acids found in corn, sunflower, and safflower oils. Canola oil and olive oil are much better choices. Trans fat is a "no-no" too, so avoid products with any "partially hydrogenated" ingredients, and buy trans fat–free margarine.

**Alcohol.** Pass on wine with dinner, at least before and during your period. Alcohol interferes with the normal hormone shifts that occur around menstruation and can increase breast tenderness.

**Salt.** Salt holds fluid in body tissues, adding to the swelling that increases breast tenderness.

**Caffeine.** Although there's no solid evidence that links caffeine with breast tenderness, some doctors still recommend dropping coffee and other caffeinated drinks, primarily because they've seen patients improve once they give them up. Try switching to caffeine-free teas and sodas for four to six months to see if you notice any difference.

### FEATURED RECIPES

**Edamame Hummus with Pita Crisps** *p. 592*
**Sweet Potato Soup** *p. 601*
**Ginger Butternut Squash Soup** *p. 602*
**Salsa Tuna Salad Sandwiches** *p. 604*
**Tomato-Roasted Mackerel** *p. 612*
**Roasted Salmon with Sautéed Greens** *p. 613*
**Springtime Quinoa** *p. 626*

# CANCER

If you think your genes spell out your risk for cancer, you're only partly right. Another part of the equation, and a big one at that, is the life you lead—in fact, a third of all cancers are directly linked to the kinds of foods people eat, how overweight they are, and how little physical activity they get. And that's regardless of whether they smoke.

When it comes to our diets, here's the hard, unpleasant truth: Just as popular American foods—cheeseburgers, french fries, super-size sodas, and the like—lead us down the garden path to heart disease, they're also tailor-made to give us cancer. Hard to swallow? Here's the good news: While you can't choose your genes, you *can* choose what to eat. In places where people consume more fish, produce, and whole grains and eat less saturated fat and fewer refined carbs, cancer rates are lower than in places where there's an abundance of processed foods, beef, and potatoes—your standard Western fare.

You don't have to move to another country to protect yourself, though. In fact, simply by eating five servings of produce a day, you could probably lower your overall cancer risk by 20 to 35 percent. Eating just four servings of whole grains a week could reduce that risk by 34 percent. Better still, walk to the grocery store to get them. Not only does physical activity help with weight maintenance, but exercise seems to independently reduce hormones believed to promote breast, colon, prostate, and uterine cancers.

## YOUR FOOD PRESCRIPTION

### A rainbow of fruits *and vegetables*

We really mean a *rainbow*. Don't limit yourself to the same old apples, oranges, and bananas. In one study, one group of women, all of whom were eating eight to nine servings of produce daily, were told to limit their choices to eight types of produce known to be high in antioxidants; another group was instructed to choose from up to 18 different kinds of fruits and vegetables. Blood tests later revealed that the group eating the wider variety had demonstrably less cancer-inducing DNA damage to their cells than those who cast a smaller net.

Most studies on diet and cancer—with one recent notable exception—have definitively linked higher fruit and vegetable consumption to lower risks of an array of cancers, including those of the breast, prostate, lung, mouth, esophagus, stomach, and colon. Johns Hopkins University researchers found that when they studied more than 6,000 adults, those who ate about five servings of produce a day lowered their risk of dying of cancer by 35 percent compared to those who ate less than one serving a day. Other research suggests that folks who make an effort to eat at least five servings of fruits and vegetables each day cut their overall cancer risk by about 20 percent.

It's not just the antioxidants at work. Fruits and vegetables contain other key substances, including fiber, which helps reduce hormones like estrogen that can promote cancer, and other plant compounds that actively protect our bodies from cancer.

Scientists are still working out the mystery of which compounds are most effective against various cancers. Many have already been identified, like the beta-carotene in carrots and sweet potatoes, the lycopene in tomatoes, the sulforaphane in broccoli, the folate in spinach, the sulfur compounds in garlic and onions, and the ellagic acid in berries. But researchers are still exploring the garden to discover others that may be just as potent.

What's clear is that these nutrients work best when they work together, so eating that rainbow we mentioned is far more effective than relying on supplements.

**Aim for:** At the very least, get 5 servings of fruits and vegetables a day, though 7 to 10 is highly recommended. And don't let the big numbers deter you—you can easily get 3 or more servings just by eating a large salad. A serving is one medium piece of fruit; 1/2 cup of fruit or vegetable juice; 1/2 cup of chopped fruit or cooked vegetables, beans, or legumes; or 1 cup of leafy vegetables.

**Helpful hint:** Steam, stir-fry, or microwave your vegetables. While nutrients can leach out when vegetables are boiled, steaming and microwaving helps conserve them.

# Broccoli *and other cruciferous vegetables*

If there's an all-star cancer fighter, it's broccoli, along with its cruciferous cousins like cauliflower, brussels sprouts, cabbage, and bok choy. These veggies are packed with very potent anticancer compounds, such as sulforaphane and other isothiocyanates, that not only flush out carcinogens—particularly those created when meats are grilled or fried—before they can damage cells but may also repair cell damage that could lead to tumor growth. In addition, they slow the growth of cancer cells that do develop and increase their self-destruction.

Eating more of these vegetables is associated with lower risk of breast, colon, prostate, and lung cancers. Other research has shown that these veggies also lower the risk of lymphoma and bladder cancer. And some researchers suspect that broccoli (particularly broccoli sprouts, which contain up to 20 to 50 times more sulforaphane than mature broccoli) may protect against stomach cancer by reducing levels of *Helicobacter pylori,* a bacterium that damages cells in the stomach lining.

**Aim for:** Four 1/2-cup servings a week.

# Whole grains

There are more reasons than you can shake a stalk at to eat more whole grains. You may not think of them as a source of antioxidants, but they are. And they contain plant estrogens called lignans, which help lower estrogen levels and encourage cancer cells to self-destruct (see the Breast Cancer entry, page 414). But there's more. Because whole grains are excellent sources of fiber and complex carbohydrates, which are digested and absorbed slowly, they don't raise blood sugar as dramatically as refined carbohydrates and sugary foods do. This keeps insulin levels low. That's important because high levels of insulin, along with its cousin, insulin-like growth factor-1, encourage cells to multiply, which can ultimately cause tumors to develop and allow cancer cells to spread.

**Aim for:** Research suggests that eating at least four servings of whole grains (such as a slice of whole-grain bread, an ounce of cereal, or 1/2 cup of rice or pasta) a week lowers overall cancer risk by 34 percent. However, to meet recommended daily fiber goals and get the protective compounds linked to overall health, it's best to eat at least three servings every day.

**Helpful hint:** A good way to have your pasta but avoid those refined carbs is to switch to whole-wheat pasta. Some brands and even some shapes taste better than others, so experiment until you find a kind you like. And don't forget to top it with plenty of garlic and veggies.

# Water

Drinking water and noncaffeinated beverages (fat-free milk, herbal tea) may help protect against bladder cancer because fluids dilute any potential carcinogens lurking in urine. Plus, the more trips you take to the loo, the less time carcinogens are in contact with the bladder lining.

**Aim for:** Drink enough fluids throughout the day so that your urine is very pale. (It will have a darker yellow tinge if you're taking B vitamins.)

# Fatty fish

If you're fishing for anticancer foods, you might try snaring a salmon (good luck with that, unless you're a bear). This famously heart-healthy fish, as well as other fish high in omega-3 fatty acids, such as albacore tuna, sardines, mackerel, and rainbow trout, may also help keep cancer at bay. Some studies already show an association between fatty fish consumption and lower risk of breast, colon, prostate, and lung cancers.

The research is far from conclusive, but if omega-3s do turn out to guard against cancer, it may be because they fight inflammation inside the body, which is thought to spur tumor growth. Getting more omega-3s protects against disease even more when you also reduce your consumption of omega-6 fats, which actively promote inflammation and are found in corn, sunflower, and safflower oils,

Also, let's not forget that eating grilled or steamed fish instead of steaks and burgers can help keep your waistline trim; weight gain is a significant risk factor for many types of cancer.

Aim for: The American Heart Association recommends two servings (8 to 12 ounces total) of fatty fish each week to protect against heart disease, which is also a good target for cancer protection.

Helpful hint: Worried about mercury and other toxins? Avoid swordfish, tilefish, shark, and king mackerel.

## FEATURED RECIPES

Broccoli Salad *p. 595*
Spinach Salad with Chickpeas *p. 597*
Ginger Butternut Squash Soup *p. 602*
Lentil-Tomato Soup *p. 603*
Mac 'n Cheese Primavera *p. 608*
Roasted Salmon with Sautéed Greens *p. 613*
Chicken in Garlic Sauce *p. 616*
Chicken-Barley Bake *p. 616*
Brown Rice Risotto *p. 625*
Mixed Berry Tart *p. 639*

# Green tea

If you want to avoid cancer, it may be time you acquired a taste for green tea, a potent source of cancer-fighting antioxidants that can protect against the DNA damage that causes cells to turn cancerous. In cell studies, one of the most important of these antioxidants, called epigallo-catechin gallate (EGCG), blocked an enzyme that cancer cells need to grow.

Aim for: To get significant anticancer benefits, you'll probably need to drink four cups a day.

# Beans *and leafy green vegetables*

Especially if you drink or smoke, consider having a green salad sprinkled with beans for lunch. Dark leafy greens like spinach, kale, and even romaine lettuce contain the cancer-fighting antioxidants lutein and beta-carotene as well as the B vitamin folate, which safeguards cells from alcohol and tobacco carcinogens. Beans are also rich in antioxidants called flavonoids, not to mention fiber.

Researchers at University College London have found that beans and other legumes, like lentils and peas, also contain a cancer-fighting compound with the tongue-twisting name of inositol pentakisphosphate, which blocks a key enzyme involved in tumor growth. It even makes some anticancer drugs work more effectively.

Aim for: At least one serving of leafy green vegetables (1/2 cup cooked or 1 cup raw) and one serving of legumes (1/2 cup) most days of the week.

Helpful hint: Sneak beans into your favorite dishes by adding rinsed canned beans to casseroles, stews, chilis, salads, salsas, and soups.

# Grapes and grape juice

You know wine's good for your heart, thanks in large part to a potent antioxidant called resveratrol. The hitch is that alcohol also promotes cancer (see the Breast Cancer entry, page 414, and the Colon Cancer entry, page 434). But there's no need to toss out the baby with the bathwater. You can get resveratrol without the alcohol by eating some grapes or drinking grape juice. Laboratory studies suggest that resveratrol, minus the alcohol, protects against breast, skin, liver, and stomach cancers as well as lymphoma and leukemia.

**Aim for:** There's no established recommendation, but having 1/2 cup of grapes or 3/4 cup of grape juice several times a week as part of your daily 7 to 10 servings of fruits and vegetables is a smart idea.

# Garlic

Whether or not garlic wards off vampires, it does seem to help ward off cancer, especially stomach and colorectal cancer. Chalk it up to garlic's powerful sulfur compounds, which flush out carcinogens before they can damage cell DNA and force cancer cells that do develop to self-destruct.

Researchers from the University of North Carolina at Chapel Hill found that people who ate an average of about five garlic cloves a week, raw or cooked, had only two-thirds the risk of colon cancer and half the risk of stomach cancer compared to people who didn't eat much garlic. The thought is that because garlic is antibacterial, along with killing cancer cells, it also kills *H. pylori,* the bacterium that damages the stomach lining, thus making it more vulnerable to cancer.

In addition, cell studies suggest that garlic works like the cruciferous vegetables in protecting cells from damage by carcinogens created when meat is cooked over open flames or high heat.

**Aim for:** Three to five cloves a week.

**Helpful hint:** Cooking deactivates garlic's therapeutic compounds. But that doesn't mean you have to eat raw garlic. One way to preserve these cancer-fighting compounds is to chop or crush the garlic and let it stand for 10 to 15 minutes before using it in cooking.

## *Spice Up Your Life*

Who says healthy food has to be bland? When you spice things up, you also add a good dose of antioxidants and other cancer-fighting phytochemicals to your meals. Many spices in the rack, like cayenne, ginger, cumin, and oregano, are considered beneficial for their antioxidant and anti-inflammatory actions. But for cancer, turmeric, the yellow spice used in Indian cooking, is a real standout.

Turmeric contains curcumin, which not only clears out carcinogens before they can wreak havoc with cell DNA but also shuts down an inflammatory protein that encourages tumor growth. Turmeric also helps block a tumor's effort to construct blood vessels it needs to survive and spread. Research suggests that turmeric may protect against colon cancer as well as melanoma, the deadliest form of skin cancer.

## NUTRITIONAL SUPPLEMENTS

**A multivitamin/mineral.** The fact is, most studies have found no connection between taking supplements and lowering your cancer risk. Indeed, some research has found that taking individual supplements of beta-carotene may actually *increase* the risk of lung cancer. Nutrition experts always advise getting your nutrients from foods because nutrients appear to work more effectively in the amounts and combinations that nature intended. That said, if you simply can't manage to eat all of the recommended servings of fruits, vegetables, and grains each day, then taking a daily multivitamin/mineral supplement to close the gap can't hurt, especially if you're over 50 and don't eat breakfast cereal or other foods fortified with vitamin $B_{12}$. **DOSAGE:** One a day.

**Vitamin D.** The sunshine vitamin may be the one exception to the "no individual supplements for cancer prevention" rule. There is a growing body of evidence to suggest that higher amounts of this vitamin—about 1,000 IU—than can be gotten from food do help reduce the risk of colon and breast cancer. Other data from the Health Professionals Follow-Up Study and the Nurses Health Study indicated that 300 IU or more of vitamin D a day lowered the risk of pancreatic cancer by more than 40 percent. **DOSAGE:** At least 400 IU daily. According to a number of studies, 1,000 IU appears to be even more protective. Check how much you're already getting from any calcium or multivitamin supplements you take, and don't forget to factor in what you may be getting from milk, fortified juice, or cereal (three servings of milk provide about 300 IU). Look at the supplement ingredient label to make sure it contains the form of D known as cholecalciferol (vitamin $D_3$), which is the more active form. Don't exceed 2,000 IU a day from both food and supplements.

## OFF THE MENU

**Saturated fats.** Already linked with many other diseases, like heart disease, saturated fat also promotes the kind of inflammation that damages cell DNA and permits tumors to build the blood vessel network that allows them to grow and spread. Saturated fat has been linked with cancers of the stomach, esophagus, breast, and colon.

**Red meats and processed meats.** Red and processed meats are associated with a host of cancers, no doubt largely because these meats are sources of saturated fat. It's also because grilling or frying meat creates carcinogens that have been linked with breast, colon, and other cancers. Data from the largest study to look at the connection between diet and cancer risk showed that eating even 5 ounces of red or processed meat a day increases the risk of colon and rectal cancers by 35 percent. The study also found that every 3.5-ounce serving of meat eaten quintuples the risk of certain gastric cancers among people who are known to be infected with *H. pylori*. An 18-year Swedish study of more than 61,000 women found that study participants who ate the most processed meats, such as bacon, salami, sausage, or hotdogs, had a 48 to 66 percent higher risk of stomach cancer.

**Sugar and refined carbohydrates.** Some cancer experts are branding sugary foods and the starchy, refined carbohydrates that quickly become sugar in the body as cancer promoters. When we overeat sugar, not only do the extra calories cause us to gain weight but sugar/refined carbohydrate consumption also raises levels of insulin and insulin-like growth factor-1, both of which can be considered "cancer food." Links have already been established between a diet high in refined carbohydrates and stomach, colon, prostate, and breast cancers. Data from the Nurses Health Study, which examined sugar intake among thousands of women, indicated that obese, sedentary women with high blood sugar who ate a lot of sweets and other refined carbohydrates had more than 2 1/2 times the risk of developing pancreatic cancer.

**Salty foods.** Salt appears to damage the stomach lining, making it more vulnerable to cancer development, especially among people infected with *H. pylori*. Studies in Eastern Europe and Japan point to a link between high consumption of salted or smoked fish and meats and an increased gastric cancer risk of between 70 and 200 percent (depending on what was eaten and how often). Reducing your salt intake along with increasing your fruits and vegetables (and of course not smoking) can prevent as many as 75 percent of gastric cancer cases.

**Alcohol.** Alcohol raises the risk of cancers of the breast, colon, esophagus, and liver. As alcohol is metabolized, free radicals and other compounds that damage DNA are produced. Too much alcohol can also raise estrogen levels and lower folate levels, which can lead to DNA damage and disrupt the body's ability to repair it. Researchers at the University of Mississippi have also found that alcohol stimulates blood vessel development in tumors, causing them to grow and spread. One laboratory study showed that animals exposed to alcohol had tumors that were twice as big as those in the control group, and the spread of cancer cells into the blood vessels was eight times greater.

Put a plate of raw vegetables on the table with every meal. It could include carrots, celery sticks, cucumber slices, cherry tomatoes, green pepper slices, and broccoli crowns. No one is excused until the plate is empty!

# CATARACTS

Get out the salad bowl and fishing lures: Fruits, vegetables, and fish appear to help stave off cataracts, cloudy coverings that can form over the lenses of the eyes as you age.

Cataracts, the leading cause of blindness worldwide, occur when proteins in the lens fray, and their debris muddies the lens.

Aging is the most common culprit behind cataracts. Heredity and ethnicity (black people have a higher risk), some medications, and other eye conditions play a role, but so does a lifetime of sun exposure, smoking, and poor nutrition. Fortunately, nutrients in certain foods help protect the eye from an array of assailants. Some nutrients throw up a natural sunscreen; others fight damaging molecules known as free radicals; and still others lower blood sugar levels, which also benefits the eyes.

## YOUR FOOD PRESCRIPTION

### Fatty fish
*and other foods high in omega-3 fatty acids*

Savoring grilled salmon or tuna at least once a week may cut your risk of cataracts by as much as 12 percent, according to a long-term Harvard study. Researchers suspect that it's the omega-3 fatty acids plentiful in fish that help protect the eyes. Although scientists haven't pinpointed why these fat building blocks help, they do know that our eye membranes are awash with them and that they're essential for visual development in embryos and infants. In other words, omega-3s are clearly important to eye health.

If you hate fish, you can get some omega-3s from plant sources such as nuts, soybeans, flaxseed, and some leafy greens.

**Aim for:** An average of 1,000 milligrams a day—the equivalent of a 4-ounce serving of salmon, 1/4 cup of walnuts, or 2 tablespoons of flaxseed several times a week.

**Helpful hint:** Skip the mayonnaise-laden tuna salad. The corn oil in mayonnaise and salad dressing may promote cataracts (see Off the Menu, below).

### Fruits and vegetables

Sunlight, cigarette smoke, air pollution, and infection—many of the culprits associated with cataract damage—all generate free radicals, unstable molecules that damage cells throughout the body, including those in the eyes. The antidote? Antioxidants, which neutralize free radicals. Where can you get them? Your fruit bowl and vegetable bin. A 10-year Harvard study found that serving yourself plenty of produce may cut cataract risk by 10 to 15 percent. Particularly strong protectors are the vitamin C in citrus fruits; the beta-carotene in carrots and other orange and yellow fruits and vegetables (plus spinach); and the vitamin E in nuts, seeds, and green leafy vegetables such as spinach.

## FEATURED RECIPES

Tropical Fruit Salad *p. 590*
Spinach Salad with Chickpeas *p. 597*
Tuna and White Bean Salad *p. 599*
Sweet Potato Soup *p. 601*
Tomato-Roasted Mackerel *p. 612*
Salmon Steaks with Peach Salsa *p. 612*
Orange Beets *p. 627*
Raspberry-Almond Muffins *p. 628*

Pay special attention to those leafy greens—spinach, kale, turnip greens, and collard greens. The antioxidant plant pigments lutein and zeaxanthin, found in abundance in these foods, accumulate in the eyes and provide excellent "eye armor." In one laboratory study, when lens cells were treated with these pigments and then exposed to ultraviolet radiation, a harmful component of sunlight, those cells showed 50 to 60 percent less damage than the untreated cells.

**Aim for:** Five to six 1/2-cup servings of vegetables and three to four 1/2-cup servings of fruits every day.

**Helpful hint:** Consider freezing fruits and vegetables you don't eat immediately. It will help prevent the loss of nutrients, especially vitamin C.

## NUTRITIONAL SUPPLEMENTS

**Omega-3 fatty acids.** Omega-3s come in fish-oil capsules and in liquids such as flaxseed oil. Buying a version with vitamin E helps prevent rancidity, as does storing the supplement in the refrigerator. **DOSAGE:** Optimal dosages aren't established, but many experts recommend 1 gram a day. If you want to take more, check with your doctor.

**A multivitamin/mineral.** The simplest way to get a mix of antioxidants is from a multivitamin/mineral supplement. **DOSAGE:** One a day.

## OFF THE MENU

**Mayonnaise and creamy salad dressings.**
If you're slathering your tuna sandwiches with mayonnaise or drowning salads in creamy dressings, you're probably undoing the good the tuna and greens do for your eyes. Mayo and creamy dressings are usually loaded with corn oil, safflower oil, and/or soybean oil, all rich in omega-6 fatty acids. In a 25-year Harvard study, researchers found that omega-6s appeared to increase the risk of cataracts. Maybe it's time to make your own mayonnaise—with olive oil.

## Sight-Saving Weight Loss

All of us know that ice cream cleaves to our waists, but now research suggests that having a bulging waistline may contribute to eye damage. In a study at Tufts University, obese women were 2 1/2 times more likely to develop a certain type of cataract than women of normal weight. It may have something to do with the effects of high blood sugar, which often goes hand in hand with weighing too much. Women with diabetes were four times more likely to have this type of lens cloudiness.

**Too much alcohol.** Here's another reason not to pass your glass too often. Several studies have found an association between alcohol and cataracts. In one, women who drank two glasses a week of any kind of alcohol bumped up their risk of the most common type of cataract by 13 percent, although they lowered the risk of a less common form. As usual, the message is that a drink or two is probably fine, but know when to say when.

**Salt and salty processed foods.** Turn in the saltshaker. According to an Australian study of almost 3,000 people, liberal sprinklers who consumed more than 1 1/4 teaspoons of salt a day were twice as likely to have cataracts as people who ate about half a teaspoon. Scientists believe that excess salt bodywide may interfere with sodium levels in the eye as well. Don't forget that much of the salt we consume comes from soups, processed meats, and the many other processed foods manufacturers load with the stuff.

# COLDS AND FLU

No doubt you've heard the old joke: If you treat a cold aggressively, it'll be gone in about seven days, but if you do absolutely nothing, it'll drag on for a full week.

Neither your doctor nor your pharmacy can do much to cure your cold. Don't bother begging for antibiotics—colds and flu are caused by viruses, so these drugs, which fight bacteria, won't help. (In the case of the flu, your doctor *does* have antiviral drugs that can cut it short if you start taking them right away.) But if conventional medicine has no cure for a cold, your grandma just might—if she has a good recipe for chicken soup.

That's right, chicken soup, along with other foods, drinks, and herbs, can ease symptoms and may even cut a cold short. In fact, follow our food and supplement prescriptions, and you may just sail through the next cold and flu season with nary a sniffle or ache. That's nothing to sneeze at!

## YOUR FOOD PRESCRIPTION

## Water, decaffeinated tea, and juices

Cold and flu bugs thrive in dried-out throats and nasal passages, but drinking plenty of fluids throughout the day can help keep your mucous membranes moist so they're better able to trap viruses. Then you can either blow them out your nose or swallow them so they're destroyed by your stomach acids before they have a chance to make you sick. Not only can this help prevent colds, but it's just as useful if you're already sick. If you find plain $H_2O$ too boring to drink, cut up some oranges and add them to a pitcher of water for flavor. Each orange also provides 50 milligrams of vitamin C.

If you have a sore throat, sip your water hot with a bit of honey (to coat your throat) and lemon (to shrink swollen throat tissues and help kill off virus cells), or add honey and lemon to tea. Gargling with warm saltwater can also ease a sore throat by clearing away dead white blood cells and increasing blood flow to the throat, which helps your body fight the infection. Or squirt saltwater into your nose to help clear out nasal mucus. Squirt one nostril, then blow your nose. Repeat with the other nostril.

**Aim for:** At least eight glasses of water or other fluids each day, and more if you have a fever.

**Helpful hint:** Orange juice is a popular "go-to" beverage during cold and flu season. If you're planning to drink up, know this: Frozen OJ contains more vitamin C than the ready-to-drink kind. That's because more of the vitamin C in juice sold in cartons or bottles is oxidized—as much as 76 percent compared to just 20 percent of C in frozen juice—and the body doesn't absorb it as well. To get the most C from your juice, grab some frozen juice concentrate from the freezer section and drink it within a week of mixing it up.

## Chicken soup

Although Grandma's favorite cold fighter hasn't yet yielded up all its healing secrets, researchers are beginning to puzzle out why it may work. For starters, hot chicken soup raises the temperature in your nose and throat, creating an inhospitable environment for viruses that prefer cooler, drier climes. Next, just like a hot, steamy shower, hot, steamy soup thins out mucus so you can more easily blow it out. Studies have proved it works better at this than plain old hot water. And finally, according to a laboratory study of both homemade and store-bought soups done at the University of Nebraska Medical Center, the soup inhibits white blood cells called neutrophils that are released in huge numbers when you have a cold. It's the congregation of these white cells that causes a cold's hallmark congestion.

**Aim for:** There's no prescribed "dosage" for chicken soup, so just enjoy a steaming bowlful when you're feeling sniffly and sneezy.

**Helpful hint:** Vegetarians don't have to miss out. In the Nebraska study, vegetable soup was just as effective for slowing neutrophil activity as soups made with chicken.

# Garlic

Those pungent cloves contain allicin, a potent antimicrobial that can fend off bacteria, viruses, and fungi.

**Aim for:** If you can stand it, chew a clove every 3 to 4 hours. You can also cut the clove into pieces and swallow them like pills. Or simply add them to your chicken soup, along with some onions. But chop garlic first and let it stand for 10 to 15 minutes before adding it to the soup. This will allow its therapeutic compounds to form.

**Helpful hint:** It's totally wacky, but one way to get children to consume garlic if they won't eat it raw is to crush two cloves in a garlic press and put one in each of their socks. As they run around, the garlic will be absorbed through their skin.

# Spices and spicy condiments

According to Ayurveda (traditional Indian medicine), cinnamon, coriander, and ginger promote sweating and are often used to help break a fever. You may also be able to unclog your stuffy nose by generously spicing up some dishes with cayenne, horseradish, or (for lovers of sushi) wasabi. Each of these condiments can shrink the blood vessels in your nose and throat to temporarily relieve congestion.

**Aim for:** As much of the spicy hot stuff as you can comfortably stand.

**Helpful hint:** Try this Ayurvedic fever reducer: In a cup of hot water, mix 1/2 teaspoon each of powdered coriander and cinnamon with 1/4 teaspoon of powdered ginger. Let it steep for 10 minutes, then drink.

For a double dose of healing foods, make a pot of garlicky chicken soup. Just add a few peeled cloves to the soup while it cooks. Remove the cooked garlic before serving the soup—and eat it, spread on toast.

## NUTRITIONAL SUPPLEMENTS

**Vitamin C.** Vitamin C really doesn't seem to help prevent a cold—although people could debate this longer than which way the roll of toilet paper should go—but there's much evidence to suggest that taking high doses of C may help shorten the time you're sick by a day or so. Vitamin C acts as an antihistamine and anti-inflammatory to help dry up a runny nose. It also improves immune function. If you think of your immune system as a high-performance vehicle, vitamin C is like high-octane fuel that makes the immune cells, such as neutrophils and macrophages, better able to find and destroy viruses. By the way, being sick (or under intense physical stress) increases the body's need for vitamin C.

For added effect, look for a C supplement that contains bioflavonoids—antioxidants found in citrus fruits, tea, and other foods. **DOSAGE:** There's no consensus about how much vitamin C, if any, to take for treating colds or flu. However, some dietitians and physicians recommend taking several grams a day in divided doses at the first sign of a scratchy throat or stuffy nose. For aggressive treatment, start with 1,000 to 2,000 milligrams every 2 hours for 8 hours, then scale back to three times a day. Be prepared, however: High doses of C can cause bowel problems, so if you experience gas or diarrhea, reduce your dose. And once you're feeling better, taper off your C consumption, rather than stop it abruptly, to avoid "rebound scurvy," a condition that may cause gums to

bleed. People who have a history of oxalate kidney stones should check with their doctors about the type of vitamin C that's best for them—a combination of buffered vitamin C and bioflavonoids doesn't appear to raise the risk of stones the way C by itself seems to.

**Zinc.** Getting zinc—one of the most critical minerals for overall immune function—right up against your mucous membranes seems to reduce the amount of time you have to endure a nasty cold, which is no doubt one reason why zinc lozenges are such popular cold fighters. A good stack of studies shows that taking zinc gluconate or acetate lozenges every 2 hours within the first two days of a cold can decrease its duration. (Just be sure to use them on a full stomach so they won't make you nauseated.) Alas, taking zinc preventively doesn't seem to do much to keep you from catching a cold. **DOSAGE:** Lozenges containing between 9 and 24 milligrams of zinc are most effective.

**Garlic.** If you just can't stomach raw garlic, don't worry: Garlic supplements seem to work just as well. A British study of 146 people found that volunteers who took a garlic supplement for 12 weeks during cold season were far less likely to get sick than those who took placebos. There were 24 colds in the garlic group compared to 65 in the placebo group. And the garlic takers who did get sick recovered about four days sooner on average than the others.

### FEATURED RECIPES

**Quick Chicken Noodle Soup** *p. 600*
**Ginger Butternut Squash Soup** *p. 602*
**Minestrone with Fava Beans** *p. 603*
**Chicken in Garlic Sauce** *p. 616*
**Roasted Root Vegetables** *p. 622*

If you take medications, particularly blood thinners like warfarin (Coumadin), check with your doctor before using garlic because it can increase drugs' blood-thinning effects. **DOSAGE:** 300 milligrams two or three times daily. Look for extracts standardized to contain at least 13 percent allicin.

**Vitamin E.** This antioxidant vitamin, another immune system booster, won't do much, if anything, to shorten a cold, but it could keep you from getting one. In one year-long, high-quality study from Tufts University, 451 adults age 65 and older were given either 200 IU of vitamin E each day or a placebo. While 74 percent of the people in the placebo group came down with at least one upper respiratory infection during the study, only 65 percent of the volunteers in the vitamin E group experienced one or more infections. **DOSAGE:** 200 IU daily.

## OFF THE MENU

**Caffeine and alcohol.** When you're battling a cold or flu, staying well hydrated helps loosen and clear out nasal congestion, so it's better to skip caffeinated drinks like coffee, caffeinated tea, and soda, which are dehydrating. The same holds true for alcohol; although it's certainly tempting to down a few drinks to help you rest when you're feeling ill, alcohol only makes dehydration worse.

**Sugary foods.** Sugary foods are like Valium to your immune system. Sugar makes your white blood cells sluggish, so they're less able to hunt down and destroy viruses. In a study at Loma Linda University in California, when volunteers consumed about 100 grams of sugar (about the amount in two cans of nondiet soda), their white blood cell activity dropped by 50 percent and stayed low for up to 5 hours. Fruit juices may be the one exception to the "no sweets" rule because they contain good immunity-boosting and infection-fighting phytochemicals—provided they're 100 percent fruit juice, not "juice drinks."

# Herbal Infection Fighters

In terms of supplements, zinc may be your best option for fighting colds, but other supplements can help, too—though not the ones you might think. Echinacea, for instance, was found to do not much at all to prevent colds or reduce their severity in two major recent studies. A better bet is *Andrographis paniculata,* found in products such as TriMune and Kold Kare. Ginseng is another smart choice; it's been shown to help with both colds and flu.

For flu, perhaps the number one supplement to try is elderberry extract, which seems to cut the severity of symptoms in half and reduce the amount of time you're sick if you take it within 48 hours after you experience your first symptoms. Elderberries contain several flavonoids, notably anthocyanidins, which help regulate immune function and reduce inflammation. In one study involving residents of an Israeli farming collective (called a kibbutz) who came down with the flu, more than 93 percent of those who took elderberry reported feeling markedly better within two days, while the majority of those taking placebos took six days to recover. For all of these supplements, follow the dosage instructions on the label.

# COLON CANCER

If you live for steak, bacon, and hotdogs, it's not just your arteries and waistline that take the hit. It's also your colon—the place all that food ends up. Some people can blame their genes, in part, for colon cancer, but the wrong diet plays a major role. On the flip side, experts estimate that making even moderate diet and lifestyle changes can prevent about 70 percent of colon cancers.

Just as smoking leads to lung cancer, the endless beef-and-potatoes buffet that is the standard Western diet may nearly quadruple a person's risk of developing the growths, called polyps, in the digestive tract that lead to colon cancer. Getting a colonoscopy, which simultaneously finds and removes polyps, when you turn 50 (earlier if you have a family history) and every 10 years after that can dramatically reduce your risk. But since most colon cancers start with a polyp, preventing the darn things in the first place is a top priority. Simple steps like serving yourself some spinach salad sprinkled with beans for lunch and piling on the broccoli or brussels sprouts at dinner can go a long way.

## YOUR FOOD PRESCRIPTION

## Beans, lentils, peas,
### *and other foods high in folate*

If colon cancer runs in your family, pile your plate high with these foods. Along with fiber, they also contain vast stores of folate, a B vitamin that protects cell DNA from damage. According to a Harvard study of nearly 89,000 women, those with a family history of colon cancer who consumed more than 400 micrograms of folate each day lowered their risk by more than 52 percent compared to women who consumed just 200 micrograms a day. You can get almost 300 micrograms just by eating 1 cup of chickpeas or cooked spinach. Fortified cereals are another terrific source, as is orange juice.

Of course, it pays to get more folate even if you don't have a family history of colon cancer. Several studies show it could cut your risk by 30 to 40 percent.

**Aim for:** 400 micrograms of folate daily. You may be getting that much already if you take a multivitamin each day or start your morning with orange juice and a fortified cereal. But you can also get there by eating at least 5 servings of whole grains each day along with 7 to 10 servings of fruits and vegetables. At least one of those servings should be dark leafy greens or legumes, like kidney beans, black beans, or chickpeas (garbanzo beans).

**Helpful hint:** Broccoli does double duty as a cancer fighter. It contains the antitumor compounds found in cruciferous vegetables as well as a fair amount of folate.

## Milk

You know the saying "milk does a body good"? Along with building strong bones, milk can help shield you from colon cancer. Data on more than a half million people showed that drinking at least 8 ounces a day lowered the risk of cancers of the colon and rectum by about 15 percent. Drink two more glasses, and your risk drops by another 12 percent.

**Aim for:** At least 8 ounces a day.

**Helpful hint:** Because saturated fat is strongly linked to tumor growth, opt for 1% or fat-free milk.

# Cruciferous vegetables

These veggies (which include broccoli, brussels sprouts, cauliflower, cabbage, bok choy, kale, parsnips, turnips, rutabagas, and kohlrabi) are among the most powerful cancer fighters in the garden. They contain an array of compounds that flush out cancer-causing substances before they cause damage to cell DNA. Studies have consistently shown that people who eat the most crucifers have half the risk of developing colon cancer compared to those who eat the least.

If you're fond of putting steaks on the grill, you'll definitely want to serve these veggies with them. Compounds in crucifers act like little scrubbing pads to clean out the carcinogens created when meats are barbecued.

**Aim for:** At least four 1/2-cup servings each week.

# High-fiber whole grains, fruits, and vegetables

The news on whether fiber protects against colon cancer flips more often than pancakes at an all-night diner. And yet, despite conflicting studies, specialists are still encouraging us to eat more than the 15 grams of fiber we typically get each day. Why? Fiber helps speed food through your system so any carcinogens you may have eaten don't linger long enough to cause trouble. And as it's digested by bacteria in the gut, compounds are formed that protect against carcinogenic bile acids, also produced during digestion.

Weighing in heavily on the pro-fiber side of the argument, data from a large study called the European Prospective Investigation of Cancer and Nutrition (EPIC) showed that people who ate the most fiber were 40 percent less likely to develop colon cancer.

It's better to get your fiber from food rather than supplements because it's not clear how much protection comes from fiber per se and how much comes from the other nutrients and plant compounds in fiber-rich foods.

**Aim for:** Between 25 and 35 grams of fiber daily. You can get close to 25 grams with three servings of whole grains—like a sandwich made with whole-wheat bread plus 1/2 cup of brown rice—and seven servings (a mere half cup each) of fruits and vegetables. To boost your fiber even more, add a few servings of legumes, nuts, seeds, and high-fiber cereal.

# Fish and chicken

As evidence of a link between red meat and colon cancer continues to mount, you may wonder what's left to eat. The answer: Fish and chicken.

Results from the EPIC study show that eating at least 10 ounces of fish (two or three servings) weekly lowers the risk of colon cancer by 30 percent compared to eating fish less than once a week. That's not so surprising. If you're eating more fish, you're eating less meat. And if you choose fatty fish like salmon or mackerel, you're also getting more omega-3 fatty acids, which help to reduce inflammation in the gut.

If you don't like fish, flock to chicken. Studies show that unlike red meat, chicken doesn't actively promote colon cancer.

**Aim for:** At least two servings of fish or chicken a week.

**Helpful hint:** Most of chicken's fat is in the skin, so remove it before you dig in.

# Turmeric

This is the spice so common in Indian food. The natural yellow pigment in turmeric, called curcumin, is considered a top anticancer agent. It's strongly anti-inflammatory, quelling inflammation that's thought to contribute to tumor growth. It also helps clean out carcinogens before they can damage cell DNA, and it helps repair any damage already done. Lab studies show this spice also helps stop the growth and spread of cancer cells that do form.

**Aim for:** There's no established recommendation; just try to use it more often in your cooking.

Helpful hint: Although the turmeric in curry powder mixes can turn your food yellow, some research suggests that several commercial curry powders don't actually contain much curcumin. It's better to use turmeric powder or, if you're using premixed curry powder, add some extra turmeric.

## Garlic and onions

Garlic may not protect you from vampires, but it can help keep colon cancer away. Both garlic and onions contain sulfides, which help to clear out carcinogens and force cancer cells that do develop to self-destruct. In the Iowa Women's Health Study, women who consumed one to two cloves of garlic per week had a 32 percent lower risk of colon cancer compared to women who rarely ate garlic. And according to a study that examined fruit and vegetable consumption among more than 650 people in South Australia, onion eaters reduced their risk by 28 to 52 percent.

Aim for: Eating a couple of garlic cloves and about 1/2 cup of onions at least a few times a week may help lower your cancer risk.

Helpful hint: If you plan to cook garlic, chop or crush the cloves first, then let them stand for 10 to 15 minutes to give the therapeutic compounds a chance to form.

### FEATURED RECIPES

**Coleslaw with Orange-Sesame Vinaigrette** *p. 594*
**Spinach Salad with Chickpeas** *p. 597*
**Simple Broccoli Soup** *p. 602*
**Ginger Butternut Squash Soup** *p. 602*
**Roasted Salmon with Sautéed Greens** *p. 613*
**Chicken in Garlic Sauce** *p. 616*
**Brussels Sprouts with Caramelized Onions** *p. 623*
**Brown Rice Risotto** *p. 625*

## Black and green tea

The next time you're jonesing for a hot cup of somethin', make tea your choice. Lab studies show that the compounds in tea help disable cancer-causing agents. They also stymie the growth of cancer cells and encourage them to self-destruct.

Among more than 35,000 women in the Iowa Women's Health study, those who drank two or more cups of tea each day were almost 30 percent less likely to develop colon cancer than those who rarely drank tea. And while the participants in this study primarily drank black tea, it's worth noting that green tea contains even more of the antioxidant compounds, called catechins, that appear to work the magic.

Aim for: Three to four cups a day.

Helpful hint: Brew your own tea. Commercial bottled teas generally contain less than 5 percent of the antioxidant compounds found in brewed tea.

### NUTRITIONAL SUPPLEMENTS

**Folic acid.** If you're not getting enough folate in your diet, fill the gap with a multivitamin. The Nurses Health Study found that women who took a daily multivitamin with folic acid (the supplement form of folate) for 15 years were 75 percent less likely to develop colon cancer than those who didn't. **DOSAGE:** 400 micrograms a day, the amount in most multivitamins.

**Calcium and vitamin D.** These bone helpers are pretty good at protecting against cancer, too. A study called the Polyp Prevention Trial found that supplementing with both lowered the risk of polyp recurrence by 18 percent. **DOSAGE:** For calcium, aim for 1,200 to 1,500 milligrams daily from food and supplements. With vitamin D, research suggests getting 1,000 IU from food and supplements combined is considered safe and likely to be beneficial.

## OFF THE MENU

**Red meat.** When it comes to colon cancer, red meat—especially processed meats like ham, hotdogs, sausage, bacon, bologna, and corned beef—is a triple threat. The saturated fat promotes inflammation, and the iron, called heme iron, aggravates the colon lining and creates carcinogenic substances. Finally, grilling or frying meat over flames or very high heat creates other cancer-causing substances.

A German study found triple (and in some cases quadruple) the risk of polyp formation among people who ate the most red meat compared to people who ate the least. The American Institute for Cancer Research recommends eating no more than 3 ounces of red meat daily.

**Sugar and refined carbohydrates.** Some cancer experts are branding sugary foods and the starchy, refined carbohydrates that quickly become sugar in the body as cancer causers. When we overeat these foods, the weight we gain puts us at risk (see "What's Weight Got to Do with It?" on this page). But a diet high in this stuff (think doughnuts and cookies but also potatoes, white bread, white rice, and sugary drinks) also increases levels of insulin and insulin-like growth factor-1, both of which can be considered "cancer food"—the more there is in your body, the more tumors grow.

One study found that women whose diets were high in refined carbohydrates were almost three times more likely to develop colon cancer.

## What's Weight Got to Do with It?

A lot. Body fat, particularly belly fat, doesn't just sit there and look bad. It produces proteins called cytokines, which crank up inflammation and lead to the kind of cell damage that encourages tumor growth. Being overweight also goes hand in hand with higher insulin levels, also linked to tumor growth. According to a study at Boston University School of Medicine, if your waist is bigger than 39 inches, you have double the risk of colon cancer. If you're also sedentary, your risk is tripled.

Excess sugar consumption also puts us in line for diabetes, which boosts the risk of colon cancer by about 40 percent.

**Alcohol.** Booze depletes folate, the B vitamin that guards against colon cancer. Imbibing also makes DNA more vulnerable to damage by carcinogens. A pooled analysis of almost 490,000 people showed that heavy drinkers are about 20 percent more likely to develop colon cancer, and a Northwestern University study of more than 161,000 adults suggested that they develop it about five years earlier. The risk is highest for people who have more than two drinks daily.

*food for thought . . .*

"Filling two-thirds of your plate with whole grains, vegetables, fruit, and legumes is an easy way to protect against colon cancer."

— Karen Collins, MS, RD, CDN, nutrition
advisor to the American Institute for
Cancer Research ■

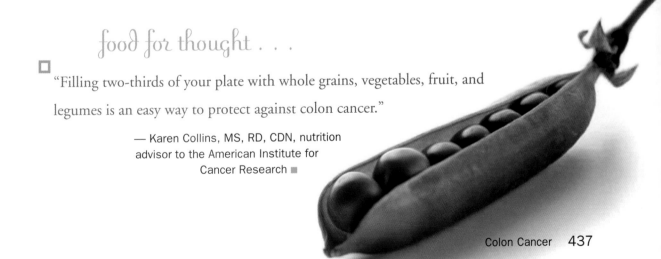

# CONSTIPATION

When your "works" are all stopped up, you want relief quicker than you can say "go." If a poor diet—one lacking fruits, vegetables, and whole grains—is a major cause of the problem, better food choices and plenty of fluids are a major part of the solution. Has traveling or stress disrupted your regularity? We'll also show you some fast-acting, short-term solutions (like a handful of prunes or a cup of coffee).

If changing your diet and getting more fluids don't help, see your doctor to find out whether a condition such as hypothyroidism may be causing the problem.

## YOUR FOOD PRESCRIPTION

### Fruits, vegetables, beans,
*and whole grains*

These are full of fiber, the key to a smooth-running digestive system. As fiber travels along the large intestine, it absorbs fluids to bulk up and soften waste material. That helps stool pass more easily through the colon, where muscle contractions move it along. Fiber is particularly dense in the skin, stems, and leaves of fruit and plants, so don't peel that apple or toss those broccoli stalks.

Dark green leafy vegetables (think spinach, broccoli, etc.) can do double duty not only because of their fiber but also because of their high magnesium content (see under Nutritional Supplements on the opposite page).

Be sure to increase your fiber slowly; a sudden jump may wreak havoc with your system.

**Aim for:** 25 to 35 grams of fiber a day. You can get more than 8 grams just by eating 1/2 cup of

cooked red beans, 5 grams from 1/4 cup of all-bran cereal, and 4.5 grams from 1/2 cup of cooked winter squash.

**Helpful hint:** A great way to get fiber is to start your day with a bowl of oatmeal topped with prunes rather than sugar.

### Prunes

Prunes (now known as dried plums) act as a mild laxative, stimulating muscles to push waste through the large intestine. Five prunes provide about 3 grams of fiber, but because prune juice is equally effective as a laxative, researchers doubt that fiber is the key. More likely, the effect is due to prunes' high content of sorbitol, a sugar alcohol.

**Aim for:** 1 cup prune juice (add 1 tablespoon lemon juice for even more effect) or four prunes a day. Stewed prunes or prunes that have soaked overnight in water may be easier to digest than the dry variety.

**Helpful hint:** Don't overdo it, or you may end up with diarrhea.

### Coffee *and other hot liquids*

Coffee gives us that "get up and go," but it also gives us the urge to "sit down and go." Part of the reason is that hot liquids help move the bowels. Coffee may also trigger intestinal muscles to contract. It's not a good long-term solution,

### FEATURED RECIPES

**Spinach Salad with Chickpeas** *p. 597*
**Roasted Broccoli with Cheese** *p. 624*
**Ginger Butternut Squash Soup** *p. 602*
**Three-Bean Chili** *p. 610*
**Hearty Vegetable Stew** *p. 608*
**Pumpkin Streusel Bread** *p. 631*
**Pear Crisp** *p. 636*

especially because coffee is a diuretic (so drink plenty of water as well), but in the short term, it should help do the trick.

Another alternative: hot water mixed with a tablespoon of lemon or lime juice. The juice stimulates the release of bile, and that can kick-start intestinal contractions.

Aim for: A cup or two of black coffee or an 8-ounce mug of hot water mixed with 2 tablespoons lemon juice.

## Water

Fiber needs water to work its magic. When we don't drink enough water, our bodies pilfer it from our waste, leaving stools hard and difficult to pass. Make water more enticing by adding sliced seasonal fruit, like strawberries, peaches, watermelon, or citrus fruits.

Aim for: Between 8 and 11 eight-ounce glasses, or 2 to 3 liters, a day.

Helpful hint: To help keep track of how much you're drinking, get a 1-liter bottle and put three rubber bands around it. Each time you refill your bottle, remove one rubber band.

## Flaxseed and psyllium

Both help to bulk up stool. Try drinking a cup of warm milk with a teaspoon of ground flaxseed mixed in before bedtime. Sprinkle 2 tablespoons flaxseed over cereal or in a fruit smoothie in the morning. And look for cereals that list psyllium as one of the first ingredients.

Aim for: 1 to 2 teaspoons a day with plenty of water.

## Salad, European-style

In Europe, many people eat their salads at the end of the meal. Adding that crunchy fiber as a finishing touch can help push the rest of the food through the digestive tract. Eating fruit an hour before or after a meal can also be helpful.

Aim for: A piece of fruit before or after lunch and a small salad at the end of dinner.

## NUTRITIONAL SUPPLEMENTS

**Magnesium.** Magnesium is a superb laxative, as anyone who's gulped down some Milk of Magnesia can attest. While nuts, seeds, and leafy dark green vegetables are good sources of magnesium, if you're really backed up, a magnesium supplement can help. **DOSAGE:** 150 to 300 milligrams twice daily.

**Fiber supplements.** If you can't get the recommended 25 to 35 grams of fiber from food, psyllium-based fiber supplements such as Metamucil can close the gap. **DOSAGE:** Start with a level teaspoon once a day in 12 to 16 ounces of water (you can add some fruit juice to help it go down easier), then drink another 16 ounces of water. Work up to 2 tablespoons daily if necessary or follow label directions.

## OFF THE MENU

**Cow's milk and other dairy products.** Sometimes an intolerance to milk protein can cause constipation. An Italian study of 65 kids with chronic constipation found that when they switched from cow's milk to soy milk, constipation cleared up for 68 percent of them. If you've increased your intake of fiber and liquids and still have a problem with constipation, try cutting dairy out of your diet for two weeks to see if it makes a difference.

**Excess protein.** Diets very high in protein—especially red meat—can contribute to constipation.

**White bread, white rice, and white pasta.** "White" foods are usually stripped of their fiber and many of their nutrients in order to produce a smooth, bland food. Although many people prefer their soft texture and mild taste, refined foods lack the fiber that our bowels need to stay regular. Ditto for most packaged foods.

**Alcohol.** It's a diuretic, and if you're constipated, you need more fluid, not less.

# DEPRESSION

You know the old expression "You are what you eat." Well, when it comes to mental health, "You feel what you eat" appears to be equally true. While we typically associate depression with a family history of the illness or devastating life events like the loss of a loved one, it may come as a surprise that what we eat—or don't eat—influences our emotional health as well.

Much of the current science has focused on the importance of getting the right balance of essential fatty acids—consuming more omega-3 fatty acids from fatty fish, walnuts, and flaxseed and fewer omega-6 fatty acids from vegetable oils like corn and canola oil and packaged and processed foods. Other research indicates that people with depression tend to have lower levels of certain B vitamins as well as the minerals selenium, iron, and zinc. It's still unclear, though, whether the nutrient deficiency causes depression or whether depression alters eating habits, which then leads to deficiency.

The diet connection may offer particular insight into postpartum depression. Women are more than twice as likely as men to experience depression, and researchers at the University of Pittsburgh are exploring the theory that nutrient depletion during pregnancy and breastfeeding (as nutrients are preferentially transferred to the growing baby), combined with a delay in the time it takes for a new mother's nutrient stores to return to prepregnancy levels, may be at least partly responsible for postpartum depression.

Depression can be serious and often requires professional help and sometimes medication. You should make changes to your diet in addition to, not instead of, getting the help you need. That said, increasing your intake of certain key nutrients may prevent depression, help ease symptoms, and even improve the effectiveness of antidepressant medications.

## food for thought . . .

"Before 1890, the ratio of omega-6 to omega-3 essential fatty acids in the American diet was 1:1. Today, it's as high as 25:1. This radically increased intake of omega-6 essential fatty acids is thought to be behind the rise of depression in the U.S."

— "Nutrition and Depression: Implications for Improving Mental Health among Childbearing Aged Women," *Biological Psychiatry,* 2005 ∎

## Salmon, mackerel, tuna,
*and other foods rich in omega-3 essential fatty acids*

In countries where fish consumption is high, such as Japan, Taiwan, and Finland, rates of depression tend to be low. Conversely, in areas where fish consumption is low, like the United States and Europe, depression rates are much higher—as much as 10 times higher. Women who rarely eat fish have more than twice the risk of developing depression compared to those who dine on "fin food" often.

**Aim for:** Although it's nearly impossible to consume enough omega-3s to treat depression through food alone (you'll need between 1 and 3 grams of omega-3s a day to lift your mood), eating more fish, such as sardines, may help protect you from developing depression in the first place. Start by eating at least two fish meals a week. If you don't like fish, add a teaspoon of ground flaxseed, another good source of omega-3s, to cereal, yogurt, or salads every day.

## Beans, spinach, fish,
*and other foods high in B vitamins*

Although all B vitamins are essential for preventing depression, most of the research has focused on folate (also known as folic acid), $B_6$, and $B_{12}$ because these vitamins are often in short supply among people with depression. Harvard researchers found that between 15 and 38 percent of people with depression are deficient in folate. While it's uncertain whether low folate levels cause depression, we do know that they can interfere with antidepressant medications, delaying symptom relief.

Women who take birth control pills or hormone replacement drugs can also be low in $B_6$ (another possible reason why women's depression rates are twice those of men), while deficiencies of $B_{12}$ are common among the elderly and among vegans who don't eat any animal proteins. Studies have yet to be done on whether eating enough B vitamin–rich foods like whole grains, lean meats, beans, and nuts can prevent or treat depression, but these foods are believed to be generally beneficial for brain health.

**Aim for:** *Vitamin $B_6$:* 1.3 to 1.5 milligrams daily. You can approach that amount with a serving (3.5 ounces) of tuna or a cup of chickpeas. Buckwheat flour is another good source. *Vitamin $B_{12}$:* 2.4 micrograms daily, which is easily gotten from a serving of beef or eggs. *Folate:* 400 micrograms daily. A cup of cooked lentils will almost get you there, and a serving of breakfast cereal (all brands are enriched with folate) will give you more than this amount. Spinach and beets are other good sources. *Thiamin:* 50 milligrams a day. Because it's not possible to get this much from food sources alone, it's a good idea to include thiamin-rich foods, like whole grains and brown rice, in your diet and get the rest from a good B-complex supplement.

## Lean meats, cheese, *and bananas*

What do these foods have in common? The amino acid tryptophan. British researchers found that taking 1,000 milligrams of tryptophan three times a day helped improve mood. Tryptophan is critical to production of the neu-

---

### Get a Whiff of This!

Sure, vanilla tastes good, but even sniffing it can help reduce anxiety, according to a study done at Memorial Sloan-Kettering Cancer Center. In the study, patients undergoing MRIs who breathed vanilla-scented air reported 63 percent less anxiety than those who breathed unscented air. Add a drop or two of vanilla to the pot before the coffee brews to fill your kitchen with the pleasing scent, or simply light some vanilla-scented candles around your home or add vanilla-scented oil to your bathwater.

rotransmitter serotonin, which regulates mood. Incidentally, increasing the available serotonin in the brain is also the goal of antidepressants like fluoxetine (Prozac), which are known as selective serotonin reuptake inhibitors (SSRIs). Other sources of tryptophan are peanuts, fish, milk, dates, and even chocolate.

Because protein is a good source of the amino acid, you can help your body make its own tryptophan by eating lean meats and other good protein sources like soy and fish.

**Aim for:** It's not possible to get as much tryptophan as the British researchers used in their study from food alone, so simply aim to include more tryptophan-rich foods in your diet. Then consider talking to your physician about getting pharmaceutical-grade tryptophan from a compounding pharmacy.

**Helpful hint:** Gobble up some turkey. Not only is it a good source of tryptophan, but it also contains those brain-critical B vitamins along with good amounts of iron, selenium, and zinc, other nutrients being studied for their connection to alleviating depression.

## Complex carbohydrates *from vegetables, fruits, legumes, and whole grains*

Carbohydrates indirectly help make serotonin. Simple carbohydrates like sugary and starchy foods and those made with white flour boost serotonin levels, too, which is why we instinctively reach for them when we're feeling blue. But these foods cause blood sugar to rise quickly

and then fall quickly. When blood sugar levels fall, so do our moods. Wild swings in blood sugar that come from eating too many of these foods stress the adrenal glands, which in turn leads to fatigue and depression. By contrast, complex carbs, like those found in whole-grain products (breads, rice, and pasta), fruits, vegetables, and legumes, boost and sustain serotonin without spiking blood sugar.

**Aim for:** 7 to 10 servings of fruits and vegetables a day. In addition, make at least three of your grain servings whole grains. Eating a bowl of high-fiber cereal in the morning and making your sandwich for lunch with two slices of whole-grain bread will get you there.

## NUTRITIONAL SUPPLEMENTS

**Omega-3 fatty acids.** These are essential for optimal functioning of brain cells and neurotransmitters, particularly serotonin. While the jury is still out on whether supplements can prevent depression, research does suggests that taking omega-3 supplements can do much to alleviate symptoms, particularly for people whose depression seems resistant to treatment.

The important omega-3 components for depression are EPA and DHA. Several double-blind, randomized controlled trials showed improvements in mood after participants took at least 1 gram a day of EPA. Omega-3 supplements also seem to enhance the effectiveness of antidepressant drugs. In a four-week study of 20 patients taking either 2 grams of EPA a day or a placebo along with their antidepressants, depression symptom ratings fell by 50 percent among those taking the EPA compared to the placebo group. **DOSAGE:** Supplements typically contain both EPA and DHA; studies show 1 gram of each daily to be effective. If higher doses are needed, check with your physician.

**B-complex vitamins.** Studies suggest that some B vitamin supplements can help regulate mood. For instance, thiamin appears to increase general feelings of well-being, and folic acid seems to improve responses to antidepressant medications. **DOSAGE:** A good B-complex

### FEATURED RECIPES

**Buckwheat Pancakes with Fruit Sauce** *p. 590*
**Spinach Salad with Chickpeas** *p. 597*
**Tuna and White Bean Salad** *p. 599*
**Lentil-Tomato Soup** *p. 603*
**Tuna Kebabs** *p. 610*
**Roasted Salmon with Sautéed Greens** *p. 613*
**Brown Rice Risotto** *p. 625*
**Orange Beets** *p. 627*

supplement daily will supply what you need. Look for formulations that contain 800 micrograms of folic acid, 50 to 100 milligrams of $B_6$, and at least 500 micrograms of $B_{12}$. Higher doses may be necessary to be therapeutic, but check with your physician.

**Selenium from a multivitamin.** This antioxidant mineral is a building block for glutathione peroxidase, an enzyme that protects nerves in the brain. It's also key for metabolizing thyroid hormone, low levels of which are known to cause depression. In studies in which participants ate a low-selenium diet, they experienced more symptoms of depression and hostility than when their diet had sufficient amounts. **DOSAGE:** Studies showed that compared to a placebo, 100 micrograms daily improved mood. Most multivitamin/mineral supplements contain 100 to 200 micrograms.

**Iron.** One of the most common nutrient deficiencies in the world, low iron is associated with fatigue, apathy, irritability, and an inability to concentrate, so it's not a big leap to consider that low levels may also play a role in depression. Research showed that postpartum depression improved among new mothers with anemia who received 125-milligram iron tablets. **DOSAGE:** Iron is a tricky supplement because too little may lead to depression, while too much can lead to heart problems. Take iron supplements only if you've been diagnosed with iron deficiency by your physician.

## OFF THE MENU

**Alcohol.** Not only does alcohol depress the central nervous system, but it (particularly hard liquor) also depletes the body of the B vitamins that are essential for brain function.

**Corn, safflower, and sunflower oils and processed foods such as chips and cookies.** These oils are high in omega-6 fatty acids, as are processed foods made with them. Although we need both omega-6s and omega-3s for optimal brain function, we need them in the correct balance, and most of us get too many omega-6s, according to many experts.

## Balance Your Blood Sugar

Dieters are often encouraged to eat small meals throughout the day to prevent the swings in blood sugar that can lead to cravings—and the binges that satisfy them. Keeping your blood sugar on an even keel is a good strategy for improving mood as well. To do it, never go more than a few hours without eating something, choose complex carbohydrates over refined grains and sugary foods, and eat some protein and healthy fats with every meal or snack (think peanut butter on whole-grain toast).

On a typical day, this might mean bran cereal topped with fruit for breakfast instead of a bagel, a sandwich on whole wheat instead of white at lunch (or a salad with beans or tuna on top instead of a sandwich), and a slice or two of roast chicken with a heap of vegetables and a half cup of brown rice for dinner instead of a big plate of spaghetti.

# DIABETES

Diabetes is more tightly wound with diet than a snake in its own coil. For instance, if you have type 2 diabetes or know someone who does, you probably know that sugary foods aren't the best for a person's blood sugar. But the story doesn't end there.

Refined carbohydrates (think white crackers, cookies, white pancakes, and other foods made with white flour—foods that quickly turn into glucose, or sugar, in the body) are equal or perhaps even greater villains. Plain old eating too much, which leads to weight gain, is another trapdoor to diabetes.

Excess calories and lots of refined carbohydrates don't exactly cause type 2 diabetes—but they don't help. Studies suggest that people who eat a lot of refined carbohydrates as well as fat (particularly animal fat) and even animal protein are at much greater risk for the disease than those who don't. In other words, a diet of steak and potatoes, burgers and fries, soft drinks, doughnuts, and premium ice cream lays down the type 2 welcome mat.

Fortunately, you can roll it back up by gradually tweaking your diet here and there. If you already have type 2 diabetes, eating smart and shedding a few pounds if you need to can help you better control your blood sugar and possibly let you reduce your doses of insulin or other medications that lower blood sugar—or even eliminate the need for them. It's as simple as choosing slower-digesting foods—like whole-wheat bread instead of white bread and beans instead of white potatoes—and eating plenty of fruits and vegetables (a key to helping many health problems). Other foods play a role, too, as you'll discover shortly.

## YOUR FOOD PRESCRIPTION

## Fruits, vegetables,
### and other foods high in antioxidants

Not only does a sweet, juicy orange or crunchy carrot taste great, especially when your energy seems to have leapt out the window, but these foods are full of fiber that slows digestion. What may be equally important is that they're also loaded with antioxidants.

The antioxidant vitamins E and C and carotenoids (nutrients found in yellow and orange fruits and vegetables) like beta-carotene appear to be particularly important for people with diabetes. In a Finnish study of more than 4,300 nondiabetic men and women whom researchers followed for 23 years, those who ate foods highest in vitamin E—leafy greens like spinach as well as seeds and nuts—had a 31 percent lower risk of developing type 2 diabetes. Those who ate the most of a type of carotenoid found in citrus fruits, red bell peppers, papaya, cilantro, corn, and watermelon cut their risk by 42 percent. Although vitamin C—abundant in citrus fruits, broccoli, and tomatoes—didn't appear to cut diabetes risk, it boosts vitamin E's power. People with diabetes are often low in both C and E.

How do antioxidants help? They neutralize unstable, cell-damaging molecules called free radicals. Research suggests that people with diabetes have more free radicals than people without the disease. Free radicals may play a role both in both causing diabetes and in exacerbating its long-term effects, such as clogged arteries and blood vessel and nerve damage. Either high blood sugar or high insulin may cause a free radical invasion.

**Aim for:** Five or six servings of vegetables and four servings of fruit every day. A serving is one medium piece of fruit; 1/2 cup of fruit or vegetable juice; 1/2 cup of chopped fruit or cooked vegetables, beans, or legumes; or 1 cup of leafy vegetables.

**Helpful hint:** Dried fruits and fruit juices are too dense in sugar to be good choices for people with diabetes, except in very small portions, and most juices lack fruit's valuable fiber. Stick with fresh whole fruit instead.

## Whole grains, beans, peas, and lentils

Whole grains and other complex carbohydrates deserve top billing on any antidiabetes menu. Oats, beans, and some fruits and vegetables are loaded with soluble fiber, which dissolves in water, forming a gel in your stomach. That slows digestion, which is critical for heading off blood sugar spikes. Soluble fiber also reduces cholesterol, lowering your risk of heart disease—the problem most people with diabetes ultimately die of. Insoluble fiber, which passes through the intestines intact and is found mostly in whole wheat and some fruits and vegetables, is also linked to lower diabetes risk.

Data collected on almost 3,000 people in the Framingham Offspring Study shows that those who ate the most cereal fiber from whole grains were the least likely to have insulin resistance, the precursor of type 2 diabetes. They were also 38 percent less likely to have metabolic syndrome, a cluster of conditions (such as obesity, high blood pressure, and high blood sugar) linked to both diabetes and heart disease, than those who ate the least fiber. And a review of studies about cereal grains found that people who ate three servings of whole grains a day were 20 to 30 percent less likely to develop type 2 diabetes than those who ate less.

## Switch to Decaf

If you love your cup of Joe, go ahead and indulge. An 11-year University of Minnesota study of almost 29,000 postmenopausal women found that those who drank more than six cups of coffee a day cut their risk of type 2 diabetes by 22 percent. But they cut their risk by 33 percent if those six cups were decaffeinated. It turns out that it's the antioxidants in coffee, not the caffeine, that protect us. Researchers believe the antioxidants (similar to those in berries and grapes) protect beta cells in the pancreas (the cells that produce insulin) from free radical damage. Also, a coffee ingredient called chlorogenic acid—also found in red wine and chocolate—appears to slow the absorption of sugar into cells.

When it comes to diabetes, legumes—beans, chickpeas, peas, lentils, and soybeans—also pack star power. Like whole grains, legumes are digested slowly, allowing a gentle rise in blood sugar and a reduced rise in insulin levels. And legumes are a wonderful source of protein, without the heart-threatening animal fat of meat. They're easy to eat more of—just open a can of low-sodium lentil or bean soup for lunch and sprinkle black beans or chickpeas on any salad.

Soybeans in particular appear to shine. In a University of Illinois study of 14 men with advanced type 2 diabetes, the participants got half their daily protein from soy protein, which significantly lowered protein in the urine—a sign of kidney damage—and raised levels of HDL, or good cholesterol. And a number of studies indicate that soy can help regulate both glucose and insulin levels.

One note of caution: Add fiber to your menu gradually, or you may end up with intestinal gas and bloating. Also, the more fiber you eat, the more liquids you should drink.

**Aim for:** 25 to 35 grams of fiber per day. A half cup of chickpeas has 10.2 grams, and 1/4 cup of bran cereal has 26. Three good ways to get more fiber are to have whole-grain cereal for breakfast (look for one with at least 5 grams of fiber per serving), switch to whole-wheat bread for sandwiches, and eat at least one bean-based meal per week.

## Cinnamon

Care for some cinnamon on your oatmeal? Studies have found that cinnamon lowers blood sugar, cholesterol (including bad cholesterol, or LDL), and triglycerides (heart-threatening fats in the bloodstream) and boosts the efficiency of insulin, all factors important in fighting diabetes and heart disease. Certain compounds in cinnamon help cells take in glucose to use as energy, as insulin does, which in turn lowers blood sugar. Cinnamon also contains manganese, a mineral that appears to help the body use blood sugar.

The results are impressive. Cinnamon appears to increase the body's ability to use glucose by 20 percent. One study showed that eating 1/4 to 1 1/4 teaspoons a day for 40 days reduced blood glucose levels by 18 to 29 percent.

**Aim for:** A half teaspoon a day is a good target. Work up to that amount slowly in case you are allergic to cinnamon.

**Helpful hint:** Can't get enough cinnamon by adding it to applesauce, oatmeal, and toast? Add 1/2 teaspoon or so to your coffee before starting the pot. You can also add it to tea. Cinnamon's also great on sweet potatoes, a smart food (in moderation) for people with diabetes.

## Peanut butter and nuts

It's time for the return of the peanut butter sandwich (this time, on whole wheat). In the Nurses Health Study of more than 80,000 women with no history of diabetes, those who ate nuts five times a week lowered their risk of type 2 diabetes by 30 percent compared to women who never ate nuts; eating peanut butter five times a week cut risk by 20 percent. Researchers aren't clear why peanuts helped. It could be the magnesium, the unsaturated fats, the fiber, or a healthier lifestyle among people who grab nuts for a snack. Monounsaturated fats, which make up

### FEATURED RECIPES

**Ultimate Spiced Nuts** p. 592
**Lentil-Tomato Soup** p. 603
**Mac 'n Cheese Primavera** p. 608
**Three-Bean Chili** p. 610
**Roasted Salmon with Sautéed Greens** p. 613
**Chicken-Barley Bake** p. 616
**Roasted Root Vegetables** p. 622
**Springtime Quinoa** p. 626
**Frozen Fruit Mousse** p. 638
**Rice Pudding** p. 638
**Mixed Berry Tart** p. 639

85 percent of the fat in most nuts, may reduce insulin resistance, so swapping carb-rich foods such as pretzels for good-fat-rich foods such as nuts is a wise move. Replacing meats with nuts occasionally is a good idea, too.

Aim for: About an ounce—a small handful—of nuts or about a tablespoon of peanut butter five times a week.

Helpful hint: Nuts are high in calories, with at least 150 per ounce. Subtract an ounce or two of meat or a serving of refined grains to keep your calories in balance when you add nuts.

# Olive oil

One of life's great justices is that olive oil tastes wonderful *and* improves health conditions, including diabetes. A number of studies have shown that it lowers blood sugar as well as heart disease risk. One of the most recent, a Spanish study of 772 people at high risk for heart disease, showed that people assigned a diet high in olive oil or nuts had significantly lower blood sugar levels, blood pressure, and cholesterol than those on a low-fat diet.

Olive oil is monounsaturated, which means it's a healthier fat than saturated fats like butter. It's also loaded with antioxidants.

Aim for: Enjoy at least a tablespoon a day in place of other oils.

Helpful hint: Olive oil can lose its valuable nutrients—beta-carotene, vitamin E, and other antioxidants—when exposed to light, so store it in a dark, cool place. If your oil turns cloudy, it's time to throw it away.

## NUTRITIONAL SUPPLEMENTS

**Vitamins C and E, zinc, and magnesium.** Antioxidants such as vitamins C and E and the mineral zinc help counter free radical damage that ups the risk of diabetes-related complications like heart disease and nerve damage. Magnesium appears to help cells use insulin. Deficiencies, which are common in people with diabetes, may promote diabetes-related eye damage. Several studies have found that taking these supplements in the dosages listed below for three months significantly lowered blood sugar levels, increased "good" HDL cholesterol, and reduced blood pressure. The nutrients can also lower infection risk, which is important since people with diabetes are more susceptible to infection than those without diabetes. **DOSAGE:** *Vitamin C:* 500 to 1,000 milligrams daily. *Vitamin E:* 400 IU daily. *Magnesium:* 300 to 600 milligrams daily. *Zinc:* 30 milligrams daily.

**Calcium and vitamin D.** A 20-year study by Boston researchers of almost 84,000 nurses, none of whom had diabetes at the study's start, found that women who took 1,200 milligrams of calcium and 800 IU of vitamin D per day had a 33 percent lower risk of developing type 2 diabetes than women who consumed much lower amounts.

Not all calcium supplements are equally well absorbed. The body absorbs the calcium from chewable supplements better than from pills. **DOSAGE:** *Calcium:* Boston researchers found that 1,200 milligrams daily lowered risk of type 2 diabetes. To improve absorption, take it in two doses, one in the morning and one at night. *Vitamin D:* 400 to 800 IU daily.

There's more to peanut butter than just sandwiches. Peanut butter can be the central ingredient in all types of sauces and glazes, including some particularly yummy Asian-style dips. It's an ingredient in many muffin, soup, and cookie recipes as well.

## Is a Glass of Wine Fine?

Uncork the Burgundy. In a 12-year Harvard study, researchers found that men without diabetes who consumed even less than one drink per day five days a week lowered their risk of type 2 diabetes by 36 percent compared to infrequent drinkers. Moderate amounts of alcohol also lower the risk of heart disease. We're not suggesting you become the new life of the party, but a little indulgence may help. Drinking alcohol by itself increases the risk of low blood sugar, so be sure to eat a meal with that glass of red or white or that beer, and include the alcohol in your calorie count. And skip those high-calorie, high-carbohydrate "umbrella-sporting" cocktails.

## OFF THE MENU

**Sugar and refined grains.** If the food on your plate looks as white as snow, it's time for a new, more colorful menu. Refining grains strips them of nutrients and often fiber. Foods made with white flour and/or sugar digest too quickly, spiking blood sugar. In fact, researchers believe that diets high in these foods lay the groundwork for type 2 diabetes by putting on pounds and increasing the risk of insulin resistance and metabolic syndrome. You don't have to deny yourself all these foods all the time, but try to cut back, slowly switching to more whole grains and higher-fiber foods. Limit yourself to one or two small desserts a week, dividing a portion with a friend. If you typically slurp down sugary sodas or fruit juice, switch to water or other calorie-free drinks.

**High-fat dairy products, red meats, margarine, and other foods high in saturated fats or trans fat.** Next time you have steak for dinner, take a look at your plate after the trimmings cool. The congealed saturated fat isn't any lovelier in your arteries, upping your risk of heart disease, a risk already high for people with diabetes. Based on data from an 18-year study of almost 6,000 women with type 2 diabetes, Harvard researchers estimate that replacing just 5 percent of the calories you get from saturated fat with calories from carbohydrates would cut the risk of heart disease by 22 percent; replacing them with monounsaturated fat (found in plant foods like olives, nuts, seeds, and avocados) would lower the risk by 37 percent.

Regardless of heart disease risk, saturated fat is just plain bad for people with diabetes. Studies show that it increases insulin resistance by increasing inflammation and making cell membranes less flexible so insulin has more trouble getting blood sugar into cells.

Trans fat is just as bad or worse. A 14-year Harvard study found that replacing even 2 percent of calories from trans fatty acids—those hydrogenated oils found in commercial cakes, cookies, and fried foods—with polyunsaturated fats, like those in corn or safflower oil, appeared to lower risk of type 2 diabetes by 40 percent.

## Should You Kiss Meat Goodbye?

A dinner of tabbouleh, sliced fresh tomatoes, and marinated chickpeas sounds tasty—and the fact that it doesn't contain meat may help control your diabetes. In a study by the Physicians Committee for Responsible Medicine and Georgetown University, researchers placed seven people with type 2 diabetes on a high-fiber, low-fat vegan diet of unrefined vegetables, grains, beans, and fruit for three months. Four other people followed the American Diabetes Association (ADA) diet, which includes lots of plant foods but also chicken and fish.

The fasting blood sugar levels of the vegans decreased 59 percent more than those of the nonvegans. The vegans also lost an average of 16 pounds, compared to 8 pounds for the nonvegans, and they needed less insulin to control their blood sugar. (The ADA group's insulin dosages didn't change.) Protein loss in the urine—a sign of diabetic kidney damage—dropped in the vegan group but got worse in the other group.

Of course, this study was very small. But in a larger, 21-year study of 26,000 Seventh Day Adventists, all vegetarians, the risk of death from diabetes was half that of the white population in the United States.

Maybe you won't scrape your plate of all animal products today—a big change from the typical Western diet—but these studies do drive home the importance of whole grains, vegetables, and other plant foods.

# DIARRHEA

When you eat, food passes through the stomach and the small intestine, accumulating liquid as it goes so that by the time waste reaches the large intestine, it's quite watery. Much of that liquid is then absorbed through the large intestine. But when triggers like bacteria or viruses interrupt that process, the intestinal walls can become inflamed, making it difficult for them to absorb liquid. The result: diarrhea.

Diarrhea usually clears up pretty quickly. To baby your bowels in the meantime, choose foods that are easy to digest and "binding" foods that help reverse the problem. Even more important is replacing lost fluids.

## YOUR FOOD PRESCRIPTION

### Apple juice, water, herbal tea,
*and other clear fluids*

Diarrhea can deplete the body of fluids and lead to dehydration. Water replenishes lost liquids, as do other clear liquids like apple juice and broths, which also help replace salts and minerals lost to diarrhea. Avoid citrus, pineapple, tomato, and other juices that you can't see through because the acid in them can irritate already inflamed intestines.

**Aim for:** Start with sips of clear liquid and work your way up to drinking a cup every half hour.

### Black tea, raspberry-leaf tea, and red tea

Tannins in tea bind the mucous membranes in the intestines and help the body absorb fluids while calming inflammation in the intestinal tract. Blackberry and raspberry-leaf teas are particularly helpful. Be sure to choose those that contain real leaves rather than just flavoring, and opt for decaffeinated teas, since caffeine is dehydrating. Red teas, now becoming more commonly available, can calm spasms in the colon.

**Aim for:** Three to four cups a day.

### Rehydration solutions

When diarrhea continues for several days, it can disrupt the balance of electrolytes, especially sodium and potassium, in the body. Without these minerals to influence the proper distribution of fluids, the body is vulnerable to dehydration, which can be serious, particularly in children. Sports drinks like Gatorade replenish electrolytes, but they pack a wallop of sugar, which can worsen diarrhea. Better choices are oral rehydration solutions, sold over the counter at pharmacies (try Pedialyte for children). You can also make your own rehydration solution:

    1 quart water
    1/4 teaspoon salt
    1/4 teaspoon baking soda
    2 tablespoons sugar or honey

Place the ingredients in a pitcher or other container and stir until the salt, baking soda, and sugar are completely dissolved.

**Aim for:** Use rehydration solutions as directed. Sip homemade solutions frequently for a total of 3 quarts daily.

### White rice

Foods such as white rice and those made with white flour, which are generally lacking in fiber, tend to constipate people who eat them a lot, which is why they'll work well for you now.

**Aim for:** Eat 1/2-cup portions until diarrhea is under control.

## Bananas

A ripe banana is often a baby's first food because it's bland and easy to digest, which also makes it a perfect snack when your "waste management system" is out of whack. Bananas also have plenty of the electrolyte potassium, which can be depleted by diarrhea.

**Aim for:** One or two a day while diarrhea persists.

## Unsweetened applesauce

Part of the BRAT (bananas, rice, applesauce, and toast) diet recommended for diarrhea, applesauce contains pectin, a fiber that helps counteract the runs by soaking up extra fluid in the intestine. Avoid raw apples, which won't do the trick.

**Aim for:** 1/4 to 1/2 cup every hour or so.

## Yogurt with active cultures

Brands that contain active cultures of beneficial bacteria can help prevent and treat diarrhea caused by "bad" bacteria. If your diarrhea is a side effect of antibiotics, which kill both good and bad bacteria, it's especially important to replenish the "good guys."

**Aim for:** 1/2 cup twice a day.

### NUTRITIONAL SUPPLEMENTS

**Probiotics.** If you don't tolerate the lactose in yogurt, consider taking probiotics to fortify the "good" bacteria in your gut that can help keep diarrhea at bay. **DOSAGE:** Take no more than one to two billion live organisms once a day. Higher doses sometimes cause intestinal discomfort.

***Saccharomyces boulardii* (SB).** Studies have shown that this yeast can help prevent traveler's diarrhea and diarrhea caused by infections and antibiotics. **DOSAGE:** 500 milligrams four times a day.

## *When Water Is a Risk*

If you're traveling to a developing country where water supplies may not be clean, follow these tips to avoid bacteria that cause diarrhea.

• Never drink tap water or use it to brush your teeth. Drink sealed water, juices and sodas or boiled drinks.

• Avoid ice, raw fruits and vegetables, and salads. You can eat fruits and vegetables that you have peeled yourself.

• Avoid raw or rare meat or fish and make sure cooked meat or fish is hot when served to you.

• Don't buy food from street vendors.

• Avoid unpasteurized milk and cheeses.

**Carob powder.** Rich in tannins that help bind the mucous membranes in the intestinal tract, carob, a legume sometimes used as an alternative to cocoa, is particularly effective for young children with diarrhea. **DOSAGE:** For children, 1 gram for every 1.5 pounds of weight, up to 15 grams, divided into three equal doses and mixed with applesauce or yogurt. For adults, a total of 15 to 20 grams per day.

### OFF THE MENU

**Doughnuts, ice cream, french fries, and other foods with a lot of fat or sugar.** Fat can be difficult to digest, and sugar can make diarrhea worse by feeding diarrhea-promoting bacteria.

**Foods and chewing gums that contain sorbitol.** Too much sorbitol, a sugar substitute used in some foods, mints, and chewing gums, can cause diarrhea.

**Milk and other dairy foods.** If you can't digest lactose, you probably develop diarrhea and bloating when you eat dairy. The sugars in milk can also worsen existing diarrhea from other causes.

**Alcohol and caffeine.** Both are diuretics.

**Vitamin C supplements.** High doses (several thousand milligrams) can trigger diarrhea.

# DIVERTICULOSIS

Imagine a bicycle inner tube freckled with weak spots that can give way, bubbling out like air-filled blisters. The same thing can happen to your large intestine, a.k.a. colon.

The weak spots in this case can give way to marble-size protruding pouches called diverticula. If you have them, you have diverticulosis.

Scientists aren't sure what causes it, but they do know the condition is more common with age. It's also more common in Western societies, where people tend to overdose on low-fiber foods like white bread and shy away from high-fiber foods like fruits, vegetables, and whole grains. In fact, diverticulosis barely existed prior to 1900, when highly refined flour was a thing of the future.

Fiber is a colon's best friend. It bulks up and softens stool so it can make a timely, smooth exit. Low-fiber diets, on the other hand, create hard, dry, small stools akin to rocks that pile up and stay put. The effort to move them out causes pressure that can damage the intestine's walls by causing those nasty pouches to form. If stool or bacteria get caught in them, trouble's knocking. You may need antibiotics or even surgery.

Rest assured, you don't have to start eating twigs and berries (well, the berries are a good idea). If you have diverticulosis, you can help prevent painful symptoms by doing something as simple as changing your breakfast cereal, snacking on fruit, and eating beans more often. You might as well take the plunge, because these are the same habits that are key to just about every other aspect of good health.

## YOUR FOOD PRESCRIPTION

## Whole grains, fruits, vegetables, *and other foods rich in fiber*

You may have rolled your eyes whenever your mother mentioned the benefits of "roughage," but fiber is remarkably critical for keeping you and your colon in good health. It can help prevent diverticulosis and, if you have the condition already, help prevent painful inflammation of the diverticula.

There are two different types of fiber, and both help. Insoluble fiber, found in most fruits, vegetables, and whole grains, absorbs water to bulk up and soften stools so they can pass easily. Soluble fiber, found in oatmeal, eggplant, lentils, apples, pears, and blueberries, dissolves in water, becoming soft and sticky in the intestine. Recently, doctors have found that it too can help prevent constipation, although they aren't sure how. It's also the kind of fiber that helps lower cholesterol.

If you're not eating much fiber now, you can easily "swell" your daily servings by switching to a breakfast cereal that contains at least 5 grams of fiber per serving; eating bread with a first ingredient listed as "whole"; switching to whole-grain pasta and brown rice; and eating more fruits, vegetables, and beans. To get the most fiber from fruits and vegetables, eat the skin on those apples and potatoes. (Consider buying organic.) An easy way to boost your vegetable and fiber intake is to eat a salad every day.

Aim for: 25 to 35 grams of fiber per day. Get there by eating 2 cups of fruit, 2 1/2 cups of vegetables, three 1-ounce servings of whole grains, and 1 cup of legumes (beans and peas).

Helpful hint: Don't add heaps of fiber to your diet all at once, or you may induce new intestinal outcries: gas and bloating. Aim to make one change a week. Start by adding an extra serving of fruit or vegetables to the menu. The following week, swap your white bread for whole wheat, and so on.

## Water, juice, *and other fluids*

As you increase the amount of fiber in your meals, it's important to also increase the amount of fluids you drink. Fiber absorbs the fluid and as a result, it bulks up and softens stools. Without enough water, fiber can cause constipation.

Aim for: Eight 8-ounce glasses a day.

### NUTRITIONAL SUPPLEMENTS

**Fiber.** Supplements that have concentrated natural fibers like psyllium husk or wheat dextrin can be useful if dietary fiber isn't doing the trick for you. Be sure to drink plenty of water when taking them so they can work properly, and don't take them for more than seven days without a physician's guidance. **DOSAGE:** Follow the label directions. Some of these supplements come in capsule form, and others are powders to be added to beverages or soft foods.

### OFF THE MENU

**Refined grains and sugary foods.** If fiber is your colon's best friend, foods that fall short on fiber, like white bread, cookies and most baked goods, packaged snack foods, and most sugary cereals, are ones you shouldn't spend much time with. Even fruit juices aren't perfect because they lack the fiber of whole fruit. It's still important to consume plenty of liquids, but after one glass of juice, favor water or herbal tea the rest of the day.

## A Questionable Nut

For years, doctors suspected that nuts and seeds could easily lodge in the pouches that line the large intestine of people with diverticulosis and cause infection. But there is no scientific evidence to support that theory, and few doctors subscribe to it anymore. In fact, nuts and seeds, including popcorn hulls, sesame and poppy seeds, and almonds, all contain fiber that may actually help people with diverticulosis. That said, each person reacts differently to foods. If you experience bloating or pain after eating certain foods, including nuts, be sure to chew them thoroughly before swallowing. If that doesn't help, avoid them.

### FEATURED RECIPES

Buckwheat Pancakes with Fruit Sauce *p. 590*
Spinach Salad with Chickpeas *p. 597*
Ginger Butternut Squash Soup *p. 602*
Hearty Vegetable Stew *p. 608*
Three-Bean Chili *p. 610*
Chicken-Barley Bake *p. 616*
Turkey Ragu with Spaghetti *p. 618*

# ECZEMA

Most of us take our birthday suits for granted, but for people with eczema, skin can be a constant source of itching and irritation. Eczema often targets babies and children, but anyone can have it. Areas on the face, wrists, hands, and inner creases of the knees and elbows dry, flake, swell, and sometimes blister. The itching is relentless, and over time, itchy patches can thicken and turn a grayish brown.

Eczema appears to have a genetic link and also seems to stem from an oversensitive immune system that produces a response just short of a true allergic reaction. That response is often to certain foods that trigger eczema or make it worse. Avoiding those foods is key, of course, but so is getting more of other foods that seem to bring relief.

## YOUR FOOD PRESCRIPTION

### Salmon, herring, anchovies, *and other foods rich in omega-3 fatty acids*

Go figure: The very creatures that sport the ultimate scaly skin are those that offer some of the best protection from eczema. Salmon and the other foods above are good sources of the omega-3 fatty acids that our bodies need to grow new skin, prevent inflammation, and stave off conditions like eczema. They're particularly rich in a key component of omega-3s known as EPA, which helps reduce skin inflammation. Studies on relieving the symptoms and causes of eczema have focused more on fish oils than on fish itself, but the evidence has convinced plenty of dermatologists to emphasize the importance of fish in the diet.

Tired of salmon? Try canned sardines, which are excellent sources of omega-3s. Sauté some onion and garlic in olive oil and add sardines canned in tomato sauce. When they're heated, pour over whole-wheat pasta and toss with lemon juice and grated Parmesan.

**Aim for:** Two to three servings of fatty fish a week. Dine on fish for dinner once or twice a week, enjoy a sandwich of canned tuna or salmon, or stuff a tomato with tuna salad.

**Helpful hint:** Some people have allergic reactions to fish that may worsen rather than relieve the symptoms of eczema. If you're prone to allergies, work with your doctor or a registered dietitian to determine whether fish is among your problem foods.

### Oolong tea

A staple in Chinese pantries, oolong tea tastes like a cross between robust black tea and more bitter green tea. In a month-long study in Japan, people with eczema who drank three cups of oolong tea felt relief from their itching

## FEATURED RECIPES

**Tuna and White Bean Salad** *p. 599*
**Open-Faced Sardine Sandwiches** *p. 604*
**Tuna Kebabs** *p. 610*
**Fish Tacos** *p. 611*
**Salmon Steaks with Peach Salsa** *p. 612*

in just one week, and 63 percent of the 118 volunteers continued to improve over the next three weeks. The researchers suspect that polyphenols (a class of antioxidants) in the tea may help repair skin. Other studies have shown that the astringent tannins in tea may also work to reduce inflammation.

Aim for: Three cups daily, made by steeping the tea in hot water for at least 3 minutes.

# Yogurt with live cultures

The beneficial bacteria in these yogurts (and other fermented foods such as kefir) benefit the immune system, especially the many immune cells located in the intestinal tract. The "good" bacteria (a.k.a. probiotics) seem to affect inflammation and stimulate the body to produce certain white blood cells and antibodies as well as various growth factors that are important for keeping the body from overreacting to allergens. Studies have indicated that probiotics are especially important for infants and children, whose immune systems are still developing. Two of these bacteria, *Lactobacillus acidophilus* and *bifidobacterium,* also help your body to better absorb nutrients, including "good" fats that help ward off eczema.

Aim for: One to two cups per day.

## NUTRITIONAL SUPPLEMENTS

**Probiotics.** A number of studies have looked closely at how probiotics may offer protection from eczema for pregnant women and infants. In Finland, researchers who studied 230 babies with eczema first removed cow's milk from the diets of the babies and their nursing mothers. They then gave half of the babies daily probiotic supplements and the rest placebos. All the infants improved, but those given the probiotics experienced a 30 percent greater improvement than those given the placebo. Researchers suspect that the beneficial bacteria help to establish a strong immune system early in a child's development. Probiotics have also been found to be effective in older children. **DOSAGE:** For babies, check with your pediatrician about

supplementing formula or breast milk with a probiotic powder. Pregnant and nursing mothers should take a one million–count capsule containing *lactobacillus* and *bifidus* twice daily.

**Omega-3 fatty acids.** Especially for kids who won't eat fish, fish-oil capsules may be the best way to get enough of the omega-3s, especially EPA, that help keep skin inflammation at bay. In one study, EPA-rich fish-oil capsules taken over three months by people with eczema eased itching and inflammation by 30 percent. **DOSAGE:** For adults, four 1-gram fish-oil capsules a day (be sure they contain EPA). You may have to take the oil for at least 12 weeks before noticing an effect. For children, look for fish oil in a liquid or chewable tablets formulated for kids. They're flavored, making them a much easier sell. Follow the dosage directions on the label.

## OFF THE MENU

**Cow's milk, eggs, wheat, soy foods, and nuts.** These trigger foods commonly cause reactions in children prone to allergies and may worsen eczema. The best way to determine if certain foods are making things worse is to follow an elimination diet in which you cut out the most likely allergens for two weeks and then reintroduce them one by one to see how your body reacts. It's best to enlist the help of a physician or registered dietitian to get the clearest results and make sure you don't end up scratching foods from your diet for no good reason.

**Coffee.** Some adults with eczema experience more dramatic symptoms when they drink coffee. It may be that the body sees coffee as an irritant. One explanation is that coffee can promote acidity in the body, which in turn can promote inflammation. Try eliminating it for three weeks to see if it helps.

**Red meat.** Because red meat contains fatty acids that promote inflammation, you may find it helpful to limit burgers, pot roasts, and the like during flare-ups.

# FATIGUE

If walking to your mailbox or making it through the day without a nap seems beyond your current energy level, you may be suffering from fatigue. It has many causes, including stress, medications, overwork, sleep difficulties, or illness. If your fatigue is chronic or extreme, ask a doctor to check you out. But once you're certain that your tiredness doesn't stem from a medical problem, it may be time to reconsider your diet. Plenty of all-too-common eating habits sap energy—and plenty of relatively simple fixes can inject more oomph into your day.

## YOUR FOOD PRESCRIPTION

### Fish, meat, dairy products, beans, *and other foods high in protein*

If you're someone who eats salads with no meat, fish, or beans for lunch and then craves an afternoon nap, snubbing protein may be your problem. Studies have shown that people who skip protein at breakfast, for instance, are more apt to be depressed, stressed, and less physically fit than those who regularly add protein to their plates. Amino acids, which make up proteins, are the body's building blocks, growing and repairing everything from blood vessels to hair. Amino acids also help increase levels of neurotransmitters that in turn boost mood and alertness. And eating protein at every meal helps ensure steady blood sugar levels—and steady energy.

**Aim for:** A good rule of thumb is simply to eat some protein with every meal. If you'd rather go by the numbers, you need 0.36 gram of protein per pound of body weight. For example, if you weigh 150 pounds, you need 54 grams of protein. One serving of beef tenderloin has 32 grams of protein; 1 cup of black beans, 15 grams; and 1 cup of milk, 8 grams.

### Red meat, molasses, beans, *and other foods high in iron*

Iron isn't just strong; it offers strength. It's essential to red blood cells, combining with protein and copper to make hemoglobin, the part of red blood cells that carries oxygen. Iron deficiency is the most common cause of anemia, leading to a low volume of red blood cells that results in fatigue. Symptoms include weakness, pallor, fatigue, and brittle nails. If you suspect anemia, check with your doctor. Most cases are caused by blood loss (for example, from a bleeding ulcer or heavy menstrual flow).

**Aim for:** The recommended amount of iron is 8 milligrams per day for men and menopausal women and 18 milligrams for menstruating women. One 3-ounce serving of beef has 3.2 grams, and a cup of soybeans provides 8.8.

**Helpful hint:** Our bodies absorb iron much better from meat than from plant foods. If you get most of your iron from vegetarian sources like beans and peas, eat them with foods like citrus fruits that are high in vitamin C, which aids iron absorption.

## FEATURED RECIPES

**Zucchini Frittata** *p. 591*

**Edamame Hummus with Pita Crisps** *p. 592*

**Spinach Salad with Chickpeas** *p. 597*

**Shrimp and Grapefruit Salad** *p. 598*

**Sweet Potato Soup** *p. 601*

**Roasted Salmon with Sautéed Greens** *p. 613*

**Chicken-Barley Bake** *p. 616*

**Creamed Spinach** *p. 624*

## Whole grains, fruits, vegetables,
### and other complex carbohydrates

Carbohydrates are the body's primary energy source, but many of us eat too many "simple" carbs that digest quickly, sending blood sugar on a wild ride that saps energy. Choose complex-carb foods like brown rice over white, an orange over a glass of orange juice, and raisin bran cereal over sugar pops to get a steady supply of energy instead of a candy-bar burst followed by a slump. In a British study of 142 people who ate high-fiber cereal at breakfast for two weeks, the volunteers had more energy, mental clarity, and less emotional upset than they did when they went back eating to their usual breakfasts.

Another reason to get your fill of whole grains: They're a good source of B vitamins. Run low on Bs, and you're apt to slump. They have many functions, including the breakdown of carbohydrates, fats, and proteins into glucose, the fuel our bodies run on. They're also involved in the production of red blood cells.

**Aim for:** In addition to the recommended 7 to 10 daily servings of fruits and vegetables, aim to get at least three carbohydrate servings from whole grains like whole wheat or brown rice. A serving of bread is one slice; a serving of rice is 1/2 cup.

## Pumpkin seeds, spinach,
### and other foods high in magnesium

Popeye's spinach habit wasn't for naught. One of its nutrients, magnesium, is essential for the production of a molecule called adenosine triphosphate, the end product of food's conversion to energy. Magnesium also relaxes muscles and aids sleep. If we don't have enough, we feel tired and weak.

**Aim for:** 400 to 420 milligrams of magnesium daily for men; 310 to 320 milligrams for women. A quarter cup of pumpkin seeds has 185 milligrams; a cup of cooked spinach has 157.

## Eat and Drink Often

Sometimes fatigue is simply a signal that you're hungry and thirsty. Eating small meals throughout the day, or three meals and two smart snacks like nuts and fresh fruit, helps keep your blood sugar stable, which fends off fatigue. Choose fresh fruit over dried, which has more sugar. Unsweetened yogurt's a great snack, too, full of protein and carbs without lots of sugar and calories.

Water is also crucial. Without it, your body works at keeping a fluid balance instead of producing energy molecules. The Institute of Medicine suggests that women consume at least 11 cups of fluids a day and men 16 cups (about 20 percent of those fluids come from food).

## Citrus fruits, peppers, broccoli,
### and other foods high in vitamin C

When 17th-century sailors swooning with scurvy sipped lemon juice, their lethargy vanished. Present-day studies have found that vitamin C deficiency is associated with fatigue. C is necessary for a healthy adrenal system, which helps prevent fatigue from physical or emotional stress. It also helps fight off infections and helps us absorb iron.

**Aim for:** The recommended amount is 75 milligrams a day for women and 90 milligrams a day for men, but more is better in this case. One red bell pepper has about twice that amount; a cup of broccoli also provides more than the quota.

**Helpful hint:** Cooking reduces vitamin C by about 25 percent, so eat some fruits and veggies raw.

## Sweet potatoes, carrots,
### and other foods high in beta-carotene

Add color to your plate, and you'll add energy to your step. Beta-carotene, the vitamin A precursor that puts the color in carrots, sweet potatoes, and spinach, helps boost a depressed immune system, often at the root of chronic fatigue. By promoting healthy cell membranes, beta-carotene boosts protection from viruses, bacteria, fungi, and allergies. It also ups the activity of T cells, which fight infections, and it's necessary for healthy red blood cells.

**Aim for:** Make five of your daily produce servings leafy dark green vegetables and yellow or orange fruits and vegetables.

**Helpful hint:** Lightly steaming (not overcooking) foods like carrots and spinach can help your body absorb their beta-carotene.

## Spinach, avocados, squash,
### and other foods high in potassium

Run short on potassium, and you risk muscle weakness and exhaustion. Studies have shown that people low on potassium have weaker hand grips than people with enough of the nutrient. In studies of chronic fatigue, potassium and magnesium supplements have returned lost zip. Potassium helps transport nutrients to cells, maintain water balance, regulate muscle contraction, and maintain a healthy nervous system and heart rate.

**Aim for:** 4,700 milligrams of potassium per day. One cup of cooked spinach has 839 milligrams; an avocado, 875; and a cup of winter squash, 896.

**Helpful hint:** Potassium decreases the excretion of calcium, so boosting your potassium intake also helps keep your bones healthy.

## NUTRITIONAL SUPPLEMENTS

**Iron.** Pregnant women and women of child-bearing age, infants, toddlers, teenage girls, and people with kidney failure are most likely to benefit from iron supplements, either because they need more iron than most people, run low on the mineral, or absorb it poorly. However, because excess iron can cause organ damage (children are especially susceptible to overdose), take supplements only under medical supervision. The doctor will probably do a blood test to determine whether you could benefit from supplements. Ferrous iron salts are the best absorbed form. **DOSAGE:** The upper limit set by the Institute of Medicine is 45 milligrams per day.

**B-complex vitamins.** Most multivitamins contain the dosages of B vitamins you need daily. **DOSAGE:** One multivitamin a day.

**Vitamin C.** People who have frequent colds or infections, who smoke, or who suffer from stress can benefit from vitamin C supplements. Vitamin C boosts the immune system and helps get rid of toxins. High doses (5,000 milligrams or more) can cause diarrhea. The National Academy of Sciences has set an upper tolerable level of 2,000 milligrams a day. **DOSAGE:** The recommended daily amounts are 75 milligrams for women, 90 milligrams for men, and 100 milligrams for smokers. Studies show that 1,000 milligrams a day may shorten a cold and lower markers of stress, such as levels of the stress hormone cortisol and high blood pressure, as well as subjective feelings of stress.

**Magnesium.** People who have digestive problems like diarrhea, malabsorption, or ulcerative colitis may need to take magnesium supplements. Physical stressors such as colds, trauma, and surgery can also lead to a magnesium deficiency, as can alcoholism and kidney disease. Chelated forms like magnesium citrate are better absorbed than nonchelated forms like magnesium oxide. **DOSAGE:** The amount varies depending on the cause of the deficiency. Check with a doctor if you suspect you are deficient. Signs include loss of appetite, nausea, and fatigue.

## OFF THE MENU

**Sugar, caffeine, and alcohol.** A dip in blood sugar may send you for a sugary pick-me-up or a caffeinated soda. Neither will do you any good in the long run. Sugar gives you a brief burst of energy, but afterward, you may feel even more tired than before.

But what about caffeine? Anyone who's awakened with their eyelids drooping by their nose would swear by it. Caffeine wakes you up by stimulating your central nervous system and increasing your heart and breathing rate. But its effect wears off, leaving you needing more. And if you consume it too late in the day, it can keep you up at night. Cut it out for a month to see if you have more energy.

Finally, how about a drink in the evening? Despite alcohol's initial boost to your spirits, it's a depressant that eventually puts you to sleep—but only for a while. You wake up later on as it withdraws from your system. The result: The life of the party drags the following day.

## The Power of Breakfast

By the time you lift your head off the pillow, your tank is on empty. Without a healthy breakfast like cereal, milk, and fruit that combines whole grains, protein, and a little fat, you'll be nodding off before noon. A number of studies show that people who eat breakfast concentrate better and are more productive than those who go without. They also tend to have better control over their weight because they're not ravenous by lunchtime.

For the typical adult, a healthy breakfast should fall between 300 and 400 calories. That's not a lot of food—and that's a good thing, particularly for those people who have a false notion that it's not a real meal if it doesn't involve cooking or serious preparation. A healthy breakfast often takes just a minute to put together, and just a few minutes to eat. So no excuses for skipping it! Here are some great options:

• A bowl of high-fiber, multigrain cereal, lots of strawberries, and low-fat milk.

• A granola bar, an apple, and a glass of cold milk.

• A cup of nonfat yogurt with fresh blueberries mixed in, and a slice of whole-wheat toast with fruit spread.

• A scrambled egg, a whole-wheat roll, fresh fruit salad, and a cup of low-fat milk.

# FOOD ALLERGIES AND SENSITIVITIES

For most people, food is a source of great pleasure. But for others, nature's bounty is more of a minefield of edible hazards—foods that trigger unpleasant side effects (usually due to a food intolerance) or even life-threatening reactions (usually due to a food allergy). The answer, of course, is to avoid the offenders while filling your plate with equally nutritious foods. But oftentimes that's easier said than done. The following advice should help.

First, let's clear up the difference between food allergies and food intolerances. If you're allergic to a food—say, nuts or shellfish—trouble usually starts almost as soon as you put down your fork (although some allergic reactions are delayed by 24 to 72 hours). You may feel your mouth and tongue itch or your tongue and throat swell. You may have trouble breathing. In the most serious scenario, you may develop a severe and sometimes fatal form of shock called anaphylaxis.

Food allergies involve an immune system reaction by antibodies called immunoglobulin E (IgE) or by immune cells called lymphocytes in the GI tract. The antibodies and immune cells are designed to protect the body from foreign invaders—in this case, particular foods.

If the immune system's not involved, you have a food intolerance or sensitivity, often caused by a problem in the metabolism or digestion of the food. Although food intolerances can affect your health, they don't pose an immediate threat to life.

Sometimes food sensitivities and allergies are hard to distinguish since symptoms overlap. Both can cause gastrointestinal trouble, including cramps, diarrhea, and nausea. Some foods, like dairy products, can elicit both true allergic reactions and nonallergic ones. The most common food allergies and sensitivities are those to wheat, gluten, dairy products, soy, eggs, peanuts, nuts, fish, and shellfish.

For both allergies and sensitivities, it's important to see a doctor for testing to confirm what you're reacting to (see "Protecting Yourself" on page 465). And obviously, part of the treatment will involve eliminating the foods that cause a reaction without sacrificing essential nutrients. Unfortunately, food allergies can't be prevented or cured, but some, like milk or egg allergies in children, diminish or even vanish with age. The good news is that most foods that cause reactions have tasty substitutes that may even broaden your palate. Who knew that millet and buckwheat could be such delicious substitutes for wheat, or that soy milk could actually boost the flavor of breakfast cereal when milk's not an option? Read on for some suggestions to keep both health and taste on your plate.

### FOR PEOPLE WHO CAN'T EAT WHEAT:

## Corn, rice, millet, barley, oats,
*and all other grains except wheat*

Relatively few people have an IgE-mediated wheat allergy beyond a very young age; many more have celiac disease and must live a gluten-free life, which means no wheat, rye, barley, or spelt (see the entry on gluten avoidance below). If you do have a wheat allergy, know that it's one of the most powerful food allergies. The first step is to stop eating wheat and any food containing it, such as wheat starch or soy sauce. To replace wheat, a good source of whole grain, choose whole, unprocessed wheat substitutes like cornmeal, brown rice, or millet, which offer the same B vitamins and fiber.

Aim for: Six to eight 1/2-cup servings daily.

Helpful hint: Spelt and kamut, lesser-known grains, are ancestral cousins of wheat that are hazardous for people with an IgE-mediated wheat allergy or celiac disease.

### FOR PEOPLE WHO CAN'T EAT GLUTEN:

## Buckwheat, flax, arrowroot, beans, millet, quinoa, rice,
*and all grains that don't contain gluten*

For people who are intolerant of gluten, a protein found in wheat, barley, kamut, rye, spelt, and triticale, baked goods are verboten. One serious form of the intolerance, celiac disease, can damage the small intestine or even be life threatening. The disease is also associated with an itchy, blistery skin rash called dermatitis herpetiformis. Even oats, which contain no gluten, can be a problem if they came in contact with gluten-containing grains during milling or storage. Fortunately, people with gluten allergy needn't go grainless. Buckwheat, corn, and other grains make excellent flours full of fiber and B vitamins. Make sure any grain you use is stored and processed in a gluten-free place.

Aim for: Six to eight 1/2-cup servings daily.

Helpful hint: Read the food label on every purchase you make. If you're still unsure whether a product contains gluten, don't eat it, and contact the manufacturer for information.

### FOR PEOPLE WHO CAN'T EAT DAIRY:

## Rice, almond, and soy milk,
*and other dairy substitutes, plus calcium-rich foods*

Milk doesn't always do a body good. It can provoke both allergies and intolerances. People with allergies react to casein or whey, which are milk protein fractions. Those with intolerances react to lactose, a sugar in cow's milk. Most of us produce enough of an enzyme called lactase to avoid a reaction to lactose, but for those who don't, lactose heads to the large intestine, where trouble begins.

In either case, the symptoms aren't pretty: Lactose intolerance causes gas and diarrhea; milk allergy can cause those GI symptoms as well as a skin rash and asthma, and it may take as long as two days for the reaction to hit, although the effects are usually more immediate. As with other foods, eliminating dairy isn't as simple as it sounds. Dairy products can lurk in unexpected places, such as breath mints, nutrition bars, and salad dressings. The less processed food you eat, the easier the job of eliminating dairy. For many of us, dairy foods are also our main source of calcium, an essential nutrient for strong bones as

### FEATURED RECIPES

**Buckwheat Pancakes with Fruit Sauce** *p. 590*
**Corn, Tomato, and Quinoa Salad** *p. 596*
**Roasted Salmon with Sautéed Greens** *p. 613*
**Brown Rice Risotto** *p. 625*
**Springtime Quinoa** *p. 626*

well as for many body functions, such as blood clotting and nerve transmission. Although drinks like rice, almond, and soy milk taste great in place of milk over cereal or in coffee, they aren't nutrient-to-nutrient matches with milk. (And most people who react to cow's milk also react to goat's milk.) So you'll want to "bone up" on foods high in calcium, such as dark leafy greens and bony sardines, as well as calcium-fortified orange juice. Yogurt is also an option, since its good-for-you bacteria produce the very enzyme needed to digest lactose.

Aim for: 1,000 to 1,200 milligrams of calcium daily, the amount in 4 ounces of tofu or 1 cup of mustard greens.

Helpful hint: Processed soy foods like soy hotdogs and sausage (but not tofu) often contain added dairy proteins, so be sure to read the label before eating any of those foods.

## FOR PEOPLE WHO CAN'T EAT EGGS:

# Fish, chicken, soybeans,
### and other low-fat proteins

Egg allergies are common in young children but are frequently outgrown. As with other food allergies, proteins are the culprits. More than half of the egg white is made of the primary protein allergen called ovalbumin; a reaction to egg yolks involves other proteins. Reactions to either part of the egg can range from mild to severe.

Eggs provide exceptional low-fat protein. Luckily, fish, chicken, and soybeans and other legumes do as well. To replace the binding, tenderizing, and leavening qualities that eggs add in baking, try ground flaxseed (it turns egg white–like when liquefied with 1/4 cup water or other liquid in a recipe), bananas, tofu, prunes, and egg replacements (if they don't contain egg whites).

Aim for: 5 to 6 ounces of protein per day.

Helpful hint: Eggs can show up not only in baked goods but also in noodles, sauces, pretzels, tartar sauce, and even wine. As always, read labels and don't eat anything you're unsure of.

## FOR PEOPLE WHO CAN'T EAT SOY:

# Meat, fish, legumes,
### and other substitutes for soy

Soy has its own problems: A handful of different proteins in soy may cause allergic reactions. To add confusion, some soy foods may cause reactions, while others may not. Soybean oil, for instance, does not contain proteins and thus may not trigger symptoms. Reactions to soy include a rash, asthma, gastrointestinal symptoms, and anaphylactic shock.

If you have to give up soy, you can still get more than your fair share of protein from fish, chicken, meat, nuts, and dairy products. One thing you can't easily get elsewhere is soy's phytoestrogens, called isoflavones, which may help protect against

*food for thought . . .*

"Up to 25 percent of adults believe they have a food allergy. Scientific studies and testing, however, find that only 1 to 2 percent of adults have a true food allergy."

— *The New Nutrition* by Felicia Busch, MPH, RD, FAD ∎

heart disease as well as certain cancers and perhaps osteoporosis. Other beans and peas offer only a small fraction of the isoflavones soybeans do, but a healthy diet full of whole grains and plenty of fruits and vegetables also provides protection against these diseases.

If you can't drink soy milk *or* cow's milk, look to almond-, oat-, and rice-based drinks as possible substitutes.

Aim for: 5 to 6 ounces of nonsoy protein per day and 3 cups of legumes weekly.

## FOR PEOPLE WHO CAN'T EAT FISH OR SHELLFISH:

# Chicken, flaxseed, walnuts,
*and other substitutes for shellfish and fish*

Nothing's fishy about an allergic reaction to fish or shellfish: It's straightforward, severe, and can even cause anaphylaxis. Seafood allergies tend to predominate in countries where people eat a lot of seafood and in people who work in the seafood industry. Unfortunately, these allergies tend to last a lifetime, and reactions can sometimes worsen with each incident. (Sufferers can sometimes become sick simply from inhaling the steam from fish as it cooks.) The reactions, which occur from 2 to 24 hours after exposure, are the classic allergy symptoms: itching, swelling, trouble breathing, upset stomach, or systemic shock.

Seafood is a delicious, low-fat source of protein. Fortunately, most people with a fish allergy can still eat shellfish, and most people with a shellfish allergy can still eat fish—and even some types of shellfish. (Some must avoid all shellfish, but most need to avoid either only the crustacean category, which includes shrimp, crab, and lobster, or only the molluscan category, which includes clams, oysters, abalone, and squid.)

Chicken, beans, and eggs can make up for the loss of protein from seafood. But fatty fish like salmon and tuna are also the best food sources of omega-3 fatty acids, powerful anti-inflammatories with heart-protecting effects. Look for these in flaxseed, walnuts, and soybeans.

Aim for: 5 to 6 ounces of protein per day and 1,000 milligrams per day of omega-3 fatty acids (the equivalent of two to four servings a week of walnuts or flaxseed).

Helpful hint: Processed foods that appear to be fishless may in fact contain seafood. Check all labels.

## FOR PEOPLE WHO CAN'T EAT PEANUTS OR TREE NUTS:

# Fish, chicken, beans, *and*
*other substitutes for peanuts and tree nuts*

Peanut and tree nut allergies are nothing to sneeze at. The most prevalent life-threatening allergies in children, they are caused by a reaction to proteins in the nut. Even a trace of nut dust can set off a reaction in a few highly sensitive individuals. Some children outgrow it, but for most, the allergy is lifelong. One theory about why it's so prevalent is that children under age 3 are given some form of nuts before their immune systems are developed enough to handle them.

Although reactions to peanuts are most common, many people who are allergic to peanuts are often also allergic to tree nuts such as cashews or almonds. Symptoms include itching, shortness of breath, swelling, and possibly anaphylactic shock.

Nuts are an excellent source of protein, healthy monounsaturated and polyunsaturated fats, and fiber. Low-fat dairy foods and chicken can replace lost protein. Fish provides both low-fat protein and healthy fats. Olive oil is also a healthy fat replacement. You can get more low-fat protein plus fiber from a plateful of beans and other legumes.

Aim for: 5 to 6 ounces of protein per day, two servings of fish per week, and 25 grams of fiber per day (about 2 cups of kidney beans).

Helpful hint: A nut isn't always a nut. Nutmeg comes from the seed of a tree, and water chestnuts are plant roots. Both are safe.

## NUTRITIONAL SUPPLEMENTS

**Calcium.** Scientists are still researching the optimal amount of calcium necessary to slow bone loss. For now, the National Academy of Sciences recommends taking the amount below. Calcium supplements also often include vitamin D, which helps the body use calcium. Vitamin K is also recommended, since it too helps calcium do its work. It's not clear how much is needed, but the Linus Pauling Institute recommends the amount commonly found in multivitamins, 10 to 25 micrograms. **DOSAGE:** *Calcium:* 1,000 to 1,200 milligrams daily. *Vitamin D:* 400 IU daily. *Vitamin K:* 10 to 25 micrograms daily.

**Omega-3 fatty acids.** Omega-3s come in fish-oil capsules or in liquids such as flaxseed oil and cod-liver oil. Buying a version with vitamin E helps prevent rancidity, as does storing the supplement in the refrigerator. People allergic to fish should not take fish-oil capsules or cod-liver oil. **DOSAGE:** Optimal dosages aren't established, but the FDA considers 1 to 3 grams daily in capsule or liquid form safe.

## OFF THE MENU

**Wheat and gluten.** Wheat and gluten allergies put the kibosh on wheat by any name: durum, semolina, kamut, rye, barley, bran, couscous, or spelt. But wheat can appear in many products without being obvious, including broth and soup bases, some candies, imitation bacon and seafood, marinades, processed meats, self-basting poultry, soy sauce, communion wafers, herbal and malt supplements, medications, and Play-Doh (a problem if it's handled).

**Dairy.** Milk and other dairy products show up in more places than Paris Hilton: breath mints, coffee whiteners, fortified cereals, protein powders, nutrition bars, and salad dressings all contain some form of dairy product. Dairy products are often used to flavor processed

Sometimes, it's not natural foods that cause a reaction, but the chemicals and additives that packaged-food makers add to them. Monosodium glutamate, a flavor enhancer, is well known for causing asthma-like reactions in some people. Sulfites and benzoic acid (both preservatives) also can cause reactions, as can some artificial colorings. So stick to fresh foods.

meats. Also, just because a product is labeled "lactose-free" doesn't mean it's dairy-free. And dairy-free doesn't necessarily mean casein- and whey-free.

**Soy.** Soy too shows up in unexpected places: baked goods containing soy flour, cereals, processed vegetables with sauce or breading, fruit drink mixes and sauces, coffee, coffee substitutes, hot chocolate, processed meats, canned soups, candies, butter substitutes, salad dressings, and condiments. Soy oil is safe. Vitamin E capsules often contain oil derived from soybeans. Like soy oil, it's probably safe, but it has not been tested.

**Eggs.** Eggs, alas, are omnipresent. If you're allergic, be wary of baked or battered foods, noodles, salad dressings, egg substitutes, marshmallows, some fat substitutes, and even some wines. If you have any doubt about a product's ingredients, call the manufacturer.

**Fish and shellfish.** Even "imitation" seafood contains fish. The basis for imitation crab, for example, is pollock, also used in imitation beef and pork products. Caesar salad dressings and steak sauces may contain anchovies, as can a delicious Italian relish called *caponata*. Producers sometimes use fish gelatin to clarify wine and coffee, but fish gelatin is clinically proven to be safe for people with fish allergies.

**Peanuts and tree nuts.** Removing peanuts and tree nuts from your diet can *drive* you nuts. Avoid all nut butters; artificial nuts (which may be peanuts reflavored with another nut); peanut or arachis oil that's been cold pressed or expeller pressed (other peanut oils are safe); Asian and African foods, which are often flavored with nuts; barbecue sauces; cereals; crackers; and a type of cold cut called mortadella (which may contain pistachios). Also avoid anything processed in the presence of nuts, such as sunflower seeds and foods sold in bakeries, ice cream parlors, and candy stores. Beanbags and other filled bags may be stuffed with nut shells. Even some cosmetics, skin creams, and craft materials may contain nuts.

## Protecting Yourself

Food sensitivities are at the least discomforting and at the worst life threatening, so knowing how best to protect yourself is important. The first step is to see a doctor or an allergist to confirm what you are sensitive or allergic to. The doctor may do a blood test called the radioallergosorbent test (RAST), which measures the amount of various antibodies in your blood, each of which indicates an allergy to a certain food. He may also give you a relatively pain-free skin test, placing a tiny amount of several allergens on your skin to see if the skin reacts.

If it's still unclear what you're reacting to, your doctor may ask you to keep a food diary, tracking foods and reactions. The doc may also ask you to eliminate probable suspects and then add them back to your plate one at a time.

Once you know which food is the villain, a nutritionist can help you figure out how best to rearrange your diet so you don't miss out on any nutrients, what hidden dangers may lurk, how to read and understand a food label, and what substitutions work best in cooking and baking. If your allergy is severe, the doctor may give you an epinephrine injection kit to carry in case of a reaction. Epinephrine, a hormone most of us know as adrenaline, reverses the effects of a severe reaction, reducing swelling in the throat and airways and keeping blood pressure steady.

# GALLSTONES

In medieval times, health was thought to depend on the four "humours," or vital fluids of the body, including bile. Too much of the liquid was believed to produce a violent temperament. Today, we know that bile doesn't make you a nasty person, but if there's too much cholesterol in your bile, you may be headed toward a nasty gallstone.

Bile is made in the liver, stored in the gallbladder, and used in the small intestine to digest fat. When you eat a greasy hamburger, the gallbladder contracts and pushes bile through a duct that connects with the small intestine. There the bile helps break down and digest the fat in that burger. But too much cholesterol in the bile can turn into trouble in the gallbladder, hardening into stones that range from the size of sugar granules to the size of plums. Some stones linger benignly in the gallbladder. But when a stone tries to pass through a duct, it can cause inflammation, intense pain, and a dangerous blockage that may require surgery.

If too much cholesterol in the gallbladder can cause stones (heredity also plays a role), it makes sense that foods that lower your cholesterol can help you dodge them. Eating smaller meals throughout the day can also help because it keeps the gallbladder contracting regularly so there's no time for the bile to form stones.

## YOUR FOOD PRESCRIPTION

### A breakfast cereal that contains psyllium

At Brandeis University in Massachusetts, when hamsters were fed diets that included psyllium, a fiber found in many natural laxatives and some breakfast cereals, they were much less likely to have gallstones. The researchers suspect that psyllium increases the amount of bile released from the gallbladder, making it less likely to build up and form stones. Psyllium is also a great source of cholesterol-lowering soluble fiber.

Aim for: 1/2 cup every morning. If nothing else, this should help you stay regular.

### Avocados, olive oil, canola oil, fish, and nuts

All fats stimulate the gallbladder to contract, but it's saturated fat from burgers and bacon that raises cholesterol and your risk of gallstones. The fat in avocados, olive and canola oils, fish, and nuts is unsaturated, so it's healthy for your gallbladder and may actually help prevent stones by stimulating the gallbladder to contract and keep bile moving.

Aim for: Try to replace most of the butter and lard in your diet with olive and canola oils, have fish or nuts in place of meat, and trade the cheese in your sandwich for a slice or two of avocado.

### Fruits, vegetables, *and whole grains high in fiber*

In the Nurses Health Study, which monitors tens of thousands of women across the United States, the women who ate the most fiber had a 35 percent lower risk of developing gallstones. Foods that offer insoluble fiber—whole-grain bread and most fruits and vegetables, for instance—appear to be particularly helpful. One study showed that people who followed vegetarian diets had a lower risk of gallstones.

Aim for: 25 to 35 grams of fiber daily. Eating 2 cups of fruit, 2 1/2 cups of vegetables, and three servings of whole grains every day will help you hit your goal.

## An evening glass of wine

Many recent studies have shown that moderate amounts of wine can help lower cholesterol and help decrease the risk of gallbladder attacks.

Aim for: One to two glasses per day (the higher amount is for men).

## Coffee

In the large National Health and Nutrition Examination Survey, women with gallstones who regularly drank between one and four cups of coffee per day reported fewer symptoms than women who passed on java.

Aim for: One to four cups a day. If you're sensitive to caffeine, drink your Joe before 3:00 in the afternoon, or cut back.

## Turmeric

The spice that gives curry its yellow hue, turmeric has been shown to help decrease inflammation in the gallbladder. Some scientists also suspect that it helps stimulate the movement of bile. If you have active stones (particularly larger ones), use turmeric with caution because it can stimulate contractions.

Aim for: A tablespoon per day. Use it in curry dishes and add it to butternut squash, pea soups, stews, and casseroles.

### NUTRITIONAL SUPPLEMENTS

**Vitamin C.** Vitamin C may help break down cholesterol in bile. One study showed that women who had higher blood levels of vitamin C were 13 percent less likely to develop gallstones. **DOSAGE:** 2,000 milligrams per day. If you develop loose stools, scale back.

**Omega-3 fatty acids.** Omega-3s can lower triglycerides in the bloodstream, and that can in turn lower cholesterol and the risk of gallstones. **DOSAGE:** 3 to 5 grams per day if you have high triglycerides.

### OFF THE MENU

**Fatty meat, fried foods, and foods with trans fat.** Foods high in saturated fat can trigger gallstone attacks. The same goes for the trans fat found in many margarines and processed foods. In the Physicians Health Study from Boston, researchers found that a high intake of trans fatty acids increased the risk of gallstones by 12 percent.

**Extreme dieting.** Rapid weight loss is one of the most common causes of gallstones. Skipping meals may also cause a shift in the balance of cholesterol and bile salts in the gallbladder.

**Sugar.** In some people, a diet packed with sweet baked goods, candy, soda, and ice cream can change their bile in a way that makes them more susceptible to gallstones. For sweet treats, look to dried fruits and fruit desserts.

**Colas.** Most dark-colored sodas contain phosphoric acid, which could soften and move gallstones. This may be dangerous if a stone moves into the duct. In general, it's smart to avoid colas. Note, however, that some natural medicine doctors believe in dissolving the stones with a "flush" of cola combined with apple juice, which contains a different type of acid. If you consider trying this, do so only under expert supervision.

### FEATURED RECIPES

**Ginger Butternut Squash Soup** *p. 602*
**Salsa Tuna Salad Sandwiches** *p. 604*
**Curried Chicken Salad Sandwiches** *p. 605*
**Hearty Vegetable Stew** *p. 608*
**Roasted Salmon with Sautéed Greens** *p. 613*
**Turkey Ragu with Spaghetti** *p. 618*
**Pear Crisp** *p. 636*

# GOUT

Many of us associate gout with excess; we think of plump kings downing steins of beer and gobbling fatty haunches of lamb. But gout is actually one of the most painful forms of arthritis, affecting rich and poor alike. Fortunately, there are medications that effectively control gout symptoms—and the right dietary changes can help, too.

Characterized by severe joint pain and tenderness, especially in the big toe, gout is caused by a buildup of uric acid, which forms crystals that nestle into the joints and inflame them. Uric acid results from the breakdown of purines, compounds in body tissues and in many foods, especially red meats and alcohol. Yes, you'll want to cut back on these to avoid gout flare-ups. However, dealing with gout doesn't have to be about nixing steak dinners and fine wines; there are also foods that offer relief.

## YOUR FOOD PRESCRIPTION

### Fresh cherries

If Little Jack Horner had had gout, he would have been better off sticking his thumb in a cherry pie. According to a USDA study at the University of California, women who ate two servings (about 1 1/2 cups) of bing cherries after fasting had significantly lower levels of uric acid in their blood and higher levels in their urine than they had before eating the cherries. The researchers found that the cherries also cut markers of inflammation. Blueberries and strawberries may also be beneficial.

**Aim for:** 1 1/2 cups a day.

**Helpful hint:** Although the California researchers used bing cherries, earlier research found black, yellow, and red sour cherries to be effective, too.

### Fresh or frozen pineapple

Slice open a pineapple and enjoy a sweet, juicy snack. Bromelain, a protein-digesting enzyme in the fruit, can help reduce the pain and inflammation of a gout attack.

**Aim for:** The amount of bromelain in each serving of pineapple varies depending on the ripeness of the fruit and its exposure to heat (we don't recommend canned pineapple for this reason). Aim for at least one serving—a half cup—a day when gout flares. To get even more bromelain, which is more plentiful in the fruit's stem, take bromelain supplements. A typical dose for gout attacks is 500 milligrams twice a day between meals.

**Helpful hint:** Eat your pineapple between meals, not with them, or the enzyme will be used up digesting your food.

### Tofu, edamame, soy milk,
*and other soy foods*

People with gout should limit animal protein, which contains purines, but soy foods are a different story. Several studies show that soy reduces uric acid, making it a terrific way to get protein and combat gout.

**Aim for:** Eating soy foods once or twice a week in place of meat or poultry is a smart idea.

### Tomatoes, bell peppers,
*and other foods rich in vitamin C*

In a two-week study at Tufts University, people who ate two bowls a day of gazpacho containing tomatoes, green bell peppers, and other vegetables high in vitamin C had significantly lower levels of uric acid than they did prior to the study; acid levels were reduced by 18 percent in men and by 8 percent in women. These foods are also rich in lycopene, an antioxidant found in red fruits and vegetables that may lower levels of uric acid.

**Aim for:** At least 72 milligrams of vitamin C daily, the equivalent of 2 cups of gazpacho, one orange, or half of a red bell pepper.

# Olive oil, canola oil, avocados,
*and other foods rich in unsaturated fats*

Several studies suggest that unsaturated fats, found in these foods, may lower uric acid levels (notice we didn't list fish, which contains purines). In a South African study, after patients with gout replaced saturated fats with unsaturated ones, their blood levels of uric acid dropped 17.5 percent after 16 weeks. Getting more of your calories from unsaturated fats may also lower insulin levels, which indirectly helps protect you from gout attacks.

**Aim for:** Up to 30 percent of your calories should come from fat, and at least 20 percent of that should be unsaturated.

**Helpful hint:** Replace butter and creamy salad dressings with olive oil.

# Water *and other nonalcoholic liquids*

Drinking plenty of fluids helps wash the uric acid out of your system.

**Aim for:** At least eight glasses a day.

# Cabbage, kale, leafy greens, celery, and carrots

These vegetables are low in purines, and because they're also low in calories and high in fiber, filling half your plate with them will help keep your weight down. A wide waistline and high levels of uric acid seem to go hand in hand.

## OFF THE MENU

**Red meat and seafood.** These are high in purines, the compounds that break down into uric acid. Organ meats like liver and sweetbreads and game meats like goose are especially packed with purines. So are fatty fish like anchovies, sardines, mackerel, and herring, as well as scallops and mussels.

Although other meats and fish, such as chicken, salmon, crab, and shrimp, have only moderate levels, you should scale back. A 12-year study of more than 47,000 men found that those who ate the most meat were 40 percent more likely to have gout; those who ate the most seafood had a 50 percent higher risk. Eat only 2- to 3-ounce servings of low-fat meats and seafood once a day or less. In fact, you may want to consider a vegetarian diet.

**Purine-rich vegetables and grains.** Asparagus, beans, peas, and cauliflower contain moderate amounts of purines. Limit them to a 1/2-cup serving a day. Whole-grain cereals, wheat germ, oatmeal, and wheat bran also contain purines; limit yourself to 1/2 to 1 cup three times a day.

**Alcohol and yeasty foods like bread and beer.** Most alcoholic drinks don't contain many purines (beer is the worst offender), but because of the way alcohol is processed in the body, all alcohol raises uric acid levels. Yeast, an ingredient in beers and many breads, does, too.

**Sugar.** Research from the University of Florida shows that large amounts of table sugar and corn syrup increase uric acid levels.

## FEATURED RECIPES

**Tropical Fruit Salad** *p. 590*
**Edamame Hummus with Pita Crisps** *p. 592*
**Roasted Cherry Tomatoes in Parmesan Cups** *p. 593*
**Coleslaw with Orange-Sesame Vinaigrette** *p. 594*
**Corn, Tomato, and Quinoa Salad** *p. 596*
**Sweet Potato Soup** *p. 601*
**Hearty Vegetable Stew** *p. 608*
**Carrot Cake with Cream Cheese Glaze** *p. 637*

# GUM DISEASE

Oysters are rumored to help steam up a romance, but did you know they help protect your gums, too? Or that a squirt of lime juice now and then can help your mouth battle bacteria?

Many factors contribute to gum disease, and poor diet is one. The mildest form is gingivitis, a buildup of bacteria in the plaque that continuously forms on teeth. The result is inflamed, bleeding gums. Usually, a professional cleaning and better brushing and flossing take care of it. Let it go, however, and the bacteria-laden plaque descends below the gumline, triggering an inflammatory response that breaks down tissues. The gums pull away from the teeth, those pockets become infected, and eventually, infection can even destroy the bone. This kind of gum disease also boosts the risk of heart disease by 15 percent. Fortunately, many nutrients that protect our gums—vitamins C and E, zinc, and folate—protect our hearts, too.

## YOUR FOOD PRESCRIPTION

## Lean beef

### *and other foods rich in zinc and vitamin $B_6$*

We're not advising you to gobble down whole sides of beef; after all, animal fat is bad for your heart. But oysters, beef, and lamb are high in zinc, a mineral with anti-inflammatory, antioxidant, and immunity-boosting powers that can battle gum disease.

Vitamin $B_6$, plentiful in beef as well as seafood, also fights gum disease. In a one-year study at Pennsylvania State University, older adults with low intakes of vitamin A and vitamin $B_6$ had persistent problems with tooth decay and gum disease.

Aim for: *Zinc:* 8 milligrams for women, 11 milligrams for men (roughly what you'd get from a roast beef sandwich). *Vitamin $B_6$:* 1.3 to 1.5 milligrams for women and 1.3 to 1.7 milligrams for men. One 3-ounce serving of tuna has 0.88 milligram; a medium potato with skin, 0.62 milligram; a banana, 0.55 milligram; and 3 ounces of top sirloin, 0.53 milligram. Many fortified cereals give you most or even all of the $B_6$ you need in one serving.

Helpful hint: Drink up that milk in your cereal bowl! After the cereal soaks, many of the vitamins, minerals, and other nutrients with which cereals are fortified end up in the milk.

## FEATURED RECIPES

**Tropical Fruit Salad** p. 590
**Broccoli Salad** p. 595
**Sweet Potato Soup** p. 601
**Beef and Broccoli Stew** p. 620
**Mac 'n Cheese Primavera** p. 610
**Orange Beets** p. 627
**Creamed Spinach** p. 624
**Springtime Quinoa** p. 626

# Whole-grain cereal with milk and a glass of orange juice

Consider this the ultimate breakfast for a healthy smile. That milk on your cereal is rich in calcium, which protects your gums. In a long-term study of 13,000 people, those who ate only half the recommended servings of calcium-rich foods doubled their risk of gum disease. Scientists speculate that calcium keeps the jawbone stronger, helping it fight invading bacteria. (Get your calcium at lunchtime, too, by eating a cup of yogurt.)

The cereal adds its own benefits. Canadian researchers have found that people who ate multiple helpings of whole grains daily were 15 percent less likely to develop gum disease, probably because whole grains tend to keep blood sugar levels lower than refined grains (like most rice and corn cereals and white bread) do. Limiting blood sugar spikes may in turn limit the production of destructive compounds called AGEs (advanced glycation end products), which inflame soft tissues like the gums.

And that glass of OJ? It's rich in vitamin C, which helps gums repair themselves. People who get enough C tend to have healthier gums than people who don't.

Aim for: Start each day with whole-grain cereal, milk, and OJ, then aim to get five to six servings of whole grains per day (a serving is a cup of whole-grain cereal, a half cup of whole-grain pasta or rice, or one slice of whole-grain bread) and 1,000 to 1,200 milligrams of calcium daily, the equivalent of a glass of fat-free milk, a cup of yogurt, and a serving of spinach and canned salmon (also good calcium sources).

# Fruits and vegetables high in antioxidants

Forget eating spinach for strong muscles—eat it for strong gums. Its beta-carotene, which converts to vitamin A in the body, is a powerful antioxidant and immunity booster. Other good sources are other dark leafy greens (including beet greens), sweet potatoes, carrots, winter squash, and yellow fruits such as cantaloupe and apricots.

To drive infections off, also look to vitamin C, which is abundant in citrus fruits, bell peppers, and broccoli, not to mention the orange juice we already mentioned.

Aim for: Five to six 1/2-cup daily servings of vegetables, especially yellow vegetables and dark leafy greens, and three to four 1/2-cup servings of fruits, especially those mentioned above.

## NUTRITIONAL SUPPLEMENTS

**A daily multivitamin.** A healthy diet should give you all the nutrients you need to protect your gums, but a multivitamin is smart insurance. Fruits and vegetables provide plenty of vitamin C, but if you smoke, you'll need more of it and other antioxidants (look for a high-antioxidant multi). Meats and fortified cereals provide zinc, but if you're undereating, drink alcohol to excess, or have a digestive disease, you may need help from the zinc in a multi. Many older Americans and people with poor diets have low levels of vitamin $B_6$ and should consider a supplement if they can't boost their levels by eating more fortified cereals, beans, or meat. The easiest and best way to get B vitamins is from a multivitamin. **DOSAGE:** One a day.

**Calcium.** If you skimp on dairy foods and dark leafy greens, calcium can help you meet your goal. **DOSAGE:** A total of 1,000 to 1,200 milligrams daily from food and supplements.

## OFF THE MENU

**Sugar.** Sugar is bacteria's friend, and bacteria are at the root of gum disease. The bacteria in plaque seize on sugar, using it to increase acid production and creating a welcome mat for more bacteria. And sugar lowers the ability of white cells to fight bacteria.

Take aim at sugary drinks. A long-term study of almost 14,000 people found that among young adults 18 to 34, those who were obese were 76 percent more likely to have gum disease than those of normal weight. Researchers suspect that sugary drinks were the culprits. Drink water instead.

# HEARTBURN

When you think of heartburn and food, your Uncle Edgar's famous five-alarm chili may come to mind. In fact, though, you'd be better off avoiding pizza, since fatty and acidic foods (think tomatoes) are actually more likely than spicy ones to trigger that searing sensation. And while you're avoiding foods that ignite heartburn, you'd do well to add some that douse the flames.

As you swallow food and liquids, muscle contractions in the throat force them down the esophagus. Think of this long tube as a chute with a trapdoor at the bottom. When you swallow food, the trapdoor—known as the lower-esophageal sphincter (LES)—swings open for a few seconds, allowing your meal to enter the stomach, then closes quickly.

Some foods and beverages cause heartburn through direct contact as they pass through the esophagus. But many others create chemical changes in the gastrointestinal tract that relax the LES after a meal, causing it to open for long periods. That allows stomach contents and digestive acids to splash upward, or "reflux," scorching the tender lining of the esophagus. In some cases, food may back up all the way into the throat, which may make you cough or taste acid and have bad breath. Foods that increase stomach acid can make heartburn worse.

The foods that fan the flames vary from one person to the next. To identify your triggers, doctors recommend eliminating potentially troublesome foods from your diet one at a time for a week or two. See a doctor or nutritionist for details.

Chronic heartburn, known as gastroesophageal reflux disease, or GERD, is a serious matter. Not only is it a painful nuisance, but frequent acid baths can produce scar tissue that may make it difficult to swallow or, in rare cases, cause cell damage that results in cancer of the esophagus. Whether heartburn is an occasional woe or a daily hassle, choosing the right foods can help you chill out.

## FEATURED RECIPES

**Edamame Hummus with Pita Crisps** *p. 592*
**Curried Chicken Salad Sandwiches** *p. 605*
**Pork Chops with Dried Fruits** *p. 620*
**Roasted Root Vegetables** *p. 622*
**Pear Crisp** *p. 636*

## YOUR FOOD PRESCRIPTION

# Whole-grain bread
### *and other high-fiber foods*

Your doctor has probably been telling you for years to add more fiber to your diet. Now there's one more reason to follow his advice. Recent research suggests that eating a lot of roughage appears to protect against heartburn. Swedish researchers found that people who ate high-fiber whole-grain bread every day had half the risk of GERD compared with people who preferred low-fiber white bread.

How does fiber help? There are several possible explanations. Some foods (such as cured meats) contain substances called nitrites, which the body may use to produce nitric oxide. This gas can cause the LES to relax, allowing caustic stomach acid to sear the lining of the esophagus. Fiber soaks up nitrites, which blocks the production of nitric oxide. Fiber also forces us to chew our food more thoroughly, and chewing releases saliva, which helps protect the esophagus. Fiber helps us to feel full with less food so we don't overeat at one sitting, which helps prevent heartburn because overeating is a common trigger.

Aim for: Many health experts and organizations recommend 25 to 35 grams of fiber per day, which you can get by eating 2 to 4 servings of fruit, 3 to 5 servings of vegetables, and 6 to 11 servings of cereal and grain foods (a serving is a slice of whole-grain bread, 1/2 cup of brown rice, or about 3/4 cup of most cereals).

Helpful hint: If your diet has been relatively low in roughage until now, suddenly adding huge servings of fiber may cause a decidedly unwelcome side effect: flatulence. Increase your fiber intake gradually.

# Dishes containing ginger, turmeric, chiles, and cinnamon

Yes, that's right, we're recommending spices for heartburn. Researchers have discovered that not only do spicy foods (at least ones that aren't greasy) *not* usually contribute to heartburn but also that certain spices can actually help. Many of them, especially ginger and turmeric (found in curry powder), combat inflammation and kill bacteria. Be sure to add the spices during cooking rather than at the end to release their full healing potential. A bonus: Spices can often take the place of seasonings high in sugar and salt and help you get more enjoyment out of low-fat foods. Spicy foods don't have to be greasy.

Of course, if a food diary or elimination diet reveals that certain spices do aggravate your heartburn, cut them out.

# Slippery elm tea

Slippery elm is also recommended for sore throats, and for the same reason: It coats mucous membranes like those in the throat and digestive tract, thanks to its mucilage. The slick stuff is a form of soluble fiber—after all, slippery elm is made from the bark of a tree. You can buy slippery elm teabags in health food stores.

Aim for: A cup when your heartburn flares.

# Gentian root tea

The dried root used to make this tea has been used for many years as a digestive bitter. You can find teabags in health food stores.

Aim for: A cup before or after meals.

# Water

It's a simple trick, but drinking a glass of water helps wash the acid in your throat back into your stomach, where it belongs. It also dilutes your stomach acid a bit.

Aim for: A small glass of water (4 to 6 ounces) when heartburn strikes.

What causes heartburn?
Fatty foods. Salty foods. Acidic foods. Alcohol.
Eating too fast. Eating too much. The path to prevention?
That's simple: Eat healthy meals, in healthy amounts,
at a healthy speed.

## NUTRITIONAL SUPPLEMENTS

**DGL tablets or wafers.** Deglycyrrhizinated licorice, or DGL, is licorice with a certain blood pressure–raising compound removed. It soothes and coats the stomach, preventing that burning feeling. **DOSAGE:** One or two chewable tablets or wafers before each meal.

**Calcium.** Many popular antacids are simply calcium supplements. While some antacids use other minerals, such as magnesium or aluminum, to neutralize stomach acid, calcium protects your bones as it battles heartburn. Take a calcium supplement, or any antacid, following a meal you suspect may trigger an attack of acid indigestion or when you feel heartburn symptoms arising. If heartburn wakes you at night, popping an antacid before bed may be wise, too. **DOSAGE:** Follow the label directions. Two to four 400-milligram tablets per day is typical. Don't exceed the recommended dose; taking too much calcium to treat heartburn may cause other GI problems, such as constipation, bloating, gas, and flatulence. (Look for a calcium supplement that also contains magnesium to sidestep the constipation problem.) It may also set you up for something known as rebound reflux. Besides, if you need frequent relief, you may require more serious medicine. Talk to a doctor if you take antacids for heartburn more than a few times a week.

## OFF THE MENU

**Tomatoes, onions, and orange juice.** Acidic foods, such as the tomatoes used to make marinara and pizza sauce, may inflame the lining of the esophagus on contact as they pass through. This explains why your favorite Italian takeout place has a Rolaids dispenser by the counter. That doesn't mean you need to ban tomatoes, which are especially good for men, but you may need to cut back. The same holds true for citrus juices, such as orange, grapefruit, and pineapple. (The fruits themselves shouldn't bother you—in fact, they contain digestive enzymes that help break down animal protein at a meal—but the juices are too concentrated.) Don't worry too much about lemons and limes; they are actually weak acids and may do more good than harm. But avoid lemonade; all the sugar may be irritating, and it feeds bacteria.

Finally, high acidity is the reason many heartburn sufferers find themselves repeating the same mantra—"Hold the onions!"—when they dine out. In one study, people with persistent heartburn were able to eat plain hamburgers without incident, but eating burgers with onions consistently produced acid indigestion and reflux. You may have better luck with cooked onions—and skip the ketchup.

**Fatty foods.** Studies show that people who consume diets high in total fat and saturated fat (the kind in dairy foods and meats) have a higher risk of GERD. Eating a juicy steak, or even a bag of peanuts, causes the body to release the hormone cholecystokinin, which

It's proven: Excess weight raises the odds of developing chronic heartburn. In fact, studies show that severely overweight people have double the risk of GERD. So if heartburn is an issue, don't just avoid trigger foods —shed a few pounds!

makes the LES go slack, allowing stomach acid to slosh upward and burn the esophagus.

Swap fatty meats for fish, which actually counters inflammation, or choose the leanest cuts, such as London broil steaks, extra-lean ground beef, and skinless chicken breasts. For flavor without added fat, grill meats instead of frying or sautéing.

Dairy products, including full-fat milk, are notorious heartburn triggers. (Ironically, until the early 1970s, many doctors instructed patients to drink milk as a way to *prevent* heartburn.) They appear to increase production of stomach acids, and they prolong the length of time that acid clings to the lining of the esophagus. Opt for fat-free milk and low-fat cheese and yogurt (buy a brand that's not overly sweetened and add your own fruit to increase the fiber). Feta and goat cheese are naturally less fatty than hard cheese.

**Alcohol, caffeine, and chocolate.** Not surprisingly, alcohol, a relaxant, loosens the LES. Caffeine appears to have a similar effect; although a few studies have exonerated coffee and tea, some heartburn sufferers say that just a few sips of hot brew—even decaf—can set off an attack. (If you still want your coffee, drink it after a meal, never on an empty stomach.) Chocolate contains fat and caffeine, so your beloved bonbons may also be causing your digestive misery.

**Salty foods.** A 2005 study found that people who reported eating salty foods more than three times a week increased their risk of GERD by 50 percent. In the same study, people who said they always sprinkle extra salt on their food were 70 percent more likely to have reflux after meals than people who never added salt. It's not clear if salt is linked to heartburn, or if salt lovers may simply have other diet habits that make them vulnerable. However, there's no harm—and plenty of benefits—in eschewing the saltshaker.

**Peppermint.** Even freshening your breath after dinner could be perilous; the menthol in peppermint causes the LES to relax.

## To Beat Heartburn, Learn to Walk and Chew Gum

Your body produces its own natural antacid: It's called saliva. The stuff that keeps your mouth moist is full of bicarbonate, a chemical that neutralizes acid. (That's why bicarbonate is an ingredient in many heartburn-relief products.) Keeping your esophagus well lubed with saliva may be enough to stifle acid indigestion. Chewing sugarless gum is one way to do it, although the sugar alcohols these gums contain make some people bloated. Other options include sucking on sugar-free lozenges or hard candy. Several studies have shown that chewing gum after a meal prevents or reduces heartburn symptoms; in one, subjects with frequent reflux who took a 1-hour stroll while working their jaws gained modest additional relief.

Need another reason to give up cigarettes? Smoking dries up saliva.

# HEART DISEASE/ HIGH CHOLESTEROL

Would you believe that eating just half a serving of fish a week can help keep you from dying of a heart attack? The catch (and we don't mean the fish): You have to actually *do it* to get the benefits!

It's pretty easy to ignore your risk of heart disease. You can't feel many of the problems that contribute to it, and if nothing hurts, the temptation to assume (or pretend) everything's fine can be overwhelming. It often takes the sudden death of a friend or relative from a heart attack to instill the fear that moves you to act. But remember, heart disease takes many years to develop, and you can't reverse it overnight. So why not start now?

If diet is one of the biggest contributors to heart disease, *changing your diet* is one of the best ways to prevent it. The big changes are fairly obvious, like laying off the bacon cheeseburgers and eating more fish, fruits, vegetables, and whole grains. But you don't have to make them all at once. Tackle a few you think you can handle, then tackle a few more. *Eating just one fruit or vegetable at every meal can significantly lower your risk of a heart attack.*

Even if you already have heart disease, the right diet can help you reverse it— something no cholesterol-lowering pill will do—by improving your cholesterol readings and taming high blood pressure, steadying blood sugar, dousing inflammation, and even taking off extra pounds. Many studies have proved it. For instance, the Lyon Diet Heart Study showed that when people with heart disease follow a Mediterranean-style diet that eschews red meats and processed foods in favor of produce; whole grains; and good fats from fish, olive oil, or nuts, they are 50 to 75 percent less likely to have repeat heart attacks compared to patients who stick with standard Western fare.

Fish anyone?

## food for thought . . .

"Almost 80 percent of cardiovascular disease could be prevented by lifestyle changes, and among the most important of these are dietary changes."

— Guy Reed, MS, MD, chief of cardiovascular medicine at the Medical College of Georgia in Augusta ■

# Fatty fish

Salmon may be the first food that comes to mind when you envision a heart-healthy diet, and for good reason. Salmon and other fatty fish, such as mackerel, sardines, and tuna, contain now-famous omega-3 fatty acids, particularly compounds known as eicosapentaenoic acid (EPA) and docosahexaenoic acid (DHA).

Consider these nature's heart medicines. According to a recent study, consuming small quantities of fish—just half a serving a week—lowers the risk of dying from cardiovascular disease by 17 percent and the risk of a nonfatal heart attack by 27 percent. Each additional weekly serving reduces the risk of dying from cardiovascular disease by another 4 percent.

Eating food with fins benefits your heart and its "plumbing" in a number of ways. Having fish for dinner once a week probably means one less meat-based meal, and that in itself helps—for instance, by keeping your cholesterol under control. But the fats in fish are themselves beneficial. They help stabilize heart rhythms to prevent arrhythmias (irregular heartbeats that can lead to heart failure, blood clots, and stroke); lower cholesterol and triglycerides; and reduce inflammation in the arteries, which was recently discovered to play a major role in heart disease. Fish eaters have levels of C-reactive protein (CRP), a marker of inflammation, that are up to 33 percent lower than those of people who don't eat fish. Because high levels of CRP have been found in heart attack patients whose cholesterol levels were normal, some heart specialists believe it may be even better than cholesterol for predicting who will develop heart disease.

**Aim for:** At least two servings of fatty fish (8 to 12 ounces total) a week. Since mercury contamination is a concern, opt for fish lower in mercury, such as salmon or canned light tuna, and steer clear of highly contaminated fish such as shark, swordfish, king mackerel, and tilefish (see "Choosing Safe Seafood" on page 325).

# A rainbow of fruits and vegetables

Most of us have nothing against fruits and veggies per se; we just don't make the effort to eat enough of them. But this statistic may send you straight to the salad bar: Research from a major survey that analyzed the connection between disease risk and fruit and vegetable consumption in more than 9,000 healthy adults showed that eating a fruit or vegetable at every meal cut the risk of dying from cardiovascular disease by 27 percent.

Need more reason to serve yourself a helping of spinach or have an apple snack? According to research from the Nurses Health Study and the Health Professionals Follow-Up Study, which looked at the eating habits of well over 100,000 men and women, people who ate eight or more servings of fruit and vegetables each day had a 30 percent lower risk of developing cardiovascular disease than people who ate fewer than two servings a day.

Fruits and vegetables are among the best sources of fiber, which lowers cholesterol and helps reduce the low-grade inflammation in our bodies that contributes to heart disease. Opt for brightly colored fruits and vegetables; they contain the most antioxidants, which counteract the damage free radicals do to arteries and help prevent the breakdown of LDL ("bad") cholesterol that leads to plaque buildup. You can't rely on supplements for your antioxidants, since they don't seem to have the same effects as food.

**Aim for:** At the very least, get 3 to 5 servings of fruits and vegetables each day (a serving is one medium piece of fruit; 1/2 cup of fruit or vegetable juice; 1/2 cup of chopped fruit or cooked vegetables, beans, or legumes; or 1 cup of leafy vegetables). But having 7 to 10 daily servings is certainly better.

**Helpful hint:** Start one meal a day with a salad or add a side of steamed spinach. If you're already eating about five servings of green vegetables a day, adding a sixth lowers heart disease risk by another 23 percent.

## Oatmeal, oat bran, legumes, beans, and peas

The secret ingredient in these foods is soluble fiber, the kind that reduces cholesterol by soaking it up so it's flushed it out of the body as waste. Studies show that diets low in fat and rich in soluble fiber can reduce total cholesterol levels by 10 to 15 percent, which in many cases may be enough to get you into the target range.

Aim for: 25 to 35 grams of fiber each day. Of that, 10 grams should be soluble fiber.

Helpful hint: Oats contain more soluble fiber than any other grain, 2 to 3 grams per serving. Having just two servings of regular oatmeal or oat bran cereal a day lowers cholesterol by 2 to 3 percent. Not into oats? A half cup of beans, legumes, or peas also contains 2 grams of soluble fiber.

## Virgin olive oil

Low-fat diets have been shown to prevent and even reverse heart disease. The problem is, they can be hard to stick with. So how can you enjoy some fat in your diet and protect your heart, too? By swapping saturated fats (like butter) for olive oil, particularly virgin olive oil.

Olives and olive oil are mainstays of the famously heart-healthy Mediterranean diet. They contain monounsaturated fat, which is healthier for the heart than saturated fat. But olives—which are fruits, after all—and their oil also contain antioxidants called polyphenols, which, research suggests, help reduce inflammation in the blood vessels and help improve cholesterol and triglyceride levels.

It's important to opt for virgin olive oil; because it's minimally processed, it retains many of the polyphenols that are stripped from more heavily processed olive oils.

Aim for: Limit yourself to no more than 2 to 3 teaspoons of oil or 24 to 30 medium olives daily. And remember, olives and olive oil are meant to replace other fats in your diet, not be added to them.

## Walnuts, almonds, and peanuts

Eating nuts in place of other fatty foods can potentially lower your risk of heart disease by up to 39 percent, according to research done at Pennsylvania State University. Although nuts contain a lot of fat, it's the monounsaturated and polyunsaturated varieties, which lower cholesterol and protect against heart disease. Nuts also seem to lower CRP and fibrinogen, both of which are markers for inflammation. Plus, they're good sources of fiber and protein as well as vitamin E, the B vitamins, magnesium, and potassium, all of which are essential for good heart health.

Aim for: An ounce of nuts at least five times a week.

Helpful hint: Almonds and walnuts lower cholesterol, but don't leave peanuts out of the mix. As sources of antioxidants go, peanuts are on a par with blackberries and strawberries. They contain good amounts of vitamin E as well as vast stores of antioxidant polyphenols. Roasted peanuts contain even more of them.

## Tofu, edamame, and soy milk

Soy foods aren't the cure-alls we once thought; they lower cholesterol only a little bit, according to reviews of recent studies. But there are still plenty of good reasons to rotate them into your diet, especially in place of meats and full-fat cheeses. The fact is, like other beans, soy is an excellent source of protein with none of the saturated fat of meat. It also contains hormone-like compounds called isoflavones that seem to help fight certain cancers.

Tasteless chunks of tofu are not your only option—although tofu really is good in stir-fries because it takes on the flavor of the sauce. You can add it to beef stir-fries to cut down on the amount of meat you use or add it to lasagna in place of some of the cheese (you won't notice it's there). But one of the simplest and tastiest ways to enjoy soy is by stocking the freezer with soybeans (also called edamame), either in or out of their shells. They make a fun, satisfying snack when you squeeze them out of their pods (thaw them first), or you can sprinkle shelled soybeans on salads or into soups.

**Aim for:** There's no official recommendation, but you can do your heart good by occasionally eating soy foods instead of meats and dairy products. When you eat tofu, choose the low-fat variety.

## Special margarines *and other foods enriched with plant sterols or stanols*

Sterols and stanols are natural compounds found in vegetables, nuts, and seeds and often added to margarines and other foods because they lower cholesterol by reducing how much you absorb from food. Swapping regular salad dressing, milk, cheese, yogurt, margarine, and orange juice for the same foods fortified with plant sterols or stanols can lower LDL cholesterol within just a few weeks.

Finnish researchers split a group of 164 adults with mild to moderately high cholesterol into two groups. Half ate a range of low-fat dairy foods with these compounds added, while the other half functioned as the control group. After six weeks, the people eating the enriched dairy foods lowered their total cholesterol by 6.5 percent and their LDL cholesterol by more than 10 percent.

**Aim for:** If you need to lower your cholesterol, aim for approximately 2 grams of plant sterols/stanols daily. In general, eating plant sterol/stanol-enriched foods in place of foods like butter or high-fat salad dressing that actively raise cholesterol is a good idea.

**Helpful hint:** Pay attention to the serving sizes listed on the labels, because the enriched margarines and salad dressings are often still high in calories. These sterols/stanols are best absorbed with a little fat, so if you opt for orange juice, drink it with a meal.

## The More Heart-Healthy Foods, the Better

All of the foods in this entry help protect against heart disease, but some provide even more protection when they're eaten together. For instance, the combination of soy protein, almonds, oats, barley, and plant sterols—dubbed the Portfolio Diet by researchers at St. Michael's Hospital in Toronto—reduced LDL in people with high cholesterol by an amazing 28 percent when eaten regularly as part of a diet low in saturated fat. By comparison, the people who followed a regular diet low in saturated fat and took a statin drug saw their cholesterol drop only slightly more (31 percent).

Another diet, dubbed the Polymeal Diet, focuses on wine, fish, dark chocolate, fruits, vegetables, almonds, and garlic, all known to lower the risk of heart disease, mainly by reducing cholesterol levels and lowering blood pressure. Data from the Framingham Heart Study and Framingham Offspring Study suggest that when these foods are eaten every day (except for fish, which is recommended just two to four times a week), they collectively lower the risk of cardiovascular disease by 76 percent.

# Wine, beer, and spirits

Red wine gets all the attention in terms of heart health, but the fact is, other types of alcohol also protect against heart disease when consumed in moderation. In general, alcohol increases HDL ("good") cholesterol, lowers LDL ("bad") cholesterol, and in some cases, reduces fibrinogen and CRP, the inflammation markers. A recent study done at the University of Florida found that older adults who have one alcoholic beverage a day were 30 percent less likely to develop heart disease. Another study of cardiac patients hospitalized after heart attacks found that study participants who averaged two drinks a day were 32 percent less likely to experience fatal heart attacks.

Red wine does offer some added benefits from plant compounds found in grape skins, such as flavonoids, which help prevent blood clots, and resveratrol, which helps lower cholesterol.

Aim for: One to two drinks a day (the higher number is for men) is the amount considered generally safe and beneficial to the heart.

Helpful hint: Not sure what constitutes a drink? It's 4 ounces of wine, 12 ounces of beer, or 1.5 ounces of hard liquor.

# Tea

You may think of fruits and vegetables when you think of antioxidants, but tea is an even better source of these disease fighters. Green tea is associated with reduced cholesterol levels and lower rates of artery blockages. But both black and green teas contain significant amounts of flavonoids, antioxidants that appear to protect against heart disease by slowing the breakdown of LDL cholesterol, preventing blood clots, and improving blood vessel function.

People who drink a cup or two of tea a day have a 46 percent lower risk of developing narrowed arteries. Upping that to three cups a day lowers the risk of having a heart attack by 43 percent and of dying from a heart attack by 70 percent. It can even help prevent a second heart attack. In a study of 1,900 patients recovering from heart attacks at Beth Israel Deaconess Medical Center in Boston, the death rate among patients who drank at least two cups of tea a day was 44 percent lower than among non-tea drinkers.

Aim for: Two to five cups of green or black tea daily.

Helpful hint: Choose green tea if you're looking for a beverage naturally low in caffeine.

# Cranberry juice

Women have long relied on cranberry juice for fending off urinary tract infections. Now research suggests that the juice, one of the richest sources of antioxidants, can also raise levels of HDL cholesterol. In a three-month study of 19 volunteers with high cholesterol, three servings of cranberry juice a day boosted their HDL cholesterol levels by 10 percent, which in turn lowered their risk of heart disease by 40 percent.

Aim for: Three 4- to 6-ounce servings a day.

Helpful hint: Opt for low-sugar cranberry juice to avoid drinking excess calories.

# Apples

An apple or two a day really may keep the cardiologist away! Apples contain bushels of antioxidants that, like statin drugs, stimulate the liver to remove harmful LDL cholesterol from the blood. In addition, the antioxidants in apples and apple juice delay the breakdown of LDL cholesterol by about 20 percent. The longer it takes for LDL to break down, the less plaque there is in the arteries.

Aim for: Two apples or 12 ounces of 100 percent apple juice a day.

Helpful hint: Go for Red Delicious, Northern Spy, or Ida Red apples. Compared to other types, they contain the most antioxidants. And be sure to eat the skin, which contains five times more antioxidants than the flesh. Buy organic apples if you're concerned about pesticide residues in the skin.

# Red grapefruit

It's great with breakfast, and it can lower your cholesterol and triglyceride levels, too. In an Israeli study of 57 men and women who had had bypass surgery and whose cholesterol levels weren't responding to statin medications, those who ate a red grapefruit a day for 30 days along with their regular meals lowered their total cholesterol by more than 15 percent, their LDL cholesterol by more than 20 percent, and their triglycerides by more than 17 percent. Because grapefruit can interact with certain medications, check with your doctor first if you're taking one or more prescription drugs.

**Aim for:** 1 cup of fresh grapefruit or 1/2 cup of 100 percent grapefruit juice a day.

# Garlic

Fresh cloves contain an antioxidant compound that gives garlic its characteristic aroma, which may explain why garlic may be helpful for reducing blood clots and artery plaque and modestly lowering cholesterol. When eaten daily along with other heart-healthy foods (see "The More Heart-Healthy Foods, the Better," page 479), garlic can help lower heart disease risk by 76 percent.

Garlic's blood-thinning properties are helpful, but if you're already taking a blood-thinning drug such as warfarin (Coumadin), or you have a blood or platelet disorder or are going into the hospital for surgery or to have a baby, talk to your doctor before consuming large amounts of garlic.

**Aim for:** Some experts suggest eating as many as two to four cloves a day.

**Helpful hint:** Although cooking can deactivate garlic's therapeutic compounds, chopping or crushing the cloves and letting the garlic stand for 10 to 15 minutes before cooking will help preserve them.

# Tomato sauce

Could eating spaghetti be good for your heart? It's possible, provided you pour on the tomato sauce. Tomatoes contain lycopene, one of the more potent antioxidants in the carotenoid family that appears to protect against heart disease by preventing the oxidation of LDL cholesterol. When researchers at the University of North Carolina at Chapel Hill looked at fat samples from nearly 1,400 men who'd had heart attacks and compared them with samples from healthy men, they found that the men who had more lycopene in their fat had about half the risk of heart attack compared to those with less lycopene.

**Aim for:** 1/2 cup twice a week.

**Helpful hint:** Cooking releases lycopene from tomatoes, which is why you'll get more of this nutrient from tomato sauce than from raw tomatoes.

Get a handsome, large mason jar—one that your hand can fit into—and fill it with a mix of roasted nuts, dark chocolate chips, and raisins. A fistful (but not more!) is not only a scrumptious afternoon snack or dessert but also a powerhouse of heart-healthy ingredients.

# Dark chocolate

Yes, you can have your wine—and chocolate—on a heart-healthy diet. Dark chocolate is full of the same antioxidants found in red wine and green tea. In fact, it contains more flavonols (a subclass of flavonoids, in case you're paying attention to the technical stuff) than tea or red wine and has about four times the catechins in tea. These compounds prevent blood clots, slow the oxidation of LDL cholesterol (making it less likely to stick to artery walls), improve blood vessel function, and reduce inflammation. Another plus for chocolate: It gives good cholesterol a slight boost.

Of course, chocolate's high in fat, but a third of that fat is stearic acid, a particular type of saturated fat that doesn't raise cholesterol, while another third is a type of monounsaturated fat that lowers cholesterol.

**Aim for:** Some research suggests that 1.5 ounces a day may reduce the risk of heart disease by 10 percent. Look for dark chocolate that contains at least 60 percent cocoa.

**Helpful hint:** Choose dark chocolate over milk chocolate. Dark chocolate, which has a higher cocoa content, contains more flavonoids, and although milk chocolate contains some, the milk actually prevents their absorption. Dark chocolate also tends to contain less sugar.

## FEATURED RECIPES

**Edamame Hummus with Pita Crisps** *p. 592*
**Updated Waldorf Salad** *p. 594*
**Turkey Ragu with Spaghetti** *p. 618*
**Salmon Steaks with Peach Salsa** *p. 612*
**Tomato-Roasted Mackerel** *p. 612*
**Turkey Cutlets with Grapefruit Salsa** *p. 617*
**Pomegranate Ice** *p. 638*
**Chocolate Fondue** *p. 634*
**Blueberry-Oat Scones** *p. 628*

## NUTRITIONAL SUPPLEMENTS

**Omega-3 fatty acids.** Along with eating fish twice a week, if you have heart disease, the American Heart Association recommends taking fish-oil supplements with EPA and DHA (the two main components of omega-3 fatty acids). These have been shown to reduce LDL cholesterol and triglycerides while also increasing HDL cholesterol. They also combat inflammation. **DOSAGE:** 1 gram daily if you have cardiovascular disease; 2 to 4 grams daily (under a doctor's supervision) if your triglycerides are elevated. Taking the supplements with food can help reduce the burping often associated with fish oils, as can choosing a fish-oil supplement that contains citrus essence.

**Coenzyme Q10.** This naturally occurring chemical boosts energy in all of the body's cells, including those in the heart muscle, which is why it's thought to protect against heart failure. Because statin medications deplete CoQ10, people taking statins should talk to their doctors about also taking CoQ10 supplements. **DOSAGE:** It will depend on which statin you're taking and at what dosage.

**Plant sterols/stanols.** The same LDL cholesterol–lowering plant sterols/stanols used to fortify some "heart-healthy" margarines can also be taken as supplements to lower cholesterol. There's no need to take them if your cholesterol is in the normal range. **DOSAGE:** 1 to 3 grams daily from food and/or supplements.

**Garlic.** Along with using fresh garlic in food, taking garlic supplements may also improve cholesterol. One study done at Pennsylvania State University showed that when men with high cholesterol took garlic supplements, they lowered their total cholesterol by 7 percent and their LDL cholesterol by 10 percent compared to volunteers taking placebos. **DOSAGE:** 600 to 900 milligrams a day is considered safe.

## OFF THE MENU

**Fatty meats, chicken skin, full-fat dairy foods, and foods containing trans fat.**
Saturated fat, found in meat, cheese, and butter, raises cholesterol and heart disease risk. So does trans fat, found in vegetable shortening, stick margarine, and many commercially fried and/or baked foods (look for the word *hydrogenated* on the label). These foods should be the first to go.

According to a Cleveland Clinic study, eating even one meal that's high in saturated fat interferes with artery elasticity and encourages plaque deposits. And data from the Nurses Health Study shows that every 5 percent increase in saturated fat intake bumps up your risk of heart disease by 17 percent. Trans fat not only raises LDL cholesterol but also lowers HDL cholesterol. In addition, some animal research suggests that eating foods high in trans fat increases belly fat, which in turn raises the risk of diabetes and heart disease.

**Sugar and refined, processed carbohydrates.**
Sugary foods and drinks have something in common with starchy foods like potatoes and refined carbohydrates like white bread and white rice. All of them are quickly broken down into sugars in the body, raising blood sugar and insulin levels. Over time, this can lead to weight gain and insulin resistance, both contributors to heart disease.

## Cutting Calories Cuts Heart Disease Risk

Can cutting calories turn back the cardiological clock? It appears so. When researchers at Washington University School of Medicine looked at 25 people who cut 600 to 1,000 calories from their daily diets (most Americans eat between 2,000 and 3,000 calories a day) for six years, their hearts looked 15 years younger than their chronological age. The people in the study were also leaner and had lower levels of inflammatory markers, cholesterol, triglycerides, and blood pressure. The study participants cut their calories by eating nutrient-dense foods and limiting empty calories from refined and processed foods and sodas.

# HEMORRHOIDS

Hemorrhoids are a real pain in the … well, you know where. Essentially varicose veins in an extremely inconvenient spot, hemorrhoids—some of which bleed and some of which don't—typically occur with chronic constipation, the result of repeated straining to go to the bathroom. (Diarrhea can aggravate hemorrhoids.) Hemorrhoids are more common with age as the muscles that help propel blood through the veins tend to weaken—especially if we become overweight and sedentary. They're also common in pregnant women because of the extra pressure the baby puts on abdominal veins and because pregnancy hormones relax blood vessels, both of which cause veins to swell.

Many of us who aren't pregnant can probably blame the problem on the typical Western diet—and the typical Western lack of exercise. What's the solution? Eat plenty of fruits, vegetables, and whole grains—foods that promote regularity—along with foods that strengthen blood vessels. Why not cook dinner tonight? You can sneak in plenty of these foods and get out of your chair for a while (sitting for long periods also contributes to hemorrhoids).

## YOUR FOOD PRESCRIPTION

## Water

If you don't drink enough water, fiber becomes a plug instead of a broom. The other thing you can do with water is sit in it, preferably with some Epsom salts added, since salt literally pulls fluid from the blood trapped in a varicose vein or hemorrhoid to reduce swelling and inflammation.

**Aim for:** Between 8 and 11 eight-ounce glasses, or 2 to 3 liters, a day.

### FEATURED RECIPES

**Broccoli Salad** *p. 595*
**Spinach Salad with Chickpeas** *p. 597*
**Lentil-Tomato Soup** *p. 603*
**Chicken-Barley Bake** *p. 616*
**Raspberry-Almond Muffins** *p. 628*
**Frozen Fruit Mousse** *p. 638*
**Mixed Berry Tart** *p. 639*

## Foods that help prevent constipation

Because hemorrhoids are mainly associated with constipation, you'll want to follow all the advice in the Constipation entry (see page 438), such as eating more fruit (particularly prunes), vegetables, and whole grains. Fiber is nature's laxative. It helps hold water in waste to bulk it up, and then it works like a broom to move it through the colon. The better the broom sweeps, the less pushing you need to do.

Fiber is helpful even when hemorrhoids require medical treatment. Danish researchers studied 92 people whose hemorrhoids were treated with a procedure called rubber band ligation (in which rubber bands are used to cut off circulation to the hemorrhoid) every 2 weeks for up to 10 weeks. Some of the patients were instructed to eat bran twice a day, while others received standard care. Not only did the bran eaters need fewer treatments to heal their hemorrhoids, but only 15 percent of them experienced recurrences compared to 45 percent of their no-bran counterparts.

Aim for: At least 25 grams of fiber a day, though 35 is preferable.

# Berries

The darker the berry, the sweeter the fruit—and the more flavonoids it contains. Flavonoids, found in many berries but also in citrus fruits and onions, help to reduce inflammation and strengthen blood vessel walls. Some research suggests they may also reduce the pain, bleeding, itching, and even the recurrence of hemorrhoids. In fact, finely ground, highly purified flavonoids called diosmin and hesperidin are the active ingredients in the French prescription hemorrhoid drug Dalfon.

Berries do double duty by helping to prevent constipation, since they're also good sources of fiber.

Aim for: Include 3/4 cup of your favorite berries, like blackberries, red raspberries, blueberries, strawberries, and even cherries, among your daily fruits and vegetables.

# Kale, spinach,
*and other foods high in vitamin K*

Vitamin K is key for helping blood clot, and eating more of these foods may benefit people who have hemorrhoids that bleed.

Aim for: The recommended amount of vitamin K is 65 micrograms for women and 80 micrograms for men, an amount that's easily gotten in a serving of bitter greens like kale, spinach, and turnip greens, as well as broccoli and even green tea.

## Tea Time?

We don't mean it's time to drink it. Tea's astringent tannins reduce inflammation, so try soaking a compress in cold black tea and applying it to the problem area. Or apply a paste made from ground elderberry and water.

## NUTRITIONAL SUPPLEMENTS

**Vitamin C.** Vitamin C can be helpful for bleeding hemorrhoids associated with constipation. It promotes healing by reducing inflammation, helping build connective tissue around the hemorrhoids, and improving the overall tone of veins. **DOSAGE:** Start with 1,000 milligrams and gradually increase the dose until stools loosen, then scale back (or you may end up with diarrhea).

**Magnesium.** Magnesium's a good laxative because it helps keep water in the stools, making them softer. See the Constipation entry for more details. **DOSAGE:** 300 to 600 milligrams daily.

**Psyllium.** Getting 25 to 35 grams of fiber each day is ideal for preventing constipation and thus hemorrhoids. But if you don't seem to be able to consume the seven servings of fruits and vegetables and three servings of whole grains that will get you there, then fiber supplements like psyllium can help close the gap. For more information, see the Constipation entry. **DOSAGE:** 1 to 3 tablespoons daily dissolved in water.

Do you have an all-day water glass? You should! At the start of each day, get out a large, clean glass, fill it up with water, and sip from it throughout the day, refilling it every time it gets empty. No excuses if you are on the go—just use a portable water bottle instead.

# HERPES

Like a sleeping giant, the herpes virus can awaken at any time. Once it's in your system, it remains there, hibernating in nerve cells until something—stress, fatigue, sun exposure, or another trigger—rouses it. Scientists have discovered that certain foods are among those triggers, nourishing the beast, while a few other foods starve it, helping to keep it dormant—the ultimate goal.

You also want to eat foods that help keep your immune system strong. That's because when you get sick, you're especially vulnerable to a herpes outbreak (either a cold sore or genital herpes), adding insult to injury. Foods that help boost the immune system also help shore up your defenses against herpes.

## YOUR FOOD PRESCRIPTION

## Dairy foods, meat, fish,
### *and other foods high in lysine*

Scientists have discovered an interesting phenomenon. Foods that contain an amino acid (a building block of protein) called arginine seem to feed the herpes virus (we'll tell you about these foods in the Off the Menu section on the next page). But adding foods that contain another amino acid, lysine, to your diet can help by blocking the action of arginine. Keeping a high ratio of lysine to arginine in your system may help keep herpes under control.

**Aim for:** Up to 3,000 milligrams of lysine, spaced throughout the day. See the table below for the lysine counts of specific foods.

### FOODS RICH IN LYSINE

| FOOD | LYSINE (MG) |
| --- | --- |
| Chicken (3 oz) | 1,800 |
| Steak (4 oz) | 1,640 |
| Flounder (3 oz) | 1,500 |
| Shrimp (3 oz) | 1,500 |
| Cottage cheese (4 oz) | 1,200 |
| Plain yogurt (1 cup) | 706 |
| Fat-free milk (1 cup) | 663 |
| Muenster cheese (1 oz) | 606 |

## Garlic

Because it's full of antioxidants, especially immunity-boosting selenium, and has antiviral power, garlic is an herb you'll want to eat liberally to boost your defenses against ailments like the common cold that wear you down and make you more vulnerable to a herpes outbreak.

**Aim for:** Use garlic liberally raw and in cooking. Cut a clove into pieces and swallow them like pills throughout the day. Stomach acids will break down the garlic and release its antioxidant power as it travels through the intestines.

**Helpful hint:** When using garlic in recipes, chop it and let it stand for 10 to 15 minutes before cooking. The waiting period allows the garlic's active compounds to develop.

## Plain yogurt with active cultures

This type of yogurt is full of beneficial bacteria that help keep the body strong by keeping the population of "bad" bacteria in check. Plus, research has found that yogurt with active cultures boosts immune cell activity. While yogurt won't directly prevent herpes, it can help keep your body healthy, making it less vulnerable to outbreaks.

**Aim for:** One cup per day. Be sure to choose yogurt with live, active cultures (look on the label for *lactobacillus, bifidus, Streptococcus thermophilus,* and *acidophilus,* among other active cultures).

# Licorice

Here's an old-fashioned remedy with some science behind it. Purchase real licorice from a health food store (not the five-and-dime variety found in candy stores). Cut it into very thin slices and place them directly on herpes sores for 10 minutes. The licorice will diminish the pain and help speed healing. An antiviral compound in licorice called glycyrrhizinic acid (GLA) is probably responsible. You can also find topical creams and ointments that contain GLA in natural foods stores.

**Aim for:** Apply fresh slices several times a day.

## NUTRITIONAL SUPPLEMENTS

**Lysine.** In a study at the University of Missouri, volunteers with a history of herpes outbreaks who took 1 gram of lysine per day for six months developed significantly fewer lesions than in the six months they didn't take the supplements. **DOSAGE:** Studies have suggested that taking between 1 and 3 grams a day is safe and effective in keeping herpes at bay. Take 1 gram three times a day without food. Caution: If you have high cholesterol, check with your doctor before taking lysine supplements over the long term. Some animal studies suggest that a high lysine-to-arginine ratio can raise cholesterol levels. Lysine also comes in creams you can apply directly to a cold sore. Look for them in natural foods stores.

**A multivitamin/mineral.** You are most vulnerable to herpes outbreaks when your immune system is stressed, which can happen to anyone who is under stress, exhausted, or undernourished. Anyone under stress may be taxing their stores of vitamin C and the B vitamins. Also, as people age, they often have difficulty absorbing certain nutrients, such as zinc and vitamin E—nutrients that keep the immune system

## Prevent Shingles at the Farmers' Market

Herpes zoster, the virus that causes chicken pox, can cause shingles later in life. This painful rash of blisters can leave you feverish and put you out of commission for weeks. If you're vulnerable to shingles, make a weekly stop at the farmers' market. A study in London showed that people who ate more than three servings of fruit a day had three times less risk of getting shingles than those who ate less than one piece per week. The researchers suspect fruit's vitamins and other nutrients help fend off shingles by keeping the immune system strong.

robust—from food. A multivitamin/mineral can help close the gap. **DOSAGE:** One per day. Alternatively, choose a multi that's designed to be taken two or three times a day, which means it will deliver a continuous supply of nutrients as the body needs them. Take it with food for best absorption.

## OFF THE MENU

**Chocolate, nuts, seeds, and gelatin.** These are rich in arginine, the amino acid that competes with more beneficial lysine in the herpes battle. Legumes (including soybeans) and whole grains are also rich in arginine, but we'd be remiss in suggesting you avoid these healthy foods. Instead, consider limiting them when you have a herpes outbreak.

### FEATURED RECIPES

**Mac 'n Cheese Primavera** *p. 608*
**Thai Roasted Shrimp** *p. 614*
**Baked Chicken with Tomatoes** *p. 615*
**Chicken in Garlic Sauce** *p. 616*
**Barbecued Flank Steak** *p. 618*

# HIGH BLOOD PRESSURE

High blood pressure usually creeps up with no warnings and no symptoms. If you don't go to the doctor very often and never check your own blood pressure, you could go for years without knowing you have it. But just because you don't feel "ill," that doesn't mean high blood pressure (a.k.a. hypertension) isn't doing harm. Doctors call it the silent killer for good reason: It's the biggest risk factor for stroke and a major contributor to heart attacks and kidney failure, as well as erectile dysfunction and even blindness.

Age, stress, and the foods we eat all conspire to raise our pressure. Fortunately, one of the easiest ways to control it is by making very simple changes to your diet—namely by eating more fruits and vegetables instead of fast food, junk food, and processed foods. That helps to naturally increase your intake of key nutrients like magnesium, potassium, and calcium, all of which lower blood pressure, and to reduce sodium consumption, which raises it. Keep your pressure in the normal range, and you lower your risk of stroke by up to 40 percent and of heart attack by up to 25 percent.

## YOUR FOOD PRESCRIPTION

### Bananas, potatoes, raisins,
*and other foods rich in potassium*

Of course, you've heard that eating less salt can help reduce high blood pressure (and in case you haven't, see Off the Menu, page 490). But what's equally important is increasing the amount of potassium you consume. When researchers looked at the biggest factors contributing to high blood pressure among people in five countries, they found that low potassium consumption accounted for 4 to 17 percent of hypertension risk. Other epidemiological studies have found that in communities where potassium consumption is generally higher, blood pressure levels are generally lower.

**FEATURED RECIPES**

**Edamame Hummus with Pita Crisps** *p. 592*
**Spinach Salad with Chickpeas** *p. 597*
**Chicken Pasta Salad** *p. 599*
**Sweet Potato Soup** *p. 601*
**Mac 'n Cheese Primavera** *p. 608*
**Almond Rice** *p. 626*
**Banana-Peanut Bread** *p. 630*
**Pear Crisp** *p. 636*
**Frozen Fruit Mousse** *p. 638*

If you can manage to increase your potassium while also decreasing your sodium—which will happen quite naturally when you eat more fruits and vegetables and fewer processed foods—you're doing even better. In one study, people who ate a diet that was low in sodium and high in potassium reduced stress-related spikes in blood pressure by 10 mmHg.

**Aim for:** 4,700 milligrams of potassium a day. You can get that much by eating the recommended 7 to 10 servings of fruit and vegetables, particularly if you focus on those listed above as high in potassium.

**Helpful hint:** Baked potatoes are especially rich in potassium, with more than 1,000 milligrams each. Skip the butter or sour cream and use a margarine-like spread fortified with plant sterols and/or stanols. You'll lower your blood pressure and your cholesterol.

## Fruits and vegetables

It's likely that you can lower your blood pressure if you do nothing else but swap some of the junk food you eat for more fruits and vegetables. That was the finding of the landmark study of nutrition and blood pressure known as Dietary Approaches to Stop Hypertension, or DASH (see "Doing the DASH," page 189). When people in the study stuck to a typical Western diet and simply increased their fruit and vegetable intake, they were able to lower their systolic blood pressure (the top number) by 2.8 mmHg (millimeters of mercury) and their diastolic blood pressure by 1.1 mmHg. Lowering your blood pressure by even a few points can substantially reduce your risk of heart attack and stroke.

**Aim for:** 7 to 10 servings of fruit and vegetables daily. A serving is one medium piece of fruit; 1/2 cup of fruit or vegetable juice; 1/2 cup of chopped fruit or cooked vegetables, beans, or legumes; or 1 cup of leafy vegetables.

**Helpful hint:** It's easier than you think to work extra fruits and vegetables into your meals. Try adding a banana or a half cup of strawberries to your morning cereal, starting dinner with a salad, and tossing a cup or two of vegetables into soups or pasta sauce. Even 1/2 cup of fruit or vegetable juice counts as a serving.

## Soy foods, beans, nuts, and seeds

Now's the time to grab a bag of edamame from your grocer's freezer and start using it. People who eat more vegetable-based protein like soy (as well as beans, legumes, nuts, and seeds) tend to have lower blood pressure compared to people who get most of their protein from animal sources like meat.

Soy contains plant estrogens that are thought to help lower blood pressure, but it's also possible the benefits come as much from what soy displaces from your diet—like meat that's high in fat and calories—as from the soy itself. Weight gain tends to raise blood pressure.

**Aim for:** About four servings of soy foods (about 25 grams) daily. A serving is a glass of soy milk, a cup of soy yogurt, one-fifth to one-quarter of a package of tofu, or about 2.5 ounces of edamame (young soybeans still in their pods).

## Low-fat and fat-free dairy foods

A glass of fat-free milk is good for the ol' bones, but did you know it's good for your blood vessels, too? Experts don't completely understand why dairy foods lower blood pressure, but they suspect that their calcium, potassium, and magnesium—all of which relax arteries and improve blood flow—play a role. Recent research suggests that people who eat more low-fat dairy products like yogurt, cheese, and low-fat or fat-free milk have lower systolic pressure as well as a lower overall risk of hypertension. The DASH studies showed that diets rich in produce and fat-free dairy foods help lower blood pressure, and another study done in Spain found that people who ate more low-fat and fat-free dairy foods had half the risk of developing hypertension compared to those who didn't eat as much.

**Aim for:** Two to three servings daily. A serving is a cup of low-fat or fat-free yogurt or fat-free milk.

## NUTRITIONAL SUPPLEMENTS

**Magnesium and calcium.** Magnesium is known to relax the arteries and improve blood pressure, but it's less clear whether supplements have the same effect as food sources like black beans, pumpkin seeds, spinach, and even halibut—all of which contain more than 100 milligrams a serving. But if you have high blood pressure and can't seem to get enough magnesium in your diet, you might consider a supplement. When Japanese researchers gave 60 people with high blood pressure magnesium supplements for eight weeks, their systolic blood pressure dropped by about 2.7 mmHg, while their diastolic reading dipped by 1.5 mmHg.

Calcium is also beneficial. If you find that you're not getting the recommended two or three servings of low-fat dairy foods each day, consider taking a calcium supplement. If you want to limit the number of pills you take, buy a calcium/magnesium combo. **DOSAGE:** 500 milligrams of magnesium and 1,000 milligrams of calcium daily from food and supplements combined.

**Omega-3 fatty acids.** Some research suggests that omega-3 fatty acids, particularly DHA, found in fatty fish like salmon, tuna, and mackerel, can modestly lower high blood pressure.

Researchers don't generally recommend taking fish-oil supplements just for blood pressure, mostly because other diet changes produce more substantial results. But if you're already taking fish oil for some other reason (to lower your triglycerides, for instance), you may find that your blood pressure also drops a bit. **DOSAGE:** At least 3 grams daily. The American Heart Association currently recommends 2 to 4 grams daily to help lower triglycerides. If you wish to take more, talk with your doctor.

## OFF THE MENU

**Sodium.** Reduce your sodium (a component of salt), and you can substantially lower your blood pressure. Both the American Heart Association and the National Heart, Lung, and Blood Institute recommend limiting salt to no more than 1 teaspoon (which contains about 2,300 milligrams of sodium) each day.

A tall order? You bet. But data from studies on the DASH Diet prove it's worth it. Reducing sodium intake to 2,300 milligrams a day can lower blood pressure by 2.1/1.1 mmHg. Cut back even more—to about 2/3 teaspoon daily—and you can drop your blood pressure by 6.7/3.5 mmHg.

Make raisins a secret ingredient in your cooking. They go well with sautéed vegetables—just add a handful near the end of cooking. Or toss into roasts of chicken, beef, or pork. They'll plump up and soften if cooked in liquid, adding both sweetness and visual surprise to your meals. And their high potassium levels can help reduce your blood pressure.

The good news is that the salt you sprinkle on after food is prepared isn't that much of a concern—provided, of course, that you're not dumping a whole shaker into every dish. It's processed foods that are the big problems; they account for about 75 percent of the sodium we consume. Many foods that you wouldn't even think of as "salty," like some cereals, contain more sodium than potato or corn chips! The best way to curb your sodium intake is to steer clear of these high-sodium processed foods. You can also follow this rule of thumb: When you check the calorie and sodium content per serving on product labels, the number of milligrams of sodium should be less than or at most equal to the number of calories.

**Alcohol.** Whether alcohol should be "off the menu" or not largely depends on how much you drink. Light to moderate drinking is considered heart healthy because it raises HDL ("good") cholesterol and makes blood less likely to form artery-blocking clots, so one drink daily for women and two drinks for men are generally considered safe. But heavy drinking will increase blood pressure—and raise your stroke risk by as much as 69 percent.

**Coffee and other caffeinated drinks.** Your morning cup of java could be giving you more of a jolt than you bargained for. Although the antioxidants in coffee may help lower the risk of heart disease and cancer, if your blood pressure is on the high side, the caffeine could make it worse. Some research done at Duke University Medical Center suggests that drinking four to five cups a day boosts stress hormones like adrenaline by about 32 percent, which in turn increases blood pressure. According to these studies, blood pressure can rise within an hour of having your morning cup of Joe, and levels stay high all day. Even so, the research is far from definitive. Data from more than 155,000 women in the Nurses Health Study found no connection between coffee drinking and hypertension, though it did find a link with regular and diet sodas.

## Doing the DASH

Following the DASH (Dietary Approaches to Stop Hypertension) Diet can lower your blood pressure by 5.5/3 mmHg. That alone is enough to reduce your heart disease risk by 15 percent and your stroke risk by 27 percent. Follow the DASH Diet and cut your salt intake to less than a teaspoon a day, and you could lower your blood pressure by 8.9/4.5 mmHg. That's the kind of reduction blood pressure medication can produce. Here's what it takes to do the DASH.

**Grains:** Six to eight servings a day, such as a slice of bread or 1/2 cup of rice, pasta, or cereal.

**Fruits and vegetables:** Four to five servings a day, such as 1/2 cup of chopped fruit or cooked vegetables, a cup of leafy vegetables, 1/4 cup of dried fruit, or 1/2 to 3/4 cup of fruit or vegetable juice.

**Low-fat/fat-free dairy:** Two to three servings a day, such as a cup of milk or yogurt.

**Lean meat, poultry, or fish:** 6 ounces a day.

**Nuts, seeds, and legumes:** Four to five servings a week, such as 1/2 cup of beans, 1/3 cup of nuts, or 2 tablespoons of peanut butter.

**Sweets and added sugars:** Less than five servings a week, such as a tablespoon of sugar or jam or 1/2 cup of sorbet.

# HIV/AIDS

Food won't cure AIDS, but the right diet can support the body so it can better handle the physical stresses of this chronic disease and the drugs used to treat it.

HIV, the virus that causes AIDS, puts an enormous strain on all of the body's systems. But eating a nutrient-packed diet—one that includes lean proteins and antioxidant-rich produce and excludes empty calories from junk food and alcohol—provides your body with the raw materials it needs to fight the virus and possibly delay its progression to AIDS. A heart-smart diet can also help manage the side effects of the anti-retroviral therapy (HAART) drugs now being used to treat HIV. (While these newer drugs allow people with HIV to live longer, they also significantly raise cholesterol levels, increasing the risk of heart disease.) In addition, key nutrients from food and supplements improve digestion so you're able to replenish what your body is using as it fights the virus and generally bolster your immune system so it can fend off the AIDS-related infections that ultimately claim lives.

## YOUR FOOD PRESCRIPTION

### Lean meats, fish, chicken, beans, *and other lean proteins*

The body needs more protein when it's fighting HIV, because many of the components of the immune system, like antibodies, are made from proteins. When there's not enough protein—which often happens with HIV because calorie needs are higher, absorption isn't always good, and appetite decreases—the immune system doesn't work as well.

That hardly means you should switch to a cheeseburger diet. Saturated fats increase the already elevated risk for heart disease that comes with HAART medications, and they increase inflammation throughout the body. Chronic inflammation is believed to be responsible for many of the long-term side effects often seen with HIV, such as osteoporosis and type 2 diabetes. Plus, certain inflammation-related substances called cytokines, which increase with saturated fat consumption, also spur the replication of HIV. So keep your protein sources lean.

Aim for: Multiply your weight in pounds by 0.6 to calculate how many grams of protein you require every day. For instance, a 200-pound man needs 120 grams. (We realize that's a tall order, equal to about 15 ounces of salmon or steak or 17 cups of soy milk daily.) A 130-pound woman needs 78 grams.

Helpful hint: Using whey protein powder is an easy way to get protein without fat. You can get 34 grams just by adding two scoops of whey protein to a breakfast shake.

### High-fiber foods

Eating plenty of fiber helps the body absorb nutrients from food. It also reduces diarrhea, a common complaint with HIV. High-fiber foods also help control some of the side effects of HAART medications, like insulin resistance, elevated cholesterol and triglyceride levels, and the tendency for fat to collect around the belly. According to a study conducted at Tufts University, HIV-positive men who ate more fiber were less likely to have fat deposits around their middles than men who ate less. In fact, eating just 1 more gram of fiber lowered the risk of acquiring belly fat by 7 percent.

Aim for: 25 to 35 grams of fiber a day. Three servings of whole grains, like a sandwich on whole-wheat bread and 1/2 cup of brown rice, and seven servings (a mere 1/2 cup each) of fruits and vegetables will almost get you to 25 grams. For more, add some beans, lentils, nuts, and high-fiber cereal.

## Fruits, vegetables,
*and other foods high in antioxidants*

HIV does enormous damage to cells, and the best way to counter that damage and protect immune cells from being eviscerated by the virus is to consume as many varieties of antioxidants as possible. Fruits and vegetables are among the best sources of a wide variety of antioxidants and other vitamins and minerals (like A, C, E, the B vitamins, iron, selenium, and zinc) that tend to be in short supply in people with HIV. Even in the early stages, HIV causes vitamin deficiencies that are associated with a more rapid progression of HIV to AIDS. Fruits and veggies will help fill the gaps.

Don't just go for the same old apples and oranges. Because antioxidants work best when they work together, the more you consume from a wide variety of brightly colored fruits and vegetables, the better.

**Aim for:** 7 to 10 servings of fruits and vegetables a day, though if you're particularly prone to HIV-related yeast infections, limit fruit because its sugars may lead to an overgrowth of yeast.

## Shiitake, maitake, and reishi mushrooms

These mushrooms contain a type of carbohydrates called beta-glucans. Some lab studies suggest that these may be beneficial for HIV because they stimulate immune cells to destroy viruses.

**Aim for:** There's no established recommendation, but including 1/2 cup of mushrooms among the fruits and vegetables you eat each day is certainly safe.

**Helpful hint:** While shiitake mushrooms can be eaten raw or cooked, reishi and maitakes are more complicated to consume. To extract their

beta-glucans, boil these mushrooms for 30 minutes to make mushroom broth. You can drink a cup a day.

## Yogurt with active cultures

Eating a few daily servings of yogurt contributes to good gut health, which helps on several fronts. When your digestive tract is in good working order, you're less likely to experience diarrhea, and you're better able to absorb the nutrients from the foods you eat. The better your digestion, the stronger your immune system will be to fight the virus and the better you'll be at tolerating the medications. In addition, yogurt relieves some of the stress on your immune system by increasing the gut's population of beneficial bacteria. These help keep microorganisms like yeast and "bad" bacteria from gaining a foothold.

**Aim for:** One to three cups a day.

## Brazil nuts
*and other foods rich in selenium*

These nuts contain vast amounts of the antioxidant mineral selenium. Research shows that for people with HIV who also have low levels of selenium, the mortality risk is 10 times higher than for those whose selenium levels are within normal ranges.

**Aim for:** 200 to 600 micrograms a day, an amount that's easily gotten from a handful of Brazil nuts. Each nut contains 75 to 100 micrograms of selenium.

### FEATURED RECIPES

**Ultimate Spiced Nuts** *p. 592*
**Lentil-Tomato Soup** *p. 603*
**Three-Bean Chili** *p. 610*
**Fish Tacos** *p. 611*
**Roasted Salmon with Sautéed Greens** *p. 612*
**Baked Chicken with Tomatoes** *p. 615*
**Chicken-Barley Bake** *p. 616*
**Raspberry-Almond Muffins** *p. 628*

# Green tea

Green tea is an excellent source of the antioxidant epigallocatechin-3-gallate (EGCG), which is thought to have some antiviral properties. At least one laboratory study found that it prevented the replication of HIV in cell cultures. Other lab research shows that EGCG inhibits Kaposi's sarcoma, a cancer that people with HIV are prone to developing.

Aim for: About four cups daily.

## NUTRITIONAL SUPPLEMENTS

**A multivitamin/mineral.** HIV attacks the intestinal cells that absorb nutrients, which can cause deficiencies that lead to impaired immune function. Low levels of vitamins A, $B_6$, $B_{12}$, and E and the minerals selenium and zinc are all associated with advancing HIV. Replenishing nutrient stores with a daily multi appears to slow the progression of HIV to AIDS. One study of HIV-positive men conducted at the University of California at Berkeley showed that taking a multi every day reduced the risk of HIV developing into AIDS by 30 percent during the six-year study. **DOSAGE:** Choose a high-potency formulation and follow the label instructions.

**B vitamins.** B vitamin deficiencies are directly linked with advancing HIV. A nine-year Johns Hopkins University study of 310 HIV-positive men found that men with normal $B_{12}$ levels took eight years to develop AIDS, while men whose $B_{12}$ was low progressed from HIV to AIDS in just four years. It's still not certain whether taking extra $B_{12}$ slows the progression of HIV, but another Johns Hopkins study with the same men found that over eight years, taking $B_1$, $B_2$, $B_6$, and niacin delayed the onset of AIDS and improved survival rates by 40 percent to 60 percent. **DOSAGE:** In the study, doses of $B_1$ and $B_2$ were five times higher than the RDA, or 7.5 milligrams of $B_1$ and 9 milligrams of $B_2$. Doses of $B_6$ were twice as high as the RDA, or 4 milligrams. The RDA for $B_{12}$ is 2 micrograms. Since these doses are higher than what's routinely recommended, check with your doctor first.

**Selenium.** When people with HIV are deficient in this antioxidant mineral, their risk of dying from AIDS is 10 times higher compared to HIV-positive people whose selenium levels are normal. **DOSAGE:** Up to 600 micrograms daily, though if you're also making an effort to eat selenium-rich foods, you may not need as much from supplements.

**Alpha-lipoic acid.** Think of this nutrient as a superantioxidant. With HIV/AIDS, higher levels of antioxidants are needed to counteract the increased oxidative stress the virus puts on the body. Alpha-lipoic acid recycles both water-soluble and fat-soluble antioxidants (vitamins A, C, and E and selenium) so they work more effectively and stay in the body longer. **DOSAGE:** 600 to 1,200 milligrams daily.

**Glutamine.** This amino acid is a natural anti-inflammatory that stops the diarrhea that frequently occurs with anti-retroviral medications. In one study, HIV-positive men who took 30 grams of glutamine a day were able to cut back on their use of antidiarrheal drugs. **DOSAGE:** 2 to 30 grams daily before meals. Take the lower dose for overall maintenance of gut health and the higher one for diarrhea.

**Probiotics.** In addition to eating yogurt that contains live bacterial cultures, you may also want to take supplements of probiotics, or friendly bacteria. Look for refrigerated probiotic formulas that contain *Lactobacillus acidophilus, L. bifidobacterium,* and *L. bulgaricus.* All three are essential because each populates a different part of the digestive tract. **DOSAGE:** 3 to 6 billion organisms a day to maintain good gut health; between 15 and 30 billion organisms a day if you have diarrhea.

**Omega-3 fatty acids.** Studies haven't conclusively proven that fish oil has a direct impact on HIV, but researchers suspect it may because inflammation appears to play a role in the replication of HIV, and the omega-3s in fish oil are natural anti-inflammatories. In one promising study, Spanish researchers reported higher CD4 cell counts, a sign of improved immune function, in HIV patients who received fish-oil supplements. Because omega-3s are also so valuable in blocking heart disease, anyone taking HAART medications should consider taking supplements. **DOSAGE:** 600 milligrams of EPA and 400 milligrams of DHA daily.

## OFF THE MENU

**Fatty meats, full-fat dairy foods, and trans fat.** Cutting back on foods rich in saturated fats and trans fat (from hydrogenated oils) not only lowers the risk of heart disease that comes with HAART medications, it may also improve immune function. In a small study at Tufts University, when 18 men with high cholesterol switched from a standard Western diet with 38 percent of calories from fat to a diet with 28 percent of calories from fat, their immune function improved by up to 29 percent.

**Alcohol.** Alcohol depresses immune function and depletes the body of B vitamins, low levels of which are linked with faster disease progression. And it's processed through the liver, which is already working hard to filter out by-products of HIV medications.

**Refined sugar.** If you're eating yogurt, fiber, and probiotics to improve digestive health, don't undo your efforts by consuming a lot of sugar, known to weaken immune function. In addition, consuming too much sugar is like inviting yeast to a banquet in your gut. Yeast overgrowth contributes to a state of low-grade, chronic inflammation that further taxes the immune system, which could be one reason HIV-positive people are more vulnerable to fungal infections of the mouth and skin.

## Build Your Own Supplement Cocktail

New research suggests that a high-potency multivitamin/mineral combined with vitamin $B_6$ (100 milligrams), alpha-lipoic acid (200 milligrams), acetyl-l-carnitine (500 milligrams), and N-acetyl-cysteine (600 milligrams)—all of which can be found at health food stores—can dramatically improve immune function. When 40 HIV-positive patients on HAART medications took either the combination supplement or a placebo twice a day for three months, the number of CD4 cells in those taking the vitamin supplement was 24 percent greater than in those taking a placebo, who showed no improvement.

# IMMUNE WEAKNESS

Are you one of those people who seem to catch whatever bug is going around? Do colds and other upper respiratory infections seem to drag on and on and bring you down lower than they should? It's true that our immune systems tend to weaken with age; that's why older people generally don't respond as well to vaccinations as younger people, and why the flu can be fatal in elderly folks. But no matter what your age, it's well within your power to boost your defenses.

The various elements of the immune system are often likened to troops in an army that protects your body. And as the Emperor Napoleon once said, "An army marches on its stomach." When we don't eat well enough (or we don't get enough sleep and exercise, or we feel stressed), that army gets sluggish. Perhaps not weak enough to sound any serious alarms, but just enough to allow bacteria, viruses, and parasites to slip through the defenses. Even minor deficiencies of key micronutrients like zinc, selenium, and iron can hamper your body's ability to fend off disease and infection.

Before the next cold and flu season comes along, consider giving your diet a "shot in the arm." That can be as simple as brightening your plate with colorful produce, enjoying a delicious shrimp dinner now and then, spicing up your meals with more garlic, and cutting back on the fatty and sugary foods that work against you.

## YOUR FOOD PRESCRIPTION

## Chicken, fish, beans, eggs, yogurt, *and other foods high in protein*

Protein is the building block for many of the immune system's key players, like antibodies and the white blood cells that search out and destroy germs and cancer cells. Many protein foods are also great sources of zinc, iron, and many B vitamins, all of which are essential for strong immune function.

The typical Western diet isn't lacking in protein, but elderly people and vegetarians in particular need to be sure they get enough. If you eat meat, pass on the greasy burgers and fried chicken and choose lean beef and skinless chicken; as you'll read later on, saturated fat and fried foods promote the kind of low-grade inflammation in the body that can be a slow drain on your immune resources.

Aim for: 3 to 4 ounces of protein—the amount in a serving of meat or fish the size of a deck of cards or in a half cup of peas—twice a day; have more if you're larger or more active than average.

Helpful hint: Sardines can be triply protective. Not only are they lean proteins but they also contain anti-inflammatory omega-3 essential fatty acids along with good amounts of zinc and selenium, two other important immunity boosters.

## Pumpkin seeds

Now you've got good reason to save those seeds when you're carving up pumpkins—a half cup contains about 6 milligrams of zinc, which is one of the most critical nutrients for overall immune function. Studies show that people who are zinc deficient (which is common with age) have a more difficult time fending off garden-variety infections.

**Aim for:** The current recommendation for zinc is 15 milligrams, though if you're prone to illness, you may want to aim for 30 milligrams daily. That's a lot of pumpkin seeds, so you may want to add some oysters or crab to your diet. Not a fan of shellfish? Dark-meat turkey is another good source, as is beef.

**Helpful hint:** You can quickly "roast" pumpkin seeds in your microwave. Put some olive oil in a microwave-safe baking dish and heat for 30 seconds. Then add the pumpkin seeds and cook on high for 7 to 8 minutes, turning every 2 minutes. Not into microwaving? You can also dry pumpkin seeds in the oven (15 minutes at 200°F).

# Brazil nuts

These nuts are nature's number one source of the immunity-supporting antioxidant mineral selenium. When we're low on selenium, our white blood cells are slower to kill off microbes and tumor cells. In addition, because selenium protects cells from free radical damage, it's been suggested that a deficiency sets the stage for harmless viruses to mutate into more aggressive strains. And with a fatigued immune system, these more dangerous viruses can then mutate and reproduce out of control. This may be why selenium-deficient HIV patients are far more likely to develop AIDS and die faster. Getting enough selenium rejuvenates immune cells so they're able to clobber the germs.

**Aim for:** Each Brazil nut contains 75 to 100 micrograms of selenium, so just one or two a day will do it because the recommended amount of selenium is relatively low—about 70 micrograms for men and 55 micrograms for women, though some experts believe 200 micrograms is more beneficial. If you tend to catch every cold going around, aim for the higher amount. You'll also find selenium in salmon, crab, and shrimp (between 34 and 40 micrograms in a 3-ounce portion).

# Yogurt with active cultures

About 70 percent of the immune system resides in your gut, so it stands to reason that a healthy gastrointestinal tract means a healthy immune system. The live cultures found in certain yogurts (be sure to check the label) work by populating your GI tract with friendly bacteria, like *Lactobacillus acidophilus,* to ward off the bad bugs. You can think of it as being like a neighborhood watch program in a small city. As in any city, good and bad elements coexist. But the more friendly bacteria you have, the less likely you are to be attacked by the nastier bugs.

**Aim for:** A cup a day.

**Helpful hint:** Opt for plain, sugar-free yogurt. Eating yogurt with sugar is counterproductive since sugar not only depresses immune function, it also attracts harmful microbes like yeast.

To get more beans in your diet, keep well-rinsed and ready-to-eat kidney or garbanzo beans in your refrigerator. Put them on the table at mealtime and add to salads and green vegetables, or just nibble on them throughout the meal.

## Tea

It's believed that one reason the Japanese have lower rates of many diseases (including cancer) is that they drink so much green tea, a major storehouse of immunity-boosting compounds, including potent antioxidants like EGCG. Some research suggests that green tea is helpful for fending off the bugs that cause flu and diarrhea, whooping cough, pneumonia, and even cavities. Even black tea appears to have immunity-enhancing properties. A small study at Harvard Medical School that examined immune function in coffee drinkers compared to tea drinkers found that when blood taken from all the study participants was exposed to *E. coli* bacteria, the tea drinkers' immune cells responded about five times faster than the coffee drinkers'. Researchers believe it's the compound L-theanine in black tea that helps to rally immune function.

**Aim for:** One to two cups daily for general health. If you're sick, try to drink three to four cups.

### FEATURED RECIPES

**Ultimate Spiced Nuts** *p. 592*
**Sweet Potato Soup** *p. 601*
**Beef in Lettuce Wraps** *p. 606*
**Roasted Salmon with Sautéed Greens** *p. 613*
**Baked Chicken with Tomatoes** *p. 615*
**Beef and Broccoli Stew** *p. 620*
**Pumpkin Streusel Bread** *p. 631*

## Garlic

Garlic's a friend of the immune system, especially when eaten raw. For starters, it's an edible antibiotic, with strong antibacterial properties. It also fights viruses. And its sulfur compounds are surprisingly rich in antioxidants. Chop or crush your garlic, then let it stand for 10 to 15 minutes to fully release its healing potential.

**Aim for:** At least a clove a day.

## A rainbow of fruits and vegetables

Brightly colored produce is a storehouse of antioxidants, substances our immune systems need in vast quantities when we're sick or under stress. Stress and sickness increase the body's production of the rogue, cell-attacking molecules known as free radicals. These molecules can damage the thymus gland, where many immune system cells are incubated. As the thymus goes, so goes the immune system. When the thymus is damaged, we become more susceptible to infections, which in turn produce more free radicals. Antioxidants help break this cycle.

Eating more fruit and vegetables is an easy way to naturally keep your body well supplied with antioxidants. But don't just go for the same old apples and oranges. Because antioxidants work best when they work together, the greater the variety of brightly colored fruits and vegetables you eat, the more types of antioxidants you consume—like the flavonoids found in red grapes and citrus fruits and the carotenoids that give carrots and sweet potatoes their bright orange color—and in turn the more effectively your immune system will function.

**Aim for:** 7 to 10 servings of fruits and vegetables a day.

**Helpful hint:** Think small, as in tiny berries. Blueberries top the USDA's list of antioxidant-packed fruits. Blackberries, strawberries, and raspberries also rate high.

## NUTRITIONAL SUPPLEMENTS

**Probiotics.** In addition to eating yogurt with live cultures, you may want to take some probiotics—active cultures in supplement form—that enhance immune function by improving digestion and nutrient absorption and preventing an overgrowth of harmful bacteria and yeast in your gut. Because quality counts, look for refrigerated formulas that contain *Lactobacillus acidophilus* and *bifidobacterium*. And check the expiration date on the bottle. For the supplement to be effective, the organisms need to be alive when you take them. **DOSAGE:** 1 to 6 billion organisms daily. If you've recently taken antibiotics, you'll want more because antibiotics wipe out a good portion of your friendly bacteria. To repopulate your GI tract, take 30 billion organisms a day for two weeks, then scale back to 10 billion a day for six months. If you experience any gastric upset, scale back further.

**Garlic.** If garlic just burns your belly, supplements may be a good option, particularly around cold and flu season. A British study of 146 people found that volunteers who took garlic supplements for 12 weeks during cold season had fewer than half the number of colds compared to people in the placebo group. And when they got sick, they recovered four days faster. *Note:* If you take a blood thinner like warfarin (Coumadin), check with your doctor first because garlic can increase the drug's anti-clotting effects. **DOSAGE:** 300 milligrams two or three times daily is generally considered safe.

**Zinc.** Zinc is essential for the development and activation of T cells, white blood cells that help fight infection. Because you may not get all the zinc you need from your diet, you may want to get more from supplements in the form of pills or lozenges. When you feel a cold coming on, suck on zinc lozenges per the package directions. Some studies suggest that getting zinc right up against your mucous membranes cuts the duration of a cold by two to three days. And according to one study, taking a zinc lozenge every day throughout cold season may lower your risk of getting sick by 25 percent.

## Should You Go Organic?

Recently, when Swedish researchers analyzed extracts from both organic and conventionally grown strawberries, not only did the organic strawberries contain more antioxidants, but when the researchers tested both extracts on colon and breast cancer cells, the organic extracts encouraged more cancer cells to destroy themselves. Organic produce generally contains higher levels of calcium, iron, magnesium, and chromium and about 30 percent more antioxidants than conventionally grown fruits and vegetables. Of course, organic foods are usually more expensive. When you can't buy organic, look for the freshest seasonal produce. The main point is to eat more fruits and vegetables, regardless of whether they're organic.

Indian cuisine is particularly rich in ingredients that bolster the immune system. Consider regular visits to an Indian restaurant, and order meals rich with lentils, chicken, dark green vegetables, and yogurt-based sauces.

Just be sure to eat something before you pop a zinc lozenge; taking zinc on an empty stomach can cause nausea. **DOSAGE:** The recommended intake for zinc is 11 milligrams a day for men and 8 for women, although some practitioners recommend taking supplements of up to 25 milligrams a day. Zinc lozenges typically contain about 23 milligrams apiece. Note that too much zinc can actually depress immune function over time; don't take more than 40 milligrams a day except when you're taking the lozenges for a cold.

**B vitamins, including folic acid.** B vitamins are involved with the production of our cellular DNA as well as many of the components of the immune system, such as antibodies and white blood cells. When we don't get enough B vitamins, we don't make enough of these infection fighters, and that leaves us vulnerable to illness. Stress depletes the B vitamins, which may help explain why we tend to get sick when we're under a lot of stress. **DOSAGE:** The B vitamins work together, and you want them all in balance, so choose a quality B-complex supplement and follow the label instructions for dosage.

**Vitamins, A, C, and E.** All of the nutrients in this vitamin "cocktail" work together to keep the immune system going strong and keep the number of immune cells high. Vitamins A and C help fortify the body's physical barriers, building collagen and strengthening the mucous membranes so germs are less able to slip through. They also rally the immune troops to do battle against germs that do make it past the barricades. Vitamin A helps C work, and it has significant antiviral activity. Vitamin C helps ensure that the body has enough infection-fighting T cells, and E partners with C to protect immune cells from free radical damage. It's also thought to enhance T-cell activity and assist in the production of antibodies. One study done at Tufts University in Boston found that when 451 senior citizens were given either 200 IU of vitamin E a day or a placebo, the volunteers taking the vitamin got fewer colds. **DOSAGE:** *Vitamin E: 200 IU daily. Vitamin A:*

5,000 to 10,000 IU daily for general maintenance. You can get this amount from a good multivitamin. If you have an upper respiratory infection, you can increase your dose to 100,000 IU for five days, then scale back to 50,000 IU for another week. Note that prolonged high doses can be toxic. If you're pregnant or trying to conceive, don't take more than 5,000 IU. Consult a healthcare practitioner before taking more than 10,000 IU for more than one week. *Vitamin C:* Recommendations vary between 250 and 1,000 milligrams a day for prevention and up to 2,000 milligrams every few hours if you get sick. Because our need for C is so high when we're fighting an infection, some physicians recommend going to "bowel tolerance," that is, taking just enough to cause loose stools and then reducing the dose.

## OFF THE MENU

**Refined sugar and starches.** Sugary and starchy foods (which convert easily into sugar in the body) deliver a double whammy to the immune system. For starters, eating sugar is like giving Valium to your white blood cells, knocking them out so they're less able to hunt down and destroy germs and cancer cells. In a study at Loma Linda University in California, when volunteers consumed about 100 grams of sugar (about the amount in two cans of soda), their white blood cell activity dropped by 50 percent and stayed low for up to 5 hours.

For fungi and cancer cells, sugar is like a champagne and caviar banquet—they just can't get enough. Sugar also encourages an overgrowth of yeast, associated with chronic yeast infections and, according to some nutritionists, digestive problems like "leaky gut syndrome," which they believe burden the immune system. Some scientists are even singling out sugar as a cancer promoter.

**Saturated fats and trans fat.** Eating less of these fats—think hamburgers, marbled red meat, and fried chicken—means better immune function. High levels of cholesterol and other blood fats, a common result of eating too many saturated and trans fat, contribute to inflammation in the body and may inhibit immune functions, including the ability of white blood cells to divide, move to areas of infection, and destroy organisms. In a small study done at Tufts University, when 18 men with high cholesterol switched from a diet in which 38 percent of the calories came from fat to a diet that included 28 percent fat, their immune function related to T-cell activity improved by up to 29 percent. Keep in mind that "good" fats like those in salmon, olive oil, avocados, and flaxseed are not thought to hamper immune function and may even improve it.

**Alcohol.** Whether alcohol is "off the menu" really depends on your state of health, along with how much and what you're drinking. While numerous studies show that light drinking has cardiovascular benefits, other research indicates that alcohol temporarily "intoxicates" your immune system, reducing the ability of all its cells to fight invading germs. This probably isn't a problem for light drinkers, but frequent imbibers take heed: Heavy drinkers are much more vulnerable to infections from bacteria (like pneumonia and tuberculosis) and viruses (including HIV, which causes AIDS), certain cancers, and infections related to traumatic injuries. In fact, people who experience such injuries while drunk are six times more likely to die from them than nondrinkers with comparable injuries.

Still, all alcohol isn't equal. While hard liquor suppresses immune function, red wine, in moderation, doesn't, perhaps because of its antioxidants.

# INFERTILITY

Creating another human being has something in common with growing a prize-winning garden: You need all the right conditions and good timing to boot. As with improving the soil in your backyard, you can help make the conditions in your body ripe for conception with the help of key food nutrients.

The reproductive system is awfully sensitive. In women, shifts in hormones, an abnormality in the reproductive organs, infection, disease, and even stress can lead to infertility. In men, the most common causes are low sperm count and slow "swimmers." Although food can't fix all fertility challenges, it can help improve your odds of fruitfulness.

## YOUR FOOD PRESCRIPTION

### Beans, spinach, *and other foods high in folate*

Women are encouraged to take folic acid supplements when they're trying to conceive because doing so helps prevent certain birth defects. But men need folic acid, too. University of California researchers found that low levels of the B vitamin may affect sperm count and density (the number of sperm per milliliter of semen). Eating foods rich in folate (the natural form) can help meet these needs.

**Aim for:** 600 micrograms of folate per day, an amount found in 1 1/4 cups of fortified cereal or 1 cup of cooked lentils plus 1 cup of cooked spinach.

**Helpful hint:** Green vegetables like spinach and cabbage can lose 40 percent of their folate during cooking, so when you can, enjoy green vegetables raw.

### FEATURED RECIPES

**Broccoli Salad** *p. 595*
**Spinach Salad with Chickpeas** *p. 597*
**Shrimp and Grapefruit Salad** *p. 598*
**Beef in Lettuce Wraps** *p. 606*
**Mac 'n Cheese Primavera** *p. 608*
**Roasted Salmon with Sautéed Greens** *p. 613*

### Fatty fish, flaxseed, walnuts, *and other foods high in omega-3 fatty acids*

The body uses omega-3 fatty acids to produce hormones called eicosanoids, which increase blood flow to the uterus, thus boosting the chances of pregnancy and facilitating fetal development. Omega-3s can also lower the risk of premature birth and low birth weight.

**Aim for:** 1,000 milligrams a day, the amount in a serving of salmon, 1/4 cup of walnuts, or 2 tablespoons of flaxseed.

**Helpful hint:** Women who are trying to conceive or are pregnant should not eat shark, swordfish, king mackerel, or tilefish because of their high mercury content.

### Lean red meat, oysters, crab, *and other foods high in zinc*

Low zinc levels translate into lowered sperm counts, less sperm movement toward the cervical goal, less semen, and even infertility. A zinc deficiency can affect a woman's fertility by lengthening her menstrual cycle, which means less frequent ovulation.

**Aim for:** In studies of men, zinc doses ranged from 220 to 500 milligrams daily. The amount in two servings of beef is only about

11 milligrams, so men should consider a supplement (see Nutritional Supplements below). The recommended amount for nonpregnant women is 8 milligrams.

# Milk, cheese, yogurt, *and other foods high in calcium and vitamin D*

At the University of Wisconsin, treatment with calcium and vitamin D restored fertility—at least in male rats. Other research shows that calcium levels increase in sperm during the last seconds before fertilization, providing the burst of energy needed to penetrate the egg. And for women, a Columbia University study found that in those with polycystic ovary syndrome, which interferes with ovulation, calcium and vitamin D helped restore normal menstruation.

Aim for: *Calcium:* 1,000 milligrams for men and 1,300 milligrams for women, the equivalent of three to four glasses of milk. *Vitamin D:* 1,000 IU daily, about the amount in two 4-ounce servings of salmon and 2 cups of milk.

# Oranges, peppers, broccoli, *and other foods high in vitamin C*

Don't skip your morning orange juice. A study of 150 infertile women showed that supplementation with 750 milligrams a day of vitamin C boosted fertility. After six months, the fertility rate in the vitamin C group was 25 percent compared to only 11 percent in the placebo group. Progesterone levels were also significantly increased in the treatment group.

Aim for: You may need a supplement to get to 750 milligrams. A cup of cooked broccoli has 100 milligrams; a cup of orange juice has 124.

## NUTRITIONAL SUPPLEMENTS

**Vitamin C.** Daily supplementation has been shown to boost fertility. **DOSAGE:** 750 milligrams a day.

**Folic Acid.** Couples should begin taking folic acid supplements as soon as they decide to conceive. **DOSAGE:** 600 micrograms a day for women and men.

**Calcium and vitamin D.** Don't take calcium supplements derived from oyster shells or bonemeal. They may contain lead, which can harm an unborn child. **DOSAGE:** *Calcium:* 1,300 milligrams daily for women; men shouldn't take supplements because they may increase the risk of prostate cancer. *Vitamin D:* 1,000 IU daily for men and women.

**Omega-3 fatty acids.** These come in fish-oil capsules and in liquids such as flaxseed oil. Buy a brand with vitamin E, which helps keep the oil from becoming rancid. **DOSAGE:** 1 gram per day.

**Zinc.** Long-term use of zinc supplements also requires taking 1 to 2 milligrams of copper daily to prevent a copper deficiency. **DOSAGE:** Some doctors recommend 100 milligrams a day for infertile men for a short time or 50 milligrams a day for more prolonged periods. But don't take more than 40 milligrams per day—the upper limit set by the National Academy of Sciences—without consulting your physician.

## OFF THE MENU

**Coffee, cola, and other foods with caffeine.** Some studies, though not others, suggest that caffeine affects fertility and may contribute to miscarriage. The theory is that it may affect ovulation by altering hormone levels. Caffeine constricts blood vessels, slowing blood flow to the uterus, which theoretically could make it harder for an egg to nestle in. It also raises the risk of insulin resistance, which can affect ovulation. On the other hand, the Organisation of Teratology Information Services, a group that studies the effects of substances on fetal development, concluded that fewer than three cups of coffee a day (300 milligrams of caffeine) probably won't influence a woman's fertility.

For men, the story's different. According to findings by Brazilian scientists, caffeine appears to make sperm nimbler.

# INFLAMMATORY BOWEL DISEASE

If you have inflammatory bowel disease (IBD), the current wisdom on how to approach it can flip your perception of what constitutes a healthy diet: Don't overdo the fiber, hold back on the spices, and think twice before you eat fruit and vegetables.

Nevertheless, research has revealed that such a diet may help alleviate some of the pain associated with IBD.

Characterized by persistent inflammation of the intestinal tract, IBD can be debilitating. Symptoms, including abdominal pain, diarrhea, appetite loss, and fatigue, can linger for weeks to years and disappear for periods of time. The two different conditions that fall under the category of IBD, Crohn's disease and ulcerative colitis, affect the GI tract in different ways. With Crohn's disease, inflammation in all layers of the intestinal wall prevents the small intestine from properly absorbing nutrients and disturbs the fine balance of water needed to usher foods along the intestine. That can lead to relentless diarrhea. Add appetite loss to the equation, and vitamin and mineral deficiencies become a real problem. With ulcerative colitis, the inner lining of the large intestine becomes inflamed, preventing the normal absorption of water from the colon, the last 5 feet of the intestine. This causes diarrhea and extreme discomfort.

More than half of people who develop IBD eventually have surgery to remove part of their intestine or correct intestinal abnormalities. That can leave the digestive tract less robust and more sensitive to swings in dietary and other irritants.

Food won't prevent or cure IBD, but the right diet may diminish symptoms. The strategy is to focus on foods that reduce inflammation, to reestablish healthy bacteria in the gut, and to pamper your intestinal tract. That means keeping a food diary to determine which foods trigger flare-ups and which seem to appease the sleeping giant. Work with your doctor to determine whether you have sensitivities to specific foods and establish whether you need supplements to replenish some of the nutrients lost during bouts of IBD.

## FEATURED RECIPES

**Salsa Tuna Salad Sandwiches** *p. 604*
**Tuna Kebabs** *p. 610*
**Tomato-Roasted Mackerel** *p. 612*
**Roasted Salmon with Sautéed Greens** *p. 613*

# Small, frequent meals rich in calories

Six small meals a day are often more easily digested than the traditional three and make it easier to get enough calories to maintain weight. People with IBD often lose significant weight, making it difficult for them to get sufficient nutrients. This is particularly true for people who have narrowed areas of the intestine as a result of IBD.

Aim for: Choose calorie-rich, nutrient-dense foods like whole grains, legumes, and nuts when your gut feels calm. During flare-ups, avoid the foods listed in Off the Menu (see page 507) and focus on those that don't worsen your problem.

# Potatoes, white rice, refined pasta, *and other low-fiber foods*

The digestive tracts of people with active IBD are often inflamed and sensitive to irritation. Smooth bland foods tend to be easier on the gut during this time. Because these foods often lack essential nutrients that we need for robust health, it's best to consult your doctor or a registered dietitian and to take a multivitamin to ensure that you're getting the nutrients you need.

# Plantain

This green banana, common in South America, may have a soothing effect on the lining of the intestine. A study from England showed that soluble fiber from plantain creates an environment that resists inflammatory bacteria. If more studies follow suit, the plantain may find a regular place on the global menu of people with IBD.

Aim for: No one knows how much plantain may be the ticket to a healthy intestine, but boiled green plantain or sautéed yellow plantain is a lovely addition to any evening meal and may help soothe some of the irritation that comes with IBD.

# Olive oil

Olive oil is rich in antioxidants called flavonoids, which protect the body's cells from daily wear and tear. Flavonoids may help reduce inflammation by neutralizing free radicals that contribute to it. One recent study showed that a combination of olive oil and fish oil reduced inflammation in the colons of rats with IBD.

Buy extra-virgin olive oil, which has the most flavonoids. For the highest quality and the most nutrient-dense oils, seek out estate oils that are produced in one region. Avoid "light" and "extra light" olive oil, which is often a mixture of less nutritious, refined olive oil and sometimes other types of lower-quality oil.

Aim for: Try to replace most of the oils in your diet with extra-virgin olive oil.

Helpful hint: Olive and canola oils are your best source of fats, but you don't necessarily need to cut out butter entirely. It's a source of butyric acid, needed to maintain a healthy mucosal lining in the gut.

# Yogurt with active cultures *and other fermented milk products*

Although the cause of IBD remains a mystery, scientists are now exploring whether an overgrowth of bacteria in the intestine may contribute to the disease. Probiotics are beneficial bacteria found in fermented milk products like yogurt, buttermilk, and kefir. Getting more of them helps keep the "bad guy" bacteria in your gut in check.

Aim for: People with IBD respond differently to different diets, so there's no blanket recommendation here. You might start by having a daily half cup of yogurt or fermented milk with live, active cultures (look on the label for *lactobacillus, bifidus, Streptococcus thermophilus,* and *acidophilus,* among other active cultures) and gradually increase the amount you eat, up to 1 1/2 cups a day. Keeping a food and symptom diary during this trial period should help you establish the optimal amount for you.

## Salmon, mackerel, walnuts,
### and other sources of omega-3 fatty acids

With inflammation at the root of the problems caused by IBD, it makes sense to seek out foods rich in omega-3 fatty acids, which battle inflammation. Salmon and other fatty fish are the very best sources. In one study, patients with Crohn's disease who ate 3.5 ounces or more of fish per day for two years lowered their chances of relapse from 58 percent to 20 percent. Flaxseed, flaxseed oil, and walnuts also contain essential fatty acids, but they aren't converted efficiently by the body to the kinds of omega-3s that fight inflammation (the kinds in fish). Still, if you don't eat fish, they're certainly better than nothing.

Aim for: Three fish meals per week.

## Water *and other fluids*

The risk of dehydration is ever present with IBD because of chronic diarrhea. Kidney problems can also result when the amount of fluids entering the body doesn't keep up with the amount leaving it. Even when you don't have symptoms, it's smart to prioritize water.

Aim for: At least eight 8-ounce glasses of water or other fluids every day. Some acidic juices like pineapple or tomato may irritate your digestive tract, so stick to clear fluids whenever possible and avoid carbonated beverages, which can contribute to bloating.

## NUTRITIONAL SUPPLEMENTS

**A multivitamin/mineral.** One of the more serious consequences of IBD is poor nutrient absorption. In fact, health-threatening deficiencies can happen when IBD is not monitored closely. **DOSAGE:** Check with your physician or dietitian to determine whether you need individual supplements or simply a high-quality multivitamin/mineral.

**Vitamin B$_{12}$.** This vitamin is absorbed in the lower part of the small intestine, an area that is sometimes surgically removed in severe cases of IBD. If you have had parts of your intestine removed, make sure that your doctor checks for vitamin B$_{12}$ deficiency. **DOSAGE:** If you're B$_{12}$ deficient, your physician can determine whether you would respond better to oral supplementation or monthly injections of B$_{12}$ to replace this vital nutrient.

**Vitamin D.** Healthy bones are dependent in part on a healthy dose of vitamin D, the nutrient that aids in calcium absorption. But people with IBD may not absorb vitamin D well because of inflammation in the small intestine. Without enough D, the bones can soften and become vulnerable to fracture, a condition called osteomalacia. Research has shown that supplementation can help prevent this condition in people with IBD. **DOSAGE:** Check with your physician for the right dosage. Most people need at least 800 IU of vitamin D per day.

Get in the habit of making fruit smoothies at home—this blender drink is almost perfect for your health and digestion. Put a cup of plain yogurt, a banana, a fistful of berries, a teaspoon of honey, and a few ice cubes into your blender and process until smooth. It's that easy!

**Vitamin K.** Researchers are just starting to look at the possibility of vitamin K deficiencies in people with IBD. Because this vitamin is crucial to bone health, ask your physician to test your K levels. Vitamin K is found in leafy greens like spinach, lettuce, and watercress as well as soybean oil. **DOSAGE:** A multivitamin usually provides enough vitamin K, but check with your doctor.

**Iron.** Sometimes IBD causes bleeding in the intestinal walls, and this blood loss can lead to iron-deficiency anemia, a condition that causes fatigue and weakness. **DOSAGE:** Let your doctor decide whether you need to take supplemental iron and in what dose.

**Omega-3 fatty acids.** These anti-inflammatory "fish fats" may help people with Crohn's disease and ulcerative colitis. An Italian study recently found that when adults with IBD took supplements that included 400 milligrams of eicosapentaenoic acid (EPA) and 200 milligrams of docosahexaenoic acid (DHA)—the two main components of omega-3s—their relapse rates were lowered by 33 percent. **DOSAGE:** A combination of 400 milligrams of EPA and 200 milligrams of DHA daily. Be sure the capsules you choose are enteric coated so they won't break down until they reach the small intestine, where they can do their anti-inflammatory work.

**Probiotics.** If an overgrowth of "bad" bacteria may be to blame for IBD, increasing "good" bacteria with probiotic supplements may help relieve symptoms, especially if you're under stress. A study in Norway showed that rats fed a diet supplemented with probiotics were much less likely than those on a normal diet to develop harmful bacteria in their digestive tracts during stressful situations. **DOSAGE:** 10 billion colony-forming units (CFU) of probiotics once or twice daily.

## OFF THE MENU

**High-fiber foods.** Bran, the outer shell of many grains, can feel like sandpaper to an intestine affected by IBD, so eat bran cereals and foods made with whole-grain flour with caution. Other high-fiber foods, such as fresh fruits and vegetables, can cause already watery stools to take on even more water, producing more diarrhea. During bouts of IBD, eliminate whole grains and most produce and steer clear of nuts, seeds, and corn, which all can cause cramping in a narrowed bowel.

When a bout of IBD has receded, you can try to slowly reintroduce these foods to see whether your body will tolerate them. Eating fiber-rich foods when you're feeling okay may even be beneficial to a bowel prone to IBD because it can encourage production of butyrate, a fatty acid that helps keep inflammation under control and the intestinal lining healthy.

**Fatty meats and fried foods.** The saturated fats in burgers and the like can increase production of hormone-like compounds called prostaglandins that contribute to inflammation. Also, when fat is poorly absorbed, it can cause gas and diarrhea. Instead of doughnuts and french fries, try to eat foods with plenty of flavor that doesn't rely on fat.

**Milk and other dairy foods.** Many people diagnosed with IBD are lactose intolerant, which means they have trouble digesting lactose, a sugar found in milk and milk products. If your symptoms tend to flare up after eating dairy, try avoiding it for several weeks. A gastroenterologist can perform a test to see if you're lactose intolerant.

**Alcohol and caffeine.** Both can irritate an inflamed gut, and they act as diuretics, the last thing you need when you're prone to diarrhea.

# INSOMNIA

If you find yourself walking around in a fog, having abandoned the dream of a decent night's sleep, you might consider padding on over to the kitchen. Grandma prescribed a glass of warm milk before bed, and modern science says she may have been onto something. Research has also discovered other "sleep medicines" hiding in your kitchen. Cheese, anyone?

The foods that appear the most effective in battling insomnia help boost chemicals that cause the body to relax, making for easier, more restful sleep. Combined with plenty of exercise and some stress reduction, they just may be the ticket to sweet dreams.

## YOUR FOOD PRESCRIPTION

## Warm milk with honey;
*turkey; cheese; peanuts; and bananas*

You've probably heard the jokes about the Thanksgiving turkey putting people to sleep, but this folk wisdom has a leg—make that two legs—to stand on. Turkey and the other foods listed above are rich in tryptophan, an amino acid that the body uses to produce serotonin, a kind of chemical lullaby, if you will. Serotonin slows nerve activity, calming the brain and spreading a "feel-good" message throughout your body. When darkness enters the picture, the brain converts serotonin to yet another hormone, melatonin, which regulates sleep.

In one recent Canadian study, when chronic insomniacs ate food bars containing 250 milligrams of tryptophan (the amount in two slices of provolone cheese, for example) plus a dose of carbohydrate, the time they spent awake during the night was decreased by 50 percent.

The reason we recommend honey with your warm milk—and the reason the study food bar included carbohydrate—is that a fast-digesting carbohydrate like honey or mashed potatoes stimulates the release of insulin, which in turn allows more tryptophan to enter the brain.

**Aim for:** Before going to bed, try a glass of warm milk with honey (heat can enhance the tryptophan effect of foods), a slice of turkey on a piece of whole-grain bread, a banana, a handful of nuts, some leftover baked beans, or a slice or two of cheese.

## Whole grains

Oatmeal, whole-grain cereals and breads, and other complex carbohydrates increase production of serotonin.

**Aim for:** Make three of your daily carbohydrate servings whole grains (one serving is a small bowl of whole-grain cereal, a slice of whole-grain bread, or a half cup of brown rice or barley, for instance). Some experts recommend a bedtime snack of a complex carbohydrate to help prevent nighttime low blood sugar, which in some people may contribute to poor sleep.

### FEATURED RECIPES

**Edamame Hummus with Pita Crisps** *p. 592*
**Ultimate Spiced Nuts** *p. 592*
**Spinach Salad with Chickpeas** *p. 597*
**Lentil-Tomato Soup** *p. 603*
**Beef in Lettuce Wraps** *p. 606*
**Turkey Cutlets with Grapefruit Salsa** *p. 617*
**Banana-Peanut Bread** *p. 630*

## Chamomile tea

Sometimes all it takes to fall asleep is going to bed with the confidence that you *will* fall asleep. The scientific evidence on chamomile tea for insomnia is thin, but many people find it relaxing, and if you think a nice warm cup of this tea before bed will help you drift off, it probably will.

**Aim for:** A cup at bedtime.

## Red meat, shellfish, tofu, lentils, *and other iron-rich foods*

If restless legs keep you awake, it's possible that you have a form of anemia caused by iron deficiency. Consult a physician to find out if you do. The doctor may prescribe supplements or a diet rich in iron to help correct the problem. Choose lean red meat for the least saturated fat, and eat it for lunch rather than dinner because its protein can counteract sleep-inducing serotonin.

**Aim for:** Women up to age 50 need about 18 milligrams of iron per day. Women 51 and older and adult men need 8 milligrams. A 3-ounce portion of sirloin packs about 3 milligrams; a half dozen oysters, 14 milligrams; and 1 cup of lentils, 7 milligrams.

**Helpful hint:** To get more iron from plant foods, which contain the less absorbable nonheme type, eat them along with a food rich in heme iron (like meat) or in vitamin C, which also helps you soak up nonheme iron.

### NUTRITIONAL SUPPLEMENTS

**A multivitamin/mineral for iron and B vitamins.** These nutrients can help you get a good night's sleep, especially if you're deficient in them. A deficiency of iron or the B vitamin folate may cause restless legs syndrome. Several of the B vitamins are important for brain function and help regulate both mood and sleep. For example, $B_6$ and niacin are directly involved in serotonin production.

Don't take more than the amount of iron in a multivitamin except under a doctor's supervision; too much can be harmful. If your

## A Fishy Solution?

Fish doesn't just help your heart; its omega-3 fatty acids (found in high concentrations in the normal brain) may also improve your mood by increasing levels of the feel-good hormone serotonin. Less depression often equals better sleep. Studies of omega-3s for insomnia have yielded mixed results, but there's no harm in eating more salmon as well as flaxseed and walnuts to see if it helps.

multivitamin makes you feel energized, take it in the earlier part of the day. **DOSAGE:** One a day.

**Magnesium.** This mineral is involved in the production of sleep-inducing serotonin, and a magnesium deficiency may also cause restless legs syndrome. The glycinate and malate forms of magnesium are less likely than citrate and hydroxide forms to cause diarrhea. **DOSAGE:** 100 to 300 milligrams before bed.

### OFF THE MENU

**Alcohol.** Even though alcohol is a sedative, you may wake up after a couple of hours, when most of the alcohol has been metabolized— that is, after the sedative effect wears off. Alcohol can also make snoring and sleep apnea worse by relaxing muscles in the airways.

**Caffeine.** Caffeine's the last thing you want in your system at night. If you're really sensitive to it, you should give it up altogether: One study showed that as little as 200 milligrams—the amount in two cups of coffee—in the morning was enough to cause sleep problems at night. Tea, cola, and chocolate also contain caffeine.

**High-fat dinners.** These can trigger indigestion and heartburn, which are difficult to sleep through.

# INSULIN RESISTANCE

It's great to be resistant to viruses, bacteria, and advertising—but not to insulin. You may never have heard of insulin resistance, but it's practically an epidemic in the United States—it's estimated that 25 percent of adults have it—thanks in large part to our aversion to exercise and our undying devotion to simple carbohydrates and processed, sugary foods. (Genes also play a role.) Insulin resistance puts you on the path to weight gain and diabetes and is now thought to contribute to heart disease, obesity, and even Alzheimer's disease.

Every time you eat your fill of french fries, scones, or sugary cereal—foods that spike your blood sugar—your body has to pump out insulin to get the sugar, or glucose, out of the bloodstream and into cells, where it can be used as fuel. Over time, repeated surges of insulin can tire out your cells' insulin receptors so they don't work as well and insulin can't be used as efficiently. The result? More and more insulin is needed to do the same job. That's insulin resistance. It's not that different from what happens when your spouse's hearing starts to go: You have to shout louder and louder to get him to change the channel (unless, of course, your beloved is simply ignoring you).

Extra insulin can raise blood pressure, cause problems with cholesterol levels, and even make it easier for certain cancers to grow. It also paves the way for weight gain. As your insulin resistance gets worse—which it will if you continue to follow the same diet—you may also develop high blood sugar, which carries its own risks.

Mild and moderate insulin resistance can be detected through a blood test that shows high levels of insulin. If you have severe insulin resistance, you may notice dark patches of skin on your neck, elbows, knees, or knuckles. You're more likely to be insulin resistant if others in your family have diabetes; if you have low levels of HDL ("good") cholesterol, high triglycerides, or high blood pressure; or if you've had diabetes during a pregnancy. African Americans and Hispanics are more at risk and so are overweight people, so shedding extra pounds is key if your pants are snug and your belt no longer goes the distance. Exercise also makes cells more "insulin-friendly," and if you have insulin resistance, you're probably not active enough. But there's no ignoring the fact that what you eat takes center stage in the development—and reversal—of this condition.

Switching to slow-digesting, high-fiber foods is the major goal; this helps keep blood sugar low so you need less insulin to bring it down. And weaning yourself from saturated fats (think marbled steak) and trans fat (think packaged snack foods and baked goods) in favor of unsaturated fats like those in fish, nuts, and olive oil can even crank up your cells' sensitivity to insulin.

# Whole grains, beans, *and other complex carbohydrates high in fiber*

When's the last time you had whole-wheat pasta, barley, or beans on your plate? These are the types of foods that digest nice and slowly, keeping blood sugar spikes in check. But most of us eat perilously few of them. The same goes for legumes: Chickpeas, soybeans, and lentils are sadly underrepresented in our dishes. Fortunately, many of us have at least gotten the message as far as whole-grain cereals are concerned and are choosing higher-fiber brands. That's good. Data collected on almost 3,000 people in the Framingham Offspring Study shows that people who ate the most cereal fiber from whole grains were much less likely to have insulin resistance than those who ate the least.

Start by making sure your morning cereal contains at least 5 grams of fiber per serving. Next, make sandwiches with whole-grain bread (check that the first ingredient on the label includes the word *whole*). Then look to add beans to your diet. A can of black bean or lentil soup makes a terrific and extremely easy lunch, and it's simple enough to throw beans or chickpeas into salads.

Aim for: 25 to 35 grams of fiber per day. A cup of cooked lentils has 16 grams, as does a cup of cooked oatmeal.

Helpful hint: If you like oatmeal, buy the real stuff, not flavored instant oatmeal, which almost always contains added sugar.

# Olives, olive oil, nuts, and avocados

All this time, you've probably thought guacamole was just party food, but when it comes to foods like avocados and nuts, party on (in moderation, of course). These foods are loaded with monounsaturated fats—fats that are actually good for you as long as you don't overdo them. (By the way, fats don't raise blood sugar; in fact, they help steady it.)

Unlike saturated fat, which raises the risk of insulin resistance, unsaturated fat can actually improve insulin sensitivity, as a Finnish study suggests. The researchers placed 31 people with impaired glucose tolerance (elevated blood sugar levels that accompany insulin resistance) on a diet high in saturated fat for three weeks. The participants were then switched to diets emphasizing monounsaturated or polyunsaturated fats—the kind in plant oils like canola oil. Those whose diet emphasized monounsaturated fats had the most improvement in blood glucose levels and insulin sensitivity.

Trying to lose weight? Don't shun fat entirely. A little bit of fat makes meals more pleasing and even helps you stay full longer. Just be sure to choose the "good" fats. Fortunately, veggies taste fantastic sautéed in olive oil, and salads are all the more appealing when topped with good stuff like nuts and seeds and olive oil–based salad dressings.

Aim for: Up to 1 tablespoon of olive oil–based salad dressing drizzled on a salad at lunch and vegetables at dinner, 1 ounce of nuts, and 1/3 cup of guacamole or a few slices of avocado every day.

Helpful hint: Instead of cheese in your sandwich, try a slice or two of avocado. Squeeze the juice from a lemon wedge over avocado slices to keep them from browning and to boost vitamin C, a powerful antioxidant, as well.

## FEATURED RECIPES

**Spinach Salad with Chickpeas** *p. 597*
**Citrus Chicken Salad** *p. 598*
**Salsa Tuna Salad Sandwiches** *p. 604*
**Three-Bean Chili** *p. 610*
**Tuna Kebabs** *p. 610*
**Turkey Ragu with Spaghetti** *p. 618*
**Springtime Quinoa** *p. 626*
**Blueberry-Oat Scones** *p. 628*
**Chocolate Fondue** *p. 634*

# Dark chocolate, green tea,
## *and other foods high in flavonoids*

Love dark chocolate? Here's your chance to indulge once in a while. Two recent Italian studies showed that people who ate a 3.5-ounce bar of dark chocolate a day significantly lowered their insulin resistance compared to those who ate white chocolate. Researchers believe that the protection may come from the high levels of flavonoids in dark chocolate (actually, in the cocoa used to make it), which have both antioxidant and anti-inflammatory properties. Dark chocolate is also high in chromium, which helps increase insulin sensitivity. But the news isn't license to gorge on chocolate. Flavonoids are also found in green tea, wine, blueberries, apples with the skin, onions, cabbage, brussels sprouts, spinach, and asparagus.

**Aim for:** 1.5 ounces of dark chocolate occasionally (buy a brand that contains 60 percent cocoa if you can find it), several cups of green tea a day, and several daily servings of citrus fruits and berries.

**Helpful hint:** Milk chocolate doesn't contain nearly as many flavonoids as dark chocolate and has more fat and calories, so make sure you satisfy your sweet tooth with the dark stuff.

# Spinach, beans, fish,
## *and other foods high in magnesium*

Beans may not be glamorous, but for people with insulin resistance, they're beauties where it counts. Studies show that low magnesium is linked with insulin resistance. People on diets rich in magnesium are also at much lower risk of type 2 diabetes than those who shun beans and leafy greens.

**Aim for:** Studies have shown doses of 300 to 400 milligrams of magnesium per day to be helpful in controlling blood sugar in people who have diabetes. A quarter cup of pumpkin seeds has 185 milligrams, and a cup of cooked spinach has 157 milligrams.

**Helpful hint:** Since some magnesium is lost in cooking, head for the salad bar.

## NUTRITIONAL SUPPLEMENTS

**Chromium.** In a six-month University of Vermont study of people with type 2 diabetes, 12 were given a glucose-lowering drug plus a placebo, and 17 took the drug plus chromium supplements. The people who took chromium had significant improvement in insulin sensitivity, better glucose control, less weight gain, and less fat around their middles than the people who took the drug and placebo. The Institute of Medicine has set no upper limit for chromium, but people with liver or kidney disease should not take high doses. Take the supplement with a meal that includes foods high in vitamin C, such as orange juice and red bell peppers, to help your body absorb the chromium. **DOSAGE:** Participants in the study took 1,000 micrograms daily.

**Magnesium.** Supplements are recommended only for people with low blood levels of magnesium in their blood, as measured by a blood test. Chelated supplements like magnesium citrate are better absorbed than nonchelated forms like magnesium oxide. (*Chelated* means the magnesium is connected to another molecule, often an amino acid.) **DOSAGE:** Studies have shown magnesium doses of 300 to 400 milligrams per day to be helpful in controlling blood glucose in people with diabetes. This is about the same as the recommended amount of 400 to 420 milligrams daily for men and 310 to 320 milligrams for women.

## OFF THE MENU

**Sugar and refined grains.** White's fine for the tennis court but not for the majority of your food. Foods made from white flour (think most baked goods and white bread), sugary foods, most rice cereals, and other such "white foods" lack the fiber of whole grains and tend to be digested quickly, spiking blood sugar and in turn bumping up insulin production. Diets high in these foods also tend to be low in nutrients and full of calories, making it easy to pile on weight, which boosts the risk of insulin resistance.

Go "whole" by switching to whole-grain breads and cereals and eating whole fruit instead of drinking fruit juice. Instead of sugary soft drinks, try club soda with a slice of lime and imagine you're on a beach in the Bahamas. Processed and refined carbohydrates also figure heavily in many packaged snack foods, so be on your guard.

**Fatty meat, full-fat dairy foods, and foods made with trans fat.** It's time to seal the cookie jar (unless you bake your own treats). You may as well pack up the baloney and salami, too. The trans fat in many baked goods and the saturated fats in meats and cheese boost the risk of heart disease—already high for people with insulin resistance—and diabetes. They may also contribute directly to insulin resistance, and they may impair your body's ability to make insulin. Saturated fats are stored in cells as damaging triglycerides. When they accumulate in cells that produce insulin, they can actually kill those cells.

A Swedish study has also shown that decreasing saturated fat by replacing it with plant fats like olive oil increases insulin sensitivity as long as fat calories aren't more than 37 percent of the diet.

**Fast food.** In a 15-year University of Minnesota study of more than 3,000 young adults, researchers found that those who ate fast food more than twice a week gained an average of 10 pounds and had a 104 percent increase in insulin resistance. Fast foods tend to be packed with hydrogenated oils and refined starches (think french fries and white hamburger buns) or sugar (think soda) that raise blood sugar. What's more, the serving sizes tend to be all too "super." The next time you feel the urge to zip through the drive-through, slam on the brakes—a healthy calorie expenditure.

## Revealing Waistlines

Did you have trouble buttoning your skirt today? That could be a sign of insulin resistance. According to a survey commissioned by the National Women's Health Resource Center, 75 percent of women participants who had a family history of diabetes or heart disease reported having a burgeoning waistline, fatigue, and cravings for carbohydrates. The most common trait among the women was fat around the middle. If a woman's waist is bigger than 34 inches, or a man's 40 inches, it's time for a visit to the doctor, more exercise, and a healthier diet focused on whole grains, fruits and vegetables, and fish.

# IRRITABLE BOWEL SYNDROME

If you have irritable bowel syndrome (IBS), you may start to feel that food is your enemy, since you never know how it's going to affect your sensitive digestive system. But don't despair! A diet tailored to your body's own quirks can make food your friend again.

In normal digestion, when you eat a meal, your esophagus, stomach, and intestine react with gentle contractions that move the food along the digestive tract. IBS changes that process, causing the contractions to sometimes speed up, sometimes slow down, and often increase in strength. The gut becomes irritated and vulnerable to any combination of the following symptoms: bloating, abdominal pain, diarrhea, constipation, or a seesawing occurrence of the latter two.

Experts used to think that IBS occurred only in the colon, the last 5 feet of the intestine. We now know that IBS occurs throughout the entire digestive tract, starting in the mouth, and affects digestion, metabolism, and the excretion of waste. To make matters worse, stress often kick-starts and aggravates the symptoms, creating a vicious cycle because simply having IBS is stressful.

Because each person's case of IBS is different, the key to relieving discomfort is to keep a food and symptom diary. That diligence will pay off in helping you identify which foods to avoid and which appear to help.

If you haven't done so already, be sure to see your doctor to make sure you really have IBS. Many IBS symptoms can be warning signs of more serious diseases.

Keep a large container of plain yogurt in the refrigerator for quick, gut-healthy breakfasts and snacks. Make instant parfaits with granola and berries; use as the base for a quick smoothie; or merely mix in a spoonful of fruit spread.

# Whole grains, legumes, nuts,
## *and other foods high in fiber*

Filling your plate with these foods, as well as fruits and vegetables, is the best way to bulk up stool and keep the colon in tiptop shape for absorbing nutrients. Some types of fiber act like a snowball, gathering waste as it "rolls" through the digestive tract, then exiting the body in stool. Others act as Mother Nature's scrub brush, helping to clean off the sides of the digestive tract so nutrients can pass through intestinal walls easily. All fiber can help diminish IBS symptoms, from gas and bloating to constipation and, ironically, even diarrhea—at least in some people.

Fiber doesn't work for everyone with IBS; in some people, it can make symptoms like gas and bloating worse. So start by increasing your fiber intake very slowly. Add an extra serving of fruit or vegetables one week (starting with cooked rather than raw); eat a serving of whole grain like wild rice, quinoa, or barley the next; and by the end of the month, switch from white pasta to a whole-grain version. Try eating more beans as well: Lentils and other small beans are often more easily digested, especially when prepared with herbs and spices that help to combat gas, such as coriander and caraway. Keep a close watch on your symptoms with your food diary, and if fiber really does make your symptoms worse, cut back again.

Don't increase your fiber intake without also increasing the amount of fluids you drink. Without enough fluids, fiber hardens and shrinks in the stool, leading to constipation.

Aim for: General guidelines call for a minimum of 25 grams fiber a day (more is better). You can get there by eating 2 cups of fruit, 2 1/2 cups of vegetables, and three servings of whole grains. For snacks, have an apple instead of pretzels; for breakfast, have whole oatmeal instead of white toast; for dinner, add fresh or frozen vegetables to your pasta sauce or soup. Spread fiber throughout the day for the best effect.

# Yogurt and fermented milk

The human digestive system is full of bacteria, some of it beneficial—helping to break down undigested foods—and some of it potentially harmful. A poor diet, antibiotics, and stress can all disrupt the ratio of "good" to "bad," bugs, leaving the gut susceptible to gas, bloating, and pain. Studies have shown that yogurt and fermented milk products like kefir, which contain live, active cultures of friendly bacteria, can help reduce the symptoms of IBS. Milk sugars in kefir and yogurt help the bacteria survive the acids in your digestive system. If you're lactose intolerant, you may want to use a probiotic supplement, too (see Nutritional Supplements, page 516).

In one study, IBS patients who drank a cup of kefir every day had less abdominal pain and discomfort than those who took placebos. The relief was on a par with the relief provided by taking two different IBS drugs.

Aim for: There's no magic target, since everyone with IBS responds differently. Start with a daily half cup of yogurt or fermented milk with live, active cultures, then gradually increase the amount, up to 1 1/2 cups a day. Use your food and symptom diary to help you determine if it's making things better.

## FEATURED RECIPES

**Tropical Fruit Salad** *p. 590*
**Ginger Butternut Squash Soup** *p. 602*
**Lentil-Tomato Soup** *p. 603*
**Roasted Salmon with Sautéed Greens** *p. 613*
**Springtime Quinoa** *p. 626*
**Raspberry-Almond Muffins** *p. 628*
**Pear Crisp** *p. 636*

## Chamomile tea

If stress contributes to your IBS symptoms, consider drinking this age-old soother. One study in England found that women who drank five cups daily for two weeks increased their levels of glycine, an amino acid associated with relief of muscle spasms. This may be why chamomile has long been used to relieve menstrual cramps. Because more women than men have IBS, and symptoms often become worse during menstruation, chamomile may offer relief to women in particular.

**Aim for:** Some people find relief with just one cup of chamomile tea, but you may want to experiment with up to five cups a day for maximum relief. Besides soothing the digestive muscles, drinking the tea will boost your fluid intake, a tactic that can help diminish constipation—another trademark of IBS.

## Caraway seed, fennel seed, cardamom, and coriander

Used since ancient times as digestive aids, these spices are known to be carminative, or helpful to digestion. Caraway and fennel seeds help keep gas and bloating under control, while cardamom and coriander also help calm intestinal spasms that can lead to diarrhea.

**Aim for:** Heat the spices in a dry pan for a minute to release the flavor and then add to stews, soups, dips, and other recipes for a boost in digestion.

### NUTRITIONAL SUPPLEMENTS
**Enteric-coated peppermint-oil capsules.** Studies on using peppermint oil for IBS are numerous. It appears to help by relaxing smooth muscles in the digestive tract, relieving gas, and by possibly putting the brakes on the growth of bacteria in the small intestine. A study from Taiwan involving 110 people with IBS found that peppermint oil reduced stomach pain by 79 percent and bloating by 83 percent. **DOSAGE:** In the Taiwan study, volunteers took one capsule three or four times daily, 15 to 30 minutes before meals.

**Probiotics.** These beneficial bacteria can help get a disrupted digestive system back on track. In one study, women with IBS who took *Bifidobacterium infantis* for four weeks experienced 20 percent less bloating and pain than those taking placebos. **DOSAGE:** Take up to 10 billion live organisms, preferably *bifidus* or *lactobacillus,* once or twice daily.

### OFF THE MENU
**Milk and dairy products.** Many people with IBS can't tolerate lactose, a sugar found in milk. Instead of digesting the lactose, bacteria in the gut produce gas, bloating, and nausea. Yogurt is one of the exceptions to the rule because the

We often blame foods for our digestive woes, but sometimes, it's what we drink that is at fault. Coffee, soda, alcohol, milk, and even orange juice can irritate a sensitive digestive tract. The best plan: Stick to water or herbal tea.

active bacteria in yogurt convert lactose to lactic acid (which gives yogurt its tart flavor). Avoid sugar-free yogurt (the sugar alcohols used as sugar substitutes can increase gas and bloating) and frozen yogurt that's been whipped (the air increases bloating). If you eliminate all dairy foods, make sure you get enough calcium from other calcium-rich foods or a supplement.

**Raw tomatoes, citrus juices, and spicy condiments.** All of these can irritate the GI tract, but not everyone reacts negatively, so keep a close eye on your body's reaction through your food journal. If you like spicy foods and are reluctant to give them up, try turning down the heat a bit. Some spices, like ginger and chile peppers, are antibacterial, so if they don't bother you, they could offer benefits. Cook with spices because heating them releases their healing potential.

**Coffee.** Coffee, even decaf, contains an enzyme that irritates the digestive tract, and irritants mean trouble to anyone with IBS. If you depend on coffee to get your bowels moving in the morning, as an alternative, consider using supplemental magnesium citrate (see "Nighttime Calming Remedy" on this page) at night. A cup of hot or warm water with a good squirt of lemon juice can also help start things moving.

**Alcohol.** Beer, wine, and spirits can all irritate the gut, making digestion painful and unpredictable. Avoid alcohol during bouts of IBS and drink only moderate amounts at other times.

**Carbonated beverages.** Any food that increases the amount of air in the gut will be a problem for someone suffering from bloating and gas. Opt for nonfizzy varieties of mineral water and other beverages.

**Diet candy and sugar-free chewing gum.** The sugar substitute sorbitol can act as a laxative, causing diarrhea and stomach pain in people with IBS. Sorbitol is used to sweeten many low-calorie products, diet candy, and chewing gum, so be sure to check ingredient labels.

## Nighttime Calming Remedy

The normal digestive process requires ongoing muscle contraction and relaxation in the gut. When we're under stress, or when we drink caffeinated drinks or use nicotine, contractions in the bowels tend to increase, throwing things off-balance and messing up the excretion process. Magnesium citrate, a muscle relaxant, can restore that balance and reduce symptoms of IBS, such as constipation, cramping, and bloating. Magnesium citrate also acts as a natural laxative; it works by drawing water into the intestine to help move waste along. Mix a 200- to 800-milligram dose of the powder in water, according to the directions on the label, and drink it warm like a tea before bed.

# KIDNEY STONES

Like a little bullet that dams up your urinary tract, a kidney stone can stop you in your tracks and leave you writhing in agony. Stones can exist silently for years, but when a stone starts to move through one of the narrow tubes from the kidneys, the pain is so intense that women who've had attacks say it's worse than the pain of labor. Unfortunately, once you've had a kidney stone, the chances are high that you'll have another.

Luckily, turning on the kitchen tap and filling up with nature's most bountiful beverage may be the simple ticket to stone prevention. Certain foods can also help by correcting the balance of salts and minerals in urine and by breaking up crystals before they wreak havoc.

## YOUR FOOD PRESCRIPTION

### Water

On any given day, the kidneys filter about 200 quarts of blood to remove salts, water, and waste products that form when the body processes food and liquids. All of this refuse passes as urine through tubes called ureters into the bladder. From the bladder, it flows through a slightly wider tube, the urethra, to exit the body when you urinate. When salts and waste overwhelm the liquid needed to flush them through the system, the waste materials clump together to form stones that can range from the size of a sugar crystal to the size of an apricot.

The more fluid you drink, the more quickly waste passes through your urinary tract, and the less likely you are to get kidney stones.

**Aim for:** At least 12 cups (3 quarts) of fluid spaced throughout the day. If the weather is hot or you're exercising and sweating, you should drink even more.

### Lemon water

A natural acid in lemons called citrate helps to break down waste in the kidneys and prevent stones from forming. In one study, when people drank 4 ounces of lemon juice combined with water, the amount of citrate released in the urine doubled.

**Aim for:** Squeeze fresh lemon juice into the water you drink over the course of the day. Aim for a total of about 4 ounces of juice (about 1/2 cup).

### Low-fat milk, cheese,
*and other calcium-rich foods*

For years, researchers thought that calcium in the diet contributed to the most common type of kidney stones, those made of calcium oxalate. People prone to these stones were consequently told to cut back on milk, cheese, and other dairy products. But the Nurses Health Study, which has been analyzing the diets of thousands

> ### FEATURED RECIPES
>
> **Open-Faced Sardine Sandwiches** *p. 604*
> **Mac 'n Cheese Primavera** *p. 608*

of women for decades, has found that the more calcium-rich foods a woman eats, the lower her risk of developing kidney stones. As a result, physicians now advise patients to eat plenty of dairy foods.

It appears that when calcium binds with salts called oxalates in the gastrointestinal tract, the oxalates never enter the bloodstream to reach the kidneys. People prone to kidney stones who take calcium supplements to improve bone strength should be careful to take them with food so the calcium can bind with the oxalates, effectively ushering them away from the kidneys.

Aim for: 1,000 milligrams of dietary calcium per day (1,200 milligrams for people over 50). Get it by drinking 3 cups of milk or having a combination of cheese, yogurt, milk, and other calcium sources like sardines.

## OFF THE MENU

**Spinach, rhubarb, chocolate, and other foods high in oxalates.** This odd trio, along with a number of other foods, contains oxalates, components of calcium oxalate kidney stones. If you have this type of stones, your physician may advise you to limit foods high in oxalates. These include the foods above as well as almonds, beets, figs, Swiss chard, and wheat bran.

**Caffeinated coffee, black tea, and cola.** Caffeine can cause problems for people prone to stones. It appears to increase the amount of calcium released in urine, increasing the likelihood that calcium will bind with oxalates to form kidney stones. Limit beverages with caffeine to two or fewer cups per day. Because black tea also contains oxalates, you may want to eliminate it altogether.

**Salt.** People who eat a lot of salt tend to excrete more calcium in their urine than they would on a low-salt diet. Again, the more calcium that passes through the kidneys, the higher the likelihood that it will bind with oxalates to form kidney stones.

Try to limit your salt intake to 2,300 milligrams a day, about a teaspoon. The best way to cut back is to watch the canned, packaged, and processed foods you eat. Some brands of canned soup, for example, pack more than 1,000 milligrams of sodium into just 1 cup. Even condiments such as ketchup and salad dressing can be loaded with sodium. Check labels and limit sodium to less than 500 milligrams per serving for savory foods and 200 milligrams per serving for sweet foods. And of course, cut back on using the saltshaker, too.

**Meat, fish, and poultry.** Some people with kidney stones have excessive acid in their urine (called uric acid) that can contribute to kidney stones. Don't confuse this with other types of acid, like citrate, that can benefit you by preventing the formation of stones in urine. If you are prone to this type of stones, your physician may suggest that you limit meat, fish, and poultry because these foods are high in purines, substances that can break down into uric acid in the body.

There are countless ways to get lemons into your diet, all of them delicious. Add lemon juice when you are cooking rice; squeeze on fresh vegetables; add to poaching liquids; roast a chicken with a pierced lemon in the cavity.

# LEG CRAMPS

Here's a new reason to drink orange juice and eat bananas: Their potassium can help ease muscle cramps.

If you've ever had a charley horse—a sharp tightening of a muscle in the calf, foot, or other part of the leg—you know how painful they can be. Because they often occur at night, they interrupt sleep. And they're more common with age.

A few smart tweaks to your diet can help. Some of the key nutrients that muscles depend on are electrolytes, minerals that work in tandem to balance the acidity and alkalinity of the body's fluids, so plan to get more calcium, potassium, and magnesium from your food. Some of the advice below should also help relieve restless legs syndrome (RLS), which causes uncomfortable sensations in the legs that are relieved only by moving.

## YOUR FOOD PRESCRIPTION

## Foods rich in calcium, potassium, and magnesium

In the right balance, these three minerals help muscles contract and relax. Having a steady supply of them helps prevent leg cramps that stem from an electrolyte imbalance. Pay special attention to magnesium; without enough, muscles can't relax after contracting—and many of us don't get enough. If you're taking a beta blocker to lower your blood pressure, check with your doctor to find out if it's the kind that depletes potassium from your system. Certain diuretics also deplete potassium and magnesium.

### CALCIUM

Aim for: Three to four servings of low-fat dairy or other calcium-rich foods, like kale and other leafy dark greens, canned salmon with bones, and fortified orange juice.

### POTASSIUM

Aim for: Daily servings of avocados, potatoes, white beans, yogurt, tomatoes or tomato juice, cantaloupe, and bananas.

### MAGNESIUM

Aim for: Plenty of legumes, seafood, nuts, whole grains, leafy green vegetables—and chocolate!

## Water and other fluids

When an athlete gets muscle cramps during a workout, it's often due to dehydration. Most of us don't work out that hard, but fluids are still critical for keeping muscle cells hydrated (allowing muscles to contract and relax smoothly) and for getting electrolytes into cells, where they can be used for energy (otherwise, these key minerals could be lost through sweating).

If your cramps tend to come during or immediately following exercise, talk with your doctor. They could be a sign of atherosclerosis, or hardening of the arteries, which lets less oxygen reach muscles.

Aim for: At least 8 eight-ounce glasses of water daily. If you exercise intensely, drink small amounts of fluid (3 to 5 ounces) every 20 minutes during workouts.

Helpful hint: Athletes who exercise strenuously for 90 minutes or more may need to reestablish their electrolyte balance with a sports drink like Gatorade.

# Tonic water

Quinine, a drug made from the bark of the chinchona tree, is prescribed by doctors in measured doses for some patients with leg cramps. It exists in small amounts in tonic water, providing it with that distinctive bitter flavor. The use of prescriptive quinine is controversial because too much can cause dizziness and dangerous blood problems, but tonic water is perfectly safe in moderate amounts.

Aim for: 8 to 16 ounces before bed.

Helpful hint: Brush your teeth after drinking tonic water at night. Like many other carbonated beverages, it often contains citric acids and sugars that can contribute to tooth decay.

## NUTRITIONAL SUPPLEMENTS

**B-complex vitamins.** In one Taiwanese study, elderly patients with severe nighttime leg cramps found significant relief when they took vitamin B-complex pills for three months. Vitamin $B_{12}$ is particularly important to the transmission of nerve impulses. **DOSAGE:** B-complex supplements vary in content, but the one used in the study contained 50 milligrams of $B_1$ (thiamin), 5 milligrams of $B_2$ (riboflavin), 30 milligrams of $B_6$, and 250 micrograms of $B_{12}$.

**Folic acid.** Some people's leg cramps may be due in part to a deficiency of folate. Women who take prenatal multivitamins (which include folic acid, the supplement form of folate) have a lower incidence of RLS, and in one study, pregnant women with the condition experienced relief after being treated with folic acid.

Check with your doctor before taking folic acid supplements, since they may mask a vitamin $B_{12}$ deficiency. **DOSAGE:** 400 to 800 micrograms per day.

**Vitamin E.** Several studies have found that E can help alleviate leg cramps. The effective dose may vary from person to person. **DOSAGE:** 30 IU, the amount typically found in a multivitamin. Dosages over 1,200 IU can cause side effects like blurred vision, dizziness, and headaches.

**Iron.** Iron-deficiency anemia can cause muscle cramps, so check with your doctor to see if you may be anemic. Women and elderly people are particularly prone to this condition. Too little iron can also cause restless legs syndrome. **DOSAGE:** For women up to age 50, 18 milligrams a day, the amount in many multivitamins formulated for women. Men should avoid iron supplements unless a physician prescribes them for diagnosed anemia. Too much supplemental iron can cause constipation, so eat plenty of fiber and drink at least 64 ounces (8 cups) of water a day to help avoid it.

**Magnesium.** There is some evidence that magnesium supplements can help pregnant women with leg cramps; if you're pregnant, check with your doctor before taking supplements. But almost everyone can do with more magnesium than they get in their diets. An extra 400 milligrams per day, taken with food, may help and certainly does no harm. The glycinate and malate forms of magnesium are less likely than citrate and hydroxide forms to cause diarrhea. **DOSAGE:** Typically, 100 to 400 milligrams per day will correct a deficiency.

## OFF THE MENU

**Caffeine.** Caffeine is a diuretic, flushing the body of fluids that the muscles need to function smoothly. It also constricts blood vessels, decreasing circulation to muscles, and interferes with the body's absorption of magnesium. If you have restless legs syndrome, definitely avoid caffeine. It increases levels of the brain chemical dopamine, and overproduction of dopamine is thought to be a cause of RLS.

---

### FEATURED RECIPES

**Tuna and White Bean Salad** p. 599
**Lentil-Tomato Soup** p. 603
**Salmon Cake Sandwiches** p. 606
**Thai Roasted Shrimp** p. 614
**Banana-Peanut Bread** p. 630

# LUNG CANCER

First things first: If you smoke, stop. Tobacco use is responsible for 87 percent of lung cancer deaths. Of course, even nonsmokers get lung cancer (and being around secondhand smoke can increase your risk by up to 30 percent).

What can you do to protect yourself, besides run screaming from cigarettes? Eat more fruits and vegetables. Swedish scientists recently found that people—smokers and nonsmokers alike—who eat a lot of vegetables have half the lung cancer risk compared to non–veggie eaters. That's because vegetables contain a grab bag of cancer-protective compounds, like the carotenoids in dark green and deep yellow, orange, and red produce. So while it's certainly not license to puff away, eating some extra broccoli, papaya, or red peppers may help you breathe a little easier.

## YOUR FOOD PRESCRIPTION

## Cruciferous vegetables

If carcinogens are like a heavy metal band that's prone to trashing hotel rooms, think of cruciferous vegetables as a crack security squad that hustles them out before they do harm. What makes vegetables like cauliflower, brussels sprouts, and especially broccoli such great bodyguards is their sulforaphane, considered one of the most potent cancer fighters found in food.

Cruciferous vegetables also contain a substance called indole-3-carbinol, which works like a cleanup crew, repairing damage that carcinogens do to cells before they can turn cancerous. No wonder some research suggests that eating more broccoli and brussels sprouts may lower the risk of lung cancer by as much as 40 percent.

**Aim for:** At least four 1/2-cup servings weekly.

**Helpful hint:** Steaming broccoli for 3 to 4 minutes, until it's crisp-tender, makes more of its sulforaphane available.

## Oranges, papayas, peaches, red bell peppers, and carrots

Notice something these foods have in common? The colors orange and red, of course. Those colors come from a type of carotenoid (an orange antioxidant pigment) called beta-cryptoxanthin that specifically seems to safeguard smokers. Results from the Singapore Chinese Health Study suggest that diets high in beta-cryptoxanthin lower lung cancer risk by about 25 percent, and by 37 percent in smokers.

**Aim for:** Include some red-orange fruits and vegetables among the 7 to 10 recommended daily servings.

## Soy foods

Some very early research suggests that as in breast cancer, estrogen may encourage the growth of lung tumors, and researchers suspect that blunting estrogen's effects may help slow or even stop lung cancer's development.

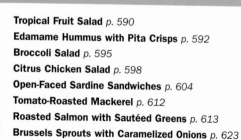

### FEATURED RECIPES

**Tropical Fruit Salad** *p. 590*
**Edamame Hummus with Pita Crisps** *p. 592*
**Broccoli Salad** *p. 595*
**Citrus Chicken Salad** *p. 598*
**Open-Faced Sardine Sandwiches** *p. 604*
**Tomato-Roasted Mackerel** *p. 612*
**Roasted Salmon with Sautéed Greens** *p. 613*
**Brussels Sprouts with Caramelized Onions** *p. 623*

Here's how it's thought to work: Lung cancer cells have estrogen receptors; you can think of them as parking spots reserved for estrogen. But soy's estrogen-like compounds (phytoestrogens called isoflavones) may block those spots so "real" estrogen can't park there. In one study of more than 3,400 people conducted at M. D. Anderson Cancer Center in Houston, volunteers who ate more foods high in phytoestrogens (soy, as well as broccoli, spinach, and carrots, which contain phytoestrogens called lignans) had about a 46 percent lower risk of lung cancer.

Aim for: Research suggests that one to three servings a day of soy foods like tofu, soy milk, and edamame (young soybeans) is enough to alter estrogen activity. If your diet is already full of fruits and vegetables, you may be able to get by with less. More isn't better when it comes to phytoestrogens, so stick with soy foods rather than isoflavone supplements.

# Salmon, sardines, mackerel, *and other foods high in omega-3 fatty acids*

Some research suggests the combination of cigarette smoke and animal fats promotes lung cancer. Substituting fish high in omega-3 fatty acids for meats appears to minimize the effect.

According to a Belgian study that examined fish consumption in 36 countries over 30 years, eating more fatty fish appeared to reduce lung cancer mortality. For instance, Hungary and Iceland both have high smoking rates, and animal fats are a big part of the diet. But fish consumption is higher in Iceland, which may explain why lung cancer deaths among men are more than three times lower there than in Hungary.

Aim for: Research suggests that two to three servings a week may help lower lung cancer risk.

# Spinach, kale, beans, *and other foods rich in folate*

If you smoke (or recently quit), load up on folate, a B vitamin that safeguards cells from tobacco carcinogens. Another study done at the

M. D. Anderson Cancer Center found that former smokers who had enough folate in their diets lowered their risk of lung cancer by 40 percent. Smoking drains folate from the body, as does alcohol consumption.

Aim for: 400 micrograms of folate each day. You may be getting that much if you take a multivitamin. But you can also get it from food if you eat at least 5 servings of whole grains each day, along with 7 to 10 servings of fruit and vegetables. At least one of those vegetable servings should be leafy dark greens or legumes. The safe upper limit for folate is 1,000 micrograms from food and supplements.

Helpful hint: Spinach packs a double anticancer punch—it's a great source of folate as well as other cancer fighters like carotenoids and phytoestrogens.

## NUTRITIONAL SUPPLEMENTS

**Vitamin C.** If someone in your family smokes, or you frequent smoky places, take some vitamin C "insurance." A study at the University of California, Berkeley, found that for nonsmokers, C supplements reduced free radical damage caused by secondhand smoke by about 11 percent. (Free radicals can alter cell DNA, which over time can cause cells to turn cancerous.) In addition, C helps vitamin E protect the lungs from cigarette damage. While smoking quickly depletes E, according to a study done at Oregon State University, taking extra C maintains E at levels typically found in nonsmokers. **DOSAGE:** 500 to 1,000 milligrams daily if you are frequently exposed to smoke.

## OFF THE MENU

**Red meat.** Several population studies suggest a link between meat (particularly if it's grilled or fried) and lung cancer. According to a National Cancer Institute study of more than 900 women, nonsmokers and former smokers who ate the most red meat had triple the risk of lung cancer compared to those who ate the least. Meat-eating smokers had nearly five times the risk.

# LUPUS

Lupus remains one of medicine's biggest mysteries. Researchers still don't fully understand exactly what triggers this autoimmune disease, but it's thought to develop when certain types of genes that may predispose someone to lupus interact with environmental factors like common viruses. The immune system gets misdirected and produces antibodies that target the body's tissues and organs. As these antibodies, called auto-antibodies, build up in various organs, inflammation results. There are several types of lupus, the most common being systemic lupus erythematosus (SLE). It can be mild, causing fatigue, joint pain, or skin rashes, or severe, affecting major organs like the kidneys.

People with lupus are always instructed to eat a healthy diet low in fat and high in fresh vegetables. But is it possible that nutrition can do more to alleviate symptoms and perhaps even stymie the disease? Since many of the medications used to treat lupus work by reducing inflammation and calming an overactive immune system, it makes sense that eating foods and taking supplements that do likewise can help, too (in addition to—not in place of—medication). Although there is no "lupus diet" per se, some very preliminary studies in animals and humans suggest that nutrition may be useful for reducing the severity of flare-ups and encouraging remission.

## YOUR FOOD PRESCRIPTION

### Fish *and other foods high in omega-3 essential fatty acids*

There's some evidence that in cultures like Japan and the Eskimo communities in Greenland, where people consume a lot of omega-3 essential fatty acids from fish, seafood, and other sources, the rates of autoimmune disease are lower than in countries where intake of omega-3s is low. That doesn't necessarily mean that fish lowers the risk of lupus, but it's worth noting that there's already a fairly well established association between high fish consumption and lower rates of conditions like depression and heart disease, so the idea isn't very farfetched.

There haven't been specific studies on eating fish to decrease lupus flare-ups, but research does suggest that taking supplements of the omega-3s EPA and DHA (found in fatty cold-water fish) reduces autoimmune disease–related inflammation and may slow the progression of disease (see Nutritional Supplements on the next page)—though it's hard to say whether this is due to the supplements or the natural ebb and flow of the disease. In a 24-week study of 52 people with SLE, researchers at the University of Ulster in Northern Ireland found that those taking 3 grams of an EPA supplement reported about a 23 percent decline in disease activity compared to those taking placebos. In a British study of 27 patients taking 20 grams daily of EPA for 34 weeks, about half the participants found it beneficial.

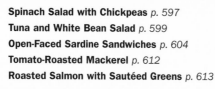

**FEATURED RECIPES**

**Spinach Salad with Chickpeas** *p. 597*
**Tuna and White Bean Salad** *p. 599*
**Open-Faced Sardine Sandwiches** *p. 604*
**Tomato-Roasted Mackerel** *p. 612*
**Roasted Salmon with Sautéed Greens** *p. 613*

Flaxseed is another source of omega-3s, particularly alpha-linolenic acid (ALA). In one very small, two-year study done in Canada, kidney function improved among eight participants who mixed 30 grams (about an ounce) of flaxseed into their daily cereal or juice.

Aim for: At least two servings of fish per week. To get the amounts of omega-3 fatty acids used in the studies, you'll need supplements.

Helpful hint: For a double anti-inflammatory whammy, choose fish like salmon, rainbow trout, and scallops. They all contain omega-3s as well as high levels of the antioxidant mineral selenium, which is also anti-inflammatory.

## Green tea

Some population studies suggest that lupus incidence is lower in countries like China and Japan, where green tea is a diet staple. One explanation may be that green tea contains potent compounds called polyphenols that are both antioxidant and anti-inflammatory. It's possible that adding green tea to your diet or even applying it directly to the skin rashes that often accompany lupus may be helpful. When green tea polyphenols were mixed with skin and salivary gland cells in lab studies done at the Medical College of Georgia, researchers noted a significant decrease in the markers for SLE.

Aim for: Because the research is still so preliminary, more studies need to be done before any definitive recommendations can be made. But it couldn't hurt to start drinking a few cups of green tea a day.

### NUTRITIONAL SUPPLEMENTS

**Omega-3 fatty acids.** Researchers are still divided over whether omega-3s are helpful for autoimmune diseases, particularly since more dramatic results are seen in animal studies than in human ones. But a small study done in India found that supplementing with EPA and DHA (which work better together than alone) appeared to induce remission in 10 patients with SLE. In other studies, when people with

## *Can a Vegetarian Diet Help?*

The answer is "probably." Research suggests that vegetarian and low-fat vegan diets (no animal products at all) significantly reduce symptoms of other chronic inflammatory diseases like rheumatoid arthritis.

Vegetarian diets usually contain less protein than meat-centered diets. Since getting too much protein puts added strain on the kidneys, a switch may help if lupus is affecting your kidneys, as it does in about 60 percent of cases. If your doctor wants you to eat less protein, this may mean you'll need to cut back on fish, too (when it comes to kidney function, protein is protein), but it's possible to get anti-inflammatory omega-3 fats from plant sources like flaxseed or from supplements.

Another reason to avoid or cut back on animal fats: They contain arachidonic acid, which stimulates inflammation.

chronic inflammatory conditions took fish oil, they were able to reduce their use of non-steroidal anti-inflammatory medications. **DOSAGE:** 3 to 6 grams of high-quality fish oil daily. Fish oil should always be refrigerated. If you find that a fishy taste or smell is "repeating" on you, it's an indication that the oil is rancid and needs to be replaced.

**Antioxidants, especially vitamin E, vitamin A, and selenium.** Some research suggests that low levels of vitamins A and E, thought to be a risk factor for rheumatoid arthritis, may also be a risk factor for lupus. Animals deficient in vitamin A seem to have more severe lupus symptoms. Although the research remains mixed, in a few small studies, supplementing with vitamin E and beta-carotene (a vitamin A precursor) seemed to relieve the rashes associated with lupus. Selenium is anti-inflammatory. In studies on mice with lupus, those fed selenium-rich diets lived longer. **DOSAGE:** *Vitamin E:* 800 milligrams of mixed tocopherols. *Beta-carotene:* The studies used 50 milligrams three times a day for a total of 150 milligrams a day. *Selenium:* 70 micrograms a day.

**Vitamin D.** Recent studies show that a deficiency of vitamin D may predispose people to a variety of autoimmune diseases. Additionally, many people in the United States, particularly in the northern states, are deficient in D. Vitamin D deficiency clearly contributes to the widespread osteoporosis that's seen in women and even men, and especially in people treated with certain lupus medications, such as steroids. Although there are no direct studies on the role of vitamin D treatment in people with lupus, we recommend D supplements. **DOSAGE:** 1,000 to 2,000 IU of D$_3$ (cholecalciferol) daily.

## OFF THE MENU

**Safflower, sunflower, and corn oils and most margarines.** These are rich in omega-6 essential fatty acids, the polyunsaturated fats believed by many experts to increase inflammation. In the United States, most of us consume far too many omega-6s and too few anti-inflammatory omega-3s. This imbalance is believed by some experts to be a contributing factor in other chronic inflammatory conditions, like rheumatoid arthritis.

In a very small study of 11 lupus patients who reduced their dietary intake of omega-6s for a year, 8 participants experienced a reduction in their symptoms. A German study of 60 people with rheumatoid arthritis gives further credence to the idea: Among those who consumed an anti-inflammatory diet, the number of tender, swollen joints decreased by 14 percent compared to those eating a standard Western diet. When the participants on the anti-inflammatory diet then added fish-oil supplements for two months, their joint swelling and pain decreased even more.

**Packaged and commercially fried foods.** These are often loaded with trans fat, which also contributes to inflammation. If the label says the product contains partially hydrogenated oils, it contains trans fat.

**Alfalfa.** Alfalfa seeds and sprouts contain the amino acid L-canavanine, which appears to aggravate lupus symptoms.

**Foods high in zinc.** You never want to become zinc deficient, because this nutrient is critical to so many body functions. But it's also one of the most effective natural immune system boosters, so if you have lupus, you may not want to take extra. Stick to the recommended amount of 15 milligrams a day and steer clear of zinc-rich foods like oysters and Brazil nuts.

**Echinacea.** Because this herb stimulates immune function, people with lupus are advised not to take it because it may initiate flare-ups. Indeed, in European countries, echinacea labels state that it's contraindicated in people with autoimmune diseases.

## DHEA: Another Solution?

Sex hormones play a role in immune function, and because estrogens are known to increase production of auto-antibodies, an imbalance in estrogen may be one reason that lupus primarily affects women. Although it's still very controversial, balancing estrogen with an androgen or male sex hormone, like the dietary supplement DHEA, may prove helpful, particularly because androgens reduce inflammation and suppress the immune system. Indeed, a California company is currently testing pharmaceutical-grade DHEA for lupus.

In a Taiwan study, 120 women with active SLE took either 200 milligrams of DHEA a day or a placebo for 24 weeks. The number of women with flare-ups was 16 percent lower in the DHEA group than in the placebo group. In other studies, participants who took DHEA were able to reduce their dosages of steroid medications.

Studies on DHEA typically used 200 milligrams a day. But there are some caveats with DHEA, so it should be used only under a doctor's supervision. DHEA boosts testosterone levels, resulting in increased acne, facial hair, and abnormal cholesterol and triglyceride profiles. Long-term use is associated with liver cancer in rats, and over time, it may even aggravate lupus symptoms. Also, because dietary supplements aren't regulated by the FDA, the amount of DHEA in over-the-counter preparations may vary from formulation to formulation and may even differ from what's stated on the label.

# MACULAR DEGENERATION

When someone says "Feast your eyes on this," he's not usually pointing to a big salad or a plate of steamed spinach. But maybe he should be. Recent studies have shown that certain foods—especially fruits and vegetables—can protect our eyes from age-related macular degeneration (AMD).

AMD is the most common cause of severe, irreversible vision loss in people 50 and older. Its target is the macula, a tiny yellow area near the center of the retina that's highly specialized to allow you to see details and provide clear central (not peripheral) vision, the kind you need to read and drive.

Although experts aren't sure what causes AMD—they now believe that heredity plays a role in many cases—it's usually characterized by a loss of pigment in the retina as well as yellowish deposits called drusen. And there's strong evidence that nutrition plays a role in preventing it. In fact, parts of the macula are actually made of certain nutrients that we get from food. Loading up your plate with the right foods won't cure AMD, but it can slow its progress and also lower your risk of developing it in the first place.

## YOUR FOOD PRESCRIPTION

### Spinach, collard greens, kale,
*and other green leafy vegetables*

One of the very best things you can do to keep your vision sharp is to eat more greens. They're loaded with lutein and zeaxanthin (pronounced zee-uh-ZAN-thin), a pair of natural plant pigments often found together in foods. These antioxidant pigments are part of the carotenoid family (think beta-carotene), and they're the only carotenoids found in the eye. Studies have found that people with high levels of lutein and zeaxanthin have as much as three times less risk of AMD than those with lower levels.

That's not so surprising, since the macula's yellow pigment is made up of lutein and zeaxanthin. Researchers believe they act as a kind of super sunscreen, protecting the retina by absorbing a damaging part of sunlight called blue light. The two antioxidants also protect the retina's cells from damaging free radicals. Zeaxanthin, the main component of the macula, may also bulk up its pigment, which in turn appears to shore up the macula's sensitivity to visual signals.

Although greens—especially cooked ones—carry the largest share of lutein and zeaxanthin, the pair is also plentiful in brightly colored fruits and vegetables like orange bell peppers, corn, persimmons, and tangerines.

**Aim for:** 6 to 10 milligrams of lutein and zeaxanthin per day—a bit more than the amount in 1/2 cup of cooked spinach or kale.

**Helpful hint:** Sauté your greens in olive oil or add some oil-based dressing to your salad. Fat helps the body absorb lutein and zeaxanthin. Indulge in a spinach omelet as well. Although eggs don't have the wealth of the two antioxidants that greens do, they have enough fat to make sure you get what's there.

## Fish *and other foods rich in omega-3 fatty acids*

Fish has been touted as a heart-healthy food, but researchers have also found that fish and other foods high in omega-3 fatty acids can lower the risk of AMD by as much as 40 percent.

The two main components of the omega-3s in fish, known as EPA and DHA, are essential for the development and function of the retina. The membranes of the photoreceptor cells—especially the rods—are also packed with DHA. It helps the membranes remain fluid, which in turn may help protein molecules in the rods respond to light. Omega-3s also help produce beneficial types of prostaglandins, hormone-like substances that affect many processes in the body, including blood flow and nerve transmission, both of which affect eye health.

Not a fish fan? Look to walnuts, flaxseed, flaxseed oil, and soybeans for alpha-linolenic acid (ALA), which the body converts (poorly, unfortunately) to DHA and EPA. ALA is essential because it can't be made by the body.

**Aim for:** 8 to 12 ounces of fatty fish a week. Too busy to grill fish? Toss a quarter cup of walnuts into a salad or add a tablespoon of ground flaxseed to oatmeal to get your daily dose of omega-3s.

**Helpful hint:** To avoid contaminants in fish, avoid swordfish, which is likely to contain mercury, and try to eat a variety of fish. Fill out your diet with more omega-3s by eating walnuts and flaxseed.

## Carrots, red bell peppers, almonds, and sunflower seeds

In a major clinical trial, the National Eye Institute has found that high doses of beta-carotene and vitamins C and E, coupled with zinc, stop or slow the progression of AMD by 19 to 25 percent. Although the effective doses were far higher than you can get from diet alone, heaping your plate with food dense in these nutrients makes sense, especially for people who already have AMD or are at increased risk for it

(such as those with a family history of the disease and possibly people with light eye color).

You'll get plenty of beta-carotene from the leafy greens we've already recommended; other great food sources are carrots and sweet potatoes. Spinach also provides vitamin E, and almonds and sunflower seeds are even better sources. For vitamin C, turn to red bell peppers, orange juice, citrus fruits, and broccoli.

Scientists aren't certain why the antioxidants in these foods protect the eyes, but they have some clues. Beta-carotene converts to vitamin A in the body, and in the retina, that's converted to a rod protein essential for the perception of light.

Like beta-carotene, vitamins C and E are powerful antioxidants that protect cells—including those in the macula—from damaging free radicals. And the mix of these antioxidants is apparently more effective than the nutrients acting singly. For example, vitamin E requires vitamin C to do its job as an antioxidant.

**Aim for:** *Beta-carotene:* 15 milligrams daily, about the amount in a sweet potato with skin or a cup of cooked spinach. You'll get even more from a cup of carrot juice. *Vitamin E:* 400 IU (about 268 milligrams) daily. This amount is virtually impossible to get from foods, especially on a low-fat diet, so you'll need help from supplements. A quarter cup of sunflower seeds has about 8 milligrams, an ounce of almonds has about 7, and a cup of cooked spinach has almost 4. *Vitamin C:* 500 milligrams daily, which you can get from a cup of orange juice plus a cup of chopped red bell pepper.

---

### FEATURED RECIPES

**Spinach Salad with Chickpeas** *p. 597*
**Sweet Potato Soup** *p. 601*
**Roasted Salmon with Sautéed Greens** *p. 613*
**Beef and Broccoli Stew** *p. 620*
**Creamed Spinach** *p. 624*
**Raspberry-Almond Muffins** *p. 628*

## Oysters, crab, beef, baked beans, *and other foods rich in zinc*

Zinc, an essential mineral found in meats (especially liver) and seafood (especially oysters), acts as vitamin A's partner, ensuring that it can be used by the body, including the retina. Scientists believe the retina's high levels of zinc help protect its membranes.

**Aim for:** 15 to 20 milligrams of zinc daily. A can of baked beans in tomato sauce contains about 14 milligrams; 3 ounces of lamb or crab, about 6 milligrams; and 3 ounces of ground beef, about 5 milligrams. If you like oysters, 3 ounces will get you to 76 milligrams of zinc.

**Helpful hint:** A serving of fortified cereal contains all the zinc you need for the day.

## NUTRITIONAL SUPPLEMENTS

**Lutein and zeaxanthin.** National Eye Institute researchers are testing doses of 10 milligrams of lutein and 2 milligrams of zeaxanthin per day. Until safe levels are established, eye doctors recommend getting these nutrients from food instead of individual supplements. **DOSAGE:** No optimal or safe level has yet been established. For now, look for a multivitamin that contains these nutrients.

**Omega-3 fatty acids.** Omega-3s come in softgel fish-oil capsules or in liquid form. Because omega-3s are sensitive to heat, light, and oxygen, store supplements in the refrigerator. Also, choose a supplement with vitamin E, which will help keep the omega-3s from becoming rancid.

As with lutein and zeaxanthin, the effective dose of omega-3 fatty acids is the subject of a current study by the National Eye Institute. The participants in the study will take 1 gram a day of fish oil or DHA, which may cause stomach discomfort or a fishy aftertaste. **DOSAGE:** Although optimal dosages aren't established, the FDA considers 1 to 3 grams daily in capsule or liquid form safe.

**Beta-carotene, vitamins C and E, and zinc.** This combination of nutrients is thus far the only proven way to halt or slow the progression of AMD. However, because some of the supplement doses evaluated by the National Eye Institute study mentioned above are high, ask your doctor whether the supplements are safe for you. According to the eye institute, only people who are at high risk for developing advanced AMD should consider taking the formulation. High doses of beta-carotene may increase the risk of cancer in smokers, and too much zinc can weaken the immune system.

Can steak be bad for your eyes? If it's fatty, the answer is yes. Animal fats boost free radical activity in your body, which can harm cells in your retinas.

If you take zinc, you should also take copper (2 milligrams a day) because high levels of zinc can cause copper deficiency. **DOSAGE:** *Vitamin C:* 500 milligrams daily. *Vitamin E:* 400 IU daily. *Beta-carotene:* 15 milligrams daily. *Zinc:* 80 milligrams of zinc oxide daily.

## OFF THE MENU

**Fatty meats, butter, and other sources of saturated fat.** Saturated fats boost free radical activity, undermining antioxidants' good work. Keep your meat choices as lean as possible and stick to small servings (3 to 6 ounces). Substitute margarine for butter, but choose a brand that doesn't contain trans fat. Cheese is another source of saturated fat, so use it sparingly and buy low-fat or part-skim cheese whenever possible. Soft cheeses like goat cheese have slightly less fat per ounce than hard types.

**Alcohol.** Too much alcohol also undermines the work of antioxidants. Alcohol forms two harmful compounds called acetaldehyde and malondialdehyde, which stoke up cellular damage by free radicals (and which make us feel so bad the day after one too many). It also depletes vitamin A, one of the antioxidants proven to slow AMD.

**Corn, sunflower, and safflower oils.** Many experts think that consuming too many of the omega-6 fatty acids in these oils—and in the many packaged foods and baked goods that contain them—undermines the beneficial effects of omega-3s, the fats in fish, walnuts, and flaxseed. In fact, research has found that omega-6s increase the risk of macular degeneration and that people who get more omega-3s and fewer omega-6s are less likely to have AMD.

## Squeezing More Nutrients from Your Food

Want to get more omega-3s from your flaxseed and more antioxidants from your spinach? Buy, store, and prepare them properly.

**Nuts and flaxseed:** Exposure to heat, light, and oxygen not only lowers the nutritive value of omega-3 fatty acids but also releases free radicals, the enemies of the retina (as well as other body tissues). Store nuts, ground flaxseed, and ground cloves (surprisingly high in omega-3s) in dark jars in the refrigerator or freezer. Buy whole flaxseed and grind it as needed; the seed's shell and the vitamin E within the seed protect the omega-3 oils from oxidation.

**Walnut and flaxseed oils:** Use these heat-sensitive oils for salads, not stir-fries.

**Leafy greens:** Leafy greens and other vegetables are highest in sight-saving nutrients right after they're picked. Buy the freshest greens you can and eat them within two days. The greener the leaves, the more packed they are with antioxidants, and leaves trump stems, so fill up on stemless outer leaves. Although cooking greens, especially in water, destroys a small percentage of some vitamins and minerals, such as vitamin C, steaming, microwaving, or stir-frying will minimize the loss. And cooking actually makes some nutrients like carotenoids more available.

**Fruits:** Once you cut them, dig in, because vitamin C is destroyed by the air exposure.

# MEMORY LOSS

If we lose our keys, we think we're losing our marbles. But in fact, everyone experiences some "recall shortfalls" from time to time. It's a normal side effect of stress, distractions, multitasking, and yes, getting older. Serious memory lapses could be a sign of dementia (see the Alzheimer's Disease entry, page 394), but plain old forgetfulness isn't usually something to fret about. The fact is, the memory usually serves us well enough even when our joints and other body parts start to go. That said, brain cells do shrink over the years, and eventually our brains make fewer chemicals called neurotransmitters that carry messages from one nerve cell to the next. Attacks from free radicals, which roam the whole body, also take their toll on brain cells over time.

Want to remember why you walked into a room? Start by walking into your kitchen. There you'll find "brain foods" rich in protective nutrients, such as antioxidants that neutralize free radicals, B vitamins that help ensure sufficient quantities of neurotransmitters, and inflammation-dousing oils and even spices. If, after adding more of these foods to your daily diet, you still can't remember the name of your dentist to make an appointment … well, you've gone too long without a cleaning.

## YOUR FOOD PRESCRIPTION

### Fruits, vegetables, nuts,
*and other foods rich in antioxidants*

Brain cells called neurons are particularly vulnerable to oxidation by free radicals. These rogue molecules attack cells much like oxygen "attacks" a freshly cut apple, turning it brown and "aging" it prematurely. Antioxidants, found in abundance in most fruits and vegetables and in nuts and beans, neutralize free radicals. When you eat enough of these foods, your brain collects antioxidants, and this offers protection to various parts of the brain, including the hippocampus, a region that's key to forming and retaining memories. Antioxidants also help prevent atherosclerosis, or hardening of the arteries, which limits the flow of oxygen and nutrients to the brain.

You can get your fill of three particularly important antioxidants—vitamins C and E and the mineral selenium—by filling your plate with fruits, vegetables, and nuts.

**Aim for:** 7 to 10 servings of fruits and vegetables a day, plus a handful of nuts almost every day.

**Helpful hint:** An ounce of almonds offers 7 milligrams of vitamin E (you need 15 milligrams daily). One kiwifruit provides 75 milligrams of vitamin C, close to your daily requirement.

### Spinach

Popeye had it right: Eating lots of spinach does make you stronger, at least mentally. Spinach-rich diets have proven particularly useful in helping patients recover motor skills like walking following a stroke or other neurological damage, and at least one enzyme in spinach has also proven effective in recovering memory in rats.

**Aim for:** Make spinach at least one of your 7 to 10 daily servings of fruits and vegetables.

**Helpful hint:** Cook or serve spinach with a drizzle of olive oil. The fat helps the body absorb fat-soluble nutrients like vitamin E from the leafy greens.

## Blueberries

When summer rolls around, there's nothing like fresh blueberries. But here's a reason to stock your freezer and eat them all year long: a better memory. The sweet blue globes are powerhouses of phytochemicals called anthocyanins—the compounds that give the berries their hue, act as strong antioxidants, and may, according to studies in aging lab animals, enhance memory. Rats did better on water maze tests after they were fed blueberry extracts over the course of eight weeks. According to the study authors, the blueberries improved age-related deficits in neuronal signaling, which translates to better message carrying between nerve cells.

Aim for: 1/2 cup a day.

## Salmon, mackerel,
### and other fish rich in omega-3 fatty acids

The brain contains tremendous amounts of fats, so it comes as no surprise that healthy fats in the diet benefit your "think tank." Brain cells are lined with omega-3 fatty acids that help reduce inflammation. These same fats help keep blood vessels elastic so oxygen and nutrients can flow upstairs unimpeded.

In a six-year study involving 4,000 Chicago residents age 65 and older, scores on cognitive function tests declined as the participants aged, but researchers found that those who ate fish twice a week or more had a 13 percent slower decline than those who ate no fish. People who ate fish once a week had a 10 percent slower decline. Other researchers have noted that high blood levels of omega-3s (the type abundant in fatty fish) are associated with preserved brain function.

Aim for: Two fish meals a week. Bake, poach, or broil fish instead of frying, or pan-fry it in a little olive oil.

## Olive oil

Researchers have linked getting a relatively high proportion of calories from monounsaturated fats like those in olive oil with lower rates of cognitive decline. This is particularly true when these fats are consumed as part of the typical Mediterranean diet (rich in vegetables, whole grains, legumes, and fish). While low-fat diets are touted for many health conditions, the brain needs these "good" fats to function well.

Aim for: 1 to 2 tablespoons a day. Use olive oil and other monounsaturated oils like canola oil in place of butter and margarine.

## Eggs

One of the few foods known to contain choline, the vitamin-like compound that cells need to function properly, eggs are particularly important in the diets of pregnant women while their babies' brains are developing. Studies have shown that rats whose mothers ate plenty of choline had stronger memories even into old age. Choline appears to be crucial to the development of the hippocampus, the memory center of the brain. Egg yolks also contain lots of vitamin $B_{12}$, which is known to help lower homocysteine. At high levels, this amino acid has been linked to cardiovascular disease that can lead to memory-impairing stroke. In fact, homocysteine is toxic to the brain and is linked to poor brain performance.

Aim for: One egg a day. If you have high cholesterol, talk to your doctor about the number of eggs appropriate for your diet.

### FEATURED RECIPES

**Zucchini Frittata** *p. 591*
**Updated Waldorf Salad** *p. 593*
**Broccoli Salad** *p. 595*
**Open-Faced Sardine Sandwiches** *p. 604*
**Tomato-Roasted Mackerel** *p. 612*
**Roasted Salmon with Sautéed Greens** *p. 613*
**Curry Seared Scallops** *p. 614*
**Blueberry-Oat Scones** *p. 628*

## Garlic

You probably think of your heart when you think about garlic and health, but your brain also benefits from these pungent cloves. Their sulfur compounds are potent antioxidants. Garlic also helps lower cholesterol and high blood pressure and reduce inflammation, three factors that increase the risk of heart disease and dementia.

**Aim for:** At least one clove a day, although more is better.

**Helpful hint:** When using garlic in recipes, chop it and let it stand for 10 to 15 minutes before cooking. The waiting period allows the garlic's active compounds to develop.

## Cinnamon

Pop a stick of cinnamon chewing gum the next time you have to take an exam or recite a poem from memory. One study showed that when volunteers chewed cinnamon gum before being tested on various tasks, they performed better than those who chewed no gum or gum of other flavors (including peppermint). Researchers hope to someday use cinnamon to help the elderly improve brain function and performance. Cinnamon also has anti-inflammatory properties that may help keep your brain sharp when you add the spice to your meals.

**Aim for:** Sprinkle cinnamon on sliced fruit, hot breakfast cereal, lattes, and even soups and stews.

## Apples

Could a daily apple in your lunch bag help sharpen your memory skills? It's possible, especially if you eat the skin, where most of the apple's quercetin is stored. In at least one study, this antioxidant proved more effective than vitamin C at protecting brain cells from oxidative damage.

**Aim for:** An apple a day, of course!

## Wine, beer, and spirits

Although too much alcohol is bad for the brain, some studies have found that people who have one to two drinks a day have a lower risk of memory loss than those who never drink. It may be because alcohol helps thin the blood, preventing clotting that can block the flow of all-important oxygen to the brain.

**Aim for:** Up to one drink a day for women, two for men. One drink is either 5 ounces of wine, 1.5 ounces of 100-proof liquor, or 12 ounces of beer.

## Curry dishes
### and other foods containing turmeric

The bright yellow spice called turmeric, used in traditional Indian curries and other dishes, gets its lovely hue from an antioxidant compound called curcumin. Animal studies have shown that curcumin helps prevent the formation of amyloid, the gummy protein buildup that can clog neural pathways in the brain. Curcumin also helps prevent oxidation and inflammation.

**Aim for:** 1 tablespoon of turmeric daily, about the amount found in two traditional curry dishes. You may also opt for up to 400 milligrams of curcumin in supplement form, but check with your doctor first.

## Tea

Want to get your fill of antioxidants? Take up a tea habit. One animal study from England has shown that the antioxidants in both black and green teas can inhibit several of the enzymes that have been linked to the progression of Alzheimer's disease. Studies also suggest that tea may help prevent the protein buildup that slows communication between neurons, damming the brain's memory channels.

**Aim for:** Scientists need to do more studies before they'll suggest just how much tea is the right amount for protecting memory. In the meantime, a few cups a day can't hurt.

## Oatmeal, high-fiber breakfast cereals, and whole grains

Where memory is concerned, the best breakfast cereal may be good old-fashioned oatmeal. In one recent study, when children ate oatmeal rather than cold cereal or no breakfast, their memory skills improved by 5 to 12 percent. In other research, the more whole grain the cereal, the more it appeared to improve memory. Scientists suspect that it may be the high fiber and protein content of oatmeal and whole-grain cereals that helps slow digestion, releasing glucose (blood sugar) more gradually into the bloodstream. The brain uses glucose as a source of energy, and a steady flow appears to help the brain retain information for tasks that require memory skills.

Aim for: One bowl of oatmeal or other cereal with at least 5 grams of fiber per serving. Top it with blueberries and toasted nuts for a real brain boost.

Helpful hint: Old-fashioned or steel-cut oats digest somewhat slower than instant oatmeal does. If you opt for instant, buy the plain (unsweetened) stuff and add your own flavorings, such as cinnamon.

## Leafy greens, lentils, fish,
*and other foods rich in B vitamins*

Folate (also known as folic acid) and vitamins $B_6$ and $B_{12}$ help lower levels of homocysteine, an amino acid in blood that has been linked to increased risk of dementia. High levels usually signify a deficiency of B vitamins. One study showed that people with high homocysteine levels and low folate levels had difficulty remembering words and details from a short story.

Aim for: A banana at breakfast; a spinach salad with chickpeas, bell pepper, and avocado at lunch; and a serving of fish at dinner should deliver the B vitamins you need for the day. Most breakfast cereals are also excellent sources of B vitamins, added by the manufacturers to replace the vitamins lost when grains are refined.

## NUTRITIONAL SUPPLEMENTS

**A multivitamin/mineral.** The brain is so complex that its proper care and feeding remain a bit mysterious. For added insurance, take a daily multivitamin to make sure that your noggin gets all the nutrients it needs. **DOSAGE:** One a day.

**Iron.** Blood depends on iron to help deliver oxygen to the brain. People with iron-deficiency anemia can have significant memory loss. **DOSAGE:** Recommended daily amounts are 18 milligrams for women up to age 50 and 8 milligrams for women 50 and older and for men. You can usually get what you need from a multivitamin formulated for your age group or gender. If you suspect you have anemia, consult your doctor to confirm your suspicion and determine the amount of iron you need to correct the problem.

## OFF THE MENU

**Fatty meats, butter, and other sources of saturated fat.** Foods rich in saturated fat are mainly responsible for raising cholesterol, which can clog arteries and prevent proper blood flow to the brain.

**White bread and flour, white rice, potatoes, and sugary foods.** These send blood sugar up and down in a hurry, but what the brain really needs is a steady supply.

# MENOPAUSE

If you break into hot sweats more often than a diva changes clothes, look to your diet for help. By eating delicious vitamin E–rich foods like almonds and leafy greens or adding edamame (green soybeans) and flaxseed to your soups and salads, you may be able to turn down those "power surges" and reduce other symptoms of menopause, like insomnia, mood swings, or depression—and boost your overall health. And unlike hormone replacement therapy, these foods won't raise your risk of breast cancer or heart disease, and they may even lower it.

## YOUR FOOD PRESCRIPTION

### Soy foods, peas, flaxseed,
*and other foods high in phytoestrogens*

Soy is no cure-all for hot flashes and other menopause complaints, but for some women, it may help. Tofu, soy milk, edadame, and soy nuts all contain estrogen-like compounds called isoflavones. In the body, these act like weaker versions of estrogen, blocking the real stuff and, the theory goes, those annoying symptoms. Results on soy for hot flashes have been mixed, but some evidence suggests that foods high in phytoestrogens, like soy, beans, and peas, may reduce hot flashes by 9 to 40 percent.

One possible reason for the mixed study results is that only 30 to 40 percent of Americans can convert isoflavones into the active form, while 90 percent of Asians and all rats (often used in studies) can. Still, it's worth giving soy foods a try for a month to see if they make a difference.

You can also get around the conversion problem by enjoying fermented soy products like miso (a paste delicious in soups) and tempeh (the healthy person's french fry; brown it and add to stir-fries). The isoflavones in fermented soy are already converted.

Flaxseed's a great choice as well because it offers a triple package of fiber, heart-healthy omega-3 fatty acids, and chemicals called lignans that reduce the risk of breast cancer. And some studies show that it helps reduce hot flashes. The best way to use flaxseed is to grind 1 to 2 tablespoons a day in a coffee grinder used just for that purpose and enjoy it sprinkled on cereal and salads and in soups.

**Aim for:** There's no recommended amount for menopause, but try replacing some of your regular milk with soy milk (try it on your morning cereal) and some of the protein in your recipes with soy protein.

### Almonds, sunflower seeds, wheat germ, leafy greens, olive oil, *and other foods high in vitamin E*

Limited research but lots of clinical evidence suggests that vitamin E may help prevent hot flashes. And a recent Tufts University study indicated that E helps prevent blood vessel blockage by keeping vessels dilated. This is important for menopausal women, whose risk of heart disease is two to three times higher than that of nonmenopausal women. Whole-grain cereals fortified with vitamin E are also excellent sources.

**Aim for:** There is no specific recommendation. Try starting your day with a bowl of whole-grain breakfast cereal sprinkled with wheat germ, and at dinner, toss a handful of sunflower seeds on top of a serving of spinach sautéed in olive oil.

**Helpful hint:** Because vitamin E requires vitamin C to remain active, toss your spinach salad with some slivered almonds, orange segments, or strawberries, and add some dried cranberries to nuts as a snack.

# Chickpeas, fish, turkey,
## and other foods high in vitamin $B_6$

If your spirits are lower than usual during menopause, consider serving yourself more fish, bananas, and other foods high in $B_6$. This vitamin spurs the production of hormones, including mood-boosting serotonin. It also helps prevent a buildup of homocysteine, an amino acid that ups the risk of heart disease. Some studies have also found that people with higher $B_6$ levels have better memory skills compared to people with lower levels.

Yams, often recommended for menopausal women, happen to be an excellent source of $B_6$. (They also contain compounds that resemble progesterone, another hormone that dips during menopause, but researchers have proven that our bodies can't use these compounds as they would progesterone.)

**Aim for:** Women need a minimum of 1.3 to 1.5 milligrams of vitamin $B_6$ daily, about the amount in a 4-ounce serving of tuna or two bananas.

**Helpful hint:** You can sneak some $B_6$ into your meal by spicing things up; turmeric, cayenne, and ginger all contain small amounts.

# Salmon, mackerel, flaxseed,
## and other foods high in omega-3 fatty acids

Fish comes packed with omega-3 fatty acids that help reduce bone loss and lower risk of heart disease; menopausal women are at greater risk for both than are premenopausal women. Flaxseed also contains an omega-3 called alpha-linolenic acid (ALA), but our bodies can convert only 5 to 10 percent of that into the forms we need, which we get directly from fish.

**Aim for:** Two to three 4-ounce servings of fish a week.

# Salmon, sardines, meat, poultry,
## and other foods high in vitamin $B_{12}$

$B_{12}$ helps the body produce neurotransmitters, chemicals that transmit nerve signals and affect mood. In fact, low levels of $B_{12}$ are associated with depression. $B_{12}$ deficiency also leads to higher levels of homocysteine, which in turn raises the risk of heart disease and stroke.

**Aim for:** At least 2.4 micrograms daily, about half the amount in a 4-ounce serving of snapper. However, the amount needed to normalize homocysteine levels—about 500 micrograms a

Create a twice-a-week fish-for-dinner habit. Simply cook fresh fillets on the stove or in the oven with olive oil, garlic, salt, and pepper, as you would a chicken breast. Then top with a simple sauce or, if you wish, just a tablespoon of salsa.

day—would be tough to get from diet alone (see Nutritional Supplements, below).

Helpful hint: Most breakfast cereals are fortified with twice the recommended daily amount of $B_{12}$.

# Beans and peas, leafy greens,
## and other foods high in folate

Several studies have shown that folate (called folic acid in supplement form) fosters heart, bone, and cognitive health by lowering levels of homocysteine. Research has also linked low levels of folate to depression. In short, this B vitamin seems an ideal match for menopausal women.

Aim for: 400 micrograms of folate daily, the amount in a bowl of fortified cereal or in 1/2 cup of sautéed spinach, 1/2 cup of chickpeas, and an ear of corn.

Helpful hint: Cooking vegetables can reduce their folate content by up to 40 percent, so enjoy raw spinach salads when you're looking for a vegetarian folate boost.

# Milk, cheese, salmon, greens,
## and other foods high in calcium

With menopause comes a higher risk of osteoporosis, so if you're not already eating plenty of calcium-rich foods, it's high time to start. The calcium in foods can't help replace bone that's already lost, but studies have shown that it does rein in the loss. To protect your heart, choose low-fat versions of dairy foods and switch to fat-free milk.

Aim for: 1,000 to 1,200 milligrams of calcium daily, about what you'll get from a cup of yogurt, an ounce or two of mozzarella cheese, and a cup of white beans.

Helpful hint: If you down a lot of sodas, you're losing calcium. Sodas contain phosphorus, another mineral that gives our bones density. But our bodies eliminate any extra phosphorus through urine—and calcium goes with it.

# Fortified milk and cereals
## and other foods high in vitamin D

The "sunshine vitamin" (which your body makes when exposed to sunlight) stimulates the absorption of calcium, especially important for menopausal women with thinning bones. Sockeye salmon is a particularly rich source of D because the fish eat a steady diet of plants that create lots of vitamin D from sunlight, as well as small sea creatures that eat those plants.

Aim for: 1,000 IU per day; 3 ounces of salmon has 425 IU.

## NUTRITIONAL SUPPLEMENTS

**Vitamin E.** It can be difficult to get enough vitamin E from foods, so a supplement may be in order to help cool hot flashes. Check the label to see if it contains mixed natural tocopherols and tocotrienols, the two most valuable groups of molecules in vitamin E. Don't buy a supplement with dl-alpha-tocopherols; this is an ineffective, synthetic form of vitamin E. You can also pop open a vitamin E soft-gel and apply the oil topically once a day for vaginal dryness. **DOSAGE:** Some doctors recommend 400 to 800 IU daily for hot flashes.

**Vitamin $B_6$.** Most people get the $B_6$ they need from their diets, although heavy drinkers and the elderly risk deficiency because of absorption difficulties. **DOSAGE:** 2 to 20 milligrams a day are typical doses for people who are deficient. Ask your doctor about the amount you should be taking, if any.

**Omega-3 fatty acids.** Omega-3s such as DHA and EPA come in soft-gel fish-oil capsules or in liquids such as flaxseed oil. Skip the flaxseed oil: It doesn't have the fiber or cancer-preventing lignans that whole flaxseed does, it's expensive, and it goes rancid. Because omega-3s are sensitive to heat, light, and oxygen, store the supplements in your refrigerator. Also, choose a supplement with vitamin E, which will help prevent rancidity. Taking the supplements with food or freezing them first can help reduce the burping often associated with fish oils. So can choosing a fish-oil supplement that contains citrus essence. **DOSAGE:** 1 gram a day of a combination of EPA and DHA is often recommended.

**Vitamin B$_{12}$.** As we age, it's harder to absorb B$_{12}$ from food. Because of that, the Institute of Medicine recommends that people over 50 take B$_{12}$ in supplement form. A study at the Cleveland Clinic Foundation found that 500 micrograms of B$_{12}$ daily, taken with B$_6$ and folic acid, normalized homocysteine levels (high levels increase heart attack risk). **DOSAGE:** 500 micrograms a day.

**Calcium.** Scientists are still researching the optimal amount of calcium necessary to slow bone loss. For now, the National Academy of Sciences recommends taking the amount below. Look for a supplement that also contains vitamin D. **DOSAGE:** 1,000 to 1200 milligrams daily, divided into two doses.

**Vitamin D.** Those of us who live in sunny climates usually get vitamin D from sunlight or by eating vitamin D–rich foods. But people who live in less sunny northern climates or who take certain medications, such as laxatives and antacids, may need a supplement boost. Ask your doctor to check your D level, especially if you live in the north. As we get older, our bodies don't convert sunlight into D as well as they once did. **DOSAGE:** 1,000 IU daily.

## OFF THE MENU

**Caffeine, alcohol, and spicy foods.** All three may crank up the ol' hot flash burner. Alcohol lowers your body temperature as you drink, especially to excess, then raises it as the alcohol leaves your system.

**Corn, sunflower, and safflower oils.** These are rich in omega-6 fatty acids that in excess are thought to cancel out the benefits of omega-3 fatty acids in fish and other foods. In a study at Purdue University, researchers found that for menopausal women who had a low ratio of omega-6s to omega-3s, bone loss was minimized.

## Should You Go Meatless?

More and more people are becoming vegetarians, and if menopausal symptoms plague you, perhaps you should consider jumping on that bandwagon. As we've noted, a diet full of the phytoestrogens in soy foods, beans, and flaxseed helps reduce hot flashes and lowers the risk of heart disease and osteoporosis. Studies have also shown that women who eat lots of fruits and vegetables have a 54 percent lower risk of stroke than women who do not. And research has shown that vegan diets (no animal products at all, including milk and eggs) help postmenopausal women lose weight and improve their sensitivity to insulin, which is important for preventing diabetes. But vegetarians who eat no meat or dairy products need to be certain they get enough vitamin B$_{12}$, calcium, and iron in their diets. Most breakfast cereals are fortified with adequate amounts of B$_{12}$ and iron, and soy milk and many brands of orange juice are fortified with calcium.

# MENSTRUAL PROBLEMS

PMS, cramps, and bloating are the price women sometimes pay for being designed with the ability to produce children. After ovulation—about halfway through the monthly cycle—the hormone progesterone increases, preparing the lining of the uterus for a fertilized egg. But about seven days before a period starts, if no egg is implanted, levels of both progesterone and estrogen drop. For many women, those seven days can bring symptoms of premenstrual syndrome, or PMS, including irritability, depression, cramping, bloating, cravings, breast pain, and headaches. For other women, problems such as heavy bleeding and cramps start with menstruation.

Ibuprofen is a godsend for many, but other helpful "medicines" come in foods, not pills. Although food isn't a cure-all for menstrual problems, women whose diets are healthful and who cut out certain foods seem to do better than others. In part, that's because some foods help balance hormones, improve mood, and diminish water retention, all of which affect how we feel during menstruation.

## YOUR FOOD PRESCRIPTION

### Dairy products *and other foods high in calcium and vitamin D*

You've probably never thought to reach for milk for your PMS, but maybe you should. In a long-term study of more than 3,000 women, researchers found that the women who drank four servings of low-fat or fat-free milk a day (or the calcium and vitamin D equivalent in fortified orange juice, low-fat yogurt, and other low-fat dairy foods) had a 40 percent lower risk of developing PMS than the women who had only one serving of milk a week. Other studies have also shown calcium's ability to curb PMS symptoms.

Researchers aren't certain why calcium and vitamin D are such a winning pair, but one theory is that PMS may stem from—or at least reveal—a lack of calcium (PMS symptoms are similar to those of calcium deficiency). And researchers do know that in women with PMS, estrogen levels tend to be higher and calcium levels lower than in women without PMS.

Vitamin D helps the body absorb calcium, and it probably affects both the brain and estrogen in ways scientists don't yet understand.

**Aim for:** 1,000 to 1,200 milligrams of calcium and 400 IU of vitamin D daily, the equivalent of four glasses of fat-free or low-fat milk.

**Helpful hint:** Be sure to drink "skinny" milk. According to researchers, women who drink fat-free or low-fat milk have a lower risk of PMS than those who drink whole milk.

### Spinach, soybeans, grains, *and other foods high in magnesium*

Munching on spinach salads and even baked goods made with whole-grain flour, buckwheat, or whole-grain cornmeal—all rich in magnesium—could help put a stop to the PMS blues. Although it's not clear how magnesium affects PMS, the nutrient is essential for dopamine production. This mood-boosting hormone also helps balance adrenal and kidney function, which in turn helps minimize fluid retention. And in a two-month British study, women who took just 200 milligrams of magnesium daily—about the equivalent of a quarter cup of almonds or two servings of spinach—had less weight gain, bloating, and breast tenderness during the second month of the study than women taking a placebo. Another study found that the ratio of magnesium to calcium was significantly lower in women with PMS than in women without it.

**Aim for:** The women in the British study took only 200 milligrams of magnesium daily, but the recommended amount is 320 milligrams. Half a halibut fillet contains 170 milligrams; a cup of whole-wheat flour, 166 milligrams; a cup of cooked spinach, 157 milligrams; and a cup of soybeans, 148 milligrams.

**Helpful hint:** Develop a yen for raw spinach. About one-third of spinach's magnesium is lost in cooking.

## Nuts, seeds, wheat germ,
*and other foods high in vitamin E*

Eating foods like almonds and sunflower seeds is never a chore, and doing so may help relieve symptoms of PMS. In a small three-month study of 46 women with PMS, those who took a daily 400 IU dose of vitamin E—admittedly the equivalent of far more nuts than you'd want to eat in one day—saw their mental and physical symptoms of PMS abate.

**Aim for:** The women in the study took 400 IU daily, an amount that's nearly impossible to get from diet alone. One tablespoon of wheat germ oil has more than 20 milligrams, and an ounce of almonds has more than 7. The recommended amount of vitamin E is 15 milligrams (about 23 IU).

## Clams, oysters, beef, soybeans,
*and other foods high in iron*

If heavy bleeding is your monthly burden, try adding more iron to your diet; too little can cause heavier flow. Lean red meat and oysters are terrific sources. One note of caution: Eating too much red meat may increase the risk of endometriosis, a painful condition in which uterine tissue grows on organs outside the uterus, such as the ovaries or fallopian tubes. In an Italian study, women who ate meat every day had double the risk of endometriosis compared to women who ate less meat and more fruits and vegetables.

**Aim for:** For women, the recommended amount of iron is 18 milligrams per day, about what you'll get from a bowl of oatmeal and a cup of soybeans.

**Helpful hint:** Women who eat low-fat vegetarian diets have fewer premenstrual symptoms than those who eat meat. But if blood flow is heavy, they need iron. The solution: Eat iron-rich beans, tofu, and spinach.

## Tofu, soy milk, flaxseed,
*and other foods with phytoestrogens*

If you snack on edamame (green soybeans) or add them to soups and salads, you may be serving up some menstrual relief. Soy and flaxseed contain phytoestrogens, plant chemicals that imitate estrogen, which may help balance hormones during menstruation. Study results are mixed, however. One Korean study found that

For dinner, steam clams—it's easy! Pour some no-iodine salt and cornmeal in cold water and soak the clams for 30 minutes. Scrub the shells and rinse thoroughly. Then steam in a mix of water, white wine, garlic, and pepper until the clams open.

soy lessened premenstrual symptoms, and in a small two-month British study of young women, soy protein significantly reduced breast tenderness and swelling compared to a placebo. Yet a Japanese study found soy had no effect.

Aim for: Try serving yourself some soy milk, edamame, or tofu a few times a week over the course of a month and see if it helps.

# Complex carbohydrates
*from whole grains, fruits, and vegetables*

Many women crave sugary carbohydrates like chocolate and ice cream before and during their periods. But instead of having a sugar fix, eating meals plump with whole grains, fruits, and vegetables may double-cross PMS symptoms, including the cramping that often accompanies heavy bleeding.

Carbohydrates boost levels of the feel-good neurotransmitter serotonin, the same one targeted by certain antidepressants. In a study at the Massachusetts Institute of Technology, researchers found that women who ate large amounts of carbohydrates became less depressed, angry, and anxious and had more stable moods than women who ate fewer carbs. Complex, or high-fiber, carbohydrates are best because they're digested more slowly than carbs that come from sugar or refined grains, so they help keep blood sugar levels stable. When blood sugar drops too low, most of us get tired and grouchy, which can worsen PMS symptoms. Complex carbs also help prevent the constipation that's common in women with menstrual cramps.

Another benefit of whole grains: They contain the mineral manganese. In a USDA study, researchers found that when women had low levels of manganese (and calcium), they had much more severe premenstrual symptoms than they did when they supplemented their diets with both minerals. Researchers aren't sure why manganese may help, but it is involved in blood clotting, and women with low levels tend to bleed more heavily than women with normal levels. Manganese also helps the body maintain normal blood sugar levels. Top-notch sources include oat bran, whole-grain wheat flour, fortified cereals, and buckwheat flour.

Include lots of citrus fruits and berries in your choices as well. Citrus fruits contain vitamin C, and berries, grapes, and cherries offer antioxidants called flavonoids, both of which help reduce heavy bleeding. An Italian study showed that women who ate lots of fresh fruit and vegetables also cut their risk of endometriosis by 40 percent.

Aim for: Three servings of whole grains a day (that's 1/2 cup of cooked oatmeal or cooked wheatberries, one slice of whole-grain bread, and 1/2 cup of whole-wheat pasta), five to six servings of vegetables, and three to four servings of fruit.

## FEATURED RECIPES

**Buckwheat Pancakes with Fruit Sauce** *p. 590*
**Edamame Hummus with Pita Crisps** *p. 592*
**Ultimate Spiced Nuts** *p. 592*
**Spinach Salad with Chickpeas** *p. 597*
**Mac 'n Cheese Primavera** *p. 608*
**Roasted Salmon with Sautéed Greens** *p. 613*
**Chicken-Barley Bake** *p. 616*
**Beef and Broccoli Stew** *p. 620*
**Zesty Cornbread** *p. 630*
**Pumpkin Streusel Bread** *p. 631*

## NUTRITIONAL SUPPLEMENTS

**Calcium and vitamin D.** Most women could benefit from a daily calcium supplement, although it's unclear whether supplements affect PMS the same way foods high in calcium and vitamin D do. **DOSAGE:** *Calcium:* 1,000 to 1,200 milligrams daily, in two doses (it's best absorbed in 500- to 600-milligram amounts). *Vitamin D:* 400 IU daily.

**Magnesium.** Several studies have found that magnesium can improve PMS symptoms. A study in Britain, for instance, found that taking 200 milligrams of magnesium a day for two months reduced fluid retention and breast tenderness. Another study found that 360 milligrams three times a day, taken from day 15 to the start of a period, helped diminish mood swings. Magnesium chloride and magnesium lactate are the easiest forms to absorb. **DOSAGE:** The studies showed an effect in doses from 200 to 1,100 milligrams a day.

**Vitamin B₆.** Several studies have found that doses of 50 to 100 milligrams can help relieve breast pain and depression related to PMS. **DOSAGE:** 50 to 100 milligrams.

## OFF THE MENU

**Salt.** Salt causes the body to retain fluids, which only adds to bloating and breast pain.

**Sugar and fat.** Sugary foods like candy bars and cake make blood sugar spike and then drop, and that rollercoaster ride can affect your mood and energy level. If you want a sweet treat, try fresh or dried fruits (these are high in calories, so just a small handful will do) instead. Their fiber slows digestion, which results in slower fluctuations in blood sugar.

Saturated fat in fatty meats and full-fat cheese cranks up production of certain prostaglandins (hormone-like chemicals) in the uterus that stimulate the muscles and can cause cramps. (Of course, as we noted earlier, heavy bleeders need the iron from these very foods. If you're a heavy bleeder with cramps, get iron from non-meat sources like oysters, beans, and spinach.)

If you're eating a lot of sugar and fat, chances are good that you weigh more than you should, and your waistline could be contributing to your menstrual problems. A University of Michigan study found that women who carry extra pounds have double the chance of longer episodes of pain compared to thinner women.

**Caffeine and alcohol.** Caffeine is a stimulant, which can lead to anxiety and mood swings, not the effect you want during menstrual periods already awash with drama. As far as alcohol goes, the University of Michigan study found that in women who had cramps, it increased their length and severity.

## Sleuthing for Hidden Salt Sources

Salt is sneakier than a cat burglar, cropping up even in foods we think of as healthy, like canned vegetables and soup, as well as more obvious sources like pizza and salty snack foods. It's also in condiments such as ketchup and barbecue sauce. Thus, even if you banish salt from the table—a great way to start cutting back—you may be eating more sodium than you think. Check food labels before you buy. The recommended daily intake of sodium is 2,300 milligrams, about 1 teaspoon.

## When You Don't Feel Like Eating

Cramps, bleeding, mood swings, and bloating aren't exactly clarion calls to dinner. But even if you don't feel like eating, you can still drink water, herbal tea, green tea, and fruit and vegetable juice. Oddly enough, drinking more fluids lessens bloating: The body releases fluid when you're well hydrated but holds on to it when you run low. And fruit and vegetable juices provide nutrients that can be helpful in reducing symptoms.

# MIGRAINE

"That no one dies of migraine seems, to someone deep into an attack, an ambiguous blessing." So Joan Didion wrote in her essay collection, *The White Album.* What causes such distress that dying doesn't seem unreasonable? That's one of the more frustrating things about migraines—headache experts aren't quite sure.

The new thinking is that people who get migraines have extra-sensitive, hyperreactive brains. Something sparks a region deep in the brain, dubbed the "migraine generator," and that unleashes a cascade of brain chemicals that inflame nerve endings, dilate blood vessels, and flood the brain with pain signals. So what's the "something" that triggers this reaction? That's even more frustrating. Almost *anything* can cause a migraine, including weather changes, strong odors, stress, loss of sleep, and certain foods and drinks. A good many migraines are also related to fluctuations in estrogen levels, which is no doubt why three times more women than men get migraines (often coinciding with their periods) and why the headaches tend to disappear during pregnancy and after menopause.

Avoiding the foods that often trigger migraines while making a point of eating those that help prevent them may reduce the number—and intensity—of headaches you get. And compared to dying, that sounds pretty good.

## YOUR FOOD PRESCRIPTION

### Fruits, vegetables, and legumes

This is good general advice, but it may be particularly helpful for women who get migraines with their periods—which may be due to a sudden drop in estrogen. The higher your overall estrogen level is to begin with, so the reasoning goes, the farther it can fall during the drop. The fiber in these foods helps by removing excess estrogen from the body along with waste, so it's not recycled back into your bloodstream.

In addition, fruits, vegetables, and legumes all contain plant estrogens that blunt the negative effects of the estrogen our bodies naturally make. Another major plus of these foods: They're low in fat. When you eat more fat, your body makes more estrogen.

**Aim for:** Getting the recommended 7 to 10 daily servings of fruit and vegetables is a great place to start.

### Fatty fish

You know it as heart-healthy fare, but salmon and other fatty fish (like mackerel, trout, and herring) just may help reduce migraines, too. These fish are rich sources of the omega-3 fatty acids EPA and DHA. Some preliminary research on these anti-inflammatory compounds done at the University of Cincinnati showed that when they

| FEATURED RECIPES |
|---|
| **Buckwheat Pancakes with Fruit Sauce** *p. 590* |
| **Spinach Salad with Chickpeas** *p. 597* |
| **Tuna and White Bean Salad** *p. 599* |
| **Ginger Butternut Squash Soup** *p. 602* |
| **Lentil-Tomato Soup** *p. 603* |
| **Roasted Salmon with Sautéed Greens** *p. 613* |
| **Beef and Broccoli Stew** *p. 620* |
| **Brown Rice Risotto** *p. 625* |
| **Almond Rice** *p. 626* |
| **Zesty Cornbread** *p. 630* |

were taken in supplement form, they appeared to reduce the frequency and severity of migraines in some people over the course of six weeks.

**Aim for:** The University of Cincinnati study used capsules containing 300 milligrams of EPA and DHA and 700 milligrams of other oils. Four 4-ounce servings of fatty fish a week would provide about the same amount of the beneficial fish oils used in the study.

## Coffee

Although caffeine may trigger migraines in some people, when a migraine strikes, a few cups of coffee do help relieve the pain. Caffeine is so effective at helping to shrink swollen blood vessels in the brain, it's one of the key ingredients (together with acetaminophen and aspirin) in over-the-counter migraine medicines like Excedrin Migraine.

**Aim for:** A cup or two when a migraine hits.

## Ginger

Research shows that this warming spice contains some potent compounds that are similar to the ones in nonsteroidal anti-inflammatory drugs. It may work against migraines by blocking inflammatory substances called prostaglandins. Ginger hasn't been rigorously tested for headache relief, but even if it doesn't stop your migraine, it should help relieve the nausea that often comes with it.

**Aim for:** There's no recommended dose for ginger, but you might start using powdered or fresh ginger liberally in cooking or ordering dishes flavored with ginger when dining out. And when a migraine strikes, drinking a glass of water with a few teaspoons of powdered ginger mixed in every few hours may help alleviate the pain. You can also suck on dried ginger candy.

## Whole grains, beans, leafy dark green vegetables, *and other foods high in magnesium*

What do these foods have in common? They're all high in magnesium, which research shows is often deficient in people who get migraines. Low levels of magnesium are thought to make the brain extra sensitive to migraine triggers.

**Aim for:** The recommended daily amount for magnesium is 280 milligrams for women and 350 milligrams for men, though if you're truly deficient, aiming for 400 to 700 milligrams daily may be better for preventing migraines.

**Helpful hint:** Roasted pumpkin seeds are among the richest sources of magnesium, with about 151 milligrams per ounce. Keep a bag in your purse, car, or desk for easy nibbling. Magnesium-rich nuts include Brazil nuts (107 milligrams per ounce) and almonds (78 milligrams per ounce). Or try some halibut, which contains 91 milligrams in 3-ounce portion, as well as a smattering of omega-3s.

Make a healing ginger tea in no time. Add about a dozen coin-size slices of fresh gingerroot to a quart of water and simmer on the stove for about 20 minutes. If you don't love the taste of fresh ginger, add orange juice and honey to your cup of tea.

## NUTRITIONAL SUPPLEMENTS

**Magnesium.** People often complain that their migraines hit when they're under stress, and a deficiency of magnesium may help explain why. Chronic stress drains our bodies of magnesium, and when levels are low, blood vessels are more likely to spasm. It's estimated that about 50 percent of people who get migraines have low magnesium levels.

When given intravenously, magnesium can completely halt a migraine, often within minutes. Researchers suspect that the mineral relaxes overexcited nerves in the brain and helps serotonin receptors block migraine pain signals. That's also how the newer migraine medications, known as triptans—sumatriptan (Imitrex) and almotriptan (Axert)—work.

Oral magnesium works well, too, but only for preventing migraines. In one three-month study, migraine frequency dropped by 42 percent in people who took 600 milligrams of magnesium, compared to 16 percent in those who took placebos. Supplementing with magnesium can even help triptan medications work better. In one small study of people who reported that Imitrex didn't relieve their migraines, the medication started working when they corrected their magnesium deficiency. The only downside to increasing magnesium is possibly some mild diarrhea. **DOSAGE:** 400 to 600 milligrams daily in divided doses. Avoid magnesium hydroxide and magnesium citrate, which are more commonly associated with loose stools.

**Riboflavin.** Researchers are still sorting out how riboflavin (vitamin $B_2$) prevents migraines, but one theory is that the brains of people with migraines simply require a little extra energy for proper function. Riboflavin increases energy production in all cells, including brain cells. In a recent German study, volunteers taking riboflavin for six months got half the migraines they normally experienced, and they were able to reduce their migraine medication. The only side effect appears to be minor gastric upset. **DOSAGE:** 400 milligrams daily. Since B vitamins work best together, take a B-complex supplement or a multivitamin and, if necessary, make up the difference in dosage with a riboflavin supplement.

**Omega-3 fatty acids.** If you can't seem to eat the four weekly servings of fish suggested above, look to fish-oil supplements to fill the omega-3 gap. **DOSAGE:** The University of Cincinnati study used 1 gram of fish oil a day in capsules that contained 300 milligrams of EPA and DHA and 700 milligrams of other oils.

**Coenzyme Q10.** Like riboflavin, CoQ10 increases cellular energy, and some preliminary research suggests it can prevent migraines. A small double-blind, placebo-controlled study of 42 people done in Switzerland found that over the three months of the study, taking CoQ10 reduced migraine frequency, duration, and accompanying symptoms such as nausea. The number of migraine attacks per month in the treatment group went from 4.4 to 3.2, compared with no change in the placebo group. The people who took CoQ10 also had shorter migraine episodes and fewer days with nausea. **DOSAGE:** 100 milligrams three times daily.

## OFF THE MENU

**Fatty foods and vegetable oils.** If you're serious about using your diet to help prevent migraines, get serious about cutting back on fat. As we mentioned earlier, eating fat increases estrogen levels, which may contribute to migraines. A small three-month study done at Loma Linda University in California found that when participants radically cut their fat intake—by 60 percent—to about 20 grams per day, they reported a 71 percent decrease in headache frequency, a 66 percent decrease in intensity, and a 74 percent decrease in duration.

This doesn't mean you should cut out fat from fish, however, since omega-3 fatty acids help to reduce inflammation and pain. Instead take aim at saturated fat (meat, cheese, butter, and ice cream). You might also start pouring olive or canola oil instead of other vegetable oils like corn, sunflower, and safflower. These oils are high in omega-6s, which may promote inflammation and worsen pain (see page 329 for more details).

**Trigger foods.** It used to be that eliminating key foods from your diet was the primary prescription for preventing migraines. Now headache experts are less sure that specific foods per se cause migraines. Rather, it may be that certain foods eaten under certain conditions tip the balance when other factors like stress, lack of sleep, or hormone fluctuations make us more vulnerable to a migraine. It's even possible that making dietary changes—any changes—has a sort of placebo effect. We feel as if we're doing *something,* and that feeling of control has a positive effect.

Still, because food sensitivity is thought to be a factor in 10 to 30 percent of migraines, it can't hurt to do a little sleuthing if you suspect that foods trigger your headaches. Oft-cited culprits include red wine, aged cheese, processed meats, dairy products, citrus fruits, wheat, chocolate, and food additives like monosodium glutamate and artificial sweeteners. Some studies show a connection with migraines; some don't. That may be because migraines are so highly individual; what triggers one person's headache may not trigger someone else's.

The best way to determine if food is affecting your migraines is to keep a food diary. When a headache hits, try to remember what you ate in the previous 12 hours. If you see a pattern, avoid that food for two or more weeks, then add it back to your diet and see if there's a change in your headache episodes. But remember, just as it's important to avoid any foods that may cause migraines, it's equally important not to skip meals, since irregular eating can bring on migraines, too.

## Two Herbs to Try

These aren't exactly foods, but since they're so potentially useful against migraines, we thought they deserved mention.

**Feverfew.** Researchers have long debated whether this popular herb really prevents migraines, but the latest study, done in Germany, suggests that it might. When the researchers tested a standardized feverfew extract against a placebo, they found that study volunteers who typically averaged five migraines a month got about two fewer migraines each month when they were taking feverfew. Feverfew preparations vary widely, so follow the package instructions for dosage.

**Butterbur.** The roots of this shrub contain anti-inflammatory and antispasmodic compounds called petasines, which may be why they're helpful for preventing migraines. In one study, when German researchers gave 108 children between 50 and 150 milligrams of butterbur root extract (depending on their weight) for four months, 77 percent of the kids reported at least a 50 percent reduction in migraines. And when 245 adults took 75 milligrams a day in a four-month study at Albert Einstein College of Medicine in New York, 68 percent of the volunteers reported getting half as many migraines as they had previously. The only downside was some occasional burping.

# NAUSEA

When you're feeling green around the gills, food is probably the last thing you want to think about. In fact, though, your kitchen may hold just the ticket to quell the queasies. The best pantry remedy, ginger, comes in forms you can carry with you to keep you safely away from that deck railing or worry-free in the backseat during a winding car ride. It's even safe for pregnant women.

## YOUR FOOD PRESCRIPTION

### Ginger

Ginger root has been used for more than 2,000 years in China to treat nausea. Scientists suspect it blocks the release of hormones that can cause irregular muscle contractions in the gut—the ones that leave you with that heaving feeling. Ginger appears particularly effective against motion sickness and morning sickness. In one study, naval cadets who were new to the open sea took either placebos or 1 gram of powdered ginger prior to a period of sailing through high waves. Those who took the ginger reported much less nausea and vomiting and fewer cold sweats than those who took the placebo.

Other studies on ginger have been less promising, but because it's safe and cheap, it's well worth a try, especially for pregnant women. In one study, symptoms of morning sickness became milder in more than half the women who took 1 gram of fresh ginger daily.

**Aim for:** For motion sickness, chew on 1 gram (about 1 tablespoon or a 1-inch piece) of peeled raw ginger or candied ginger several hours prior to travel and every 4 hours while traveling. Or take two capsules of powdered ginger every 4 hours for a full day before traveling and throughout the trip. For morning sickness, take 1 gram of fresh or candied ginger daily. You can also drink a cup of ginger tea every few hours. Avoid powdered ginger because it may be less safe in large quantities for pregnant women.

**Helpful hint:** For some people, ginger is more effective when taken on an empty stomach.

### Flat soda and clear fruit juices

Remember staying home from school with the stomach flu while your mother coaxed you to drink ginger ale or flat cola? In small quantities, sweet liquids like these or like apple or grape juice seem to calm the stomach, and they provide some energy when you can't eat. They're absorbed into the bloodstream quickly, yet they have no fiber to activate stomach acid and digestive tract contractions that could stimulate nausea. Coconut water (not to be confused with coconut milk), with its wealth of potassium, is like nature's Gatorade, and island cultures often turn to it as a remedy for nausea. Look for it in health food stores.

**Aim for:** Small sips. Don't drink too much at once. If carbonation bothers your stomach, let sodas go flat before drinking.

### Ice pops

Cold liquids can be a godsend to pregnant women. When you can't keep anything else in your stomach, sucking on frozen fruit juice cubes (make your own in an ice cube tray) or

### FEATURED RECIPES

**Quick Chicken Noodle Soup** *p. 600*
**Almond Rice** *p. 626*
**Pomegranate Ice** *p. 638*

fruit-based ice pops can replace some of the liquids and energy that you've lost.

Aim for: A few fruit-based ice pops a day may pave the path to a slightly larger meal. Avoid those that contain artificial sweeteners, some of which may woresn nausea in some people.

## Olives and lemons

These quickly dry saliva from the mouth, and that can help tone down nausea. The acid in lemons also triggers the formation of bicarbonate in the stomach, helping neutralize intestinal acids and calm gas and bloating that may intensify nausea.

Aim for: Suck an olive when nausea strikes or add lemon juice to hot or room-temperature water and sip it.

## Clear, salty broths

Chicken broth, vegetable broth, and miso soup all sit easily on the stomach and provide nutrition during episodes when most foods just aren't appealing.

Aim for: 1/2 cup of broth every 2 hours.

## Crackers, toast, and dry cereal

These dry snacks soak up the saliva in your mouth and some of the acid in your stomach. Many women in the first trimester of pregnancy can't get out of bed before eating a cracker or two.

Aim for: Eat oyster crackers, saltines, plain toast, and other mild, crunchy foods throughout the day as tiny snacks.

## Chamomile, lemon balm, and peppermint teas

Chamomile, known for its muscle-relaxing qualities, can help calm spasms in the stomach. Peppermint can help digestion by calming the stomach's muscle contractions (the reason that after-dinner mints became popular), and its menthol can anesthetize the stomach wall,

an effect that may reduce nausea. Some studies have even shown that sniffing a cloth dotted with peppermint oil can help to reduce postsurgical nausea.

Aim for: Sip tea throughout the day for hydration and nausea relief.

## Mints and lemon drops

Many cancer patients undergoing chemotherapy find that sucking on a mint or a piece of hard lemon candy can take the edge off nausea.

Aim for: Use as needed.

### NUTRITIONAL SUPPLEMENTS

**Vitamin B$_6$.** When it comes to morning sickness, a number of studies have shown that vitamin B$_6$ can help calm that green feeling. The vitamin can break down hormones that may lead to nausea and vomiting. Some studies suggest it works best when combined with ginger.

Caution: Some B vitamin supplements can actually trigger nausea. Take them with food unless directed otherwise. **DOSAGE:** 25 milligrams every 8 hours, with food. Consult your obstetrician about a dose that's appropriate beyond that in your prenatal multivitamin.

### OFF THE MENU

**Fatty foods.** The stomach needs more time to digest foods high in animal fat, such as dairy and meat, and that means digestive acids linger longer, making symptoms worse for anyone prone to nausea.

**Green tea.** On an empty stomach, green tea can trigger nausea in some people. Sip it with food if that's true for you, and take a pass on green tea supplements.

**Iron supplements.** Some people who take iron to treat or prevent iron-deficiency anemia experience nausea as a side effect. If you do, ask your doctor about lowering your dose.

# OBESITY

Despite the cliché of jolly fat folks, obesity is not funny. Being obese, defined as having a body mass index (or BMI, a measurement of body fat) of 30 or greater, can lead to heart disease, stroke, high blood pressure, diabetes, and even some forms of cancer. Millions of people are obese, and the number is growing.

You may think the answer is simple: Eat less. But the usual means of weight loss people try—starving themselves or going on fad diets—simply do not work. Some researchers speculate that when we lose weight, fat cells shrink, lessening the amount of leptin, an appetite suppressor, that pours into the blood. When leptin falls below the level genes are programmed for, the brain releases other hormones that increase hunger. This is what dieters know as the rebound effect; they lose weight, only to gain it all back and then some.

In ancient times, such mechanisms helped humans survive famine and predators. Today, the predators chasing us are the marketers who push fast food and other high-calorie, high-fat eats. We're easy targets since we're hardwired to eat (and store) fat.

If you can manage to ignore the siren songs of ever-present vending machines and fast-food joints, though, there's good news: You *can* eat enough to feel plenty full, without taking in too much fat or too many calories. In fact, in a study of 38 common foods, researchers found that high-protein and high-fiber foods were much more satisfying than high-fat foods. Cakes and cookies and other fatty foods were the least satisfying, which may account in part for why we end up gobbling down such big portions when we eat them.

If you want to really enjoy what you're eating, focus on flavorful—and above all, filling—foods. Enjoy fiber- and nutrient-rich whole-grain rice, tabbouleh salad, and vegetable soup instead of nutrient-stripped white rice or bagels, fat-filled potato salad, or cream of corn soup. Losing weight doesn't mean going hungry; it means eating well.

food for thought . . .

"Skipping breakfast isn't as bad as eating 5 pounds of bacon, but day to day, it's one of the worst things someone with a weight problem can do."

— Bruce A. Barton, PhD, president and CEO, Maryland Medical Research Institute, Baltimore

# Breakfast

Skipping breakfast is a lot like skipping rope: neither gets you anywhere. Although lots of people think they'll cut calories by cutting breakfast, the opposite is true. Studies show that eating breakfast helps you consume fewer total calories for the day. One national U.S. health and nutrition survey found that men who eat breakfast weigh about 6 pounds less than men who skip it; women weigh 9 pounds less. And a 10-year study of almost 2,400 adolescent girls showed that those who ate any kind of breakfast had lower BMIs than girls who did not. People who eat cereal for breakfast have lower BMIs than people who skip breakfast or dine on meat and eggs.

# Whole grains, beans, fruits,
### *and other foods high in fiber*

Eat a bowl of brown rice topped with chickpeas and sautéed vegetables for lunch, and it's likely you won't want another bite until supper. High-fiber foods like these have few calories, little fat, and lots of bulk, which keeps you full. They're also digested slowly, which means your blood sugar stays at an even keel instead of rapidly spiking and falling, which leaves you hungry again in no time. Whole grains also provide nutrients, such as magnesium and vitamin $B_6$, that many weight-loss diets are deficient in. A great way to get a good dose of fiber is to start your day with high-fiber cereal.

Aim for: 25 to 35 grams of fiber per day. A cup of chickpeas has about 12 grams, and 1/2 cup of bran cereal has more than 8.

Helpful hint: If whole grains put you off, ease yourself into the idea by adding them in small amounts. For instance, mix half your usual cereal with a half serving of whole-grain cereal and add some brown rice to white rice. Gradually increase the amount of whole grains as your taste buds adjust.

# Fresh greens, raw vegetables,
### *and other salad foods*

Head for the salad bar. Greens and raw vegetables like carrots, zucchini, and broccoli are remarkably low in calories but high in water and slow-digesting fiber, so they tend to fill you up.

Squelching your appetite isn't the only reason to frequent the produce section. In a study of almost 18,000 people, researchers found that those who ate salads often had higher levels of vitamins C and E, folate, and carotenoids, important for overall health, than people who had fewer salads. Researchers have also found that people who eat a vegetarian diet weigh an average of 3 to 20 percent less than meat eaters. And a study at George Washington University School of Medicine found that overweight women on a low-fat plant-based diet who were allowed to eat as much as they wanted lost an average of 12 pounds in 14 weeks compared with 8 pounds in the control group.

Aim for: Five to six servings of greens and other nonstarchy vegetables a day.

Helpful hint: If you hate vegetables, begin by adding them to foods you like: a handful to a serving of rice or pasta, sliced tomatoes with your eggs, a cup of spinach to noodle soup.

## FEATURED RECIPES

**Zucchini Frittata** *p. 591*
**Ultimate Spiced Nuts** *p. 592*
**Spinach Salad with Chickpeas** *p. 597*
**Hearty Vegetable Stew** *p. 608*
**Tuna Kebabs** *p. 610*
**Chicken in Garlic Sauce** *p. 616*
**Turkey Cutlets with Grapefruit Salsa** *p. 617*
**Springtime Quinoa** *p. 626*
**Frozen Fruit Mousse** *p. 638*

# Fish, chicken, beans,
## and other foods high in protein

Researchers are discovering intriguing information about protein and its effect on weight. A study by British researchers shows that high-protein foods like these help trigger the release of PYY, a hormone known to reduce hunger. In a study of 9 obese and 10 normal-weight men, researchers distributed three types of meals: high protein, high carbohydrate, and high fat. All the men said that the protein meal best satisfied their hunger, and those meals also spurred the highest release of PYY.

We're not advising a high-protein, low-carb diet (short-term studies of these diets do show improved weight loss, but the diets don't seem to have any advantage over other diets in the long term), just that you make it a point to eat some protein with every meal and preferably every snack, too.

Other studies have shown that people on high-protein diets that are also rich in "slow-burning" carbohydrates low on the glycemic index (such as fruits and vegetables, beans, and whole-wheat pasta) are less hungry and lose more weight than people on low-protein, high-carbohydrate diets.

Getting enough protein when you're dieting also helps you lose fat, not muscle. For instance, in a small 10-week study, one group of women ate 9 to 10 ounces of protein a day for 10 weeks and a reduced amount of carbohydrates. The control group ate about half that amount of protein and about a third more carbohydrates. Although both groups took in the same number of calories and lost about 17 pounds, the women on the higher-protein diet lost 2 more pounds of fat and 1 less pound of muscle than the control group.

Don't overdo protein, though. People with type 2 diabetes, which often affects the obese, are at greater risk for kidney disease, and overeating protein may increase the problem.

**Aim for:** A good source of protein at every meal. Women should get at least 5 1/2 ounces of protein a day and men 6 1/2 ounces, or

about 20 percent of daily calories. One ounce of protein is equivalent to 1 ounce of chicken, lean cuts of beef and pork, or fish; 1/4 cup of cooked dried beans; one egg; 1 tablespoon of peanut butter; or 1/2 ounce of nuts or seeds.

**Helpful hint:** You can get plenty of protein without upping your intake of saturated fat. Rice and beans, peanut butter and whole-grain bread, and hummus and whole-grain pita bread are all combinations that provide complete protein.

# Nuts

Nuts are crunchy, salty—and no longer forbidden. Even though nuts are fatty, they may help you shed pounds, according to a number of studies. Researchers believe that the healthy fat in nuts helps people feel full, and the protein may use up calories as it digests. Large population studies have found that people who eat nuts regularly have lower BMIs than those who don't.

In a study of 65 obese adults at City of Hope National Medical Center in Duarte, California, for example, one group added 3 ounces of almonds to a 1,000-calorie liquid diet; another group added complex carbohydrates like popcorn or baked potatoes. Both groups ate roughly the same number of calories and amount of protein, but the almond diet had more than double the fat, primarily healthy monounsaturated fat. Over 24 weeks, the people on the almond diet reduced their weights and body mass indexes by 18 percent compared with 11 percent in the carbohydrate group. Both groups lowered blood sugar, insulin levels, and insulin resistance, which can lead to weight gain—but almost all the diabetic participants in the almond group were able to control their blood sugar on less medication, compared to only half of those in the carb group.

**Aim for:** An ounce, or a small handful, a day in place of a high-carb snack.

**Helpful hint:** If you crave something sweet and crunchy, mix nuts with dried fruit for a delicious treat.

## Dairy products
*and other foods high in calcium*

Here's a reason to drink milk your mom didn't know: It may help you lose weight. Purdue University researchers found that people who got 1,300 to 1,400 milligrams of calcium a day from dairy products had less body fat after 18 months. And researchers at the University of Tennessee have found much the same thing.

Calcium, it turns out, may play a part in how fat is broken down and stored. The more calcium in a fat cell, the more fat it burns. In a study of obese adults, one group ate three 6-ounce servings of fat-free yogurt containing 1,100 milligrams of calcium per day. The other group ate one serving of dairy food containing 400 to 500 milligrams of calcium per day. Both groups also reduced their daily calories by 500. The yogurt group lost an average of more than 14 pounds compared to an average loss of 11 pounds in the low-calcium group. The yogurt group also lost 81 percent more fat from their stomachs. Although studies have found low-fat dairy foods most effective, calcium from other sources, like broccoli or fortified orange juice, works, too.

Despite the positive studies, the jury is still out on this issue. While we wait for final answers, though, eating three servings of low-fat dairy products a day remains a healthy choice.

**Aim for:** 1,000 to 1,200 milligrams daily, about the equivalent of 1 cup of yogurt plus 2 cups of fat-free milk.

**Helpful hint:** If a plain glass of milk doesn't tempt you, try other options, such as low-fat cheese on a sandwich, a midmorning latte made with fat-free milk, or oatmeal cooked with low-fat milk instead of water.

## Why "Naked" Foods Win

If nuts are good for you, pecan pie must be even better! Sound too good to be true? It is. A handful of pecans contains 200 calories; a slice of pecan pie has 700. Likewise, sweet potatoes, wonderfully healthy on their own, are anything but when smothered in butter and brown sugar. In other words, just because a food in its natural form is good for you doesn't mean it's still good for you when it's sweetened, dressed up, or fried. Fish loses its benefits when battered and fried, as does spinach when creamed. When you dine out, think "naked" food. Ask for fish and meats broiled without butter, steamed vegetables without the sauce, and so on. And if you must have pie, make it pumpkin—without the whipped cream.

# Eggs

Start your day sunny side up. A single egg has 1 ounce of high-quality protein and 14 essential nutrients, such as zinc, iron, and vitamins A, D, E, and $B_{12}$. Best of all, it contains only 85 calories. And since eggs are high in protein, it makes sense that they keep you full. In a study at St. Louis University in Missouri, 30 overweight women ate breakfasts of either two eggs and toast with a bit of jam or a bagel (chock full of "fast-digesting" carbohydrates) with cream cheese and a small serving of yogurt. Both breakfasts contained the same number of calories, but the egg breakfast had more protein and fewer carbohydrates. The egg group reported feeling fuller before lunch and ate 163 fewer calories at lunch than the bagel group, and they ate 418 fewer calories than the bagel group by the end of the day.

Aim for: Even if you have high cholesterol, experts say you can safely eat three or four eggs yolks per week (and all the egg whites you want). Dozens of studies have found that it's saturated fat, not cholesterol, that has the greatest effect on blood cholesterol.

## NUTRITIONAL SUPPLEMENTS

**Calcium.** According to the USDA, most of us don't get enough calcium from our diets, making calcium supplements a smart bet. Calcium in chewable or chelated form, such as calcium citrate, is better absorbed than calcium carbonate but is more expensive. Both types are adequate. Take calcium carbonate with food. **DOSAGE:** 1,000 to 1,200 milligrams a day.

## OFF THE MENU

**Commercial baked goods, fast food, and other processed foods high in fat and sugar.** Foods loaded with sugar and refined grains like white flour can cause blood sugar to spike and crash, leaving us hungry again in no time. White potatoes have a similar effect. A survey about fast foods—fatty cheeseburgers and fries and sugar-filled drinks—found that on days when young people ate fast foods, they consumed an average of 187 more calories than those who didn't eat those foods, an addition that amounts to about 6 extra pounds a year.

What about those low-fat cookies? Just say no. Manufacturers often add more sugar to replace the fat. Overeating sugary foods, even if they don't contain fat, increases the production of insulin, leading to excess insulin in the blood. Although normal amounts of insulin usually curb appetite, researchers are beginning to understand that the relationship between excess insulin and other hormones that influence appetite may be altered in overweight people in ways that promote both overeating and fat storage.

**Sugary drinks.** It's easy to drink far more calories than you might think. In one large Harvard study, researchers found that women who went from drinking one or fewer soft drinks per week to one or more a day gained an average of 11 pounds in four years. Even fruit juice—with or without added sugar—can be a problem if you drink too much. You're better off eating whole fruits. According to a study of 2,800 children at the University of Pennsylvania, those already tending toward plumpness who regularly drank fruit juice gained an average of 1/4 pound per month, unlike children who ate whole fruits.

If you're a coffee drinker, stick with coffee instead of "coffee drinks." Add sugar and whipped cream to a latte, and you're adding as many as 250 calories. Order a full-fat latte, and you're swigging double the calories of a version made with fat-free milk.

## Addicted to Food?

Reaching inside the cookie jar has always been irresistible. Now scientists think they know why. According to researchers, compulsive eating appears to be regulated by the part of the brain that controls emotions, the same part that stirs up cravings in drug addicts. That may explain why some people eat not out of hunger but out of an urge to soothe themselves. Exciting preliminary research suggests that obese people may have significantly more activity in regions of the brain that control sensations in the lips, tongue, and mouth, which may mean that obese people are more sensitive to food's pleasurable qualities, a possible reason for overeating.

## Selling Satisfaction

When scientists discover, food companies respond. The new food fad, it appears, spotlights foods—shakes, drinks, snacks—that keep us feeling full. Most combine protein and fiber, two nutrients that keep hunger pangs at bay longer than fat and with far fewer calories. The reason for the fad: Most people feel hungry and deprived when they diet. These foods aim to wipe out those feelings. Of course, you can do this on your own by choosing foods high in fiber and eating some protein with every meal.

# OSTEOPOROSIS

A mug of milk and strong bones go hand in hand. But dairy products aren't the skeleton's only pals. To stay strong, bones need other minerals, vitamins, and proteins as well—all of which the right diet can provide in ample amounts.

Our bones are living tissue, constantly breaking down and rebuilding. By about age 30, however, the breakdown of bone outpaces its building, and our bones lose density, particularly a spongy-looking interior structure called trabecular bone that gives bones strength. Over time, bones may become excessively fragile, resulting in fractures related to osteoporosis. Women's risk of the disease is four times higher than men's, in part because they have less bone mass to begin with. Menopausal women lose bone two to four times faster than they did before menopause, the result of a decline in bone-protecting estrogen. That rate slows down eventually, but the decline continues.

Diet won't rev up bone replacement, but along with regular exercise, it can help us hold on to the precious bone we have.

## YOUR FOOD PRESCRIPTION

### Dairy products
*and other foods high in calcium*

Our bodies contain 2 to 4 pounds of calcium, 99 percent of it in our teeth and bones. Calcium, along with other minerals, hardens the protein fibers that make up our bones. Eating foods high in calcium—dairy foods, bony sardines and salmon, leafy greens like spinach, and dried beans—may help minimize the inevitable bone loss that comes with aging. For one thing, keeping calcium levels up lowers the amount of calcium our bodies have to borrow from bones to accommodate other essential functions like blood clotting, nerve transmission, and muscle contraction.

Don't worry if you're lactose intolerant, a condition that makes it hard to digest dairy products. Bulk up instead on other calcium-rich foods. Orange juice with added calcium is another good source.

**Aim for:** 1,000 to 1,200 milligrams of calcium daily, the equivalent of eating the following foods in the course of a day: a cup of low-fat yogurt, a glass of fat-free milk, and a serving each of spinach and canned salmon. Spread your calcium intake throughout the day in amounts of 500 milligrams or less for the best use of the calcium you consume.

**Helpful hint:** While spinach and chard contain a lot of calcium, they also contain calcium oxalate, a salt that makes the calcium less available to your body. Pair them with foods rich in vitamin C so your body can absorb more of the calcium.

## FEATURED RECIPES

**Edamame Hummus with Pita Crisps** *p. 592*
**Spinach Salad with Chickpeas** *p. 597*
**Open-Faced Sardine Sandwiches** *p. 604*
**Mac 'n Cheese Primavera** *p. 608*
**Roasted Salmon with Sautéed Greens** *p. 613*
**Baked Chicken with Tomatoes** *p. 615*
**Orange Beets** *p. 627*
**Banana-Peanut Bread** *p. 630*

## Salmon, sardines,
### and other foods high in vitamin D

Without vitamin D, our bodies absorb only 10 to 15 percent of the calcium we take in. When calcium levels drop, vitamin D activates to help our bodies absorb more calcium and reduce the amount we excrete.

Many people don't get enough D, especially if they spend less than 10 or 15 minutes a day in the sun without sunscreen. (Sunlight triggers D production in our skin.) But one serving of salmon is all you need for a daily dose.

Aim for: 400 to 800 IU of vitamin D per day; 3 ounces of salmon has 425 IU, and a glass of fortified milk or OJ has 100 IU.

Helpful hint: Most milk, cereal, and orange juice are fortified with vitamin D.

## Dark green leafy vegetables
### and other foods high in vitamin K

Vitamin K, found mostly in green leafy vegetables like kale, spinach, and beet greens, may be important for bone formation. Some studies have found that people who have high levels of K have lower risk of hip fracture, higher bone density, and less loss of calcium in urine. That's because vitamin K activates a bone protein that secures calcium within the bone.

Aim for: 90 to 120 micrograms of vitamin K daily, about the amount in 2 tablespoons of chopped parsley and a quarter of the amount in 1/2 cup of spinach.

## Fruits, vegetables, beans, and nuts

Long-term studies at Tufts University in Boston have shown that people who eat plenty of fruits and vegetables—most of which are rich in potassium and magnesium—have significantly less bone loss than those who have lower intakes of these foods. The reason: When the body has an excess of acid—usually the result of eating meat and other animal protein—the body depends on fruits and vegetables full of potassium and magnesium to neutralize it. Without those nutrients, the body borrows calcium from our bones to do that work.

Fruits and vegetables high in potassium, like bananas and tomatoes, also protect bones by counteracting calcium loss caused by high-salt diets. In a University of California study, when 60 women were given a high-salt diet, their calcium loss increased by 42 milligrams a day. But when they added potassium, calcium loss decreased to 8 milligrams. Studies have also shown that if you consume adequate amounts of calcium, you can be less concerned about your salt intake.

Leafy greens, beans, nuts, and whole grains have hefty doses of magnesium, essential for bone strength; 50 percent of your body's magnesium supply lies within your skeleton.

Aim for: *Potassium:* 4,700 milligrams daily. Avocados, bananas, oranges, and tomatoes are just a few of the fruits and vegetables that offer 300 milligrams per serving. *Magnesium:* 320 milligrams daily. Enjoy a cup of cooked oatmeal for breakfast, a handful (1/4 cup) of almonds as an afternoon snack, a 4-ounce serving of salmon, and a half cup of sautéed spinach for dinner, and you're all set.

Helpful hint: Eat fresh fruits and vegetables whenever possible instead of canned. Canning destroys potassium.

## Black tea

It turns out that a nice cup of tea isn't as meek as it sounds. In a Chinese study of more than 1,000 people, tea drinkers who'd been indulging in an average of three to four cups a day for 10 years or more had 0.5 to 5 percent higher bone density than non–tea drinkers, a significant difference when it comes to bones. It turns out that tea contains several compounds, including fluoride and tannins, that may benefit bone. So fire up the kettle and say hip, hip, hurray!

Aim for: Three to four cups a day.

Helpful hint: Add some milk to each cup, and you'll boost bone-building calcium as well.

# Soy, fish, chicken,
## *and other foods high in protein*

Several studies have found that people who eat diets moderately rich in protein and take calcium/vitamin D supplements lose less bone density over three years than those with low-protein diets who don't take supplements. The tricky thing is that too much protein—more than 30 percent of daily calories—weakens bones, particularly if calcium intake is low.

Try to get some of your protein from soy (think tofu, edamame, and soy milk). Soy is a rare alkaline protein, which helps lower acid content in the blood—a good thing for your bones. Research also shows that protein from soy foods may help reduce bone loss in menopausal women.

**Aim for:** About 20 percent of your daily calories should come from protein.

## NUTRITIONAL SUPPLEMENTS

**Calcium.** Scientists are still researching the optimal amount of calcium necessary to slow bone loss. Some studies suggest we need only 550 milligrams a day. Others suggest that a high intake doesn't stop osteoporosis. Longer studies are needed, but for now, the National Academy of Sciences recommends taking the following amount. **DOSAGE:** 1,000 to 1,200 milligrams daily in two doses.

**Vitamin D.** Those of us who live in sunny climates usually get enough vitamin D by exposing our skin (without sunscreen) to sunlight for about 15 minutes each day or by eating vitamin D–rich foods. But those in less sunny northern climates may need a supplement boost. Ask your doctor if any medication you are taking affects vitamin D absorption. **DOSAGE:** 400 to 800 IU daily. Check your multivitamin; many brands contain up to 400 IU. Many calcium supplements contain vitamin D as well.

**Potassium.** In 2004, the Institute of Medicine raised the recommended level of potassium to 4,700 milligrams daily, in part to reduce the risk of bone loss. However, experts suggest that no one take supplemental amounts of potassium beyond what's in a multivitamin unless supervised by a doctor. **DOSAGE:** The dose in a multivitamin, which usually doesn't exceed 99 milligrams; take potassium supplements only under medical supervision.

**Magnesium.** There are various forms of magnesium supplements, and some calcium supplements come with both vitamin D and magnesium. Magnesium chloride and magnesium lactate are the most easily absorbed forms. Many elderly people and those with gastrointestinal diseases may require magnesium supplements, but most people get enough magnesium from a healthy diet. **DOSAGE:** 320 milligrams a day.

## OFF THE MENU

**Piles of protein.** When protein exceeds 30 percent of calories a day, it can hurt your bones, although the type of protein also matters. Sulfur in animal proteins increases the acid content of blood, and without enough alkaline

Each evening after dinner, brew yourself a pot of decaf tea. It will stay warm in a ceramic teapot for hours. Sip a cup throughout the evening. It's not only healthy, but wonderfully calming. And it keeps you from noshing as well.

fruits and vegetables, the body rebalances itself by borrowing calcium from bones.

**Salty foods.** Too much salt pulls calcium out of bones. In fact, according to one study, women on a month-long high-salt (9 grams a day) diet lost 42 milligrams more calcium than they did on a low-salt (2 grams a day) diet. Cut back on naturally salty foods like anchovies as well as processed foods, which are often loaded with salt. Eat lots of potassium-rich foods like bananas, which help offset salt's calcium-leaching effect, and eat plenty of high-calcium foods to replace what's lost. The Institute of Medicine recommends no more than 3.8 grams of salt daily.

**Too much alcohol.** Drinking to excess undermines bone health. For one thing, too much alcohol can interfere with the body's use of calcium and vitamin D. And it boosts the excretion of magnesium, a mineral essential for bone strength. In men, excess alcohol also lowers testosterone, which can interfere with bone building. In women, frequent overindulgence may lead to irregular menstrual cycles, which raises osteoporosis risk.

Still, you don't always have to skip the wine-and-cheese party. Several studies have found that *moderate* drinking may give bone density a boost. In small amounts, alcohol helps convert testosterone (which women have, too) into estradiol, a form of estrogen that helps prevent bone loss.

**Caffeine.** You may want to pass on that third or fourth cup of Joe. A Swedish study of more than 31,000 women ages 40 to 76 found that four or more cups of coffee daily increased the risk of bone fractures, particularly in women who took in too little calcium. Yet another study found that more than three cups of coffee a day increased the risk of osteoporosis in both men and women by 82 percent. The reason: Caffeine increases the amount of calcium we lose in urine, and it may also interfere with the absorption of calcium and vitamin D. If you can't give up caffeine, get enough calcium and vitamin D from foods to counteract any losses.

## Dieting? You May Be Losing More Than Pounds

Losing and regaining as few as 10 pounds may be a problem for your bones. In a Canadian study of more than 1,000 men and women ages 25 to 96, those whose weight rose and fell several times had significantly greater risk of bone fractures than those whose weight did not fluctuate. Researchers believe that weight loss may lead to decreases in estrogen and progesterone, both of which help preserve bone. Weight loss also increases cortisol, a hormone that, in excess, makes calcium harder for the body to absorb. There are some studies that show if you exercise and consume enough calcium and vitamin D while losing weight, you can minimize bone loss.

# PROSTATE CANCER

For men living in Western societies, prostate cancer may seem inevitable. Although it's relatively uncommon in men under 45, by age 80, between 70 and 90 percent of American men have it. In fact, it's the most common type of cancer in men. The average age of diagnosis is 72.

Of course, you can't change your age. You also can't alter your family history (if your father, brother, or son had prostate cancer, your risk is higher) or race (prostate cancer is more prevalent among African Americans). But growing evidence suggests that you can dramatically reduce your risk of this cancer—and slow its progression if you already have it—simply by making moderate changes in your diet. It's worth noting that in Asian countries, where consumption of soy, fish, and produce is high and red meat and dairy consumption is low, rates of prostate cancer are more than 10 times lower than in Western countries, where plates are filled with red meats and fatty dairy foods.

The good news is that most prostate cancers are slow growing. In fact, with early detection, many doctors just take a wait-and-see approach rather than attacking the cancer immediately. The trick is careful monitoring. Screening tests used include the PSA (prostate specific antigen) blood test and digital rectal exams.

But why sit back and wait for trouble to happen? By improving your diet, you can take a big step toward delaying the cancer's development or inhibiting its growth. In other words, by eating more foods like tomatoes and broccoli, you can make prostate cancer something you live with rather than die from.

## YOUR FOOD PRESCRIPTION

## Tomatoes and tomato products

If the color pink (think pink ribbons) symbolizes the fight against breast cancer, the color red actually *fights* prostate cancer! An antioxidant called lycopene, which gives tomatoes their fire-engine hue, helps prevent prostate cancer or slow its growth. Lycopene (a member of the carotenoid family, like beta-carotene) does this by preventing free radicals from damaging cells, including the all-important DNA inside. DNA damage is what leads healthy cells to turn cancerous. Some research suggests that the lycopene in about two daily servings of tomato sauce or juice curbs DNA damage by 28 percent. What does that mean for men? Well, in the Health Professionals Follow-Up Study, an ongoing study of the diet and lifestyle habits of 50,000 men, guys who ate at least two servings of tomato sauce a week lowered their prostate cancer risk by 23 percent.

**Aim for:** A half-cup of cooked tomatoes twice a week appears to help prevent prostate cancer. Even if you've already been diagnosed, eating cooked tomatoes frequently may slow the progression of the disease. Although about 85 percent of our lycopene comes from tomatoes, watermelon, red grapefruit, and guava are also good sources.

**Helpful hint:** Although all tomatoes contain lycopene, when they're cooked with a little oil, the lycopene becomes more available, which is why tomato sauce is such a good way to increase your intake. To give your sauce even more cancer-fighting punch, add cruciferous vegetables like broccoli, kale, and cauliflower, which have proven anticancer compounds.

## Tofu, soy milk, *and other soy foods*

People in Asian countries tend to eat a lot of soy, and they don't get prostate cancer as often as we do. Coincidence? Probably not. Tofu and other soy foods contain estrogen-like compounds called isoflavones that are thought to delay the development and growth of cancer cells and encourage them to "do the right thing" by destroying themselves.

In a three-month study at the Cancer Research Center of Hawaii, blood levels of prostate specific antigen (PSA), a marker that signals the possibility of prostate cancer, dropped 14 percent in men who ate two servings of soy a day. Another study of more than 12,000 men conducted at Loma Linda University in California found that men who consumed more than one serving of soy milk each day were 70 percent less likely to have prostate cancer than men who never drank it.

**Aim for:** At least one to two servings of soy foods daily, such as a cup of soy milk or a half cup of tofu. Unprocessed soy foods like tofu, soy nuts (roasted soybeans), and soy milk retain more of their isoflavones than processed soy products such as soy-based deli "meats" and soy "bacon."

**Helpful hint:** Edamame, very young soybeans still in their pods, are another excellent way to get more soy into your meals. You can find them in your supermarket freezer section. Steam them lightly and toss them with a little salt for a healthy snack, or add them to stir-fries.

## Green tea

In test-tube studies, a powerful compound in green tea called epigallocatechin gallate (EGCG) blocks many processes involved with cancer development and growth. Population studies suggest it may protect against several cancers, including those of the prostate, stomach, colon, and breast. Some research has found no benefit for people with cancer. But one Chinese study found that men who drank more than three cups of tea a day (almost all of it green tea) dropped their risk of prostate cancer by over 70 percent. Those who consumed the most green tea had about 85 percent less risk than those who consumed the least. More research is under way, so stay tuned.

**Aim for:** Two to four cups a day if you enjoy the light flavor of this delicate tea, which is also rich in antioxidants.

Tomato sauce isn't just for spaghetti. Use it on chicken, fish, pork, or beef; add it to omelettes or on fried eggs; mix it into soups; stew vegetables in it. You can even add tomato sauce to the cooking liquid for rice, couscous, or lentils!

# Pomegranate juice

It makes your mouth pucker—and it may help shield you from cancer. Pomegranate juice is chock-full of colorful plant chemicals called polyphenols, the same chemicals that make grape skins red and lend brilliant colors to autumn leaves. Polyphenols are powerful antioxidants, and that's probably why pomegranate juice is shaping up to be an important cancer fighter.

According to some very early but promising studies, the polyphenols in the juice appear to slow cancer cell growth and encourage cancer cells to kill themselves off. They also lower PSA levels. In a two-year study conducted at UCLA, 48 prostate cancer patients drank 8 ounces of pomegranate juice each day. Researchers found that PSA levels dropped in more than 30 percent of the men—in some cases by up to 85 percent. More significantly, cancer progression was delayed in more than 82 percent of the men.

**Aim for:** An 8-ounce glass daily.

**Helpful hint:** Since weight control and reducing sugar consumption are part of prostate cancer prevention, it's best to drink pomegranate juice instead of high-calorie beverages like sodas, not in addition to them.

## FEATURED RECIPES

**Roasted Cherry Tomatoes in Parmesan Cups** *p. 593*
**Tuna Kebabs** *p. 610*
**Tomato-Roasted Mackerel** *p. 612*
**Turkey Ragu with Spaghetti** *p. 618*
**Beef and Broccoli Stew** *p. 620*
**Brussels Sprouts with Caramelized Onions** *p. 623*
**Roasted Broccoli with Cheese** *p. 624*
**Pomegranate Ice** *p. 638*

# Salmon, mackerel, sardines, herring, *and other fatty fish*

Surely by now someone's told you to eat more fish—maybe your doctor, who's looking out for your heart. But shopping at the seafood counter more often can also protect your prostate—if you buy the right kinds of fish. In a Swedish study that followed more than 6,000 men for 30 years, those who ate moderate amounts of fatty fish—rich in omega-3 fatty acids—lowered their risk of prostate cancer by 30 percent, while non–fish eaters had a two- to threefold higher risk of developing it. *Note:* Try to get your essential fatty acids from your plate, not a pill. So far, research shows prostate protection from eating fish, but not from taking fish-oil supplements.

**Aim for:** Three 3- to 4-ounce servings of fatty fish a week. If you've already been diagnosed with early-stage prostate cancer, eating even two fish meals a week may lower the risk of further cancer growth by 17 percent.

# Broccoli, brussels sprouts, *and other cruciferous vegetables*

If you're going to grill a steak, be sure to serve a side of broccoli with it. Why? Grilling meat creates cancer-causing substances, such as heterocyclic amines, which damage cells. Vegetables like broccoli, brussels sprouts, and cabbage contain several anticancer compounds that actually help rid the body of these substances before they have a chance to damage cells.

Consider this experiment: In one study, men ate six 1/2-cup servings of broccoli and brussels sprouts each day for 12 days. On the 12th day, the men each had a steak. Next, the guys went 12 days without eating any cruciferous vegetables, and then they each had another steak. After each phase, researchers analyzed the volunteers' urine for heterocyclic amines. What they found was that when the men ate their veggies, they were able to dump more of these carcinogens from their bodies as waste than when they just ate the steaks.

Even if you aren't a big fan of grilling, you'll still do well to get more of these cancer fighters onto your plate. Data from the Health Professionals Follow-Up Study showed that eating five or more servings of cruciferous vegetables a week lowers your risk of developing prostate cancer by up to 20 percent.

**Aim for:** At least four to five 1/2-cup servings a week.

**Helpful hint:** Look for broccoli sprouts at the market. They're among the most concentrated amounts of sulforaphane, one of broccoli's cancer-fighting compounds, with 20 to 50 times as much as mature broccoli.

## Garlic and onions

Are you a garlic lover? Good! "The stinking rose" does far more than add flavor to food. Garlic, onions, and their cousins (known as allium vegetables), like scallions, shallots, and chives, may help prevent tumors by eliminating cancer-causing substances before they can damage cells. They also encourage cancer cells to self-destruct.

When researchers from the National Cancer Institute looked at how much garlic and other allium vegetables men in Shanghai, China, consumed, they found that those who ate at least 10 grams of these vegetables (1 to 1 1/2 tablespoons of chopped onions or scallions) each day lowered their risk of developing prostate cancer by 49 percent compared to men who consumed much less. Men who ate at least five cloves of garlic a week lowered their risk by 53 percent.

**Aim for:** About one garlic clove or 1 to 2 tablespoons of onion most days of the week.

**Helpful hint:** Put a few garlic cloves through a press, then add them to low-fat salad dressings, tuna salad, and even potato salad. If you'd rather have your garlic cooked, chop the cloves and let them stand for 10 minutes to give the therapeutic compounds a chance to form. Then sauté the garlic and add it to tomato sauce to give it some extra cancer-fighting punch.

### NUTRITIONAL SUPPLEMENTS

**Vitamin E.** If you're a smoker, you should consider taking vitamin E supplements. A study designed to look at antioxidants and lung cancer found that the vitamin wasn't helpful against lung cancer, but among smokers who took 50 milligrams (about 75 IU) daily, it did cut the risk of getting prostate cancer by 32 percent and reduced the risk of dying from it by 41 percent. More recently, a National Cancer Institute study of more than 29,000 men found that smokers who took more than 400 IU of vitamin E daily for eight years cut their prostate cancer risk by 71 percent compared to smokers who didn't take E. *Note:* Vitamin E appears to protect only smokers and former smokers who quit within the previous 10 years. It seems to have no effect on non-smokers. **DOSAGE:** Studies have shown benefit for smokers with doses ranging from 50 to 400 IU per day, which must be taken with food to be properly absorbed. However, if you have uncontrolled high blood pressure or take anti-coagulant medications (blood thinners), you

Garlic has a powerful odor when raw, but cooking mellows the flavor considerably. Get in the habit of adding a teaspoon of chopped garlic to almost everything you cook on the stove—be it chicken, fish, vegetables, stir fries, sauces, soups, or stews.

shouldn't take vitamin E without close medical supervision because of the risk of stroke or hemorrhage.

**Selenium.** This antioxidant mineral has an impressive track record when it comes to prostate cancer, not only for preventing it but also for slowing its progression. One study designed to examine selenium and recurrent skin cancer found that while selenium had no effect on skin cancer, it did cut the risk of prostate cancer in half. Selenium supplements appear to work most effectively for men who have low levels to start with. Men with normal levels may not get any additional benefits from supplements. **DOSAGE:** Up to 200 micrograms daily.

**Antioxidant combinations.** Antioxidants tend to work better when they work together, and an eight-year study of the health effects of antioxidants in more than 5,000 French men suggests that a combination of vitamin C, vitamin E, beta-carotene, selenium, and zinc may protect men from certain cancers, including prostate cancer. Men who had normal PSA levels when the study started and took this combination of supplements were half as likely to develop prostate cancer as men who were given a placebo. However, among men whose PSA levels were already elevated, the supplement combo seemed to have the opposite effect—the men taking the antioxidants tended to develop more prostate cancer than those taking a placebo. **DOSAGE:** The men in the study were given 120 milligrams of vitamin C, 30 milligrams (45 IU) of vitamin E, 6 milligrams of beta-carotene, 100 micrograms of selenium, and 20 milligrams of zinc. If you take more than one supplement, be sure to tally up the amounts in each to make sure you aren't overdoing it. Taking too much of both vitamin E and selenium poses risks, and consuming more than 100 micrograms of zinc a day has been linked to greater prostate cancer risk.

## OFF THE MENU

**Fatty meats and dairy foods.** The scientific jury is still debating whether meat itself is linked with prostate cancer; some research suggests it is, while other studies find no connection. But the way meat is prepared may provide some additional clues. When it's fried, grilled, or otherwise cooked until very well done, carcinogens form, and that could explain meat's tentative link to prostate cancer risk. Indeed, one study found that men who ate more than 2 1/2 ounces per week of very well done meat faced a 40 percent greater risk of prostate cancer.

While the meat connection is still likely to be debated for some time, eating a lot of saturated fat (which mainly comes from meats and whole-milk dairy products) *is* linked with increased prostate cancer risk. It may be that eating a lot of dairy also means consuming a lot of calcium, and some scientists believe that excess calcium (more than 1,500 milligrams a day, or about five servings of dairy) is believed to increase prostate cancer risk.

Beyond the calcium link, saturated fat is also known to promote inflammation within the body, which damages cell DNA (remember, damaged DNA can lead to cancer) and stimulates the formation of blood vessels that allow tumors to grow and spread. Inflammation has already been linked with cancers of the stomach, esophagus, and colon, so it's not hard to believe that it contributes to prostate cancer, too. In fact, in one study of more than 1,000 men, higher saturated fat consumption was linked with more than double the risk of aggressive prostate tumors.

Saturated fat also raises cholesterol levels, another cause for concern. High cholesterol provides the raw materials for creating the hormones (like testosterone) that promote prostate cancer growth. Substantially cutting back on saturated fats may lower your risk. A small study recently showed that eating a vegan diet (no meat, dairy foods, or other animal products) that limited fat to just 10 percent of calories helped delay cancer progression among 93 men with early-stage prostate cancer. During the year-long study, PSA levels dropped by an average of 4 percent among the vegans, indicating a slowdown in the cancer's development. But among the control group, PSA levels rose by an average of 6 percent.

**Sugar and refined carbohydrates.** If you're a big fan of doughnuts, sweet desserts, and "white" foods like white bread and bagels, listen up. These easily digested carbohydrates boost insulin levels, which also raises levels of insulin-like growth factor-1, which in turn promotes tumor growth. An elevated insulin level is also one of the central problems in metabolic syndrome, a collection of symptoms that includes a large waist measurement, high blood pressure and triglycerides, and low HDL cholesterol. According to a 13-year Finnish study of 1,880 men, those who had metabolic syndrome at the start of the study were nearly twice as likely to develop prostate cancer as men without metabolic syndrome. Among overweight men, the risk was three times higher. Men with metabolic syndrome are also more likely to die from prostate cancer if they get it.

Swapping "white" foods and sugary foods for whole grains in your diet may prevent and even reverse insulin resistance. The fiber in foods like whole-grain cereals and breads slows the digestion of carbohydrates and thereby reduces blood sugar spikes, keeping insulin levels low. Still, you don't want to go overboard on carbohydrates—even the healthy ones—because controlling carbohydrate portions is an important part of controlling both your weight and blood sugar.

## One More Reason to Slim Down

The connection's not so obvious, but lugging around extra pounds raises your risk of prostate cancer. Not only does excess body fat produce hormones and inflammation associated with tumor growth (indeed, obesity may promote the development of a more aggressive form of prostate cancer, one that's more likely to recur and more likely to be fatal), but research now suggests that obesity may be connected to more advanced cancer because being overweight makes tumors harder to detect.

Heavy men tend to have larger prostates and lower PSA levels, which can yield false negatives on screening tests; tumors are missed in up to 25 percent of cases. Cancer also recurs more frequently in obese men. A study conducted at the M. D. Anderson Cancer Center in Houston found that men who were obese at age 40 had more than double the risk of prostate cancer recurrence after surgery than men of average weight.

# PROSTATE ENLARGEMENT

If you're like many men over 50, you may have trouble "going"—maybe you go too frequently, or you often feel as if you have to go, but when you try, not much happens.

The problem is most likely an enlarged prostate or, as doctors call it, benign prostatic hyperplasia (BPH). The prostate is a small, walnut-size gland located behind the bladder that adds fluid to semen just before orgasm. After age 50, hormonal changes, such as a drop in testosterone and a rise in other hormones such as prolactin, stimulate the prostate to grow. This puts the squeeze on the urethra, the tube that carries urine out of the bladder, which is why urinating becomes such a problem.

The goal of any treatment is to shrink the prostate and improve urinary function. Prescription medications can accomplish this, but the right diet can also help.

## YOUR FOOD PRESCRIPTION

### Lean beef, oysters, pumpkin seeds, *and other foods rich in zinc*

The prostate contains more zinc than any other body part. Nutritionally oriented physicians routinely recommend that men with enlarged prostates get more zinc in their diets. Zinc is thought to help by reducing prolactin secretion; this indirectly blocks 5-alpha-reductase, an enzyme that converts testosterone into another form that causes prostate growth. Prescription medications for prostate enlargement inhibit the same enzyme.

### FEATURED RECIPES

**Edamame Hummus with Pita Crisps** *p. 592*
**Beef in Lettuce Wraps** *p. 606*
**Tuna Kebabs** *p. 610*
**Eggplant Lasagna** *p. 609*
**Salmon Steaks with Peach Salsa** *p. 612*
**Pumpkin Streusel Bread** *p. 631*

**Aim for:** 30 milligrams of zinc daily. You can get nearly three times this amount in a 3.5-ounce serving of fresh oysters, or try pumpkin seeds, with about 8 milligrams in a half cup.

**Helpful hint:** You can "roast" pumpkin seeds in your microwave. Put some olive oil in a microwave-safe baking dish and heat for 30 seconds. Then add the pumpkin seeds and cook on high for 7 to 8 minutes, turning them every 2 minutes.

### Tofu, edamame, soy milk, and soy nuts

Soy foods are a good source of weak estrogen-like plant compounds called isoflavones, which help prevent prostate growth by blocking 5-alpha-reductase. Choose whole soy foods like tofu, soy milk, and soy yogurt; they contain more isoflavones than processed products like soy lunchmeats.

**Aim for:** There's no set recommendation, but eating a few servings of soy foods a week is a good goal.

## Salmon, flaxseed,

*and other sources of omega-3 fatty acids*

Omega-3 essential fatty acids are naturally anti-inflammatory. Men who consume adequate amounts tend to have smaller prostates, stronger urine flow, and less urine retention in their bladders.

Aim for: The same foods that promote a healthy heart also promote a healthy prostate—yet another reason to follow the American Heart Association's recommendation to eat at least two fish meals a week.

### NUTRITIONAL SUPPLEMENTS

**Zinc.** Along with getting more zinc in your diet, you might consider a supplement. In one small study of 19 men done at Cooke County Hospital in Chicago, zinc supplements reduced prostate size in 14 of the men, and all of them reported improved urinary symptoms. **DOSAGE:** A standard dose is 30 milligrams above what's in your multi (most contain about 15 milligrams). However, if you're taking a multi and increasing your food sources of zinc, you may not need more. Getting more than 100 milligrams daily for an extended period can depress the immune system and increase the risk of prostate cancer. Because zinc interferes with copper absorption, people taking zinc for more than a month should make sure they also get 2 milligrams of copper a day.

**Essential fatty acids.** Along with reducing cholesterol and inflammation, both of which appear to contribute to prostate growth, the essential fatty acids (EFAs) gamma-linolenic acid (GLA) and eicosapentaenoic acid (EPA) also block 5-alpha-reductase, the enzyme that triggers prostate growth, according to a test-tube study at the University of California, Davis. **DOSAGE:** There's no established dosage for prostate health, so look for a reputable product and follow label instructions for dosage. Take your EFAs with vitamin E (400 IU) to prevent the fatty acid oxidation that can actually lead to prostate disease.

## Old Man's Friend

Saw palmetto has long been a popular remedy for prostate problems. But despite its reputation for slowing prostate growth, improving urine flow, and reducing urgency, the scientific evidence is mixed. Recently, a study of 225 men published in the *New England Journal of Medicine* reported that saw palmetto was no better than a placebo for alleviating BPH symptoms. But this Florida palm hasn't been known as "old man's friend" for nothing. An earlier analysis of 18 trials with more than 3,000 men showed that, compared to placebos, saw palmetto improved weak urinary flow by up to 50 percent. The typical dosage is 160 milligrams twice a day. Note that the full benefits can take several months to kick in.

Saw palmetto is sometimes used in conjunction with pumpkin seed extract (480 milligrams a day taken in three doses), a natural source of the beta-sitosterols that help improve urinary flow.

### OFF THE MENU

**Foods high in saturated fat, trans fat, cholesterol, and sugar.** The same poor eating habits that damage the heart also damage the prostate. Studies suggest that being overweight and having elevated cholesterol, blood pressure, and blood sugar puts you at risk for prostate problems. Researchers from the University of California, San Diego, found that obese men were three and a half times more likely to have enlarged prostates than were slimmer men. They also found a strong connection between high blood sugar—which some of these foods contribute to—and prostate growth.

**Alcohol.** Alcohol, especially beer, is a diuretic, the last thing you want when you're already making many trips to the bathroom. Alcohol also depletes key nutrients for prostate health, like zinc.

# PSORIASIS

If anyone's ever told you to "get a thicker skin," they probably weren't thinking about psoriasis. But that's just what the condition does to a person. A faulty immune system tricks the body into producing extra skin cells that build up and create thick, unsightly scaly patches.

Over the course of a month, the top layer of normal skin sloughs off and makes room for fresh new cells. In psoriasis, that new skin growth is speeded up so dramatically that the body has no time to shed the old skin cells, so they pile up like multiple layers of paint that flake and peel on the exterior of a house.

Dermatologists aren't sure just why the immune system causes the body to react this way. There's no cure, which is all the more reason to look to your diet for foods that can help ease symptoms, including natural inflammation fighters and plenty of fresh fruits and vegetables with important nutrients for healthy skin.

## YOUR FOOD PRESCRIPTION

## Salmon and other fatty fish

Just as creamy moisturizers can help relieve itchy skin, the right fats in your diet are like lotion that you apply from the inside out. Oily fish like salmon, mackerel, and herring provide omega-3 fatty acids that help to quell inflammation. One study from London compared the effect of eating 6 ounces of white fish (lacking in omega-3s) daily for six weeks to eating a similar portion of oily fish. The oily fish improved the symptoms of psoriasis in patients by 15 percent, while the white fish provided little to no relief.

**Aim for:** Two to three 3- to 4-ounce servings of fatty fish per week.

## Tomatoes, carrots, spinach,
### *and other vegetables high in beta-carotene*

When researchers in Italy compared the diets of 316 people with psoriasis to the diets of 366 people without it, they found that eating carrots, tomatoes, and other foods high in beta-carotene helped decrease the risk of developing psoriasis. Beta-carotene is converted to vitamin A in the body, where it helps maintain the tissues that make up skin. Other good sources are pumpkin, sweet potatoes, winter squash, cantaloupe, and beet greens.

**Aim for:** Follow the advice to eat 7 to 10 servings of fruits and vegetables a day, and make sure as many as possible are rich in beta-carotene.

## The Mediterranean diet

Call it the Fountain of Youth, but the Mediterranean diet, consisting mainly of fresh fruits and vegetables, fish, chicken, whole grains, and olive oil, has been linked to a number of health benefits, including relieving psoriasis. Researchers in Hawaii tracked the symptoms of psoriasis in five patients who followed a diet featuring many of the foods in the

### FEATURED RECIPES

**Ginger Butternut Squash Soup** *p. 602*
**Tuna Kebabs** *p. 610*
**Tomato-Roasted Mackerel** *p. 612*
**Roasted Salmon with Sautéed Greens** *p. 613*
**Brown Rice Risotto** *p. 625*
**Orange Beets** *p. 627*
**Pumpkin Streusel Bread** *p. 631*

Mediterranean diet. After six months, all five had improved significantly.

Aim for: In the study, the patients ate fresh fruits and vegetables and moderate amounts of fish, chicken, and olive oil, and they avoided highly processed foods like potato chips as well as refined carbohydrates like white bread.

# Turmeric

Studies have linked turmeric, the spice that gives curry its yellow hue, to reduced inflammation in a number of conditions, including psoriasis.

Aim for: 1 tablespoon daily. Add it to stews, soups, and stir-fries.

# Lemon juice

Could squeezing lemon juice into the water you drink help your skin? Some natural health practitioners think so.

By way of some rather complicated chemistry, weak acids like lemon juice (despite its mouth-puckering taste, it is actually a weak acid) are thought to create a friendly environment for beneficial bacteria in the intestinal tract that help support a healthy immune system and lessen its burden. These acids may help against autoimmune conditions in other ways as well. On the other hand, some people report that *avoiding* lemons, oranges, and pineapples, among other acidic fruits, helps improve their psoriasis.

Aim for: Squeeze lemon juice into your drinking water for several weeks to see how it affects your skin. If it seems to make things worse, take it off the menu.

## NUTRITIONAL SUPPLEMENTS

**Omega-3 fatty acids.** Studies keep stacking up on the benefits of omega-3s—especially the type known as EPA—for skin conditions. **DOSAGE:** Most studies indicate that 6 grams per day will produce results. Make sure the product you buy contains EPA. It may take several months to see an effect.

**A multivitamin/mineral.** Studies have shown that people with psoriasis are often deficient in the antioxidant mineral selenium as well as vitamin D. Taking a multivitamin will help reverse any problems associated with inadequate intake of either nutrient. It's best to stick with a multi for selenium, as it can be toxic at high doses. **DOSAGE:** One a day.

## OFF THE MENU

**Bread and other foods made with gluten-containing grains.** Many people who have an allergy to gluten, a protein in wheat, oats, rye, and barley, have flare-ups of psoriasis after eating anything made from these grains. Avoid foods with gluten for at least three weeks to see if it makes a difference in your skin.

**Red meat.** Red meats contain a fatty acid that can worsen inflammation.

**Alcohol.** Heavy drinkers have a higher incidence of psoriasis than moderate drinkers or people who abstain from alcohol.

Have an indoor Mediterranean picnic for dinner. Put out platters of raw vegetables, olives, low-fat cheese, good-quality tuna, dry-roasted nuts, and pita bread. Then nibble to your health's and heart's content.

# SINUSITIS

If there's ever a time to grate some ginger or chop up some chile peppers, it's when you have a sinus infection. Get these infections often? Serve yourself more fruits and vegetables to take advantage of their immunity-boosting antioxidants.

If you've suffered through sinus infections, just thinking about them can make your face tender and your head ache. Sinuses, the air-filled cavities in your forehead and cheeks and behind the bridge of your nose, produce thin mucus that drains through narrow ducts into the nasal cavity. Because of their many delicate blood vessels, sinuses are particularly vulnerable to inflammation. Sinusitis is actually inflammation of the membrane that lines the sinus and nasal passages. It can spring from hay fever, a cold, or just about anything that irritates your nasal passages.

The inflammation alone can cause painful, tender eyes, cheeks, and nasal passages; headaches; and even earaches. When congestion builds up along with it, mucus can't drain into the nasal cavity. The lingering congestion provides a perfect breeding ground in the sinuses for infectious bacteria and viruses. Not only are sinus infections painful, they are also notoriously long-lived and difficult to clear up, even with antibiotics—a good reason to thin the mucus and encourage drainage with foods.

## YOUR FOOD PRESCRIPTION

## Chiles, onions, horseradish,
*and other foods that make your nose run*

Draining mucus is a sure way to relieve sinus pressure and pain, and these foods should do the trick. Chiles, in their many varieties, can make grown men weep and sniffle. The fire comes from capsaicin, a compound so powerful it can numb pain receptors. It can also numb nerve receptors, helping to arrest inflammation. You can add chiles to your meals or simply sprinkle on some cayenne pepper.

Onions and garlic have "bite" and contain compounds that reduce inflammation. Horseradish, a pungent root that makes great cocktail sauce for boiled shrimp, is also a terrific sandwich spread. Radishes, round little flavor bombs from the mustard family, have a sharp bite that packs a punch in salads. If you get sinus infections often, consider planting radish seeds in your garden. They sprout quickly and tend to be the first crop harvested from the spring garden. Plant a row every few weeks for a continuous supply.

Also opt for spicy dishes that are traditional to Indian or Cajun cooking. A good old-fashioned bowl of spicy chili can do the trick, too.

**Aim for:** Enough to make your nose run.

**Helpful hint:** If you overdo the heat from chile peppers at a meal, eat bread with butter or drink milk to relieve the burning. The fat in these foods breaks down the capsaicin and coats the mouth, blocking the burn.

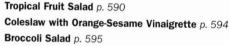

### FEATURED RECIPES

**Tropical Fruit Salad** *p. 590*
**Coleslaw with Orange-Sesame Vinaigrette** *p. 594*
**Broccoli Salad** *p. 595*
**Quick Chicken Noodle Soup** *p. 600*
**Three-Bean Chili** *p. 610*
**Fish Tacos** *p. 611*
**Raspberry-Almond Muffins** *p. 628*
**Zesty Cornbread** *p. 630*

# Red bell peppers, kiwifruit,
*and other foods rich in vitamin C*

Vitamin C is crucial for keeping the immune system in top form, and better immune function means fewer colds, flus, and even allergies that can provoke congestion and sinusitis. Studies suggest that people who are prone to sinus infections have low blood levels of antioxidants. So keep your kitchen stocked with citrus fruits and red bell peppers as well as C-rich greens, including broccoli and brussels sprouts. Papayas and raspberries are other good sources of C.

Aim for: Five to six 1/2-cup servings of vegetables and three to four 1/2-cup servings of fruits every day.

# Hot liquids

Sip hot tea with lemon or a steaming bowl of chicken soup (or any soup made with clear broth) to get the "juices" in your head flowing. While you're at it, breathe in the steam for the benefits of warm, moist heat without taking a shower. Grate ginger, an anti-inflammatory, into your tea or broth for an added benefit. To make ginger tea, grate a large piece of ginger into a pot containing 1 pint of water and simmer for 15 minutes. Strain, then drink. You can also use the tea and a clean cloth to make a hot, moist compress to apply to your sinuses.

Aim for: Several cups a day.

# Tea and water

The more fluids you take in, the thinner the mucus in your nasal passages will be. It's best to avoid sugary liquids like juice because they can promote the growth of yeast, linked to sinusitis.

Aim for: 8 to 10 glasses of liquids every day.

# Nuts, greens, sweet potatoes,
*and other foods rich in vitamin E*

Of the many antioxidants recently found to boost health, vitamin E has proven particularly effective in helping to reduce inflammation. You can get it from kale, sweet potatoes, canola oil, almonds, wheat germ, and sunflower seeds—all foods that have a bevy of health benefits, so eat up.

Aim for: At least 15 milligrams of vitamin E daily (roughly the amount in 1 ounce of almonds plus a cup of cooked spinach), although many experts recommend 200 milligrams or more per day, which you'd need a supplement to get.

## NUTRITIONAL SUPPLEMENTS

**Vitamin C.** Because it boosts the immune system, vitamin C can be a true ally in preventing the triggers that lead to sinusitis, like colds and hay fever. Choose a C supplement with bioflavonoids for even more immunity-boosting power. **DOSAGE:** 1,000 to 3,000 milligrams per day. If you experience diarrhea as a side effect, cut back. To keep your blood levels of C high throughout the day, divide your dosage in half, taking 500 to 1,500 milligrams of C in the morning and the same amount in the evening.

**Vitamin E.** It can be difficult to get much vitamin E from your diet unless you eat a lot of nuts, seeds, and vegetable oils. It can't hurt to take an E supplement, as long as you stay within the dosage recommendations. **DOSAGE:** 200 to 400 IU daily. To help your body absorb this fat-soluble vitamin, take it with a snack or meal that contains some fat.

## OFF THE MENU

**Dairy products.** Many people find that milk, cheese, and other dairy foods are mucus forming, although scientists are still duking this one out. If you feel that dairy products make your congestion worse, skip them when you have sinus problems. If you find you have to permanently cut them from your diet to get relief, be sure to make up your calcium needs with other calcium-rich foods and a supplement.

**Alcohol.** Alcohol swells nasal and sinus membranes, the last thing you want when you have a sinus infection.

# STROKE

You know that a diet of butter, bacon, burgers, and processed foods puts you on a fast track to a heart attack, but it also increases your risk of a stroke, which is also caused by narrowed arteries—in this case, blood vessels that feed the brain. (A small percentage of strokes, called hemorrhagic strokes, are caused not by clogged arteries but by ruptured ones.) Since the underlying problems are similar, so are the solutions, like not smoking, renewing your gym membership, and of course, changing your diet, which, by the way, can help control high blood pressure, considered the leading modifiable risk factor for stroke. (Also, as with heart disease, there are some factors, like age, gender, and race, that you can't do anything about—so why not act on the ones you *can* influence?)

A massive study of thousands of women, called the Nurses Health Study, showed that eating the typical Western-style diet increased stroke risk by 58 percent, whereas consuming more whole grains, fruits, vegetables, and fish—the same foods that guard against so many other diseases—lowered that risk by 30 percent. Here's where to start. (Hint: Buy a bunch of bananas at the store and plan a spinach salad topped with tuna for tomorrow's lunch.)

## YOUR FOOD PRESCRIPTION

## The DASH Diet

One of the most important ways to protect yourself from stroke is to lower your blood pressure. When your pressure is higher than 140/90 mmHg (millimeters of mercury), your stroke risk doubles. And for every 20 mmHg increase in systolic pressure (the first number in your blood pressure reading) or 10 mmHg increase in diastolic pressure (the second number), your risk doubles yet again.

The DASH (Dietary Approaches to Stop Hypertension) Diet, which is low in saturated fat and cholesterol and high in fiber, low-fat and fat-free dairy foods, and fruits and vegetables, has been shown to decrease blood pressure by 5.5/3.0 mmHg, which is enough to cut your stroke risk by 27 percent. Go a step further and reduce your sodium intake to about 2/3 teaspoon of salt a day, and you can lower your pressure by 8.9/4.5 mmHg. That's about the same reduction you can get by taking a single blood pressure medication.

Even on their own, the foods that make up the DASH Diet are potent stroke fighters. Eating plenty of whole-grain fiber lowers risk by about 40 percent, and other research shows that eating fruit and vegetables daily reduces it by 20 to 40 percent. While you're "doing the DASH," you can lower your blood pressure another 4 points or so by getting some regular exercise, maintaining a healthy weight, and moderating your alcohol intake (see Off the Menu, page 576). For more information about this diet, see the High Blood Pressure entry, page 488.

## Oats, almonds, soy foods, and cholesterol-lowering margarine

How does a nice, steaming bowl of cholesterol-lowering oatmeal sound, or a snack of crunchy almonds (excellent sources of vitamin E)? Have you discovered soy milk or edamame—young green soybeans, great in soups and salads or eaten right out of their pods—yet? These are three of the foods that make up a cholesterol-

Blueberries are extraordinarily healthy, but their growing season is short. The solution: Buy large amounts when in season, wash thoroughly, then freeze in airtight containers. Use the berries year-round as a topping, in smoothies, or in your cooking.

lowering regimen known as the Portfolio Eating Plan, developed by researchers in Toronto. When eaten as part of a total diet that's low in saturated fat, this combination of foods appears to reduce LDL ("bad") cholesterol levels by 28 percent, almost as much as a statin drug does. (For more information on the meal plan as well as recipes, visit http://portfolioeatingplan.com.)

It's not clear whether high cholesterol levels contribute as much to strokes as they do to heart attacks, but there's good reason to suspect they may. Some research suggests that lowering cholesterol levels with statin medications can reduce stroke risk by about 25 percent. It follows that lowering your cholesterol through diet would also help.

High cholesterol contributes to plaque buildup in blood vessels around the brain, paving the way for an ischemic stroke, the most common kind. In fact, for women under age 55, having high cholesterol seems to increase the risk of dying from a stroke by about 23 percent, even if they don't have cardiovascular disease. Even more frightening: Elevated cholesterol increased stroke deaths among younger African American women by a whopping 76 percent.

Now, to get your LDL cholesterol below the 100 mg/dl level that's recommended for people with multiple risks for cardiovascular disease (below 70 mg/dl for those at very high risk), you may still need a statin, but following a cholesterol-lowering diet is a good place to start.

Aim for: The Portfolio plan calls for eating the following each day: about a handful of almonds; 20 grams of soluble fiber from foods such as oats, barley, and certain fruits (to get there, you'll need to eat 1 cup each of oatmeal, beans, strawberries, and mashed sweet potatoes

and one apple); 50 grams of soy protein (the equivalent of a whopping five or more servings of soy foods); 2 grams of plant sterols from sterol-enriched margarine; and five to nine daily servings of fruits and vegetables. Of course, even if you don't follow this plan exactly, you're bound to see benefits from adding more of these foods to your diet.

## Blueberries, sweet potatoes, artichokes, *and other foods rich in antioxidants*

One reason fruits and vegetables are so helpful against stroke is that they're such good sources of antioxidants, which help reduce inflammation and prevent plaque buildup in the arteries. They also improve blood flow by helping blood vessels dilate.

Aim for: 7 to 10 servings of fruits and vegetables a day. One serving is one medium piece of fruit; 1/2 cup of fruit or vegetable juice; 1/2 cup of chopped fruit or cooked vegetables, beans, or legumes; or 1 cup of leafy vegetables.

### FEATURED RECIPES

**Buckwheat Pancakes with Fruit Sauce** *p. 590*
**Updated Waldorf Salad** *p. 594*
**Tuna and White Bean Salad** *p. 599*
**Sweet Potato Soup** *p. 601*
**Mac 'n Cheese Primavera** *p. 608*
**Roasted Salmon with Sautéed Greens** *p. 613*
**Creamed Spinach** *p. 624*
**Blueberry-Oat Scones** *p. 628*
**Pumpkin Streusel Bread** *p. 631*

## Bananas, baked potatoes, white beans, *and other foods rich in potassium*

Here's a great reason to pack a banana with your lunch: Bananas are loaded with potassium, and experts think one of the reasons the DASH Diet works so well is that it provides plenty of this mineral. Research shows that eating a diet low in potassium (less than 1.5 grams a day) increases stroke risk by 28 percent. The Health Professionals Follow-Up Study found that participants who ate nine daily servings of potassium-rich fruits and vegetables, like potatoes, prunes, and raisins, as well as the foods listed above, lowered their stroke risk by 38 percent compared to people who ate just four servings daily.

Aim for: 4.7 grams (4,700 milligrams) of potassium daily, an amount you can get by eating 7 to 10 servings of potassium-rich fruits and vegetables each day. One baked potato, a cup of white beans, a cup of canned tomatoes, and a cup of winter squash contain about 1,000 milligrams.

## Beans, spinach, *and other foods rich in folate*

Beans aren't just good for your heart; they're also good for protecting your brain. That's because they're rich in the B vitamin folate (a.k.a. folic acid). According to a 20-year study of nearly 10,000 adults, eating a diet rich in folate lowers the risk of stroke by 20 percent. Here's more intriguing evidence: Researchers who looked at the number of strokes in the United States before and after food manufacturers began fortifying flour with folic acid to prevent birth defects found 10 to 15 percent fewer stroke deaths in the three years after fortification began than in the three years before.

Aim for: 400 micrograms of folate daily, which you can get from a half cup of pinto beans plus a cup of cooked spinach.

## Low-fat milk

If you've stopped drinking milk, it may be time to start again. There's an excellent reason that low-fat and fat-free dairy foods are mainstays of the DASH Diet—they're good sources of potassium, magnesium, and calcium, all of which naturally lower blood pressure. Indeed, a study of men in Puerto Rico found that hypertension was half as prevalent among milk drinkers as among those who didn't drink it. So it makes sense that if milk (and dairy foods) lowers blood pressure, it would also reduce the risk of stroke. In fact, a 22-year study of more than 3,100 Japanese men in the Honolulu Heart Study found that those who drank at least two 8-ounce glasses of milk a day had half the risk of stroke compared to non–milk drinkers.

Aim for: Two to three 8-ounce servings daily.

Few vegetables contain as many healing nutrients as spinach. At least once a week, sauté fresh spinach and garlic in olive oil and season with pepper and a dash of lemon juice. It's the perfect dinner side dish, for both taste and health.

Helpful hint: Not everyone loves a glass of cold milk, so if you'd prefer not to drink yours straight, remember that all the milk you consume—in coffee and on cereal, for example—counts toward your daily goal. And because saturated fat is linked to cardiovascular disease in general, opt for 1 percent or fat-free milk.

# Barley, buckwheat, cornmeal,
### and other magnesium-rich foods

The same study that found that potassium-rich foods decreased stroke risk also showed that a diet higher in magnesium-rich foods reduced risk by 30 percent, even if you don't have high blood pressure.

Aim for: 500 milligrams of magnesium a day. You can get there by eating a cup of black beans, a cup of spinach, a serving of halibut, and an ounce of pumpkin seeds.

## Salmon *and other fatty fish*

You know it's good for your heart, so you should be eating fish like salmon anyway. If you are, you're probably protecting yourself from stroke. For starters, by eating more fish, you're automatically eating less red meat and processed meats like sausage, hotdogs, bacon, or lunchmeat, and that means you're eating less arterty-clogging saturated fat.

It's also possible that the omega-3 fats in fish like tuna, mackerel, and salmon also improve blood flow by reducing inflammation in the arteries and making blood less likely to clot. A 12-year study done at Harvard Medical School of nearly 5,000 adults age 65 and older found that eating fish one to four times a week lowered stroke risk by 27 percent.

Aim for: The American Heart Association recommends at least two servings of oily fish (8 to 12 ounces total) a week. Since mercury contamination is a concern, opt for types lower in mercury, such as salmon and canned light tuna, and steer clear of highly contaminated fish such as shark, swordfish, king mackerel, and tilefish.

## Getting the Salt Out

Trying to cut back on sodium? The good news is that you can still add some salt to your food when you prepare it. As long as you're not dumping a shakerful into every dish, table salt isn't that much of a worry. Rather, it's processed foods that are the big concern, since they account for about 75 percent of the sodium we consume. In fact, many foods that you wouldn't even think of as "salty," like cereals, contain more sodium than potato chips! The best way to curb your sodium intake is to steer clear of these high-sodium processed foods. You can also follow this rule of thumb: When you check the calorie and sodium content per serving on product labels, the number of milligrams of sodium should be less than or at most equal to the number of calories.

## NUTRITIONAL SUPPLEMENTS

**Omega-3 fatty acids.** Although fish-oil supplements aren't specifically recommended to prevent strokes, there's reason to suspect they may be helpful because they lower levels of triglycerides. These blood fats, which contribute to blood vessel blockages, are shaping up to be an independent risk factor for stroke. Research indicates that heart patients who have triglyceride levels above 200 mg/dl have a 30 percent increased risk of stroke. **DOSAGE:** The American Heart Association recommends taking 2 to 4 grams of eicosapentaenoic acid (EPA) and docosahexaenoic acid (DHA) a day to lower elevated triglycerides. Taking the supplements with food can help reduce the burping often associated with fish oils. So can choosing a fish-oil supplement that contains citrus essence.

**Folic acid and vitamin B$_{12}$.** These B vitamins may lower stroke risk by reducing levels of homocysteine, an amino acid that can damage arteries. While high doses aren't recommended, if you're not getting enough from your diet, make sure your multivitamin fills the gap. **DOSAGE:** *Folic acid:* 400 micrograms daily. *Vitamin B$_{12}$:* 2 micrograms daily.

## OFF THE MENU

**Sodium.** Excess sodium raises blood pressure, which in turn increases stroke risk. In a study of more than 29,000 adults in Japan, men whose diets were highest in sodium had more than twice the risk of dying from strokes compared to men who ate low-sodium diets. For women, the death rate from stroke was 70 percent higher in those who consumed the most sodium than in those who ate less.

Reducing your sodium intake substantially lowers both your blood pressure *and* your stroke risk. Both the American Heart Association and the National Heart, Lung, and Blood Institute recommend limiting sodium intake to no more than 2,300 milligrams each day—the equivalent of 1 teaspoon of salt. According to research from studies on the DASH Diet, doing so lowers blood pressure by 2.1/1.1 mmHg. Cut back even more—to about 2/3 teaspoon daily—and you can drop your blood pressure by 6.7/3.5 mmHg. That's helpful because even a 5-point drop in pressure reduces your stroke risk by 27 percent. See "Getting the Salt Out" on page 575 for tips on lowering your sodium intake.

**Saturated fat, cholesterol, refined sugar, and refined flour.** In other words, the stuff that makes up the typical Western diet. All of these are known contributors to heart disease, so it's no surprise that they boost stroke risk as well—by as much as 58 percent. The grease factor increases fatty deposits in the arteries that can lead to blockages. Refined flour and sugar raise blood sugar and insulin levels, which in turn raise stroke risk by increasing fat levels in the blood, thickening artery walls, and increasing blood pressure and inflammation. If you're overweight or have high blood pressure, a Western-style diet becomes even more problematic: The Nurses Health Study found that obese women who followed such a diet had double the risk of stroke; women with high blood pressure had triple the risk, and smokers had quadruple the risk.

**Heavy drinking.** Alcohol is tricky, and whether it raises your stroke risk depends largely on your drinking habits. Light to moderate drinking (two drinks daily for men and one for women) actually lowers stroke risk by 28 percent, probably by boosting HDL cholesterol—the good kind—and making blood less likely to clot. Yet, if you have three or four drinks a day, your risk suddenly goes up by 42 percent. Toss back five, and it jumps by 69 percent. Heavy drinking raises blood pressure, thickens the blood, interferes with heart rhythm, and reduces blood flow to the brain. If you've already had a stroke, it may be best to give up the goblet and stick to club soda.

## Insulin Resistance: A Hidden Stroke Risk

Do you have a spare tire around your middle? Have high blood sugar, high triglycerides, or high blood pressure? You may have a condition called insulin resistance syndrome, which puts you at significantly increased risk for a stroke. If you do have it, your stroke risk increases by 78 percent if you're a man and 100 percent if you're a woman.

Insulin resistance is typically associated with developing diabetes (see the Diabetes entry, page 444). But now research suggests that being insulin resistant (even without diabetes) raises stroke risk by increasing the assault on the arteries.

What is insulin resistance syndrome (which also goes by the names metabolic syndrome and syndrome X)? Rather than being a single disease, it's a collection of health problems that includes excess belly fat (a measurement of more than 35 inches around the waist for women and 40 inches for men); elevated triglycerides (over 150 mg/dl) and blood sugar (over 110 mg/dl); high blood pressure (over 130/85 mmHg); and low HDL cholesterol (under 40 mg/dl for women and 50 mg/dl for men). If you have any three of these conditions, you have insulin resistance syndrome. And while there may be some debate about what to call this condition, there's no doubt about its dangers.

Eating more fruits, vegetables, and whole grains—the core formula for stroke prevention—will also help you combat insulin resistance.

# ULCERS

Before you reach for a glass of milk to soothe your ulcer pain, read this: Much of what we used to "know" about ulcers has been proven wrong. Most ulcers aren't caused directly by stress but by the bacterium *Helicobacter pylori,* which is why ulcers today are often treated with antibiotics along with an acid suppressor. Spicy foods don't cause ulcers either—in fact, chile peppers are used in some countries to treat them—although these foods can worsen the pain if you're not used to eating them. And milk, once considered an ulcer soother, won't do any good and may even make things worse.

*H. pylori,* a bug with a spiral shape, can screw itself into the mucosal lining that protects the digestive tract. Once there, it weakens the mucus produced by the stomach and the duodenum (the first part of the small intestine) and exposes the delicate lining to digestive acids. What begins as irritation can quickly develop into sores along the walls of the esophagus, small intestine, and stomach. In advanced ulcers, sores can become so severe that they burn a hole in the tissue.

Researchers estimate that almost 80 percent of the people in the world carry *H. pylori* in their bodies. Obviously, not all of them develop ulcers. Sometimes it takes another factor to pave the way. An all-too-common one is the regular use of painkillers such as aspirin and ibuprofen, known as nonsteroidal anti-inflammatory drugs (NSAIDs). Over time, these can inflame and irritate the linings in the GI tract and often trigger *H. pylori* into action. Because NSAIDs also block the production of hormones that protect the stomach lining, digestive acids can begin their damage, and soon afterward, ulcers make themselves known. Once an ulcer takes up residence, stress, diet, alcohol, caffeine, and smoking can aggravate it.

While antibiotics are often necessary to kill off *H. pylori,* certain foods also wield power against the bugs. Others can help strengthen the digestive tract's own protective bacteria, making it less inviting to *H. pylori.* And once an ulcer has taken hold, foods that help to rebuild the lining of the stomach can aid in healing.

Tired of the same old salad? Cut the amount of lettuce in half and replace with thinly sliced cabbage. Add broccoli or cauliflower crowns, berries, grapes, or pear slices. Then change to a yogurt-based dressing. Your new salad will be as delicious as it is healthy.

# Honey

Modern medicine has finally caught on to a folk remedy that has been used for centuries. Because honey fights bacteria, hospitals and clinics sometimes apply it to burns and other open wounds. For the same reason that it can help heal a skin ulcer, honey may help thwart *H. pylori*. Researchers from New Zealand tested honey made from the nectar of the Manuka flower on bacteria from biopsies of gastric ulcers and found that the honey inhibited bacterial growth. Other researchers have been successful in using other types of honey to halt the growth of *H. pylori*.

**Aim for:** The research on honey is young, so a specific recommendation has yet to be made. Start by taking a tablespoon of raw, unprocessed honey in the morning and at night to calm a fiery belly. Spread it on toast or a cracker to keep it in the stomach longer. Because *H. pylori* is slow growing, be sure to keep up your honey regimen until ulcer symptoms are long gone.

# Slippery elm tea

Slippery elm coats the stomach just as it does a sore throat, bringing some relief, albeit short-lived, from ulcer pain.

**Aim for:** Several cups throughout the day.

# Broccoli, brussels sprouts, cauliflower, and kale

These cruciferous vegetables all contain sulforaphane, a compound that appears to squelch *H. pylori*. In one study, after patients who tested positive for the bacteria ate a half cup of broccoli sprouts twice daily for seven days, 78 percent tested negative for the bacteria. Other studies, on mice, have shown that sulforaphane extracts can successfully destroy the bacteria in the mice's digestive tracts.

**Aim for:** We'll have to wait for studies to show just how much broccoli you would have to eat to help cure ulcers. Until then, consider eating a cup a day of broccoli, raw or cooked, or broccoli sprouts. Not only will the broccoli begin to battle your ulcer, but it will also provide more than a day's worth of vitamin C and a generous amount of fiber, two more allies in the fight against ulcers.

# Cabbage

Scientists think that it may be the amino acid glutamine that gives cabbage its anti-ulcer punch. Glutamine helps to fortify the mucosal lining of the gut and to improve blood flow to the stomach, meaning it not only helps prevent ulcers but can also speed healing of existing sores.

**Aim for:** Eat 2 cups of raw cabbage daily. Add it to salads, coleslaw, and wraps. You can also drink raw cabbage juice, sold in health food stores. Drink a quart a day for three weeks if you can stand it.

# Yogurt with active cultures

Foods like yogurt and kefir (fermented milk) contain "good" bacteria that can inhibit *H. pylori* and may help ulcers heal faster. In one large study in Sweden, people who ate fermented milk products like yogurt at least three times a week were much less likely to have ulcers than people who ate yogurt less often.

**Aim for:** Have a cup of yogurt, kefir, or another fermented milk product with live, active cultures at least once a day. Avoid sweetened varieties, which are less effective.

## FEATURED RECIPES

**Coleslaw with Orange-Sesame Vinaigrette** *p. 594*
**Broccoli Salad** *p. 595*
**Hearty Vegetable Stew** *p. 608*
**Chicken-Barley Bake** *p. 616*
**Springtime Quinoa** *p. 626*
**Blueberry-Oat Scones** *p. 628*

## Plantain

This large, green, banana-like fruit is starchy and sticky in texture. It helps to soothe inflamed and irritated mucous membranes and has some anti-bacterial properties to boot. Studies on rats with ulcers caused by daily aspirin use have shown that unripe green plantain can both prevent the formation of ulcers and help to heal them. Plantain works its magic best when it's unripe.

Aim for: Until human studies determine the amount that might help, use the fruit as they do in Latin America, where green plantain is eaten boiled like a potato. Avoid fried plantain, as the fat can aggravate ulcers.

## Fruits, vegetables, whole grains, *and other foods high in fiber*

Add another star to fiber's crown. Besides keeping you regular, fiber has a role in keeping ulcers at bay, especially those in the duodenum. A number of studies have found that people who eat high-fiber diets have a lower risk of developing ulcers. In the Physicians Health Study from Harvard, researchers looked at the diets of 47,806 men and found that those who ate 11 grams or more of fiber from vegetables had a 32 percent lower risk of developing duodenal ulcers.

Scientists aren't sure how fiber helps, but it may be thanks to the fact that it slows the emptying of the stomach and thus reduces the amount of time the stomach lining and duodenum are exposed to digestive acids. Soluble fiber, the kind found in oats, beans, barley, peas, and pears, also forms a slippery goo in the stomach that acts as a barrier between the stomach lining and corrosive stomach acids.

Aim for: General health guidelines suggest getting 25 to 35 grams of fiber a day.

## NUTRITIONAL SUPPLEMENTS

**DGL tablets or wafers.** Strong-tasting licorice made from the root of the licorice plant contains a number of compounds that help soothe irritated, inflamed mucosal tissue. Licorice also stimulates the lining of the stomach and small intestine to produce more mucus, which may help sores heal faster. It may also have some antibacterial properties against *H. pylori*.

In a recent animal study on rats with ulcers, licorice-coated aspirin cut the number of ulcers in half. A separate study compared the effect of licorice extract with that of cimetidine (Tagamet), a common ulcer medication, on 100 patients with chronic ulcers. The researchers found that both treatments cured 90 percent of the ulcers after 12 weeks.

Unfortunately, the licorice candy most commonly sold today won't do the trick because it contains little or no real licorice, so you'll need to go to a health food store for chewable supplements (not capsules). Because real licorice can cause high blood pressure, it's important to get deglycyrrhizinated licorice (DGL), which has been processed to eliminate the problem. **DOSAGE:** One or two tablets or wafers before meals and at bedtime.

**Probiotics.** Probiotics—the "good" bacteria found in yogurt and other fermented milk products—may help heal your ulcer faster and could even help prevent future ulcers. Several studies have shown that one bacterium in particular, *Lactobacillus gasseri,* is especially effective in helping to protect the gastrointestinal tract.

If you're taking antibiotics for your ulcer, it's a good idea to take probiotics as well, since antibiotics wipe out both the bad and good bacteria in your system, and eliminating good bacteria can have unwanted side effects, such as diarrhea. **DOSAGE:** Take no more than one to two billion live organisms once a day. Higher doses sometimes cause intestinal discomfort. Choose a supplement with multiple strains, including *L. gasseri.*

## OFF THE MENU

**Milk.** Once considered the perfect therapy for ulcers because it was thought to coat and calm the stomach, milk is now on the list of foods to avoid. Research has shown that in fact, milk increases rather than neutralizes stomach acids. Any additional acid in the gut can irritate existing ulcers.

**Spicy foods.** People who eat spicy diets loaded with chile peppers are actually less likely to develop ulcers, probably because many spices contain compounds that kill bacteria. But if you already have an ulcer, it's best to steer clear of the fiery stuff, which may increase ulcer pain because they can irritate the exposed sores.

**Fatty foods.** The higher the fat content of your dinner, the more stomach acid is needed to digest it, and the acids can irritate ulcers.

**Coffee and alcohol.** Caffeine and alcohol stimulate the release of stomach acids that can crank up ulcer pain. (Nicotine has the same effect, so add this to your reasons to quit smoking.) Alcohol can also irritate and wear down the mucosal lining of the stomach.

**Calcium carbonate supplements.** Ironically, the very acids that stimulate ulcer pain help protect your gut from *H. pylori* when you don't have an ulcer, so taking antacids such as calcium carbonate supplements (the form found in Tums) may work against you in the long run. If you want to take calcium for your bones, take it in the form of calcium citrate, which doesn't cause these problems.

## Say Hello to Aloe?

If you're looking around your kitchen for ways to help soothe and heal an ulcer, consider the aloe plant on the counter. Better yet, go to the health food store for some aloe vera juice, which helps heal the lining of the digestive tract. Take 1/4 to 1/2 cup three times a day for a month. Make sure you don't get the leaf exudate (sometimes just called aloe), which is a laxative. Aloe juice may also help stop the bleeding of a bleeding ulcer because of its astringent, or drying, effects.

# URINARY TRACT INFECTIONS

No one thinks much about their personal plumbing until something goes awry. If that something is a urinary tract infection, or UTI, you don't need a plumber—but you may need antibiotics. See your doctor if you suspect you have a UTI. If you get frequent UTIs, there are steps you can take to help prevent them.

UTIs start at the end of the urinary tract. The urethra, a tube only about 2 inches long, carries urine from your bladder out of the body. The trouble starts when gastrointestinal bacteria, often of the *Escherichia coli* variety, stick to the walls of the urethra and begin to multiply, leading to an infection. The result is a burning sensation when you urinate, along with the urge to urinate even when you don't need to go. You may also feel pressure above your pubic bone or in the rectum. If the infection moves up the urinary tract into the bladder or even farther, into the kidneys, the condition becomes trickier and more serious, causing pain in the sides and back as well as nausea and fever.

The best way to prevent a UTI is to prevent problem bacteria from clinging to the lining of the urethra. Your doctor will explain that one way to do this to urinate after sex. Two simple beverages can also do the trick (read on for details).

## YOUR FOOD PRESCRIPTION

## Cranberry and blueberry juice

Doctors used to think that it was acidity that made cranberries so effective in treating UTIs, but other acidic juices like pineapple don't work. (And increasing the acidity of urine by taking vitamin C supplements also appears to have little or no effect, although the practice became popular in recent years.) Now research hints that an antioxidant compound in cranberries and blueberries called epicatechin may work directly on bacteria like *E. coli*, affecting the tendrils on their surface. The bacteria essentially become boats without anchors and are no longer able to attach to the lining of the urethra walls. Cranberry compounds also appear to weaken bacteria cells.

A study from Finland involving 150 women prone to UTIs found that those who drank cranberry juice daily for 12 months experienced a 20 percent reduction in infections. In a study in Massachusetts, scientists found that more intense cranberry products like whole cranberries and pure cranberry juice (rather than cranberry juice cocktail) were particularly effective at quashing the bacterial threat.

If you have kidney stones made of oxalate, note that one small study suggests that cranberry extract tablets may contribute to the stones. Also, drinking more than a liter of juice a day over a long period may increase the risk of uric acid kidney stones. Check with your doctor before starting a cranberry regimen.

Aim for: Three 8-ounce glasses of pure unsweetened cranberry or blueberry juice. You can often find this type of juice in the natural foods section of your supermarket. Avoid cranberry juice cocktail, which is loaded with added sugar—something bacteria thrive on! Because the unsweetened stuff is so tart, some people prefer to take cranberry extract tablets (see Nutritional Supplements, below).

Helpful hint: Like all acidic juices, cranberry juice can erode tooth enamel. Be sure to brush your teeth after drinking it.

## Water

Drinking plenty of water keeps urine diluted so bacteria have less chance to group together and cause problems. It also stimulates you to urinate more often, helping to flush the walls of the urethra, where bacteria may be clinging.

Aim for: At least 8 to 10 eight-ounce glasses of water per day. If you exercise or live in a humid, hot environment, drink even more.

## Plain yogurt with active cultures

Yogurts that contain live bacterial cultures help keep up your gut's population of "good" bacteria, which in turn keep "bad" bacteria in check. Studies on whether yogurt and other natural sources of "good" bacteria, like kefir (fermented milk), can help to prevent UTIs have had mixed results. It may be that the abundant added sugar in some yogurts cancels the effect of the probiotic bacteria. But eating some yogurt every day can't hurt, and if you have to take antibiotics for a UTI, it may help you avoid a yeast infection, which antibiotics sometimes trigger. Keep eating yogurt for two weeks following your last dose of antibiotics to keep up with the continued effect of the medication.

Aim for: A cup a day. Stick to plain yogurt with live, active cultures and without the sugar that feeds "bad" bacteria.

## NUTRITIONAL SUPPLEMENTS

**Cranberry extract.** Although most of the studies that offer evidence to support the power of cranberry in preventing UTIs have been conducted using cranberry juice, a recent study from Finland suggests that cranberry extract tablets work just as well. **DOSAGE:** One 400-milligram tablet twice daily.

**Probiotics.** *Acidophilus* and *bifidobacteria* are the two main probiotics ("good" bacteria) that can help support a healthy immune system if you're not eating enough yogurt. They're sometimes combined in supplements. **DOSAGE:** Follow the dosage instructions on the label.

## OFF THE MENU

**Sugary foods and beverages.** Cookies, candy, soda, and other foods and drinks made with refined sugar or high-fructose corn syrup create an environment in which bacteria thrive and multiply, making infection more likely. Try to stick to natural sources of sugar like fresh fruits.

**Coffee, tea, cola, and alcohol.** All of these beverages can irritate the bladder and make a UTI more likely.

If you find cranberry juice hard to drink on its own, then dilute it with an equal amount of club soda and add a squeeze of lime or lemon juice for flair. Or you can mix it with other fruit juices that will counter its tart, unsweetened flavor.

# WRINKLES

A face can tell a thousand stories, both happy and sad, but most of us would rather not have our histories written out in wrinkles.

As we age, the surface layer of the skin thins. The layer beneath the surface also loses collagen—skin's scaffolding—and elastin, fibers that give skin its bounce. Far beneath the surface, fat cells also shrink. The result? Wrinkling and sagging. You can blame some of this on exposure to the sun. Ultraviolet rays damage the skin and generate unstable molecules called free radicals that wreak further havoc by breaking down collagen. Smoking and air pollution have a similar effect.

The body fights back with its own antioxidants, which neutralize free radicals, but getting more antioxidants from foods as sweet and delicious as berries increases your protection when the damage starts to overwhelm the body's natural defenses.

## YOUR FOOD PRESCRIPTION

### Skinless chicken, fish, beans, nuts, *and other lean protein foods*

Protein helps repair cells that have suffered free radical damage. When protein is digested, it breaks down into amino acids, the building blocks of cells. Having plenty of amino acids available helps to speed the repair and regeneration of skin cells and collagen.

Aim for: Lean protein at every meal.

### Olive oil

Olive oil is chock-full of oleic acid, one of the fatty acids that keep cell membranes fluid and therefore make skin supple. Olive oil also has small amounts of other essential fatty acids that fight inflammation. Yet another benefit comes in the form of vitamin E and polyphenols, a class of antioxidants that protect skin from free radical damage.

Aim for: Choose olive oil for most of your dishes that include oil.

Helpful hint: Opt for 100 percent extra-virgin oil, which is the least refined and has the most antioxidants. Drizzle it over sautéed and steamed vegetables. Heating the oil as little as possible helps retain its healing properties.

### Garlic

The "stinking rose" offers much more than essential flavor for cooking; it also brings a wealth of skin-protective polyphenols to your plate.

Aim for: Keep a clean garlic press at the ready and add minced garlic—especially raw—to as many of your dishes as possible. You can also eat a garlic clove, chopped into several pill-size pieces, every day.

Helpful hint: After you chop garlic, let it stand for 10 to 15 minutes before using it in cooking. The waiting period allows the garlic's active compounds to develop.

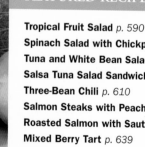

### FEATURED RECIPES

**Tropical Fruit Salad** *p. 590*
**Spinach Salad with Chickpeas** *p. 597*
**Tuna and White Bean Salad** *p. 599*
**Salsa Tuna Salad Sandwiches** *p. 604*
**Three-Bean Chili** *p. 610*
**Salmon Steaks with Peach Salsa** *p. 612*
**Roasted Salmon with Sautéed Greens** *p. 613*
**Mixed Berry Tart** *p. 639*

## Blueberries, blackberries, raspberries, and strawberries

For tiny fruits, berries pack more antioxidant punch than any other fruit or vegetable tested. Next in line? Red apples with the peel. All these fruits work beautifully to help protect skin from the damage that leads to wrinkles. Citrus fruits are also rich in antioxidants.

Aim for: A cup of berries a day. Blend them into fruit smoothies, add them to breakfast cereal, and use them in pancake or muffin batter.

## Green tea

Thanks to its impressive storehouse of polyphenols, green tea is high on the list of skin-friendly beverages.

Aim for: Four cups throughout the day. If you're sensitive to caffeine, drink your last cup before 3:00 in the afternoon.

## Salmon, mackerel, *and other fatty fish rich in omega-3 fatty acids*

No doubt you've already heard what omega-3 fatty acids can do for your heart, but a nice piece of broiled salmon can also do wonders for your skin. The omega-3s provide a wealth of protection by keeping cell membranes fluid.

Aim for: At least two 4-ounce servings of fatty fish per week.

## Vegetables and beans

Add these foods to the fish and olive oil we already mentioned, and you're really feeding your skin the foods it needs to achieve that youthful smoothness. When researchers in Australia compared the diets and wrinkles of hundreds of people in Australia, Greece, and Sweden, they found that those who ate more vegetables, beans, fish, and olive oil had the fewest wrinkles. The researchers suspect it was a combination of monounsaturated fats, antioxidants, and lean protein that did the trick.

Aim for: Five to six 1/2-cup servings of a range of vegetables daily. In addition, sprinkle beans on salads, enjoy bean-based soups, and plan a bean-based meal such as chili once a week.

## Water

Skin cells need a bounty of fluid to keep their membranes supple and receptive to the nutrients that keep them healthy. Take out a half-gallon pitcher and fill it with water. That's the very least you ought to drink in a day to keep your skin smooth and hydrated. If you're sweating because of physical activity or being outside in hot weather, you should drink even more.

Aim for: At least 8 to 10 eight-ounce glasses per day.

### NUTRITIONAL SUPPLEMENTS

**Vitamin E.** Vitamin E has long been linked to a glowing complexion because its protective antioxidants help to heal damaged skin. Parents rub vitamin E oil on their babies' sensitive skin and bottoms for the same reason that cosmetic companies add it to lotions and other facial products. **DOSAGE:** Up to 400 IU a day.

**Omega-3 fatty acids.** These fatty acids, especially EPA, combat skin inflammation, and one study showed that EPA applied topically helped to improve collagen and elastin fibers in the skin. We're not suggesting that you apply EPA to your skin; more research is needed before dermatologists can make that kind of recommendation. But taking fish-oil supplements may go a long way toward preventing wrinkles. **DOSAGE:** Four 1-gram capsules a day.

### OFF THE MENU

**Coffee.** Some health professionals believe that coffee contributes to wrinkles by increasing stress hormones like adrenaline and noradrenaline.

**Sugar.** It's time to kick that cake and candy bar habit. Several studies indicate that consuming sugary foods and beverages like sodas can damage collagen, the protein that supports skin.

# YEAST INFECTIONS

Ask a baker about yeast, and you'll hear stories of the miracles it creates in the oven—airy pastries and crusty breads that can make you swoon. But ask a woman who has had a yeast infection, and you'll hear a very different tale. Having too much of a certain type of yeast in your body can make you miserable, leaving you itching and irritated in the most intimate places.

The moist, dark areas of your body—the mouth, vagina, and rectum—are full of beneficial bacteria that help protect against infection, as well as fungi that normally cause no problems. But certain conditions change that balance, killing off beneficial bacteria that keep yeast populations in check. Common culprits include pregnancy and diabetes, both of which can change the acidity of the vagina, making it more vulnerable to infection, and antibiotics, which can wipe out the good bacteria that protect the body from more harmful bacteria. The result? Fungus of the *Candida* variety, the type behind most yeast infections, can take over. Oral thrush, a white, itchy, sensitive rash in the mouth, and vaginal yeast infections, with their burning itch and discharge, commonly crop up as a result.

Yeast infections can be stubborn, recurring even after successful treatment with medicines and antifungal creams. For that reason, prevention is the best option, and you can start with that yogurt in the refrigerator. Eating foods that strengthen the immune system is also smart because they may help fortify your body against many types of infection, so you might avoid the antibiotics that make you vulnerable to yeast infections. (See the Immune Weakness entry on page 496 for more advice.)

## YOUR FOOD PRESCRIPTION

## Garlic

Garlic's a powerful bacteria fighter—in fact, it was used to help wounds heal back in World War I. But the "stinking rose" also fights fungi. When scientists in Iran added extracts of pure garlic and onion to samples of *C. albicans*, the fungus that causes most yeast infections, the garlic and onion kept it from growing.

Only recently have scientists discovered that garlic's little bulbs are packed with antioxidants, so eating plenty of garlic should also help keep your immune system running at full steam.

**Aim for:** Two cloves per day. Garlic is most effective when eaten raw, so chop some and add it to salads, salsa, and pasta dishes, or simply chew the cloves if you can bear it.

## Yogurt with active cultures

This fermented dairy product is chock-full of "good" bacteria. When more of these bugs take up residence in your body, there's less room for

### FEATURED RECIPES

**Edamame Hummus with Pita Crisps** *p. 592*
**Greens with Creamy Garlicky Dressing** *p. 596*
**Simple Broccoli Soup** *p. 602*
**Chicken in Garlic Sauce** *p. 616*

yeast to multiply and cause trouble. In one study on women with recurring yeast infections, yogurt proved particularly helpful. For six months, the women ate a daily 8-ounce serving of yogurt with the active culture *Lactobacillus acidophilus*. For the next six months, they ate no yogurt at all. During the yogurt period, the women experienced 30 percent fewer yeast infections.

Aim for: 8 ounces of plain yogurt a day. Make sure you choose yogurt with live, active cultures, particularly *L. acidophilus*. Avoid sweetened yogurts because sugar can worsen a yeast infection.

## NUTRITIONAL SUPPLEMENTS

**Garlic.** If you don't want to risk the scent-ual side effects of garlic, consider a no-odor garlic supplement. A word of warning: Theoretically, garlic may increase the risk of bleeding and should be used under a doctor's supervision by anyone taking a blood-thinning medication, such as warfarin (Coumadin). Garlic can also irritate the gastrointestinal tract and should be used with caution by people with infectious or inflammatory GI conditions. **DOSAGE:** 500 milligrams three times a day for up to six weeks.

**Probiotics.** If you can't eat enough yogurt, or if it doesn't seem to be working as quickly as you'd like, try supplementing with probiotics, the very bacteria found in yogurt. Probiotics teem with live, active cultures that aid digestion and keep the body's population of good bacteria at healthy numbers. They have shown such promise in fighting yeast infections in both the vagina and mouth that some doctors recommend taking them whenever you start a course of antibiotics that may make you vulnerable to yeast infections.

Several studies have found particular benefits from the probiotic *L. rhamnosus*, often listed on labels as *Lactobacillus GG*, which can survive the digestive acids in the gut better than others. *L. acidophilus*, which is more common and much less expensive, has also shown promise.

A study on premature babies found that when their breast milk was supplemented with probiotics for the first six weeks of life, the infants' risk of yeast infections in their mouths, a common problem, decreased by 20 percent. **DOSAGE:** Usually 1 tablespoon of liquid probiotic culture or one or two capsules a day. Take the dose between meals when digestive acid production is at its lowest and be sure to follow the product's dosing instructions for best results. Check with your pediatrician before giving your infant probiotics.

Probiotics should be taken for at least two weeks after finishing a course of antibiotics to ensure that your good bacteria reach effective levels.

## OFF THE MENU

**Sugary foods, sugary drinks, and alcohol.** Yeasts love sugars—in fact, they thrive on them. To starve the troublemakers, make a conscious effort to cut back. That means avoiding fruit juices, sweetened breakfast cereals, ice cream, and desserts as well as anything made with high-fructose corn syrup, like soft drinks and packaged cookies or candy. Try to satisfy your sweet tooth with fruits like cherries, grapes, and fresh apricots or, better yet, have some sweet, crunchy carrots.

You should also avoid alcohol if you have a yeast infection, because yeasts feed on it.

**White bread, white rice, and white potatoes.** Refined grains and starches raise the level of blood sugar (glucose) in the body, and yeasts feed on glucose. Switch to high-fiber foods like whole-wheat bread, brown rice, and whole-grain pasta and cereal. Choose sweet potatoes over white potatoes whenever possible because they have less effect on blood sugar.

**Yeasty foods.** Mushrooms and yeast breads contain yeast that may cause yeast fungi to flourish in the body. Avoid them if you're on antibiotics, under stress, sick, or pregnant—all conditions that make you more vulnerable to a yeast infection.

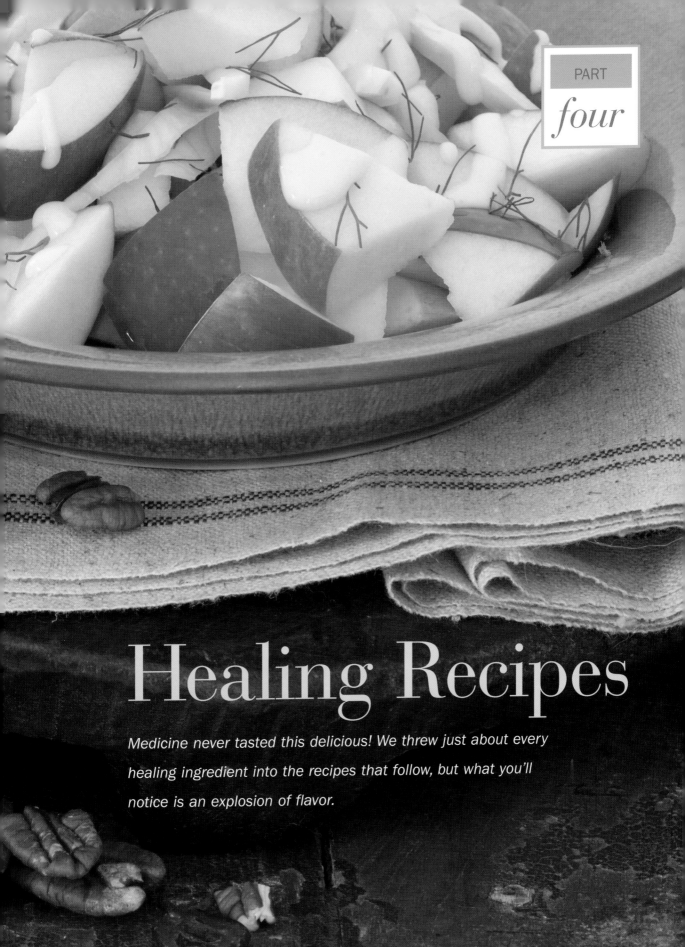

# Healing Recipes

*Medicine never tasted this delicious! We threw just about every*
*healing ingredient into the recipes that follow, but what you'll*
*notice is an explosion of flavor.*

# Tropical Fruit Salad  Serves 6

**Prep Time** • 20 minutes

1 cup low-fat vanilla yogurt

1 teaspoon grated lime zest

2 red grapefruits

2 kiwifruits, peeled and cut into thin wedges

2 bananas, sliced

1 small cantaloupe or large papaya, seeded and cut into chunks

2 tablespoons crystallized ginger

Fresh and flavorful, this salad features antioxidant-rich fruits blended with ginger and lime for a scrumptious breakfast treat. Don't forget that bananas and cantaloupe are both loaded with blood pressure–lowering potassium.

1. In a small bowl, combine the yogurt and lime zest.

2. Over a large bowl, cut the grapefruits into sections, then place in the bowl. Squeeze the membranes over the bowl to release the juice. Add the kiwis, bananas, cantaloupe, and ginger. Toss to blend.

3. To serve, divide the fruit among 6 bowls. Top each with 1 1/2 tablespoons of the yogurt mixture.

164 calories, 4 g protein, 37 g carbohydrates, 7 g fiber, 1 g total fat, 1 g saturated fat, 4 mg cholesterol, 39 mg sodium

# Buckwheat Pancakes with Fruit Sauce  Serves 5

**Prep Time** • 5 minutes
**Cook Time** • 20 minutes

3 apples, pears, or plums, cored and sliced

1/3 cup pure maple syrup

1 cup buckwheat flour

1/3 cup brown rice flour

2 tablespoons brown sugar

1 teaspoon baking powder

1/2 teaspoon baking soda

1/2 teaspoon salt

1/2 teaspoon cinnamon

3/4 cup milk

2 tablespoons canola oil

2 eggs

Here's a gluten-free recipe that tastes great! Buckwheat isn't a cereal like wheat and rice but actually a fruit seed related to rhubarb and sorrel. Its nutty flavor makes these a step up from plain white pancakes.

1. Heat a nonstick skillet coated with cooking spray over medium heat. Add the apples and cook, turning, until just tender, 5 minutes. Add the syrup and reduce the heat to low to keep warm.

2. In a large bowl, whisk together the buckwheat flour, rice flour, brown sugar, baking powder, baking soda, salt, and cinnamon. In a measuring cup, whisk together the milk, oil, and eggs. Stir into the flour mixture just until blended.

3. Heat a griddle or nonstick skillet coated with cooking spray over medium heat. Drop the batter by 2 tablespoons onto the griddle to form pancakes. Cook until browned on the bottom and bubbles form on top, 3 minutes. Turn and cook until the bottoms are browned and the pancakes are firm to the touch, 3 minutes. Place on a plate and cover to keep warm. Repeat with the remaining batter. Serve with the fruit syrup.

328 calories, 7 g protein, 54 g carbohydrates, 7 g fiber, 10 g total fat, 2 g saturated fat, 88 mg cholesterol, 283 mg sodium

# Zucchini Frittata  Serves 6

**Prep Time** • 5 minutes
**Cook Time** • 5 minutes

4 eggs

4 egg whites

1/4 cup grated Parmesan cheese

1/4 teaspoon salt

2 tablespoons olive oil

1 clove garlic, minced

2 small zucchini, shredded

2 roasted red peppers, cut into
  thin strips

Eggs, a stellar source of protein, will start your day off right. Here, only half the yolks are used to keep down the cholesterol and fat.

1. Preheat the oven to 400°F. In a medium bowl, whisk together the eggs, egg whites, cheese, and salt.

2. Heat the oil in a large ovenproof nonstick skillet over medium heat. Add the garlic and cook just until tender, 1 minute. Add the zucchini and peppers and cook 1 minute. Pour in the egg mixture and cook until the bottom of the frittata is set, 3 minutes. Bake until set, 10 minutes.

138 calories, 9 g protein, 5 g carbohydrates, 1 g fiber, 9 g total fat, 2 g saturated fat, 144 mg cholesterol, 331 mg sodium

# Edamame Hummus with Pita Crisps Serves 8

**Prep Time** • 20 minutes
**Cook Time** • 10 minutes

4 pita breads (8 inches),
  halved crosswise

1/2 teaspoon cumin

2 cups shelled edamame

1/4 cup sesame tahini

3 tablespoons lemon juice

2 cloves garlic, mashed

1/2 teaspoon salt

2 tablespoons extra-virgin olive oil

This unique hummus features edamame (green soybeans) instead of the traditional chickpeas. Tahini is a paste made from ground sesame seeds that's similar to peanut butter. Sesame seeds are a great source of manganese and copper and a good source of magnesium as well as sterols, plant compounds that help lower cholesterol.

1. Preheat the oven to 350°F. Place the pita halves on a cutting board and lightly coat with cooking spray. Sprinkle with the cumin and cut each into 8 wedges. Place on a baking sheet and bake until lightly browned, 10 minutes. Transfer to a rack and let cool.

2. Meanwhile, place the edamame in a medium saucepan, add enough water to cover, and bring to a boil over medium-high heat. Cook until very tender, 10 minutes. Drain and rinse under cold water. Let cool slightly.

3. In a food processor, combine 1/3 cup water and the edamame, tahini, lemon juice, garlic, and salt. Process until smooth. With the motor running, gradually add the oil and blend until combined. Serve with pita wedges.

212 calories, 9 g protein, 24 g carbohydrates, 5 g fiber, 10 g total fat,
1 g saturated fat, 0 mg cholesterol, 333 mg sodium

# Ultimate Spiced Nuts Serves 18

**Prep Time** • 5 minutes
**Cook Time** • 20 minutes

1 medium egg white

2 cups mixed nuts, such as Brazil
  nuts, walnuts, pecans, and
  almonds

1/2 cup pumpkin seeds

1 tablespoon brown sugar

2 teaspoons ground ginger

1/2 teaspoon ground nutmeg

1/2 cup dried cranberries

Just 1/4 cup of this high-protein snack will give you the afternoon boost to get through the day. But don't reserve nuts just for snacking. Try sprinkling some on a tossed salad, fruit salad, or frozen yogurt.

1. Preheat the oven to 350°F. In a large bowl, whisk the egg white, then add the nuts and seeds. With a rubber spatula, toss to coat. Add the brown sugar, ginger, and nutmeg and stir until well blended. Stir in the cranberries. Spread onto 2 ungreased baking sheets with sides and bake until browned, 20 minutes.

129 calories, 4 g protein, 6 g carbohydrates, 2 g fiber, 11 g total fat,
1 g saturated fat, 0 mg cholesterol, 0 mg sodium

# Roasted Cherry Tomatoes in Parmesan Cups Serves 4

**Prep Time** • 10 minutes
**Cook Time** • 17 minutes

1 wedge (4 ounces) Parmesan
   cheese, coarsely shredded

2 packages (10 ounces each)
   cherry tomatoes (2 cups)

2 tablespoons extra-virgin olive oil

1/4 cup basil leaves, cut into
   thin strips

Be sure to use Parmesan cheese for this recipe; a richer cheese such as pecorino or Romano may have too much fat to hold a shape. When shredding the cheese, use the section of your shredder with the largest holes.

1. Preheat the oven to 375°F. Line a baking sheet with parchment paper. Place 3 tablespoons cheese on the paper and, with a spoon, spread into a 6-inch circle. Repeat with the remaining cheese to make 6 circles. Bake until lightly browned around the edges, 6 minutes.

2. Meanwhile, place 4 custard cups or small shallow bowls upside down on a countertop. Working one at a time, carefully remove the hot cheese circles from the baking sheet and place over the cups. Let stand to form cups and cool completely.

3. Place the tomatoes in a roasting pan and drizzle with the oil. Roast until the tomatoes split, 10 minutes. Add the basil, tossing to blend.

4. Place a Parmesan cup on each of 4 plates. Divide the tomatoes equally among the cups and serve immediately.

173 calories, 10 g protein, 4 g carbohydrates, 1 g fiber, 14 g total fat, 5 g saturated fat, 20 mg cholesterol, 394 mg sodium

# Updated Waldorf Salad Serves 6

**Prep Time** • 3 hrs, 20 minutes

1/2 cup yogurt cheese (see below)

3 tablespoons pure maple syrup

1 1/2 tablespoons Dijon mustard

1/4 teaspoon salt

4 medium apples, quartered, cored, and cut into chunks

1 small head fennel, coarsely chopped

1/4 cup dried cranberries

1/3 cup toasted nuts, such as walnuts or almonds

Forget the fat-laden, mayonnaise-coated salads of days gone by. Here you'll find a delicious dressing made from low-fat yogurt spiked with mustard and maple syrup. Turn this tasty salad into a light meal or lunch by adding 8 ounces cooked chicken, turkey, or fish.

**1.** In a medium bowl, whisk together the yogurt cheese, syrup, mustard, and salt. Add the apples, fennel, cranberries, and nuts and toss to coat well.

169 calories, 3 g protein, 32 g carbohydrates, 5 g fiber, 4 g total fat, 1 g saturated fat, 2 mg cholesterol, 196 mg sodium

## Yogurt Cheese

When replacing mayonnaise or sour cream with yogurt, it's best to drain a bit of the liquid from the yogurt. To do so, simply line a sieve with a large coffee filter or 2 layers of white paper towels (be sure to avoid printed ones). Set the sieve over a large bowl and place 1 cup low-fat plain yogurt in the filter. Refrigerate for about 3 hours. This will yield 1/2 cup yogurt cheese.

# Coleslaw with Orange-Sesame Vinaigrette Serves 6

**Prep Time** • 50 minutes

1/4 cup fresh orange juice

2 tablespoons rice wine vinegar

1 tablespoon grated fresh ginger

1 clove garlic, minced

1/2 teaspoon salt

2 tablespoons dark sesame oil

1 head Napa cabbage, shredded

3 carrots, shredded

1 bunch scallions, thinly sliced

2 tablespoons sesame seeds, toasted

Like broccoli, cabbage is a strong anticancer food, and here's a delicious way to eat more. Napa cabbage, also known as Chinese cabbage, differs from the round, waxy heads of green and red cabbage. Napa cabbage heads are elongated, with tender, ruffled leaves and a mild flavor.

**1.** In a large bowl, stir together the orange juice, vinegar, ginger, garlic, and salt. Whisk in the oil. Add the cabbage, carrots, and scallions and toss to coat well. Let stand for 30 minutes or refrigerate for 2 hours. Sprinkle with the sesame seeds before serving.

98 calories, 2 g protein, 9 g carbohydrates, 3 g fiber, 6 g total fat, 1 g saturated fat, 0 mg cholesterol, 229 mg sodium

# Broccoli Salad Serves 6

**Prep Time** • 20 minutes

1/4 cup balsamic vinegar

2 tablespoons Dijon mustard

2 tablespoons honey

1/4 teaspoon salt

1/4 teaspoon black pepper

2 tablespoons flaxseed oil

2 tablespoons extra-virgin olive oil

2 heads broccoli

1 small red onion, cut into thin wedges

1/2 cup whole almonds, toasted and coarsely chopped

1/2 cup dried cranberries

4 ounces chèvre goat cheese, crumbled

If raw broccoli florets are too strong for you, steam them for 4 minutes, then rinse in cold water and drain well before adding to the salad.

1. In a large bowl, whisk together the vinegar, mustard, honey, salt, and pepper. Whisk in the flaxseed and olive oils until well blended. Set aside.

2. Remove the florets from the broccoli and add to the vinaigrette. Trim the ends of the stalks and, with a vegetable peeler, peel off the thick outer layer. Shred the stalks with a food processor or by hand.

3. Add the shredded stalks, onion, almonds, and cranberries to the bowl and toss to coat well. Top with the cheese.

333 calories, 12 g protein, 33 g carbohydrates, 7 g fiber, 20 g total fat, 4 g saturated fat, 9 mg cholesterol, 303 mg sodium

# Corn, Tomato, and Quinoa Salad Serves 4

**Prep Time** • 20 minutes
**Cook Time** • 15 minutes

1 cup quinoa, rinsed well

1/2 teaspoon salt

1/4 cup lime juice

1 tablespoon olive oil

1 tablespoon flaxseed oil

1 teaspoon honey (optional)

1/8–1/2 teaspoon crushed
    red pepper

1 cup fresh or thawed frozen
    corn kernels

1 tomato, seeded and chopped

1 avocado, peeled, seeded,
    and chopped

Known as the super grain, quinoa is considered a complete protein and is higher in unsaturated fat and lower in carbohydrates than other grains. When preparing quinoa, be sure to rinse it well to remove the bitter saponin coating.

1. Heat 2 cups water in a medium saucepan over medium heat. Add the quinoa and salt and bring to a simmer. Reduce the heat to low, cover, and simmer until the liquid is absorbed and the quinoa is tender, 15 minutes. Transfer to a large bowl and let cool for 15 minutes.

2. Meanwhile, in a measuring cup, whisk together the lime juice, olive oil, flaxseed oil, and red pepper.

3. Add the corn, tomato, and avocado to the quinoa. Drizzle with the vinaigrette and toss to coat well.

345 calories, 8 g protein, 44 g carbohydrates, 7 g fiber, 17 g total fat, 2 g saturated fat, 0 mg cholesterol, 310 mg sodium

# Greens with Creamy Garlicky Dressing Serves 6

**Prep Time** • 3 hours, 10 minutes

1/2 cup yogurt cheese
    (see page 292)

1 tablespoon extra-virgin olive oil

1 tablespoon balsamic vinegar

1 tablespoon lemon juice

2 tablespoons minced fresh herbs,
    such as basil, cilantro, or
    parsley

2 cloves garlic, minced

1/4 teaspoon salt

6 cups mixed greens

No need to give up creamy salad dressings. Yogurt, rich in beneficial bacteria, forms the base of this dressing, and flavorful ingredients—garlic, basil, and balsamic vinegar—make it delicious.

1. Place the yogurt cheese in a small bowl and whisk in the oil, vinegar, lemon juice, herbs, garlic, and salt.

2. Place 1 cup greens on each of 6 salad plates. Top with 2 tablespoons of the dressing.

59 calories, 3 g protein, 5 g carbohydrates, 1 g fiber, 3 g total fat, 1 g saturated fat, 2 mg cholesterol, 141 mg sodium

# Spinach Salad with Chickpeas Serves 4

**Prep Time** • 10 minutes
**Cook Time** • 20 minutes

2 medium onions, cut into
    1/2-inch slices

1 can (15 ounces) chickpeas,
    drained, rinsed, and patted dry

1/4 cup lemon juice

2 tablespoons flaxseed oil

1 tablespoon olive oil

1 clove garlic, minced

1/2 teaspoon salt

1/4 cup crumbled feta cheese

1 package (5 ounces) baby spinach

2 apples, cored and sliced

2 tablespoons ground flaxseed

Forget the heavy spinach salads loaded with fat and cholesterol. Fresh and delicious, this crunchy salad is packed with antioxidants, fiber, and cancer-fighting ingredients.

1. Preheat the oven to 400°F. Coat a baking sheet with sides with olive oil cooking spray. Add the onion slices and coat each with the spray. Roast for 10 minutes. Add the chickpeas and roast until the onions are tender and browned, 10 minutes.

2. Meanwhile, in a measuring cup, whisk together the lemon juice, flaxseed oil, olive oil, garlic, and salt. Stir in the cheese.

3. Place the spinach in a large bowl and toss with the onions, chickpeas, apples, and flaxseed. Drizzle with the vinaigrette.

292 calories, 9 g protein, 37 g carbohydrates, 10 g fiber, 14 g total fat, 3 g saturated fat, 8 mg cholesterol, 476 mg sodium

# Shrimp and Grapefruit Salad Serves 4

**Prep Time** • 15 minutes

1 red grapefruit

1 teaspoon Dijon mustard

1/2 teaspoon salt

1/4 teaspoon black pepper

2 tablespoons olive oil

1 large head romaine lettuce, shredded (about 6 cups)

1 Hass avocado, peeled, pitted, and chopped

1 pound peeled deveined cooked large shrimp

Grapefruit isn't just for breakfast. It helps boost the antioxidants in this salad while forming a delicious vinaigrette.

1. Working over a large bowl, section the grapefruit, letting the juice drip into the bowl. Place the sections in a small bowl. Squeeze the membranes over the large bowl to release any juice (you should have 1/4 cup).

2. Whisk the mustard, salt, and pepper into the juice. Whisk in the oil. Add the lettuce, avocado, shrimp, and grapefruit. Toss gently to coat well.

317 calories, 31 g protein, 15 g carbohydrates, 7 g fiber, 16 g total fat, 2 g saturated fat, 229 mg cholesterol, 656 mg sodium

# Citrus Chicken Salad Serves 4

**Prep Time** • 3 hours, 10 minutes
**Cook Time** • 18 minutes

1/4 cup orange juice

2 tablespoons lemon juice

2 tablespoons lime juice

1 clove garlic, minced

4 boneless skinless chicken breast halves

2 tablespoons olive oil

1 package (4 ounces) mixed baby greens

1 red bell pepper, seeded and cut into thin strips

1 orange, cut into sections

Citrus makes the calcium in greens like spinach more available to the body. Here, citrus juices—orange, lemon, and lime—blend with garlic to make a delicious marinade. While the chicken grills, the marinade is thickened, creating a flavorful salad dressing.

1. In a zipper-seal plastic bag, combine the orange juice, lemon juice, lime juice, and garlic. Add the chicken and turn to coat. Seal the bag and refrigerate for 1 to 3 hours.

2. Preheat the broiler or grill. Coat a broiler pan or grill rack with cooking spray. Remove the chicken from the marinade, reserving the marinade. Broil or grill the chicken until a thermometer inserted in the center of the breasts reaches 160°F, 15 minutes.

3. Meanwhile, in a small saucepan over high heat, bring the marinade to a boil and cook for 3 minutes. Remove from the heat and whisk in the oil.

4. Divide the greens, bell pepper, and orange equally among 4 plates. Slice the chicken, place on the salads, and drizzle with the marinade.

241 calories, 29 g protein, 13 g carbohydrates, 4 g fiber, 9 g total fat, 1 g saturated fat, 68 mg cholesterol, 123 mg sodium

# Chicken Pasta Salad Serves 4

**Prep Time** • 10 minutes
**Cook Time** • 10 minutes

6 ounces whole-wheat pasta shells

2 tablespoons low-fat canola
    mayonnaise

2 tablespoons low-fat plain yogurt

2 tablespoons red wine vinegar

2 tablespoons grated
    Parmesan cheese

1 clove garlic, minced

3 cups shredded cooked
    chicken breasts

1 cup grape or cherry
    tomatoes, halved

1/4 cup Kalamata olives, cut
    into thin strips

2 cups baby arugula

Pasta salad gets a healthy makeover with whole-wheat pasta and nutrient-rich vegetables like tomatoes and arugula. Opt for canola mayonnaise the next time you shop to add omega-3 and omega-6 fatty acids to your diet.

1. Cook the pasta according to package directions. Drain well but do not rinse.

2. Meanwhile, in a large bowl, whisk together the mayonnaise, yogurt, vinegar, cheese, and garlic. Add the chicken, tomatoes, olives, and arugula and toss gently to coat.

3. When the pasta has drained, let cool slightly, about 2 minutes. Add to the chicken mixture and toss to coat.

408 calories, 36 g protein, 36 g carbohydrates, 5 g fiber, 13 g total fat, 2 g saturated fat, 84 mg cholesterol, 228 mg sodium

# Tuna and White Bean Salad Serves 4

**Prep Time** • 15 minutes

1/3 cup tomato juice

3 tablespoons lemon juice

2 tablespoons olive oil

1 tablespoon chopped fresh basil
    or 1 teaspoon dried basil

1/4 teaspoon salt

1 can (6 ounces) tuna, drained

1 can (15 ounces) white beans,
    drained and rinsed

1 medium cucumber, peeled,
    seeded, and chopped

1/4 cup pitted Kalamata olives,
    chopped

6 cups mixed salad greens

Delicious salad dressings don't have to be laden with fat. Vitamin-rich tomato juice is the base for this delightful dressing.

1. In a measuring cup, whisk together the tomato juice, lemon juice, oil, basil, and salt.

2. In a medium bowl, toss the tuna, beans, cucumber, olives, and 1 tablespoon of the vinaigrette.

3. Divide the greens equally among 4 plates. Top with 1/4 of the tuna mixture and drizzle with the vinaigrette.

206 calories, 18 g protein, 20 g carbohydrates, 7 g fiber, 9 g total fat, 1 g saturated fat, 13 mg cholesterol, 597 mg sodium

# Quick Chicken Noodle Soup Serves 6

**Prep Time** • 10 minutes
**Cook Time** • 25 minutes

2 tablespoons olive oil

3/4 pound boneless skinless
  chicken breasts, cut into
  1-inch pieces

1 large onion, chopped

2 cloves garlic, chopped

2 carrots, chopped

1 red bell pepper, chopped

1 teaspoon dried thyme

1 carton (32 ounces) chicken broth

8 ounces whole-grain spaghetti,
  broken into 2-inch pieces

Perfect for a last-minute supper or to ward off a winter cold, this flavorful soup will hit the spot. Garlic, onion, carrots, and bell pepper add flavor and healing properties, while the spaghetti is reminiscent of the noodle soup of days gone by.

1. Heat the oil in a large saucepan over high heat. Add the chicken and cook, stirring, until browned, 5 minutes. With a slotted spoon, transfer to a bowl.

2. Add the onion to the saucepan and cook until lightly browned, 5 minutes. Add the garlic, carrots, bell pepper, and thyme. Cook, stirring, until lightly browned, 3 minutes. Add the broth and 1 cup water, the chicken, and any drippings in the bowl and bring to a boil. Add the spaghetti and cook for 8 minutes or until tender.

275 calories, 20 g protein, 37 g carbohydrates, 7 g fiber, 6 g total fat,
1 g saturated fat, 33 mg cholesterol, 345 mg sodium

# Chicken Curry Soup Serves 6

**Prep Time** • 15 minutes
**Cook Time** • 30 minutes

2 tablespoons olive oil

2 onions, chopped

4 large carrots, chopped

1 russet potato, peeled and finely
  chopped

1 tablespoon mild curry powder

1 carton (32 ounces) low-sodium
  chicken broth

1 pound boneless skinless chicken
  breasts, cut into thin strips

1/2 small head cauliflower, cut into
  florets (2 cups)

1 cup frozen peas, thawed

You'll want to eat this warming soup because it's comforting and delicious, but you'll get a bonus: the anticancer properties of turmeric, found in curry powder, and cauliflower. With its creamy carrot base, this soup is a meal in itself. Round it out with a whole-grain pita or bread.

1. Heat the oil in a large saucepan over medium heat. Add the onions and carrots and cook, stirring, until lightly browned, 5 minutes. Add the potato, curry powder, 1 cup broth, and 1 cup water. Cover and cook for 10 minutes or until the vegetables are tender.

2. Remove from the heat and let cool slightly, 5 minutes. Place in a food processor or blender and process until smooth.

3. Return the mixture to the saucepan and add the remaining broth and the chicken and cauliflower. Bring to a boil, reduce the heat to medium-low, and simmer until the chicken is cooked and the cauliflower is tender, 15 minutes. Add the peas and cook until heated through, 3 minutes.

260 calories, 25 g protein, 26 g carbohydrates, 6 g fiber, 7 g total fat,
1 g saturated fat, 44 mg cholesterol, 230 mg sodium

# Sweet Potato Soup Serves 6

**Prep Time** • 10 minutes
**Cook Time** • 30 minutes

2 tablespoons olive oil

2 cloves garlic, minced

1 large onion, chopped

1 red bell pepper, seeded
and chopped

1 teaspoon ground ginger

1 teaspoon allspice

4 cups low-sodium vegetable or
chicken broth

2 large sweet potatoes, peeled and
cut into 1-inch pieces

1 can (14 ounces) diced tomatoes

1/2 cup natural peanut or
almond butter

1 package (16 ounces) frozen
shelled edamame

5 ounces baby spinach

This rich, creamy dish is thickened with peanut butter, which adds delicious flavor and stellar nutrition. Packed with chunks of vegetables and seasoned with ginger and allspice, it's sure to become a favorite.

1. Heat the oil in a large saucepan over medium-high heat. Add the garlic, onion, and bell pepper and cook until lightly browned, 5 minutes. Add the ginger and allspice and cook for 1 minute.

2. Stir in the broth, sweet potatoes, and tomatoes and bring to a boil. Reduce the heat to low, cover, and simmer until the potatoes are just tender, 15 minutes.

3. Place the peanut butter in a small bowl. Whisk in about 1 cup of the simmering broth. Return to the saucepan and add the edamame and spinach. Cook until the edamame is cooked through, 10 minutes.

405 calories, 20 g protein, 40 g carbohydrates, 10 g fiber, 20 g total fat, 3 g saturated fat, 0 mg cholesterol, 303 mg sodium

# Ginger Butternut Squash Soup Serves 4

**Prep Time** • 20 minutes
**Cook Time** • 45 minutes

2 tablespoons olive oil

1 large onion, chopped

2 cloves garlic, minced

1 teaspoon turmeric

1 butternut squash
    (2–2 1/2 pounds), peeled,
    seeded, and cubed

4 cups vegetable or chicken broth

2 large apples, peeled, cored,
    and chopped

1 tablespoon grated fresh ginger or
    1 teaspoon ground ginger

1/2 teaspoon salt

Sweet butternut squash is delicious pureed with apple and ginger, and this soup is a perfect way to get the inflammation-fighting properties of ginger and turmeric. For a lovely presentation, swirl a dollop of plain yogurt on top before serving.

1. Heat the oil in a large saucepan over medium heat. Add the onion and cook, stirring, until lightly browned, 4 minutes. Stir in the garlic and turmeric and cook for 1 minute. Add the squash and broth and bring to a boil.

2. Reduce the heat to low, cover, and simmer until the squash is just tender, 20 minutes. Add the apples, ginger, and salt and cook until the squash and apples are very tender, 10 to 20 minutes. Remove from the heat and let cool for about 10 minutes.

3. Working in batches, place the mixture in a food processor or blender and process until smooth.

267 calories, 4 g protein, 51 g carbohydrates, 10 g fiber, 8 g total fat,
1 g saturated fat, 0 mg cholesterol, 762 mg sodium

# Simple Broccoli Soup Serves 4

**Prep Time** • 20 minutes
**Cook Time** • 1 hour, 40 minutes

1 bulb garlic

1 bunch broccoli

2 tablespoons olive oil

1 large onion, chopped

1 carton (32 ounces) vegetable or
    chicken broth

1 russet potato, peeled
    and chopped

1/2 cup low-fat plain yogurt

You'd never know this vitamin-rich soup is low in fat. Instead of heavy cream, a potato and roasted garlic thicken it. If you'd like to make it really special, top with a sprinkling of low-fat cheddar cheese.

1. Preheat the oven to 400°F. Cut the top 1/4 inch off the garlic to expose the cloves. Wrap in a double thickness of foil and bake until very tender and browned, 1 hour.

2. Meanwhile, remove the florets from the broccoli and chop coarsely. Peel and chop the stalks.

3. Heat the oil in a large saucepan over medium heat. Add the onion and cook until lightly browned, 5 minutes. Add 3 cups broth, the broccoli, and the potato. Bring to a boil, then reduce the heat to low, cover, and simmer until the broccoli stalks and potato are very tender, 30 minutes.

4. Squeeze the garlic into a food processor. Add the hot broccoli mixture and puree until smooth. Return to the saucepan and add the remaining broth and 1 cup water. Simmer to blend flavors, 10 minutes. Top each serving with a dollop of yogurt.

247 calories, 9 g protein, 37 g carbohydrates, 7 g fiber, 8 g total fat,
1 g saturated fat, 2 mg cholesterol, 512 mg sodium

# Lentil-Tomato Soup Serves 8

**Prep Time** • 10 minutes
**Cook Time** • 50 minutes

6 teaspoons olive oil

3 ounces sliced Canadian bacon, cut into matchsticks

3 carrots, sliced

2 celery stalks, sliced

1 onion, chopped

2 cloves garlic, minced

1 teaspoon chili powder

1/2 teaspoon dried oregano

1/2 teaspoon ground cumin

1/2 teaspoon salt

1 can crushed tomatoes (28 ounces), with juice

1 1/2 cups lentils, sorted and rinsed

2 cups low-fat plain yogurt

Low-fat Canadian bacon adds smoky flavor to tomato soup packed with lycopene and studded with high-fiber, protein-rich lentils.

1. Heat 1 teaspoon oil in a stockpot over medium heat. Add the bacon and cook, stirring constantly, until well browned, 3 minutes. Transfer to a plate.

2. Add the remaining 5 teaspoons oil to the pot and heat. Add the carrots, celery, and onion and cook, stirring, until well browned, 5 minutes. Add the garlic, chili powder, oregano, cumin, and salt. Cook for 2 minutes, stirring constantly.

3. Add the tomatoes and juice, lentils, and 6 cups water and bring to a boil. Reduce the heat to medium-low, partially cover, and simmer until the lentils are tender, 30 to 40 minutes.

4. To serve, ladle the soup into 8 bowls and top each with 1/4 cup yogurt and a few strips of bacon.

256 calories, 15 g protein, 38 g carbohydrates, 9 g fiber, 6 g total fat, 1 g saturated fat, 9 mg cholesterol, 506 mg sodium

# Minestrone with Fava Beans Serves 8

**Prep Time** • 10 minutes
**Cook Time** • 25 minutes

2 tablespoons olive oil

2 carrots, sliced

2 celery stalks, sliced

1 medium onion, chopped

2 zucchini, halved and sliced

1 red bell pepper, chopped

1 carton (32 ounces) vegetable or chicken broth

2 cans (14 1/2 ounces each) diced tomatoes with basil, garlic, and oregano

2 cups whole-grain rotelle, penne, or shell pasta

1 can (19 ounces) fava beans, drained and rinsed

Parmesan cheese (optional)

Using flavored diced tomatoes saves you time when making this hearty soup. The flavors are rich and make a lovely base for vegetables, pasta, and beans.

1. Heat the oil in a stockpot over medium heat. Add the carrots, celery, and onion and cook, stirring, until the onion is soft and translucent, 5 minutes. Add the zucchini and bell pepper and cook, stirring, until lightly browned, 2 minutes.

2. Add the broth, tomatoes, and 2 cups water and bring to a boil. Add the pasta, then reduce the heat to low and simmer until the pasta is cooked, 12 minutes.

3. Stir in the beans and cook until heated through, 2 minutes. Sprinkle each serving with cheese, if desired.

229 calories, 9 g protein, 42 g carbohydrates, 7 g fiber, 4 g total fat, 1 g saturated fat, 0 mg cholesterol, 634 mg sodium

# Salsa Tuna Salad Sandwiches Serves 2

**Prep Time •** 20 minutes

1/2 cup salsa

2 tablespoons low-fat canola mayonnaise

1/2 teaspoon lime or lemon juice

1 can (6 ounces) water-packed tuna, drained

4 slices whole-grain bread

1/2 avocado, peeled, pitted, and sliced

Salsa adds flavor and moisture to canned tuna without any added fat. The avocado adds unexpected creaminess and richness—not to mention "good" fats.

1.  Drain the salsa by placing it in a sieve over a bowl for about 10 minutes. Shake the sieve to release any remaining liquid.

2.  In a small bowl, stir together the salsa, mayonnaise, and lime juice. Add the tuna and mix well.

3.  Spread 1/2 of the tuna mixture onto 2 slices of bread. Top each with 1/2 of the avocado slices and top with another slice of bread.

350 calories, 27 g protein, 35 g carbohydrates, 14 g fiber, 13 g total fat, 1 g saturated fat, 26 mg cholesterol, 644 mg sodium

# Open-Faced Sardine Sandwiches Serves 2

**Prep Time •** 5 minutes
**Cook Time •** 3 minutes

1 tablespoon low-fat canola mayonnaise

1/2 teaspoon fresh lemon juice

1/4 teaspoon grated lemon zest

2 slices (each 3/4 inch thick) whole-grain bread, such as 12-grain

1 small tomato, cut into 4 slices

1 can (3 3/4 ounces) sardines in olive oil

2 slices (2 ounces) low-fat Jarlsberg cheese

Here's a sandwich that features sardines—one of the best nondairy sources of calcium if you buy them with the bones, and an excellent source of omega-3 fatty acids. The lemon's fresh flavor blends with the nutty taste of the cheese to create a delicious warm sandwich.

1.  Preheat the broiler. In a small bowl, combine the mayonnaise, lemon juice, and zest. Spread half of the mixture onto each slice of bread.

2.  Top each slice with 1/2 of the tomatoes, sardines, and cheese. Place on a broiler pan or baking sheet and broil until the cheese melts, about 3 minutes.

228 calories, 20 g protein, 17 g carbohydrates, 5 g fiber, 9 g total fat, 1 g saturated fat, 72 mg cholesterol, 637 mg sodium

# Curried Chicken Salad Sandwiches Serves 4

**Prep Time** • 10 minutes

1/4 cup low-fat plain yogurt

2 tablespoons low-fat canola
    mayonnaise

1 1/2 teaspoons curry powder

1 teaspoon honey

1/4 teaspoon salt

2 cups chopped cooked chicken
    (8 ounces)

1 apple, cored and chopped

2 celery stalks, chopped

4 lettuce leaves

2 whole-grain pita breads
    (8 inches), halved

Make all your creamy salads healthier by replacing most of the mayonnaise with low-fat yogurt, leaving just 2 tablespoons of mayo. Here, blended with curry powder and honey, tender chicken is combined with apple and celery for a delicious light lunch.

1. In a large bowl, whisk together the yogurt, mayonnaise, curry powder, honey, and salt. Add the chicken, apple, and celery.

2. Place a lettuce leaf in each pita half and fill with 1/4 of the chicken salad.

253 calories, 23 g protein, 27 g carbohydrates, 4 g fiber, 6 g total fat, 1 g saturated fat, 53 mg cholesterol, 440 mg sodium

# Salmon Cake Sandwiches Serves 4

**Prep Time** • 45 minutes
**Cook Time** • 6 minutes

2 egg whites

1/4 cup mild salsa

1/4 cup low-fat canola mayonnaise

1/2 teaspoon ground cumin

1/4–1 teaspoon hot red pepper sauce

2 pouches (7 ounces each) salmon, patted dry

1 cup fresh whole-wheat bread crumbs

4 whole-wheat sandwich rolls

4 lettuce leaves

1 large tomato, cut into 4 slices

If you find the flavor of salmon a bit too strong, try this sandwich made with salmon sold in a pouch, which has a mild, subtle flavor. If, however, you love the bold flavor of canned salmon, use a 14 3/4-ounce can instead of the pouches.

1. Drain the salsa by placing it in a sieve over a bowl for about 10 minutes. Shake the sieve to release any remaining liquid.

2. Line a baking sheet with parchment paper. In a medium bowl, whisk the egg whites. Stir in the salsa, mayonnaise, cumin, and red pepper sauce. Add the salmon and bread crumbs and gently fold in just until combined. Shape the mixture into 4 cakes, place on the baking sheet, and refrigerate for at least 30 minutes.

3. Coat a nonstick skillet with cooking spray. Add the cakes and cook over medium heat, turning once, until browned and crisp, about 6 minutes.

4. Place a lettuce leaf on each roll. Top with a salmon cake and a tomato slice.

367 calories, 30 g protein, 39 g carbohydrates, 6 g fiber, 11 g total fat, 1 g saturated fat, 81 mg cholesterol, 779 mg sodium

# Beef in Lettuce Wraps Serves 4

**Prep Time** • 5 minutes
**Cook Time** • 11 minutes

3 tablespoons hoisin sauce

2 tablespoons wine vinegar

1 tablespoon soy sauce

1 teaspoon toasted sesame oil

1/2 teaspoon ground ginger

1 pound lean ground beef

4 scallions, chopped

2 carrots, shredded

1 clove garlic, minced

12 Bibb or Boston lettuce leaves

What fun—using lettuce in place of bread to hold this warm, flavorful filling. Great for when you're looking for a light lunch, and kids will love them, too!

1. In a small bowl, whisk together the hoisin sauce, vinegar, soy sauce, oil, and ginger.

2. In a nonstick skillet over medium heat, cook the beef until browned, 5 minutes. Add the scallions, carrots, and garlic and cook until tender, 3 minutes. Stir in the hoisin mixture and cook until it thickens and flavors are blended, 3 minutes.

3. Place 3 lettuce leaves on each of 4 plates and fill with the beef mixture.

201 calories, 24 g protein, 13 g carbohydrates, 3 g fiber, 6 g total fat, 2 g saturated fat, 61 mg cholesterol, 619 mg sodium

# Mac 'n Cheese Primavera Serves 8

**Prep Time** • 15 minutes
**Cook Time** • 1 hour

16 ounces whole-grain pasta, such as penne, rotelle, or elbows

2 bunches broccoli, cut into florets (4 cups)

1 large red bell pepper, chopped

2 carrots, sliced

4 cups low-fat milk

1/4 cup cornstarch

1 teaspoon mustard powder

16 ounces shredded low-fat (2%) extra-sharp cheddar cheese

1/4 cup wheat germ

Here's a low-fat dish bursting with richness, flavor—and calcium. Tossing high-fiber vegetables with whole-grain pasta makes this comfort food good for your health as well as your soul.

1. Preheat the oven to 350°F. Coat a 9 x 13-inch baking pan with cooking spray.

2. Cook the pasta according to package directions, adding the broccoli, bell pepper, and carrots during the last 2 minutes of cooking. Drain and return to the pot.

3. Meanwhile, in a medium saucepan, whisk together the milk, cornstarch, and mustard. Bring to a simmer over medium heat. Add the cheese and cook until the cheese melts and the sauce thickens, 3 minutes. Pour over the pasta and toss to coat. Pour into the pan and sprinkle with the wheat germ. Bake until bubbling, 45 minutes.

427 calories, 27 g protein, 61 g carbohydrates, 7 g fiber, 8 g total fat, 5 g saturated fat, 24 mg cholesterol, 94 mg sodium

# Hearty Vegetable Stew Serves 6

**Prep Time** • 5 minutes
**Cook Time** • 30 minutes

2 tablespoons olive oil

2 onions, chopped

2 celery stalks, chopped

2 carrots, chopped

2 cloves garlic, minced

1 tablespoon balsamic vinegar

1 1/2 pounds precut, preseeded butternut squash

8 ounces green beans, halved

3 1/2 cups chicken broth

1/2 teaspoon rubbed sage

1 red bell pepper, chopped

2 cups sliced shiitake mushrooms

1 tablespoon Dijon mustard

1 tablespoon honey

This nourishing stew is a snap to make because you can chop some of the vegetables while it's cooking. The stew will be almost ready by the time you're finished chopping.

1. Heat the oil in a large saucepan or Dutch oven over medium heat. Add the onions and celery and cook until lightly browned, 3 minutes. Add the carrots and garlic and cook for 2 minutes. Add the vinegar and stir to break up the brown bits, 1 minute.

2. Add the squash, beans, broth, and sage and bring to a simmer. Cook until the squash is almost tender, 15 minutes. Add the bell pepper and mushrooms and simmer until the vegetables are tender, 5 to 10 minutes.

3. In a small bowl, whisk together the mustard and honey. Stir into the stew until well blended.

170 calories, 4 g protein, 31 g carbohydrates, 7 g fiber, 5 g total fat, 1 g saturated fat, 0 mg cholesterol, 325 mg sodium

# Eggplant Lasagna Serves 12

**Prep Time** • 15 minutes
**Cook Time** • 1 hour, 15 minutes

2 tablespoons olive oil

1 large onion, chopped

2 cloves garlic, minced

1 tablespoon Italian seasoning

2 cans (14 ounces each)
    diced tomatoes

1 can (28 ounces) tomato sauce

1 small eggplant (12 ounces),
    peeled and cut into 1-inch
    pieces

1/4 teaspoon salt

1 container (16 ounces) lite silken
    tofu, drained

2 large eggs

1 cup grated Parmesan cheese

9 no-boil lasagna noodles

1 package (8 ounces) shredded
    part-skim mozzarella cheese

Even though it's not especially rich in vitamins and minerals, eggplant is surprisingly high in antioxidants. It's also an excellent replacement for meat. Here, the eggplant is roasted to mellow any bitterness, blending beautifully with garlic, onions, and tomato for a wholesome, stick-to-your-ribs meal.

1. Preheat the oven to 400°F. Heat the oil in a large saucepan over medium-high heat. Add the onion and cook until tender, about 5 minutes. Add the garlic and Italian seasoning and cook for 1 minute. Add the tomatoes and tomato sauce and bring to a simmer. Reduce the heat to low and simmer until the flavors are blended, 40 minutes.

2. Meanwhile, coat a baking sheet with sides with olive oil cooking spray. Add the eggplant, coat with cooking spray, and sprinkle with the salt. Roast, turning occasionally, until browned, 30 minutes.

3. In a food processor, combine the tofu, eggs, and cheese and puree until smooth.

4. Coat a 9 x 13-inch baking dish with cooking spray. Spread 1 cup sauce on the bottom of the dish and arrange 3 lasagna noodles on top. Spread 1/2 of the tofu filling over the noodles, followed by 1/2 of the eggplant. Top with 1 1/2 cups sauce and 1/2 cup mozzarella. Repeat with another layer, then top with the remaining noodles, sauce, and mozzarella.

5. Cover with foil and bake for 1 hour. Remove the foil and bake until heated through, about 15 minutes. Let cool slightly before serving.

229 calories, 15 g protein, 23 g carbohydrates, 3 g fiber, 10 g total fat,
4 g saturated fat, 51 mg cholesterol, 852 mg sodium

# Three-Bean Chili Serves 8

**Prep Time** • 10 minutes
**Cook Time** • 7 hours, 15 minutes

3 carrots, sliced

3 celery stalks, sliced

2 cloves garlic, minced

1 large onion, chopped

1 can (28 ounces) crushed tomatoes

1 jar (16 ounces) salsa

2 teaspoons chili powder

1 teaspoon ground cumin

1 can (15 1/2 ounces) kidney beans, drained and rinsed

1 can (15 ounces) black beans, drained and rinsed

1 can (15 ounces) white beans, drained and rinsed

1 green bell pepper, chopped

1 red bell pepper, chopped

Every ingredient here is loaded with vitamins, minerals, antioxidants, and fiber. Even better, this simple dish cooks in a slow cooker while you're off living life! To change the flavors, vary the types of salsa—chipotle for a spicy, smoky flavor; roasted garlic for pungent flavor; or mild for just a hint of spice.

1. Place the carrots, celery, garlic, onion, tomatoes, salsa, chili powder, and cumin in a 3 1/2- to 4-quart slow cooker. Cover and cook on high until the vegetables are tender, 5 to 7 hours.

2. Stir in the beans and bell peppers and cook, uncovered, on high until the chili thickens slightly and the peppers are tender, 15 minutes.

299 calories, 19 g protein, 58 g carbohydrates, 20 g fiber, 2 g total fat, 0 g saturated fat, 0 mg cholesterol, 712 mg sodium

# Tuna Kebabs Serves 4

**Prep Time** • 35 minutes
**Cook Time** • 5 minutes

1/4 cup lime juice

1 tablespoon olive oil

1 clove garlic, minced

1 teaspoon grated fresh ginger

1/4 teaspoon salt

1 1/2 pounds tuna steaks, cut into 1 1/2-inch squares

1 pint cherry tomatoes

6 scallions, cut into 2-inch pieces

These mouthwatering kebabs cook up in a jiffy and look pretty on your plate. Fresh tuna, abundant in omega-3s, is very different from the canned variety. Firm and dense, tuna steaks have meaty texture and a milder taste.

1. In a small shallow dish, combine the lime juice, oil, garlic, ginger, and salt. Add the tuna and turn to coat. Let stand 30 minutes, turning once. Place 8 wooden skewers in water and soak for 30 minutes.

2. Preheat the broiler or grill. Lightly coat a broiler pan or grill rack with cooking spray. Alternately thread the tuna, tomatoes, and scallions onto the skewers. Broil or grill, turning once, until the tuna is opaque, 5 minutes.

304 calories, 40 g protein, 7 g carbohydrates, 2 g fiber, 12 g total fat, 3 g saturated fat, 65 mg cholesterol, 226 mg sodium

# Fish Tacos Serves 4

**Prep Time** • 20 minutes
**Cook Time** • 7 minutes

1 tablespoon olive oil

2 cloves garlic, minced

1 teaspoon ground cumin

1/2 teaspoon salt

3 tablespoons lime juice

1 1/2 pounds halibut fillets

1 ripe mango, peeled, seeded,
and chopped

1/2 small red bell pepper, seeded
and finely chopped

1/2 jalapeño pepper, seeded,
deveined, and finely chopped
(wear gloves when handling;
they burn)

1/4 cup chopped cilantro (optional)

8 soft corn tortillas (6 inches)

1 cup shredded lettuce

Here's a truly fun way to enjoy fish. The mango's sweetness marries well with spicy peppers, creating a refreshing salsa. Mangoes are deliciously rich in beta-carotene, vitamin C, potassium, and fiber and contain an enzyme with stomach-soothing properties. Even the corn tortillas are rich in antioxidants.

1. Preheat the broiler. Coat a broiler pan with cooking spray. In a medium bowl, combine the oil, garlic, cumin, salt, 1 tablespoon lime juice, and the fish and toss to coat. Let stand 15 minutes.

2. In a small bowl, combine the mango, bell pepper, jalapeño, cilantro, if desired, and the remaining 2 tablespoons lime juice. Set aside.

3. Wrap the tortillas in foil. Remove the fish from the marinade and place on the broiler pan. Broil until opaque, 3 to 6 minutes. Transfer to a plate and place the tortillas in the oven to warm slightly, 1 minute. Flake the fish.

4. Top the tortillas with equal amounts of lettuce, fish, and salsa.

380 calories, 39 g protein, 36 g carbohydrates, 5 g fiber, 9 g total fat,
1 g saturated fat, 54 mg cholesterol, 430 mg sodium

# Salmon Steaks with Peach Salsa Serves 4

**Prep Time** • 15 minutes
**Cook Time** • 8 minutes

2 peaches, peeled, seeded, and chopped

1 red bell pepper, seeded and chopped

1 jalapeño pepper, seeded, deveined, and minced (wear gloves when handling; they burn)

1 clove garlic, minced

1/2 teaspoon salt

1/2 teaspoon black pepper

2 tablespoons honey

2 tablespoons lime juice

4 salmon steaks (about 1 1/2 pounds)

2 tablespoons olive oil

If peaches aren't in season, substitute frozen (not in syrup) peaches or another seasonal fruit, such as cantaloupe, plums, pears, grapes, or pineapple.

1. In a small bowl, combine the peaches, bell pepper, jalapeño, garlic, 1/4 teaspoon salt, 1/4 teaspoon black pepper, and the honey and lime juice. Toss to coat well and set aside.

2. Sprinkle both sides of the salmon with the remaining 1/4 teaspoon salt and 1/4 teaspoon black pepper. Heat the oil in a large nonstick skillet over high heat. Add the salmon and cook, turning once, until browned and seared, 4 minutes. Reduce the heat to medium-low and cook until opaque, 3 to 4 minutes. Serve with the salsa.

439 calories, 35 g protein, 17 g carbohydrates, 2 g fiber, 26 g total fat, 5 g saturated fat, 100 mg cholesterol, 393 mg sodium

# Tomato-Roasted Mackerel Serves 4

**Prep Time** • 5 minutes
**Cook Time** • 10 minutes

1 pound mackerel fillets

2 tablespoons low-fat canola mayonnaise

1/4 cup basil leaves

2 large tomatoes, sliced

1/2 teaspoon salt

1/4 teaspoon black pepper

Tired of salmon? Mackerel is also a fantastic source of omega-3 fatty acids. Its strong flavor is mellowed by mayo and flavorful tomato and basil. Baking the tomatoes brings out more of their lycopene.

1. Preheat the oven to 400°F. Place the fish on a baking sheet and spread with the mayonnaise. Layer the basil and tomatoes on top of each fillet and sprinkle with the salt and pepper. Bake until the fish is just opaque, 5 to 10 minutes depending on thickness.

268 calories, 22 g protein, 4 g carbohydrates, 1 g fiber, 18 g total fat, 4 g saturated fat, 79 mg cholesterol, 450 mg sodium

# Roasted Salmon with Sautéed Greens Serves 4

**Prep Time** • 5 minutes
**Cook Time** • 10 minutes

1/4 cup balsamic vinegar

2 tablespoons brown sugar

1 teaspoon mustard powder

1/2 teaspoon salt

1 1/4 pounds salmon, cut into
   4 pieces

1 tablespoon olive oil

1 large red onion, cut into
   thin strips

8 ounces baby spinach

Balsamic vinegar adds natural sweetness to savory dishes. It gets its dark color and sweetness from aging in barrels, like wine. For dishes where you'd like the flavor without the dark brown color, opt for white balsamic vinegar.

1. Preheat the broiler or grill. In a small bowl, combine the vinegar, brown sugar, mustard, and salt. Brush 1/2 of the mixture over the salmon. Broil or grill until opaque, 4 to 5 minutes, brushing with the vinegar mixture after 2 minutes.

2. Meanwhile, heat the oil in a large skillet over medium heat. Add the onion and cook until lightly browned, 2 minutes. Cover and cook until tender, 2 minutes. Add the spinach and cook, stirring, until almost wilted, 1 minute. Add the remaining vinegar mixture and cook, stirring, until the spinach is wilted and the sauce thickens slightly, 1 minute.

3. Divide the spinach mixture equally among 4 dinner plates. Top each serving with a piece of salmon.

356 calories, 31 g protein, 13 g carbohydrates, 2 g fiber, 20 g total fat, 4 g saturated fat, 84 mg cholesterol, 428 mg sodium

# Curry-Seared Scallops Serves 4

**Prep Time** • 5 minutes
**Cook Time** • 15 minutes

1/2 cup low-fat plain yogurt

2 teaspoons cornstarch

1 1/2 pounds sea scallops

1 tablespoon curry powder

1/2 teaspoon salt

3 tablespoons olive oil

1 package (10 ounces) grape or
    cherry tomatoes, halved

6 scallions, sliced

You'll never believe this creamy dish is good for you! Antioxidants abound in this dish of delicately sweet sea scallops cooked in curry with tomatoes and scallions. Healthful yogurt creates a sauce you'd swear was made with heavy cream. Serve over cooked brown rice or quinoa if you like.

1. In a small bowl, combine the yogurt and cornstarch and set aside. Place the scallops in a medium bowl, sprinkle with the curry powder and salt, and toss to coat well.

2. Heat 2 tablespoons oil in a large nonstick skillet over medium-high heat. Add the scallops and cook, turning to brown all sides, until well browned and opaque, 3 to 6 minutes. With tongs or a slotted spoon, transfer to a plate.

3. Add the remaining 1 tablespoon oil to the skillet and reduce the heat to low. Add the tomatoes and scallions and cook until tender and lightly browned, about 4 minutes.

4. Return the scallops to the skillet along with the yogurt mixture. Cook until thickened and heated through, 2 minutes.

287 calories, 31 g protein, 12 g carbohydrates, 2 g fiber, 13 g total fat, 2 g saturated fat, 58 mg cholesterol, 595 mg sodium

# Thai Roasted Shrimp Serves 4

**Prep Time** • 5 minutes
**Cook Time** • 15 minutes

1 can (14 ounces) lite coconut milk

1 cup low-sodium vegetable or
    chicken broth

2 tablespoons low-sodium
    soy sauce

1/4–1/2 teaspoon green
    curry paste

1 pound peeled deveined shrimp

8 scallions, thinly sliced

1 large tomato, seeded and
    chopped

1 tablespoon lime juice

2 cups cooked brown rice or quinoa

Lite coconut milk varies from the thick, sweet crème of coconut used in desserts and cocktails. Lower in fat but full of rich flavor, it cools the heat of spicy curry paste and creates a quick, flavorful shrimp dish in minutes.

1. In a large saucepan, whisk together the coconut milk, broth, soy sauce, and curry paste. Bring to a boil over medium-high heat. Add the shrimp and scallions and cook until the shrimp is opaque, 5 minutes.

2. Remove from the heat and stir in the tomato and lime juice. Serve over the rice.

311 calories, 23 g protein, 31 g carbohydrates, 3 g fiber, 9 g total fat, 6 g saturated fat, 168 mg cholesterol, 516 mg sodium

# Baked Chicken with Tomatoes Serves 4

**Prep Time** • 10 minutes
**Cook Time** • 15 minutes

1 egg

1/2 teaspoon salt

1/2 cup toasted Brazil nuts or blanched almonds, finely chopped

1/3 cup wheat germ

4 boneless skinless chicken breast halves

2 tablespoons olive oil

2 cups grape or cherry tomatoes, halved

1 teaspoon dried basil

Extraordinarily rich in the antioxidant trace mineral selenium, Brazil nuts add crunch and health to chicken breast crust. Here, they're blended with wheat germ, which is loaded with vitamin E and folate, for a flavorful, rich crust.

1. Preheat the oven to 425°F. Coat a baking sheet with cooking spray.

2. Place the egg and salt in a shallow dish and whisk with 1 tablespoon water. In another shallow dish, combine the nuts and wheat germ. Dip the chicken breasts into the egg and then the nut mixture. Place on the baking sheet and coat with cooking spray. Bake, turning once, until a thermometer inserted in the center reaches 160°F, 15 minutes.

3. Meanwhile, heat the oil in a large skillet over medium-high heat. Add the tomatoes and basil and cook until just browned, 3 minutes. Serve with the chicken.

371 calories, 34 g protein, 10 g carbohydrates, 4 g fiber, 22 g total fat, 5 g saturated fat, 121 mg cholesterol, 391 mg sodium

# Chicken-Barley Bake Serves 4

**Prep Time** • 5 minutes
**Cook Time** • 1 hour, 5 minutes

2 tablespoons olive oil

1 onion, chopped

1 clove garlic, minced

1 cup pearled barley

1 1/2 cups chicken broth

1 cup orange juice

1 teaspoon dried thyme, crushed

1/2 teaspoon salt

4 skinless bone-in chicken breast halves

1/2 cup dried cranberries

1 orange, washed and sliced (optional)

With a robust nutty flavor, barley's so high in soluble fiber that it can lower high cholesterol and even help stabilize blood sugar. Blended here with orange and cranberry, it becomes a tasty base for roasted chicken breasts.

1. Preheat the oven to 350°F. Coat a 9 x 13-inch baking pan with cooking spray.

2. Heat the oil in a large skillet over medium heat. Add the onion and garlic and cook until tender, 2 minutes. Add the barley and cook for 2 minutes. Add the broth, orange juice, thyme, and salt and bring to a boil. Carefully pour into the baking pan. Top with the chicken breasts, cover, and bake for 45 minutes.

3. Uncover and stir the cranberries into the barley mixture. If desired, top each chicken breast with 1 or 2 orange slices. Bake until the chicken is cooked and the barley is tender, 15 minutes.

451 calories, 34 g protein, 58 g carbohydrates, 10 g fiber, 10 g total fat, 2 g saturated fat, 68 mg cholesterol, 548 mg sodium

# Chicken in Garlic Sauce Serves 4

**Prep Time** • 5 minutes
**Cook Time** • 13 minutes

2 tablespoons olive oil

4 boneless skinless chicken breast halves

4 cloves garlic, minced

1/4 cup white wine or white balsamic vinegar

1 3/4 cups chicken broth

Help prevent heart disease with this dish bursting with garlic. Serve over brown rice with steamed broccoli on the side for a scrumptious meal in minutes.

1. Heat the oil in a large skillet over medium heat. Add the chicken and cook until browned on both sides, 5 minutes. Transfer to a plate.

2. Add the garlic to the skillet and cook until just tender, 2 minutes. Add the wine and cook, stirring to loosen the brown bits, 3 minutes. Add the broth and return the chicken and any accumulated juices to the skillet. Cook until a thermometer inserted in the center of the chicken reaches 160°F, about 5 minutes.

214 calories, 28 g protein, 3 g carbohydrates, 0 g fiber, 8 g total fat, 1 g saturated fat, 68 mg cholesterol, 268 mg sodium

# Turkey Cutlets with Grapefruit Salsa Serves 4

**Prep Time** • 10 minutes
**Cook Time** • 3 minutes

2 ruby red grapefruits, sectioned
   and chopped

1/2 small red bell pepper, seeded
   and minced

4 scallions, chopped

1 tablespoon olive oil

1/2 teaspoon sugar

1 pound turkey breast cutlets

1/4 teaspoon salt

1/4 teaspoon black pepper

Always reach for red grapefruits, which are not only a great source of vitamin C but are also rich in lycopene. Here, they blend with crunchy bell pepper and pungent scallions for a flavorful medley that's perfect atop browned turkey cutlets.

1. In a small bowl, combine the grapefruit, bell pepper, scallions, oil, and sugar. Set aside.

2. Season the cutlets with the salt and pepper. Coat a large skillet with cooking spray and heat over medium heat. Add the cutlets, in batches if necessary, and cook until browned on both sides and cooked through, 3 minutes. Transfer to a plate and top with the salsa.

203 calories, 29 g protein, 13 g carbohydrates, 3 g fiber, 4 g total fat,
0 g saturated fat, 45 mg cholesterol, 256 mg sodium

# Turkey Ragu with Spaghetti Serves 6

**Prep Time** • 15 minutes
**Cook Time** • 1 hour, 15 minutes

2 tablespoons olive oil

2 carrots, finely chopped

1 onion, finely chopped

1 red bell pepper, finely chopped

2 cloves garlic, minced

1 pound ground turkey breast

1/2 cup white wine or chicken broth

1 can (28 ounces) crushed tomatoes

1 can (6 ounces) tomato paste

1 teaspoon Italian seasoning

12 ounces whole wheat spaghetti

1/2 cup low-fat milk

Where's the beef? You'll never miss it in this hearty tomato sauce studded with vegetables and ground turkey. Ground turkey, a low-fat substitute for ground beef, works best when bathed in a healthful, flavorful sauce.

1. Heat the oil in a large saucepan over medium heat. Add the carrots, onion, and bell pepper and cook until lightly browned, 5 minutes. Add the garlic and turkey and cook, stirring, until the turkey is no longer pink, 5 minutes. Add the wine and cook until the liquid is absorbed, 4 minutes.

2. Add the tomatoes, tomato paste, and Italian seasoning. Reduce the heat to low, cover, and simmer until well blended, 1 hour.

3. About 15 minutes before serving, cook the spaghetti according to package directions.

4. Remove the sauce from the heat and stir in the milk. Serve over the hot pasta.

437 calories, 32 g protein, 66 g carbohydrates, 13 g fiber, 7 g total fat, 1 g saturated fat, 31 mg cholesterol, 470 mg sodium

# Barbecued Flank Steak Serves 4

**Prep Time** • 6 hours, 5 minutes
**Cook Time** • 13 minutes

2 cloves garlic, grated

1 small onion, grated

1/2 cup tomato sauce

2 tablespoons red wine vinegar

2 tablespoons brown sugar

1 tablespoon Worcestershire sauce

1/4 teaspoon salt

1 pound flank steak

It may be lower in fat than many other cuts of beef, but flank steak, an excellent source of protein, vitamins, and minerals, is bursting with rich flavor. Marinated in a healthy homemade barbecue sauce, it's sure to be a crowd pleaser.

1. In a large zipper-seal bag, combine the garlic, onion, tomato sauce, vinegar, brown sugar, and Worcestershire. Add the steak, seal the bag, and turn to coat. Refrigerate for 6 hours or overnight.

2. Preheat the broiler or grill. Remove the steak from the marinade, reserving the marinade. Broil the steak 2 to 3 inches from the heat source or grill until a thermometer inserted in the center reaches 145°F for medium-rare, 13 minutes. Transfer to a cutting board.

3. Meanwhile, place the marinade in a small saucepan, bring to a boil, and cook for 4 minutes. Slice the steak and serve with the sauce.

219 calories, 25 g protein, 11 g carbohydrates, 1 g fiber, 8 g total fat, 3 g saturated fat, 40 mg cholesterol, 415 mg sodium

# Herb-Crusted Roast Beef Serves 12

**Prep Time** • 15 minutes
**Cook Time** • 1 hour, 5 minutes

1 top round beef roast (about
   3 pounds), trimmed of all
   visible fat

5 cloves garlic, minced

1 tablespoon olive oil

1 teaspoon dried basil

1 teaspoon dried thyme

1 teaspoon mustard powder

1 teaspoon salt

1 teaspoon black pepper

Yes, roast beef can be healthy! Top round is a very tender yet lean roast—delicious topped with garlic, basil, thyme, and mustard.

1. Preheat the oven to 350°F. Rinse the meat and pat dry. Place on a rack in a large roasting pan.

2. In a small bowl, combine the garlic, oil, basil, thyme, mustard, salt, and pepper. Rub the mixture over the meat.

3. Roast until a thermometer inserted in the center reaches 145°F for medium-rare or 160°F for medium, 55 to 65 minutes. Transfer to a cutting board and let stand for 10 minutes before slicing.

169 calories, 26 g protein, 1 g carbohydrates, 0 g fiber, 6 g total fat, 2 g saturated fat, 62 mg cholesterol, 264 mg sodium

# Beef and Broccoli Stew Serves 4

**Prep Time** • 10 minutes
**Cook Time** • 35 minutes

4 tablespoons olive oil

1 pound top round steak, cut into
1-inch pieces, then halved

1/4 teaspoon black pepper

1/4 teaspoon cayenne pepper

2 onions, cut into wedges

1 clove garlic, mashed

1 tablespoon minced fresh ginger

1/4 cup low-sodium soy sauce

3 1/2 cups low-sodium beef broth

3 carrots, cut into 2-inch julienne
strips

1 bunch broccoli, cut into florets

2 tablespoons cornstarch mixed
with 2 tablespoons water

This hearty stew contains an unexpected taste twist—inflammation-fighting ginger—and cooks in no time, making it a favorite for weeknight meals. Serve with cooked brown rice or crusty whole-grain bread.

1. Heat 2 tablespoons oil in a large saucepan over high heat. Season the meat with the black pepper and cayenne. Add 1/2 of the meat to the saucepan and stir-fry until no longer pink, 2 minutes, then transfer to a bowl. Repeat with the remaining meat.

2. Add the onions to the saucepan and cook until lightly browned, 4 minutes. Stir in the garlic and ginger and cook for 1 minute.

3. Add the soy sauce and broth and bring to a boil over high heat. Reduce the heat to medium-low, add the carrots and broccoli, and cook until crisp-tender, 10 minutes.

4. Add the beef and any drippings from the bowl. Stir in the cornstarch mixture and cook until thickened, 2 minutes.

429 calories, 31 g protein, 29 g carbohydrates, 7 g fiber, 22 g total fat, 5 g saturated fat, 70 mg cholesterol, 997 mg sodium

# Pork Chops with Dried Fruits Serves 4

**Prep Time** • 5 minutes
**Cook Time** • 30 minutes

4 boneless pork chops (about
1 pound)

1/4 teaspoon salt

1/4 teaspoon black pepper

2 tablespoons olive oil

1 medium onion, finely chopped

1 1/4 cups apple cider or juice

1 package (6 ounces) dried sliced
apples

1/2 cup pitted prunes

1 tablespoon fresh thyme or
1 teaspoon dried thyme

Simmering boneless pork chops and dried fruits in apple cider creates a succulent, creamy sauce. Lovely enough to serve to guests, this simple dish is rich in fiber and low-fat protein.

1. Sprinkle the chops with the salt and pepper. Heat 1 tablespoon oil in a large skillet over medium-high heat. Add the chops and cook, turning once, until browned on both sides, 4 minutes. Transfer to a plate and keep warm.

2. Add the remaining 1 tablespoon oil to the skillet. Add the onion and cook until lightly browned, 4 minutes. Add the cider and bring to a simmer, stirring to loosen the browned bits. Return the chops to the skillet and add the apples, prunes, and thyme. Reduce the heat to medium-low, cover, and simmer until the chops reach 160°F on an instant-read thermometer, about 10 minutes.

404 calories, 21 g protein, 51 g carbohydrates, 4 g fiber, 12 g total fat, 3 g saturated fat, 59 mg cholesterol, 491 mg sodium

# Harvest Pork Roast Serves 8

**Prep Time** • 30 minutes
**Cook Time** • 1 hour, 15 minutes

1 butternut squash (about 2 pounds), peeled, seeded, and cut into 2-inch pieces

2 red onions, cut into wedges

2 large red bell peppers, seeded and cut into 2-inch pieces

2 tablespoons olive oil

1 teaspoon salt

1 teaspoon black pepper

1 teaspoon ground ginger

1/2 teaspoon ground allspice

1/2 teaspoon ground cinnamon

1 boneless pork loin roast (about 2 pounds)

2 cups apple cider

When company's coming, serve this roast spiked with health benefits from the vegetables as well as the spices. Red onions, red bell peppers, and butternut squash tossed in ginger olive oil are a powerhouse of nutrients and are bursting with great flavor.

1. Preheat the oven to 400°F. Place the squash, onions, and peppers in a large roasting pan. Drizzle with the oil, sprinkle with 1/2 teaspoon salt and 1/2 teaspoon black pepper, and toss to coat well. Set aside.

2. In a small bowl, combine the ginger, allspice, and cinnamon and stir to blend well. Remove 1 teaspoon spice mixture, place in a small saucepan, and set aside.

3. Add the remaining 1/2 teaspoon salt and 1/2 teaspoon black pepper to the bowl with the spice mixture. Rub the mixture over the meat and place the meat on a rack in the pan. Roast until the vegetables are tender and an instant-read thermometer inserted in the center of the meat reaches 150°F, about 1 hour.

4. Meanwhile, add the cider to the saucepan with the spice mixture. Bring to a boil over high heat and cook until thick and syrupy and reduced to about 1/2 cup, about 40 minutes.

5. When the meat is cooked, transfer to a cutting board and let stand for 10 minutes. Pour 1/2 of the cider mixture over the vegetables in the pan and toss to coat well. Roast for 5 minutes. Serve with the meat. Use the rest of the cider mixture as gravy.

294 calories, 25 g protein, 25 g carbohydrates, 4 g fiber, 11 g total fat, 3 g saturated fat, 73 mg cholesterol, 360 mg sodium

# Shiitake Green Beans  Serves 4

**Prep Time** • 5 minutes
**Cook Time** • 12 minutes

1 pound green beans, trimmed

2 tablespoons olive oil

8 ounces shiitake mushrooms, cleaned and stems removed

1 clove garlic, minced

1 tomato, seeded and chopped

1/2 teaspoon salt

Shiitake mushrooms deserve a place on your plate thanks not only to their rich, earthy flavor but also to their immunity-boosting qualities. Here, they blend with tomato to turn ordinary green beans into a tasty dish.

1. Bring 2 inches of water to a boil in a large saucepan over high heat. Insert a steamer basket and add the beans. Cover and cook over medium heat until bright green and crisp-tender, 4 minutes. Transfer to a serving plate and keep warm.

2. Meanwhile, heat the oil in a large skillet over medium-high heat. Add the mushrooms and cook, stirring, until browned and tender, 5 minutes. Add the garlic, tomato, and salt and cook, stirring, until the tomato is tender and the mixture forms a sauce, 3 minutes. Spoon over the green beans.

109 calories, 3 g protein, 11 g carbohydrates, 5 g fiber, 7 g total fat, 1 g saturated fat, 0 mg cholesterol, 300 mg sodium

# Roasted Root Vegetables  Serves 4

**Prep Time** • 10 minutes
**Cook Time** • 40 minutes

1 pound carrots, peeled and sliced diagonally into 1/2-inch pieces

1 pound parsnips, peeled and sliced diagonally into 1/2-inch pieces

2 tablespoons olive oil

1 tablespoon grated fresh ginger

1 teaspoon ground cinnamon

1/2 teaspoon salt

Parsnips and carrots are related, and although both are good sources of fiber, they're nutritionally different. Carrots burst with beta-carotene, while parsnips are rich in potassium. Roasting with ginger and cinnamon lends them both an especially savory flavor.

1. Preheat the oven to 400°F. Place the carrots, parsnips, oil, ginger, cinnamon, and salt in a large roasting pan and toss to coat well. Roast, turning occasionally, until tender and browned, 40 minutes.

199 calories, 3 g protein, 33 g carbohydrates, 9 g fiber, 7 g total fat, 1 g saturated fat, 0 mg cholesterol, 361 mg sodium

# Brussels Sprouts with Caramelized Onions Serves 4

**Prep Time** • 10 minutes
**Cook Time** • 20 minutes

1 pound brussels sprouts, trimmed and halved

2 tablespoons olive oil

1 medium white onion, halved lengthwise and sliced

1 medium red onion, halved lengthwise and sliced

1 tablespoon fresh thyme, chopped, or 1 teaspoon dried thyme

1/2 teaspoon salt

1 tablespoon white balsamic vinegar

Brussels sprouts fight cancer, and their soluble fiber should help lower your cholesterol, too. But their taste may be too strong for some. Here, sweet, tender onions beautifully mellow their flavor.

1. Bring 1 inch of water to a boil in a large saucepan over medium-high heat. Insert a steamer basket, reduce the heat to medium, and add the sprouts, Cover and cook until crisp-tender, about 7 minutes.

2. Meanwhile, heat the oil in a medium saucepan over medium heat. Add the onions and cook, stirring occasionally, until browned, about 4 minutes. Add the thyme and salt, then reduce the heat to low, cover, and cook until very tender and browned, 10 minutes. Stir in the vinegar.

3. Place the sprouts in a serving dish, top with the onion mixture, and toss to coat.

141 calories, 5 g protein, 18 g carbohydrates, 6 g fiber, 7 g total fat, 1 g saturated fat, 0 mg cholesterol, 333 mg sodium

# Roasted Broccoli with Cheese Serves 4

**Prep Time** • 5 minutes
**Cook Time** • 15 minutes

1 pound broccoli, cut into spears

3 tablespoons olive oil

2 cloves garlic, minced

1 teaspoon red pepper flakes

1/4 teaspoon salt

1/4 cup shredded Romano cheese

Roasting softens the characteristic taste of this nutritional superstar. Here it's tossed with garlic, hot red pepper, and olive oil for a simple, flavor-loaded side dish.

1. Preheat the oven to 425°F. Place the broccoli in a large roasting pan, drizzle with the oil, and sprinkle with the garlic, red pepper flakes, and salt. Toss to coat well. Roast until tender and browned, 15 minutes. Sprinkle the hot broccoli with the cheese.

162 calories, 6 g protein, 8 g carbohydrates, 3 g fiber, 13 g total fat, 3 g saturated fat, 8 mg cholesterol, 273 mg sodium

# Creamed Spinach Serves 4

**Prep Time** • 5 minutes
**Cook Time** • 11 minutes

2 tablespoons olive oil

1 large onion, halved and thinly sliced

1/2 cup vegetable or chicken broth

10 ounces baby spinach

2 ounces reduced-fat cream cheese

1/4 cup shredded Romano cheese

1/2 teaspoon ground nutmeg

Spinach may have made Popeye strong, but it'll do a lot more for you. It's jam-packed with the B vitamin folate—a cancer fighter—and carotenoids such as lutein, which helps prevent macular degeneration. Here, it's delicious tossed in a light cream sauce prepared with just a touch of reduced-fat cream cheese.

1. Heat the oil in a large skillet over medium heat. Add the onion and cook until lightly browned, 5 minutes. Add the broth and cook for 1 minute. Add the spinach and cook, stirring, until wilted, 3 minutes. Stir in the cream cheese and Romano and cook, stirring, until well blended and creamy, 3 minutes.

178 calories, 7 g protein, 14 g carbohydrates, 5 g fiber, 12 g total fat, 4 g saturated fat, 14 mg cholesterol, 328 mg sodium

# Brown Rice Risotto Serves 4

**Prep Time** • 10 minutes
**Cook Time** • 1 hour

2 tablespoons olive oil

1 medium onion, chopped

1 medium red bell pepper, seeded
  and chopped

1 cup brown rice, preferably short
  or medium grain

1 clove garlic, minced

1/2 teaspoon turmeric

3 1/2 cups low-sodium
  chicken broth

1/3 cup grated Romano cheese

Whole-grain brown rice mimics Arborio rice in this hearty dish reminiscent of risotto. The turmeric adds great color as well as anti-inflammatory benefits.

1. Preheat the oven to 425°F. Heat the oil in a large ovenproof saucepan or Dutch oven over medium heat. Add the onion and bell pepper and cook for 3 minutes. Add the rice, garlic, and turmeric and cook until the rice is shiny and coated with oil, 2 minutes. Add the broth and bring to a boil.

2. Cover and bake until the broth is absorbed and the rice is just tender, about 55 minutes. Top with the cheese, then cover and let stand for 5 minutes.

305 calories, 8 g protein, 43 g carbohydrates, 3 g fiber, 11 g total fat,
3 g saturated fat, 10 mg cholesterol, 220 mg sodium

# Almond Rice Serves 6

**Prep Time** • 5 minutes
**Cook Time** • 55 minutes

2 tablespoons olive oil

1 medium onion, chopped

1 clove garlic, minced

1 cup brown rice

1/2 cup wild rice

1 cup orange juice

1 teaspoon ground ginger

1/2 cup toasted almonds, chopped

1/2 cup raisins

For a change of pace, try short-grain brown rice in this dish. It has a chewier texture and nuttier flavor than long-grain brown rice and can be used interchangeably with it.

1. Heat the oil in a medium saucepan over medium heat. Add the onion and garlic and cook until just beginning to brown, 3 minutes.

2. Add the brown and wild rice, 1 1/2 cups water, and the orange juice and ginger. Bring to a boil, then reduce the heat to low, cover, and simmer until the rice is tender, 50 minutes. Stir in the almonds and raisins.

317 calories, 7 g protein, 53 g carbohydrates, 4 g fiber, 10 g total fat, 1 g saturated fat, 0 mg cholesterol, 8 mg sodium

# Springtime Quinoa Serves 6

**Prep Time** • 10 minutes
**Cook Time** • 25 minutes

1 cup quinoa, rinsed and drained

1/2 teaspoon salt

1 tablespoon olive oil

1 small red onion, halved and cut into thin slices

1/2 cup vegetable or chicken broth

1 pound asparagus, cut into 2-inch pieces

1 cup fresh or thawed frozen peas

High-fiber, protein-rich quinoa has a nutty flavor and a creamy, fluffy texture. It can easily replace white rice in dishes and cooks in half the time of brown rice. Here, it's tossed with healthful vegetables that are most delicious when fresh in the spring.

1. In a small saucepan over high heat, bring the quinoa, salt, and 2 cups water to a boil. Reduce the heat to low, cover, and simmer until all the water is absorbed, 15 minutes.

2. Meanwhile, heat the oil in a large nonstick skillet over medium heat. Add the onion and cook until lightly browned, 4 minutes. Add the broth, asparagus, and peas and cook until crisp-tender, 5 minutes. Stir in the quinoa.

171 calories, 8 g protein, 28 g carbohydrates, 5 g fiber, 4 g total fat, 1 g saturated fat, 0 mg cholesterol, 262 mg sodium

# Pasta with Walnut Cream Sauce Serves 4

**Prep Time** • 10 minutes
**Cook Time** • 10 minutes

8 ounces whole-grain penne, fusilli, or farfalle pasta

1 cup walnuts, toasted

1–3 cloves garlic, mashed

1/4 cup basil leaves

2 tablespoons olive oil

1/2 cup low-fat evaporated milk

1/4 cup grated Parmesan cheese

Walnuts are the base of this creamy pesto-like sauce that's so rich and delicious you'd swear it was loaded with heavy cream. Serve over whole-grain pasta, and you have a high-fiber, omega-3–rich side dish that's sure to become a favorite.

1. Cook the pasta according to package directions.

2. Meanwhile, place the nuts, garlic, and basil in a food processor or blender and process until the nuts are finely chopped. Add the oil and milk and pulse until well blended.

3. Toss the sauce with the hot pasta and sprinkle with the cheese.

479 calories, 16 g protein, 49 g carbohydrates, 4 g fiber, 26 g total fat, 4 g saturated fat, 9 mg cholesterol, 115 mg sodium


# Orange Beets Serves 6

**Prep Time** • 15 minutes
**Cook Time** • 55 minutes

1 1/2 pounds beets with greens (about 4 medium beets)

1 tablespoon olive oil

1 clove garlic, minced

1/2 teaspoon salt

3 tablespoons orange marmalade

1 tablespoon white wine vinegar

1/4 teaspoon black pepper

If you've only had beets from a can, give fresh ones a chance. They're mild, delicious, and sure to become a favorite. Here, flavorful, folate-rich beets are tossed with sautéed beet greens, high in beta-carotene, and bathed in a sweet marmalade sauce.

1. Preheat the oven to 350°F. Trim the greens from the beets and set aside. Fold a 36-inch piece of foil in half crosswise. Scrub the beets and place in the center of the foil. Sprinkle with 1 teaspoon water and seal the foil around the beets. Roast until tender, about 45 minutes. Let cool for 15 minutes, then remove the skins and cut each beet into 8 wedges.

2. Meanwhile, trim the stems from the beet greens, wash the greens, and cut into 1-inch strips. While the beets are cooling, heat the oil in a skillet over medium-high heat. Add the garlic and cook for 1 minute. Add the greens and 1/4 teaspoon salt and cook, stirring constantly, until wilted, 2 minutes. Transfer to a serving dish.

3. Add the marmalade, vinegar, pepper, and the remaining 1/4 teaspoon salt to the skillet and cook until hot and bubbling. Add the beets and toss to coat well. Transfer to the serving dish and toss with the greens.

75 calories, 1 g protein, 13 g carbohydrates, 2 g fiber, 2 g total fat, 0 g saturated fat, 0 mg cholesterol, 253 mg sodium

# Blueberry-Oat Scones Serves 12

**Prep Time** • 10 minutes
**Cook Time** • 15 minutes

1 cup whole oats, ground

1 cup whole-wheat pastry flour

1/4 cup sugar

2 teaspoons baking powder

1/2 teaspoon baking soda

1/2 teaspoon salt

1 cup low-fat plain yogurt

2 tablespoons canola oil

1/2 pint blueberries

1 teaspoon grated lemon zest

A great way to add the fiber and wholesomeness of whole oats to foods is by grinding it into flour. Here, half of the wheat flour is replaced by ground oats.

1. Preheat the oven to 400°F. Lightly coat a baking sheet with cooking spray.

2. In a large bowl, whisk together the ground oats, flour, sugar, baking powder, baking soda, and salt. In a measuring cup, stir together the yogurt and oil.

3. Make a well in the center of the flour mixture and add the yogurt mixture. Add the blueberries and lemon zest and stir just until blended.

4. Drop by 1/4 cups onto the baking sheet. Bake until lightly browned, 12 to 15 minutes.

112 calories, 3 g protein, 18 g carbohydrates, 2 g fiber, 3 g total fat, 0 g saturated fat, 2 mg cholesterol, 255 mg sodium

# Raspberry-Almond Muffins Serves 12

**Prep Time** • 10 minutes
**Cook Time** • 20 minutes

2 cups whole-wheat pastry flour

1 cup almonds, toasted and finely chopped

2 tablespoons wheat germ

1 tablespoon baking powder

1/2 teaspoon salt

1 cup soy milk

1/2 cup honey

1 egg

3 tablespoons canola oil

1 teaspoon vanilla extract

1/4 teaspoon almond extract (optional)

1 cup fresh or frozen raspberries

Use baked goods like these scrumptious muffins, bursting with antioxidants (almonds are a surprising source), to sneak some soy milk into your diet. You can substitute it equally for dairy milk.

1. Preheat the oven to 400°F. Lightly coat a 12-cup muffin pan with cooking spray.

2. In a large bowl, whisk together the flour, almonds, wheat germ, baking powder, and salt. In a medium bowl, whisk together the milk, honey, egg, oil, and vanilla. Add the almond extract, if desired.

3. Make a well in the center of the flour mixture and add the milk mixture. Stir just until blended, then gently fold in the raspberries. Pour the batter into the muffin pan.

4. Bake until a wooden pick inserted in the center of a muffin comes out clean, 20 minutes.

198 calories, 5 g protein, 29 g carbohydrates, 4 g fiber, 8 g total fat, 1 g saturated fat, 0 mg cholesterol, 246 mg sodium

**Blueberry-Oat Scones and Raspberry-Almond Muffins** Breads and Baked Goods 629

# Banana-Peanut Bread Serves 10

**Prep Time** • 10 minutes
**Cook Time** • 20 minutes

3 very ripe medium bananas, mashed (about 1 cup)

1/2 cup natural peanut butter

2 eggs

1 tablespoon canola oil

1 1/2 cups whole-wheat pastry flour

1/2 cup whole oats, ground

1/4 cup sugar

2 tablespoons ground flaxseed

2 teaspoons baking powder

1/2 teaspoon baking soda

1/2 teaspoon salt

Spice up your banana bread with peanut butter! It adds protein, vitamins, monounsaturated fat, and great flavor to this bread, also a good source of fiber.

1. Preheat the oven to 350°F. Lightly coat a 5 x 9-inch loaf pan with cooking spray.

2. In a medium bowl, stir together the bananas, peanut butter, eggs, and oil. In a large bowl, whisk together the flour, oats, sugar, flaxseed, baking powder, baking soda, and salt.

3. Make a well in the center of the flour mixture, add the banana mixture, and stir just until moistened. Place in the pan.

4. Bake until a wooden pick inserted in the center comes out clean, 40 to 50 minutes. Transfer to a rack and let cool for 5 minutes, then remove from the pan and let cool completely.

234 calories, 7 g protein, 31 g carbohydrates, 4 g fiber, 9 g total fat, 1 g saturated fat, 42 mg cholesterol, 351 mg sodium

# Zesty Cornbread Serves 8 *(See photograph, p. 337)*

**Prep Time** • 20 minutes
**Cook Time** • 30 minutes

4 tablespoons canola oil

1 small red bell pepper, seeded and chopped

1 jalapeño pepper, seeded, deveined, and minced (wear gloves when handling; they burn)

1 small onion, chopped

1 clove garlic, minced

1 cup cornmeal

1 cup whole-wheat pastry flour

2 teaspoons baking powder

1/2 teaspoon salt

1 cup soy milk

1 egg, beaten

Cornmeal is a grain (a whole grain if you buy whole cornmeal) that's quite rich in folate and iron. Try preparing this bread the old-fashioned way—baked in a cast-iron skillet. Not only is cooking in cast iron delicious and easy, it adds iron to the food.

1. Preheat the oven to 375°F. Coat a 9-inch square baking pan with cooking spray.

2. Heat 1 tablespoon oil in a medium skillet over medium heat. Add the bell pepper, jalapeño, and onion and cook until lightly browned, 4 minutes. Add the garlic and cook for 1 minute. Remove from the heat.

3. In a large bowl, stir together the cornmeal, flour, baking powder, and salt. In a measuring cup, combine the milk, egg, and remaining oil. Make a well in the center of the cornmeal mixture, add the milk and pepper mixtures, and stir just until blended. Place in the pan.

4. Bake until a wooden pick inserted in the center comes out clean, 30 minutes.

205 calories, 6 g protein, 27 g carbohydrates, 3 g fiber, 9 g total fat, 1 g saturated fat, 26 mg cholesterol, 310 mg sodium

# Pumpkin Streusel Bread — Makes 2 loaves

**Prep Time** • 25 minutes
**Cook Time** • 50 minutes

## Topping

1/3 cup pumpkin seeds

2 tablespoons packed brown sugar

2 teaspoons canola oil

## Bread

1 can (15 ounces) pumpkin puree

1 cup soy milk

1/2 cup canola oil

4 large eggs

1 cup packed brown sugar

3 1/2 cups whole-wheat
   pastry flour

1/4 cup ground flaxseed

4 teaspoons baking powder

2 teaspoons ground cinnamon

1 teaspoon ground ginger

1/2 teaspoon freshly
   ground nutmeg

3/4 teaspoon salt

You'd never know this delicious, sweet bread offers so many health benefits. Pumpkin seeds, also known as pepitas, are loaded with magnesium, and canned pumpkin is just about the best source of beta-carotene on Earth. We've even sneaked some flaxseed into this bread.

1. Preheat the oven to 350°F. Coat two 4 x 8-inch loaf pans with cooking spray.

2. *To make the topping:* In a small bowl, stir together the pumpkin seeds, brown sugar, and oil. Set aside.

3. *To make the bread:* In a medium bowl, combine the pumpkin, milk, oil, eggs, and brown sugar. In a large bowl, combine the flour, flaxseed, baking powder, cinnamon, ginger, nutmeg, and salt.

4. Make a well in the center of the flour mixture, add the pumpkin mixture, and stir just until blended. Place in the pans and top with the pumpkin seed mixture, pressing the seeds gently into the top.

5. Bake until a wooden pick inserted in the center comes out clean, 50 minutes. Transfer to a rack and let cool for 10 minutes, then remove from the pans and let cool completely.

226 calories, 5 g protein, 31 g carbohydrates, 3 g fiber, 9 g total fat,
1 g saturated fat, 42 mg cholesterol, 252 mg sodium

# Cinnamon-Raisin Coffee Cake Serves 12

**Prep Time** • 1 hour, 40 minutes
**Cook Time** • 30 minutes

1 cup low-fat granola with almonds

1 cup yogurt cheese (see page 292)

1 cup sugar

3 eggs

1/3 cup canola oil

1 tablespoon vanilla extract

1 teaspoon ground cinnamon

1 1/2 teaspoons baking powder

1 teaspoon baking soda

1/2 teaspoon salt

2 1/4 cups whole-wheat pastry flour

1/2 cup raisins

Nutrient-rich yogurt replaces the butter of typical coffee cakes, but you'll never notice in this moist, tender treat. The cinnamon helps lower blood sugar, and the raisins offer blood pressure–lowering potassium.

1. Preheat the oven to 350°F. Coat a Bundt pan with cooking spray. Sprinkle the granola into the bottom of the pan.

2. In a large bowl, whisk together the yogurt cheese, sugar, eggs, oil, vanilla, and cinnamon. Stir in the baking powder, baking soda, and salt. Add the flour and whisk until well blended, then fold in the raisins. Pour into the pan.

3. Bake until a wooden pick inserted in the center comes out clean, 30 minutes. Transfer to a rack and let cool for 10 minutes, then remove from the pan and let cool completely.

279 calories, 7 g protein, 45 g carbohydrates, 3 g fiber, 8 g total fat, 1 g saturated fat, 55 mg cholesterol, 333 mg sodium

# Chocolate-Almond Biscotti Makes 4 dozen

**Prep Time** • 3 hours
**Cook Time** • 1 hour

2 1/2 cups whole-wheat pastry flour

3/4 cup sugar

2 teaspoons baking powder

1 teaspoon ground cinnamon

1 teaspoon salt

1 1/2 cups whole almonds

6 ounces bittersweet chocolate (60% or higher cocoa content), chopped

4 large eggs

These low-fat cookies are bursting with flavor. Packed with almonds, which are a great source of vitamin E, and drizzled with antioxidant-rich chocolate, they're perfect with an after-dinner cup of coffee.

1. Preheat the oven to 350°F. Line a baking sheet with parchment paper. In a large bowl, whisk together the flour, sugar, baking powder, cinnamon, and salt. Stir in the almonds and 2/3 of the chocolate.

2. Beat the eggs in a small bowl, then stir into the flour mixture. Place the dough on a lightly floured surface and knead until smooth. Cut in half and shape each piece into a log 12 inches long and 3 inches thick. Place on the baking sheet and bake until the outside seems firm and puffed, 30 minutes. Transfer to a rack and let cool completely, 2 hours.

3. With a serrated knife, cut the logs crosswise into slices about 1/2 inch thick. Place the slices on their sides on the parchment-lined baking pan and bake, turning once, until crisp and lightly browned, 30 minutes. Transfer to a rack and let cool for 30 minutes.

4. Meanwhile, place the remaining chocolate in a small bowl and microwave on low until almost melted, 1 minute. Stir until melted completely. Drizzle over the biscotti.

80 calories, 2 g protein, 10 g carbohydrates, 1 g fiber, 4 g total fat, 1 g saturated fat, 18 mg cholesterol, 75 mg sodium

# Chock-Full Chocolate Chip Cookies Makes 5 dozen

**Prep Time** • 15 minutes
**Cook Time** • 50 minutes

1 1/2 cups whole-wheat
    pastry flour

1 cup whole oats, ground

1/3 cup cocoa powder

1 teaspoon baking soda

1/2 teaspoon salt

1 cup nonhydrogenated butter-
    replacement stick margarine

1/2 cup granulated sugar

1 cup packed light brown sugar

2 eggs

1 tablespoon vanilla extract

1 cup bittersweet chocolate chips
    (60% or higher cocoa content)

1 cup raisins

1 cup walnuts, coarsely chopped

Yes, you can have your chocolate and eat it, too! The darker the chocolate, the healthier it is, so these cookies boast both cocoa powder and 60% cocoa chips. To make them even tastier and healthier, raisins and nuts are added with the chocolate chips.

1. Preheat the oven to 350°F. In a medium bowl, whisk together the flour, oats, cocoa, baking soda, and salt.

2. In a large bowl, with an electric mixer at medium speed, beat the margarine with the granulated and brown sugar until light and fluffy, 2 minutes. Add the eggs and vanilla and beat until smooth. Beat in the flour mixture until combined. Stir in the chocolate chips, raisins, and walnuts. Drop by teaspoons onto a baking sheet.

3. Bake until browned, 10 minutes. Let cool on the baking sheet for 2 minutes, then transfer to a rack and let cool completely.

97 calories, 1 g protein, 12 g carbohydrates, 1 g fiber, 5 g total fat,
2 g saturated fat, 7 mg cholesterol, 77 mg sodium

# Chocolate-Pecan Torte Serves 16

**Prep Time** • 2 hours, 20 minutes
**Cook Time** • 40 minutes

1 1/2 cups pecan halves

1 cup sugar

6 ounces bittersweet chocolate
   (60% or higher cocoa content)

6 eggs, separated

1/4 cup cocoa powder

1/3 cup orange juice

1 teaspoon grated orange zest

Confectioners' sugar (optional)

Orange sections (optional)

This rich cake, loaded with antioxidants, tastes best the day after baking, so whenever possible, make it ahead of time. Store, covered, at room temperature for a few days or freeze any extra for future use.

1. Preheat the oven to 350°F. Coat a 10-inch springform pan with cooking spray. Place the pecans and 1/2 cup sugar in a food processor and pulse until finely ground. Add the chocolate and pulse until ground. Set aside.

2. In a large bowl, with an electric mixer on high speed, beat the egg whites until foamy. Continue to beat, gradually adding the remaining 1/2 cup sugar, until stiff, glossy peaks form.

3. In another bowl, with the same beaters, beat the egg yolks until thick, about 4 minutes. Add the cocoa, orange juice, and zest and beat until well blended. Fold in the pecan mixture. Stir in 1/4 of the egg whites, then fold in the rest in 2 batches. Pour into the pan.

4. Bake until a knife inserted in the center comes out clean, 40 minutes. Transfer to a rack and let cool completely, 2 hours, then cut around the cake and release the sides of the pan. Sprinkle the torte with confectioners' sugar and top with oranges, if desired.

205 calories, 4 g protein, 21 g carbohydrates, 2 g fiber, 14 g total fat, 4 g saturated fat, 79 mg cholesterol, 25 mg sodium

# Chocolate Fondue Serves 10

**Prep Time** • 5 minutes
**Cook Time** • 10 minutes

1 cup low-fat evaporated milk

1/4 cup sugar

1/4 cup cocoa powder

1 tablespoon vanilla extract

1/2 package (6 ounces) bittersweet
   chocolate chips (60% or higher
   cocoa content)

Fruit is only made healthier when dipped in this fondue, made with antioxidant-rich bittersweet chocolate. Serve surrounded by apple or pear wedges, thick banana slices, orange sections, whole strawberries, and pineapple chunks for dipping.

1. In a small saucepan, whisk together the milk, sugar, cocoa, and vanilla until well blended. Add the chocolate chips.

2. Place over low heat and cook, stirring occasionally, until melted, 10 minutes. Pour into a fondue pot or small slow cooker set on low.

128 calories, 3 g protein, 20 g carbohydrates, 1 g fiber, 5 g total fat, 3 g saturated fat, 4 mg cholesterol, 33 mg sodium

# Carrot Cake with Cream Cheese Glaze Serves 12

**Prep Time** • 1 hour, 20 minutes
**Cook Time** • 35 minutes

1/2 cup applesauce

2/3 cup granulated sugar

2 large eggs

2 tablespoons canola oil

1 teaspoon vanilla extract

1 1/4 cups whole-wheat
    pastry flour

1 teaspoon baking soda

1 teaspoon ground cinnamon

1/2 teaspoon salt

1 1/2 cups shredded carrots
    (3 large)

1/2 cup chopped walnuts

1 ounce low-fat cream cheese

2 tablespoons low-fat milk

2–3 tablespoons
    confectioners' sugar

You'll never notice that this dense, flavorful cake is low in fat and made with healthful ingredients. What you will notice is how delicious and moist it is and how quickly it disappears from the plate.

1. Preheat the oven to 350°F. Coat a 9-inch round cake pan with cooking spray. In a small bowl, whisk together the applesauce, sugar, eggs, oil, and vanilla.

2. In a large bowl, whisk together the flour, baking soda, cinnamon, and salt. Make a well in the center, add the applesauce mixture, and stir just until blended. Stir in the carrots and walnuts. Pour the batter into the pan.

3. Bake until a wooden pick inserted in the center comes out clean, 35 minutes. Transfer to a rack and let cool for 10 minutes, then remove from the pan and let cool completely, 1 hour.

4. Meanwhile, in a small bowl, whisk together the cream cheese and milk until well combined. Add 2 tablespoons confectioners' sugar and whisk until smooth, adding more sugar if the glaze is too thin. Place the cake on a serving plate and drizzle with the glaze.

160 calories, 3 g protein, 23 g carbohydrates, 2 g fiber, 6 g total fat, 1 g saturated fat, 37 mg cholesterol, 236 mg sodium

# Pear Crisp Serves 6

**Prep Time** • 10 minutes
**Cook Time** • 30 minutes

4 cups sliced pears (about
    5 medium)

1/2 cup prunes, chopped

1/4 cup packed brown sugar

1 tablespoon chopped
    crystallized ginger

1 tablespoon lemon juice

2 cups low-fat granola

3 tablespoons pure maple syrup

A great way to sneak prunes into a dessert, this sweet, flavorful crisp is bursting with fiber, with pears being a terrific source. The prunes are blended with the pears, sugar, and ginger and topped with a simple crunchy topping.

1. Preheat the oven to 350°F. In a large bowl, combine the pears and prunes. Sprinkle with the brown sugar, ginger, and lemon juice and toss gently to coat. Place in a 9-inch pie plate.

2. In a small bowl, toss the granola with the maple syrup. Sprinkle over the pear mixture, pressing into the pears. Bake until bubbling in the center and the pears are tender, 30 minutes.

322 calories, 4 g protein, 75 g carbohydrates, 6 g fiber, 3 g total fat, 0 g saturated fat, 0 mg cholesterol, 96 mg sodium

# Frozen Fruit Mousse Serves 4

**Prep Time** • 5 minutes

1 cup cold low-fat evaporated milk

2 tablespoons confectioners' sugar

1 teaspoon grated orange zest

2 cups frozen strawberries

Looking for a light, sweet treat? Here's a spoonable way to get all the health benefits of berries when they're out of season.

1. In a measuring cup, combine the milk, sugar, and orange zest.

2. Place the strawberries in a food processor and pulse just until shaved. With the motor running, gradually add the milk mixture just until the ingredients come together. Serve immediately.

88 calories, 5 g protein, 15 g carbohydrates, 2 g fiber, 1 g total fat, 1 g saturated fat, 10 mg cholesterol, 70 mg sodium

# Pomegranate Ice Serves 4

**Prep Time** • 4 hours, 10 minutes

2 cups pomegranate-blueberry juice (100% juice)

1/4 cup lime juice

2 tablespoons sugar

Packed with antioxidants, this delicious dessert is refreshing on a hot summer's night or after a spicy meal. Use any blend of pomegranate juice as long as it's 100% juice.

1. In a 9-inch square metal baking pan, whisk together the pomegranate juice, lime juice, and sugar until the sugar dissolves. Freeze for 1 hour, then stir to blend in any frozen portions. Freeze, stirring every 45 minutes to incorporate frozen portions, until the mixture has a uniform slushy consistency and ice crystals form, about 4 hours.

98 calories, 1 g protein, 25 g carbohydrates, 0 g fiber, 0 g total fat, 0 g saturated fat, 0 mg cholesterol, 15 mg sodium

# Rice Pudding Serves 4

**Prep Time** • 5 minutes
**Cook Time** • 1 hour, 35 minutes

3 cups vanilla soy milk

2/3 cup brown rice

1/2 teaspoon ground cinnamon

1/4 teaspoon salt

2 eggs, at room temperature, lightly beaten

1/2 cup raisins

1/2 cup chopped nuts, such as Brazil nuts, almonds, or walnuts

Who doesn't love creamy, comforting rice pudding? This one serves up health benefits that most don't. Soy milk, used here, can easily be substituted for dairy milk in all baked goods.

1. In a medium saucepan over medium heat, combine the soy milk, rice, cinnamon, and salt. Bring to a simmer, then reduce the heat to low, cover, and simmer for 1 1/2 hours. Remove from the heat and let cool for 5 minutes.

2. Stir 1/2 cup of the rice mixture into the eggs, stirring constantly. Gradually stir back into the rice mixture. Cook over low heat, stirring constantly, until thickened, 5 minutes. Stir in the raisins and nuts. Serve warm or refrigerate and serve cold.

354 calories, 13 g protein, 50 g carbohydrates, 4 g fiber, 12 g total fat, 1 g saturated fat, 106 mg cholesterol, 256 mg sodium

# Mixed Berry Tart Serves 12

**Prep Time** • 2 hours, 20 minutes
**Cook Time** • 40 minutes

1/4 cup ice water, without ice

3 tablespoons low-fat plain yogurt

1 cup whole-grain pastry flour

1/2 cup all-purpose flour

1 tablespoon + 1/3 cup sugar

1/4 teaspoon ground cinnamon

1/4 teaspoon salt

7 tablespoons nonhydrogenated butter-replacement stick margarine

5 cups mixed berries, such as blueberries, raspberries, and strawberries

2 tablespoons cornstarch

1 tablespoon lemon juice

Confectioners' sugar (optional)

Sweet berries and flaky crust add up to an irresistible dessert rich in antioxidants and fiber. Use a blend of berries or just one type. Vary the flavors with lime juice instead of lemon juice and ginger instead of cinnamon.

1. In a measuring cup, whisk together the water and yogurt. In a food processor, combine the pastry and all-purpose flour, 1 tablespoon sugar, cinnamon, and salt. Add the margarine and pulse until the mixture resembles coarse crumbs. With the motor running, gradually add the yogurt mixture and process just until the ingredients come together. Gather the dough into a ball. Wrap in plastic and refrigerate for at least 2 hours.

2. Preheat the oven to 350°F. In a large bowl, combine the berries, cornstarch, lemon juice, and 1/3 cup sugar and toss gently.

3. Shape dough into 6 small balls. Roll out each ball on a lightly floured work surface to about a 6-inch circle. Using 6 4-inch tartlet pans with removable bottoms, line the pans with the dough. Evenly distribute the fruit mixture into the pans.

4. Bake until the filling is bubbling and crust is browned, 15 to 20 minutes. Transfer to a rack for 15 minutes. Remove from pans and cool completely. Each tartlet is 2 servings. Dust with confectioners' sugar.

165 calories, 3 g protein, 26 g carbohydrates, 3 g fiber, 7 g total fat, 3 g saturated fat, 0 mg cholesterol, 128 mg sodium

# Recipe List

## Breakfasts

Buckwheat Pancakes with Fruit Sauce, 590
Tropical Fruit Salad, 590
Zucchini Frittata, 591

## Appetizers and Snacks

Edamame Hummus with Pita Crisps, 592
Roasted Cherry Tomatoes in Parmesan Cups, 593
Ultimate Spiced Nuts, 592

## Salads

Broccoli Salad, 595
Chicken Pasta Salad, 599
Citrus Chicken Salad, 598
Coleslaw with Orange-Sesame Vinaigrette, 594
Corn, Tomato, and Quinoa Salad, 596
Greens with Creamy Garlicky Dressing, 596
Shrimp and Grapefruit Salad, 598
Spinach Salad with Chickpeas, 597
Tuna and White Bean Salad, 599
Updated Waldorf Salad, 594

## Soups

Chicken Curry Soup, 600
Ginger Butternut Squash Soup, 602
Lentil-Tomato Soup, 603
Minestrone with Fava Beans, 603
Quick Chicken Noodle Soup, 600
Simple Broccoli Soup, 602
Sweet Potato Soup, 601

## Sandwiches

Beef in Lettuce Wraps, 606
Curried Chicken Salad Sandwiches, 605
Open-Faced Sardine Sandwiches, 604
Salmon Cake Sandwiches, 606
Salsa Tuna Salad Sandwiches, 604

## Main Dishes

Baked Chicken with Tomatoes, 615
Barbecued Flank Steak, 618
Beef and Broccoli Stew, 620
Chicken-Barley Bake, 616
Chicken in Garlic Sauce, 616
Curry Seared Scallops, 614
Eggplant Lasagna, 609
Fish Tacos, 611
Harvest Pork Roast, 621
Hearty Vegetable Stew, 608
Herb-Crusted Roast Beef, 618
Mac 'n Cheese Primavera, 608
Pork Chops with Dried Fruits, 620
Roasted Salmon with Sautéed Greens, 613
Salmon Steaks with Peach Salsa, 612
Thai Roasted Shrimp, 614
Three-Bean Chili, 610
Tomato-Roasted Mackerel, 612
Tuna Kebabs, 610
Turkey Cutlets with Grapefruit Salsa, 617
Turkey Ragu with Spaghetti, 618

## Sides

Almond Rice, 626
Brown Rice Risotto, 624
Brussels Sprouts with Caramelized Onions, 623
Creamed Spinach, 624
Orange Beets, 627
Pasta with Walnut Cream Sauce, 627
Roasted Broccoli with Cheese, 624
Roasted Root Vegetables, 622
Shiitake Green Beans, 622
Springtime Quinoa, 626

## Breads and Baked Goods

Banana-Peanut Bread, 630
Blueberry-Oat Scones, 628
Chock-Full Chocolate Chip Cookies, 633
Chocolate-Almond Biscotti, 632
Cinnamon-Raisin Coffee Cake, 632
Pumpkin Streusel Bread, 631
Raspberry-Almond Muffins, 628
Zesty Cornbread, 630

## Desserts

Carrot Cake with Cream Cheese Glaze, 636
Chocolate Fondue, 634
Chocolate-Pecan Torte, 634
Frozen Fruit Mousse, 638
Mixed Berry Tart, 639
Pear Crisp, 636
Pomegrante Ice, 638
Rice Pudding, 638

# index

diverticulosis and, 453
food substitutes for, 463
for gallstones, 466
for heart disease, 476, 478, 479, 481
for high blood pressure, 489, 491
for insulin resistance, 511
for memory loss, 532
for menstrual problems, 541
myth about, 351
for obesity, 552
for osteoporosis, 557
for sinusitis, 571
storing and using, 531
Ultimate Spiced Nuts, 592
for wrinkles, 584
*see also specific nuts*

## O

oat bran, 334, 337–338
for heart disease, 478
oats, oatmeal, 336, 337, 338, 362, 364,
399, 409, 445, 452, 461, 469,
479, 508, 511, 535
Blueberry-Oat Scones, 628
for heart disease, 478
for stroke, 572–573
as wheat substitute, 461
obesity, 324, 326, 337, 484, 550–555
arthritis and, 403
breast cancer and, 414, 419
cancer and, 424
cataracts and, 429
colon cancer and, 437
dementia and, 394
gum disease and, 470
high-protein diets and, 338
inflammation and, 330, 331, 437
insulin and, 510
prostate cancer and, 565
olive oil, 317, 319, 321, 322, 330, 348,
350, 360, 365, 389, 407, 415,
421, 429, 463, 497, 501
Alzheimer's disease and, 394, 395
breast cancer and, 417
for diabetes, 447
extra-virgin, 350, 365, 417
for gallstones, 466
for gout, 469
for heart disease, 318, 348, 350, 365,
447, 476, 478
for IBD, 505
for insulin resistance, 511
for memory loss, 533
for menopause, 536–537
storing of, 318

virgin, 478
for wrinkles, 584
olives, 354, 448, 478, 511, 549
omega-3 fatty acids, 325, 329, 330,
360, 379, 395, 397, 415, 417,
424
acne and, 388
ADHD and, 410–411
for allergies, 392
for AMD, 529, 530
arthritis and, 400, 402
asthma and, 405
autoimmune diseases and, 326–327
benefits of, 318, 319, 321, 322, 328
for BPH, 567
breast tenderness and, 420, 421
cataracts and, 428, 429
controlling inflammation with, 323–327,
331, 390, 415, 463, 496
depression and, 440, 441, 442, 443
eczema and, 454, 455
for food allergies and sensitivities, 464
for gallstones, 467
for heart disease, 477, 483
for high blood pressure, 490
HIV/AIDS and, 494–495
for IBD, 507
for infertility, 502, 503
lung cancer and, 523
for lupus, 524–526
for memory loss, 533
for menopause, 536, 538–539
for migraine, 544–546
for prostate cancer, 562
for psoriasis, 568–569
sources of, 318, 320, 347, 363, 367,
383, 390, 405, 420, 441, 454, 463,
477, 502
for stroke, 575–576
for wrinkles, 585
*see also* fish, fish oil
omega-6 fatty acids, 318, 325, 329–
330, 331, 390, 403, 407, 415,
421, 424, 429, 440, 443, 526,
531
onions, 343, 346, 395, 485
allergies and, 390, 391
for arthritis, 402
for asthma, 404, 405
Brussels Sprouts with Caramelized
Onions, 623
colon cancer and, 436
heartburn and, 474
for prostate cancer, 563
for sinusitis, 570

Oolong tea, *see* tea, Oolong
orange juice, 341, 395, 401, 406, 434,
457, 462, 479
frozen vs. ready-to-drink, 430
for gum disease, 470
heartburn and, 474
oranges, 334, 343, 369, 401, 413, 430,
444, 457, 469, 493
for acne, 389
Coleslaw with Orange-Sesame
Vinaigrette, 594
for infertility, 503
for lung cancer, 522
Orange Beets, 627
oregano, 350, 392, 425
osteoarthritis, 327, 340, 400, 401
osteomalacia, 506
osteoporosis, 344, 463, 492, 556–559
oxidative stress, 341, 344
oysters, 325, 388, 463, 470, 497, 530,
541
for BPH, 566

## P

pancakes, Buckwheat Pancakes with
Fruit Sauce, 590
pancreatic cancer, 348, 426
papaya, 346, 395, 444, 522
Parkinson's disease, 348
parsnips, 435
pasta:
Chicken Pasta Salad, 599
Eggplant Lasagna, 609
Mac 'n Cheese Primavera, 608
Pasta with Walnut Cream Sauce, 627
Turkey Ragu with Spaghetti, 618
pasteurization, 362, 373
peaches, 393, 439, 522
Salmon Steaks with Peach Salsa, 612
peanut butter, 317, 351, 363, 443
for diabetes, 446–447
peanut oil, 330
peanuts, 321, 363, 410, 413, 442
allergies to, 460, 463, 465
food substitutes for, 463
for heart disease, 478
Peanut-Banana Bread, 630
pears, 452
breast tenderness and, 421
Pear Crisp, 636
peas, 334, 346, 395, 424, 463, 469
colon cancer and, 434
for diabetes, 445–446
for heart disease, 478
for menopause, 536, 538

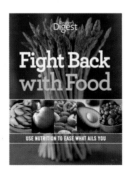